"The editors deserve our gratitude for having assembled these wide-ranging essays. They offer fascinating perspectives on a topic that could hardly be more important for humanity—but which has received far less systematic attention than it merits. Let's hope this book will raise awareness of these possible catastrophes, and thereby help ensure a safer world."

—Martin Rees, Astronomer Royal, University of Cambridge, and Centre for the Study of Existential Risk
Author of *If Science Is to Save Us, Our Final Hour, From Here to Infinity*, and *On the Future*

"How did ancient societies crash or reinvent themselves? Can we learn from that? History rhymes. For the ones interested in the search for patterns, this book is a treasure trove."

—Marten Scheffer, Wageningen University and Santa Fe Institute
Author of *Critical Transitions in Nature and Society*

"This must-read volume on collapse presents twenty original contributions from some of the best thinkers on the topic. The chapters explore collapse theory, case studies on individual historical collapses, and how things might change for humanity in the future. Collapse is considered from a range of perspectives: theoretical, historical, ecological, and modeling, providing an important multidisciplinary introduction. It will keep the increasingly important debate on collapse and transformation in the spotlight for some time to come."

—Guy D. Middleton, University of Newcastle upon Tyne
Author of *Understanding Collapse: Ancient History and Modern Myths*

How Worlds Collapse

As our society confronts the impacts of globalization and global systemic risks—such as financial contagion, climate change, and epidemics—what can studies of the past tell us about our present and future? *How Worlds Collapse* offers case studies of societies that either collapsed or overcame cataclysmic adversity. The authors in this volume find commonalities between past civilizations and our current society, tracing patterns, strategies, and early warning signs that can inform decision-making today. While today's world presents unique challenges, many mechanisms, dynamics, and fundamental challenges to the foundations of civilization have been consistent throughout history—highlighting essential lessons for the future.

Miguel A. Centeno is Musgrave Professor of Sociology at Princeton University and Executive Vice Dean of Princeton University's School of Public and International Affairs. He is founder and co-director of the Princeton Institute for International and Regional Studies (PIIRS) Global Systemic Risk research community.

Peter W. Callahan is a graduate of Princeton University who earned his MS in Geography and Environmental Studies from the University of New Mexico. He is a researcher at Princeton's PIIRS Global Systemic Risk research community where his scholarly interests include the study of socio-ecological systems, historical systemic risks, sustainable development, and renewable energy policy and technology.

Paul A. Larcey is co-director of the PIIRS Global Systemic Risk research community at Princeton University. Larcey's work with the UK's innovation agency focuses on key emerging technologies including life sciences, quantum technologies, and AI. He has worked in corporate research, venture capital, and global industrial sectors at board and senior levels and studied engineering, materials science, and finance at London, Oxford, and Cambridge Universities.

Thayer S. Patterson is coordinator and a founding member of the PIIRS Global Systemic Risk research community at Princeton University. Following his studies in economics and mechanical engineering at Yale, and finance at Princeton's Bendheim Center for Finance, his research has focused on the causes and consequences of catastrophic systemic risk.

How Worlds Collapse

*What History, Systems, and Complexity
Can Teach Us About Our Modern World and
Fragile Future*

**Edited by Miguel A. Centeno,
Peter W. Callahan, Paul A. Larcey,
Thayer S. Patterson**

Routledge
Taylor & Francis Group

NEW YORK AND LONDON

First published 2023
by Routledge
605 Third Avenue, New York, NY 10158

and by Routledge
2 Park Square, Milton Park, Abingdon, Oxon, OX14 4RN

Routledge is an imprint of the Taylor & Francis Group, an informa business

Library of Congress Cataloging-in-Publication Data
Names: Centeno, Miguel Angel, 1957- editor.
Title: How Worlds Collapse/edited by Miguel A. Centeno [and three others].
Description: New York, NY: Routledge, 2023. | Includes bibliographical references and index.
Identifiers: LCCN 2022036785 | ISBN 9781032363257 (hbk) | ISBN 9781032363219 (pbk) | ISBN 9781003331384 (ebk)
Subjects: LCSH: Disasters–History. | Emergency management–History. | Emergency management–Decision making. | Social systems–History.
Classification: LCC D24 .H555 2023 | DDC 363.34/8068–dc23/ eng/20221122
LC record available at https://lccn.loc.gov/2022036785

ISBN: 978-1-032-36325-7 (hbk)
ISBN: 978-1-032-36321-9 (pbk)
ISBN: 978-1-003-33138-4 (ebk)

DOI: 10.4324/9781003331384

Typeset in Bembo
by Deanta Global Publishing Services, Chennai, India

Cover image: Shutterstock, Ancient Roman town in Palmyra, Syria

For Deborah Nichols

Contents

Acknowledgement   xii

Authors   xiv

Introduction   1
MIGUEL A. CENTENO, PETER W. CALLAHAN, PAUL A. LARCEY, AND
THAYER S. PATTERSON

SECTION 1
Theory and Insights of Historical Collapse   3

1 **Globalization and Fragility: A Systems Approach to Collapse**   5
MIGUEL A. CENTENO, PETER W. CALLAHAN, PAUL A. LARCEY, AND THAYER S.
PATTERSON

2 **How Scholars Explain Collapse**   25
JOSEPH A. TAINTER

3 **Diminishing Returns on Extraction: How Inequality and**
Extractive Hierarchy Create Fragility   37
LUKE KEMP

4 **Collapse, Recovery, and Existential Risk**   61
HAYDN BELFIELD

SECTION 2
Historical and Archaeological Investigations of Collapse   93

5 **"Mind the Gap": The 1177 BCE Late Bronze Age Collapse**
and Some Preliminary Thoughts on Its Immediate Aftermath   97
ERIC H. CLINE

6 The End of "Peak Empire": The Collapse of the Roman, Han, and Jin Empires   108
WALTER SCHEIDEL

7 Collapse and Non-collapse: The Case of Byzantium ca. 650–800 CE   124
JOHN HALDON

8 *Fluctuat Nec Mergitur*: Seven Centuries of Pueblo Crisis and Resilience   146
TIMOTHY A. KOHLER, R. KYLE BOCINSKY, AND DARCY BIRD

9 Episodes of the Feathered Serpent: Aztec Imperialism and Collapse   167
DEBORAH L. NICHOLS AND RYAN H. COLLINS

10 The Black Death: Collapse, Resilience, and Transformation   191
SAMUEL K. COHN, JR.

11 The Cases of Novgorod and Muscovy: Using Systems Thinking to Understand Historical Civilizational Response to Exogenous Threats   206
MIRIAM POLLOCK, BENJAMIN D. TRUMP, AND IGOR LINKOV

12 Resilience of the Simple?: Lessons from the Blockade of Leningrad   236
JEFFREY K. HASS

SECTION 3
Systemic Collapse Insights from Ecology, Climate, and the Environment   259

13 Climate Change and Tipping Points in Historical Collapse   261
TIMOTHY M. LENTON

14 Conservation of Fragility and the Collapse of Social Orders   282
JOHN M. ANDERIES AND SIMON A. LEVIN

15 Resilience and Collapse in Bee Societies and Communities   296
CHRISTINA M. GROZINGER AND HARLAND M. PATCH

SECTION 4

Future Systemic Collapse and Quantitative Modeling   313

16   **Producing Collapse: Nuclear Weapons as Preparation to End Civilization**   315
ZIA MIAN AND BENOÎT PELOPIDAS

17   **From Wild West to Mad Max: Transition in Civilizations**   333
RICHARD BOOKSTABER

18   **Phase Transitions and the Theory of Early Warning Indicators for Critical Transitions**   358
GEORGE I. HAGSTROM AND SIMON A. LEVIN

19   **The Lifespan of Civilizations: Do Societies "Age," or Is Collapse Just Bad Luck?**   375
ANDERS SANDBERG

20   **Multipath Forecasting: The Aftermath of the 2020 American Crisis**   397
PETER TURCHIN

Index   417

Acknowledgement

The Editors would like to acknowledge and thank the many people who helped make this volume possible.

First, the Office of the Dean for Research at Princeton University supported the creation of our Global Collaborative Network on Historical Collapse, specifically Pablo Debenedetti, Anastasia Vrachnos, Aly Kassam-Remtulla, and Claire Hu. Their endorsement of this research initiative allowed us to gather together the scholars who contributed presentations, ongoing conversations, and collaborations that produced the works within this volume.

Next, the Princeton Institute for International and Regional Studies (PIIRS) for the creation of—and ongoing support for—the PIIRS Global Systemic Risk research community. This great team has included Mark Beissinger, Stephen Kotkin, Deborah Yashar, Susan Bindig, David Jarvis, Jayne Bialkowski, Nicole Bergman, Carole Dopp, Rachel Golden, Karen Koller, Pooja Makhijani, Nita Mallina, Julia Panter, Tim Waldron, and Nikki Woolward.

At the Princeton School of Public and International Affairs, Amaney Jamal, Cecilia Rouse, Todd Bristol, Pamela Garber, Meghann Kleespie, Heather Evans, Nancy Everett, and Nancy McCollough. And in the Department of Sociology, Mitch Duneier, Donna DeFrancisco, Amanda Rowe, Cindy Gibson, and Eric Altman. In the Office of the Vice Provost, Paul LaMarche, Amy Bristol, Cynthia Gorman, and Jill Alves for their continued support of PIIRS Global Systemic Risk.

Simon Levin at Princeton, Johan Rockström at the Potsdam Institute for Climate Impact Research, and Carl Folke and Victor Galaz at the Stockholm Resilience Centre who have worked tirelessly to advance the science and mitigation of systemic risk. Their leadership in our collaborative research partnership has been invaluable.

We are grateful to Kathryn W. Davis and Shelby M.C. Davis for providing pioneering support in 2010 for the study of catastrophic systemic risk at Princeton. Sean Brennan and Tom Quirk at Princeton have championed the mission of the PIIRS Global Systemic Risk project all along the way. And Carl Robichaud and Steve Del Rosso at the Carnegie Corporation of New York were instrumental in their early understanding of the importance of—and their support for—the study of critical systemic threats in 2010.

A special thank you to Arka Mukherjee for his profound curiosity, vision, and generosity. Without his support for—and participation in—the PIIRS Global Systemic Risk research community, this work would not have been possible.

We thank Dean Birkenkamp at Routledge Press for his stewardship, guidance, and inspiration throughout this project. His support for this topic and his understanding of the importance of multidisciplinarity allowed us to assemble these diverse perspectives into this volume.

And finally, we would like to thank all the authors and members of this Global Collaborative Network on Historical Collapse who, through their work, have advanced this academic subfield that has lamentably become increasingly relevant in our modern times.

Authors

John M. Anderies	Arizona State University—School of Human Evolution and Social Change; School of Sustainability
Haydn Belfield	University of Cambridge—Centre for the Study of Existential Risk (CSER)
Darcy Bird	Washington State University—Anthropology Max Planck Institute for Geoanthropology
R. Kyle Bocinsky	University of Montana—Society and Conservation; Montana Climate Office Desert Research Institute Crow Canyon Archaeological Center
Richard Bookstaber	Fabric RQ
Peter W. Callahan	Princeton University—PIIRS Global Systemic Risk research community
Miguel A. Centeno	Princeton University—Sociology; School of Public and International Affairs; PIIRS Global Systemic Risk research community
Eric H. Cline	George Washington University—Classical and Ancient Near Eastern Studies; Anthropology; Capitol Archaeological Institute
Samuel K. Cohn, Jr.	University of Glasgow—Medieval History University of Edinburgh—Institute for Advanced Studies in the Humanities
Ryan H. Collins	Dartmouth College—Anthropology; Neukom Institute for Computational Science
Christina M. Grozinger	Penn State University—Entomology; Center for Pollinator Research; Insect Biodiversity Center; Huck Institutes of the Life Sciences
George I. Hagstrom	Princeton University—Ecology and Evolutionary Biology; High Meadows Environmental Institute

John Haldon — Princeton University—History; Climate Change and History Research Initiative

Jeffrey K. Hass — University of Richmond—Sociology and Anthropology
St. Petersburg State University—Economics

Luke Kemp — University of Cambridge—Centre for the Study of Existential Risk (CSER)

Timothy A. Kohler — Washington State University—Archaeology and Evolutionary Anthropology
Santa Fe Institute
Crow Canyon Archaeological Center
University of Durham—Archaeology

Paul A. Larcey — Princeton University—PIIRS Global Systemic Risk research community

Timothy M. Lenton — University of Exeter—Global Systems Institute; Geography

Simon A. Levin — Princeton University—Ecology and Evolutionary Biology; High Meadows Environmental Institute

Igor Linkov — US Army Corps of Engineers—US Army Engineer Research and Development Center
Carnegie Mellon University—Engineering and Public Policy

Zia Mian — Princeton University—Program on Science and Global Security

Deborah L. Nichols — Dartmouth College—Anthropology

Harland M. Patch — Penn State University—Entomology; Center for Pollinator Research; Insect Biodiversity Center; Huck Institutes of the Life Sciences

Thayer S. Patterson — Princeton University—PIIRS Global Systemic Risk research community

Benoît Pelopidas — Sciences Po—Nuclear Knowledges, Center for International Studies (CERI)

Miriam Pollock — US Army Corps of Engineers—US Army Engineer Research and Development Center

Anders Sandberg — University of Oxford—Future of Humanity Institute
The Institute for Futures Studies

Walter Scheidel — Stanford University—Humanities; Classics; History

Joseph A. Tainter — Utah State University—Environment and Society, College of Natural Resources

Benjamin D. Trump — US Army Corps of Engineers—US Army Engineer Research and Development Center

Peter Turchin — Complexity Science Hub Vienna—Social Complexity and Collapse

Introduction

Miguel A. Centeno, Peter W. Callahan,
Paul A. Larcey, and Thayer S. Patterson

In our era of heightened division and polarization, a powerful concern that unites us is the perception that modern civilization may be on a trajectory toward fragility, systemic shocks, or even *collapse*. From the rise of crypto-currencies to the increasing popularity of dystopian novels and apocalyptic movies, civilizational collapse seems like *the* issue of our time. With a potentially global impact, this collective fear has attracted a broad audience. Modern catastrophes have contributed to this anxiety, as recent crises like the COVID-19 pandemic, supply chain disruptions, the global financial crisis, and the Russian invasion of Ukraine bring our vulnerabilities into sharper focus.

The timing of this volume is inspired by this sense of urgency, and we believe it advances an important perspective. To anticipate the future, we look to lessons from the past to discover patterns, themes, and shared characteristics of doomed civilizations that might offer warning signs for modern collapse. Our study of historical systemic collapse is in the spirit of Santayana's cautionary exhortation—by understanding how and why our predecessors failed, we hope to adopt greater resilience in our modern systems.

Over the past three years, the Princeton Institute for International and Regional Studies (PIIRS) Global Systemic Risk research community at Princeton University hosted conferences around the themes of historical collapse and systemic fragility. Formed in 2013 as a collaborative and multidisciplinary scholarly project, PIIRS Global Systemic Risk has worked to identify the risks that emerge from the unprecedented levels of global complexity, interconnectivity, and interdependency that are key characteristics of our modern world. A consistent theme throughout this project has been that formidable risks to our globalized systems are accelerating and that widespread systemic failure would be catastrophic.

The conferences on historical systemic collapse convened a global collaborative network of archaeologists, historians, sociologists, ecologists, physicists, mathematicians, and scholars of collapse from around the world to seek a better understanding of how and why systems, populations, and ultimately societies collapse. With the goal of sharing insights, theories, and methodologies

DOI: 10.4324/9781003331384-1

across academic fields, scholars sought to move beyond disciplinary walls and silos that traditionally separate efforts that could benefit from cross-pollination. Inspired by shared curiosity across disciplines, collaborators explored how our understanding of today can be enhanced by multidisciplinary explorations of collapse.

This volume is the product of these conferences and presents the work of 31 authors involved in the effort. Each chapter stands alone as a work of scholarship in its own right, but together, they begin to paint a picture of what systemic collapse can look like in its many, varied, and nuanced forms. This volume presents both macro- and micro-level perspectives on collapse. Some chapters present philosophical investigations and meta-analyses at high levels across the entire chronology of civilizational collapses, while others demonstrate the importance of analysis within the collapse of a specific civilization or system.

Reflecting the multidisciplinary influences and scope of the analyses, the chapters in this volume are organized into four broad sections based on themes. The first section presents an introduction to important theories, mechanisms, and literature relevant to the study of collapse, and features debates within and around the discipline. The second section explores case studies from historical civilizations with close analysis of characteristics and events that precipitate fragility and collapse. The third section focuses on ecology and the environment, and identifies examples, concepts, and methodologies that are useful in the study of systemic collapse. In the final section, authors present quantitative modeling and other methods of conceptualizing systemic and civilizational failure.

We believe this field of historical systemic collapse is rich with potential for influential discoveries, developments, and academic insights, with the ultimate goal of mitigating collapse and the tragic human costs in death and suffering seen throughout history. We hope that many of the ideas and multidisciplinary perspectives in this volume serve as an inspiration to attract a greater number of scholars to this field as we collectively seek to better understand how worlds collapse.

Section 1

Theory and Insights of Historical Collapse

The first section of this volume introduces readers to perspectives on the study of systems and explores theories of collapse causality. The authors present literature surveys and analyses within the field of collapse and examine how collapse studies could borrow insights and understanding from other relevant disciplines.

In the first chapter of this section, produced by the editors of this volume, we seek to combine concepts from our study of complexity science, globalization, and systemic risk with our work within this scholarly collaboration on historical collapse. Viewing historical societies through the lenses of systems theory and complexity, we analyze how social systems reflect the structure and dynamics of complex adaptive systems. In this way, a complex society can be seen as an interdependent and interactive system of systems—economic, financial, agricultural, water, energy, and transportation, among others—each adding layers of complexity and fragility. Drawing on insights of systemic risk from multiple disciplines, we discuss systemic properties and phenomena that contribute to either a society's downfall or to its ability to withstand shocks and recover from failure. Mindful of the prospect of a modern collapse, we believe that applying systems theory to past collapses will be relevant to understanding the fragilities within our increasingly interdependent, technologically advanced, and complex global systems.

In the second chapter, Joseph Tainter begins with a wide-ranging literature review of collapse scholarship. Noting that scholars have been interested in identifying causes of collapse for over 3,000 years, Tainter identifies key themes and patterns from this extensive literature, and names ten categories into which all explanations of collapse can be divided. He observes how a contemporary lens can impact research of the past and argues that scholars of collapse are often "influenced by, and sometimes attempt to influence, contemporary social issues," and that explanations thus "wax and wane in popularity according to the issues of the day." In his classification of collapse theories, Tainter finds that a plurality of the explanations offered by historians elides human agency, encompassing causes that he variously refers to as "*deus ex machina*," "bolt from the blue," or "just bad luck." Cautioning against such biases and fatalistic explanations, Tainter galvanizes scholars to uncover each

DOI: 10.4324/9781003331384-2

civilization's role in its own collapse by seeking more nuanced and systemic casualties, writing, "surely we can do better."

In his seminal book, *The Collapse of Complex Societies* from 1988, Tainter presented his theory of diminishing returns on complexity, which claims that civilizational collapses can be attributed to society reaching an untenable level of complexity and interconnectivity. Tainter argues that while complexity is beneficial for the growth and development of a society, once it reaches a certain threshold, the costs and risks outweigh the benefits. Luke Kemp recognizes Tainter's hypothesis as "perhaps the foremost unifying theory of societal aging," and in the third chapter of this section, he provides a challenge and alternative to Tainter's theory. Kemp argues that diminishing returns on "extraction"—not "complexity"—is a more accurate way to characterize collapse causality. Here, Kemp focuses on how societal institutions extract capital from citizens and the environment—such as through taxation, conscription, confiscation, and energy depletion—arguing that inefficiencies and mismanagement of these extractive practices are the real precipitators of collapse. He argues that over-extraction of capital results in inequality, corruption, intraelite struggle, lower energy return on investment, and weakened societal stabilizing structures, resulting in a more fragile state vulnerable to collapse. He concludes by arguing that this shift in thinking means that societal collapse is not inevitable and that rather than fighting an "unwinnable battle" against the inexorable decline of energy return on investment, societies can instead "reach true, lasting stability ... by building more inclusive institutions that are democratically proactive to emerging problems."

In the final chapter of this section, Haydn Belfield provides a comparative analysis of methodologies employed in the fields of existential risk and collapse studies. While both fields study low-probability catastrophic events, existential risk scholars typically examine only cases involving human extinction or those that would change humanity's long-term trajectory. Collapse scholars, on the other hand, focus on societal failures after which there is potential for human reorganization and recovery. Belfield argues, however, that even if society recovers after a collapse, the consequences could still be permanent and severe. In this way, he shows that both collapse and existential risk studies should find common ground around the potential impact on humanity's long-term trajectory. Through his survey of perspectives, theories, and methodologies in both fields, Belfield presents a prescription for greater collaboration, synergy, and understanding between these two increasingly relevant disciplines.

1 Globalization and Fragility

A Systems Approach to Collapse

Miguel A. Centeno, Peter W. Callahan,
Paul A. Larcey, and Thayer S. Patterson

[T]he decline of Rome was the natural and inevitable effect of immoderate greatness. Prosperity ripened the principle of decay; the causes of destruction multiplied
with the extent of conquest; and as soon as time or accident had removed the
artificial supports, the stupendous fabric yielded to the pressure of its own weight.
The story of its ruin is simple and obvious; and instead of inquiring why the Roman
empire was destroyed, we should rather be surprised that it had subsisted so long.
—Edward Gibbon, *The History of the Decline and Fall of the Roman Empire* (1788)

1.1 Introduction

There is a specter haunting globalization and modern life: The potential for
widespread civilizational collapse. Stories of dystopian fiction and apocalyptic
futures have never been more popular, with audiences flocking to big-budget
disaster movies (Roberts 2020). Our world is existentially anxious because
we sense that our trajectory is not sustainable (Ord 2020). Even the most
optimistic possibilities of scientific and technological progress cannot guarantee our collective ongoing stability and prosperity. Global systemic shocks
like 9/11, the Global Financial Crisis, COVID-19, and the Russian invasion of Ukraine, together with increased actual or threatened aggression from
other global actors, have heightened awareness of the fragility of our increasingly globalized and interdependent way of living. Such developments have
brought the magnitude of these fragilities into sharper focus and have caused
some to advocate for a retreat from globalization, claiming that its dangers
outweigh the benefits (Altman 2020; Greber 2022). Regardless of these concerns, however, international interdependence continues and along with it, so
do the risks.

With the goal of understanding this precariousness of our modern world,
we offer a lens through which to investigate "failures" in history and examine whether there are insights from systemic risk that can illuminate patterns
of historical collapse. A certain teleological triumphalism dominates modern
social science where victors wrote their histories and survivorship biases lead
us to focus on the civilizations that remain standing. We see value in also
examining the reverse view by attempting to learn from failed civilizations.

DOI: 10.4324/9781003331384-3

We may have access to insights that past doomed societies lacked—self-aware-ness of our own trajectory toward destruction, access to historical hindsight, and an understanding of themes and patterns that have led to systemic failures in societies. We seek to identify systemic causes and mechanisms for break-down that can provide historians with a systemic perspective for analyzing the past and can allow these past collapses to serve as cautionary tales for our present and future.

This chapter begins with a discussion of hubris as a theme in social develop-ment. We then present a summary of the structure of globalization as a com-plex adaptive system. We follow by defining collapse, then move on to its most significant causes. The penultimate section discusses some of the mechanisms through which isolated failures could lead to systemic collapse. We end with consideration of robustness, resilience, and the governance required to avoid risk and mitigate failures, with the goal of creating a more stable civilization today.

1.2 The Enemy Is Us

> We have met the enemy and he is us.
>
> —Walt Kelly 1971

Hubris has been a cautionary theme in mythology, literature, and religion throughout history. Humans have a habit of taking a few successes as a sign of continued and future prosperity, often extrapolating it into a perception of infallibility. This has led to the construction of ever-taller edifices on fragile foundations. Standing nearly twice the height of the Empire State Building, Dubai's Burj Khalifa may serve as a contemporary analog to the Tower of Babel. What would possess us to build something so incongruous with its natu-ral environment, surrounded by a set of environmentally unsustainable desert city-states? Believing that we have it all under control and that tomorrow will be just like today, we create crucial systems on which we depend, neglecting to design into them the robustness and resilience to survive crises. (Pastor-Satorras et al. 2015; Taleb 2007).

We argue that this overconfidence also characterizes globalization (Brauer 2018). Over the last half-century, our complex global system has emerged as a set of tightly coupled interactions that together allow for the continued flow of information, money, goods, services, and people. We have clear evidence that in many ways—environmental hazards aside for the moment—globalization has in fact been largely beneficial for humans collectively. Life expectancy has increased globally by more than two decades since 1960 (Roser, Ortiz-Ospina, and Ritchie 2013), and there is continuing evidence that the science of longevity will sharply accelerate (Oeppen 2002; Kannisto et al. 1994). We now produce enough food to feed the planet and enjoy an unprecedented economic and tech-nological standard of living. Like a Roman during the reign of the Antonines, we can look around us and marvel at what we have created (Birley 2000).

Much of this advancement has come through our ability to create systems that are technologically advanced, complex, interdependent, and constructed at massive scale. Expansive networks of telecommunication, transportation, energy, agriculture, and trade, among others, have facilitated this progress, but have given rise to new and unprecedented risks (Manheim 2020; Oughton et al. 2018). We see these networks as complex adaptive systems (CAS), where the interactions of components create new dynamics that cannot be explained by the characteristics of the constituent parts. Because of this complexity, the risks associated with maintaining CAS are non-linear and impossible to predict (Helbing 2009). Emergent risks in such a system are the threats that originate not in any single component, but rather from the collective structure and dynamics of the system in its entirety. In the case of CAS, the risk of systemic failure when looking at the whole may be far greater than when the system is viewed simply as the sum of its parts (Crucitti, Latora, and Marchiori 2004). This is particularly true of "systems-of-systems" that rely on the coordination of various domains. The agricultural system, for example, relies on networks of finance, trade, water, labor, energy, electricity, transportation, communications, and others to efficiently plant, grow, harvest, transport, and sell foodstuffs in a globalized society (Centeno, Callahan, and Patterson 2015; Nyström et al. 2019). A miscoordination or deliberate interference in any of these underlying and interdependent systems could be catastrophic (Ibrahim et al. 2021).

Globalization requires the continuous flow of people, money, commodities, goods, services, and the cooperation of vast numbers of individuals (Danku, Perc, and Szolnoki 2019; Foreman-Peck 2007). COVID-19 has shown us that none of us is isolated from the rest of the globe and the impact of unpredictable world events. A novel virus can rapidly emerge to bring down economies, influence elections, and humble even the most powerful. Even with warnings, foresight, and suggested mitigation strategies, overconfidence and failure of imagination enabled such a deadly scenario (Cambridge Centre for Risk Studies 2019; Epstein 2009; Nuzzo et al. 2019).

We now live in a global system-of-systems where a failure in one part could lead to disaster across the whole structure. The sheer quantity and breadth of possible interactions require a shift in our analysis of interdependence. Moreover, we have added a pursuit of optimization and efficiency to this complex system, which leads to short-term gains but lays the foundation for longer-term catastrophe (Centeno et al. 2015). Global systems, much like the Burj Khalifa, are wonders to behold, but the increase in complexity and tight coupling makes a "normal accident" ever more likely and more dangerous (Perrow 1984; Ledwoch et al. 2018). That is, we have created systems that we can never truly comprehend, whose risk profiles we cannot understand (Wildavsky and Dake 1990), over which no one has responsibility, and on which we have staked our continued survival.

Our hubris lies not only in our overconfidence in our increasingly fragile systems, but more so in our belief that our twenty-first-century civilization is immune to the tragic fates of fallen societies in history. While our modern societies and the systems upon which they rely exist at a scale, scope, and degree of complexity far greater than their historical counterparts, the mechanisms of systemic failure and collapse remain the same. In this way, lessons from the past that relate to fundamental systemic characteristics still remain relevant today. Because of the unimaginable magnitude of potential contemporary collapse, the study of past systems to gain greater insight into our present and future is more urgent and compelling than ever.

1.3 Looking to History

One constant throughout recorded history is that even the most apparently powerful and successful civilizational systems inevitably break down. History has repeatedly demonstrated that the second law of thermodynamics applies to human-created systems: We cannot escape entropy—the inexorable trend toward greater chaos in nature (Meyer and Ponthiere 2020; Gleick 2011). Consequently, no form of social order is eternal.

Several years ago, we (the editors of this book) began a scholarly project on Global Systemic Risk at Princeton University. We sought to bring insights from complexity (Holovatch, Kenna, and Thurner 2017), systems theory (Miller and Page 2007), and network theory (Barabási 2002) to identify: (1) how the systems of globalization work and (2) the risks associated with this global complexity. We understood that it was important not just to analyze the systems and identify key vectors, but also to imagine how it might all come apart (Vespignani 2010). We began to see that the risks to our increasingly interconnected and globalized systems are substantial and that widespread failure could be catastrophic. To anticipate the future, we looked to lessons from the past to discover shared characteristics of doomed civilizations, which might offer warning signs for modern collapse.

What do previous "falls of empire" have to teach us about how we might best prepare for an uncertain and potentially perilous future (Tainter 1988; Middleton 2013; Taleb 2012)? In this chapter, we look to our experience from our study of global systemic risk and systemic collapse to provide insights and perspectives that historians may apply to their study of historical collapse.

1.4 Defining Systemic Collapse

To understand "systemic collapse," we begin with a standard definition of a system: "a regularly interacting or interdependent group of units forming a unified whole" (Merriam-Webster). Modern complexity and technology only accelerate this interactive interdependence. In our study of collapse, we are interested in how the structure and dynamics of a system decline over time—how this "unified whole" decreases in scale, scope, or cohesion, and how the central axis of action of the system moves from the system itself to its constituent parts.

If there is one central theme in the collapse literature, it is that there is notable disagreement about methodology of study, and even the meaning of the term "collapse" (Middleton 2013; Yoffee 2005; Yoffee and Cowgill 1988; Haldon et al. 2020). One area of debate is what exactly constitutes a collapse. Another debate, or criticism, revolves around how our historical view of collapse tends to be influenced by multiple cognitive biases—cultural bias, availability bias, confirmation bias, etc. Another critique is that speaking only of collapse introduces failure bias and ignores comparable scenarios where civilizations survived hardships and shocks and thereby conceals or ignores significant elements of robustness and resilience that are important to identify (Nicoll and Zerboni 2020). We have to also address *what* exactly collapses. One standard focus is the level of social complexity of a society (e.g., level of interdependence, control, or coordination) (Renfrew 1973; Tainter 1988). Another is the level of political control or simple performance measures, such as nutrition or life expectancy (van Zanden et al. 2014).

We recognize that the term "collapse" is somewhat ambiguous with different definitions across academic disciplines. In this analysis we propose borrowing the usage of the term "collapse" from the literature on networks, systems, and complexity. In these fields, collapse refers to the disaggregation and breaking apart of a connected network. A collapsing complex system breaks down or fragments into smaller units requiring less order, complexity, coordination, and organization to function. The systemic dynamics are thus reduced on a macro scale. This view of collapse from complexity science is consistent with Joseph Tainter's view of sociopolitical collapse as "a rapid simplification, the loss of an established level of social, political, or economic complexity" (Tainter 1988; Tainter 2006). The best question for such network analyses may be: Has the system lost a significant part of its aggregate functionality (Hernández-Lemus and Siqueiros-García 2013)?

In this type of analysis, what collapses is not necessarily an entire society or civilization, but instead the larger organizational framework (Yoffee 2005; Kauffman 1993). In other words, for many citizens of the society, life goes on, just not at the same level of complex interdependence. So, for example, while the complex systems of the Maya civilization collapsed, the late-classic Maya city-states decentralized and became smaller agglomerations of farmers, allowing elements of the Maya way of life to endure. Similarly, the radius of collapse may also differ such that the failure of some systemic elements does not imply the collapse of the entire *status quo ante*. The Western Roman Empire became a collection of much smaller political units—with significantly fewer interactions between them—yet the Eastern portion maintained its structure and societal identity in a semblance of its former self for a further thousand years (Mango 2002).

Within the collapse literature, there is discussion about the importance of the temporality or speed and timescale of collapse. While the "rapidity" of systemic simplification is an important element of many definitions, some scholars argue that collapse can also take place over longer timescales. Once a tipping point toward collapse is reached, the breakdown of that society's interconnectivity begins, whether it takes decades, as in Mycenaea, or centuries, as in the case of the Maya (Middleton 2017).[1] Many of the systemic mechanisms we discuss in this chapter are applicable to historical examples of disaggregation and fragmentation that take place over both short- and long-term periods, and we believe that insights from both of these timescales could be relevant to our modern times.

Distinct from collapses, however, are *declines*, which are inevitable in gradual cycles of rise and decline. The two may have very different causes. In distinguishing a collapse from a decline, most discussions of collapse focus on a dramatic event, moment, or tipping point when key indicators begin to mark social fragmentation and breakdown. For our purposes, we identify collapse as a clear inflection point followed by a significant and perceptible reduction in any combination of: (1) level of organization, (2) spatial reach, and (3) socioeconomic complexity of a system. (cf. Haldon et al. 2020, 1–3, 15). A collapse may mark the dramatic end of one system, creating the conditions for another system to form in its place.

For a society's fragmentation to be relevant to our discussion of collapse, it must have significant long-term consequences or costs. That is, social collapse must involve the loss of basic structure or function, or at the very least a decline in critical measures such as nutrition, life expectancy, or peace. Ibn Khaldûn's term *asabiyyah*, meaning "group feeling" or "social cohesion," might represent the antithesis of collapse. Interestingly, in 1377, Ibn Khaldûn wrote in his *Muqaddimah* that all social systems have collapse written into their structures and that the cycles of rise and decline may be inevitable (Ibn Khaldûn 2015).

It is important to recognize that a society or civilization can experience a major crisis without experiencing a collapse. While the Global Financial Crisis of 2008 was a systemic shock with significant costs, it did not precipitate a collapse of the entire financial system (Coggan 2020, 338–347). The "Second 30 Years War" (1914–1945), however, did produce a collapse in the global, social, and political order (Ferguson 2006). This last example also serves as a reminder that one person's collapse may be another's opportunity; in the case of barbaric regimes, collapse is widely welcomed by the oppressed. Similarly, the collapse of nineteenth-century colonial empires might have been lamented in some parts of the world but celebrated in others. This phenomenon where some constituencies suffer from collapse while others benefit has guided civilizational history. Similarly, within evolutionary biology, a parallel dynamic of collapse and rise has determined the path dependency of life on Earth through cycles of species mass extinction and emergence (Richter 2015). For example, perhaps the most dramatic collapse of all, caused by an asteroid 65 million years ago, was certainly a disaster for the dinosaurs, but it provided an ecological opening for mammals.[2]

Another perspective on collapse can be gained by analyzing collapse—and the systemic transformations that follow—more objectively and descriptively as ecological phenomena with niches disappearing and appearing. In ecological systems, for example, "collapse" or "release" is a critical phase of cyclical regeneration, which allows for new reorganization as different feedbacks and competition within the system allow for new systemic characteristics to emerge with regrowth (Gunderson and Holling 2002). While a forest fire is devastating for the *status quo ante*, it creates opportunity for a new cycle of growth, making sunlight and nutrients available for the smaller organisms that seed the early phase of ecosystem cyclicality (Burkhard, Fath, and Müller 2011).

1.5 Identifying the Causes of Collapse

Given the intractable complexity of many historical civilizational systems, it is often difficult to reach consensus on the causes of various collapses. Historian Alexander Demandt famously counted 210 different explanations given for the collapse of the Roman Empire (1984). Others argue that the Roman Empire never truly collapsed but instead fragmented and slowly faded away (Brown 1978).[3] An influential explanation for the cause of collapse is Tainter's theory on diminishing returns on complexity, which argues that civilizations begin to fall once the benefits of their societal complexity are outweighed by the costs (Tainter 1988). More recently, environmental change has become a frequent explanation for the collapse of certain complex societies (Middleton 2017). As with any tragic denouement, it may be impossible to string together the various episodes, mistakes, and challenges that might have led to the loss of *asabiyyah*. Each observer might choose a different critical moment, decision, or causal variable that precipitated a downfall.[4]

Generally, we can distinguish between three broad categories of explanations for collapse: Purely exogenous, purely endogenous, and a combination of both exogenous and endogenous. Narratives of purely exogenous causality describe when a shock from outside a system is entirely responsible for its downfall. Volcanic eruptions, earthquakes, and sudden climate shifts have been devastating in human history and are often associated with collapse (Bostrom and Cirkovic 2008; Ord 2020). Similarly, much of history is the story of human invasion, conquest, and brutality; each of these would be viewed as an exogenous cause by the civilizations conquered. For example, conquest and colonization by those like Alexander the Great, Genghis Khan, or nations of Western Europe often meant the collapse of long-established civilizations in those conquered lands.

By contrast, narratives of collapse that focus entirely on endogenous causes posit that some societal failures would happen regardless of outside forces or pressures. Like Gibbon's view on Rome, whose "stupendous fabric yielded to the pressure of its own weight," some societies have internal characteristics, which make them vulnerable to failure (1788). Viewing these societies as complex adaptive systems, we can see that these endogenous vulnerabilities are products of how the society is organized, governed, and complexly integrated. As a civilization advances in its growth phase, the structure and dynamics of critical underlying systems—economic production and trade, food and water, communications, and travel, among others—evolve into CAS as well. These CAS are interconnected and interdependent, forming systems-of-systems that weave this weighty fabric and can experience failure absent any precipitating exogenous shock. The most relevant causes of collapse may not be the specific factors that initiate the process, but rather the structure that allows perturbation and contagion to amplify through the system as in a chemical reaction.

Thus, collapse may not be precipitated by the failure of any single component, but instead by the unexpected dynamic interactions of countless nodes in a complex network. Instead of individual causes, we might better focus on the systemic mechanisms that escalate local challenges into existential crises that lead to collapse.

Endogenous failures can originate from impracticalities of systemic scale and complexity or can have sociological or political origins. Systems can depend too much on a tightly knit and complex base, which cannot endure forever, or the society can lose the political authority or social cohesion required for its function. Other human elements that can generate endogenous fragilities include corruption, loss of legitimacy or trust, unsustainable inequality, shortsightedness driven by hyperbolic discounting, overuse of resources, misplaced faith in the reliability of advanced technologies, and an overemphasis on efficiency. Vulnerabilities can appear when a sclerotic bureaucracy and corrupt elite fail to properly maintain critical systems. Similarly, the inability of political authority to guarantee safety and security can lead to societal fragmentation, resulting in a loss of economies of scale—if not a complete breakdown of systems. Tainter's theory of decreasing returns on complexity is a prominent explanation for increasing endogenous fragility (1988). In other writing on endogenous elements of collapse, Peter Turchin identifies "principal components" of societal organization and dynamics that may explain crises and outcomes (2016).

The third narrative of collapse puts the culpability for failure on some combination of both exogenous and endogenous elements. Here, an exogenous shock—environmental, financial, military, epidemiological, et cetera—stresses a society, its structures, and its systems beyond the breaking point. Exogenous explanations alone, while salient and dramatic, can neglect the importance of internal systemic characteristics that enabled, accelerated, or perpetuated the collapse. Depending on the internal systemic structure, an external shock, which might be easily survivable by one system, could be a death sentence for another. Thus, of greater relevance than the exogenous shock itself are the endogenous differences between the two systems that explain these disparate results. In this way, viewing collapse as simply the consequence of unlucky exogenous shocks makes for an unsatisfying account (Bailey 2011). In our highly engineered modern complex systems, these internal vulnerabilities are even more determinative to system survival. As these vulnerabilities are within our agency to influence, they are particularly worthy of our study. It may not be possible to avoid exogenous shocks from earthquakes, asteroids, droughts, or plagues, but with foresight and understanding, societal systems can be designed with greater resilience to withstand these shocks.

1.6 Systemic Mechanisms of Collapse

Recognizing that endogenous systemic characteristics are critical to many explanations of collapse, we now turn toward systems theory and complexity science to identify mechanisms that can propagate systemic—and therefore societal—fragmentation and failure. Just as all ecological and human-made systems share components and behaviors that allow for growth or development (Siskin 2016; Kauffman 2013), societies throughout history share common systemic structures that enabled their evolution. As a society develops, however, the systemic properties that were critical to its growth could provide the pathways for its rapid unraveling. Here, we explore some of these critical systemic mechanisms of collapse.

1.6.1 Tipping Points

Every complex social system contains thresholds beyond which social cohesion falls apart. These tipping points are the levels of tolerance within a system that, when exceeded, mark the rapid transition to a new state or equilibrium. For societies, this could be the moment when longstanding behaviors of individuals, groups, or the society as a whole suddenly have more drastic consequences than expected. This is a result of inertia, force, stress, or momentum building up that leads to a phase change, causing the system to transition into a different equilibrium structure or dynamics. Tipping points can serve as gateways of opportunity or pathways to failure (Milkoreit et al. 2018). Examples of tipping points with negative consequences include the proverbial final straw breaking a camel's back or a rubber band stretched beyond its breaking point: After a minor additional stress, it loses its functionality. An example of a tipping point that leads to greater systemic resilience is that of herd immunity—after a population reaches a certain threshold of immunity, the vectors of transmission become vanishingly small, effectively reducing the probability of further outbreak. The key in all instances is the persistence or irreversibility of the transformation (Dakos et al. 2019; Bentley et al. 2014).

It may well be impossible to predict a tipping point, or even identify it *post hoc*, because it may be contextual—only becoming critical under certain circumstances. The most frequent examples of tipping points may be found at the start of wars where antagonism, fears, and perceived injustices lead to the creation of a spiral into violence. In Thucydides' account of the negotiations between Sparta and Athens, the debate in Corinth may be seen as the tipping point leading to the resolution of the Thucydides Trap (Robinson 2017). Or consider a doomsday weapon *à la Dr. Strangelove*, established precisely as a public "red line," or "line in the sand," the crossing of which begins a chain reaction that cannot be stopped. Caesar's crossing of the Rubicon can be regarded as one such tipping point. Again, the central lesson from tipping points is that an apparently small perturbation can set off a series of events that leads to irreversible change, or in the worst scenario, collapse.

1.6.2 Feedback Loops

Stable social systems are fundamentally cooperative and reciprocal, with systemic dynamics that reinforce (or undermine) this social cohesion through feedback loops. These are structures that use the measure of output from a process to determine the subsequent input back into the beginning of the cycle (Martin 1997). Feedback loops are critical to the nature and behavior of a system and can determine how the system responds to—and manages— shocks. *Positive* feedback loops, for example, magnify systemic perturbations, while *negative* feedbacks work to dampen the impact of these shocks, leading to greater stability in the system (Miller and Page 2007, 50–52; Ashby 1956, 53–54; B. Walker and Salt 2006, 164). These feedback effects can have significant systemic consequences as positive loops drive change away from the current equilibrium toward new steady or stable states, while negative loops work to resist that change and reinforce the current steady state.

When studying instances of historical collapse, it may be important to identify feedback loops, with either positive feedback loops causing a stable society to spiral into disorder, or negative feedback loops enabling a social system to absorb otherwise catastrophic shocks (Turchin 2005).

Many incentive systems are forms of feedback loops: As a result of a certain level of performance, rewards or punishments are determined for the next round, in a game theoretic framework (Yang, Neal, and Abdollahian 2017). The human nervous system (Lessard 2009) is an example of a feedback loop where we are encouraged or discouraged from certain forms of behavior by signals of pleasure or pain. An important characteristic of feedback loops is the time lag that dictates the speed of the loop. In the case of the nervous system, the lag is relatively short, but in large and complex human or ecological systems, the lag can take up to years, generations, or even longer.

Within social systems, social norms and institutionalized rules are forms of feedback loops, as they determine responses to individual actions. Certain feedback loops are critical to establishing stable equilibria. For example, in complex economic systems and markets, the relationship between supply, demand, and price may be seen as a constantly iterative loop of inputs and outputs, feeding back on each other to arrive at an equilibrium price and quantity. Similarly, in the struggle against chaos and entropy, an equilibrium of peace and prosperity in a civilization can be maintained through feedback loops driven by social norms.

1.6.3 Contagions

The COVID-19 pandemic made the phenomenon of contagion spreading through networks far too familiar, and highlighted the inexorable systemic risk inherent in globalization (Smil 2019). From a network science perspective, contagion involves the passing of objects, effects, or characteristics from one node to another, transmitted through contact or a systemic connection: A person may infect a group by coughing, someone shouting "Fire!" may lead to the spread of alarm or panic, or the failure of one part of a system may lead to malfunction elsewhere or even of the whole. Similar to tipping points and feedback loops, contagion might also be considered beneficial if the result is considered valuable. The "viral" diffusion of a new invention or technology can be an example of a beneficial contagion. The replication and propagation of information through memetics is an example of how ideas can spread within and between societies through the process of diffusion and contagion (Lynch 1996). While contagion of concepts and inventions can benefit society, risk of collapse can increase with the spread of ideas that undermine social order and social cohesion. In highly connected societies, the mechanism of contagion allows shocks that would otherwise be isolated to one sector or region to propagate and potentially lead to collapse.

1.6.4 Cascades

A cascade—or uncontrollable domino effect—might be best thought of as a combination of tipping points and contagion. When a node reaches a tipping point and fails, that failure can be transmitted to neighboring nodes through the links or connections in the system. This can trigger second-order failures, which can in-turn precipitate a sequence of breakdowns, causing an uncontrollable chain reaction, or cascade. As the regular dynamics of the system spiral out of control, the structure of a highly connected system can allow the cascade to increase exponentially in both speed and magnitude. In this way, complex systems can contain within them leverage that increases the magnitude of the failure at each step in the cascade (Rocha et al. 2018, Watts 2002, Buldyrev et al. 2010).

Perhaps the best-known cascading failures in our modern systems are within highly coupled energy infrastructures. Widespread blackouts, for example, often involve a domino effect of overloaded electrical infrastructure as transformers and transmission lines begin to fail (Korkali et al. 2017). In political systems, the assassination of Franz Ferdinand in 1914 is perhaps the most infamous instance in modern history of a cascading failure. Interdependent nations tightly coupled through alliances designed to increase geopolitical systemic resilience created pathways and dynamics for a cataclysmic cascading failure. One domino fell and ultimately led to a world-transforming global conflict (Clark 2014).

1.6.5 Synchronous Failures

While complex systems may be designed to survive individual localized failures, a certain number of such failures occurring simultaneously could overwhelm any system. Such a "perfect storm" of events is considered a synchronous failure. Probability theory dictates that random events will eventually occur simultaneously, or at least in close proximity of time or location. This clustering of failures, or the simultaneous and synergistic interaction of several failures, may result in a challenge unimagined by designers, and for which the system is not prepared (Homer-Dixon et al. 2015).

Charles Perrow's concept of a "normal accident" illustrates how such an apparently innocuous confluence of events can lead to catastrophe (Perrow

1984). In tightly coupled and complex systems, two apparently unrelated events can lead to a disastrous outcome. Natural disasters are particularly dangerous because they often precipitate the simultaneous failure of various social systems. The response to the failure of one part of a system might then lead to a strain in another part that leads to systemic breakdown.

Synchronous failures are particularly threatening because no individual or society can prepare for the infinite number of disastrous combinations and consequences (West 2017). We might be able to create mechanisms to deal with individual problems, but in the face of multiple failures, resources may be taxed beyond their limits. In the case of complex systems, the interaction of failures may lead to consequences not expected from each failure in isolation. Invaded societies weakened by novel pathogens found themselves fighting two battles instead of one. While either invasion or pandemic may have been manageable shocks on their own, the confluence of both could serve as a *coup de grâce*.

1.6.6 Cycles

The notion of civilizational or biological cycles is central to behavioral and natural sciences. The organic cycle of growth and decay is one that dominates our planet (Walker, Packard, and Cody 2017). Death and decomposition make new biological life possible, and within the "adaptive cycle," a systemic collapse can provide opportunity for a new type of ecosystem to take root (Gunderson and Holling 2002). For over a half-century, economic policy has been guided by attempts to regulate the cyclical nature of inflation and unemployment, booms, and busts. The central notion of Keynesianism is to avoid the deep troughs of the cycle through monetary and fiscal intervention (Skidelsky 2018). Many civilizations have experienced secular cycles of expansion, stagflation, crisis, and depression (Turchin and Nefedov 2009). Ecological systems experience oscillating cycles of population growth and decline based on factors such as predator–prey dynamics (Volterra 1928). Similarly, climate systems experience natural cycles through the activity of sunspots and astronomical interactions, resulting in temperature fluctuations and drought. These cycles in environmental systems can be catastrophic for civilizations that are unexpectedly deprived of food or water (Parker 2013).

Many societies, such as the Mexica, organized their lives in accordance with a calendar of rise and decline (Boone 2007). Cultures and religions have embraced the notion of reincarnation reflecting their faith in the inevitability of the cycle of life, death, and rebirth. Since at least the Enlightenment—or even the Renaissance—European and associated societies have sought to escape the inevitability of cyclicality and have constructed the expectation of linear progress. While this aspirational desire to transcend cyclicality may facilitate economic and social dynamism (Sweezy 1943), it also makes cyclical decline unexpected and threatening.

Cyclicality implies a natural rise and inevitable fall; understanding this universality should inspire a humility that every civilization could—at any moment—be at its apex. Much like Shelley's *Ozymandias*, even the mightiest civilizations that expected to prosper eternally ultimately transformed, declined, or collapsed (Shelley 1818).

1.7 Robustness and Resilience

The limits of systems will inevitably be tested through exogenous shocks, endogenous characteristics, and emergent properties that threaten failure. The concepts of robustness and resilience have migrated from engineering and ecology into all disciplines in which systems are studied. These concepts describe how vulnerabilities caused by the aforementioned systemic mechanisms can be prevented, and systemic fragilities can be mitigated (Evans and Reid 2013; Levin and Lubchenco 2008). Robustness often refers to the capacity of any system—a human body, a city, a tropical forest, or even a civilization—to withstand shocks and disruptions (Walker and Cooper 2011). Resilience often describes the ability of a system to be flexible and adaptable in order to survive and recover after a brief failure.[5] For example, a robust city could have levees to keep floodwaters at bay, while a resilient one would have infrastructure in place to quickly rebuild after a disaster. A robustness approach to regulation might focus on preventing failures in our logistical, economic, infrastructural, or epidemiological systems, while a resilience approach might design triage protocols, contingencies, and recovery plans to mitigate the damage and accelerate the return to normal operation.

In the design or engineering of systems, robustness and resilience are often in tension and represent a series of tradeoffs: While it is best to be both strong *and* adaptable, physical realities often force the prioritization of one over the other. Building each requires significant resources, and both cannot be maximized. The ideal systemic design or evolution will weigh, balance, and combine these two qualities to achieve a "golden mean" depending on preferences and contexts. It is in these tradeoffs and balances that we find challenging policy dilemmas.

Systemic resilience and robustness are "public goods" that are eroded by a lack of fiduciary planning and maintenance. This erosion leads to fragilities in the system, making collapse through endogenous mechanisms more likely. One short-sighted behavior creating systemic fragility is the focus on ever-increasing efficiency, where cost savings and just-in-time management have replaced redundancy, slack, and reserves. Such overemphasis on efficiency creates greater systemic interdependence of nodes in a network through increased reliance on suppliers, making modern systems more fragile and susceptible to collapse. Other oversights of fiduciary planning can give rise to negative externalities, such as in the "tragedy of the commons" where short-run self-interest—rather than coordination and cooperation—can lead to systemic failure (Hardin 1968).

Another example of short-term optimization that threatens robustness and resilience occurs when decision-makers within systems focus primarily on their relationships with those to whom they are immediately connected, neglecting to consider the inherent endogenous systemic risks beyond the control of any one participant. An example from the financial system occurs when each participant verifies the credit-worthiness of just their own trading partners and counterparties, ignoring the reality that other more distant members of the network could fail, causing an unavoidable chain reaction of contagion—such as a bank run—to propagate through the system (Gorton and Metrick 2012).

Governance strategies should include an awareness of the mechanisms of collapse and the managerial failures that threaten the viability of our modern systems. Though they come at the cost of efficiency, systemic features like reserves, redundancies, contingencies, and diversification can bolster resilience and robustness, and reduce over-dependence on heavily trafficked choke points or "too big to fail" trading partners. Similarly, design elements that act like firewalls or circuit breakers within a system can counteract system dynamics that would otherwise lead to collapse. Resilience and robustness can be prioritized through regulations and standards that incentivize more prudent—if less efficient—systemic organization.

1.8 Conclusion

Globalization at an ever-increasing scale and level of complexity is a modern tale of hubris. Building increasingly technologically advanced, interconnected, and interdependent systems without an awareness of the risky mechanisms inherent in their design will inexorably lead to endogenous failures and potential collapse. These risks of globalization have brought us to our study of systemic risk, and to our interest in learning insights about systemic collapse from history.

At first glance, one may find few similarities between ancient civilizations and our modern globalized present. When we see these civilizations as complex adaptive systems, however, we can begin to recognize patterns, structures, and dynamics that have remained consistent through the centuries. Mechanisms like tipping points, feedback loops, contagions, cascades, synchronous failures, and cycles that can be responsible for systemic collapse are fundamental characteristics of any complex adaptive system, and can therefore serve as a useful common denominator from which to examine collapses through the ages. We offer this systemic framework for the study of historical collapse with the belief that these common mechanisms will help illuminate and expose relevant vulnerabilities in historical systems. In the end, our hope is that we may learn from past societies and civilizations and allow our modern systems to benefit from lessons of systemic failure that historians may share with us. As the weight of our modern civilizational fabric grows, and as the strains increase, we believe these insights could inform how we see our own systemic vulnerabilities and help to build a more robust and resilient future.

Notes

This chapter is a continuation in our study of historical systemic collapse, with earlier analysis published in Izdebski, Haldon, and Filipkowski (2022: 59–74).

1 Guy Middleton hints at this debate in his book *Understanding Collapse: Ancient History and Modern Myths*, saying "the Mycenaean collapse was fairly rapid, taking place probably over a few decades, whereas the Maya collapse took place over as much as three centuries, which has led to some wondering why it is termed a collapse at all" (Middleton 2017, 342)

2 Among some scholars, there remains some discomfort with the asteroid theory, with others focusing on the volcanic activity in the Deccan Plateau (Keller, Sahni, and Bajpai 2009).

3 A similar argument has flared concerning the Meghalayan Age beginning around 2200 BC with disputes about the extent of global civilizational collapse (Middleton 2018).

4 For an excellent overview of the literature on causes of collapse, see Haldon et al. 2020.

5 As a note on usage, the terms robustness and resilience are often defined differently in different fields, such as ecology and engineering. While engineering often separates robustness and resilience into two distinct concepts, scholars within ecology often combine the meanings of both robustness and resilience into the term "resilience" (Bak 1996; West 2017; Barabási 2016; Holme 2019; Broido and Clauset 2019). In this chapter, we adopt the engineering perspective in our analysis here to reflect the human agency involved in constructing elements of robustness and resilience in human-made systems upon which civilizations rely.

References

Altman, Steven A. 2020. Will Covid-19 Have a Lasting Impact on Globalization? *Harvard Business Review*, May 20, 2020.

Ashby, W. Ross. 1961. *An Introduction to Cybernetics*. First edition. London: Chapman & Hall, Ltd.

Bailey, Mark. 2011. Risk and Natural Catastrophes: The Long View. In *Risk*, edited by Layla Skinns, Michael Scott, and Tony Cox, 131–158. New York: Cambridge University Press.

Bak, Per. 1996. *How Nature Works: The Science of Self-Organized Criticality*. First edition. New York: Springer-Copernicus.

Barabási, Albert-László. 2002. *Linked: The New Science of Networks Science of Networks*. First edition. Cambridge, MA: Perseus Books Group.

———. 2016. *Network Science*. First edition. Cambridge: Cambridge University Press.

Bentley, R. A., Eleanor J. Maddison, P. H. Ranner, John Bissell, Camila C. S. Caiado, Pojanath Bhatanacharoen, Timothy Clark, et al. 2014. Social Tipping Points and Earth Systems Dynamics. *Frontiers in Environmental Science* 2: 35.

Birley, A. R. 2000. Hadrian to the Antonines. In *The Cambridge Ancient History, Volume 11: The High Empire, A.D. 70–192*, edited by Alan K. Bowman, Dominic Rathbone, and Peter Garnsey, Second edition, 11: 132–94. The Cambridge Ancient History. Cambridge: Cambridge University Press.

Boone, Elizabeth Hill. 2007. *Cycles of Time and Meaning in the Mexican Books of Fate.* Illustrated edition. Austin, TX: University of Texas Press.

Bostrom, Nick, and Milan M. Ćirković, eds. 2008. *Global Catastrophic Risks.* First edition. Oxford: Oxford University Press.

Brauer, Daniel. 2018. Theory and Practice of Historical Writing in Times of Globalization. In *Philosophy of Globalization,* edited by Concha Roldán, Daniel Brauer, and Johannes Rohbeck, 397–408. Boston, MA: Walter de Gruyter.

Brown, Peter. 1978. *The Making of Late Antiquity.* First edition. Cambridge, MA: Harvard University Press.

Buldyrev, Sergey V., Roni Parshani, Gerald Paul, H. Eugene Stanley, and Shlomo Havlin. 2010. Catastrophic Cascade of Failures in Interdependent Networks. *Nature* 464(7291): 1025–8.

Burkhard, Benjamin, Brian D. Fath, and Felix Müller. 2011. Adapting the Adaptive Cycle: Hypotheses on the Development of Ecosystem Properties and Services. *Ecological Modelling* 222(16): 2878–90.

Cambridge Centre for Risk Studies. 2019. *Cambridge Global Risk Index 2019: Executive Summary.* Cambridge: Cambridge Centre for Risk Studies.

Centeno, Miguel A., Manish Nag, Thayer S. Patterson, Andrew Shaver, and A. Jason Windawi. 2015. The Emergence of Global Systemic Risk. *Annual Review of Sociology* 41(1): 65–85.

Centeno, Miguel, Peter Callahan, and Thayer Patterson. 2015. *Systemic Risk in Global Agriculture: Conference Report.* Princeton, NJ: Princeton PIIRS Global Systemic Risk & Columbia Agriculture and Food Security Center.

Clark, Christopher. 2013. *The Sleepwalkers: How Europe Went to War in 1914.* First edition. New York: Harper.

Coggan, Philip. 2020. *More: The 10,000-Year Rise of the World Economy.* First edition. London: Economist Books.

Crucitti, Paolo, Vito Latora, and Massimo Marchiori. 2004. Model for Cascading Failures in Complex Networks. *Physical Review: Part E* 69(4): 045104.

Dakos, Vasilis, Blake Matthews, Andrew P. Hendry, Jonathan Levine, Nicolas Loeuille, Jon Norberg, Patrik Nosil, Marten Scheffer, and Luc De Meester. 2019. Ecosystem Tipping Points in an Evolving World. *Nature Ecology and Evolution* 3(3): 355–62.

Danku, Zsuzsa, Matjaž Perc, and Attila Szolnoki. 2019. Knowing the Past Improves Cooperation in the Future. *Scientific Reports* 9(1): 262.

Demandt, Alexander. 1984. *Der Fall Roms: Die Auflösung des Römischen Reiches Im Urteil der Nachwelt (The Fall of Rome).* First edition. Munich: C.H. Beck.

Epstein, Joshua M. 2009. Modelling to Contain Pandemics. *Nature* 460(7256): 687.

Evans, Bradley, and Julian Reid. 2013. Dangerously Exposed: The Life and Death of the Resilient Subject. *Resilience: International Policies, Practices and Discourses* 1(2): 83–98.

Ferguson, Niall. 2006. *The War of the World: History's Age of Hatred.* First edition. London: Penguin.

Foreman-Peck, James. 2007. European Historical Economics and Globalisation. *Journal of Philosophical Economics* 1(1): 23–53.

Gibbon, Edward. 1788. *The Decline and Fall of the Roman Empire.* London: A. Strahan and T. Cadell.

Gleick, James. 2011. *The Information: A History, a Theory, a Flood.* First edition. New York: Pantheon.

Gorton, Gary B., and Andrew Metrick. 2012. Securitized Banking and the Run on Repo. *Journal of Financial Economics* 104(3): 425–51.

Greber, Jacob. 2022. Does Ukraine Crystallise the Reality That Globalisation Is Dead? *Australian Financial Review*, March 4, 2022, Section: Politics.

Gunderson, Lance H., and C. S. Holling, eds. 2002. *Panarchy: Understanding Transformations in Human and Natural Systems*. Washington, DC: Island Press.

Haldon, John, Arlen F. Chase, Warren Eastwood, Martín Medina-Elizalde, Adam Izdebski, Francis Ludlow, Guy Middleton, Lee Mordechai, Jason Nesbitt, and B. L. Turner. 2020. Demystifying Collapse: Climate, Environment, and Social Agency in Pre-modern Societies. *Millennium* 17(1): 1–33.

Hardin, Garrett. 1968. The Tragedy of the Commons. *Science* 162(3859): 1243–8.

Helbing, Dirk. 2009. Managing Complexity in Socio-economic Systems. *European Review* 17(2): 423–38.

Hernández-Lemus, Enrique, and Jesús Siqueiros-García. 2013. Information Theoretical Methods for Complex Network Structure Reconstruction. *Complex Adaptive Systems Modeling* 1(1): 1–22.

Holme, Petter. 2019. Rare and Everywhere: Perspectives on Scale-Free Networks. *Nature Communications* 10(1): 1016.

Holovatch, Yurij, Ralph Kenna, and Stefan Thurner. 2017. Complex Systems: Physics beyond Physics. *European Journal of Physics* 38(2): 023002.

Homer-Dixon, Thomas, Brian Walker, Reinette Biggs, Anne-Sophie Crépin, Carl Folke, Eric F. Lambin, Garry D. Peterson, et al. 2015. Synchronous Failure: The Emerging Causal Architecture of Global Crisis. *Ecology and Society* 20(3): 6.

Ibrahim, Sherwat E., Miguel A. Centeno, Thayer S. Patterson, and Peter W. Callahan. 2021. Resilience in Global Value Chains: A Systemic Risk Approach. *Global Perspectives* 2(1): 27658.

Izdebski, Adam, John Haldon, and Piotr Filipkowski. 2022. *Perspectives on Public Policy in Societal-Environmental Crises: What the Future Needs from History*. Cham, Switzerland: Springer.

Kannisto, Väinö, Jens Lauritsen, A. Roger Thatcher, and James W. Vaupel. 1994. Reductions in Mortality at Advanced Ages: Several Decades of Evidence from 27 Countries. *Population and Development Review* 20(4): 793–810.

Kauffman, Stuart A. 1993. *The Origins of Order: Self-Organization and Selection in Evolution*. First edition. New York: Oxford University Press.

———. 2013. Evolution beyond Newton, Darwin, and Entailing Law: The Origin of Complexity in the Evolving Biosphere. In *Complexity and the Arrow of Time*, edited by Charles H. Lineweaver, Paul C. W. Davies, and Michael Ruse, 1–24. Cambridge: Cambridge University Press.

Keller, G., A. Sahni, and S. Bajpai. 2009. Deccan Volcanism, the KT Mass Extinction and Dinosaurs. *Journal of Biosciences* 34(5): 709–28.

Kelly, Walt. 1972. *Pogo: We Have Met the Enemy and He Is Us*. First edition. New York: Simon & Schuster.

Korkali, Mert, Jason G. Veneman, Brian F. Tivnan, James P. Bagrow, and Paul D. H. Hines. 2017. Reducing Cascading Failure Risk by Increasing Infrastructure Network Interdependence. *Scientific Reports* 7(1): 44499.

Ledwoch, Anna, Alexandra Brintrup, Jörn Mehnen, and Ashutosh Tiwari. 2018. Systemic Risk Assessment in Complex Supply Networks. *IEEE Systems Journal* 12(2): 1826–37.

Lessard, Charles S. 2009. *Basic Feedback Controls in Biomedicine*. First edition. San Rafael, CA: Morgan and Claypool Publishers.

Levin, Simon A., and Jane Lubchenco. 2008. Resilience, Robustness, and Marine Ecosystem-Based Management. *BioScience* 58(1): 27–32.

Lynch, Aaron. 1996. *Thought Contagion: How Belief Spreads Through Society – The New Science of Memes*. New York: Basic Books.

Mango, Cyril, ed. 2002. *The Oxford History of Byzantium*. New York: Oxford University Press.

Manheim, David. 2020. The Fragile World Hypothesis: Complexity, Fragility, and Systemic Existential Risk. *Futures* 122: 102570.

Martin, Leslie A. 1997. *An Introduction to Feedback*. White Paper: D-4691. Cambridge, MA: Massachusetts Institute of Technology.

Meyer, Patrick, and Gregory Ponthiere. 2020. Human Lifetime Entropy in a Historical Perspective (1750–2014). *Cliometrica* 14(1): 129–67.

Middleton, Guy D. 2013. That Old Devil Called Collapse. *E-International Relations* (blog). February 6, 2013.

———. 2017. *Understanding Collapse: Ancient History and Modern Myths*. New York: Cambridge University Press.

———. 2018. Bang or Whimper? *Science* 361(6408): 1204–5.

Milkoreit, Manjana, Jennifer Hodbod, Jacopo Baggio, Karina Benessaiah, Rafael Calderón-Contreras, Jonathan F. Donges, Jean Denis Mathias, Juan Carlos Rocha, Michael Schoon, and Saskia E. Werners. 2018. Defining Tipping Points for Social-Ecological Systems Scholarship: An Interdisciplinary Literature Review. *Environmental Research Letters* 13(3): 033005.

Miller, John H., and Scott Page. 2007. *Complex Adaptive Systems: An Introduction to Computational Models of Social Life*. Princeton, NJ: Princeton University Press.

Nicoll, Kathleen, and Andrea Zerboni. 2020. Is the Past Key to the Present? Observations of Cultural Continuity and Resilience Reconstructed from Geoarchaeological Records. *Quaternary International*, ArchaeoLife and Environment, 545: 119–27.

Nuzzo, Jennifer B., Lucia Mullen, Michael Snyder, Anita Cicero, and Thomas V. Inglesby. 2019. *Preparedness for a High-Impact Respiratory Pathogen Pandemic*. Baltimore: The Johns Hopkins Center for Health Security.

Nyström, Magnus, J.-B. Jouffray, Albert V. Norström, Beatrice Crona, Peter Søgaard Jørgensen, Stephen R. Carpenter, Örjan Bodin, Victor Galaz, and Carl Folke. 2019. Anatomy and Resilience of the Global Production Ecosystem. *Nature* 575(7781): 98–108.

Oeppen, Jim, and James W. Vaupel. 2002. Broken Limits to Life Expectancy. *Science* 296(5570): 1029–31.

Ord, Toby. 2020. *The Precipice: Existential Risk and the Future of Humanity*. Hachette Books.

Oughton, Edward, Will Usher, Peter Tyler, and Jim W. Hall. 2018. Infrastructure as a Complex Adaptive System. *Complexity* 2018: 3427826.

Parker, Geoffrey. 2013. *Global Crisis: War, Climate Change and Catastrophe in the Seventeenth Century*. New Haven, CT: Yale University Press.

Pastor-Satorras, Romualdo, Claudio Castellano, Piet Van Mieghem, and Alessandro Vespignani. 2015. Epidemic Processes in Complex Networks. *Reviews of Modern Physics* 87(3): 925–79.

Perrow, Charles. 1984. *Normal Accidents: Living with High-Risk Technologies*. New York: Basic Books.

Renfrew, Colin. 1973. *Explanation of Culture Change: Models in Prehistory*. Pittsburgh, PA: University of Pittsburgh Press.

Richter, Vivian. 2015. The Big Five Mass Extinctions: Mass Extinctions Where More Than 75% of the Species Disappear. *COSMOS*, July 6, 2015.

Roberts, Adam. 2020. *It's the End of the World: But What Are We Really Afraid of?* London: Elliott & Thompson.

Robinson, Eric W. 2017. Thucydides on the Causes and Outbreak of the Peloponnesian War. In *The Oxford Handbook of Thucydides*, edited by Ryan K. Balot, Sara Forsdyke, and Edith Foster. New York: Oxford University Press.

Rocha, Juan C., Garry Peterson, Örjan Bodin, and Simon Levin. 2018. Cascading Regime Shifts within and across Scales. *Science* 362(6421): 1379–83.

Roser, Max, Esteban Ortiz-Ospina, and Hannah Ritchie. 2013. Life Expectancy. *Our World in Data*, May 23, 2013.

Shelley, Percy Bysshe. 1818. *Ozymandias. The Examiner*, London. January 11, 1818.

Siskin, Clifford. 2016. *System: The Shaping of Modern Knowledge*. First edition. Cambridge, MA: The MIT Press.

Skidelsky, Robert. 2018. *Money and Government: The Past and Future of Economics*. New Haven, CT: Yale University Press.

Smil, Vaclav. 2019. *Growth: From Microorganisms to Megacities*. First edition. Cambridge, MA: The MIT Press.

Sweezy, Paul M. 1943. Professor Schumpeter's Theory of Innovation. *The Review of Economics and Statistics* 25(1): 93–6.

Tainter, Joseph A. 1988. *The Collapse of Complex Societies*. First edition. Cambridge: Cambridge University Press.

———. 2006. Social Complexity and Sustainability. *Ecological Complexity* 3(2): 91–103.

Taleb, Nassim Nicholas. 2007. *The Black Swan: The Impact of the Highly Improbable*. Annotated edition. New York: Random House.

———. 2012. *Antifragile: Things That Gain from Disorder*. First edition. Random House.

Turchin, Peter. 2005. Dynamical Feedbacks between Population Growth and Sociopolitical Instability in Agrarian States. *Structure and Dynamics* 1(1).

———. 2016. *Ages of Discord: A Structural-Demographic Analysis of American History*. Chaplin, CT: Beresta Books.

Turchin, Peter, and Sergey A. Nefedov. 2009. *Secular Cycles*. Princeton, NJ: Princeton University Press.

van Zanden, Jan Luiten, Joerg Baten, Marco Mira d'Ercole, Auke Rijpma, Conal Smith, and Marcel Timmer, eds. 2014. *How Was Life?: Global Well-Being since 1820*. Paris: Organisation for Economic Co-operation & Development Publishing.

Vespignani, Alessandro. 2010. The Fragility of Interdependency. *Nature* 464(7291): 984–5.

Volterra, Vito. 1928. Variations and Fluctuations of the Number of Individuals in Animal Species Living Together. *ICES Journal of Marine Science* 3(1): 3–51.

Walker, Brian, and David Salt. 2006. *Resilience Thinking: Sustaining Ecosystems and People in a Changing World*. Washington, DC: Island Press.

Walker, Jeremy, and Melinda Cooper. 2011. Genealogies of Resilience: From Systems Ecology to the Political Economy of Crisis Adaptation. *Security Dialogue* 42(2): 143–60.

Walker, Sara I., N. Packard, and G. D. Cody. 2017. Re-conceptualizing the Origins of Life. *Philosophical Transactions of the Royal Society, Series A: Mathematical, Physical and Engineering Sciences* 375(2109): 20160337.

Watts, Duncan J. 2002. A Simple Model of Global Cascades on Random Networks. *Proceedings of the National Academy of Sciences of the United States of America* 99(9): 5766–71.

West, Geoffrey. 2017. *Scale: The Universal Laws of Growth, Innovation, Sustainability, and the Pace of Life in Organisms, Cities, Economies, and Companies.* First edition. New York: Penguin Press.

Wildavsky, Aaron, and Karl Dake. 1990. Theories of Risk Perception: Who Fears What and Why? *Dædalus* 119(4): 41–60.

Yang, Zining, Neal Patrick deWerk, and Mark Abdollahian. 2017. When Feedback Loops Collide: A Complex Adaptive Systems Approach to Modeling Human and Nature Dynamics. In *Advances in Applied Digital Human Modeling and Simulation*, edited by Vincent G. Duffy, 317–27. Cham, Switzerland: Springer.

Yoffee, Norman. 2005. *Myths of the Archaic State: Evolution of the Earliest Cities, States, and Civilizations.* New York: Cambridge University Press.

Yoffee, Norman, and George L. Cowgill, eds. 1988. *The Collapse of Ancient States and Civilizations.* First edition. Tucson: University of Arizona Press.

2 How Scholars Explain Collapse

Joseph A. Tainter

2.1 Collapse Explanations in Historical Perspective

Archaeology and history have long been uncertain about how to understand collapses. These disciplines have predominantly had a progressivist narrative. Archaeologists and historians are socialized members of complex societies. We have been raised in the ideology of modern industrial societies, which emphasizes progress. So we write about how our ancestors tamed fire, developed agriculture, invented the wheel and writing, established metallurgy and cities, and created states all the while improving human life. Much of this narrative resembles what anthropologists term ancestor myths. Ancestor myths validate a contemporary social order by presenting it as a natural, and sometimes heroic, progression from a simpler and less desirable past to the idealized way that we live today. Within this narrative, collapses and dark ages have presented troubling contradictions to the story of humanity's continual progress. If the arc of history leads to inexorable improvement of the human condition, how could that trajectory ever be interrupted? Equally troubling, if collapses happened in the past, could one happen again?

It is difficult to pinpoint when collapse studies began. Much depends on how one defines the term. It is common to look to Edward Gibbon's *The Decline and Fall of the Roman Empire* (1776–1788) as the progenitor of modern collapse literature. Gibbon considered the ends of both the Western and Eastern Roman empires. He thereby subsumed two different historical processes—loss of political unity and overall simplification in the West versus replacement of one empire with another in the East—under the single term "decline and fall." This problem of terminology gives an early hint of why collapse has been so difficult to explain. Another hint is given by what may be Gibbon's greatest insight: The wonder is not that Rome fell, he repeatedly wrote, but that it lasted so long. Such an institution, Gibbon thought, was intrinsically impermanent.

Other authors in Gibbon's era addressed decline and fall. C. F. Volney ascribed collapse to greed and class conflict. As a result of greed and class conflict, he wrote:

> a holy indolence spread over the political world; the fields were deserted, empires depopulated, monuments neglected and deserts multiplied;

DOI: 10.4324/9781003331384-4

ignorance, superstition and fanaticism combining their operations, overwhelmed the earth with devastation and ruin.

(Volney 1793: 51)

Charles-Louis Montesquieu advanced an argument based on morality: Roman
power derived from Roman virtue, which declined when the Romans
advanced beyond Italy (1968).

The great Arab historian Ibn Khaldun, in the fourteenth century, continued the ancient tradition of considering history to be cyclical (1958 [original
1377–1381]). Dynasties, he thought, have a natural life span like individuals.
In the course of dynastic succession, rulers become ever more addicted to
luxuries and security. Taxes are raised to pay for these. Whereas at the beginning of a dynasty large revenues are received from small assessments, at the
end of a dynasty this situation is reversed. When taxes are low, the population
is more productive and the tax yield is greater. Yet as the dynasty evolves,
increased spending on luxuries leads to higher taxes. Eventually taxes become
so burdensome that productivity first declines, and then is stifled. As more
taxes are enacted to counter this, the point is finally reached where the polity
is destroyed by desert nomads.

The greatest cyclical theorist was the Greek historian Polybius. In the second
century BC, he predicted the fall of the Roman Empire some 600 years before
it actually happened. Societies, to ancient historians like Polybius, develop like
the biological cycle through growth, maturity, senescence, and death. It was
thus no challenge to predict that Rome would eventually fall.

The biological analogy of societal evolution was common in the ancient
world. It appears in Plato's *Laws*, no doubt based on long-established thinking.
Although long in disrepute, cyclical theory has been resurrected recently by
the population biologist Peter Turchin (2003), who bases his approach on Ibn
Khaldun. C. S. Holling's Resilience Theory (e.g., 2001) is a nuanced update
to cyclical theory. In Resilience Theory, the basic model derives from forest
succession rather than from the growth and death of organisms.

Norman Yoffee (1988) has pointed to early Mesopotamian literature that
may be the earliest surviving ancestral explanation of collapse. In considering
the fall of Sargon of Akkad and of the Third Dynasty of Ur, the decline of
empires was ascribed by Mesopotamian writers to the impiousness of rulers,
and to marauding enemies sent by the gods as punishment. Cities flourish
under good kings but suffer under impious ones. This gives 3,000 years of
ancestry to writings about collapse and related processes.

Shortly later we find literature in China ascribing the problems of the
Western Chou dynasty (1122–771 BC) to a similar cause: the failure of rulers.
This is expressed in the poem *Shao-min*:

> Compassionate Heaven is arrayed in anger
> Heaven is indeed sending down rain,
> Afflicting us with famine,

So that the people are all wandering fugitives;
In the settled regions and on the border all is desolation.
Heaven sends down its web of crime;
Devouring insects weary and confuse men's minds,
Ignorant, oppressive, negligent,
Breeders of confusion, utterly perverse;
These are the men employed to tranquilize our country.
...
Oh! Alas!
Among the men of the present day,
Are there not still some with the old virtue?

(Hsu and Linduff 1988: 283–284)

Collapse theories often express ideals and criticisms of the social world (Carr 1961: 37). These theories are influenced by, and sometimes attempt to influence, contemporary social issues. During the tumultuous eighteenth century, for example, Giambattista Vico (Bergin and Fisch 1948) and C. F. Volney (1793)) attributed collapse to factionalism and conflict, while Gibbon (1776–1788) saw in the Roman collapse a failure of leadership. In the aftermath of World War I, the German Spengler foresaw the decline of the West (1962 [original 1918, 1922]), while the expatriate academic Rostovtzeff (1926) perceived in the Roman collapse a foretaste of the Russian Revolution. The moral uncertainty of the twentieth century influenced Toynbee's (1962) emphasis on internal discord in spiritual values. Many writers today link collapse to environmental resources, with failure brought on by anthropogenic degradation, climate change, or a combination of factors including these. Where the explanation focuses on environmental damage a collapse is like a Greek tragedy: The protagonist brings on self-destruction. The message of this literature is that tragedy is avoidable with foresight and moral behavior.

There are many strands in collapse theories, strands that persist through the centuries and millennia of collapse literature (Tainter 1988). While these strands do seem to persist, they wax and wane in popularity. Since collapse is commonly seen as a failure, someone must be responsible. A theme common among earlier writers is that an individual or group did not rule properly or fulfill a responsibility, and so an empire fell or a dynasty perished. Usually the failure is attributed to the paramount ruler. Ibn Khaldun's (1958 [original 1377–1381]) theory of cyclical dynastic succession in medieval North Africa is a classic of this genre. The causal force in this framework, as noted, is the changing morality of rulers.

Kings and emperors have frequently legitimized their rule by claiming a role as divine intermediaries (e.g., Netting 1972). They are thus responsible for the weather and a good harvest (much as presidents and prime ministers today are considered responsible for a good economy). Poor weather and a failed harvest would indicate that the ruler had not fulfilled this responsibility. The history of China illustrates this attitude. Widespread catastrophes, failures of crops, and unrest were taken as signs that a dynasty had lost the Mandate of Heaven, which legitimized rule (Lattimore 1940; Fairbank, Reischauer, and Craig 1973). The loss of the Mandate of Heaven was a signal that a dynasty's end was near. The final years of the Western Chou Dynasty (1027–771 BC), for example, produced remarkable literature on the many disturbances unfolding simultaneously. One poem related the natural catastrophes of the times.

> Grandly flashes the lightning of the thunder;
> There is a want of rest, a want of good.
> The streams all bubble up and overflow.
> The crags on the hill-tops fall down.
> High banks become valleys;
> Deep valleys become hills.
> Alas for the men of this time!
> Why does (the King) not stop these things?
>
> (Hsu and Linduff 1988: 281)

A variant of this approach is that kings and emperors may not be exclusively to blame for collapse. The fault rather belongs to entire social strata, particularly the elites. Tenney Frank, for example, ascribed the Roman failure to a lack of vision on the part of the landed gentry: Their willingness during the Republic to betray the peasantry for large slave estates and to accept the monarchy for personal safety (1940: 304). Christopher Caudwell indicted soil impoverishment by large estates and the general demoralization of the exploited class (1971: 55). Arthur Boak and William Sinnigen singled out the fact that:

> Rome failed to develop an economic system that could give to the working classes of the Empire living conditions sufficiently advantageous to encourage them to support it devotedly and to reproduce in adequate numbers.
>
> (1965: 522)

Samuel Dill also cited the economic weakness of the Roman class system but believed that collapse was due to the ruin of the middle class and the municipalities (1899: 245).

There is a long history within anthropology and other social sciences of scholarly interest in the environmental dimensions of social life (e.g., Forde 1934; Hack 1942; Kroeber 1939; Steward 1938; Thomas 1956; Wissler 1917). This interest has naturally found expression in the study of collapse (e.g., Cooke 1931; Sanders 1962, 1963; Adams 1981; Culbert 1988). In general the literature of this strand postulates that collapses result from shortages of resources, brought on by normal environmental variation, abrupt climate shifts, or human damage. This approach to understanding collapse is experiencing a renaissance of popularity. Contemporary discussions of our own sustainability and sustainable development frequently postulate that ancient societies collapsed because they degraded their environments (e.g., Brown 2001; Heinberg 2003, 2004; Ponting 1991), justifying the concern that today's societies could collapse for the same reason. Academics have responded to this popular movement with books and papers addressing human–environment interactions over the long term (e.g., Chew 2001, 2007; Costanza et al. 2007; Costanza, Graumlich, and Steffen 2007; Fagan 2000; Flenley and Bahn 2002; McIntosh, Tainter, and McIntosh 2000a, 2000b; Redman 1999; Redman et al. 1999; Tainter 2000; van der Leeuw 1998, 2000; van der Leeuw and Redman 2002). Much of this recent professional literature seeks explicitly to connect historical research to current environmental concerns.

An environmental focus, though, requires adjustments in the assignment of blame. It is expectable that collapses in the days of rule by kings and emperors were attributed to the failings of leaders or the class from which they came. In the days of democracy and mass consumption, though, blame is not so easily narrowed. The people themselves must be responsible for collapse, so it is thought. This is so whether the collapse occurred in the past or is merely foretold.

Louis West (1933) offered an early attribution of collapse to the masses. West wrote in an age when economic concerns outweighed environmental ones, and when capitalism and socialism vied for supremacy. The weakness leading to the Roman collapse, according to West, came not from the elites but from the parasitical poor:

> In a word, the poor and the army [of Rome] had eaten up the capital of the thrifty, and the western half of Europe sank into the dark ages, from which it did not emerge until the thrifty and energetic could again safely use their abilities in wealth-producing activities.
>
> (West 1933: 106)

Whereas collapses were once attributed to impious or selfish rulers, or in West's view to indolent masses, in today's framework the sin is gluttony: Ancient societies collapsed because they overshot the carrying capacities of their environments, degrading their support bases in the process. And since it happened to past societies, it could happen to us too (Ponting 1991; Brown 2001; Flenley and Bahn 2002; Heinberg 2003, 2004; Diamond 2005). According to contemporary literature, the next collapse will come because all of us have consumed too many goods, eaten too much, traveled too far, and produced too many children. The Greek tragedy unfolds even as numerous Cassandras warn us to mend our ways.

There is, however, another strand of thought that holds humans blameless. Collapses happen. J. B. Bury (1923) once argued that there was no systematic reason for the fall of Rome. It resulted from a series of contingent events—the irruption of the Huns, Roman mismanagement, weak emperors, and employment of barbarians in the army, all occurring over a short time. In other literature the factor precipitating collapse is thought to have been a change in climate:

Cold, heat, or drought deprived a society of the resources it required, and collapse ensued. Both scholars and the public find climate change to be perpetually attractive as an explanation of cultural change. It offers a simple solution to complicated problems. Ellsworth Huntington (1915, 1917) pioneered this line of inquiry. He was followed a few decades later by Nels Winkless and Iben Browning, who published a semi-popular book titled *Climate and the Affairs of Men* (1975). (Iben Browning, a zoologist by training, later gained notoriety when he predicted that a catastrophic earthquake would strike New Madrid, Missouri, around 2–3 December 1990. It didn't happen.) Archaeologists and climatologists have postulated that climate change forced collapses and abandonments in cases as far-flung as Old Kingdom Egypt (e.g., Butzer 1976), Mycenaean Greece (e.g., Carpenter 1966), the American Southwest (e.g., Reed 1944), and Highland Mesoamerica (e.g., Weaver 1972). Hubert Lamb, in a magisterial work (1982), traced the cultural effects of climate change across much of the globe. As it has become clear that climate change will affect our own way of life, scholars have recently found that climate affected ancient civilizations from Mesopotamia (Weiss et al. 1993), to Peru (Binford et al. 1997), Greenland (McGovern 1994), and the Maya Lowlands (Hodell, Curtis, and Brenner 1995; deMenocal 2001; Haug et al. 2003). Here, too, the implicit message concerns anthropogenic degradation, if indirectly: Past societies were destroyed by abrupt climate change, although for them it was unforeseeable. We, however, must take care not to cause such a change ourselves.

2.2 Is There a Common Trend in Current Collapse Explanations?

Collapse studies clearly have a long history, involving a plethora of explanations. The literature on collapse has become vast, especially since 1988. Is it possible to synthesize from this literature common explanatory themes, or even a consensus? Fortunately two studies have considered collapse cases in breadth, and to some extent in depth. These are the studies by Tainter (1988) and Middleton (2017). As listed in Table 2.1, 18 cases can be extracted from these works, to which I add a recent study of the collapse of Cahokia in the American Midwest (Tainter 2019). For these 19 cases of collapse, 64 explanations have been advanced. The 64 explanations can be condensed into 10 themes, as follows:

1. Climate change (the Egyptian First Intermediate Period, Akkad, the Harappans, the Mycenaeans, the Hittites, the Western Roman Empire, Teotihuacan, Tiwanaku, the Maya, Chaco Canyon).
2. Invaders/external conflict (Akkad, the Third Dynasty of Ur, the Western Chou Dynasty, the Harappans, the Minoans, the Mycenaeans, the Hittites, the Western Roman Empire, the Maya, Teotihuacan, Easter Island, Akkad).
3. Revolt/rebellion (the Egyptian First Intermediate Period, Akkad, Monte Albán, the Mycenaeans, Teotihuacan, the Maya).

Table 2.1 Collapse Cases (After Tainter [1988, 2019] and Middleton [2017]).[a]

Old Kingdom Egypt	Teotihuacan
Akkad	The Classic Maya
The Third Dynasty of Ur	Tiwanaku
The Harappans	Huari
Minoan Crete	Easter Island (Rapa Nui)
Mycenaean Greece	Chaco Canyon
The Hittites	Cahokia
The Western Roman Empire	The Abbasid Caliphate
Monte Albán	The Ik
The Western Chou Dynasty	

[a] Two cases considered by Middleton—Moche and Angkor—are not included here since they were not collapses. Easter Island (Rapa Nui) is included, although its collapse appears to have occurred in the historic period, due to European contact (Mulrooney et al. 2010).

4. Intra-societal conflict (the Egyptian First Intermediate Period, Akkad, the Third Dynasty of Ur, the Harappans, Minoan Crete, Teotihuacan, the Western Roman Empire, the Maya, Huari, the Mycenaeans, Easter Island).
5. Environmental deterioration (other than climate change) (the Harappans, the Maya, Easter Island, the Third Dynasty of Ur, the Western Roman Empire, the Abbasid Caliphate, Cahokia, the Ik).
6. Catastrophes (e.g., epidemics, plagues, earthquakes, volcanoes) (the Minoans, the Mycenaeans, the Western Roman Empire, the Maya, Teotihuacan).
7. Change in trade patterns (the Mycenaeans, the Hittites, the Maya).
8. Mystical (e.g., religious/ideological change; dysfunctional belief systems; ethics; cyclical theory; concepts such as "decadence;" loss of faith in rulers) (the Western Roman Empire, Teotihuacan, Huari, the Maya).
9. Economics of complexity (the Western Roman Empire, the Maya, Chaco Canyon, Cahokia).
10. Chance concatenation of events (the Western Roman Empire).

There are some clearly favored explanations in this list, as follows:

- –Invaders/external conflict (12 explanations)
- –Intra-societal conflict (11 explanations)
- –Climate change (10 explanations)

Many scholars explain collapse as resulting suddenly and surprisingly from outside a society, a "bolt from the blue," rather than searching for systematic explanations or cross-cultural regularities. In the list above we can see the following:

- –Climate change (10 explanations)
- –Invaders (12 explanations)

- -Catastrophes (5 explanations)
- -Chance concatenation of events (1 explanation)

The literature thus reveals 28 explanations that might be characterized as the *deus ex machina* theory of collapse. The term derives from the ancient, classical theater in which, if a plot became too complicated to resolve, a god would descend on a machine and sort everything out. In collapse studies, the god from the machine is some bolt from the blue, an unforeseeable occurrence such as a change in climate that clarifies a complicated and mysterious historical event. Forty-four percent (28/64) of collapse explanations fall within this theme. Another way of characterizing the *deus ex machina* theory of collapse is that at least a plurality of scholars believe that *collapse is just bad luck*.

2.3 Concluding Remarks

Misia Landau (1984) observed that descriptions of human biological evolution have a narrative structure like myths or folk tales. In such stories, the hero starts from humble beginnings, just as humans began as merely another unassuming primate. The hero undergoes various trials, acquiring new capabilities in the process—just as humans acquired an opposable thumb, upright posture, and a large brain. The hero finally triumphs—as did humans—although this triumph is often not the end of the story. In this narrative structure, we can also see our ancestor myths about the evolution of complex societies. Human society began as small, humble, and threatened. But through heroic efforts, we discovered fire and agriculture and invented the wheel, metallurgy, cities, and civil society. These new capabilities facilitated the emergence of civilization, making humanity triumphant over nature. The hero—humanity—had achieved its quest. In many myths, though, the hero is destroyed through pride or hubris. Just so, civilizations have collapsed, often through their own faults, and many people worry that it could happen again.

I noted at the beginning of this chapter that collapse explanations wax and wane in popularity according to the issues of the day. As related above, in the eighteenth century, Volney, Gibbon, and their contemporaries saw collapse as resulting from the sort of factionalism occurring in their time, which the drafters of the American Constitution tried to counter. Collapse explanations were influenced by the world wars. During the Cold War, we had theories attributing collapse to elite mismanagement, class conflict, and peasant revolts. The environmental movement brought attention to environmental degradation in ancient societies. As global warming became an issue, scholars of the past began to discover that ancient societies collapsed due to climate change. If elite consumption once caused collapses, today the reason must be mass consumerism. The trend cannot stop there. Given recent developments in the public arena, inevitably someone must propose that societies are made vulnerable to collapse by inequality and "the 1%." In fact, some authors already have. Such a model has been proposed by Motesharrei, Rivas, and Kalnay (2014). Their research was sponsored by that bastion of historical inquiry, NASA's Goddard Space Flight Center, and was based on sociological research published in obscure physics journals (Kloor 2014).

Collapse theories are influenced by contemporary issues. They are influenced by our need for an ancestor myth, which the phenomenon of collapse seems to contradict. They are even influenced by the structure of folk tales. These influences will never end. After 3,000 years of literature on collapse and related phenomena, we cannot fail to be disappointed that 44% of collapse explanations answer the question "What causes collapse?" with the reply "Nothing in particular, just bad luck."

Surely we can do better.

Acknowledgment

I am pleased to express my appreciation to Walter Scheidel and Temis Taylor for comments on an earlier version of this chapter.

References

Adams, Robert M. C. 1981. *Heartland of Cities*. Chicago: Aldine.

Bergin, Thomas Goddard and Max Harold Fisch, trans. 1948 [1744]. *The New Science of Giambattista Vico* (3rd edition). Ithaca: Cornell University Press.

Binford, Michael W., Alan L. Kolata, Mark Brenner, John W. Janusek, Matthew T. Seddon, Mark Abbott and Jason H. Curtis. 1997. Climate Variation and the Rise and Fall of an Andean Civilization. *Quaternary Research* 47(2): 235–248.

Boak, Arthur E. and William G. Sinnigen. 1965. *A History of Rome to A.D. 565* (5th edition). New York: MacMillan.

Brown, Lester R. 2001. *Eco-economy: Building an Economy for the Earth*. New York: Norton.

Bury, J. B. 1923. *History of the Later Roman Empire*. London: MacMillan.

Butzer, Karl W. 1976. *Early Hydraulic Civilization in Egypt*. Chicago: University of Chicago Press.

Carpenter, Rhys. 1966. *Discontinuities in Greek Civilisation*. Cambridge: Cambridge University Press.

Carr, Edward Hallett. 1961. *What Is History?* London: MacMillan.

Caudwell, Christopher. 1971. *Further Studies in a Dying Culture*. New York: Monthly Review Press.

Chew, Sing C. 2001. *World Ecological Degradation: Accumulation, Urbanization, and Deforestation 3000 B.C.–A.D. 2000*. Walnut Creek: AltaMira.

Chew, Sing C. 2007. *The Recurring Dark Ages: Ecological Stress, Climate Changes, and System Transformation*. Lanham: AltaMira.

Cooke, C. Wythe. 1931. Why the Mayan Cities of the Peten District, Guatemala, Were Abandoned. *Journal of the Washington Academy of Sciences* 21(13): 283–287.

Costanza, Robert, Lisa J. Graumlich and Will Steffen (eds.). 2007. *Sustainability or Collapse? An Integrated History and Future of People on Earth*. Dahlem Workshop Report 96. Cambridge: The MIT Press.

Costanza, Robert, Lisa J. Graumlich, Will Steffen, Carole Crumley, John Dearing, Kathy Hibbard, Rik Leemans, Charles Redman and David Schimel. 2007. Sustainability or

Collapse: What Can We Learn From Integrating the History of Humans and the Rest of Nature? *Ambio – A Journal of the Human Environment* 36(7): 522–527.

Culbert, T. Patrick. 1988. The Collapse of Classic Maya Civilization. In *The Collapse of Ancient States and Civilizations*, edited by Norman Yoffee and George L. Cowgill, pp. 69–101. Tucson: University of Arizona Press.

deMenocal, Peter B. 2001. Cultural Responses to Climate Change During the Late Holocene. *Science* 292(5517): 667–673.

Diamond, Jared. 2005. *Collapse: How Societies Choose to Fail or Succeed*. New York: Viking.

Dill, Samuel. 1899. *Roman Society in the Last Century of the Western Empire* (2nd edition). London: MacMillan.

Fagan, Brian. 2000. *The Little Ice Age: How Climate Made History, 1300–1850*. New York: Basic Books.

Fairbank, John K., Edwin O. Reischauer and Albert M. Craig. 1973. *East Asia: Tradition and Transformation*. Boston: Houghton Mifflin.

Flenley, John and Paul Bahn. 2002. *The Enigmas of Easter Island* (2nd edition). Oxford: Oxford University Press.

Forde, C. Darryl. 1934. *Habitat, Economy and Society: A Geographical Introduction to Ethnology*. London: Methuen.

Frank, Tenney. 1940. *An Economic Survey of Ancient Rome, Volume V: Rome and Italy of the Empire*. Baltimore: Johns Hopkins Press.

Gibbon, Edward. 1776–1788. *The Decline and Fall of the Roman Empire*. New York: Modern Library.

Hack, John T. 1942. The Changing Physical Environment of the Hopi Indians of Arizona. *Papers of the Peabody Museum of American Archaeology and Ethnology* 35(1).

Haug, Gerald H., Detlef Günther, Larry C. Peterson, Daniel M. Sigman, Konrad A. Hughen and Beat Aeschlimann. 2003. Climate and the Collapse of Maya Civilization. *Science* 299(5613): 1731–1735.

Heinberg, Richard. 2003. *The Party's Over: Oil, War and the Fate of Industrial Societies*. Gabriola Island: New Society Publishers.

Heinberg, Richard. 2004. *Power Down: Options and Actions for a Post-carbon World*. Gabriola Island: New Society Publishers.

Hodel, David A., Jason H. Curtis and Mark Brenner. 1995. Possible Role of Climate in the Collapse of Classic Maya Civilization. *Nature* 375(6530): 391–394.

Holling, C. S. 2001. Understanding the Complexity of Economic, Ecological, and Social Systems. *Ecosystems* 4(5): 390–405.

Hsu, Cho-yun and Katheryn M. Linduff. 1988. *Western Chou Civilization*. New Haven: Yale University Press.

Huntington, Ellsworth. 1915. *Civilization and Climate*. New Haven: Yale University Press.

Huntington, Ellsworth. 1917. Climatic Change and Agricultural Exhaustion as Elements in the Fall of Rome. *Quarterly Journal of Economics* 31(2): 173–208.

Ibn Khaldun. 1958. *The Muqaddimah: An Introduction to History*, translated by Franz Rosenthal. Pantheon, New York.

Kloor, Keith. 2014. Judging the Merits of a Media-Hyped 'Collapse' Study. Discover, March 21. Online: http://blogs.discovermagazine.com/collideascape/2014/03/21/judging-merits-media-hyped-collapse-study/#.V8ib1W25xZg.

Kroeber, Alfred L. 1939. *Cultural and Natural Areas of Native North America*. Berkeley: University of California Press.

Lamb, H. H. 1982. *Climate, History and the Modern World*. London: Methuen.

Landau, Misia. 1984. Human Evolution as Narrative. *American Scientist* 72: 262–268.

Lattimore, Owen. 1940. *Inner Asian Frontiers of China.* Boston: Beacon Press.

McGovern, Thomas H. 1994. Management for Extinction in Norse Greenland. In *Historical Ecology: Cultural Knowledge and Changing Landscapes.* Carole L. Crumley ed., pp. 127–154. Santa Fe: School of American Research Press.

McIntosh, Roderick J., Joseph A. Tainter and Susan Keech McIntosh (eds.). 2000a. *The Way the Wind Blows: Climate, History, and Human Action.* New York: Columbia University Press.

McIntosh, Roderick J., Joseph A. Tainter and Susan Keech McIntosh. 2000b. Climate, History, and Human Action. In *The Way the Wind Blows: Climate, History, and Human Action.* Roderick J. McIntosh, Joseph A. Tainter and Susan Keech McIntosh eds., pp. 1–42. New York: Columbia University Press.

Middleton, Guy D. 2017. *Understanding Collapse: Ancient History and Modern Myths.* Cambridge: Cambridge University Press.

Montesquieu, Charles Louis. 1968. *Considerations on the Causes of the Greatness of the Romans and Their Decline,* translated by David Lowenthal. Ithaca: Cornell University Press.

Motesharrei, Safa, Jorge Rivas and Eugenia Kalnay. 2014. Human and Nature Dynamics (HANDY): Modeling Inequality and Use of Resources in the Collapse or Sustainability of Societies. *Ecological Economics* 101: 90–102.

Mulrooney, Mara A., Thegn N. Ladefoged, Christopher M. Stevenson and Sonia Haoa. 2010. Empirical Assessment of a Pre-European Societal Collapse on Rapa Nui (Easter Island). In *The Gotland Papers: Selected Papers From the VII International Conference on Easter Island and the Pacific: Migration, Identity, and Cultural Heritage.* P. Wallin and H. Martinsson-Wallin eds., pp. 141–154. Visby: Gotland University Press.

Netting, Robert M. 1972. Sacred Power and Centralization: Aspects of Political Adaptation in Africa. In *Population Growth: Anthropological Implications.* Brian Spooner ed., pp. 219–244. Cambridge: Massachusetts Institute of Technology Press.

Ponting, Clive. 1991. *A Green History of the World.* New York: St. Martin's.

Redman, Charles L. 1999. *Human Impacts on Ancient Environments.* Tucson: University of Arizona Press.

Reed, Erik K. 1944. The Abandonment of the San Juan Basin. *El Palacio* 51: 61–74.

Rostovtzeff, M. 1926. *The Social and Economic History of the Roman Empire.* Oxford: Oxford University Press.

Sanders, William T. 1962. Cultural Ecology of the Maya Lowlands, Part I. *Estudios de Cultura Maya* 2: 79–121.

Sanders, William T. 1963. Cultural Ecology of the Maya Lowlands, Part II. *Estudios de Cultura Maya* 3: 203–241.

Spengler, Oswald. 1962. *Decline of the West,* edited by Helmut Werner, translated by Charles Francis Atkinson. New York: Vintage.

Steward, Julian H. 1938. Basin-Plateau Aboriginal Sociopolitical Groups. Bureau of American Ethnology, *Bulletin* 120.

Tainter, Joseph A. 1988. *The Collapse of Complex Societies.* Cambridge: Cambridge University Press.

Tainter, Joseph A. 2000. Global Change, History, and Sustainability. In *The Way the Wind Blows: Climate, History, and Human Action.* Roderick J. McIntosh, Joseph A. Tainter and Susan Keech McIntosh eds., pp. 331–356. New York: Columbia University Press.

Tainter, Joseph A. 2019. Cahokia: Urbanization, Metabolism, and Collapse. *Frontiers in Sustainable Cities* 1(6). http://doi.org/10.3389/frsc.2019.00006.

Thomas, William L., Jr. (ed.). 1956. *Man's Role in Changing the Face of the Earth*. Chicago: University of Chicago Press.

Toynbee, Arnold J. 1962. *A Study of History*. Oxford: Oxford University Press. .

Turchin, Peter. 2003. *Historical Dynamics: Why States Rise and Fall*. Princeton: Princeton University Press.

van der Leeuw, Sander E. 1998. Introduction. In *The Archaeomedes Project: Understanding the Natural and Anthropogenic Causes of Land Degradation and Desertification in the Mediterranean Basin*. S. E. van der Leeuw ed., pp. 2–22. Luxembourg: Office for Official Publications of the European Communities.

van der Leeuw, Sander E. and the Archaeomedes Research Team. 2000. Land Degradation as a Socionatural Process. In *The Way the Wind Blows: Climate, History, and Human Action*. Roderick J. McIntosh, Joseph A. Tainter and Susan Keech McIntosh eds., pp. 357–383. New York: Columbia University Press.

van der Leeuw, Sander E. and Charles L. Redman. 2002. Placing Archaeology at the Center of Socio-natural Studies. *American Antiquity* 67(4): 597–605.

Volney, C. F. 1793. *The Ruins; or Meditations on the Revolutions of Empires*. New York: Calvin Blanchard.

Weaver, Muriel Porter. 1972. *The Aztecs, the Maya, and Their Predecessors*. New York: Seminar Press.

Weiss, H., M.-A. Courty, W. Wetterstrom, F. Guichard, L. Senior, R. Meadow and A. Curnow. 1993. The Genesis and Collapse of Third Millennium North Mesopotamian Civilization. *Science* 261(5124): 995–1004.

West, Louis C. 1933. The Economic Collapse of the Roman Empire. *The Classics Journal* 28: 96–106.

Winkless, Nels and Iben Browning. 1975. *Climate and the Affairs of Men*. New York: Harper's Magazine Press.

Wissler, Clark. 1917. *The American Indian; an Introduction to the Anthropology of the New World*. New York: D. C. McMurtrie.

Yoffee, Norman. 1988. The Collapse of Ancient Mesopotamian States and Civilization. In *The Collapse of Ancient States and Civilizations*. Norman Yoffee and George L. Cowgill eds., pp. 44–68. Tucson: University of Arizona Press.

3 Diminishing Returns on Extraction

How Inequality and Extractive Hierarchy Create Fragility

Luke Kemp

3.1 Introduction: The Iatrogenic Theory of Collapse

Do societies lose resilience over time? Joseph Tainter's theory of diminishing returns on complexity (TDRC) answers yes (Tainter 1988, 1995, 2011). The theory rests on four key points:

- First, complex societies are problem-solving organizations that gain in socio-political complexity to address problems.
- Second, increased socio-political complexity entails an energy cost.
- Third, building socio-political complexity to solve problems eventually reaches a point of declining marginal returns. The costs of complexity grow faster than the benefits.
- Fourth, the diminishing returns result in economic decline and popular disaffection, leaving a complex but vulnerable society, which is unable to cope with new challenges.

Socio-political complexity, past a certain point, becomes "iatrogenic": As with many medical treatments, the cure can become worse than the disease. Tainter defines collapse as a rapid, significant loss of an established level of socio-political complexity (Tainter 1988). For the purposes of this chapter, I define collapse in this case as the relatively rapid (within decades), significant, and enduring loss of population and physical capital, and an accompanied failure of the state (including its ability to maintain a monopoly on violence and taxation) and change in political identity. It is (at least historically) primarily an elite and urban problem, and one that can be less damaging, perhaps barely noticeably or even beneficial in some cases, for most of the population outside of palatial centers (Haldon, Chase, et al. 2020). It is a rare but real phenomenon in human history.

Tainter focuses on two specific pathways that lead from diminishing returns to crisis. The first is economic decline: As societies lose their budget, they also lose their ability to respond to new crises. They lack a buffer of resources to address new shocks, whether they be invasion or climate change. The second

DOI: 10.4324/9781003331384-5

is mass disaffection and discontent. Non-elite workers are expected to do more and more for either the same, or less, benefit (Tainter 1988).

TDRC is perhaps the foremost unifying theory of societal aging (a loss of resilience over time). There is much to admire in it. It meshes well with both human ecological work on socio-economic metabolism and complexity theory. It coincides with modern-day concerns about an "energy cliff" due to the declining Energy Return on Investment (EROI) (Hall, Balogh, and Murphy 2009) of fossil fuels, knowledge of tipping points (Lenton 2011), and provides a theory that is amenable to modeling. The emphasis that collapse is an (often adaptive) disaggregation into smaller political units is a point that both collapse proponents and skeptics can agree on.

TDRC also echoes other emerging theories of societal collapse and resilience. Some have suggested through complexity modeling that increases in complexity can lead to a condition of "self-organized criticality," which is precariously unstable (Brunk 2002). Others have pointed toward the accumulation of regulatory feedbacks over time as slowly engraining fragility in complex systems from the biological to the social (Anderies and Levin 2023). Most recently, empirical analysis using the Seshat Databank (Turchin et al. 2015) suggests that there could be a general scale threshold: societies need to develop greater information processing, such as writing, to move beyond a certain size. Some have even tried to develop a general biophysical theory and model of societal collapse based on Tainter's hypothesis (Bardi, Falsini, and Perissi 2019).

Yet, as a theory, it can be improved on by considering multiple factors of resilience and decay (Butzer 2012; Middleton 2012) as well as the role of politics and power. In this chapter, I revise TDRC to create a more nuanced, political, and empirical theory. I will begin by outlining some of the key problems with the theory, present a revised theory of "Diminishing Returns on Extraction," and highlight how diminishing returns apply to the specific category of empires.

In short, TDRC has a partly correct diagnosis, but faulty theoretical foundations. TDRC confuses complexity with hierarchy, and makes a problematic assumption that states are rational problem-solvers of collective problems with collective solutions. A more realistic picture is that states build capital, not complexity. Their problem-solving efforts address largely elite-selected problems with elite-derived benefits. Tainter is right to highlight diminishing returns on energy and resource extraction. For empires and expansionary states, this includes diminishing returns on conquest. For elites, this is accompanied by declining returns on economic development, inequality, corruption, and oligarchy. These drive intra-elite competition and further state capture, hollowing out the state. Eventually, the state falls alongside elites.

The underlying dynamic is one of extractive political systems. All states are extractive in the sense of taking a certain share of resources from their populace. This exists on a spectrum, and extractive institutions here refers to those which are marked by more exclusive political arrangements, which result in decisions and resource distributions that disproportionately benefit a small elite at the expense of wider society. Collapse is a case of diminishing returns on extraction.

3.2 The Problems of TDRC

TDRC is elegant and compelling in its simplicity. Despite this, it faces several problems as a unifying theory of societal collapse.

First, complexity is a vague concept and TDRC conflates its characteristics with the attributes of state hierarchies. If we use a more intuitive and sensible definition of complexity, it becomes clear that states increase complexity in some areas and decrease it in others. We should instead focus on capital, which is more easily, precisely measured and correlates with energy use.

Second, different lines of evidence suggest that economic complexity and large-scale coordination do not require a state hierarchy.

Third, states rarely efficiently and rationally address collective problems. Instead, efforts are often wasteful, avoid the most pressing problems, or are counterproductive. We should be careful not to naturalize or glorify the state and its problem-solving (Yoffee 2019).

Fourth, states are not uniform in their political structure and goals. These differences lead to widely disparate levels of vulnerability and resilience.

3.2.1 Capital, Not Complexity

Complexity in systems has several common characteristics, but no consensus definition. Key indicators often include the diversity and interconnectivity of parts, non-linear behavior, the presence of feedback loops, and scale. Socio-political complexity also lacks an official definition, but Tainter provides a useful one: "Complex societies are problem-solving organizations, in which more parts, different kinds of parts, more social differentiation, more inequality, and more kinds of centralization and control emerge as circumstances require" (Tainter 1988). This has some overlap with the typical notions of complexity, but differs most in its emphasis on inequality, centralization, and control (sometimes termed "information processing"). It is, rather, a closer description of hierarchy.

There is a tension between complexity in the broad sense, and this definition of socio-political complexity. Scholars of complexity are split on what defines a hierarchy and its role in complex systems, particularly given its apparent tension with common ideas of emergence, self-organization, and distributed control (Lane 2006). Synchronized swarm behavior in schools of fish and flocks of birds are the more usual fare for complexity studies rather than top-down chains of command.

I suggest we rely on a definition of complexity that aligns with its usage in the field of complex systems. Collective dynamic systems exhibit nonlinear and difficult-to-predict behaviors due to the interconnectivity and diversity of their constituent parts. Hence, the complexity of these systems can be defined and measured by this diversity and interconnectivity. Scale is an amplifier: it allows for greater degrees of interconnectivity and diversity. Measuring an overall level of complexity will be partly a subjective judgement. Agrarian states appear to have had a greater diversity in occupations and economic goods than stateless foragers. Stateless hunter-gatherers had more diverse diets, movement patterns, and individual skillsets (Scott 2017). Calculating an overall level of complexity will depend on how much we value the complexity of certain domains, and which ones can be tracked.

I define states as centralized institutions that coercively extract resources from, and impose rules on, a territorially circumscribed population. Note that Tainter's characteristics of complexity—centralization, control, and inequality —are fundamental markers of the state. They are not however, attributes of the more broadly used and common-sense definition of complexity (scale and interconnectivity of parts leading to nonlinear and difficult-to-predict behavior). Hence there appears to be a confusion between complexity and the state.

Statehood does not exist as an on–off switch. It exists by degradations. This is particularly apparent in the earliest states such as Mesopotamian city-states and pre-dynastic Egypt (Stevenson 2016), which were marked more by varying, fluctuating degrees of centralization and hierarchy. Permanent coercive hierarchies did eventually rise, but it was not a single, clear causal trajectory. There were multiple pathways as well as reversals. This distinction between statehood and socio-political complexity is crucial. States should not be confused with complexity. They are a particular template for political organization that can reduce and increase complexity in different domains.

The imposition of a state hierarchy has frequently shrunk rather than grown socio-political complexity. James C. Scott's influential Seeing Like a State argues that state hierarchies simplify the world to make it legible and controllable (Scott 1999). A multitude of languages and dialects are replaced by a common standard tongue. The numerous contextual names of an individual are stamped out in favor of a single surname for purposes of taxation, census tracking, and conscription. That is, even though government bureaucracy and institutions may become larger, more interconnected, and more diverse, there is a decrease in the linguistic and social diversity. Often, resistance to such simplification and attempts to "shackle the leviathan" of the state (Acemoglu and Robinson 2020) are perhaps more likely to induce an overall increase in socio-political complexity rather than top-down homogenization.

Capital is a more useful measurement for the TDRC. If we are interested in what states tend to accumulate over time to address new problems and what correlates to energy usage, then it is economic capital. I define capital in the same way as Thomas Piketty: A saleable, tangible, or intangible asset that can be owned and receives a monetary return[1] (Piketty and Zucman 2014). This definition of capital only includes humans when they are traded as slaves. In pre-monetary societies, a monetary return can be replaced by a general material return based on exchange value. This provides a much more precise and measurable idea than broader notions of capital that includes social, natural, or human capital.

Other forms of capital are more difficult to estimate over time and follow less simple trajectories. Take, for instance, social capital. One of the most famous definitions of social capital comes from Putnam, who views it as networks of relationships, trust, and norms that facilitate cooperation for mutual benefit (Putnam 1993).

While other definitions vary, they share many of these common characteristics of interpersonal ties and norms such as reciprocity. While there are no deep historical measurements of social capital, it appears dubious that it has experienced the same exponential growth as economic capital has since the Neolithic revolution. The most recent evidence suggests that modern foragers have extensive networks of social relationships across bands and with non-kins. For many individuals, up to 90% of relations were not kin-based (Bird et al. 2019). This maintenance between tight, small-scale groups and much larger social networks suggests that in terms of social capital, modern and ancient foragers may not differ substantially from contemporary city-dwellers (Wengrow 2019).

It is hard to definitively show that the Western Roman Empire was more diverse and interconnected than the Germanic "barbarians" to the North, with their multiple dialects, diverse customs, intricate overlapping social relations, and deliberative assemblies. It did, however, undoubtedly possess far more capital.

Economic capital also more closely tracks what Tainter and others are most concerned about: Energy capture. Tainter has put forward the case that complexity precedes and drives resource and energy consumption (Tainter 2006b). This is not straightforward to address due to the ambiguity of defining, let alone measuring, complexity.[2] However, the relationship between economic capital and energy use is clear. Most recent systematic reviews and evidence suggest that GDP, a decent proxy for levels of economic capital and activity, is innately tied to energy use (Hickel and Kallis 2020; Haberl et al. 2020).

Complexity should not be confused with hierarchy. Hierarchies by nature are intended to simplify relations. States have likely made some areas of life, such as economic activity and bureaucracy, more complex while simplifying others, such as languages, measurements, ecology, politics, and many social practices.

For understanding collapse and diminishing returns, it would be more prudent to focus on states and capital accumulation. Capital has an easily measured and proven relationship with energy use and leaves a clear archaeological footprint. Complexity does not.

It is reflective of emerging evidence that complexity does not inherently need hierarchy, nor does problem-solving always need increased energy or economic capital.

3.2.2 Economic Complexity Without Hierarchy

The idea that state hierarchies drove complexity is a standard narrative. Across the vast expanse of history, the rise of states has tended to result in undeniable, long-term trends of increasing energy capture, information processing, population density, and sheer population (Marcus 2008; Morris 2010). It remains unclear which of the variables drove which, including whether population scale and density pushed ecological exploitation and energy extraction (Ellis et al. 2018). These also are not synonymous with complexity. As noted earlier, stateless foragers likely possess greater complexity than large states in certain areas, including diets, individual skills, and ecology.

Even if we narrow our lens to just the diversity and interconnectedness of economic activities, it is difficult to contend that complexity required state-level hierarchies. Scholars have recently challenged the state-complexity link, drawing on examples such as seasonal foragers in the Upper Paleolithic, early cities, the Celts, and nomadic pastoralists. Complex grave goods that would have required thousands of hours of work, monumental public works made of mammoth bones, megalithic stone works requiring coordinated workforces and detailed design (most famously in Göbekli Tepe), and seasonal variation between hierarchal structures and more distributed forager groups were present during the Upper Paleolithic (Wengrow and Graeber 2015). None of these should be conflated with complexity writ large; they are simply the most archaeologically visible proxies for certain areas of complexity. That is, they are useful proxies for the diversity and interconnectedness of forms of labor and economic activity, not of political practices, languages, or social relations.

Many of the earliest cities display aspects of complexity (coordinated and interconnected labor, long-distance trade, as well as diverse jobs, skills, and social practices) without centralized hierarchy (Wengrow 1972). For the large, ancient city of Teotihuacan, evidence of egalitarianism has been sidelined due to the persistent belief that economic complexity and large-scale urbanism require centralization. This has led scholars to undertake mathematical modeling to prove an idea that should be uncontroversial: That large-scale cooperation in the city could have been distributed and self-organized (Froese, Gershenson, and Manzanilla 2014). In Mesopotamia, while the earliest states were "fragile and short-lived," (Scott 2017) the cities they sought to conquer and bind were remarkably resilient (Yoffee and Seri 2019). Even when states did reign, the actual responsibilities of urban governance appear to have largely been decentralized (Van De Mieroop 1999). The Harappan is perhaps the most notable contradiction to the evolutionary state hypothesis. This cultural zone of settlements is exceptional in its size (encompassing multiple large urban sites), trade networks extending into Mesopotamia, longevity (at least 800 years during the "mature" phase), and slow decline over multiple centuries rather than abrupt collapse (Middleton 2017). Despite all this long-lasting urbanization and economic complexity, there is little evidence that it required a state-based hierarchy. As the most recent review of the evidence summarized:

> Urbanization, collective action, and technological innovation are not driven by the agendas of an exclusionary ruling class and can occur in their total absence. The priest-king is dead. The Indus civilization was egalitarian, but this is not because it lacked complexity; rather, it is because a ruling class is not a prerequisite for social complexity (Green 2020).

These are provisional and contested findings. Such is true of much in ancient archaeology. Evidence of hierarchy could be archaeologically invisible, and absence of evidence is not evidence of absence. While further work is needed, it provides an important, promising data point.

In the modern world, there also seems to be no iron rule that higher complexity requires more hierarchy. In Bali, the traditional, complex, and large-scale water irrigation management system has existed since the eleventh century by not just operating outside of the state but deliberately evading state control (Wengrow 2017). There are similar long-lived, complex, and sustainable irrigation management structures in Amazonia, the Maya Lowlands, Angkor, and West Africa characterized by cooperation, heterarchy, and specialized occupations rather than hierarchy (Scarborough and Lucero 2010). These are notable since coordinated labor for irrigation was one of the original proposals for why states were a functional adaptation.

The evidence suggests a more nuanced picture of the links between certain indicators of economic complexity and hierarchy. As archaeologist David Wengrow noted while drawing on the work of anthropologist Jack Goody: "[T]here was no universal or law-like connection between urban life, state sovereignty, and bureaucracy. These are instead parts of a distinct 'package' of developments that coalesced under a particular set of historical circumstances." (Wengrow 2015) The exact relationship between these elements remains unclear. There is a still speculative, tenuous, and emerging picture that cities, trade, and specialization tend to have their roots in some particular, localized needs for integration. States and hierarchy were more frequently the outcomes of coercive efforts to capitalize on the opportunity presented by the large labor-grain concentrations that urbanism offered (Scott 2017). Trade preceded the flag, and the town square preceded the king.

The earliest states often simplified many domains of life, a point that archaeologists have made for aesthetic labor (in the Neolithic Near East) (Wengrow 2001) and administration (Yoffee 2016). States frequently increased complexity in some domains while simplifying others. It is a complex picture (pun intended).

3.2.3 Broken Returns

Viewing societies as problem-solving entities that build complexity to address new problems is enticing. It is alluringly simple and easy to model. But if we assume that states build complexity for problem-solving, the question arises: Whose problems and for whose benefit? This unravels into several problems.

First, there is the issue that problem-solving often does not require increasing net complexity (or capital), and often would benefit from reducing it. Abolishing fossil fuel subsidies, for instance, would incur a range of benefits, not least of which would be tackling climate change, and overall would likely reduce at least bureaucratic complexity.

Second, many problems are better addressed by reducing energy use. Energy efficiency would reduce overall energy demand, reduce emissions, and offer significant net-economic benefit (World Resources Institute 2014), particularly due to alleviating the health and productivity impacts of air pollution (Haines 2017). A new modeling exercise suggests that the world could meet the basic material needs of a population three times the current size by 2050 while simultaneously shrinking energy demand to the level of the 1960 (Millward-Hopkins et al. 2020). The idea that solving new problems inevitably requires increasing complexity, information processing, or energy (Tainter 2011) is fortunately wrong. That said, relentlessly accumulating and controlling capital does need energy and bureaucracy.

Third, the problems that states seek to address often do not coincide with collective welfare. What problems were the mammoth undertakings of the construction of pyramids, ziggurats, or the Forbidden City attempting to solve? The most obvious answer is strengthening the legitimacy of the state and the claim of the ruler. It is harder to make the case that these led to improvements in collective wellbeing. Tainter does factor in popular disaffection, but this is tied to a declining return on energy investment resulting in overwork or over-taxation (Tainter 1988). Yet, throughout history, many rebellions and revolutions that have disrupted or upended states were built on legitimate grievances of inequality and oppression, as well as often being overtaxed and overworked (Lawson 2019).

Fourth, hierarchies frequently avoid and actively ignore pressing problems, a fact that should be all too clear in the modern world of financial fragility and climate change. Indeed, there are entire books on "agnotology," the intentional creation of doubt and ignorance by the powerful, whether it be by big oil, big tobacco (Oreskes and Conway 2010), or big pharma (Goldacre 2014). Some complex industries, such as advertising, seem to be largely devoted to creating problems (such as a lack of self-esteem) to stimulate demand (Hickel 2020). Swathes of modern jobs appear to be useless or socially harmful (Graeber 2018). The problems that states identify and act on are more often than not the product of power-elites, whose actions often reflect private more than public interest (Haldon, Eisenberg, et al. 2020).

Fifth, states were never solely rational enterprises created to allow collective problem solving for the public good. The more likely story is that they were more often vehicles of bondage for elite benefit. Tainter does note that the truth of the origins of states likely lies somewhere between "integrationist" and "conflict" theories (Tainter 1988). Others have framed this as the "social contract" and "predatory" theories of state formation (Vu 2010). States do, of course, provide additional capacities and, on occasion, public goods, which has often led institutional economists to favor the integrationist theory. Despite this, the circumstantial evidence in the earliest states—punishment for flight from states, enslavement, wars of capture, and revolts—all suggest that centralized state hierarchies have tended to be coercive rather than enjoying widespread support (Scott 2019). As noted earlier, urbanism, trade, and specialization were likely "integrationist" to address local problems, but centralized states were the opportunistic, exploitative endeavor that often arose from the concentration of capital and people.

The earliest states arose not just in areas where agrarianism (usually in floodplains) was easy, but also where easily taxable cereal grains or other sources of conveniently appropriated capital were present. They were coercive apparatuses: Walls were frequently about keeping the citizens in rather than keeping invaders out (Lattimore 1962; Scott 2017). Indeed, the geographical placement of early states in alluvial floodplain valleys suggests that the prevention of an escape route was critical to enacting the "cage of civilization" (Mann 1986). Many early laws and stratified administrations were not acts of complexity to address agreed collective action problems, but rather devices to allow for taxation, conscription, and, when needed, confiscation of property and capital (Scott 2017).

This emphasis on control and coercion carries on to later states. The Hellenistic states were formed through sustained warfare marked by numerous atrocities in the wake of the break-up of the Macedonian Empire (Linklater 2016). Similarly, the earliest nation states in Europe occurred as aristocratic rulers looked to impose their authority domestically after setting their borders through warfare (Elias 2012). None of this is to say that warfare was the only source of state formation and bureaucratic centralization. Elite politics and ideology also played a role. But the apparatus of the state throughout history was primarily predatory. Until as late as 1800, up to three-quarters of the global population was likely held in some form of bondage (Hochschild 2006). All of this has underpinned a long history of citizen evasion and resistance against states (Scott 2008, 1990).

In short, states have generally been macro-parasites on their populace. Or, as Olson termed them, "stationary bandits" (Olson 2000). Elites and states, particularly within empires, tend to have a tense but often symbiotic relationship in which the state provides stability and protection, while elites aid with local administration and extraction.

This is neither inevitable nor an absolute rule. States tend to be wealth-destroying in the absence of meaningful political constraints (Murtazashvili and Murtazashvili 2020). One of the greatest triumphs of modernity has been the increased levels of accountability and limitations placed on states.

Even in the past, with fewer restraints, states could provide public goods. This was especially the case when there were democratic constraints and a wide, balanced fiscal base across the population. It is, of course, in the short-term interest of state elites to appease the population enough to prevent rebellion and allow for long-term rent extraction. Sometimes, they were simply incidental. The roads of the Western Roman Empire were helpful for travel and trade, but they were originally built for the movement of the military to quickly reach battle fronts and put down rebellions. In most cases, the roads were constructed by the legionnaires for the legionnaires. This follows a long-term trend of empires generally aiding trade by providing protected transportation and communication infrastructure (Mann 1986). In cases where "good governments" were acting for the public good, there was still a tendency for eventual moral lapses and corruption to eventually result in extractive practices and decline (Blanton et al. 2020).

Any theory of diminishing returns should account for the unequal distribution of returns. If states' actions to build capital and grow are wasteful or counterproductive, then we can expect there to be less of a clear "Kuznets Curve" to energy and returns. It also means that there should be far greater flexibility for states to avoid and delay diminishing returns. That is, there should be significant scope for redistribution of returns and democracy in selecting the right problems to improve the return/cost ratio. State responses and resilience, after all, are just as important as contributors to collapse and decline (Butzer and Endfield 2012).

This lens of empirical political economy can give firmer grounds for a theory of diminishing returns. Tainter does partly address this more political analysis of state collapse, commenting that: "[I]f exploitation and misadministration are normal aspects of hierarchy, then it is difficult to see these as sources for the collapse of hierarchies" (Tainter 1988). The exact same logic can be applied to TDRC: *If energy capture and increasing complexity are normal parts of societies, then it is difficult to see these as sources for the collapse of complex societies.* The reason why energy capture can be seen to contribute to collapse despite being a normal phenomenon is it changes over time. So do political practices and their returns.

3.2.4 Structure

Collapse is best tied to clear, discrete political units such as states (Middleton 2017). However, TDRC has been applied to an array of societal forms beyond the state. As shown in Table 3.1, these societal forms range from non-state agrarian groups such as Rapa Nui (Easter Island), through collections of city-states or a cultural zone (the Lowland Maya), to sprawling empires (the Western Roman Empire). Notably, the case of the Rapa Nui was, according to the most recent evidence, not a case of endogenous ecocide and collapse, but rather colonization and slave raids (Hunt 2006; DiNapoli et al. 2020). It is fine to apply TDRC to different units of analysis, but we need to be clear why we think they are comparable and note the

Table 3.1 An Overview of Theory of Diminishing Returns on Complexity (TDRC) Case Studies

Case study	Polity structure	Proxies of complexity used in studies	(Non-exhaustive) non-complexity contributors to collapse
The Western Roman Empire[3]	Empire	Currency debasement, army size, and territory	Climate change,[4] hostile migration, disease,[5] inequality and elite overproduction,[6] deforestation, diminishing returns from gold and silver mines
The Lowland Maya[7]	City State Complex	Monuments, population, and state of the land	Climate change,[8] warfare
Cahokia[9]	Hierarchical Regional Polity	Public works	Climate change, deforestation
Rapa Nui (Easter Island)[10]	Complex Agrarian-Forager Chiefdom	Population, resource use	Colonial slave raids and disease,[11] deforestation due to Palm Rat infestation[12]
Chaco Canyon[13]	Hierarchical Regional Polity	Public works	Climate change, inequality.

similarities and differences between them. For instance, diminishing returns on conquest is relevant to the case of an empire (and has been regularly used for the case of the Western Roman Empire), but is not pertinent for an isolated non-state agrarian group like the Rapa Nui.

3.2.5 Diminishing Returns on Extraction: A Theory of Hierarchical Decline

Politics is a necessary ingredient for any accurate theory of social systems. For TDRC this means incorporating the problems of hierarchy. This shift can help integrate other key theories of collapse into TDRC. These include corruption, imperial overstretch (conquest), inequality, intra-elite competition (Turchin and Nefedov 2009), elite mismanagement (Blanton et al. 2020), an inability to address impending problems (Diamond 2011; Johnson 2017), and declining returns from technology and economic development. This approach also marries it to leading institutional theories of modern-day state growth and failure, which pinpoint extractive institutions as the key cause (Acemoglu and Robinson 2013; Acemoglu et al. 2003). I term this overarching idea the Theory of Diminishing Returns on Extraction (DROE). Hierarchies tend to increase economic capital over time, feeding inequality and corruption, pitting elites against one another, and constructing sclerotic institutions that struggle to address impending problems when they conflict with vested elite interests. As Tainter rightly notes, this is accompanied by diminishing returns on energy (although it does not always follow a straightforward trajectory). Economic and technological development also experience declining returns, although it is unclear how much of this is a natural phenomenon or how much is driven by state capture and elite mismanagement. For expansionist states, conquest also produces greater costs and fewer benefits over time. Below, I work through each of these contributors to DROE.

3.2.5.1 Conquest

Conquest and military expansion are a natural impulse of an extractive hierarchy. It neutralizes threats, provides a new source of extraction, and can create domestic stability by providing an infusion of new resources. It can even be a necessary source of legitimacy. This was the case for the Chingissid world order created by Genghis Khan (and many subsequent orders), which depended on universal conquest and military success (Zarakol 2022). Yet, conquered territories require maintenance, and tend to create new enemies and frontiers of conflict. Conquests further afield from the core have even higher logistical costs. More resources are required by the military and diverted from productive sectors. All of this contributes to a pattern of diminishing returns leading to fiscal decline, and eventually fragmentation, or even collapse. This is the idea of imperial overstretch. An overreached leviathan faces spiraling costs to maintain its security and military advantage, eventually leading to relative economic, and then military, decline. This was common across modern empires, including the Spanish, Ottoman, Portuguese, and British. Both budget deficits and military spending increased until either fragmentation or decline set in (Kennedy 2010).

3.2.5.2 Corruption

Elite mismanagement is a recurring motif in examples of societal decline and collapse. Typically, corruption and poor decisions from elites have been identified as a constraint on responses to crises, rather than the primary driver of decline. Two of the rare clear-cut cases of environmental over-shoot—the Abbasid Caliphate and Third Dynasty of Ur—involved bungled responses from rulers (Tainter 2006a), alongside general state fragility. These factors were as much to blame as environmental degradation and, of course, contributed to ecological deterioration. Rife corruption was a consistent source of rebellion and even collapse throughout the history of imperial dynasties in China. In many cases, such as the Ming dynasty, the Mughal Empire, The High Roman Empire, and the Republic of Venice, even "good" governments that were providing public services often eventually drifted toward oligarchy and frayed the social contract, ending in decline (Blanton et al. 2020).

In the modern world, the corrosive influence of corruption is becoming increasingly clear. As Mueller has shown, whistleblowing in countries such as the USA has reached a Golden Age not because of any renewed collective moral compass, but due to the sheer scale of fraud in finance, the military, pharmaceuticals, and government (Mueller 2019).

3.2.5.3 Economic Development

Technology is a key driver of long-run economic development. This is both a key empirical finding and tenet of "endogenous growth theory." Yet, there are signs that innovation and invention become more difficult over time. As the easiest, high-benefit discoveries and ideas are exhausted, scientists and entre-preneurs must expend more effort for incremental improvements. This appears to be the case in the USA where the average number of patents-per-inventor has decreased since the 1970s (Strumsky, Lobo, and Tainter 2010). One recent paper makes the case that ideas are getting harder to find. In the USA, research productivity is declining in almost all sectors. The rate of decline is around 50% every 13 years (Bloom et al. 2020).

There are several different explanations for falling productivity on research investments. One could be that as the lowest-hanging fruit are already discov-ered, follow-on innovations simply require more investment and effort. Other reasons mesh well with the theory of diminishing returns on extraction. These include environmental and resource inputs becoming more costly, and industries suffocating innovation by adopting "defensive" research and development to pro-tect their rent (Dinopoulos and Syropoulos 2007). This echoes other explanations for broader declining economic returns on productivity and profits due to wage suppression and elites redirecting investment away from productive sectors toward finance and coercion (Van Bavel 2016; Wallerstein 2000).

3.2.5.4 Inequality

We now have an abundance of evidence for both the dynamics and corrosive impacts of economic inequality. In the presence of surplus capital accumulation and the intergenerational transmission of wealth, inequality tends to increase inexorably over time until a great act of violence—a "great leveller" of rebellion, mass-mobilization warfare, pandemic, or state failure—strikes (Scheidel 2017). In recent times, this is due to returns on wealth increasing more quickly than wages over time (Piketty 2017). There are also ideological roots, with each polity using ideology to explain, justify, and reinforce its inequalities (Piketty 2020). The amount of surplus capital and its disconnection from labor appear intricately tied to the level of inequality. This is supported by the markedly lower levels of inequality in the New World compared to the Old World, with the former lacking ox-drawn plows (Bogaard, Fochesato, and Bowles 2019). Wealth inequality has a well-documented connection to poorer mental health, higher interpersonal violence, and a suite of other social woes (Wilkinson and Pickett 2009, 2019). Inequality and corruption within hierarchies appear to have a bi-directional relationship: They often feed each other, creating a feedback loop (Gupta and Abed 2002; Policardo and Carrera 2018; You and Khagram 2005). As inequality increases, it places greater general stress on society, while corruption drains both the legitimacy of the state and its revenue. In short, societal fragility rises alongside wealth inequality and corruption.

3.2.5.5 Intra-elite Competition

Cyclical change in structural demographics has been advanced as a quantifiable and predictable way of understanding and even forecasting socio-political violence (Turchin and Nefedov 2009; Goldstone 2016). While many historians loathe a cyclical theory, these ideas have proven impressive in back-casting and perhaps even forecasting numerous cases (Goldstone 2017). In short, population growth over time causes real wages to decrease (due to an oversupply of labor), rents and elites' incomes to increase, and the number of elites to swell. This leads to rising inequality as well as "elite overproduction": An oversupply of economic elites relative to high-status positions. This leads to intra-elite competition with aspiring elites fighting over scarce positions. While this theory is unlikely to be a panacea, or applicable to all cases, the potential for political and social turmoil to be spurred by struggling elites against a backdrop of inequality is persuasive.

3.2.5.6 Energy Return on Investment (EROI)

Societies can be thought of as a trophic chain of energy. All material flows can be reduced to the basic universal currency of energy. Even grain, the basic constituent of tax and trade, is simply captured solar energy. The extraction of most energy faces a principle of diminishing returns where the most easily accessible and abundant sources are used first. Each marginal unit of energy extracted becomes increasingly costly: We need to go further abroad for land to cultivate and dig deeper for the next oil well. This is commonly measured by the energy return on energy invested (EROI). The EROI of fossil fuels has been steadily declining. The EROI of replacement renewable energy sources is improving but still lags significantly behind fossil fuels (Gupta and Hall 2011). This has led to fears of an energy cliff (Hall, Balogh, and Murphy 2009) or energy wall (Jarvis 2018) to growth.

Since most activities can be converted to energy, the EROI can be thought of much more widely and include energy captured through conquest (booty, land, and slaves). Some have pointed toward this wider conception of EROI as the best indicator for TDRC and linked it to the case of the Western Roman Empire, which faced declining return on conquests as well as agriculture (Homer-Dixon 2008). There can be declining EROIs on agriculture due to environmental degradation as well as climate change. In the case of the Indus, the switch to more drought-tolerant crops meant lower yields, which was at least one (albeit likely minor) contributor to their de-urbanization (Petrie 2019).

3.2.5.7 Oligarchy and Broken Feedbacks

Concentration of power and decision-making buffers elites from social and environmental change and often creates incentives to ignore unfolding problems. This is an endemic mark across many cases of transformation and collapse. In the Ottoman Empire, fiscal restructuring during a period of drought and climate change aimed to pacify local elites rather than alleviate the hardships of the farming base. This forced migration into cities caused social conflict and degraded the tax base. The empire knew that the farmers needed relief, but instead chose to please elites, severely contributing to the empire's eventual demise. (Izdebski, Mordechai, and White 2018). Similarly, the decline of the Caracol city-state in the lowland Maya was as much about elite action (or inaction) as it was climate change. The state had previously faced drought, but this time, economic policies worsened inequality, triggering internal conflict (Haldon et al. 2018). The disregarding of environmental deterioration and the prioritizing of elite interests were as influential as environmental change. The practice continues today. CEOs and national leaders regularly practice "strategic ignorance" of corruption and ill practice within firms and governments to ensure legal non-liability and plausible deniability (McGoey 2019).

In many cases, elite interests will lead to the proliferation of ineffective but bureaucratically costly policies. This is evidenced in modern-day environmental policy, which is marked by "treaty congestion" (Anton 2012) and regulatory bloat, with often limited effectiveness. Regulators want to placate the public with shows of action but avoid addressing the problems to assuage economic elites. Regulations multiply, but the problems remain unresolved.

The robustness-fragility tradeoff (Anderies and Levin 2023) is inevitable in such a situation.

Oligarchy, in this case, is largely synonymous with the idea of "state capture." Elites use their wealth to buy political power, prevent regulation, and control the apparatus of the state. They are inherently conservative and seek to uphold the status-quo to protect their own interests (Van Bavel 2019). All of this prevents adaptation and degrades resilience. It is especially true when the most powerful industries engaging in state capture are also the ones creating the greatest risks that society faces. This is likely the case with both the fossil fuel industry and the "stalker complex" of big tech and intelligence agencies (Kemp 2021).

In the language of systems thinking, oligarchy and elite decision-making tend to weaken and delay the information and motivation necessary to take corrective responses—the "negative feedbacks" that maintain equilibrium. Impending problems are either not seen due to hierarchy and bureaucracy, covered up, or actively ignored until it is too late. This is similar to a recent "social hubris" theory of collapse: That ancient societies frequently foresaw their demise but were too arrogant and/or proud to build resilience or adapt (Johnson 2017). The commonality is that responses are delayed, distorted, or averted due to vested interests and actions (Table 3.2).

The phenomenon of diminishing returns on extraction can be summarized as: *[I]nequality, corruption, intra-elite competition, impaired regulatory feedbacks*

Table 3.2 The Different Dimensions of Diminishing Returns

Variable	Dynamic
Conquest	Benefits can be dispersed across elites, commoners, and the state, depending on governance and inequality. Follows a trend of diminishing returns.
Corruption	Benefits accrue to elites, with costs shared across the state and commoners. Often increases over time alongside inequality.
Economic Development	Benefits can be dispersed across elites, commoners, and the state, depending on governance and inequality. Both technological and economic development appear to follow a pattern of diminishing returns.
Energy Return on Investment (EROI)	Benefits are usually dispersed across elites, commoners, and the state, depending on governance and inequality. EROI for environmental and resource extraction tends to decrease over time without significant innovation.
Inequality	Benefits accrue to elites with costs shared across the state and commoners. Increases over time due to dynamics of capital accumulation until a great leveler (or more rarely policy intervention) occurs. Tends to be driven further by oligarchy and corruption.
Intra-Elite Competition	Tends to increase cyclically over-time due to structural-demographic changes and changes in capital accumulation.
Oligarchy and Broken Feedbacks	Increases over time driven by inequality, corruption and in some cases, economic expansion (such as in the case of imperial immolation). The end result is state/regulatory capture.

increase over time. These occur alongside diminishing returns on conquest (for empires in particular), energy and resource extraction, and economic development, eventually creating state capture, instability, fiscal drain, and fragility. Elites tend to take a larger share of extractive benefits until state decline or collapse sets in. Then, returns on extraction begin to diminish for elites as well, who depend on the coercive framework provided by the state.

Most of the contributors to DROE have some form of diminishing returns, although with different returns to different parts of society. Inequality only truly provides returns to the elites. Eventually, even they suffer diminishing returns. Other dynamics identified here, such as economic development and innovation, can, in principle, bring broader benefits, but also tend to follow a pattern of declining returns. Each of these is interconnected. For instance, intra-elite competition is best thought of as an outcome of declining returns on inequality, EROI, and economic development.

The important point is that the overarching theory of diminishing returns on extraction refers to returns for the state and economic elites.

This is by no means a complete picture of state decline and collapse. It does not account for the early mortality that befell many states. The earliest states were tenuous constructs, and even today, many artificial states born of colonialism have proved to be brittle. As Yofee, McAnany, and Cowgill note, "concentrations of power in early civilizations were typically fragile and short-lived." (Yoffee and Cowgill 1991; McAnany and Cowgill 2009)

It should also be noted that any declining returns on energy and environmental extraction were often highly shaped by external factors. As noted above, the declining returns on crop yields faced by the Indus Valley population were the result of adaptation to climate change, rather than any law of diminishing returns. In the case of the collapse of the Akkadian Empire, the threat of advancing Amorite forces compelled the administration to work the cultivators so hard that most resisted or fled (Scott 2017).

It is worth pausing here to address one of the most common critiques of "conflict" accounts of state decline. It is in the interest of elites and the state to maintain and provide for the welfare of the population they rely on (Tainter 1988). This assumes a long-sighted, rational view that few possess, and overlooks that state administrations and elites are often locked in competition within groups (intra-elite competition), between each other (corruption), and with other states. This heightens the pressure toward extraction. This competitive state creates a kind of "attractor state" where further exploitation faces less friction than remedying actions. For instance, efforts toward long-lasting distribution have always faced heated opposition throughout history and have almost always failed (Scheidel 2017). In contrast, worsening taxes or conscription are as regular as rain. Importantly, the empirical findings around the social degrading effect of inequality are not contingent on the standard of living, but rather on the relative level of inequality (Wilkinson and Pickett 2009).

None of these factors—corruption, inequality, declining EROI, or weakened feedbacks—is intrinsic to complex social systems. Nor is hierarchy an inherent part of complex social systems. Instead, states face a range of diminishing economic, political, and environmental returns as they build capital through extraction. Each of these relationships—between capital accumulation and inequality, inequality and corruption, structural and demographic change, and inequality and broken feedbacks—is well-established empirically. It is largely a process of "politicide" (Scott 2017) that has often coincided with more external shocks such as climate change, war, disease, and natural disasters. Which effects predominate, and how long they take to arise, will vary by the extractive political form. Empires provide one clear and exemplary case of how diminishing returns on extraction occur given a particular political logic.

3.2.6 Imperial Immolation

Empires present a societal structure that is particularly prone to one type of diminishing returns: Diminishing returns on militaristic expansion. Empires are large polities composed of previously sovereign territories and states that are formally and informally controlled to extract value (Doyle 1986; Taagepera 1978). This can be either through direct conquest of territory or effective economic control of resources. The latter has been the basis for branding the modern-day USA as a form of new imperialism (Harvey 2005). In both cases, the empire requires coercion for the extraction of value for the imperial heartland. It needs military power.

Empires are run autocratically at a geopolitical level, and the main benefits of conquest tend to be concentrated. This is clear in Hobson's criticisms of British imperialism: "Although the new Imperialism has been bad business for the nation, it has been good business for certain classes and certain trades within the nation" (Hobson 1902). There are, of course, spillover benefits to citizens more widely, especially those within the imperial core. The capture of the treasury of Macedonia in 167 BCE allowed the Western Roman Empire to eliminate taxes in Rome. Such benefits, whether they be in booty, captives, or new resources, tend to diminish as the costs of maintenance pile up, new wars become costlier, and enemies multiply.

Imperial expansion tends to career into fiscal decline, and eventually fragmentation or collapse. The thesis of Paul Kennedy's *Rise and Fall of Great Powers* is that overstretch and an inability to maintain a costly military leviathan eventually lead to relative economic, and then military, decline (Kennedy 2010). This was common across modern empires including the Spanish, Ottoman, Portuguese, and British. Both budget deficits and military spending increased until either fragmentation or decline set in.

Such a dynamic is also apparent in the Western Roman Empire, where economic problems were compounded by reforms over the course of the fourth century, in which the military and land taxes doubled while the bureaucracy swelled (Tainter 2015). In many of these cases, dwindling resources compounded the declining returns on imperialism. For Rome, silver and gold mines, particularly in Spain, required deeper, costlier excavation (Edmondson

1989). To make matters worse, industrial activity and mining were disrupted by the third-century crisis (McConnell et al. 2018). This was accompanied by intra-elite struggles, civil war, rampant inequality, and the eventual intersection of exogenous shocks such as climate change (Büntgen et al. 2016) and disease (Harper 2017) (although the severity of the Justinian Plague is questionable) (Mordechai et al. 2019). Corruption and elite mismanagement were present in key events during the decline of Rome, including the beginning of the Gothic War with the mistreatment of refugee Goths by Commander Lupicinus (Middleton 2017). All of the markers of diminishing returns on extraction were manifest in Rome, not just simply debt. As Walter Scheidel notes in a later chapter in this volume, the process of imperial decay in Rome fits fairly well with the theory of diminishing returns on extraction (Scheidel 2023).

Understanding and studying this process of what I term *imperial immolation* will require a more detailed case study analysis and analysis of empires as a category. Notably, existing studies of the lifespan of empires (Arbesman 2011) based on data gathered from 3000 BCE to 600 CE (Taagepera 1978, 1979) suggests an ageless distribution. This may suggest that any theory of overreach is false as the risk of imperial disaggregation would, if such a theory were accurate, rise over time. However, the problem is that the data is confounded by cases of early conquest (even growing empires can be defeated before overreach sets it) and that it is ambiguous as to when the deleterious effects of imperial overreach set in. Importantly, empires can and do take corrective actions to avert decline, as was the case of the Byzantine Empire (Haldon, Eisenberg, et al. 2020). In short, more work is needed, but empires and the process of imperial immolation provide the clearest case study of diminishing returns on extraction. Empires are, after all, an extractive political apparatus.

3.3 Conclusions

This chapter revises Tainter's diminishing returns on complexity into a theory of diminishing returns on extraction. It is a broader framework with different foundations in how it sees complexity and problem-solving.

Cases of decline and collapse typically involve stratified states. State gains in capital are not rationally or collectively decided; they are mainly a result of elite preferences. There are diminishing returns on energy and resource extraction, although these vary based on social practices and political forms. This is accompanied by declining returns for elites on corruption, economic development, inequality, and oligarchy, eventually leading to intra-elite competition. Conquest also undergoes a pattern of diminishing returns, although this is most applicable to empires (imperial immolation), and not necessarily generalizable to all states.

Moving from complexity to extraction is not just a change in rhetoric. It shifts the frame in which we try to address the problem of declining societal resilience. The solutions no longer appear to be just in the domain of seeking new technical innovations to stave off diminishing returns on complexity, or the acquisition of new sources of energy to keep EROI high. Instead, it places the emphasis on institutional fixes. If the issue is diminishing returns on both social and environmental extraction, then the way forward is much more about social transformation: The implementation of deliberative democracy to improve negative feedbacks, the reduction of wasteful expenditure and regulation, the leveling of wealth disparities, the separation of wealth and political power, and potentially even economic degrowth.

This could be viewed as cause for celebration: We are no longer doomed to frantically grasp for one technological stopgap after another in an unwinnable battle against an eventually diminishing EROI. Instead, societies can reach true, lasting stability if citizens can "shackle the leviathan" (Acemoglu and Robinson 2020) by building more inclusive institutions that are democratically proactive to emerging problems.

Returns on energy and economic development will continue to be an important consideration, as will the wise and prudent use of resources to address genuine social problems, rather than elite capital accumulation. These are problems not of complexity, but of extractive political systems.

Acknowledgment

I would like to extend my gratitude to Miguel Centeno, Peter Callahan, Thayer Patterson, and Paul Larcey for the kind offer to participate in the Princeton symposium and this volume. Many thanks to Walter Scheidel, John Haldon, Zia Mian, Benjamin Hunt, Nathaniel Cooke, Catherine Richards, Haydn Belfield, Sabin Roman, Carla Zoe Cremer, and Tilman Hartley for their useful comments on earlier drafts.

Notes

1 This paraphrases Piketty and Zucman's definition of "capital" on pages 1264-1265.
2 If one defines or measures complexity by energy use, then it of course becomes a circular argument.
3 Tainter 1988; Roman and Palmer 2019; Homer-Dixon 2008.
4 Büntgen et al. 2016.
5 Harper 2017.
6 Turchin and Nefedov 2009.
7 Roman et al. 2018.
8 Aimers and Hodell 2011; Bazy and Inomata 2017.
9 Tainter 2019.
10 Roman et al. 2017.
11 DiNapoli et al. 2020.
12 Diamond 2011.
13 Tainter 1988.

References

Acemoglu, D., Johnson, S., Robinson, J. and Thaicharoen, Y. 2003. Institutional Causes, Macroeconomic Symptoms: Volatility, Crises and Growth. *J. Monet. Econ.* 50(1), 49–123.

Acemoglu, D. and Robinson, J. A. 2013. *Why Nations Fail: The Origins of Power, Prosperity, and Poverty.* Currency.

Acemoglu, D. and Robinson, J. A. 2020. *The Narrow Corridor: States, Societies, and the Fate of Liberty.* Penguin Books.

Aimers, J. and Hodell, D. 2011. Societal Collapse: Drought and the Maya. *Nature* 479(7371), 44–45.

Anderies, J. and Levin, S. 2023. Conservation of Fragility and the Collapse of Social Orders. In: *How Worlds Collapse: What History, Systems, and Complexity Can Teach Us about Our Modern World and Fragile Future.* (eds. Centeno, M., Callahan, P., Larcey, P., and Patterson, T.) 282–295. Routledge.

Anton, D. 2012. "Treaty Congestion" in International Environmental Law. In: *Routledge Handbook of International Environmental Lobby* (eds. Alam, H. and Bhuiyan, J. H.) 651–665. Routledge.

Arbesman, S. 2011. The Life-Spans of Empires. *Hist. Methods* 44(3), 127–129.

Bardi, U., Falsini, S. and Perissi, I. 2019. Toward a General Theory of Societal Collapse: A Biophysical Examination of Tainter's Model of the Diminishing Returns of Complexity. *Biophys. Econ. Resour. Qual.* 4, 1–9.

Bazy, D. and Inomata, T. 2017. Multiple Waves of Political Disintegration in the Classic Maya Collapse: New Insights from the Excavation of Group D, Ceibal, Guatemala. *J. Archaeol.* 42(2), 82–96.

Bird, D. W., Bird, R. B., Codding, B. F. and Zeanah, D. W. 2019. Variability in the Organization and Size of Hunter-Gatherer Groups: Foragers Do Not Live in Small-Scale Societies. *J. Hum. Evol.* 131, 96–108.

Blanton, R. E., Feinman, G. M., Kowalewski, S. A. and Fargher, L. F. 2020. Moral Collapse and State Failure: A View from the Past. *Front. Pol. Sci.* 2, 8.

Bloom, N., Jones, C. I., Van Reenen, J. and Webb, M. 2020. Are Ideas Getting Harder to Find? *Am. Econ. Rev.* 110(4), 1104–1144.

Bogaard, A., Fochesato, M. and Bowles, S. 2019. The Farming-Inequality Nexus: New Insights from Ancient Western Eurasia. *Antiquity* 93(371), 1129–1143.

Brunk, G. G. 2002. Why Do Societies Collapse? A Theory Based on Self-Organized Criticality. *J. Theor. Polit.* 14(2), 195–230.

Büntgen, U. et al. 2016. Cooling and Societal Change During the Late Antique Little Ice Age from 536 to Around 660 AD. *Nat. Geosci.* 9(3), 231–236.

Butzer, K. W. 2012. Collapse, Environment, and Society. *Proc. Natl. Acad. Sci. U.S.A.* 109(10), 3632–3639.

Butzer, K. W. and Endfield, G. H. 2012. Critical Perspectives on Historical Collapse. *Proc. Natl. Acad. Sci. U.S.A.* 109(10), 3628–3631.

Diamond, J. 2011. *Collapse: How Societies Choose to Fail or Succeed.* Penguin Books.

DiNapoli, R. J., Rieth, T. M., Lipo, C. P. and Hunt, T. L. A. 2020. A Model-Based Approach to the Tempo of "Collapse": The Case of Rapa Nui (Easter Island). *J. Archaeol. Sci.* 116, 1–10.

Dinopoulos, E. and Syropoulos, C. 2007. Rent Protection as a Barrier to Innovation and Growth. *Econ. Theor.* 32(2), 309–332.

Doyle, M. 1986. *Empires.* Cornell University Press.

Edmondson, J. C. 1989. Mining in the Later Roman Empire and Beyond: Continuity or Disruption? *J. Rom. Stud.* 79, 84–102.

Elias, N. 2012. *On the Process of Civilization: Sociogenetic and Psychogenetic Investigations.* University College Dublin Press.

Ellis, E. C., Magliocca, N. R., Stevens, C. J. and Fuller, D. Q. 2018. Evolving the Anthropocene: Linking Multi-level Selection with Long-Term Social–Ecological Change. *Sustain. Sci.* 13(1), 119–128.

Froese, T., Gershenson, C. and Manzanilla, L. R. 2014. Can Government Be Self-Organized? A Mathematical Model of the Collective Social Organization of Ancient Teotihuacan, Central Mexico. *PLOS ONE* 9(10), e109966.

Goldacre, B. 2014. *Bad Pharma: How Drug Companies Mislead Doctors and Harm Patients.* Macmillan.

Goldstone, J. A. 2016. *Revolution and Rebellion in the Early Modern World: Population Change and State Breakdown in England, France, Turkey, and China, 1600–1850.* Routledge.

Goldstone, J. A. 2017. Demographic Structural Theory: 25 Years On. *Cliodynamics* 8(2), 85–112.

Graeber, D. 2018. *Bullshit Jobs: A Theory.* Simon & Schuster.

Green, A. S. 2020. Killing the Priest-King: Addressing Egalitarianism in the Indus Civilization. *J. Archaeol. Res.* doi:10.1007/s10814-020-09147-9.

Gupta, A. K. and Hall, C. A. S. 2011. A Review of the past and Current State of EROI Data. *Sustainability* 3(10), 1796–1809.

Gupta, S., Abed, G. and Alonso-Terme, R. 2002. Does Corruption Affect Income Inequality and Poverty? *Econ. Gov.* 3(1), 23–45.

Haberl, H. et al. 2020. A Systematic Review of the Evidence on Decoupling of GDP, Resource Use and GHG Emissions, Part II: Synthesizing the Insights. *Environ. Res. Lett.* 15(6), 65003.

Haines, A. 2017. Health Co-benefits of Climate Action. *Lancet Planet. Heal.* 1(1), e4–e5.

Haldon, J., Chase, A., Eastwood, W., Medina-Elizalde, M., Izdebski, A., Ludlow, F., Middleton, G., Mordechai, L., Nesbitt, J., and Turner, B. L. 2020. Demystifying Collapse: Climate, Environment, and Social Agency in Pre-modern Societies. *Millennium* 17(1), 1–33.

Haldon, J., Mordechai, L., Newfield, T., Chase, A., Izdebski, A., Guzowski, P., Labuhn, I., and Roberts, N. 2018. History Meets Palaeoscience: Consilience and Collaboration in Studying past Societal Responses to Environmental Change. *Proc. Natl. Acad. Sci. U. S. A.* 115(13), 3210–3218.

Haldon, J., Eisenberg, M., Mordechai, L., Izdebski, A. and White, S. 2020. Lessons from the past, Policies for the Future: Resilience and Sustainability in past Crises. *Environ. Syst. Decis.*, 1–11. doi:10.1007/s10669-020-09778-9.

Hall, C. A. S., Balogh, S. and Murphy, D. J. R. 2009. What Is the Minimum EROI That a Sustainable Society Must Have? *Energies* 2(1), 25–47.

Harper, K. 2017. *The Fate of Rome: Climate, Disease, and the End of an Empire (The Princeton History of the Ancient World).* Princeton University Press.

Harvey, D. 2005. *The New Imperialism.* OUP.

Hickel, J. 2020. *Less Is More: How Degrowth Will Save the World.* William Heinemann.

Hickel, J. and Kallis, G. 2020. Is Green Growth Possible? *New Polit. Econ.* 25(4), 469–486.

Hobson, J. A. 1902. *Imperialism: A Study.* Cosimo Classics.

Hochschild, A. 2006. *Bury the Chains: Prophets and Rebels in the Fight to Free an Empire's Slaves.* Houghton Mifflin Harcourt.

Homer-Dixon, T. 2008. *The Upside of Down: Catastrophe, Creativity, and the Renewal of Civilization.* Island Press.

Hunt, T. L. 2006. Rethinking the Fall of Easter Island. *Am. Sci.* 94(5), 412–419.

Izdebski, A., Mordechai, L. and White, S. 2018. The Social Burden of Resilience: A Historical Perspective. *Hum. Ecol. Interdiscip. J.* 46(3), 291–303.

Jarvis, A. 2018. Energy Returns and the Long-Run Growth of Global Industrial Society. *Ecol. Econ.* 146, 722–729.

Johnson, S. A. 2017. *Why Did Ancient Civilizations Fail?* Routledge.

Kemp, L. 2021. Agents of Doom: Who Is Creating the Apocalypse and Why. *BBC Future* (online newsletter).

Kennedy, P. 2010. *The Rise and Fall of the Great Powers: Economic Change and Military Conflict from 1500 to 2000*. Vintage.

Lane, D. 2006. Hierarchy, Complexity, Society. In: *Hierarchy in Natural and Social Sciences* (ed. Pumain, D.) 81–119. Springer.

Lattimore, O. 1962. *Studies in Frontier History: Collected Papers 1928–1958*. Oxford University Press.

Lawson, G. 2019. *Anatomies of Revolution*. Cambridge University Press.

Lenton, T. M. 2011. Early Warning of Climate Tipping Points. *Nat. Clim. Chang.* 1(4), 201–209.

Linklater, A. 2016. *Violence and Civilization in Western States-Systems*. Cambridge University Press.

Mann, M. 1986. *The Sources of Social Power: Volume 1: A History of Power from the Beginning to AD 1760*. Vol. 1. Cambridge University Press.

Marcus, J. 2008. The Archaeological Evidence for Social Evolution. *Annu. Rev. Anthropol.* 37(1), 251–266.

McAnany, P. A. and Yoffee, N. 2009. *Questioning Collapse: Human Resilience, Ecological Vulnerability, and the Aftermath of Empire*. Cambridge University Press.

McConnell, J. R. et al. 2018. Lead Pollution Recorded in Greenland Ice Indicates European Emissions Tracked Plagues, Wars, and Imperial Expansion During Antiquity. *Proc. Natl. Acad. Sci. U. S. A.* 115(22), 5726–5731.

McGoey, L. 2019. *The Unknowers: How Strategic Ignorance Rules the World*. Zed Books.

Middleton, G. D. 2012. Nothing Lasts Forever: Environmental Discourses on the Collapse of Past Societies. *J. Archaeol. Res* 20(3), 257–307.

Middleton, G. D. 2017. *Understanding Collapse: Ancient History and Modern Myths*. Cambridge University Press.

Millward-Hopkins, J., Steinberger, J. K., Rao, N. D. and Oswald, Y. 2020. Providing Decent Living with Minimum Energy: A Global Scenario. *Glob. Environ. Change* 65, 102168.

Mordechai, L. et al. 2019. The Justinianic Plague: An Inconsequential Pandemic? *Proc. Natl. Acad. Sci. U.S.A.* 116(51), 25546–25554.

Morris, I. 2010. *Why the West Rules—for Now: The Patterns of History and What They Reveal About the Future*. Profile Books.

Mueller, T. 2019. *Crisis of Conscience: Whistleblowing in an Age of Fraud*. Riverhead Books.

Murtazashvili, J. and Murtazashvili, I. 2020. Wealth-Destroying States. *Public Choice* 182(3–4), 353–371.

Olson, M. 2000. *Power and Prosperity: Outgrowing Communist and Capitalist Dictatorships*. Basic Books.

Oreskes, N. and Conway, E. M. 2010. *Merchants of Doubt: How a Handful of Scientists Obscured the Truth on Issues from Tobacco Smoke to Global Warming*. Bloomsbury Press.

Petrie, C. A. 2019. Diversity, Variability, Adaptation and "Fragility" in the Indus Civilization. In: *The Evolution of Fragility: Setting the Terms* (ed. Yoffee, N.) 109–133. McDonald Institute for Archaeological Research.

Piketty, T. 2017. *Capital in the Twenty-First Century*. Belknap Press.

Piketty, T. 2020. *Capital and Ideology*. Harvard University Press.

Piketty, T. and Zucman, G. 2014. Capital Is Back: Wealth-Income Ratios in Rich Countries 1700–2010. *Q. J. Econ.* 129(3), 1255–1310.

Policardo, L. and Carrera, E. J. S. 2018. Corruption Causes Inequality, or Is It the Other Way Around? An Empirical Investigation for a Panel of Countries. *Econ. Anal. Policy* 59, 92–102.

Putnam, R. 1993. The Prosperous Community: Social Capital and Public Life. *Am. Prospect* 13(4), 249–262.

Roman, S. and Palmer, E. 2019. The Growth and Decline of the Western Roman Empire: Quantifying the Dynamics of Army Size, Territory, and Coinage. *Cliodynamics* 10(2), 1–23.

Roman, S., Bullock, S. and Brede, M. 2017. Coupled Societies Are More Robust against Collapse: A Hypothetical Look at Easter Island. *Ecol. Econ.* 132, 264–278.

Roman, S., Palmer, E. and Brede, M. 2018. The Dynamics of Human–Environment Interactions in the Collapse of the Classic Maya. *Ecol. Econ.* 146, 312–324.

Scarborough, V. L. and Lucero, L. J. 2010. The Non-hierarchical Development of Complexity in the Semitropics: Water and Cooperation. *Water Hist.* 2(2), 185–205.

Scheidel, W. 2017. *The Great Leveler: Violence and the History of Inequality from the Stone Age to the Twenty-First Century.* Princeton University Press.

Scheidel, W. 2023. The End of 'Peak Empire': The Collapse of the Roman, Han, and Jin Empires. In: *How Worlds Collapse: What History, Systems, and Complexity Can Teach Us about Our Modern World and Fragile Future* (eds. Centeno, M., Callahan, P., Larcey, P., and Patterson, T.) 108–123. Routledge.

Scott, J. C. 1990. *Domination and the Arts of Resistance: Hidden Transcripts.* Yale University Press.

Scott, J. C. 1999. *Seeing Like a State: How Certain Schemes to Improve the Human Condition Have Failed.* Yale University Press.

Scott, J. C. 2008. *Weapons of the Weak: Everyday Forms of Peasant Resistance.* Yale University Press.

Scott, J. C. 2017. *Against the Grain: A Deep History of the Earliest States.* Yale University Press.

Scott, J. C. 2019. Response to Commentaries on *Against the Grain. J. Peasant Stud.* 46(4), 885–892.

Stevenson, A. 2016. The Egyptian Predynastic and State Formation. *J. Archaeol. Res.* 24(4), 421–468.

Strumsky, D., Lobo, J. and Tainter, J. A. 2010. Complexity and the Productivity of Innovation. *Syst. Res. Behav. Sci.* 27(5), 496–509.

Taagepera, R. 1978. Size and Duration of Empires: Growth-Decline Curves, 3000 to 600 B.C. *Soc. Sci. Res.* 7(2), 180–196.

Taagepera, R. 1979. Size and Duration of Empires: Growth-Decline Curves, 600 B.C to 600 A.D. *Soc. Sci. His* 3(3–4), 115–138.

Tainter, J. A. 1988. *The Collapse of Complex Societies.* Cambridge University Press.

Tainter, J. A. 1995. Sustainability of Complex Societies. *Futures* 27(4), 397–407.

Tainter, J. A. 2006a. Archaeology of Overshoot and Collapse. *Annu. Rev. Anthropol.* 35(1), 59–74.

Tainter, J. A. 2006b. Social Complexity and Sustainability. *Ecol. Complexity* 3(2), 91–103.

Tainter, J. A. 2011. Energy, Complexity, and Sustainability: A Historical Perspective. *Environ. Innov. Soc. Transit.* 1(1), 89–95.

Tainter, J. A. 2015. Collapse and Sustainability: Rome, the Maya and the Modern World. *Archaeological Pap. Am. Anthropol. Assoc.* 24, 201–214.

Tainter, J. A. 2019. Cahokia: Urbanization, Metabolism, and Collapse. *Front. Sustain. Cities* 1.

Turchin, P. and Nefedov, S. A. 2009. *Secular Cycles.* Princeton University Press.

Turchin, P. et al. 2015. Seshat: The Global History Databank. *Cliodynamics: J. Quant. Hist. Cult. Evol.* 5, 77–107.

Van Bavel, B. 2019. Power Concentration and State Capture: Insights from History on Consequences of Market Dominance for Inequality and Environmental Calamities. *UN Human Development Report 2019*, 60.

Van Bavel, B. 2016. *The Invisible Hand?: How Market Economies Have Emerged and Declined Since AD 500*. Oxford University Press.

Van de Mieroop, M. 1999. The Government of an Ancient Mesopotamian City: What We Know and Why We Know so Little. In: *Priests and Officials in the Ancient Near East* (ed. Watanabe, K.) 139–161. Universitätsverlag C. Winter.

Vu, T. 2010. Studying the State Through State Formation. *World Polit.* 62(1), 148–175.

Wallerstein, I. 2000. Globalization or the Age of Transition? *Int. Sociol.* 15(2), 249–265.

Wengrow, D. 1972. The Origins of Civic Life: A Global Perspective. In: *Prehistory and Protohistory of Ancient Civilizations* (eds. Frangipane, M. and Manzanilla, L. R.) 1–44. Gangemi Editore International.

Wengrow, D. 2001. The Evolution of Simplicity: Aesthetic Labour and Social Change in the Neolithic Near East. *World Archaeol.* 33(2), 168–188.

Wengrow, D. 2017. Avoiding the Pestilence of the State: Some Thoughts on Niche Construction, Heritage, and Sacred Waterworks. *Archaeol. Int.* 20, 137.

Wengrow, D. 2019. Rethinking Cities, from the Ground Up. *Medium.* Available at: https://medium.com/whose-society-whose-cohesion/rethinking-cities-from-the-ground-up-73d92059b15f#ednref3.

Wengrow, D. and Graeber, D. 2015. Farewell to the "Childhood of Man": Ritual, Seasonality, and the Origins of Inequality. *J. R. Anthropol. Inst.* 21(3), 597–619.

Wilkinson, R. and Pickett, K. 2009. *The Spirit Level: Why Greater Equality Makes Societies Stronger*. Bloomsbury Publishing.

Wilkinson, R. and Pickett, K. 2019. *The Inner Level: How More Equal Societies Reduce Stress, Restore Sanity and Improve Everyone's Well-Being*. Penguin Books.

World Resources Institute: Global Commission on the Economy and Climate. 2014. *Better Growth, Better Climate: The New Climate Economy Report*, 2–33. World Resources Institute.

Yoffee, N. 2016. The Power of Infrastructures: A Counternarrative and a Speculation. *J. Archaeol. Method Theor.* 23(4), 1053–1065.

Yoffee, N. 2019. Introducing the Conference: There Are No Innocent Terms. In: *The Evolution of Fragility: Setting the Terms* (ed. Yoffee, N.) 1–7. McDonald Institute for Archaeological Research.

Yoffee, N. and Cowgill, G. L. 1991. *The Collapse of Ancient States and Civilizations*. University of Arizona Press.

Yoffee, N. and Seri, A. 2019. Negotiating Fragility in Ancient Mesopotamia: Arenas of Contestation and Institutions of Resistance. In: *The Evolution of Fragility: Setting the Terms* (ed. Yoffee, N.) 183–196. McDonald Institute for Archaeological Research.

You, J.-S. and Khagram, S. 2005. A Comparative Study of Inequality and Corruption. *Am. Soc. Rev.* 70(1), 136–157.

Zarakol, A. 2022. *Before the West: The Rise and Fall of Eastern World Orders*. Cambridge University Press.

4 Collapse, Recovery, and Existential Risk

Haydn Belfield

4.1 Introduction

Around 2000 BCE, regarding the devastation of the Old Kingdom, Ankhtifi wrote:

> The whole of Upper Egypt died of hunger and each individual had reached such a state of hunger that he ate his own children.
>
> (Grimal & Shaw, 2001)

It must have felt like the end of the world—the end of civilization, humanity itself.

This ghastly image had an echo 4000 years later, after the Trinity test in 1945 when humanity first gained the capability to end the entire human story, in Oppenheimer's famous statement, quoting from the Bhagavad-Gita:[1]

> I am become death, destroyer of worlds.
>
> (Hijiya, 2000)

These statements are about two horrors: collapse in the first and existential risk in the second. Collapse and existential risk share many similarities, as among the worst things human civilization can do to itself. However, the two fields that study these topics—collapse studies and existential risk studies—have surprisingly few overlaps.

The field of collapse studies seeks to understand historical societal collapses. The chapters in this volume explore both particular case studies, such as the Late Bronze Age or the Western Roman Empire, and theoretical causal mechanisms and relationships, such as diminishing returns on complexity and elite overproduction. The field of collapse studies has tended to draw mostly on history and archaeology, with significant interest from complexity scholars and the social sciences more broadly.

Existential risk studies seeks to understand and mitigate events and processes that threaten the destruction of humanity's longterm potential (Ord, 2020)—that could "either annihilate Earth-originating intelligent life or permanently

DOI: 10.4324/9781003331384-6

and drastically curtail its potential" (Bostrom, 2002). It is particularly concerned, therefore, with human extinction and changes to humanity's longterm trajectories. It has tended to draw more on the physical sciences (such as space, nuclear, biology, and machine learning) with significant interest from philosophers working on population ethics.

The histories of the two fields have several similarities (Beard & Torres, 2020). Both had early precursors (Gibbon, 1789; Shelley, 1826; Toynbee, 1934; Wells, 1897). In the post-war era, groups of concerned scientists such as the Club of Rome and the Bulletin of Atomic Scientists raised attention to both fields. In the 1990s and 2000s, both collapse (Diamond, 2005; Homer-Dixon, 2007; Tainter, 1988; Turchin, 2003) and existential risk (Bostrom, 2002; Leslie, 1996; Posner, 2004; Rees, 2003) experienced increased academic and popular interest.

In recent years, there has been some limited interaction between the two. For example, my own group, the Centre for the Study of Existential Risk at the University of Cambridge, is "dedicated to the study and mitigation of risks that could lead to human extinction or civilisational collapse." In February 2018, I organized a Workshop on Modelling Societal Collapse with Prof. Jared Diamond. There has also been useful work done by the Global Catastrophic Risk Institute (Baum et al., 2019; Maher & Baum, 2013), and indeed the Princeton Institute for International and Regional Studies (PIIRS) Global Systemic Risk research community at Princeton University. However, this has been recent and partly motivated by a recognition of this very gap.

Yet overall, current collaboration is limited. The two disciplines rarely cite one another or attend one another's conferences. Few academics, centers, research programs, and agendas, or seminar series and conferences cover both. Key topics from each field (such as system dynamics or anthropogenic risks) take time to travel across the two. This is strange for two relatively small fields that both study low-probability, high-impact catastrophic events, share certain methodologies and interests (such as complex adaptive systems), and could learn a lot from one another. Why do these two fields not collaborate more?

I suggest that a key reason for this apparent disconnect has been a remarkably sanguine attitude toward the prospect of recovery following a collapse of contemporary global civilization from leading existential risk scholars. This has contributed to, and been matched by, a relative lack of interest on the part of collapse scholars in recovery from a contemporary collapse.

There are many possible motivations to be concerned about a contemporary collapse. It would be terrible for the present generation. The suffering and death of billions would be an unprecedented tragedy. It would also be deeply unjust, as those in precarious situations in the developing world who have contributed least to the risk would likely be the main victims (Mitchell & Chaudhury, 2020).

However, a key motivation for many existential risk scholars is "longtermism," the moral view that we should be particularly concerned with ensuring that the long-run future goes well (Beckstead, 2013; Greaves & MacAskill,

2019). This does not deny the suffering and death that would accompany a collapse. But it does say the most important thing is how the long run goes.

Longtermists have reason to be concerned, as the effects of collapse might not be limited to the present generation. If a collapse were "permanent" (Bostrom, 2013), it could lead to all future possible generations living in a worse state. At the extreme, collapse could lead to extinction, if humanity is unable to prevent natural risks such as asteroids or uses weapons of mass destruction (WMD). Extinction would mean that all future generations would never exist (Parfit, 1984). This betrayal of the future would also be a betrayal of the past. The unbroken chain of generations, each passing on the baton to the next—surviving, growing, and learning—would come to an end.[2]

However, many scholars are confident that collapse would not have these effects—that the likelihood of recovery is high. For example, in his new book that aims to be the standard introduction to the field, Toby Ord stated:

> I think that even if civilization did collapse, it would likely recover.[3]
> (Ord, 2020)

This view is shared by other leading scholars (Bostrom, 2002; Hanson, 2008;; Paul Christiano, 2018; Shulman, 2020). If collapse will likely be followed by a rapid recovery, then from a longtermist perspective it might not destroy humanity's longterm potential. Collapse could be a regrettable, sad episode but zooming out, only a momentary blip—barely perceptible in humanity's steady rise.[4]

Is this true? Is collapse not that important?

In this chapter, I argue that while a credible argument can be made for the likelihood of recovery, we should not be sanguine. Even from a longtermist perspective, a collapse could destroy humanity's longterm potential. We cannot yet confidently rule out the prospect of permanent collapse or extinction—and we have good reasons to be concerned that a global civilization that recovered may have much worse prospects. In turn, I discuss the prospects for survival from a catastrophe and "technical recovery," a concept I will introduce, before turning to what effect a collapse could have on our prospects. There is a kaleidoscope of contemporary collapse scenarios, depending on the hazards involved, scale, severity, and speed. The best this chapter can offer are some high-level considerations. Nevertheless, the central claim that collapse is not particularly relevant to existential risk is deeply questionable. Finally, I end with some suggestions for lessons the two fields could learn from one another, and for fruitful collaborations.

4.2 A Contemporary Collapse: Characteristics and Contributing Factors

The conceptualization of "collapse" is highly contested, but I use it to refer to a process of societal and political disaggregation (relatively rapid, over years or decades) to a less complex, enduring form, typically associated with economic loss, state collapse,[5] and large-scale migration or death. It is the end of a particular complex form of social organization and cooperation. Most scholars across the two fields agree that a collapse of current global civilization is possible. By "civilization," I refer to contemporary global society—the complex adaptive system formed by the interdependent economic, political, military, and cultural networks that link states and communities (Centeno et al., 2015). A "contemporary collapse," then, would be a global process of disaggregation, to a fragmented, simpler form, likely accompanied economic loss, widespread state collapse, and large-scale migration or death

We could operationalize this in a number of ways. For example, the "social development index," includes energy capture, urbanism, information processing, and war-making capacity (Morris, 2013). Other proxies associated with economic and technological capacity include population, gross world product (GWP), material culture production, percentage of people in various classes of occupations, or proxies for complexity such as trade, communication, and political and diplomatic contact over large distances. On a more normative dimension, one could also consider average and total wellbeing, healthy life years (Quality-Adjusted Life Years, or QALYs), the Human Development Index (HDI), the Genuine Progress Indicator (Kubiszewski et al., 2013), the Weighted Index of Social Progress (Estes, 2019), or percentage living in slavery or living in democracies. I will not specify particular proxies, as it is not central to my argument.

4.2.1 Characteristics of a Contemporary Collapse

What would a contemporary collapse look like? Too often, the assumption has been a simplistic, charismatic "return to foraging," but this seems implausible.

It has become common in "big history" to separate human history into three stages: "foragers, farmers and fossil fuels" (Morris et al., 2015). While this may be defensible as a short summary of human history, it has contributed to simplistic visions of collapse. Writing on the prospects of a contemporary collapse has sometimes fallen into these simplistic terms, imagining progress simply reversed with humanity being "knocked back" to a "previous stage"—especially that of "hunter-gatherers"[6] (Hanson, 2008; Mitchell & Chaudhury, 2020). Popular media (books and films such as *The Road*) have encouraged this imaginary.

However, historical collapses have rarely led to foraging. Foraging is a highly skilled lifestyle, and many areas are now unsuited to it due to human land use. Societies would not necessarily need to, or be able to, transition from farming and industry. The process of losing technological and manufacturing capacity—like the loss of the ability to construct monumental architecture in historical collapses—might be measured in decades or centuries.

Historical collapse is more often associated with deurbanization and a return to the fields, decentralization and state failure, disaggregation and local rule, and sometimes anarchy and violence—that is to say warlordism (McMahon, 2020). On a global scale, in the post-Industrial Revolution era, this would be unprecedented. However, there are some regional examples of industrialized societies that exhibit similar features—civil wars with state failure. Not all civil wars look like collapse. Some civil wars are concentrated in particular regions, with for example the capital being relatively untouched by violence—such as Angola, Sri Lanka, or Sudan. This can even be the case when warfare is widespread—during the Russian Civil War, several armies showed complex social organization. However, some civil wars have state failure and local warlordism. Possible examples include 1920s China, the Second Congo War, the Syrian War, the Somalian War, or the Afghanistan War. We can usefully consider these modern cases alongside pre-modern collapses such as Late Bronze Age or Western Roman Empire.

4.2.2 Contributing Factors to a Contemporary Collapse

What could contribute to a contemporary collapse? Collapse scholars have explored in-depth factors that contributed to historical societal collapses, and possible contemporary analogues of those factors. However, they have explored relatively less well new anthropogenic risks. Collapse studies is rooted in studies of agrarian societies, but contemporary society faces new, and potentially more concerning risks.

Collapse scholars have explored human factors, environmental factors, and factors associated with systemic structure and system dynamics. When discussing contemporary society, they have emphasized inequality, power centralization, and political polarization at the national level (intra-state), and fragmented global governance at the international level (Turchin, 2003). This has been placed in the context of climate change, resource depletion, the sixth mass extinction, and ecological tipping points (Diamond, 2005). The COVID-19 pandemic has shown the potential of natural pandemics as a "shock" (Ehrenreich, 2020). Scholars have discussed network architecture and systemic characteristics such as tightly coupled just-in-time supply chains with little slack (Homer-Dixon, 2007). The position of critical nodes, such as transport links and reliance on a small number of "breadbaskets" has been emphasized, as have feedback loops such as between the food–water–energy nexus and conflict (Janetos et al., 2017).

However, collapse scholars have been more limited in their exploration of the unprecedented hazards and shocks contemporary society faces. Existential risk scholars suggest that, at a global level, in addition to the "natural" risks all previous generations have faced from asteroids and supervolcanic eruptions to climactic shifts, the current generation now faces a new class of anthropogenic risks. Since the beginning of the Anthropocene, human civilization has gained the ability to destroy itself: nuclear weapons, biological weapons, anthropogenic climate change, and risks from emerging technologies such as artificial intelligence (AI) or synthetic biology.

Existential risk scholars have been particularly interested in these unprecedented anthropogenic risks, which significantly raise the stakes of a contemporary collapse. These risks may dwarf those that previous generations faced. First, unlike earthquakes or famines, they are global in scope. Second, their severity may be worse. Humans as a species have a track record of tens of thousands of years of surviving natural risks (Ord, 2020; Sandberg, 2018). The track record of anthropogenic risks only lasts a few decades. This is captured by Lord Rees' statement:

> Our Earth has existed for 45 million centuries, but this century is special: it's the first when one species, ours, has the planet's future in its hands.
>
> (Rees, 2003)

Risks from nuclear war (Xia et al., 2020; Scherrer et al., 2020) or anthropogenic climate change (Weitzman, 2009; Xu & Ramanathan, 2017) will be familiar to many. However, we now face a set of emerging risks that could also pose a significant threat: those around biotechnologies and AI.[7] Rapidly advancing capabilities in these fields are likely to produce much social benefit but also raise new risks. Global governance for anthropogenic risks is limited and diffuse, with many gaps (Kemp & Rhodes, 2020).

One particular biotechnological concern is an engineered pandemic with a combination of transmission, incubation, and lethality much worse than that produced by nature (Adalja et al., 2018). This risk could emerge from state bioweapons programs (Carus, 2015, 2017), terrorist groups (Yuki et al., 2011), or accidental release from academic or corporate groups (Lipsitch & Inglesby, 2014). For example, a single postdoctoral researcher recently produced a complete synthesis of a horsepox virus, which is similar to history's deadliest disease, smallpox (Koblentz, 2017). An engineered pandemic could threaten global society in a way that, for example, the 1918 Influenza ("Spanish Flu") was unable to (Millett & Snyder-Beattie, 2017; Schoch-Spana et al., 2017).

Concerns with AI and machine learning can be categorized into safety, security, and structural concerns (Zwetsloot & Dafoe, 2019). Safety concerns are that as global society becomes increasingly dependent on increasingly advanced AI systems, accidents could be catastrophic (Bostrom, 2014; Russell, 2019). Security concerns include new physical, political, and cybersecurity risks from states and non-state groups (Brundage et al., 2018; Payne, 2018). Especially concerning are lethal autonomous weapons, those that can autonomously identify, select, and kill targets without meaningful human intervention or control (Boulanin & Verbruggen, 2017). These could be a new weapon of mass destruction (Russell et al., 2018), a concern raised by an Open Letter signed by over 3700 AI and robotics researchers and over 20,000 others (Future of Life Institute, 2015). Structural concerns include arms races, quicker escalation, destabilizing the geopolitical order, and destabilizing nuclear deterrence (Cave & ÓhÉigeartaigh, 2018; Dafoe, 2018; Geist & Lohn, 2018; Horowitz et al., 2018). These three categories all threaten global society.

A contemporary collapse is predictable and preventable. Contributing factors include those highlighted by collapse and existential risk scholars respectively. A collapsed state for global society might be characterized by state failure and warlordism—a general decentralization, disaggregation, and fragmentation.

4.3 Three Pathways from Collapse

In the previous section, we explored what could lead to a contemporary collapse, and the possible characteristics of the collapsed state. We now turn to what happens next. How could collapse destroy humanity's longterm potential?

There are three ways collapse could permanently impact humanity, the first two of which are clear: if humanity went extinct during the period of collapse, or if humanity never recovered. The third is less clear, but by no means less worrying: that the global society that recovers could be much worse for humanity's longterm potential. I will examine each of these outcomes (see Figure 4.1) in turn.

4.3.1 Extinction

One possible outcome of a collapse is that humanity goes extinct. A traumatized, fractured world population after a collapse maybe not be able to survive for long.

Collapse is a major risk factor—far greater, I would argue, than for example great power war. It increases the chance of extinction from a range of hazards. During the process of breakdown, WMD such as nuclear weapons or bioweapons are more likely to be used by states, or to fall out of state control.[8] While in the collapsed state, humanity would be less able to respond to natural hazards (such as asteroid impact) or environmental hazards (such as climate change). In a disaster risk reduction framework, collapse increases humanity's exposure and vulnerability to hazards, and reduces its resilience.

A contemporary collapse would differ from pre-industrial cases due to deepened interdependence, the existence of WMD, and the "hyperconnected, hypercomplex, hypercoupled" nature of modern society (Kemp, 2019a, 2019b). Humanity may have climbed high up a "rungless ladder"—while

Figure 4.1 Three Negative Possible Outcomes of Civilizational Collapse.

historic societies fell only a small distance, modern societies may reach "terminal velocity." Around 1% of the UK workforce is currently employed in agriculture (DEFRA, 2020). As Centeno et al. argue in Chapter 1 of this volume, unlike previous collapses where people could respond by either returning to the fields or "exiting" the territory (Hirschman, 1970), modern globalization means that there would be no simple escape from a global collapse. This unprecedented nature is most concerning. A single collapse could be one too many.

Assessing the likelihood of survival can be split into two stages: surviving the initial crisis/catastrophe and surviving the condition of collapse.

For the first stage, key factors are the size, spread, and connectivity of the global population. There are seven billion people, spread across the world in every biome/ecoregion (Olson et al., 2001). The majority of those people are clumped together in cities (Matt Boyd, Nick Wilson , 2022). However, some of these people are very isolated. There exist many places that, while not designed to be "bunkers," serve that purpose, such as nuclear submarines, oil rigs, and cruise ships on the ocean, and isolated rural communities on land (Beckstead, 2015b). There are thousands of people in uncontacted groups, tens of thousands on oil rigs, and hundreds of thousands on cruise ships—an estimated one million seafarers at sea at any time (CruiseMarketWatch, 2020; Holmes, 2013; Statista, 2017; Westgarth, 2020).

Most of the hazards we face would likely not kill everyone.[9] Nuclear winter could drastically harm food production; however, some modeling suggests the worst effects could be concentrated in the Northern hemisphere, and for a period of years rather than decades (Coupe et al., 2019). Climate change could render large parts of the world uninhabitable, due to lack of arable land or average temperatures being above "wet bulb temperature," but this would not be the entirety of the world, and a "Venus effect" is unlikely (Lynas, 2020). Engineered pandemics could infect and kill large parts of the world population, but face an evolutionary trade-off between infectivity and lethality (Adalja et al., 2018), and the hurdle of reaching everyone in the world. Even considering interconnected or cascading risks, it is simply very hard to kill eight billion people—to get everyone.

During the collapsed condition of global society, a key problem would likely be hunger. For the second stage, key factors are the total number of people, the quantity and quality (perishability and accessibility) of food stores, and the ability to grow new food. Feeding the global population requires immense systems of chemical processing, land management, and transportation. The global food system does not have much slack—there are only food stores for up to 12 months if 12 months if waste, animal feed, and biofuels are reduced to near zero (Rivers, et al. 2016).

However, depending on the lingering effects of the crisis, this "grace period" should be long enough to focus on food production (Dartnell, 2014). Even if humanity were unable to grow crops using sunlight, prospects for "resilient foods" (such as mushrooms grown on felled trees) seem surprisingly positive—though ramping up production would be complex, and it would be more effective and easier to have capacity in place before a collapse (Baum et al., 2015; Denkenberger & Pearce, 2016).

A substantial number of people seem likely to survive, and they may be clustered around functional refuges or productive agricultural regions. For example, even if 99.9% of the current world population died or were separated and only 0.1% of the survivors were grouped together, that would still leave the population of New Zealand—which as a major food exporter is certainly capable of autarchic self-sufficiency (Matt Boyd, Nick Wilson , 2022). Indeed, borrowing from conservation, some have argued for remarkably small "minimum viable populations" for humans—in the thousands (Li & Durbin, 2011; Lynch et al., 1995) or even hundreds (Hey, 2005).

Nevertheless, a collapse of a global, industrialized society is unprecedented. We cannot be sure that extinction would not follow. The probability of extinction is low, but not imperceptibly low—it is not a rounding error from 0%. For example, humanity could be unlucky and be hit by a low-probability natural existential hazard while collapsed. Extinction following collapse is a slim but serious possibility.

4.3.2 No Recovery

Another possible outcome is that humanity does not recover from a collapse. To assess the probability of this I will define a "technical recovery," assess the positive and negative factors through the lens of capital theory, and conclude that technical recovery seems likely, but by no means certain.

"Recovery" is a vague term, as it could cover a range of different variables of interest. I will use "technical recovery" to mean a return to the technological and economic level of the current civilization. As discussed above, this can be operationalized in different ways, for example, energy capture, urbanism, information processing, and war-making capacity (Morris, 2013). Rather than specify particular proxies, I will rely on a general assessment of technological and economic output.

For now, I am deliberately excluding a normative or political aspect of recovery. As I am using the term, a "technical recovery" is compatible with a range of outcomes including a range of total, average, and distributions of welfare and wellbeing; and a range of state numbers, sizes, and political regime types. This will be important for the next section.

A range of literature is concerned with prospects for recovery. In the early Cold War, a slew of reports (for example, from the RAND Corporation) attempted to assess the USA and USSR's prospects after a nuclear war (Hirshleifer, 1963, 1965, 1966; Winter, 1963). Other, more recent, relevant literature addresses post-conflict and post-disaster response, reconstruction, and state building and development. These national-level state failures in a globalized world can offer small-scale analogies to a global collapse.[10] We have several recent examples of successful (such as Timor-Leste or Sierra Leone) and less successful (such as Libya or Congo) post-conflict transitions (Howard, 2014; Onoma, 2014). The average is 15–30 years to transition from fragility to resilience (World Bank, 2011), though it should be noted this is with substantial external support in the form of aid, trade, and even "neo-trusteeship" (Fearon & Laitin, 2004), which would not apply in a global collapse.

Notably, however, the field of collapse studies has not been particularly concerned with addressing this question. Research has addressed robustness and resilience, but has been focused on collapse, rather than recovery (Butzer, 2012).

To assess the likelihood of a global "technical recovery," we can draw on capital theory. Theories of long-run economic growth typically rely on models of capital stocks (Cass, 1965; Mankiw et al., 1992; Solow, 1956). Global capital stocks can be categorized into physical, social, human, and natural capital. From the perspective of these capital theories, longterm economic growth (and social development) depends upon the management, combination, and use of these capital stocks (Tzachor, 2020).

We can assess the capital stocks likely available in a post-collapse world to assess its prospects for technical recovery.[11] Indeed, further work could compare that to the capital stocks available at various points of interest, such as 10,000 years ago at the transition to agriculture, cities, and states; or at the transition to the industrial revolution 250 years ago. The better the stocks, the more likely the recovery. For example, humanity was able to develop from the first farmers to our current civilization before: If the capital stocks available in a post-collapse world were better than the stocks existing at the time of the agricultural revolution, then we can be more confident that humanity will be able to repeat its earlier progress. The comparison would also be relevant to an assessment of speed—whether development would be faster in a post-collapse recovery than what was experienced in human history. It would also be relevant to an assessment of the likelihood of multiple recoveries.

Physical (or "manufactured" or "produced") capital refers to "material goods or fixed assets which contribute to the production process rather than being the output itself" (Goodwin, 2003). A post-collapse world would have an abundance of physical capital: Transport infrastructure such as roads, bridges, and tunnels; factories with a variety of machinery; and industrial farms with pesticides and agricultural equipment (Dartnell, 2014). Even a small town in most parts of the world would have metal tools, rubber tires, plastic containers, and internal combustion engines—though physical capital may be becoming more complex and interdependent, requiring specialized skills to maintain (compare an old car to a modern hybrid). The crops we plant and animals we raise are more productive than even those of a hundred years ago, and dramatically so compared to those first domesticated.

Human capital refers to individuals' knowledge, skills, health, and motivation. The world population is well-educated and skilled compared to human history. Over 80% of the world population has had some formal basic education, compared to less than 20% in 1820 (Roser & Ortiz-Ospina, 2013).

Literacy, numeracy, and specialized skills would be important in an industrial recovery. Humanity's collective knowledge includes many topics in science, technology, engineering and mathematics, and medicine. Knowledge of the germ theory of disease, electromagnetism, or crop rotation would be very useful in recovery.

An individual's knowledge is lost if they die without passing it on to the next generation. However, a post-collapse world would be in a much better situation than, for example, Renaissance Europeans relying on Arabic translations and scraps found in monasteries. Google Books estimates there are at least 146 million books in the world, and this is likely an underestimate (Taycher, 2010). Even a small town in most parts of the world would have homes with books and often a library, with histories, maps, science textbooks, and guides.

Average human health is remarkable, with life expectancy the highest in history. Many of the current population are vaccinated against common diseases, and many diseases are much less prevalent than at any point in history. Indeed smallpox, possibly the biggest killer in human history, has been eradicated (Hopkins, 2002). A post-collapse world does not need to worry about that particular disease. However, increased interaction with new environments has led to novel zoonoses. HIV/AIDS, for example, could be challenging in a world without good diagnostics and antiretrovirals.

As to motivation, the demonstration effect would be powerful in a post-collapse world. For example, many people in medieval Europe did not think of progress as possible. Even in the early modern period, the possibilities of an industrial society were not foreseen—it was not clear for example to Song China that it was worthwhile to invest in coal production and textile manufacturing (Morris, 2010). Many simple and useful improvements, like the flying shuttle, were not invented until the Industrial Revolution (Howes, 2017). A post-collapse world would be able to see very visibly what had been created before, and that progress and an industrial society were possible.

Social capital refers to collective institutions such as organizations and norms, the strength of interpersonal networks and connections, and levels of trust in institutions and one another. Social capital is the strongest predictor of recovery from small-scale disasters (Aldrich, 2012). It might also be important in a contemporary collapse. Several durable institutions and identities may survive. These include the "imagined communities" (Anderson, 2006) of countries and religions, along with the institutions of the state (with the armed forces being particularly important) and the organized religions tied to them. Even smaller institutions like particular universities, companies, unions, or political parties could plausibly survive. This social capital would likely increase the probability of recovery by diminishing conflict and creating a structure and leadership for rebuilding. Other enduring norms could include even more ideological notions of democracy, freedom, and equality (as I will go on to discuss in the next section).

Natural capital refers to natural assets such as soil, ecologies, water, ores, fossil fuels, and climate. It is here where the picture is much more mixed. There are still huge stocks of natural capital, but they have been significantly depleted over the last 250 years since the industrial revolution.

One of the biggest questions for recovery relates to fossil fuels. The pessimistic argument goes as follows: A post-collapse industrialized economy relies on easily accessible fossil fuels, and most of the easily accessible fossil fuels have been used, so a post-collapse industrialized economy is unlikely. These premises seem persuasive, but we can question both.

On the first premise, humanity has experienced only one industrial revolution, and fossil fuels did enable and sustain it. However, a recovery of industrial society based on renewable resources such as biomass and hydropower could be possible (Dartnell, 2014). Indeed, the historic industrial revolution may have been possible based on wind, water, and charcoal (Dartnell, 2015; LePage, 2014). Such a recovery would likely be easier if humanity transitions to a low or no-carbon economy this century, as is planned.

The second premise doubts the availability of easily accessible fossil fuels. In the past, fossil fuels were remarkably accessible. Coal mining was possible in shallow, unsophisticated mines. Petroleum seeps produced lakes of oil in some parts of North America where one could dip in and fill a jug (Yergin, 1991). We now have deep-sea oil rigs, in inhospitable locations, drilling kilometers down. Less impressionistically, energy companies use a measure of "energy returned on energy invested" (EROEI ratio). This has declined—for example, for finding oil and gas in the USA from 1200:1 in 1919 to 5:1 in 2007 (Guilford et al., 2011; Hall et al., 2014). However, while that may be the case, there still are large stocks of fairly accessible fossil fuels. Examples include open-pit mines for coal,[12] or some Saudi oil fields. Both would be accessible and transportable with limited technology.

While the pessimistic fossil fuel argument should carry weight, it does not completely rule out the prospects for a technical recovery.

The situation with metals and minerals is similar to that for fossil fuels. There are suggestions that humanity is running out of various metals such as cryolite, phosphorus, or "rare earths" (such as europium, indium, rhenium, tellurium, terbium, dysprosium, and neodymium) (Alonso et al., 2012). Mining operations have become more complex, extending to remote areas including the sea floor and the far Arctic. However, while it may be more costly to access them from mining, there would be abundant supplies of humanity's physical capital or waste that could be recycled and redeployed. Moreover, many of the most commonly used metals such as copper, iron, lead, or manganese do not face the constraints of rare earths. The initial stages of recovery could be more dependent on commonly accessible metals and minerals, and rarer metals and minerals could become constraints later in recovery, when humanity's extractive capabilities would be larger.

The world's ecosystems, and their capacity to provide ecosystem goods and services such as food and clean water, have degraded since the industrial revolution, and continue to degrade. This includes substantial pollinator loss, soil degradation, and biodiversity loss (IPBES, 2019). There is significant uncertainty around tipping points, and the interactions between these systems and quantitative assessments of the consequences of ecosystem regime shifts are limited. Some indicative studies suggest costs in the hundreds of billions of dollars in China (K. Zhang et al., 2016) or 4–8% of GDP in desertifying developing countries (D'Odorico et al., 2013). It may be significantly harder to recover with these degraded ecosystems. However, if left alone rapid ecosystem recovery may be possible (Jones & Schmitz, 2009).

Natural capital should arguably include a stable, hospitable climate. We may have transitioned from the relatively stable, benign-temperature climate of the Holocene to the much more unpredictable and warmer Anthropocene (Zalasiewicz et al., 2019). All historical development (from the first settled farms to now) occurred during the Holocene. While humanity is very adaptable, we cannot be certain that a global industrial society could re-emerge during the Anthropocene.

Finally, the lingering effects of humanity's effect on the climate lead to a discussion of other lingering effects our current civilization might have in a post-collapse world. This includes especially the lingering effects of any global catastrophe—such as nuclear winter or biological weapons. These would make recovery harder.

Overall then, a capital theory approach suggests that the prospects for a technical recovery are positive. However, there are two key uncertainties. The first is about the extent to which natural capital has degraded. It is unclear whether the apparent advantages of physical, human, and social capital can compensate for these disadvantages. Second, as discussed before, is that a global collapse is unprecedented and creates unavoidable uncertainty—we cannot be sure. While the probability of a technical recovery may be high, dangerous uncertainties remain.

4.3.3 A Range of Recoveries

I have argued that, while dangerously uncertain, extinction is unlikely and recovery is likely. However, there is another key reason to be concerned about collapse—that is the range of possible recoveries. I have previously been considering recovery in a technical sense, but now I reintroduce the normative and political aspects.

The basic argument is that a range of global societies is compatible with a "technical recovery." These could vary substantially in their geopolitical situation—especially in dominant regime types, and rates of scientific and social progress. I will use the term "positive recovery" to refer to recovery to a world "at least as good" as the current one, by which I mean one with ongoing scientific and social progress and a relatively favorable geopolitical situation.[13] I will use the term "negative recovery" to refer to recovery to a world with less or no scientific and social progress, and a less favorable geopolitical situation.[14] A positive recovery is valuable from a longtermist perspective as a negative recovery would increase extinction risk and would be more likely to impose their misguided values on future generations. However, the likelihood of a "positive recovery" is uncertain and possibly low.

One widely used (though "ideal type") typology of regime types includes democracy, authoritarianism, and totalitarianism (Linz, 2000). Democracies are typified by widespread participation by—and responsiveness to—citizens, with governmental offices typically filled as a consequence of free and fair elections (though they could also rely more on sortition, deliberative, or direct democracy) (Cheibub et al., 2010; Dahl, 1971; Schmitter & Karl, 1991; Schumpeter, 1976). Authoritarian regimes can be distinguished from totalitarian regimes by the degree of pluralism tolerated, the centrality of ideology, and the degree of mobilization of the population (Linz, 2000). I would also include the massive and/or arbitrary use of terror, such as secret police, camps, purges, show trails, and collective punishment (Arendt, 2006, 2011; cf. Linz, 2000). The classic examples are Hitler, Mao, and Stalin, but could also include for example North Korea, Khmer Rouge Cambodia, and Rwanda during the genocide.[15]

Democracies dominate contemporary global society. By "dominate" I mean that a majority of the world's population lives in them (Roser, 2019), they form the majority of states (Magaloni & Kricheli, 2010), and perhaps most importantly, they have by far the preponderance of economic, "soft," and military power (IISS, 2020). However, the world could instead be dominated by authoritarian or totalitarian regimes. I will focus in particular on totalitarian regimes, as they are the most concerning and make my argument clearest.

4.3.3.1 Why Could It Be Worse?

A world dominated by totalitarian states would be more incompetent, more war-prone, less cooperative, and more inhibitive of progress than one dominated by democratic states. Our current world is not particularly competent, peaceful, cooperative, or progressive—a totalitarian-dominated world would be worse. It would increase the risk of another collapse and extinction and could shape the future toward less desirable trajectories (Beckstead, 2013).

Totalitarian states are incompetent. They are bad at forecasting and dealing with disasters (Caplan, 2008).[16] This can be seen most clearly in the great famines of Communist China and the USSR, in which millions died (Applebaum, 2017; Becker, 1996; Dikötter, 2010; Snyder, 2010). In comparison, functioning multiparty democracies rarely, if ever, experience famines (Sen, 2010). "Established autocracies" (or "personal"/"sultanist") are particularly bad, as there are few checks or restraints on arbitrary rule and the whims and ideology of the single individual, even from other elites (Svolik, 2012). From the inside, the "inner circle" around Mao, Stalin, and Hitler seems incredibly chaotic, with elites strongly incentivized to conceal information and encouraged by the autocrat to squabble and feud—so they are divided (Conquest,

1992; Kershaw, 2008; Zhang & Halliday, 2006). If totalitarian states are worse at addressing social, environmental, and technological problems, then a world dominated by them would likely be worse at responding to risks of collapse and extinction.

A world dominated by totalitarian states is more likely to have major wars. States with near-universal adult suffrage rarely (if ever) go to war with one another (Barnhart et al., 2020), so a world dominated by democracies has fewer wars. Miscalculation might be a particular problem for totalitarian states due to personalization and disincentives for accurate information, leading to well-known strategic disasters such as Hitler and Stalin's blunders in World War II (Bialer, 1970; Noakes & Pridham, 2001), or at a smaller level, Saddam Hussein's rejection of diplomacy (Atkinson, 1993). War makes collapse and extinction more likely, by raising the chance of weapons of mass destruction being used.

Linked to this, totalitarian states are less cooperative than democratic states. While cooperation is possible (Ginsburg, 2020), their internal norms are characterized by paranoia and treachery, and their lack of transparency limits their ability to credibly commit to agreements. This is bad for all risks that require cooperation such as pandemics or climate change (Tomasik, 2015).

Finally, continued social and scientific progress is likely to reduce risks of collapse and extinction. Social progress could reduce global inequality and other risk factors. Scientific progress could help address natural risks and climate change (Sandberg, 2018), differentially increase defensive rather than offensive power (Garfinkel & Dafoe, 2019), and solve safety challenges in AI or biotechnology (Russell, 2019). However, as we will now discuss totalitarian states would likely inhibit social progress.

A central question from a longtermist perspective is: Which values should shape the future? I would argue that we should prefer it to be shaped by liberal democratic values. This is not to say that the current democracy-dominated world is perfect—far from it. The fate of billions of factory-farmed animals or hundreds of millions of people in extreme poverty makes that abundantly clear. However, democracies have two advantages. First, democracies have space for cosmopolitan values such as human rights, plurality, freedom, and equality. These are better than those that characterize life under totalitarianism: Fear, terror, subjection, and secrecy. Second, they have within themselves the mechanism to allow progress. In the last 100 (or even 50) years, the lives of women, LGBT people, religious minorities, and non-white people have dramatically improved. Our "moral circle" has expanded, and could continue to expand (Singer, 1981). The arc of the moral universe is long, but given the right conditions, it might just bend toward justice (King, 1968). A global society dominated by these values, and with the possibility of improving more, has a better longterm potential. A totalitarian-dominated world, on the other hand, would reduce the space for resistance and progress—distorting the human trajectory.

We should be particularly concerned about "bottlenecks" at which values are particularly important—where there is a risk of "locking-in" some particular set of (possibly far from optimal) values. While they are currently far-off, future technologies such as artificial general intelligence, space settlement, life extension (of autocrats), or much better surveillance could enable lock-in (Caplan, 2008).[17]

Conditional on them avoiding new catastrophes, world orders dominated by totalitarians could be quite long-lasting (Caplan, 2008). Democracies can undermine authoritarian and totalitarian regimes through the following ways: Control, including conquest; contagion through proximity; and consent, promoting receptivity toward democratization (Whitehead, 2001). Democracies can actively undermine these regimes through war, sanctions, hosting rebellious exiles, or sponsoring internal movements. Passively, through contagion, they offer a demonstration that a better, more prosperous life is possible. For example, in the final years of the USSR, ordinary Soviet citizens were able to see that the West had a higher standard of living—more innovation, more choice, and more consumer goods. The elites were able to read books from the outside, and travel—Gorbachev's contacts and friendships with European politicians may have made him more favorable to social democracy (Brown, 1996). Democracies can undermine the will and capacity of the coercive apparatus (Bellin, 2004). However, in a world not dominated by democracies, all these pressures would be far less.

A world in which, say, totalitarian regimes emerged as dominant after World War II (for example if the USA was defeated) could be self-reinforcing and long-lasting, like the self-reinforcing relationship of Oceania, Eurasia, and Eastasia (Orwell, 1949). Orwell's fictional world is characterized by constant low-grade warfare to justify emergency powers and secure elites, and with shifting alliances of convenience as states bandwagon and balance, thereby preventing any resolution. A totalitarian-dominated world order could be rather robust, perhaps for decades or even centuries.

A long-lasting totalitarian-dominated world would extend the period of time humanity would spend with a heightened risk of collapse or extinction, as well as increased potential for distortion of the human trajectory and the possibility that a "lock-in" event may occur. This example illustrates the possibility of a "negative recovery," resulting in a trajectory with less or no scientific and social progress and a less favorable geopolitical situation, which would threaten the destruction of humanity's longterm potential.

4.3.3.2   The Likelihood of a Negative Recovery

Within the range of possible recoveries, how likely is a "positive recovery" compared to a "negative recovery"? Let us start with an illustrative thought experiment, which I will call "Reroll the 100-Sided Die."

Imagine that we could measure global societies by how well they are set up for future progress and flourishing, and score them on a scale of 1–100. The

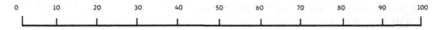

Figure 4.2 Reroll the 100-sided Die.

lowest number indicates that the society is worst-positioned for the future, while 100 means the society is best-positioned. If our current global society were to collapse, we can then ask where the recovered society might fall on this range. So, "restarting" civilization is akin to starting again and ending up with another society. We can visualize this uncertainty about our potential trajectory after collapse as rerolling a 100-sided die (see Figure 4.2).

This raises two questions. First, we can ask whether the configuration of our current society is better than average, i.e., higher than 50 on this scale. I discuss this above, but I tentatively suggest the answer is yes, given how totalitarian and authoritarian global societies could raise extinction risk or inhibit progress. Second, recovery could be completely random, and one might end up any-where on the range. This would be particularly bad if there are more possibili-ties below our current configurations than desirable ones above our current state (Rozendal, 2019). Thus, since there are more societies "below" us, a recovery could "revert to the mean" and likely position us less effectively for humanity's future. Furthermore, there might be particular reasons that recov-ery to a society "below" us might be more likely, as we will go on to discuss. In this thought experiment, value is fragile, recovery is risky, and we should not "reroll the 100-sided die."

We can assess the likelihood of a positive recovery by considering posi-tive and negative factors. Positive factors include history, the current status of democracies, and some democratization theories. Negative factors include plausible counterfactuals, the unprecedented nature of a collapse, and some theories of totalitarianism. I will consider the positive and negative factors together in turn.

First, the actual history of the world since the industrial revolution has been one in which democracies have emerged as dominant. One might expect the same result after a collapse and recovery. Against this, there are several plau-sible counterfactuals—nearby "possible worlds" (Lewis, 1986)—of totalitarian dominance. While acknowledging the methodological challenges of counter-factuals, it seems plausible, for example, that if the USA did not enter World War II or had been defeated, three totalitarian states would dominate Eurasia, and perhaps the world (Ferguson, 2000).

Second, democracies are currently dominant. If institutions are rela-tively durable, it could be that in democracies, democratic institutions sur-vive a collapse and recovery and are able to exploit their surviving physical infrastructure for economic and military advantage. Against this, as I have emphasized throughout, there is essentially no precedent for a collapse of global industrialized society. A collapse could disproportionately affect lead-ing democracies, for example, through a nuclear exchange or a collapse involving advanced AI. Power balances could shift during recovery, as rapid industrialization in totalitarian countries is possible (Conquest, 1992; Zhang & Halliday, 2006).

Third, some theories suggest that certain historical trends over the previous 200–300 years might have favored democracy. Bellicist theories of early modern Europe often emphasize the tax-raising and hence war-fighting advantages of states with representative institutions (Ertman, 2010; Tilly, 1992). Class-based theories of the first wave of democratization in 1800s Europe have a sense of inevitability to them—that economic growth favored the middle classes, who then pushed for more democracy (Acemoglu & Robinson, 2005; Ansell & Samuels, 2014; Moore, 1967). In classic modernization theory, levels of social and economic development (such as industrialization, urbanization, and literacy) were thought to favor democratization (Lipset, 1959). If these theories are correct, and if these historical trends were associated with a technical recovery after a collapse, then we might expect democracies to be favored.

Against this, we can consider other trends that could also be associated with collapse. I have argued that a contemporary collapse might resemble modern "failed states," warlordism, and civil war. In China, the Revolution led to the "Warlord Era," and the Chinese Civil War (punctuated by World War II)—from which the Chinese Communist Party emerged victorious (Zhang & Halliday, 2006). In Russia, World War I, and the Revolution were followed by the Russian Civil War—from which the Bolsheviks emerged victorious (Conquest, 1992). Similarly, the Second Congo War led to substantial warlordism and human rights abuses (International Rescue Committee, 2008). This is by no means a necessary condition: Hitler was appointed by the constitutional president (albeit in the context of extensive paramilitary violence) (Noakes & Pridham, 1998). But it is indicative. The political forces that emerge out of collapsing states and civil war can be far from democratic. Collapse could produce conditions that favor authoritarianism or totalitarianism (Beeson, 2010; Fritsche et al., 2012; Homer-Dixon, 2007; Martin, 1990; Oreskes & Conway, 2014).

In addition, an influential recent thread in the democratization literature emphasizes contingency and agency on behalf of political actors (Capoccia & Ziblatt, 2010; Linz, 1978; O'Donnell & Schmitter, 1986; Ziblatt, 2017). The post-war flowering of democracy may have only been possible by a war-caused reduction in inequality, maintained for only a few decades by social democracy (Piketty & Goldhammer, 2017; Scheidel, 2017). From this perspective, choice and chance strongly influence whether democratization occurs. The main takeaway from this discussion is to raise uncertainty. We might not be able to say with any confidence ahead of time what regime type may emerge as dominant. This adds further support to the suggestion that we should not "reroll the 100-sided die."

I have argued that survival and technical recovery after a collapse seem likely but that we cannot be sure of that. The probability of a positive recovery is even more uncertain, could be low, and is therefore particularly concerning.[18]

4.4 Collapse, Recovery, and Existential Risk: Implications, Shared Lessons, and Fruitful Collaboration

I have argued that anthropogenic risks could contribute to a contemporary collapse. Such a collapse could destroy humanity's longterm potential. The probabilities of it leading to extinction, or of there being no recovery, are low but not low enough to rule out. Moreover, collapse and recovery could lead to trajectory changes that limit humanity's longterm potential.

If this argument is correct, it suggests implications for the two fields of collapse studies and existential risk studies: Changing the priorities and focus of each. The fields can draw substantive, methodological, and political lessons from one another. The subject of a contemporary collapse should be central to both fields, and there should be extensive collaboration between the two.

One implication for existential risk studies is that they should change their risk assessment, and therefore the hazards they prioritize.

Currently, existential risk scholars tend to focus on events and processes for which a fairly direct, simple story can be told about how they could lead to extinction. We can see this *within* hazards, for example, a focus on which engineered pandemics could not just collapse civilization but make humanity extinct. We can see it even more strongly *across* hazards, for example, the focus on artificial general intelligence. For example, Ord (2020) provides his rough best estimates of the chance that within the next 100 years various "sources" lead to a catastrophe that destroys humanity's potential. He assigns a 1 in 1000 chance to nuclear war, climate change, and other environmental damage—but 1 in 30 to engineered pandemics, and 1 in 10 to unaligned AI. This follows straightforwardly from his sanguine view of collapse and recovery.

However, if there is a substantial probability that collapse could destroy humanity's longterm potential, this should change one's view of catastrophic risks: Climate change, nuclear war, and broad biological risks should become more important. This is especially the case as for each hazard, the probability of an outright extinction event is much smaller than the probability of a global catastrophe. Total risk from global catastrophes is then at least "in the same ballpark" as total risk from potential outright extinction events (Beckstead, 2015).

From collapse studies, scholars of existential risk can draw several useful insights.

Studying the future possibility of a contemporary collapse is hard. Causal identification is not possible, as one cannot carry out an experiment, and one cannot draw on observational data on a contemporary collapse that has not occurred. However, historical societal collapses can offer crucial case studies for process tracing, and data for quantitative analysis.

One lesson is that collapses are usually multi-causal. Several "external" shocks typically occur in a similar period. "Internal" factors matter too—very similar shocks can affect societies very differently depending on their internal structure and leadership. When complex adaptive systems shift equilibria, several causes are normally at play. This can be seen in historical societal collapses but also in ecological regime shifts (Zhang et al., 2016) and mass extinction events (Barnosky et al., 2011).

This should shift existential risk from a narrow "hazard focussed" approach, considering, e.g., nuclear weapons in a siloed way. Scholars should consider hazards alongside exposure and vulnerability for a fuller assessment of risk. Contemporary global society relies on a large number of critical systems, such as agriculture, transport, and communications. The failure of these systems could lead to, and indeed constitute, collapse (Avin et al., 2018; Centeno et al., 2015; Cotton-Barratt et al., 2020; Liu et al., 2018). A vulnerability-based approach is emerging as best practice in the private sector, and to some extent in government—this should be extended to existential risk as a whole (Hilton & Baylon, 2020).

One implication for collapse studies is that they should increase their interest in recoveries.

While there has been useful research on recoveries (Homer-Dixon, 2007) it is fair to say that the field has largely focused on collapse, with less theorizing about recoveries. However, if the form of recovery from collapse is indeed highly important, then as a topic it should become a more central question of interest. Case studies of recovery may be more limited than collapses, as collapses can lead to invasion and displacement, but there are still useful case studies to explore, for example in Mesopotamia or the Puebloan Southwest (McMahon, 2020). This difference in emphasis can even occur while keeping the focus squarely on historical examples.

From existential risk studies, scholars of collapse can draw on extensive discussion of contemporary risks, and a certain political urgency.

When considering a contemporary collapse, collapse scholars can draw on extensive research on anthropogenic risks, such as nuclear war, engineered pandemics, and other sociotechnical risks. They can also draw on futures methodologies which existential risk scholars are more familiar with, such as participatory futures and horizon scans (Kemp et al., 2020), expert elicitation surveys (Grace et al., 2018), evidence synthesis, extrapolating data trends, or scenario-planning and exercises (Avin, 2019).

When considering historical societal collapses, some historians often take a measured view. The societies that collapsed were often highly unequal or exploitative, collapse may have made little difference to—or even have been an improvement for—much of the population (Scott, 2009, 2017). "Collapse" could be viewed as a natural part of a society's life cycle, or a process of transformation (McAnany & Yoffee, 2010; Middleton, 2017). In any case, it happened a long time ago, and one should keep a historian's objectivity. This sanguinity is an odd point of agreement with many in existential risk. But if applied to our current society, it is mistaken. A contemporary collapse would likely result in large-scale mortality. It would be a moral disaster—as Joseph Tainter says, "the worst catastrophe in history" (Ehrenreich, 2020). Most collapse scholars recognize that.

However, despite widespread recognition of that ethical importance, collapse scholars have been limited in making concrete recommendations and seeing them through to impact. Collapse is a fascinating intellectual topic. But a key reason to study it is to have more information about whether *our* system might collapse and know what we could do to reduce that chance. The field of collapse studies is an important discipline and should ideally produce policy recommendations. Contemporary global society needs to act to reduce the risk of collapse. Existential risk scholars have been rather more active in making recommendations to governments, foundations, and companies and achieving change (Brundage et al., 2018, 2020; Farquhar et al., 2017; Hilton & Baylon, 2020).

4.4.1 Collaboration Between Collapse and Existential Risk Scholars

If a contemporary collapse is indeed possible, and could be disastrous, then it should become more of a focus for both fields. This subject of common interest suggests key interdisciplinary research questions and several underexplored priorities for international society.

There are many promising lines of inquiry for further research. The probabilities for which I have argued could be critically assessed and challenged, and better probabilities for collapse, survival, technical recovery, and positive recovery could be proposed. Researchers could elucidate causal pathways for how global collapse could lead to extinction. Researchers could conduct a more thorough accounting of likely post-collapse capital stocks, and to what extent advantages in one can compensate for disadvantages in others. This could be extended to consider the possible speed of technical recovery, or whether multiple recoveries are plausible. Researchers could extend theories of democratization and authoritarianism to explore positive recovery and the question of what can be done to increase its probability. What are the leading contributing causes to the possibility of a contemporary collapse? What lessons can we draw from historical recoveries? What are the problems with applying lessons from agrarian to industrial societies, and can they be resolved? This chapter has been an early, rough attempt to grapple with such questions. Exploring contemporary collapse and recovery—and what we can do about them—is a rich and fruitful ground for interdisciplinary research.

Priorities for national governments, international organizations, and philanthropists could include research, awareness-raising, and advocacy around collapse and recovery. Policy responses could aim to decrease the probability of collapse, e.g., reducing nuclear stockpiles and investing in prevention and resilience; increase the probability of survival, e.g. investments in alternative foods; increase the probability of technical recovery, e.g., stockpiling fossil fuels instead of burning them, or lessening ecosystem degradation; or increase the probability of positive recovery, e.g., making Cold War-type recovery plans to increase the probability of democratic institutions enduring. The most secure, ethical, and perhaps the cheapest option is prevention—reducing the probability of contemporary collapse.

Collapse studies and existential risk studies tackle some of the most important and urgent issues in our world. Exchange between these fields has been unfortunately limited. I have argued that this can be partly attributed to a mistaken confidence in the prospects for recovery after a contemporary collapse, and therefore a relative lack of interest from both fields in this topic. However, a contemporary collapse could destroy humanity's longterm potential. Contemporary collapse and recovery should therefore be a key topic for these two fields. They have much to learn from and do together. This chapter is hopefully one small contribution toward that goal.

Acknowledgement

For discussions and useful suggestions, I would like to thank the editors and Marty Anderies; my colleagues at the Centre for the Study of Existential Risk, especially Luke Kemp, Jaime Sevilla, Catherine Richards, Natalie Jones, Matthijs Maas, Tom Hobson, and Sabin Roman; the participants in the Modelling Societal Collapse Workshop, especially Jared Diamond and Lewis Dartnell; Seth Baum and Gregory Lewis; Felicity McDermott; Nick Beckstead; Toby Ord; Anders Sandberg; Andrew Snyder-Beattie; and Luisa Rodriguez.

Notes

1 Possibly apocryphal, certainly apocalyptic.
2 Ord (2020), following Burke (1790).
3 See also: "a thousand years hence [a collapse] may be considered just one of several dark episodes in the human story" or "the Black Death … suggests that triggering the collapse of civilization would require more than 50 percent fatality in every region of the world. Even if civilization did collapse, it is likely that it could be re-established." (Ord, 2020, p.40)
4 When discussing the twentieth-century events smaller in scale than a collapse, Nick Bostrom says: "If we look at global population statistics over time, we find that these horrible events of the past century fail to register. … Calamities such as the Spanish flu pandemic, the two world wars, and the Holocaust scarcely register (If one stares hard at the graph, one can perhaps just barely make out a slight temporary reduction in the rate of growth of the world population during these events)." (Bostrom, 2013).
5 The loss of a monopoly on legitimate violence (Weber, 1918).
6 "Forager" is replacing "hunter-gatherer" in the literature and is the term I will use (Güldemann et al., 2020).
7 One could also include geoengineering, especially the possibility of a "termination shock" following an abrupt end to solar radiation management (Baum et al., 2013; Parker & Irvine, 2018).
8 In 1991, the Soviet coup plotters seized the "nuclear briefcase" (Tsypkin, 2004). Similar concerns have been raised about Pakistani nuclear security (Nuclear Threat Initiative, 2020).
9 Outside of natural disasters that would kill everyone on Earth (such as a gamma ray burst [Sandberg, 2018]), and agents that are trying to kill everyone, such as misaligned artificial general intelligence (Bostrom, 2014).
10 Though it could be that a globalized system is good at buffering against and recovering from small shocks, but vulnerable to amplifying large ones (Scheffer et al., 2012).
11 This approach is suggested but not implemented in Hanson (2008).

12 Though these could flood.

13 This distinction draws on Beckstead (2015), but is extended and applied to collapse specifically, rather than global catastrophes. Beckstead is particularly concerned about "derailing progress." He offers two general concerns, that "mechanisms of civilizational progress are not understood" and "there is essentially no historical precedent for" global catastrophes; and two specific concerns, that a global catastrophe could "could degrade the culture and institutions necessary for scientific and social progress" and/or "upset a relatively favorable geopolitical situation."

14 This leaves open the possibility of an "even better recovery," to a situation with greater progress and a better geopolitical situation than currently. However, as I will go on to argue, I believe that possibility is unfortunately unlikely.

15 I will not distinguish between extreme left and extreme right (Gregor, 2000).

16 Advocates of "authoritarian capitalism" might question to what extent this applies to authoritarian regimes. However, even if some cherry-picked authoritarians might appear competent in some domains, this does not change the overall assessment that authoritarian states are worse than democracies at dealing with ecological problems (Wurster, 2013). In the response to COVID-19, authoritarian China has not fared better than democratic South Korea or New Zealand.

17 See also the distinction between enforced, undesired, and desired dystopias, figure 5.2, p. 154 (Ord, 2020).

18 It has been suggested (Hanson, 2008) in an analogy to the astronomical waste argument (Bostrom, 2003), that the *speed* of recovery is unimportant compared to the *probability* of recovery. I would go further and say it is the *type* of recovery that is the crucial consideration.

References

Acemoglu, D., & Robinson, J. A. (2005). *Economic Origins of Dictatorship and Democracy*. Cambridge University Press. https://doi.org/10.1017/CBO9780511510809.

Adalja, A., Watson, M., Toner, E., Cicero, A., & Inglesby, T. (2018). The Characteristics of Pandemic Pathogens. Johns Hopkins Center for Health Security. https://www.centerforhealthsecurity.org/our-work/publications/the-characteristics-of-pandemic-pathogens.

Aldrich, D. P. (2012). Building Resilience. University of Chicago Press. https://press-uchicago-edu.ezp.lib.cam.ac.uk/ucp/books/book/chicago/B/bo13601684.html.

Alonso, E., Sherman, A. M., Wallington, T. J., Everson, M. P., Field, F. R., Roth, R., & Kirchain, R. E. (2012). Evaluating Rare Earth Element Availability: A Case with Revolutionary Demand from Clean Technologies. *Environmental Science and Technology*, 46(6), 3406–3414. https://doi.org/10.1021/es203518d.

Anderson, B. R. O. (2006). *Imagined Communities: Reflections on the Origin and Spread of Nationalism* (Rev. ed.). Verso.

Ansell, B. W., & Samuels, D. (2014). *Inequality and Democratization: An Elite-Competition Approach*. Cambridge University Press.

Applebaum, A. (2017). *Red Famine: Stalin's War on Ukraine*. (First United States Edition). Doubleday.

Arendt, H. (2006). *Eichmann in Jerusalem: A Report on the Banality of Evil*. Penguin Books. https://ebook.yourcloudlibrary.com/library/fmplib-document_id-d4ntr9.

Arendt, H. (2011). *The Origins of Totalitarianism*. Houghton Mifflin Harcourt.

Atkinson, R. (1993). *Crusade: The Untold Story of the Persian Gulf War*. Diane Pub Co.

Avin, S. (2019). Exploring Artificial Intelligence Futures. *Journal of AI Humanities*, 2, 171–193. https://doi.org/10.17863/CAM.35812.

Avin, S., Wintle, B. C., Weitzdörfer, J., Ó hÉigeartaigh, S. S., Sutherland, W. J., & Rees, M. J. (2018). Classifying Global Catastrophic Risks. *Futures, 102*, 20–26. https://doi.org /10.1016/j.futures.2018.02.001.

Barnhart, J. N., Trager, R. F., Saunders, E. N., & Dafoe, A. (2020). The Suffragist Peace. *International Organization*, 1–38. https://doi.org/10.1017/S0020818320000508.

Barnosky, A. D., Matzke, N., Tomiya, S., Wogan, G. O. U., Swartz, B., Quental, T. B., Marshall, C., McGuire, J. L., Lindsey, E. L., Maguire, K. C., Mersey, B., & Ferrer, E. A. (2011). Has the Earth's Sixth Mass Extinction Already Arrived? *Nature, 471*(7336), 51–57. https://doi.org/10.1038/nature09678.

Baum, S. D., Armstrong, S., Ekenstedt, T., Häggström, O., Hanson, R., Kuhlemann, K., Maas, M. M., Miller, J. D., Salmela, M., Sandberg, A., Sotala, K., Torres, P., Turchin, A., & Yampolskiy, R. V. (2019). Long-Term Trajectories of Human Civilization. *Foresight, 21*(1), 53–83. https://doi.org/10.1108/FS-04-2018-0037.

Baum, S. D., Denkenberger, D. C., Pearce, J. M., Robock, A., & Winkler, R. (2015). Resilience to Global Food Supply Catastrophes. *Environment Systems and Decisions, 35*(2), 301–313. https://doi.org/10.1007/s10669-015-9549-2.

Baum, S. D., Maher, T. M., & Haqq-Misra, J. (2013). Double Catastrophe: Intermittent Stratospheric Geoengineering Induced by Societal Collapse. *Environment Systems and Decisions, 33*(1), 168–180. https://doi.org/10.1007/s10669-012-9429-y.

Beard, S., & Torres, P. (2020). Identifying and Assessing the Drivers of Global Catastrophic Risk. https://globalchallenges.org/assessing-the-drivers-of-global-catastrophic-risk -final/.

Becker, J. (1996). *Hungry Ghosts: Mao's Secret Famine.* The Free Press.

Beckstead, N. (2013). *On the Overwhelming Importance of Shaping the Far Future.* Rutgers.

Beckstead, N. (2015a, August 13). The Long-Term Significance of Reducing Global Catastrophic Risks. The GiveWell Blog. https://blog.givewell.org/2015/08/13/the -long-term-significance-of-reducing-global-catastrophic-risks/.

Beckstead, N. (2015b). How Much Could Refuges Help Us Recover from a Global Catastrophe? *Futures, 72*, 36–44. https://doi.org/10.1016/j.futures.2014.11.003.

Beeson, M. (2010). The Coming of Environmental Authoritarianism. *Environmental Politics, 19*(2), 276–294. https://doi.org/10.1080/09644010903576918.

Bellin, E. (2004). The Robustness of Authoritarianism in the Middle East: Exceptionalism in Comparative Perspective. *Comparative Politics, 36*(2), 139. https://doi.org/10.2307 /4150140.

Bialer, S. (1970). *Stalin and His Generals: Soviet Military Memoirs of World War II.* Souvenir.

Bostrom, N. (2002). Existential Risks: Analyzing Human Extinction Scenarios. *Journal of Evolution and Technology, 9*(1). https://nickbostrom.com/existential/risks.html.

Bostrom, N. (2003). Astronomical Waste: The Opportunity Cost of Delayed Technological Development. *Utilitas, 15*(3), 308–314. https://doi.org/10.1017/ S0953820800004076.

Bostrom, N. (2013). Existential Risk Prevention as Global Priority: Existential Risk Prevention as Global Priority. *Global Policy, 4*(1), 15–31. https://doi.org/10.1111/1758 -5899.12002.

Bostrom, N. (2014). *Superintelligence: Paths, Dangers, Strategies* (1st ed.). Oxford University Press.

Boulanin, V., & Verbruggen, M. (2017). Mapping the Development of Autonomy in Weapon Systems. SIPRI. https://www.sipri.org/publications/2017/other-publications /mapping-development-autonomy-weapon-systems.

Brown, A. (1996). *The Gorbachev Factor.* Oxford University Press.

Brundage, M., Avin, S., Clark, J., Toner, H., Eckersley, P., Garfinkel, B., Dafoe, A., Scharre, P., Zeitzoff, T., Filar, B., Anderson, H., Roff, H., Allen, G. C., Steinhardt, J., Flynn, C., hÉigeartaigh, S. Ó., Beard, S., Belfield, H., Farquhar, S., ... Amodei, D. (2018). *The Malicious Use of Artificial Intelligence: Forecasting, Prevention, and Mitigation.* arXiv:1802.07228 [cs]. http://arxiv.org/abs/1802.07228.

Brundage, M., Avin, S., Wang, J., Belfield, H., Krueger, G., Hadfield, G., Khlaaf, H., Yang, J., Toner, H., Fong, R., Maharaj, T., Koh, P. W., Hooker, S., Leung, J., Trask, A., Bluemke, E., Lebensold, J., O'Keefe, C., Koren, M., ... Anderljung, M. (2020). Toward Trustworthy AI Development: Mechanisms for Supporting Verifiable Claims. arXiv:2004.07213 [cs]. http://arxiv.org/abs/2004.07213.

Burke, E. (1790). *Reflections on the Revolution in France* (1st ptg. edition). Yale University Press.

Butzer, K. W. (2012). Collapse, Environment, and Society. *Proceedings of the National Academy of Sciences, 109*(10), 3632–3639. https://doi.org/10.1073/pnas.1114845109.

Caplan, B. (2008). The Totalitarian Threat. In Nick Bostrom and Milan M. Cirkovic *Global Catastrophic Risks.* Oxford University Press 504–519.

Capoccia, G., & Ziblatt, D. (2010). The Historical Turn in Democratization Studies: A New Research Agenda for Europe and Beyond. *Comparative Political Studies, 43*(8–9), 931–968. https://doi.org/10.1177/0010414010370431.

Carus, W. S. (2015). The History of Biological Weapons Use: What We Know and What We Don't. *Health Security, 13*(4), 219–255. https://doi.org/10.1089/hs.2014.0092.

Carus, W. S. (2017). A Century of Biological-Weapons Programs (1915–2015): Reviewing the Evidence. *The Nonproliferation Review, 24*(1–2), 129–153. https://doi.org/10.1080/10736700.2017.1385765.

Cass, D. (1965). Optimum Growth in an Aggregative Model of Capital Accumulation. *The Review of Economic Studies, 32*(3), 233. https://doi.org/10.2307/2295827.

Cave, S., & ÓhÉigeartaigh, S. S. (2018). An AI Race for Strategic Advantage: Rhetoric and Risks. *Proceedings of the 2018 AAAI/ACM Conference on AI, Ethics, and Society,* 36–40. https://doi.org/10.1145/3278721.3278780.

Centeno, M. A., Nag, M., Patterson, T. S., Shaver, A., & Windawi, A. J. (2015). The Emergence of Global Systemic Risk. *Annual Review of Sociology, 41*(1), 65–85. https://doi.org/10.1146/annurev-soc-073014-112317.

Cheibub, J. A., Gandhi, J., & Vreeland, J. R. (2010). Democracy and Dictatorship Revisited. *Public Choice, 143*(1–2), 67–101. https://doi.org/10.1007/s11127-009-9491-2.

Christiano, P. (2018, June 7). Sending a Message to the Future. The Sideways View. https://sideways-view.com/2018/06/07/messages-to-the-future/.

Conquest, R. (1992). *Stalin: Breaker of Nations* (Repr). Penguin.

Cotton-Barratt, O., Daniel, M., & Sandberg, A. (2020). Defence in Depth against Human Extinction: Prevention, Response, Resilience, and Why They All Matter. *Global Policy, 11*(3), 271–282. https://doi.org/10.1111/1758-5899.12786.

Coupe, J., Bardeen, C. G., Robock, A., & Toon, O. B. (2019). Nuclear Winter Responses to Nuclear War between the United States and Russia in the Whole Atmosphere Community Climate Model Version 4 and the Goddard Institute for Space Studies ModelE. *Journal of Geophysical Research: Atmospheres,* 2019JD030509. https://doi.org/10.1029/2019JD030509.

CruiseMarketWatch. (2020). 2021 Worldwide Cruise Line Passenger Capacity. *CruiseMarketWatch.* https://cruisemarketwatch.com/capacity/.

Dafoe, A. (2018). *AI Governance: A Research Agenda.* Centre for the Governance of AI Future of Humanity Institute University of Oxford.

Dahl, R. (1971). *Polyarchy: Participation and Opposition* Yale University Press.

Dartnell, L. (2014). *The Knowledge: How to Rebuild Our World from Scratch.* The Penguin Press.

Dartnell, L. (2015, April 13). Could We Reboot a Modern Civilisation without Fossil Fuels? Aeon. https://aeon.co/essays/could-we-reboot-a-modern-civilisation-without-fossil-fuels

DEFRA. (2020). *Agriculture in the UK 2019.* Department for Environment, Food and Rural Affairs Department of Agriculture, Environment and Rural Affairs (Northern Ireland) Welsh Government, Knowledge and Analytical Services The Scottish Government, Rural and Environment Science and Analytical Services.

Morgan Rivers, Michael Hinge, Juan B. García Martínez, Ross J. Tieman, Victor Jaeck, Talib E. Butt, David C. Denkenberger (2016). *Feeding Everyone No Matter What: Managing Food Security after Global Catastrophe* Academic Press .

Diamond, J. M. (2005). *Collapse: How Societies Choose to Fail or Succeed.* Viking.

Dikötter, F. (2010). *Mao's Great Famine: The History of China's Most Devastating Catastrophe, 1958–1962* (1st U.S. ed). Walker & Co.

D'Odorico, P., Bhattachan, A., Davis, K. F., Ravi, S., & Runyan, C. W. (2013). Global Desertification: Drivers and Feedbacks. *Advances in Water Resources, 51,* 326–344. https://doi.org/10.1016/j.advwatres.2012.01.013.

Ehrenreich, B. (2020, November 4). How Do You Know When Society Is About to Fall Apart?. New York Times. https://www.nytimes.com/2020/11/04/magazine/societal-collapse.html.

Ertman, T. (2010). *Birth of the Leviathan: Building States and Regimes in Medieval and Early Modern Europe.* Cambridge University Press.

Estes, R. J. (2019). The Social Progress of Nations Revisited. *Social Indicators Research, 144*(2), 539–574. https://doi.org/10.1007/s11205-018-02058-9.

Farquhar, S., Halstead, J., Cotton-Barratt, O., Schubert, S., Belfield, H., & Snyder-Beattie, A. (2017). *Existential Risk: Diplomacy and Governance.* Global Priorities Project.

Fearon, J. D., & Laitin, D. D. (2004). Neotrusteeship and the Problem of Weak States. *International Security, 28*(4), 5–43.

Ferguson, N. (Ed.). (2000). *Virtual History: Alternatives and Counterfactuals* (New e. edition). Basic Books.

Fritsche, I., Cohrs, J. C., Kessler, T., & Bauer, J. (2012). Global Warming Is Breeding Social Conflict: The Subtle Impact of Climate Change Threat on Authoritarian Tendencies. *Journal of Environmental Psychology, 32*(1), 1–10. https://doi.org/10.1016/j.jenvp.2011.10.002.

Future of Life Institute. (2015, July 28). Open Letter on Autonomous Weapons. Future of Life Institute. https://futureoflife.org/open-letter-autonomous-weapons/.

Garfinkel, B., & Dafoe, A. (2019). How Does the Offense-Defense Balance Scale? *Journal of Strategic Studies, 42*(6), 736–763. https://doi.org/10.1080/01402390.2019.1631810.

Geist, E., & Lohn, A. J. (2018). How Might Artificial Intelligence Affect the Risk of Nuclear War? RAND Corporation. https://www.rand.org/pubs/perspectives/PE296.html.

Gibbon, E. (1789). *The History of the Decline and Fall of the Roman Empire* (Vol. 1–7). AMS Press.

Ginsburg, T. (2020). Authoritarian International Law? *American Journal of International Law, 114*(2), 221–260. https://doi.org/10.1017/ajil.2020.3.

Goodwin, N. R. (2003). *Five Kinds of Capital: Useful Concepts for Sustainable Development, 3,* 14.

Grace, K., Salvatier, J., Dafoe, A., Zhang, B., & Evans, O. (2018). When Will AI Exceed Human Performance? Evidence from AI Experts. Arxiv:1705.08807 [Cs]. http://arxiv .org/abs/1705.08807.

Greaves, H., & MacAskill, W. (2019). *The Case for Strong Longtermism* (Working Paper No. 7–2019; GPI Working Paper). Global Priorities Institute. https://static1.squarespace.com /static/5506078de4b02d88372eee4e/t/5f1704905c33720e61cd3214/1595344019788/ The_Case_for_Strong_Longtermism.pdf.

Gregor, A. J. (2000). *The Faces of Janus: Marxism and Fascism in the Twentieth Century*. Yale University Press.

Grimal, N., & Shaw, I. (2001). *A History of Ancient Egypt* (Repr). Blackwell.

Guilford, M. C., Hall, C. A. S., O'Connor, P., & Cleveland, C. J. (2011). A New Long Term Assessment of Energy Return on Investment (EROI) for U.S. Oil and Gas Discovery and Production. *Sustainability*, *3*(10), 1866–1887. https://doi.org/10.3390/ su3101866.

Güldemann, T., McConvell, P., & Rhodes, R. A. (Eds.). (2020). Hunter-Gatherer Anthropology and Language. In *The Language of Hunter-Gatherers* (1st ed., pp. 3–48). Cambridge University Press. https://doi.org/10.1017/9781139026208.002.

Hall, C. A. S., Lambert, J. G., & Balogh, S. B. (2014). EROI of Different Fuels and the Implications for Society. *Energy Policy*, *64*, 141–152. https://doi.org/10.1016/j.enpol .2013.05.049.

Hanson, R. (2008). Catastrophe, Social Collapse, and Human Extinction. In Nick Bostrom and Milan M. Cirkovic *Global Catastrophic Risks* (p. 15). Oxford University Press.

Hey, J. (2005). On the Number of New World Founders: A Population Genetic Portrait of the Peopling of the Americas. *PLOS Biology*, *3*(6), e193. https://doi.org/10.1371/ journal.pbio.0030193.

Hijiya, J. A. (2000). The 'Gita' of J. Robert Oppenheimer. *Proceedings of the American Philosophical Society*, *144*(2), 123–167.

Hilton, S., & Baylon, C. (2020). Risk Management in the UK: What Can We Learn from COVID-19 and Are We Prepared for the Next Disaster? Centre for the Study of Existential Risk. https://www.cser.ac.uk/resources/risk-management-uk/.

Hirschman, A. O. (1970). *Exit, Voice, and Loyalty: Responses to Decline in Firms, Organizations, and States*. Harvard University Press.

Hirshleifer, J. (1963). Disaster and Recovery: A Historical Survey. https://www.rand.org/ pubs/research_memoranda/RM3079.html.

Hirshleifer, J. (1965). *Economic Recovery* (P-3160). RAND Corporation.

Hirshleifer, J. (1966). Disaster and Recovery: The Black Death in Western Europe. https:// www.rand.org/pubs/research_memoranda/RM4700.html.

Holmes, B. (2013, August 22). How Many Uncontacted Tribes Are Left in the World? *New Scientist*. https://institutions-newscientist-com.ezp.lib.cam.ac.uk/article/dn24090 -how-many-uncontacted-tribes-are-left-in-the-world/.

Homer-Dixon, T. F. (2007). *The Upside of down: Catastrophe, Creativity, and the Renewal of Civilization*. A. A. Knopf Canada.

Hopkins, D. R. (2002). *The Greatest Killer: Smallpox in History, with a New Introduction*. University of Chicago Press.

Horowitz, M., Kania, E. B., Allen, G. C., & Scharre, P. (2018). Strategic Competition in an Era of Artificial Intelligence. Center for a New American Security. https:// www.cnas.org/publications/reports/strategic-competition-in-an-era-of-artificial -intelligence.

Howard, L. M. (2014). Kosovo and Timor-Leste: Neotrusteeship, Neighbors, and the United Nations. *The Annals of the American Academy of Political and Social Science, 656*(1), 116–135. https://doi.org/10.1177/0002716214545308.

Howes, A. (2017).The Relevance of Skills to Innovation during the British Industrial Revolution, 1547-1851 *The Spread of Improvement: Why Innovation Accelerated in Britain 1547–1851*, Working Paper, Brown University .

IISS. (2020, February 14). The Military Balance 2020. IISS. https://www.iiss.org/press/2020/military-balance-2020.

International Rescue Committee. (2008). *Mortality in the Democratic Republic of Congo: An Ongoing Crisis* International Rescue Committee.

IPBES. (2019). *Summary for Policymakers of the Global Assessment Report on Biodiversity and Ecosystem Services* (Summary for Policy Makers). Zenodo. https://doi.org/10.5281/ZENODO.3553579.

Lili Xia, Alan Robock, Kim Scherrer, Cheryl S. Harrison, Benjamin Leon Bodirsky, Isabelle Weindl, Jonas Jägermeyr, Charles G. Bardeen, Owen B. Toon & Ryan Heneghan (2020). A Regional Nuclear Conflict Would Compromise Global Food Security. *Proceedings of the National Academy of Sciences, 117*(13), 7071–7081. https://doi.org/10.1073/pnas.1919049117.

Janetos, A., Justice, C., Jahn, M., Obersteiner, M., Glauber, J., & Mulhern, W. (2017). *The Risks of Multiple Breadbasket Failures in the 21st Century: A Science Research Agenda* (p. 28). The Frederick S. Pardee Center for the Study of the Longer-Range Future.

Jones, H. P., & Schmitz, O. J. (2009). Rapid Recovery of Damaged Ecosystems. *PLOS ONE, 4*(5), e5653. https://doi.org/10.1371/journal.pone.0005653.

Kemp, L. (2019a, February 19). Are We on the Road to Civilisation Collapse? BBC Futures. https://www.bbc.com/future/article/20190218-are-we-on-the-road-to-civilisation-collapse.

Kemp, L. (2019b, May 21). Civilisational Collapse Has a Bright Past – But a Dark Future. Aeon. https://aeon.co/ideas/civilisational-collapse-has-a-bright-past-but-a-dark-future.

Kemp, L., Adam, L., Boehm, C. R., Breitling, R., Casagrande, R., Dando, M., Djikeng, A., Evans, N. G., Hammond, R., Hills, K., Holt, L. A., Kuiken, T., Markotić, A., Millett, P., Napier, J. A., Nelson, C., ÓhÉigeartaigh, S. S., Osbourn, A., Palmer, M. J., … Sutherland, W. J. (2020). Bioengineering Horizon Scan 2020. *ELife, 9*, e54489. https://doi.org/10.7554/eLife.54489.

Kemp, L., & Rhodes, C. (2020). The Cartography of Global Catastrophic Governance. Global Challenges Foundation. https://www.cser.ac.uk/resources/cartography-global-catastrophic-governance/.

Kershaw, I. (2008). *Hitler.* Allen Lane.

King, M. L. (1968). *Remaining Awake Through a Great Revolution: Speech given at the National Cathedral* Congressional Record.

Koblentz, G. D. (2017). The De Novo Synthesis of Horsepox Virus: Implications for Biosecurity and Recommendations for Preventing the Reemergence of Smallpox. *Health Security, 15*(6), 620–628. https://doi.org/10.1089/hs.2017.0061.

Kubiszewski, I., Costanza, R., Franco, C., Lawn, P., Talberth, J., Jackson, T., & Aylmer, C. (2013). Beyond GDP: Measuring and Achieving Global Genuine Progress. *Ecological Economics, 93*, 57–68. https://doi.org/10.1016/j.ecolecon.2013.04.019.

LePage, M. (2014, October 15). What Would a World without Fossil Fuels Look Like? *New Scientist.* https://www.newscientist.com/article/mg22429910-700-what-would-a-world-without-fossil-fuels-look-like/.

Leslie, J. (1996). *The End of the World: The Science and Ethics of Human Extinction.* Routledge.

Lewis, D. K. (1986). *On the Plurality of Worlds.* B. Blackwell.

Li, H., & Durbin, R. (2011). Inference of Human Population History from Individual Whole-Genome Sequences. *Nature, 475*(7357), 493–496. https://doi.org/10.1038/nature10231.

Linz, J. J. (1978). *Crisis, Breakdown & Reequilibration.* Johns Hopkins University Press.

Linz, J. J. (2000). *Totalitarian and Authoritarian Regimes.* Lynne Rienner Publishers.

Lipset, S. M. (1959). Some Social Requisites of Democracy: Economic Development and Political Legitimacy. *American Political Science Review, 53*(1), 69–105. https://doi.org/10.2307/1951731.

Lipsitch, M., & Inglesby, T. V. (2014). Moratorium on Research Intended to Create Novel Potential Pandemic Pathogens. *MBio, 5*(6), e02366-14. https://doi.org/10.1128/mBio.02366-14.

Liu, H.-Y., Lauta, K. C., & Maas, M. M. (2018). Governing Boring Apocalypses: A New Typology of Existential Vulnerabilities and Exposures for Existential Risk Research. *Futures, 102,* 6–19. https://doi.org/10.1016/j.futures.2018.04.009.

Lynas, M. (2020). *Our Final Warning: Six Degrees of Climate Emergency* HarperCollins Publishers.

Lynch, M., Conery, J., & Bürger, R. (1995). Mutational Meltdowns in Sexual Populations. *Evolution, 49*(6), 1067–1080. https://doi.org/10.1111/j.1558-5646.1995.tb04434.x.

Magaloni, B., & Kricheli, R. (2010). Political Order and One-Party Rule. *Annual Review of Political Science, 13*(1), 123–143. https://doi.org/10.1146/annurev.polisci.031908.220529.

Maher, T., & Baum, S. (2013). Adaptation to and Recovery from Global Catastrophe. *Sustainability, 5*(4), 1461–1479. https://doi.org/10.3390/su5041461.

Mankiw, N. G., Romer, D., & Weil, D. N. (1992). A Contribution to the Empirics of Economic Growth. *The Quarterly Journal of Economics, 107*(2), 407–437. https://doi.org/10.2307/2118477.

Martin, B. (1990). Politics after a Nuclear Crisis. *The Journal of Libertarian Studies, IX*(2), 69–78.

McAnany, P. A., & Yoffee, N. (Eds.). (2010). *Questioning Collapse: Human Resilience, Ecological Vulnerability, and the Aftermath of Empire.* Cambridge University Press.

McMahon, A. (2020). Early Urbanism in Northern Mesopotamia. *Journal of Archaeological Research, 28*(3), 289–337. https://doi.org/10.1007/s10814-019-09136-7.

Middleton, G. D. (2017). *Understanding Collapse: Ancient History and Modern Myths.* Cambridge University Press.

Millett, P., & Snyder-Beattie, A. (2017). Existential Risk and Cost-Effective Biosecurity. *Health Security, 15*(4), 373–383. https://doi.org/10.1089/hs.2017.0028.

Mitchell, A., & Chaudhury, A. (2020). Worlding Beyond 'The' 'End' of 'the World': White Apocalyptic Visions and BIPOC Futurisms. *International Relations.* https://doi.org/10.1177/0047117820948936.

Moore, B. (1967). *Social Origins of Dictatorship and Democracy: Lord and Peasant in the Making of the Modern World* Beacon Press.

Morris, I. (2010). *Why the West Rules—For Now: The Patterns of History, and What They Reveal about the Future* (1st ed.). Farrar, Straus and Giroux.

Morris, I. (2013). *The Measure of Civilization: How Social Development Decides the Fate of Nations.* Princeton University Press.

Morris, I., Seaford, R., Spence, J. D., Korsgaard, C. M., Atwood, M., Macedo, S., & Morris, I. (2015). *Foragers, Farmers, and Fossil Fuels: How Human Values Evolve.* Princeton University Press.

Noakes, J., & Pridham, G. (Eds.). (1998). *Nazism 1919–1945: A Documentary Reader. Vol 1: The Rise to Power 1919–1934.* (New edition with index, reprinted, Vol. 1). University of Exeter Press.

Noakes, J., & Pridham, G. (Eds.). (2001). *Nazism 1919–1945: A Documentary Reader. Vol 3: Foreign Policy, War and Racial Extermination* (New edition with index and revised chapters, reprinted, Vol. 3). University of Exeter Press.

Nuclear Threat Initiative. (2020). *NTI Nuclear Security Index Fifth Edition* (No. 5; NTI Nuclear Security Index). Nuclear Threat Initiative.

O'Donnell, G. A., & Schmitter, P. C. (1986). *Transitions from Authoritarian Rule. Tentative Conclusions about Uncertain Democracies.* Johns Hopkins University Press.

Olson, D. M., Dinerstein, E., Wikramanayake, E. D., Burgess, N. D., Powell, G. V. N., Underwood, E. C., D'amico, J. A., Itoua, I., Strand, H. E., Morrison, J. C., Loucks, C. J., Allnutt, T. F., Ricketts, T. H., Kura, Y., Lamoreux, J. F., Wettengel, W. W., Hedao, P., & Kassem, K. R. (2001). Terrestrial Ecoregions of the World: A New Map of Life on Earth. *BioScience, 51*(11), 933. https://doi.org/10.1641/0006-3568(2001)051[0933:TEOTWA]2.0.CO;2.

Onoma, A. K. (2014). Transition Regimes and Security Sector Reforms in Sierra Leone and Liberia. *The Annals of the American Academy of Political and Social Science, 656*(1), 136–153. https://doi.org/10.1177/0002716214545445.

Ord, T. (2020). *The Precipice: Existential Risk and the Future of Humanity.* Bloomsbury.

Oreskes, N., & Conway, E. M. (2014). *The Collapse of Western Civilization: A View from the Future.* Columbia University Press.

Orwell, George. (1949). *Nineteen Eighty-Four.* London: Secker & Warburg.

Parfit, D. (1984). *Reasons and Persons.* Clarendon Press.

Parker, A., & Irvine, P. J. (2018). The Risk of Termination Shock From Solar Geoengineering. *Earth's Future, 6*(3), 456–467. https://doi.org/10.1002/2017EF000735.

Payne, K. (2018). *Strategy, Evolution, and War: From Apes to Artificial Intelligence.* Georgetown University Press.

Piketty, T., & Goldhammer, A. (2017). *Capital in the Twenty-First Century* Harvard University Press.

Posner, R. A. (2004). *Catastrophe: Risk and Response.* Oxford University Press.

Rees, M. J. (2003). *Our Final Hour: A Scientist's Warning: How Terror, Error, and Environmental Disaster Threaten Humankind's Future in This Century – on Earth and Beyond.* Heinemann.

Roser, M. (2019). Democracy. Our World in Data. https://ourworldindata.org/democracy.

Roser, M., & Ortiz-Ospina, E. (2013). Primary and Secondary Education. Our World in Data. https://ourworldindata.org/primary-and-secondary-education.

Rozendal, S. (2019). Uncertainty about the Expected Moral Value of the Long-Term Future: Is Reducing Human Extinction Risk Valuable? University of Groningen. http://www.sieberozendal.com/wp-content/uploads/2020/01/Rozendal-S.T.-2019-Uncertainty-About-the-Expected-Moral-Value-of-the-Long-Term-Future.-MA-Thesis.pdf.

Russell, S., Aguirre, A., Conn, A., & Tegmark, M. (2018, January 23). Why You Should Fear "Slaughterbots"—A Response—IEEE Spectrum. IEEE Spectrum: Technology, Engineering, and Science News. https://spectrum.ieee.org/automaton/robotics/artificial-intelligence/why-you-should-fear-slaughterbots-a-response.

Russell, S. J. (2019). *Human Compatible: Artificial Intelligence and the Problem of Control.* Viking.

Sandberg, A. (2018). Human Extinction from Natural Hazard Events. In A. Sandberg (ed.), *Oxford Research Encyclopedia of Natural Hazard Science.* Oxford University Press. https://doi.org/10.1093/acrefore/9780199389407.013.293.

Scheffer, M., Carpenter, S. R., Lenton, T. M., Bascompte, J., Brock, W., Dakos, V., van de Koppel, J., van de Leemput, I. A., Levin, S. A., van Nes, E. H., Pascual, M., & Vandermeer, J. (2012). Anticipating Critical Transitions. *Science, 338*(6105), 344–348. https://doi.org/10.1126/science.1225244.

Scheidel, W. (2017). *The Great Leveler: Violence and the History of Inequality from the Stone Age to the Twenty-First Century.* Princeton University Press.

Scherrer, K. J. N., Harrison, C. S., Heneghan, R. F., Galbraith, E., Bardeen, C. G., Coupe, J., Jägermeyr, J., Lovenduski, N. S., Luna, A., Robock, A., Stevens, J., Stevenson, S., Toon, O. B., & Xia, L. (2020). Marine Wild-Capture Fisheries after Nuclear War. *Proceedings of the National Academy of Sciences.* https://doi.org/10.1073/pnas.2008256117.

Schmitter, P. C., & Karl, T. L. (1991). What Democracy Is. . . And Is Not. *Journal of Democracy, 2*(3), 75–88. https://doi.org/10.1353/jod.1991.0033.

Schoch-Spana, M., Cicero, A., Adalja, A., Gronvall, G., Kirk Sell, T., Meyer, D., Nuzzo, J. B., Ravi, S., Shearer, M. P., Toner, E., Watson, C., Watson, M., & Inglesby, T. (2017). Global Catastrophic Biological Risks: Toward a Working Definition. *Health Security, 15*(4), 323–328. https://doi.org/10.1089/hs.2017.0038.

Schumpeter, J. A. (1976). *Capitalism, Socialism, and Democracy* (5th ed.; with a new introduction by Tom Bottomore). Allen and Unwin.

Scott, J. C. (2009). *The Art of Not Being Governed: An Anarchist History of Upland Southeast Asia.* Yale University Press.

Scott, J. C. (2017). *Against the Grain: A Deep History of the Earliest States.* Yale University Press.

Sen, A. (2010). *Poverty and Famines: An Essay on Entitlement and Deprivation.* Oxford University Press.

Shelley, M. (1826). *The Last Man.*

Shulman, C. (2020, May 31). Experience Curves, Large Populations, and the Long Run. *Reflective Disequilibrium* (blog). http://reflectivedisequilibrium.blogspot.com/2020/05/experience-curves-large-populations-and.html.

Singer, P. (1981). *The Expanding Circle: Ethics and Sociobiology.* Farrar, Straus & Giroux.

Snyder, T. (2010). *Bloodlands: Europe between Hitler and Stalin* (Nachdr.). The Bodley Head.

Solow, R. M. (1956). A Contribution to the Theory of Economic Growth. *The Quarterly Journal of Economics, 70*(1), 65. https://doi.org/10.2307/1884513.

Statista. (2017). Number of Offshore Rigs Worldwide 2010–2017. Statista. https://www.statista.com/statistics/307146/number-of-offshore-rigs-worldwide/.

Svolik, M. W. (2012). *The Politics of Authoritarian Rule.* Cambridge University Press.

Tainter, J. A. (1988). *The Collapse of Complex Societies* (23. print). Cambridge University Press.

Taycher, L. (2010, August 5). Books of the World, Stand up and Be Counted! All 129,864,880 of You. http://booksearch.blogspot.com/2010/08/books-of-world-stand-up-and-be-counted.html.

Tilly, C. (1992). *Coercion, Capital, and European States, AD 990–1992* (Rev. pbk. ed). Blackwell.

Tomasik, B. (2015, August 29). How Would Catastrophic Risks Affect Prospects for Compromise? Center on Long-Term Risk. https://longtermrisk.org/how-would-catastrophic-risks-affect-prospects-for-compromise/.

Toynbee, A. (1934). *A Study of History* (Vol. 1–12) Oxford University Press .

Tsypkin, M. (2004). Adventures of the Nuclear Briefcase: A Russian Document Analysis. *Strategic Insights, 3*(9). https://web.archive.org/web/20040923072304/http://www.ccc .nps.navy.mil/si/2004/sep/tsypkinSept04.asp.

Turchin, P. (2003). *Historical Dynamics: Why States Rise and Fall.* Princeton University Press.

Tzachor, A. (2020). *A Capital Theory Approach Should Guide National Sustainability Policies.* https://doi.org/10.17863/CAM.52719.

Matt Boyd, Nick Wilson Island refuges for surviving nuclear winter and other abrupt sunlight-reducing catastrophes Risk Analysis 04 December 2022 https://doi-org.ezp.lib .cam.ac.uk/10.1111/risa.14072.

Weber, M. (Ed.). (1918). *Wissenschaft als Beruf, Politik Als Beruf* (1. Aufl., [1. Dr.]). Klett-Schulbuchverl.

Weitzman, M. L. (2009). On Modeling and Interpreting the Economics of Catastrophic Climate Change. *Review of Economics and Statistics, 91*(1), 1–19. https://doi.org/10.1162 /rest.91.1.1.

Wells, H. G. (1897). The Extinction of Man. In *Certain Personal Matters.* William Heinemann.

Westgarth, G. (2020, November 1). An SOS for the Stranded Seafarers Who Ship Global Trade. Financial Times. https://www.ft.com/content/bb6dca79-d918-406d-886e -162d40cf41c4.

Whitehead, L. (Ed.). (2001). *The International Dimensions of Democratization: Europe and the Americas* (Expanded ed.). Oxford University Press.

Winter. (1963). *Economic Viability After Thermonuclear War: The Limits of Feasible Production* (RM-3436-PR). RAND Corporation.

World Bank. (Ed.). (2011). *World Development Report 2011: Conflict, Security and Development.* World Bank.

Wurster, S. (2013). Comparing Ecological Sustainability in Autocracies and Democracies. *Contemporary Politics, 19*(1), 76–93. https://doi.org/10.1080/13569775.2013.773204.

Xu, Y., & Ramanathan, V. (2017). Well Below 2°C: Mitigation Strategies for Avoiding Dangerous to Catastrophic Climate Changes. *Proceedings of the National Academy of Sciences, 114*(39), 10315–10323. https://doi.org/10.1073/pnas.1618481114.

Yergin, D. (1991). *The Prize: The Epic Quest for Oil, Money, and Power.* Simon & Schuster.

Yuki, H., Hough, L., Sageman, M., Danzig, R., Kotani, R., & Leighton, T. (2011). Aum Shinrikyo: Insights Into How Terrorists Develop Biological and Chemical Weapons. Center for a New American Security. https://www.cnas.org/publications/reports/aum -shinrikyo-insights-into-how-terrorists-develop-biological-and-chemical-weapons.

Zalasiewicz, J., Waters, C., Williams, M., & Summerhayes, C. (Eds.). (2019). *The Anthropocene as a Geological Time Unit: A Guide to the Scientific Evidence and Current Debate.* Cambridge University Press.

Zhang, K., Dearing, J. A., Tong, S. L., & Hughes, T. P. (2016). China's Degraded Environment Enters A New Normal. *Trends in Ecology and Evolution, 31*(3), 175–177. https://doi.org/10.1016/j.tree.2015.12.002.

Zhang, R., & Halliday, J. (2006). *Mao: The Unknown Story.* Vintage Books.

Ziblatt, D. (2017). *Conservative Parties and the Birth of Modern Democracy in Europe.* Cambridge University Press. https://doi.org/10.1017/9781139030335.

Zwetsloot, R., & Dafoe, A. (2019, February 11). Thinking about Risks From AI: Accidents, Misuse and Structure. Lawfare. https://www.lawfareblog.com/thinking-about-risks-ai -accidents-misuse-and-structure.

Section 2

Historical and Archaeological Investigations of Collapse

As we continue our investigation of historical collapse, we now turn to authors with expertise in archaeology and history. From the Late Bronze Age to the twentieth century, the case studies presented in this section explore a wide range of endogenous and exogenous causes of collapse and resilience. Organized chronologically, the eight chapters in this section give an expansive view of historical collapse, incorporating concepts of systems thinking and complexity science in their analyses.

The section begins with the work of Eric Cline and his analysis of Late Bronze Age societal collapse in the Mediterranean and ancient Near East. He shows that this collapse was very much a systemic one, as the degree of interconnectedness between spatially separated communities helped create a cascading effect when a series of disruptions such as earthquakes, climate change, and external aggression caused massive trade route dislocations and social breakdown. Disturbingly, Cline describes this collapse as a "black swan event" that was not preventable or predictable, and one that required a further 400 years for these societies to return to their previous degree of sophistication.

In the second chapter, Walter Scheidel contrasts the collapse of the Western Roman Empire with that of Han China, and argues that both exhibited what he refers to as "peak empire" in the first or second centuries AD. Both societies had shown considerable resilience during and after periods of rapid expansion. Equally, both showed similar patterns of internal decay, perhaps exacerbated by a global cooling period affecting agricultural outputs. These pressures in turn gave rise to large non-state-affiliated military bodies that would eventually be impossible for any central authority to control and led to the fragmentation of both societies into smaller autonomous units. Scheidel notes that in the decay of both the Han and Roman empires, increasing wealth and power concentration among elites slowly hollowed out state authority—offering a cautionary lesson to observers of emerging fragilities in our contemporary systems.

Next, the contribution by John Haldon covers both the collapse and non-collapse of Byzantium ca. AD 650 and demonstrates that collapse is not a straightforward and linear concept. His thesis is also one of resilience rather than total collapse. From an analysis of geographic reach and military defeat, Haldon notes that the Byzantines saw a dramatic loss of empire, production,

DOI: 10.4324/9781003331384-7

and revenues in the mid-AD 600s, yet many societies before them proved extremely resilient to severe challenges. Haldon argues that total systemic collapse is rare in complex societies due to the linked and nested multi-scale subsystems that are constantly and almost imperceptibly changing. More broadly for the study of collapse, Haldon raises intriguing questions regarding whether a true collapse occurred, how we might frame and demarcate the collapse time period, and what criterion or biases we may use in these judgments.

In their analysis of Pueblo society during AD 600–1300, in what is now the US Southwest, Timothy Kohler, Kyle Bocinsky, and Darcy Bird draw on multidisciplinary insights from systems theory, archaeology, biology, and climate science—among other fields—to uncover statistical and causal relationships between climate effects and collapse. In a civilization with concentrated dependence on maize as its source of agricultural sustenance, the impacts of aridity on crop yields were mitigated by the societal fabric of the Pueblo communities. Nevertheless, they were also subject to periodic collapses or transformations. Climates unfavorable to maize production, along with loss of resilience due to social factors—such as increasing wealth inequality—tipped these societies toward new stable states, resulting in transformations that were often accompanied by disaggregation, violence, and culture change.

In the next chapter, Deborah Nichols and Ryan Collins explore cases of collapse, adaptation, and persistence in the history of the Mexico basin. Focusing mainly on the periods surrounding Spanish invasion, they examine the multiple factors that led to the dissolution of the "Triple Alliance," or Aztec empire. They show how epidemics, internal politics, ecology, and other factors resulted in waves of depopulation and other fragilities, and explore some systemic structures and elements of Nahua life that showed significant resilience and continuity, even after the empire crumbled. Nichols and Collins provide a rich and detailed historical survey of indigenous peoples of the region and remind us of the complex mechanisms that can be at play in collapse.

Samuel Cohn, in his analysis of the impact of the Black Death in Europe, shows that even during the chaotic period of the Middle Ages, some societies in the region displayed considerable resilience. Contrary to the long-held historical view, Cohn uses new data sets to show that the global shock from this pandemic triggered the transformation of Western European societies rather than their collapse. The successive waves of the pandemic created a degree of resilience that allowed socio-political-economic transformations to occur that a single devastating event would not have.

Applying concepts from the study of complex systems, Miriam Pollock, Benjamin Trump, and Igor Linkov explore the impacts of Mongol rule on Kievan Rus' and Muscovy in the early Middle Ages. Here, the authors highlight the importance of interconnections and feedback loops within and between societies and how such complexity succeeded or failed in building resilience to exogenous shocks of invasion and subjugation. Fundamentally, they show that the Muscovite system was more resilient to collapse through its flexibility and willingness to adapt to the Mongol "governing model." By contrast, the Kievan Rus' political system was unable to adapt to a new political environment and thus exhibited more fragility.

This section on history and archaeology concludes with a chapter from Jeffrey Hass, which focuses on the Nazi blockade of Leningrad in the Second World War. By comparison with the other studies included in this section, Hass shows what fragility and resilience can look like in a more localized society during a more compressed time period. Examining innovations at the meso and micro levels of the social system, Hass identifies some key ways in which resilience was fostered in Leningrad. He explores how this besieged city, cut off from the world through an exogenous force, largely maintained its sense of order and resisted collapse.

In the previous section, Joseph Tainter noted that nearly half of the major works in the field of historical collapse argue that many civilizational failures are ultimately the product of bad luck. Tainter finds this explanation limiting and unsatisfying and urges scholars to search for non-stochastic causality in their research and analysis. We believe the authors in this section have succeeded in this endeavor by uncovering complex and nuanced causes of collapse throughout history, providing valuable lessons and insights for a more resilient modern civilization.

5 "Mind the Gap"

The 1177 BCE Late Bronze Age Collapse and Some Preliminary Thoughts on Its Immediate Aftermath

Eric H. Cline

5.1 Introduction and Background

I was asked to participate in this volume, and in the initial conference on "Historical Systemic Collapse," because of my book *1177 BC: The Year Civilization Collapsed*, which originally came out in 2014 and is now available in a revised edition (Cline 2014, 2021). Its focus is on the end of the Late Bronze Age, just after the beginning of the twelfth century BCE, in the Mediterranean and ancient Near East—essentially the area from what is now modern Italy in the west to modern Afghanistan in the east and from the region of modern Turkey in the north to Egypt in the south.

This geographical region was home to a thriving, and interconnected, group of societies or civilizations during much of the second millennium BCE, from approximately 1700 BCE to just after 1200 BCE. Among these were the Mycenaeans on mainland Greece; the Minoans on Crete; the Cypriots on Cyprus; the Hittites in Anatolia and the northern Levant; the Egyptians, who controlled both Egypt and the southern Levant; the Canaanites in what is now Israel, Lebanon, Syria, and Jordan; and the Mitanni, Assyrians, and Babylonians in Mesopotamia.

However, soon after 1200 BCE, all of these societies experienced to varying degrees a catastrophic Collapse (with a capital "C," as it is referred to in the scholarly literature), bringing an end to this "globalized for its time" era. The Collapse did not happen overnight for everyone, of course, although it did for some, but taken as a whole, it took place over the course of the twelfth century BCE. Within two or three generations at most, and by 1100 BCE at the absolute latest, the interconnected world as they had known it was completely gone and the individual societies had to fend for themselves. Some collapsed and disappeared; others proved more resilient and were able to transform and otherwise survive, but almost always in a new permutation.

In other words, the connected network that had been in place for several centuries by that point in the Mediterranean and ancient Near East broke apart. We now see disaggregation where there had previously been unity, as well as the fragmentation of the previously complex globalized society into smaller units; less order, less complexity, less coordination, and less organization

DOI: 10.4324/9781003331384-8

became the order of the day. In fact, this fits well with Tainter's definition of collapse: "Collapse is fundamentally a sudden, pronounced loss of an established level of sociopolitical complexity" (Tainter 1988: 193). Tainter also elaborated on what happens after such a collapse, noting that

> The flow of information drops, people trade and interact less, and there is overall lower coordination among individuals and groups. Economic activity drops…while the arts and literature experience such a quantitative decline that a dark age often ensues. Population levels tend to drop, and for those who are left, the known world shrinks.
>
> (Tainter 1988: 193)

However, we also need to keep in mind, as scholars such as Cumming and Peterson have said, that "Collapse and resilience are two sides of the same coin; collapse occurs when resilience is lost, and resilient systems are less likely to collapse" (Cumming and Peterson 2017: 696; see now also Haldon et al. 2020). It should not be surprising, therefore, to note that there were varying degrees of success and that it took different lengths of time for each of the societies to begin the process of recovery—it was a gap lasting anywhere from a few decades to several centuries, during what is frequently referred to as the world's "first Dark Age" in the early first millennium BCE.

It is not until the eighth century BCE, nearly 400 years later, that we can begin to once again speak of an interconnected network spanning the same region. By that time, however, some of the players were different or at least had transitioned and transformed: for example, the Greeks now lived in city-states such as Athens and Sparta, in the same territory on mainland Greece where once the Mycenaeans had lived; Israel and Judah were now kingdoms established in place of the previous Canaanites in the southern Levant, with the Phoenicians and Philistines as their erstwhile neighbors, and sometime enemy, in the case of the latter; and the Neo-Assyrians were on their way to reconquering and reclaiming much of the Near East as their own.

All of the above has been known to scholars for decades, if not a century or more. However, the question of what actually caused the Collapse has not ever been answered to everyone's satisfaction, despite numerous attempts at an explanation. When I was an undergraduate, majoring in classical archaeology, I was taught that there were no fewer than six or seven hypotheses that had been suggested over the years for what had brought the Bronze Age Mycenaeans, on mainland Greece, to an end. These range from drought to invaders and a whole host of other suggestions in between (see, e.g., Carpenter 1968). However, just a few years later, as a graduate student studying the ancient Near East, I learned that it wasn't only the societies in the Aegean which had collapsed; it was virtually everyone else too, all across the ancient Near East, including the Egyptians, the Hittites, the Assyrians, and so on. Moreover, the scholars studying the ancient Near East blamed the Collapse on something else entirely, for the Egyptian records speak of an invasion by groups collectively known as the Sea Peoples, who overran everyone and everything that was in their way, including Hittites, Canaanites, and the Cypriots as well. In fact, according to the Egyptian records, the Sea Peoples defeated everyone in the Eastern Mediterranean except for the Egyptians themselves, to whom they lost not once but twice (in 1207 BCE and 1177 BCE).

The Sea Peoples are named specifically in the Egyptian inscriptions as including individual groups identified as the Shardana (or Sherden), Shekelesh, Weshesh, Ekwesh, Denyen, Teresh, and Peleset, among others. Some of them had been mentioned in earlier Egyptian records, including the Shardana who apparently fought as mercenaries both for and against the Egyptians in various previous engagements, such as the battle of Qadesh in 1279 BCE, during which the Hittites and the Egyptians fought to a draw.

Overall, it has been a scholarly guessing game, for the past century or more, as to exactly who these groups were and where they came from. It is generally thought now, for example, that the Shardana are likely to have come from the region of Sardinia and the Shekelesh from Sicily, but that has not been definitively determined. The others are even more shadowy, except for the Peleset, who have long been thought to be the Philistines, mentioned in the Bible and known archaeologically from the region of modern Israel and Gaza.

And that, to paint things with a very broad brush and with the exception of a book or two and a few conferences that have been held over the years (e.g., Drews 1993; Ward and Joukowsky 1992; Oren 2000), is essentially where things stood until about 20 years ago, when Amos Nur and I resurrected the idea that earthquakes should possibly be added into the mix (Nur and Cline 2000, 2001). Then, about a decade ago, in 2010, David Kaniewski and his team, as well as subsequently others, first began to come up with hard evidence, at least by proxy, that there had been climate change and a severe megadrought all across the region for up to 300 years, starting in about 1200 BCE (cf. Kaniewski et al. 2010 and subsequent publications, including Kaniewski et al. 2013, 2015, and 2019).

So, when Rob Tempio of Princeton University Press asked me to write a book about the Collapse, I began looking again at the things that I had first studied decades ago and realized that there was still no consensus as to what had caused it. There were, however, now even more ideas and suggestions—though still ranging from drought and famine to invaders and a cutting of the international trade routes—as well as other overarching publications, such as Joseph Tainter's 1988 volume on the collapse of complex societies (Tainter 1988).

In the end, after considering all of the various hypotheses one after another, I suggested in *1177 BC* that it was "all of the above"—namely, a systems collapse (as defined by Renfrew 1978, 1979) that had been caused by a perfect storm of interacting factors, drivers, and stressors, any one of which would probably have been survivable on its own, but the combination of which proved lethal. Moreover, not all of the societies went down at the exact same time, or for the same reason, or to the same extent, but they were so interdependent that they were all impacted by the events and most fell within a few decades of each other. The Collapse was catastrophic enough that the world would not see another such calamity until the fall of the Roman Empire some 1,500 years later.

It is for this reason, namely a unique occurrence of a multi-societal collapse that took place in the ancient world—and one which most members of the general public have never heard of—that my studies have a role to play in this volume. Moreover, even though the Collapse took place more than 3,000 years ago, there were enough similarities between their world back then and our world today, as well as enough similarities between the problems that ultimately caused their demise and the problems that we have in our world today, that I believe studying the events that lead to their collapse is more than just an exercise of reviewing ancient history. In fact, learning from what happened to them may be more relevant than ever, especially if we continue down the path of global warming, climate change, and pandemic(s) without further thought as to where that might lead us.

5.2 Analysis and Synthesis

As already mentioned briefly above, I believe that there are quite a number of different stressors or drivers that contributed to the Collapse of the end of the Bronze Age. Some are environmental factors; some are human factors, many of which stemmed directly from the environmental factors; and still others are factors from the failure of the network that had been in place.

For example, in terms of natural environmental factors, we now have pretty good evidence that earthquakes contributed to the destruction of a number of the sites that were abandoned at the end of the Bronze Age. These range from cities like Mycenae on the Greek mainland to Troy in Anatolia to a number of different sites in Canaan (i.e., in modern Israel and Jordan). Admittedly, it can frequently be difficult to identify a city destroyed by an earthquake as opposed to one destroyed by warfare, but previous scholars have acknowledged a number of characteristics that are usually observable in an earthquake-ravaged city. These include items such as skeletons of people lying underneath collapsed walls; walls that have been knocked off kilter or are otherwise askew; keystones that have slipped into arches; and so on. It is also worthwhile pointing out that much of this entire region is home to active seismic faults, including the North Anatolian Fault Line and the one that runs up the Great Rift Valley through the Dead Sea and the Sea of Galilee. Other fault lines are found in the Aegean; Mycenae itself is built directly on top of an active fault.

Another environmental factor for which we now have good scientific evidence, albeit through proxy data, is a mega-drought that lasted between 150 and 300 years. The data come from a variety of sources, including lake sediments, stalagmites in caves, and pollen from cores taken in dried-up lagoons, in areas across the Aegean and Eastern Mediterranean, from Greece and Turkey to Israel, Iran, and Iraq. There is also now evidence of drought in northern

Italy ca. 1200 BCE, which had long been presumed, but now seems to have been confirmed (Kristiansen 2018).

Hand-in-hand with this goes evidence for famine, which comes primarily from texts found at Hattusa in Anatolia, the capital city of the Hittites, and Ugarit in northern Canaan, on the coast of what is now modern Syria. These can get quite dramatic, with the Hittite king stating at one point that "it is a matter of life and death." In another text, found at Ugarit, a businessman stated plaintively, "If you do not quickly arrive here, we ourselves will die of hunger. You will not see a living soul from your land."

In terms of human factors, we have both archaeological and textual evidence for invaders and warfare. The textual evidence is especially compelling, ranging from the inscriptions cited above, left to us by the Egyptian pharaohs Merneptah and Ramses III, which described the battles fought against the Sea Peoples, to texts found at Ugarit noting that enemy ships had been sighted as well as the fact that invaders had overrun a nearby port city (Ras ibn Hani) and were advancing upon Ugarit itself. The latter texts were found in the ruins of Ugarit, which had been burned and destroyed, with the structural debris piled up more than a meter deep in places and with arrowheads embedded in the walls of buildings.

Just as with earthquakes, it can be difficult to determine exactly who destroyed a specific city, even when it's clear that it was destroyed by humans rather than by Mother Nature. For example, there is some question as to who destroyed the city of Hazor in Canaan. One school of thought is that it was destroyed by invaders, along the lines of the biblical story which attributes the destruction to Joshua and the incoming Israelites. Another school of thought is that the city was only partially destroyed, most likely as the result of an internal rebellion by the inhabitants of the city who were starving because of the effects of the drought and accompanying famine. Regardless, it is clear that the human factors are intertwined with the environmental factors, in large part because it seems likely that neither the migrations and invasions nor the internal rebellions would have necessarily occurred if it were not for the climatic problems and associated difficulties.

As a result of all of the above factors and stressors, problems also developed in the systemic structure of the globalized network that had connected all of these various societies during the previous centuries in the Bronze Age. None of these societies were self-sufficient; all of them depended upon the others for both raw materials and finished goods. For example, much of the silver probably came from mainland Greece, e.g., the Laurion mines; most of the gold came from Egypt, courtesy of Egyptian control over Nubia and Sudan; while copper came from Cyprus and tin came principally from the Badakhshan region of what is now modern Afghanistan.

Therefore, when the international trade routes were likely cut as a result of both the environmental factors, such as climate change and earthquakes, and the human factors, such as migration and invasions, access to these raw materials was probably severely curtailed, leading to immediate problems. Without tin, for instance, one could not make bronze, a factor which most likely destabilized to some extent the sociopolitical, economic, and military systems that had been in place for centuries by that time, and which may have led directly to the need to turn to the use of iron.

It is often erroneously stated that the Hittites had a monopoly on iron, which they did not. It is also a common misconception that the Sea Peoples were able to be so successful in their invasions because they possessed iron weapons, while the inhabitants of the Aegean and Eastern Mediterranean did not. This, however, is not correct either; the initial experiments with iron and then its subsequent implementation and widespread use did not fully begin until after the collapse at the end of the Bronze Age, motivated most likely by necessity more than anything else.

5.3 Governance and Mitigation

Overall, as mentioned above, the Collapse took about a century, likely two to three generations at most, to fully bring the Bronze Age globalized world in these areas to an end. In some areas, however, the destructions happened so rapidly—within days, weeks, or months at most, especially in the instances of being attacked by invaders—that they are not fully reflected in the texts that have been left to us. Indeed, the textual materials at Ugarit seem to indicate that it was almost "business as usual" until just before the end, when both the famine and invaders seem to have hit nearly simultaneously.

As a result, we do not have any written records documenting administrative or societal collapse at either the highest or lowest levels in any of these sites or even the overall kingdom or empire; just mentions of famine and invaders at places like Ugarit. We can only presume, from the events that occurred, what must also have happened in places like the Greek mainland, where the Mycenaean administrative structure seems to have collapsed and was only partially remembered in some of the later titles, such as "basileus," that remained in use during the subsequent re-emergence of Greece following the Dark Ages. Here, in Greece, it seems quite clear that the surviving inhabitants essentially lost everything during the Collapse and had to rebuild their society basically from scratch.

However, at the same time, it is also clear that some societies were able to prove more resilient than others—a fact which is documented in their written records—and that some may have had only a partial collapse, i.e., perhaps administratively but not economically, or suffering a loss of population but not societal integrity. We may think here specifically of the Assyrians, who managed to continue through much of the twelfth century BCE, as if not much had impacted them. Their king was still in place, as was, apparently, the upper echelon of their administration and society. This, though, seems to have been a temporary situation, for they were finally impacted by the Collapse toward the beginning of the eleventh century BCE and did not climb back up again until some 200 years later, when they began to expand once again during the ninth century BCE.

The other areas under consideration fall somewhere between the two extremes of Greece on the one hand and Assyria on the other. Egypt, Anatolia, the Levant, Cyprus, and Italy/Sicily/Sardinia each had their own response to what had taken place and differed in whether it involved a total rebuilding of the sociocultural, political, and economic aspects of the civilization, as opposed to a simpler transformation or even new groups of people establishing themselves (such as the Israelites, Philistines, and Phoenicians). Cyprus, for example, survived by transforming to a new normal, to a greater or lesser degree; its inhabitants seem to have reorganized the political system and may have even begun to focus on manufacturing and exporting iron rather than bronze in the aftermath of the Collapse.

In contrast, the Hittites in Anatolia essentially failed to adapt and disappeared, leaving only remnants of the original inhabitants and cultures on the outskirts of the original territory, i.e., the Neo-Hittites in northern Syria and southeastern Turkey (now sometimes referred to as the Syro-Hittites or Syro-Anatolians). New groups took over the main portion of the original territory, including the Urartians who based their new kingdom in eastern Anatolia and even further east, above what is now modern Iraq. Clearly, everybody in this widespread region, from Italy to Iraq and Iran in modern terms, was trying to recover from the same Collapse, but each society followed their own individual route to recovery, or not.

We also do not have any information whatsoever about whether preventative measures were taken, except insofar as we can glean from proxy data. For example, a recent study has shown that the Egyptians apparently took some pre-emptive steps in the region that they controlled in Canaan, ranging from planting new types of crops to breeding their cattle to be hardier in a drought situation (Finkelstein et al. 2017). It would be nice if we could attempt to distinguish between managerial failures on the one hand and structural failures on the other and determine whether it is possible to blame inept leadership among the many other possible factors, but the data simply are not detailed enough, or even available in some areas, for such analyses.

Thus, we are left with a series of questions, especially concerning whether this collapse was predictable, preventable, or inevitable. I would argue that it was not predictable and that it was essentially a black swan event, defined as "unexpected and low-probability events with massive repercussions" (Taleb 2007). I would also argue that it was probably neither preventable nor inevitable. The various societies had been fairly happily interacting in a globalized network for several centuries by this point, as mentioned above, and there is no reason to suspect that they would not have continued to do so, had this series of unfortunate events not unexpectedly occurred.

In the revised/updated version of *1177 BC*, as well as in other conference papers, I have recently asked whether there is any evidence that the various entities (Hittites, Mycenaeans, Egyptians, etc.) *knew* that they were collapsing. That is to say, were any of them aware that they were part of a much larger Collapse and that their way of life was threatened? Offhand, I can't think of any such indications, but would we necessarily find such in the archaeological record? Furthermore, had they known, or realized, that they were collapsing, is there anything that they could have done to stop it or even reverse it, perhaps before they reached a tipping point? In fact, we may well ask if they ever even realized that they had reached the point of no return before it was too late (see, e.g., Scheffer et al. 2009, 2012). To put it another way, in the spirit of this volume, were there any Early Warning Signs (EWS) of an approaching critical transition in their complex system(s) (see Levin and Hagstrom's chapter [Chapter 18] in this volume)?

Personally, I think that there is little that they could have done about it, even if they had recognized what was transpiring, especially in the face of such a "perfect storm" of catastrophes coming one after the other. Perhaps they could have done a better job of banding together to support each other in a time of crisis, but we cannot know this for certain. As for the robustness or fragility of the system in place, I do not think that any of these societies were somehow fragile. In fact, they had already been robust for centuries, and—as I have mentioned above—the data that are available to us (especially in the form of textual records, but also actual imported objects found in situ at various sites) indicate that the various communities, such as Ugarit, appear to have still been thriving, and trading with each other, right up until the problems began to hit. So, why weren't they able to survive? Why weren't they resilient?

The answer to such a question is complicated, as I have just indicated above: some were resilient, while others were not. Some were able to survive pretty much as is, like the Assyrians; others transformed themselves, like the Cypriots who appear to have altered their political structure. Some not only survived but flourished, albeit in an altered state, like the Canaanites in the area of modern Lebanon who emerged as the Phoenicians—one might refer to them as "anti-fragile," to borrow a phrase from Taleb (2014), or perhaps as the *alpha* part of an Adaptive Cycle, in which they took advantage of the disorder and chaos to flourish when others were failing—it seems clear that they actually benefited from the Collapse. But still others were unable to adapt and essentially disappeared, like the Mycenaeans on mainland Greece, the Minoans on Crete, and the Hittites in central Anatolia. As mentioned, they were replaced by new city-states in Greece, and new kingdoms and peoples in the Near East, such as Israel and Judah, Urartu, and the Arameans, as well as some small pockets of people who survived, such as the Neo-Hittite petty kingdoms in northern Syria.

5.4 Insights, Relevance, and Applicability

As for the applicability of all of this to today, I see some current trends that give me pause and perhaps even cause for concern for ourselves in the coming years, decades, and/or beyond. As I have described in *1177 BC*, many of the same problems that contributed to the Collapse at the end of the Bronze Age in the Aegean and Eastern Mediterranean are with us again today. Not only do we have drought, famine, earthquakes, migrations, civil wars and internal unrest, and other stressors around the globe, but we now also have a worldwide pandemic, which is an additional factor that they do not seem to have had at the end of the Bronze Age (though there was one ca. 1340 BCE, 150 years before the Collapse, that devastated the Hittite Empire and the royal family).

We are, however, in a position today where we can address these problems and potentially mitigate the damage. In other words, unlike the Hittites and others in the twelfth century BCE, we are able to address these growing calamities head on, if we choose to do so. However, as I have said at the very end of the revised edition of *1177 BC*, it remains to be seen whether we are wise enough to do that.

In his recent essay for the BBC, Luke Kemp said that

> The collapse of our civilization is not inevitable. History suggests it is likely, but we have the unique advantage of being able to learn from the wreckages of societies past. ... We will only march into collapse if we advance blindly. We are only doomed if we are unwilling to listen to the past.
>
> (Kemp 2019)

I agree with him almost entirely and would note that we are perhaps in a better position than any other society in history to note Early Warning Signs and approaching tipping points. However, I would also point out that every society and civilization during the history of humankind so far has eventually collapsed and that there is no reason to think that we will be any different, in either the short term or the long run. In my opinion, when speaking about the potential collapse of our current society, it is not a matter of "if," but rather "when." And the timing of the "when" is up to us, perhaps for the first time in the history of humanity.

Acknowledgment

I would like to thank Miguel Centeno, Peter Callahan, Paul Larcey, and Thayer Patterson for the invitation to participate in the original conference and for the subsequent invitation to contribute to this volume, as well as for comments made by the participants in both the original conference in April 2019 and the follow-up in December 2020. References have been kept to a minimum throughout this current contribution, since much of the material in this chapter is an abbreviated version of the data and discussions that appear in a fuller form in Cline 2014 (and in the revised edition, i.e., Cline 2021), where one will also find complete references and a substantial bibliography. Additional portions represent initial thoughts stemming from research for the forthcoming sequel, which will be published by Princeton University Press.

References

Carpenter, R. 1968. *Discontinuity in Greek Civilization*. New York: W. W. Norton and Co.

Cline, E. H. 2014. *1177 BC: The Year Civilization Collapsed*. Princeton, NJ: Princeton University Press.

Cline, E. H. 2021. *1177 BC: The Year Civilization Collapsed*. Revised and Updated Edition. Princeton, NJ: Princeton University Press.

Cumming, G. S., and G. D. Peterson. 2017. Unifying Research on Social–Ecological Resilience and Collapse. *Trends in Ecology & Evolution* 32(9): 695–713. http://doi.org /10.1016/j.tree.2017.06.014.

Drews, R. 1993. *The End of the Bronze Age: Changes in Warfare and the Catastrophe ca. 1200 B.C.* Princeton, NJ: Princeton University Press.

Finkelstein, I., D. Langgut, M. Meiri, and L. Sapir-Hen. 2017. Egyptian Imperial Economy in Canaan: Reaction to the Climate Crisis at the End of the Late Bronze Age. *Egypt and the Levant* 27: 249–259.

Haldon, J., A. F. Chase, W. Eastwood, M. Medina-Elizalde, A. Izdebski, F. Ludlow, G. Middleton, L. Mordechai, J. Nesbitt, and B. L. Turner II. 2020. Demystifying Collapse: Climate, Environment, and Social Agency in Pre-modern Societies. *Millennium* 17(1): 1–33.

Kaniewski, D., J. Guiot, and E. Van Campo. 2015. Drought and Societal Collapse 3200 Years Ago in the East Mediterranean: A Review. *WIREs Climate Change* 6: 369–382. http://doi.org/10.1002/wcc.345.

Kaniewski, D., N. Marriner, J. Bretschneider, G. Jans, C. Morhange, R. Cheddadi, T. Otto, F. Luce, and E. Van Campo. 2019. 300-Year Drought Frames Late Bronze Age to Early Iron Age Transition in the Near East: New Palaeoecological Data from Cyprus and Syria. *Regional Environmental Change*. https://doi.org/10.1007/s10113-018-01460 -w.

Kaniewski, D., E. Paulissen, E. Van Campo, H. Weiss, T. Otto, J. Bretschneider, and K. Van Lerberghe. 2010. Late Second–Early First Millennium BC Abrupt Climate Changes in Coastal Syria and Their Possible Significance for the History of the Eastern Mediterranean. *Quaternary Research* 74(2): 207–215.

Kaniewski, D., E. Van Campo, J. Guiot, S. Le Burel, T. Otto, and C. Baeteman. 2013. Environmental Roots of the Late Bronze Age Crisis. *PLOS ONE* 8/8: e71004.

Kemp, L. 2019. Are We on the Road to Civilisation Collapse? BBC Future. https://www .bbc.com/future/article/20190218-are-we-on-the-road-to-civilisation-collapse.

Kristiansen, K. 2018. The Rise of Bronze Age Peripheries and the Expansion of International Trade 1950–1100 BC. In *Trade and Civilisation: Economic Networks and Cultural Ties, From Prehistory to the Early Modern Era*, ed. K. Kristiansen, T. Lindkvist, and J. Myrdal, 87–112. Cambridge: Cambridge University Press.

Nur, A., and E. H. Cline. 2000. Poseidon's Horses: Plate Tectonics and Earthquake Storms in the Late Bronze Age Aegean and Eastern Mediterranean. *Journal of Archaeological Science* 27(1): 43–63.

Nur, A., and E. H. Cline. 2001. What Triggered the Collapse? Earthquake Storms. *Archaeology Odyssey* 4/5: 31–36, 62–63.

Oren, E. D., ed. 2000. *The Sea Peoples and Their World: A Reassessment*. Philadelphia, PA: University of Pennsylvania.

Renfrew, C. 1978. Trajectory Discontinuity and Morphogenesis: The Implications of Catastrophe Theory for Archaeology. *American Antiquity* 43(2): 203–222.

Renfrew, C. 1979. Systems Collapse as Social Transformation. In *Transformations: Mathematical Approaches to Culture Change*, ed. C. Renfrew, and K. L. Cooke, 481–506. New York: Academic Press.

Scheffer, M., J. Bascompte, W. A. Brock, V. Brovkin, S. R. Carpenter, V. Dakos, H. Held, E. H. van Nes, M. Rietkerk, and G. Sugihara. 2009. Early-Warning Signals for Critical Transitions. *Nature* 461/3(7260): 53–59. http://doi.org/10.1038/nature08227.

Scheffer, M., S. R. Carpenter, T. M. Lenton, J. Bascompte, W. Brock, V. Dakos, J. van de Koppel, I. A. van de Leemput, S. A. Levin, E. H. van Nes, M. Pascual, and J. Vandermeer. 2012. Anticipating Critical Transitions. *Science* 338/344(6105): 344–348. http://doi.org/10.1126/science.1225244.

Tainter, J. A. 1988. *The Collapse of Complex Societies*. Cambridge: Cambridge University Press.

Taleb, N. N. 2007. *The Black Swan: The Impact of the Highly Improbable*. London: Penguin.

Taleb, N. N. 2014. *Antifragile: Things That Gain from Disorder*. Paperback Edition. New York: Random House.

Ward, W. A., and M. S. Joukowsky, eds. 1992. *The Crisis Years: The 12th Century B.C. from Beyond the Danube to the Tigris*. Dubuque, IA: Kendall/Hunt Publishing Co.

6 The End of "Peak Empire"

The Collapse of the Roman, Han, and Jin Empires

Walter Scheidel

6.1 Introduction

I discuss the fall of the western half of the Roman empire in the fifth century CE and the dismantling of the Han empire and the short-lived successor regime of Jin in the third and early fourth century CE. I focus on the process of the unraveling of centralized authority, rather than on the more prolonged transformation and (most notably in the Roman case) decay of imperial institutions of governance that followed (for which see Wickham 2005; Lewis 2009; Scheidel 2019: 227–253). Due to space constraints, I confine my discussion to the breakdown of hierarchy and control at the level of empire without exploring its impact on constituent elements from households to local communities and regions.[1]

These events have long attracted attention well beyond academia. The fall of the western Roman empire in particular is often viewed as a paradigmatic case of the collapse of a deeply entrenched major power. Its causes continue to be debated: One modern survey counts more than 200 different explanations that have been put forward (Demandt 1984: 695). The Han collapse reversed more than 400 years of large-scale political unification in East Asia and set off "dynastic cycles" of serial concentration and abatement of imperial power in China that continued into the twentieth century.

Neither the western Roman empire nor the Han and Jin empires were simply conquered by external challengers. Internal decay was a critical element and powerful driver of the eventual demise of these polities. This makes them especially suitable case studies of societal collapse because they highlight the complex interplay of multiple factors in precipitating this outcome.

These collapse events are also significant because they ended the period of what I call "peak empire." As far as we can tell, in the first two centuries CE, a larger share of the entire world population was ruled by the three largest empires that existed at the time than at any other point in history (Scheidel 2021: 102). This extreme level of concentration was driven in the first instance by Chinese and Roman state formation. Its reversal ended a long-term trend toward an ever-greater degree of political consolidation, which was replaced by an overall pattern of repeated re-concentration and abatement that is still ongoing.

DOI: 10.4324/9781003331384-9

6.2 Background

In the most basic terms, the Roman and Han empires had much in common (Scheidel 2009, 2019: 221–227). They both arose through the conquest of multiple and diverse entities, from several sizable precursor kingdoms to diverse smaller-scale societies. At their peak (in the first or second century CE) each controlled at least four million square kilometers of land (and more if we include peripheral zones of influence) and some 60–70 million people. Both empires experienced a short period of internal division due to civil war (in the 40s/30s BCE in Rome and in the 20s CE in China) as well as a somewhat longer tripartite division (in the 260s/270s CE in Rome and from the 220s to 270s CE in China, wrapped up by the Jin dynasty). In both cases, the half of each empire that was more exposed to peripheral challengers from less settled areas fell first: The western half of the Roman empire in the fifth century CE and the northern half of the post-Han Jin empire at the beginning of the fourth century CE. Rump states survived in the east and south, respectively.

6.2.1 Rome[2]

The Roman empire grew from tiny beginnings in the fourth century BCE into a pan-Mediterranean empire that by the first century CE had also massively expanded into its continental European hinterland all the way to Britain. This polity was highly stable for a long time. In the first century BCE, when Rome was still ruled by an aristocratic oligarchy, several episodes of civil war did not lead to lasting fragmentation. Instead, this domestic disorder gave rise to a monarchical system of government that heavily relied on a large standing army of some 400,000 soldiers who were deployed mostly along the frontiers. Routine governance was provided by the local elites of some 2,000 urban communities, overseen by members of the central imperial aristocracy who served as governors and senior military commanders, and by enslaved or freed members of the imperial household who performed essential administrative functions.

In the third century CE, the empire underwent a 50-year period of serious political instability that coincided with, and was to a significant extent triggered by, novel challenges from mostly Germanic tribal confederations to the north and the Iranian empire of the Sasanians in the Middle East. These disturbances culminated in a temporary fracturing of the empire into three regional entities (260–274 CE) that was overcome by military force. This crisis encouraged organizational reforms that may have played a role in preserving the full territorial reach of the empire for more than another century (see Section 6.3.1). Even so, military conflicts among rival claimants to emperorship repeatedly broke out during the fourth century CE, especially in the European part of the empire.

From the 370s CE, Germanic groups that were settled within the empire began to assert a degree of effective autonomy, undermining the imperial state's claim to a monopoly on organized violence. The Germanic Goths, who had entered the empire after being displaced by the advance of the nomadic Huns across the eastern Eurasian steppe, played a crucial role in this process.

Beginning in 395 CE, the eastern and western halves of the empire were consistently run by separate emperors and courts. Conditions in the western half of the empire rapidly deteriorated in the first decade of the fifth century CE, as multiple campaigns by different Germanic groups coincided with violent internal conflict among incumbents and usurpers. In 410 CE, the original capital city of Rome was sacked by the Visigoths. While the western Roman court managed to settle some Germanic groups on provincial land and turn them into allies, others retained effective autonomy. This was especially true of the Vandals, which after traversing Gaul and the Iberian Peninsula established a separate kingdom in North Africa in the 430s CE, thereby depriving the imperial center of vital material resources (see Sections 6.3.4.1 and 6.3.4.2).

This made it harder for that center to organize resistance to Hunnic incursions into Gaul and Italy in the 450s CE, and more generally to compensate allied Germanic groups for their cooperation. In the 460s and 470s CE, the western empire unraveled into multiple polities run by Germanic leaders and their followers. To various degrees, the principal successor regimes of the Ostrogoths (Italy), Franks (Gaul), Visigoths (Iberian Peninsula), and Vandals (North Africa) relied on Roman-style institutions of governance, which took up to several centuries fully to erode.

Meanwhile, the eastern half of the empire, centered on Constantinople, survived intact, deflecting incursions from central Europe and benefiting from the temporary weakness of its Iranian competitor farther east. Yet this was merely a temporary reprieve: In the sixth and seventh century CE, the eastern empire came close to succumbing to pressures from Slavs and Avars in southeastern Europe and of Iranians and Arabs in the Middle East (see John Haldon's chapter [Chapter 7] in this volume).

6.2.2 China[3]

At the end of the third century BCE, the Han empire took over the Qin empire, which had been formed by conquering the other major kingdoms or "Warring States" in northeastern and eastern China during the 220s BCE. The Han dynasty (202 BCE–220 CE) came to control much of present-day China (except for Manchuria, Inner Mongolia, and the far southwest), including large swathes of Xinjiang as well as northern Vietnam and Korea. This empire maintained a high degree of territorial integrity well into the late second century CE. Up to that point, the dynasty's rule was only briefly challenged between 9 and 30 CE.

Following a template established in the Warring States period (fifth to third century BCE), the Han empire was organized as a monarchy that relied on salaried officials to perform administrative functions. Around 130,000–150,000 officials were directly recruited and deployed by the imperial center.

They, in turn, oversaw the activities of lower-ranked officials who controlled the local communities from which they were drawn. Standing military forces were far less numerous than in the Roman empire but were boosted by levies as required. Unlike in the Roman empire, the civilian bureaucracy was formally separated from regular military commands and eclipsed the latter in terms of power and status.

The imperial authorities extracted revenue by taxing output as well as civilian and military labor. The state periodically organized empire-wide censuses to count the population and assess its resources. Whereas under the Western Han dynasty (202 BCE to 9 CE), military conscription and corvée duties for civilians were widespread, these practices were scaled back or (in the case of conscription) even abolished after the restoration of the regime (as the Eastern Han dynasty) in the late 20s CE.

Throughout its existence, the Han empire faced pressure from confederations of mobile pastoralist populations in the eastern Eurasian steppe, known as the Xiongnu and Xianbei. Even though, from the late third to the mid–first century BCE, the Xiongnu greatly scaled up their reach and achieved a degree of centralized coordination by mimicking Han imperial institutions, their presence did not pose an existential threat to the empire. Later on, the Han empire fostered divisions among the steppe groups in order to protect the frontier, and repeatedly admitted some of them to its territory. In the second century CE, encroachment by the tribal Qiang on the northwestern frontier created renewed pressures.

In the end, the Han empire succumbed to internal conflicts rather than foreign invasion. In 184 CE, massive religiously inspired peasant uprisings organized by renegade elements of the gentry—the Yellow Turban Rebellion in the central regions of the empire and the Five Pecks of Rice Rebellion in Sichuan—destabilized imperial rule. Efforts to suppress these violent movements involved the creation of powerful military commands that concentrated large resources in the hands of a few leaders. A flare-up of factional strife at the imperial court in 189 CE led one of these leaders to seize the capital and others to establish control in various provinces. At that point, the empire ceased to function as a unified polity: The abdication of the last Han ruler in 220 CE was a mere formality. The period from 190 to 220 CE was taken up by shifting coalitions and conflicts among rival warlords that culminated in the formation of three successor states headed by separate emperors: Wei, based in the original imperial core in the Central Plain; Shu, in Sichuan; and Wu, centered on the lower Yangzi valley.

Superior in terms of size and manpower, Wei conquered Shu in 263 CE and Wu in 280 CE, re-establishing imperial unity under the Jin dynasty. This brittle polity incorporated several semi-nomadic groups that had moved in from the steppe and came to play an outsized role in military affairs. In an arrangement that was meant to balance competing interests, political and military power (aside from a large Inner Army at the empire's core) was dispersed among a number of princes of the ruling dynasty who controlled regional commands and large fiefs. The conventional separation of civilian and military administration was abandoned. This strategy soon proved ineffective when a massive civil war between different contenders (known as the "War of the Eight Princes" of 301–307 CE) destabilized the empire. This conflict triggered interventions and uprisings by the incorporated steppe groups. Between 308 and 316 CE, Xiongnu forces defeated Jin armies and destroyed the imperial capitals of Luoyang and Chang'an.

While the Jin dynasty retained control over the southern half of the empire, northern China (including the original core areas of the Han and Jin empires) came to be contested between a series of fairly ephemeral polities that were set up by competing coalitions of warriors drawn from the steppe frontier and adjacent peripheral zones. The Chinese historiographical tradition conventionally recognizes 16 northern states that existed between 304 and 460 CE. Only some of them were present at any one time: The co-existence of between three and five states was the norm for most of this period. In this respect, the overall degree of fragmentation resembled conditions in what had been the western half of the Roman empire in the late fifth and sixth centuries CE. By the same token, the survival of the southern Jin empire offers a close analogy to that of the eastern Roman empire.

6.3 Factors in Imperial Collapse

6.3.1 General Dynamics

Both empires were characterized by competition between the center and elites over control of surplus and the producers of surplus, especially the peasantry. The Roman empire had always relied on fairly autonomous local elites for tax assessment and local collection, which ensured loyalty but limited the center's ability to increase revenue. After the third century CE crisis, efforts were made to bolster revenue collection and expand the number of salaried state agents. Even so, it appears that in the fourth and fifth century CE, landlords in the western half of the empire were able to expand their control of the peasantry and shield it from conscription and taxation, thereby constraining the center's ability to mobilize manpower and resources.

In keeping with Joseph Tainter's theory of diminishing returns on complexity, adding layers of complexity increased the burden on the system (Tainter 1988; cf. Luke Kemp, Chapter 3 in this volume). After the third-century CE crisis, the Roman center doubled the number of provinces, separated civilian and military functions, hired some 30,000 salaried officials, and created intermediate supra-provincial administrative structures (vicariates and superordinate prefectures) and supra-provincial military commands (under *comites*) with their own personnel. Transient secondary courts for junior co-rulers added to the burden.

Overall, opportunities for rent-seeking became more widely dispersed in late antiquity. The employment of additional civil servants increased burden on the population, while growing privileges for the newly coopted Christian Church cut into revenues that were available to the state. Overall, this decreased the state's share of the surplus while alienating commoners.

These trends coincided with internal divisions. The de facto division of the empire in 395 CE made it harder to coordinate efforts and resource flows and to concentrate them in particular hotspots, which had been common practice in previous centuries. Because of the uneven distribution of threats and clientelistic practices, this disproportionately weakened the western empire while favoring the eastern one. The effects of this organization division were amplified by recurrent conflicts between contenders and usurpers that further obstructed coordination and also reduced the military's ability to focus on external threats.

Following practices established in the Warring States period, the Western Han regime periodically pursued measures to check the influence of landowning elites and preserve the autonomy of smallholders in order to count, tax, and mobilize them directly. Han rule was restored in the late 20s CE thanks to the support of large landlords. Thus, the Eastern Han period was characterized by greater and growing aristocratic power, which resulted in patronage protection of peasants and choked off access by state authorities. In addition, conscription was abolished. The third century CE in particular witnessed the growth of large estates and clientelism that gave rise to private armies, all of which filled the void left by receding state power.

By creating larger provinces, the eastern regime superimposed a new layer of administrative organization on the traditional two-tier system of commanderies and counties. In some ways, the creation of extraordinary regional military commands to address the risings of the 180s CE echoed the division of the Roman empire into several prefectures and consolidated military commands, albeit in a much more ad hoc fashion. In the Han case, these novel power concentrations enabled intervention in the imperial center that led to armed conflict among contenders for influence or supreme power. We may view this as a simplification of hierarchical structures that improved command and control capabilities at the regional level while undermining the superordinate imperial edifice.

Census records indicate that the three successor states and the Jin regime were unable to restore levels of registration and thus taxation that had been maintained in the pre-crisis Han empire. In addition, the deployment of multiple princes of the dynasty in different regions, endowed with their own courts and military forces, simultaneously increased opportunities for administrative rent-seeking, channeled resources away from the imperial center, and prepared the ground for internal conflict and effective territorial division.

All of this is consonant with a key element of Peter Turchin's demographic-structural theory (Turchin and Nefedov 2009, and Turchin's chapter in this volume): The late Roman empire, the eastern Han dynasty, and the Jin regime all experienced elite overproduction that intensified conflict over status and rents.[4] This in turn chimes well with Luke Kemp's emphasis on the role of diminishing returns on extraction: The principal drivers of hierarchical decline—corruption, inequality, intra-elite competition, and oligarchy—were all abundantly present, and environmental factors may also have depressed energy returns on investment (see Luke Kemp, Chapter 3 in this volume).

6.3.2 Environmental Factors

Both the first serious crisis of the Roman empire and the partitioning of the Han empire in the third century CE coincided with a temporary cooling phase and more generally with the onset of less stable climatic conditions in the northern hemisphere (Harper and McCormick 2018). Various indices point to lower temperatures in the first half of the fifth century CE, precisely the period when the western Roman empire transitioned from stability to decay. A period of heightened volcanic activity followed in the sixth and especially the seventh century CE, when the eastern empire suffered massive loss of territory. While it seems reasonable to suspect that climate change adversely affected the volume and predictability of agricultural production and might also have influenced southward migratory movement by peripheral groups (in central and eastern Europe and the steppe), the scale and impact of any such effects continue to be uncertain and much debated.

In the late second and the mid–third century CE, the Roman empire was struck by unprecedentedly severe pandemics (of an uncertain nature but probably involving smallpox) that modern researchers have linked to various signs of economic problems at the time (Harper 2017). However, no similarly prominent disease events are reported for the fifth century CE, when the western empire collapsed. A massive wave of bubonic plague (from 541 CE) postdated this process by several generations but probably contributed to the subsequent weakening of the eastern empire.

References to seven epidemic outbreaks in China between 151 and 185 CE have been conjecturally linked to the destabilization that commenced at that time. The fact that the first leader of the cataclysmic Yellow Turban Rebellion of 184 CE propagated faith healing may lend some support to this idea. The collapse of the Jin empire in the early fourth century CE coincided with the spread of smallpox, which was then for the first time clinically described in the Chinese medical tradition. In both cases, the scale and impact of these disease events are impossible to assess.

6.3.3 Systemic Structure

6.3.3.1 Network Architecture

In the Roman empire, the existence of large standing armies that were routinely commanded by aristocrats was a source of both resilience and instability: The former because it helped balance competing interests and enabled the empire to respond quickly to domestic and external challenges, and the latter because it provided usurpers with ready means of power projection. Rulers were never able fully to discourage such usurpations. Dependence on decentralized revenue collection by local elites and—especially in the fourth and fifth century CE—on cooperative intermediation by large landowners who also acted as patrons of rural communities constrained revenue collection by the imperial center. In times of stress, such groups could withhold cooperation and curtail revenue flows to the central authorities.

The Han empire gained stability by separating the civilian bureaucracy from the military, and by relying more than the Romans on salaried state agents who were deployed outside their areas of origins. Socialization within a shared Confucianism-inflected elite culture that emphasized imperial unity and the merits of state service was expected to suppress particularism and ensure loyalty. However, most salaries were very modest in real terms, elite aspirants were frequently able to obtain office through patronage or simony, and rent-seeking behavior was endemic among officials. Despite a somewhat deeper penetration of local society by state agents than in the Roman empire, the bureaucratic apparatus was heavily concentrated at the imperial court and in provincial centers and largely relied on local notables to manage towns and villages. This limited the infrastructural power of the state.

The creation of major military commands to deal with the crisis of the 180s CE shifted power from the civilian administration to the military in novel and untested ways. At the same time, different court factions (such as titled officials and eunuchs), whose interests had previously been balanced, resorted to violence to achieve their objectives, prompting intervention by the new military commanders. Together, these deviations from established practice destabilized and ultimately shattered the architecture of governance.

Under Jin, by contrast, competitive fragmentation was already baked into the system from the outset, as princes controlled large regions and military assets. This helps account for the unusually rapid demise of the re-unified empire.

6.3.3.2 Key Players

At the level of the individual, in the Roman, Han, and Jin cases, leaders of large military forces acted as key players in the process of imperial unraveling. In the 190s CE, effective control over the Han empire was divided among approximately 20 rival warlords who claimed portions of its territory. Following some reconsolidation in northern China under one of these warlords from 200 to 207 CE, his efforts to restore the empire's territorial integrity were thwarted by a coalition of the principal southern warlords. I have already noted the later segmentation of the Jin domain among rival princes.

In the fourth century CE, the western Roman empire experienced several usurpations that often led to large-scale combat between Roman forces. In the early fifth century CE, multiple usurpations created opportunities for encroachment by Germanic forces and settlers which set in motion the gradual erosion of central governance.

At the group level, the insertion of heavily militarized elements from outside the empire added an element of instability that played a crucial role in the eventual demise of the western Roman and Jin systems. The Jin regime, already riven by dynastic conflict, was brought down by a revolt of a coalition of Xiongnu who had been settled in the northwestern part of the empire while maintaining their own organization and cavalry forces.

In the Roman case, the Germanic groups that entered the empire were not particularly large but came to exercise outsized influence thanks to their spatial positioning within the western provinces. In 409 CE, the Vandals invaded the Iberian Peninsula, a region that had long been sheltered from external pressure and served as a critical source of net revenue. The Visigoths, settled as Roman allies in southwestern Gaul in 418 CE, expelled them in coordination with the Roman state, soon effectively replicating the Vandal occupation. The Vandal takeover of the most resource-rich parts of Roman North Africa (centered on present-day Tunisia) and later also Sicily further deprived the imperial center of revenue.

6.3.4 System Dynamics

6.3.4.1 Flows

The functioning of the Roman empire depended on the steady flow of resources between three different zones: The capital (or later capitals); developed and sheltered regions along the Mediterranean basin (present-day Italy, southern Spain, southern France, Tunisia, western Turkey, northwestern Syria, Lebanon, and above all Egypt) that yielded much more revenue than their protection absorbed; and frontier zones (in Britain, along the Rhine and the Danube, and in eastern Turkey and Syria) where much of the military was concentrated. Net revenue from the second zone was exported to the center(s) and the frontiers to fund the court(s) and above all the military, which absorbed the majority of state income.

To some extent, these tributary flows were counterbalanced by reciprocal trade flows, whereby the tax-exporting provinces sold goods to the center and the frontiers to earn back specie for further tax payments. Thus, fiscal demands boosted long-distance trade (Hopkins 1980).

The administrative division of the empire in 395 CE curtailed east-west transfers. More importantly, the introduction of either overtly hostile or nominally allied but increasingly autonomous Germanic forces into key tax-exporting regions such as the Iberian Peninsula (from 409 CE), southern Gaul (from 418 CE), North Africa (from 429 CE), and Sicily (from 469 CE) gradually eroded the western empire's fiscal base. Owing to its reliance on the fiscal infrastructure, interregional commercial exchange declined as well, reducing state revenue from tolls. This steady erosion of fiscal capacity undermined the center's ability to fund defense, punish defectors and purchase the cooperation of outside parties such as Germans and Huns.

Although the fiscal history of late Han and Jin China is less well known, we have to assume that the rise of regional warlords likewise disrupted revenue flows to the central authorities. Even though a large share of total revenue was always retained in the regions that generated that revenue, the metropolitan bureaucracy would have relied on resource transfers from other regions, in addition to income from the capital's hinterland and nearby imperial domains. For what it is worth, similar processes of fiscal erosion are documented for later Chinese history, most notably for the Tang dynasty after the mid-eighth century CE and the terminal phases of the Yuan and Ming dynasties.

6.3.4.2 Feedback Loops

In the western Roman empire during the fifth century CE, the gradual lack of central control over vital tax-exporting regions triggered a death spiral or cascading failure. Dwindling revenues diminished the center's ability to make credible protection commitments to provincials and especially to local elites. This, in turn, encouraged further Germanic encroachment that changed the incentive structure of local elites, encouraging them to defect from an imperial center that was no longer able to guarantee protection in exchange for taxation or to punish defectors. Moreover, the Germanic groups that took over a growing share of the territory operated with lower overhead than the established imperial governance structure that required support for the court, several secondary administrative centers, and rent-seeking officials. This added to the appeal of defection. Overall, imperial power structures were undermined by a feedback loop of internal conflict (among rival contenders), external pressure and infiltration (by Germanic groups), and domestic defection (by local elites).

In the late Han period, population pressure and elite capture of rural populations caused high inequality and popular discontent that triggered peasant uprisings. Epidemics and famine may have contributed to these events and lent them a millenarian religious dimension. The emergency concentration of military assets to combat these movements undermined the position of the central authorities and allowed local elites to re-orient their loyalties to regional powerholders when it was expedient and to seek greater autonomy whenever it was possible. These developments resulted in more entrenched regionalism and enhanced plutocratic power within regions. This militated against imperial unity and more generally reduced state capacity.

The short-lived Jin restoration did not overcome these obstacles. It failed when conflict within the top echelon of the ruling class triggered armed intervention and separatism by previously settled steppe groups that later proved unable to maintain cohesive and durable polities of their own. This created an environment (in northern China) in which power was dispersed among thousands of fortified settlements run by local gentry clans, balancing military coalitions of steppe groups that were spatially concentrated around transient political centers and struggled to project power across the territories they sought to claim.

6.3.5 Risks and Shocks

6.3.5.1 Sources

In all the cases under review, the risks faced by imperial polities were largely endogenous. The Roman system of relying on the compliance of highly autonomous local elite bodies to govern the empire and raise revenue had been entrenched for centuries and proved largely impervious to efforts to modify it in favor of greater centralization and efficacy. The dispersion of military power among elite leaders that were capable of challenging incumbents also had a long pedigree.

In late Han China, the relative novelty of large military commands meant that no effective strategies were in place to contain or balance them. Throughout Chinese history, popular uprisings—driven by elite exploitation and Malthusian factors—played a major role in destabilizing the imperial order and ushering in the demise of particular dynasties. Thus, the rebellions of the 180s CE were merely one episode in a long series of comparable events that stretched from the third century BCE into the modern era.

Infiltration and intervention by armed "barbarian" elements are likewise best classified as endogenous factors. From the first century BCE onward, Roman-German relations across the frontier-sustained patronage ties, military conflicts, commercial relations, and human capital transfers that cumulatively and in the long term enabled the Germans to improve their organizational and military capabilities. The Roman empire sought to manage the resultant pressure through a mixture of violent suppression, subsidies, resettlement, and recruitment of members of peripheral groups into the Roman military. The main difference between the fifth century CE and previous centuries is that in the former, these strategies finally failed. However, the gradual strengthening and insertion of peripheral groups had been a longer-term process and was in the final analysis an inevitable by-product of the gravitational pull of the empire's resources on these groups.

Much the same was true in East Asia. Throughout its existence, the Han empire had employed a wide range of strategies—such as violent confrontation, diplomacy, subsidies, cooptation, and resettlement—to manage and defuse pressure from mobile populations along and beyond its northern steppe frontier. While these groups did not play a crucial role in the demise of the Han regime, they dealt a fatal blow to the Jin state in a way that is broadly comparable to the aggregate impact of Vandal, Gothic and Frankish operations on Roman territory during the fifth century CE.

Insofar as exogenous shocks can be identified, they were limited to the domains of climate and disease, as discussed in Section 6.3.2. The appearance of the Huns in eastern Europe in the fourth century CE is the only likely exception. By putting pressure on Germanic populations closer to the Roman empire, their westward migration added an external and meaningfully exogenous element to Roman–German relations that amplified existing challenges to Roman control.

6.3.5.2 Speed

In the Han and Roman cases, risks had been building up over the long run. By the 180s CE, the power of large landlords in China had been steadily growing for some 150 years, and factionalism at the imperial court had also been intensifying over time. While it is difficult to track the processes that prompted the popular uprisings in the 180s CE, it is likely that they were tied up with long-term trends such as rising inequality driven by elite capture and Malthusian dynamics. As noted above, infiltration by external groups had likewise been going on for centuries.

At critical junctures, however, shocks unfolded quite rapidly. At the beginning of 395 CE, the Roman empire had still been ruled by a single emperor and had not faced any acute challenges from external competitors. Within the next 15 years, the western provinces were riven by usurpations, Vandals and allied groups invaded Gaul and the Iberian Peninsula, Britain appears to have been abandoned, Italy was attacked by two separate Germanic confederations, and Visigoths sacked the city of Rome. This concatenation of events set in motion the cascading failure that took up the following 70-odd years (see Section 6.3.4.2) and that the central authorities were unable to arrest.

The Han regime unraveled with even greater speed. Only five years separated the outbreak of the principal popular uprisings in 184 CE from the seizure of the imperial capital Luoyang by one of the warlords and the effective end of Han dynastic power in 189 CE. And ten years after the competition among the princes of Jin escalated into open warfare in 301 CE, the rebellious Xiongnu captured and destroyed the imperial capital city of Luoyang.

All these breakdowns of central control were as violent as they were sudden and can be identified as the relevant tipping points for the ensuing collapses. But this suddenness was deceptive: The disruptive trends noted above had existed for generations or even centuries.

6.4 Governance and Mitigation

6.4.1 Nature of Governance

Both the Roman and Han empires relied on long-established structures of imperial rule. Neither one of these systems permitted hereditary governorships or regional self-rule. Roman governance was more decentralized, relying as it did on a large degree of management of individual cities and their hinterlands by local elites and maintaining only a very modestly sized salaried bureaucracy. The Han system, by contrast, adhered to the "higher-end" governance model of the Warring States period that emphasized more overt centralization and employed salaried state agents more widely.

In practice, these differences must not be overrated: The Han empire also drew on resident notables to manage local affairs, and the Roman authorities were able to fall back on a large standing army in dealing with administrative tasks. Some convergence took place over time, as the later Roman empire, especially in the fourth century CE, embarked on centralizing reforms and built up a larger salaried bureaucracy whereas Eastern Han rulers granted local and regional elites more leeway in managing people and resources.

Overall, the processes of political decay described in this chapter were too pervasive to be attributed in any significant way to idiosyncratic personal agency. Actors generally behaved in ways that were consistent with established modi operandi, such as latent disloyalty and opportunistic usurpation by Roman senior military commanders and factional conflict within the Han and Jin elite.

6.4.2 Failure of Prevention

Following the crisis of the third century CE, Roman rulers sought to shore up state capacity and stability by separating civilian and military chains of command, increasing functional differentiation within the armed forces, expanding the ranks of salaried state agents, introducing additional layers of administrative hierarchy, reforming the currency system, and codifying legal rules. The Eastern Han period, by contrast, did not witness similarly ambitious reform attempts.

In the end, this need not have made a real difference: Given how rapidly the integrity of the western Roman empire deteriorated in the early fifth century CE (see Section 6.3.5.2), it is not at all clear that these measures had substantively increased its resilience. Although the eastern Roman empire, which had been subject to the same measures, survived, it remains doubtful to what extent this outcome can be attributed to these measures rather than unrelated factors such as geography and geopolitical conditions. Its subsequent near-failure in the seventh and early eighth century CE suggests that the eastern empire was just as vulnerable once put under more significant pressure.

The western half of the Roman empire might have fared better if it had not been effectively separated from the more economically developed and better-protected eastern provinces. Tax exports and military transfers from those regions could have shored up defenses in the northwestern reaches of the empire. However, this potential benefit of imperial unity would have been hard to foresee. The resurgence of Iranian power in the third and fourth centuries CE used to absorb large resources on the empire's eastern frontier, an experience that would have made it impossible to anticipate the temporary abatement of this pressure in the fifth century CE that freed up some of these resources.

Only plausible counterfactuals should be considered here. When viewed in context, far-reaching preventative measures that might in theory have

staved off collapse, such as military mass mobilization of the general population or comprehensive suppression of Germanic infiltration, do not fall
in this category.

The same applies to the Han and Jin empires. Once massive popular uprisings erupted, the rapid concentration of military power was the most promising response. As analogous events in later periods of Chinese history show, the
political fallout from such sudden interventions was generally hard to manage:
In the second half of the eighth century CE, the Tang empire experienced
similar regionalization of political and military power in the wake of a major
rebellion. Only in the early second millennium CE was the Song regime able
to ensure centralized civilian control over the military.

6.4.3 Predictability

All these collapse events were inevitable in the banal sense that no pre-modern
empires lasted forever. More specifically, the aforementioned lack of plausible
alternatives speaks against the notion that these events were readily preventable.

In the Roman case, the temporary fracturing of the empire in the 260s and
270s CE had already highlighted serious structural weaknesses. The extent of
subsequent organizational and institutional reform and the relative stability of
the empire for much of the fourth century CE may well have created a false
impression that these weaknesses had been successfully addressed. This would
have made it even harder if not impossible for contemporaries to predict the
onset of cascading failure in the early fifth century CE.

The Han regime successfully weathered disturbances at the end of the
third century BCE and in the 20s CE, and gradually learned how to manage threats from the steppe. Thus, even as the sudden dislocations of the
180s CE would have arrived unexpectedly, they might initially have been
viewed as yet another challenge to be overcome, rather than as the beginning of the end for the unified empire. It is only in retrospect that the
Han demise seemed overdue: The average lifespan of the four later major
dynasties of Tang, Song, Ming, and Qing was a little less than 300 years, a
watermark the Han system had already reached an entire century before the
crisis of the 180s CE struck.

6.5 Lessons

Superficial analogies between the fall of Rome and the fate of the United States
or the "West" have long been a staple of popular writing in the media and
elsewhere but must be treated with caution, especially as they sometimes take
a xenophobic turn by likening immigration from lower-income countries to
the so-called Migration of the Peoples into the western Roman empire and its
subsequent downfall.

Even so, the lessons of ancient history retain some relevance even today.
In both the Han and Roman cases, the hollowing out of the state by elite

constituencies that sought to capture policy-making and withhold resources from the central authorities was a key driver of system decay and collapse. American society has long displayed similar symptoms: Witness the scale of plutocratic influence on the political process and its success in curtailing taxation on large incomes and fortunes, which has contributed to rising inequality and social division.

In the end, the history of ancient Rome and China, just like the history of most if not all states in world history, was in no small part shaped by competition for power and resources between central authorities and certain elite groups. These dynamics mediated societal resilience and decay and contributed to episodes of state collapse. They are still present today and are now also closely intertwined with environmental challenges, shaping as they do political responses to climate change.

Although our own incomparably greater dependence on interconnectivity and differentiation of function exposes our societies to shocks that traditional subsistence economies would have found easier to weather, more recent development also provides some reasons for guarded optimism. Formal inclusion of the general population in the political process offers opportunities for combating elite capture. In societies that lack comparable arrangements, most notably China, novel surveillance capabilities may stymie a return of popular uprisings, which used to be a major driver of state collapse in that part of the world. The enormous increase in the stock of useful knowledge that has occurred since late antiquity provides us with tools for managing crises that were not available at the time.

The most important lesson might be the fact that as far as we know, nobody at the time anticipated the (relatively rapid) demise of the western Roman or Han imperial systems. Even though concepts of cyclical historical change existed at the time, universal empire, boosted to a scale previously unknown in history, might well have seemed stable and possibly eternal. Its demise reminds us that even an order that seems deeply entrenched can unravel with little advance warning.

Notes

1 I closely follow the chapter template the editors circulated in August 2020 and I keep references to a bare minimum: Relevant scholarship is extensive, especially on the Roman side.

2 Bang 2021 offers the most recent concise analysis of Roman imperial history. Woolf 2012 is an accessible survey. For recent syntheses of the fall of the western Roman empire, see Heather 2006; Goldsworthy 2009; Kulikowski 2019.

3 See Twitchett and Loewe 1986; Lewis 2007; and more briefly Lewis 2021 for the history of the Han period, and Lewis 2009; Dien and Knapp 2019 for the Jin dynasty and the subsequent period of fragmentation.

4 In the Eastern Han case, Malthusian pressures in society more generally probably also played a role, whereas the western part of the Roman empire in late antiquity did not go through a full "secular cycle" of growth and abatement (Baker 2011, who rightly stresses the role of elite overproduction and infighting).

References

Baker, David C. 2011. "The Roman Dominate from the Perspective of Demographic-Structural Theory." *Cliodynamics* 2(2): 217–251.

Bang, Peter Fibiger. 2021. "The Roman Empire." In Bang, Peter Fibiger, Bayly, C. A., and Scheidel, Walter, eds. *The Oxford World History of Empire, Vol. 2: The History of Empires*. New York: Oxford University Press: 240–289.

Demandt, Alexander. 1984. *Der Fall Roms: Die Auflösung des römischen Reiches im Urteil der Nachwelt*. Munich: C. H. Beck.

Dien, Albert E., and Knapp, Keith N., eds. 2019. *The Cambridge History of China, Vol. 2: The Six Dynasties, 220–589*. Cambridge: Cambridge University Press.

Goldsworthy, Adrian. 2009. *How Rome Fell: Death of a Superpower*. New Haven, CT: Yale University Press.

Harper, Kyle. 2017. *The Fate of Rome: Climate, Disease, and the End of an Empire*. Princeton, NJ: Princeton University Press.

Harper, Kyle, and McCormick, Michael, eds. 2018. "Reconstructing the Roman Climate." In Scheidel, Walter, ed. *The Science of Roman History: Biology, Climate, and the Future of the Past*. Princeton, NJ: Princeton University Press: 11–52.

Heather, Peter. 2006. *The Fall of the Roman Empire: A New History of Rome and the Barbarians*. Oxford: Oxford University Press.

Hopkins, Keith. 1980. "Taxes and Trade in the Roman Empire (200 B.C. – A.D. 400)." *Journal of Roman Studies* 70: 101–125.

Kemp, Luke. 2023. "Diminishing Returns on Extraction: How Inequality and Extractive Hierarchy Create Fragility." In: *How Worlds Collapse: What History, Systems, and Complexity Can Teach Us about Our Modern World and Fragile Future*. New York, NY: Routledge.

Kulikowski, Michael. 2019. *The Tragedy of Empire: From Constantine to the Destruction of Roman Italy*. Cambridge, MA: Harvard University Press.

Lewis, Mark Edward. 2007. *The Early Chinese Empires: Qin and Han*. Cambridge, MA: Harvard University Press.

Lewis, Mark Edward. 2009. *China between Empires: The Northern and Southern Dynasties*. Cambridge, MA: Harvard University Press.

Lewis, Mark Edward. 2021. "The First East Asian Empires: Qin and Han." In Bang, Peter Fibiger, Bayly, C. A., and Scheidel, Walter, eds. *The Oxford World History of Empire, Vol. 2: The History of Empires*. New York: Oxford University Press: 218–239.

Scheidel, Walter. 2009. "From the 'Great Convergence' to the 'First Great Divergence: Roman and Qin-Han State Formation and Its Aftermath." In Scheidel, Walter, ed. *Rome and China: Comparative Perspectives on Ancient World Empires*. New York: Oxford University Press: 11–23.

Scheidel, Walter. 2019. *Escape from Rome: The Failure of Empire and the Road to Prosperity*. Princeton, NJ: Princeton University Press.

Scheidel, Walter. 2021. "The Scale of Empire: Territory, Population, Distribution." In Bang, Peter Fibiger, Bayly, C. A., and Scheidel, Walter, eds. *The Oxford World History of Empire, Vol. 1: The Imperial Experience*. New York: Oxford University Press: 91–110.

Tainter, Joseph A. 1988. *The Collapse of Complex Societies*. Cambridge: Cambridge University Press.

Turchin, Peter, and Nefedov, Sergey A. 2009. *Secular Cycles*. Princeton, NJ: Princeton University Press.

Twitchett, Denis, and Loewe, Michael, eds. 1986. *The Cambridge History of China, Vol. I: The Ch'in and Han Empires, 221 B.C., Vol. A.D. 220*. Cambridge: Cambridge University Press.

Woolf, Greg. 2012. *Rome: An Empire's Story*. New York: Oxford University Press.

Wickham, Chris. 2005. *Framing the Early Middle Ages: Europe and the Mediterranean, 400–800*. Oxford: Oxford University Press.

7 Collapse and Non-collapse

The Case of Byzantium ca. 650–800 CE

John Haldon

The extent to which environmental and climatic changes, whether sudden high-impact events or more subtle gradual changes, impact human responses in the past has an enduring interest, both because of the situation in which human society finds itself in the twenty-first century and because of the value of comparison with the past and the question of whether or not historical developments might help us understand our present and our future. The degree to which societal perceptions of such changes affected behavioral patterns and explanatory rationalities in premodernity, for example, has obvious relevance, as does the question as to whether, and if so to what extent, were past societies able to manage risk and implement mitigating strategies? In the same vein, the ways in which historical cultures perceived and understood what we might recognize as systemic transformations have particular interest. Does our use of the term "collapse" help or hinder understanding major civilizational transformations or transitions in the past? As a historian, I find on the whole that the term collapse is both overused and misunderstood, which leads both to serious misrepresentation among non-specialists about the ways in which historical transformations took place, as well as an over-dramatization of historical change.

Before we can generalize about historical collapse(s) and draw out any general patterns, it is obviously essential to study a range of historical cases and, crucially, to examine them in detail and to try to pinpoint the causal mechanisms at work. We need to find out how the societies in question worked as complex systems, what degree of resilience or brittleness they display when confronted by potentially existential challenges, and in which aspects or combination of aspects that resilience is located; we need also to find out—if we have the evidence—how the people who inhabited and constituted those systems responded to various types of societal or environmental stress or pressure, and why, because that is also a fundamental element in societal responses to stress and challenge, whether long- or short-term. To exemplify this approach, this chapter looks at one particular case at a particular stressful point in its history, the medieval eastern Roman empire—Byzantium—in the seventh to eighth century CE.

DOI: 10.4324/9781003331384-10

7.1 Theoretical and Methodological Framework

Past human societies have largely been remarkably resilient in the face of severe challenges. They were well able to manage known environmental risks—seasonal challenges resulting from poor weather, for example, occasional flooding or short-term drought: Explanations for such events, and ways of mitigating their impacts, were part of the annual cycle of life. But major instances of any of these—such as multi-decadal drought, for example—could overburden a society's capacity to absorb the shock. At the same time, the configuration of social and political structures has always been impacted by such challenges in many different ways, with substantial implications for development pathways—for example, the different medium-term outcomes of the Black Death in England and France, or western and eastern Europe, illustrative of socio-environmental asymmetries in which different degrees of socio-political complexity and population density precondition the potentials for inherent resilience under stress.

Threats and challenges to the stability and integrity of a past social system can be defined both objectively, by an external or a modern observer on the basis of a set of agreed criteria, and subjectively, by the inhabitants of the society in question, or their successors. "Objective" does not necessarily mean unbiased or free of subjective assumptions, of course. But it does mean a perspective outside of the members and value system of the society being observed. Both need to be kept in mind, since perceptions and understanding determine responses and reactions, and because the logic and rationality of past social–cultural systems, even those out of which our own have developed, were often very different from our own. Historical research in the broadest sense (thus including archaeological research, for example) can reveal the extent to which rulers and elites, or farmers and producers, for example, responded to challenges in both shorter- and longer-term timescales. But it is important to bear in mind that in the pre-modern/pre-scientific world, moral and religious responses *were* at one and the same time practical responses, even if to our way of thinking this may not be obvious. Instituting religious processions in a city to protect it from pestilence or earthquake, for example, may not have reduced the mortality consequent upon such events, yet it may have reinforced social cohesion—and thus sectoral resilience—allowing the urban community to survive (Haldon et al. 2020: 9–11; Haldon et al. 2021).

The study of history is above all about how and why things changed through time. Fundamental to this is the question of the relationship between agency and structure—about the relationship between what people believed about themselves and the world they inhabited (and how they perceived it) and how this affected their actions upon and within it. At the level of historical grand narratives and large-scale comparative work, such aspects often get pushed into the background. Yet the degree to which key ideas are shared or not across a society as a whole is fundamental, and the extent to which the beliefs and ideology of the dominant political elite are relevant or not for the day-to-day interests and identities of the mass of the population has a crucial impact on social cohesion. Whether in times of stress or not, these are significant factors in how a given state system and the society upon which it is built organizes its control of resources or whether it has the internal strength or flexibility to weather particular political, social, or economic moments or longer periods of pressure. It is only by taking all these various elements into account and disentangling the overlaps, linkages, and mutual interactions that we can hope to glimpse something of the mechanisms behind societal responses (Goldstone and Haldon 2009: 11–15).

In the following I will look at one socio-cultural system, the early medieval East Roman empire (the Byzantine empire) through the lens of a complex adaptive systems approach (Levin et al. 2013; Scheffer 2009; also Haldon et al. 2020: 14–15) that takes social systems as linked or nested multi-scale subsystems (Gunderson et al. 2002; Holling 2001) in which cycles of change and adaptation at sub-systemic level intersect with larger, slower processes. In consequence, catastrophic system-wide change at the higher level only takes place when there is a coincidence in the level of vulnerability or fragility among all or most of the different adaptive cycles from which the system as a whole is composed. Without such a convergence, there can be no breakdown or collapse (Cumming and Peterson 2017). But societal sub-systems—whether institutional structures for energy capture, religious-ideological structures, kinship relationships, property and inheritance arrangements—are constantly changing, usually imperceptibly so for the human agents who constitute them through social praxis, as they evolve, i.e., as they move through the phases of their own cycle. In so doing they act to maintain the form of a system over the long term, thus facilitating a built-in elasticity and capacity for adaptation without fundamental change. This conceptual model offers an appropriate heuristic framework through which to understand processes of historical societal transformation (Haldon and Rosen 2018; Walker et al. 2004) and in particular the ways in which elements of a system can transform or break down while the basic shape and trajectory of the system as a whole is preserved.

An important aspect of this is the observation that the more complex a system becomes, the finer the balance between its mutually interdependent parts and the greater the potential for disequilibrium when one feature becomes unstable, generating a domino-effect breakdown of the whole (e.g., Dark 2016; Tainter 2006, 2000, 1988). This approach is useful in thinking about a large-scale systemic breakdown in, for example, patterns of trade and exchange, as well as in respect of international political systems (Sherratt 2003: 53–54; Bell 2006: 15). Yet complex systems may also demonstrate great flexibility, and the key to such resilience is another important element in any historical research program (e.g., Rosen 2007); by the same token, below the level of a system as a whole its sub-elements can survive because they retain resilience and are less dependent on the general system for their integrity. The counterpart to system is "conjuncture," that is to say, the processual moments experienced by the set of relationships described by the term "system" which impose the pressures that promote change or shifts. Since the basic structural dynamics of a societal system contribute to the types of collapse to which it may be subject, approaches to collapse and resilience that unites structure and process are the only reasonable way to understand societal transformation, especially when allowances are made—as I would argue they must be—for individual human agency and belief systems (Cumming and Petersen 2017; Haldon et al. 2020; also Anderies 2006; Berkes and Ross 2016; Gunderson and Holling 2002).

Looked at from this perspective, total systemic collapses—the synchronic breakdown of a whole socio-economic system—were rare even in cases of severe environmental stress. System transformations there certainly were, but these entailed incremental breakdowns of specific sub-systems within the totality of social–cultural relations, often as part of centuries-long processes. Such processes did indeed result in systemic transformation which we can describe as a transition from one state to another, but use of the term collapse gives a fundamentally misleading impression of the complex processes that were in fact involved (Haldon et al. 2020). While I will not pursue the definitional issue here, it seems to me that a major flaw in many attempts to describe the "collapse" of past societies is the absence of temporality—over what period of time did processes of change or disruption take place, and what were the agents' perception of such processes and how aware were they or how did they understand the changes they witnessed.

Historians and archaeologists with only very limited or no written archives at their disposal have come to rely increasingly on the new methodologies from the paleosciences to help in reconstructing both events and processes. But the chronological resolution and scale of the evidence offered by these disciplines are often far too coarse for the construction of a more refined historical account of societal change (Izdebski et al. 2016). The result has generally been that the historical—human—timescale fades into the background; the archaeological timescale becomes generalized to approach and conform with the coarser chronologies of the paleosciences; and the result has frequently been a dramatic compression of complex historical processes under an all-embracing single rubric—"collapse." The more distant the events being described, and the less qualitative the "historical" data at our disposal, the easier and perhaps more severe this process of compression and conflation becomes (Caseldine 2012).

Recent work on "trauma culture" and on the ways in which human agents in contemporary or near-contemporary societies respond to events suggests that most people cannot recognize a "collapse" when they are inside it and that such developments are generally defined as such only after they have taken place. It is therefore crucial to consider the perceptions of those who experienced the historical changes we are studying when we conceptualize broader historical events and narratives (Odorico 2018; Kaplan 2005; Caruth 1996; Sewell 1996; Fussel 1975). The "fall of the Roman empire" is a case in point: We might wish to talk in terms of collapse or fall, but for most of the people who populated the late Roman world, the occasional (and for most, distant) calamity was neither unusual nor unexpected, whether this was a series of failed harvests or a barbarian incursion. We should not lose sight of the fact that our perception of what happened has been formed to a very large extent by the ideologically loaded accounts of a tiny number of elite writers. This does not invalidate their testimony, but it does mean that they can hardly be representative of the vast mass of people in the Roman empire. Indeed, archaeology indicates a very slow process of incremental cultural and societal transformation, varying in pace and degree from region to region over many decades, punctuated by sudden, dramatic events in different regions at different times and across several generations. By the time the empire had actually faded away in the west, in the later fifth century, most people had never experienced the "real" empire. Instead, they had become acclimatized to the evolving moment—indeed what was experienced was generally interpreted in a way that let people perceive the old world continuing under new management (Lewit 2009; Ando 2008; Bowes and Loseby 2005). Dramatic and fundamental transformations accompanied by violence, bloodshed, and extensive human suffering there were; but they took place over an extended period of many decades, in different regions at different times. And while fundamental transformations at various levels certainly took place, to produce in the end a very different political and civilizational context, this long-term and complex series of regionally varied processes can hardly be called a collapse (given the implication of rapidity and totality this usually imparts) except at a very high level of generality, without doing serious injustice to the actual course of events, the causal interrelationships, and the complexity of the societies and local cultures that comprised the Roman world.

7.2 The Unpredictable Survival of an Empire

How societies in the past responded to stress depends on three key sets of conditions: Their complexity (the degree of interdependency across social relationships and structures), their institutional and ideological flexibility, and their systemic redundancy, all of which together determine the resilience of the system. Of course, such conditions do not exist in isolation but combine and recombine in innumerable historical configurations, so historians have to reduce this to ideal-typical models. The case of the medieval East Roman empire illustrates both common general patterns as well as subtle differences from other cases, and how such variation can lead to different or diverging developmental pathways. For the period from the early seventh- and well into the eighth century CE, it offers a good illustration both of the complex and dynamic interplay between environment, social and political institutions, cultural identities, and religion, and the ways in which these interacted to increase resilience in the face of an extreme challenge to the empire's survival.

The dominant power in the Mediterranean in the sixth century, with territory stretching from southern Spain and N. Africa in the west and south across to the Syrian desert in the east, its political power collapsed in the first half of the seventh century following wars with the Sasanian empire in Iraq and Iran and then with the expanding Arab-Islamic empire. Between ca. 634 and 642, the empire lost some 75% of its territory and an equivalent portion of its annual revenue (Maps 1 and 2). This can legitimately be termed "collapse" given the short timeframe and the extent of the empire's territorial shrinkage, even if limited to territorial control only. The fact of its survival in the face of such catastrophic loss and of its later recovery, to go onto the offensive in the later ninth and tenth centuries and recover its position as the dominant eastern Mediterranean power, has traditionally been ascribed to the leadership of certain of its emperors, such as Heraclius (610–641 CE) who, it used to be thought, introduced an entirely new system of military recruitment and finance; or to the fact of internecine fighting and civil war in the new Arab-Islamic polity during the later 650s, 660s, and 680s; or to the "simplification" of state administration; or to a combination of some or all of these (Tainter 2000, for example). In fact, there are many other factors, including environmental aspects, for which only recently has evidence become available.

Societies as adaptive systems embody five key sets of properties:

1. The nature and quality of the available natural capital (water, agrarian and pastoral resources, people).
2. The nature and quality of the available physical capital (labor, infrastructure).
3. The human capital (in terms of skills, competencies, attributes, including belief systems).
4. The ways in which a social system organizes its institutions and entitlements (that is to say, who has access to and/or control over resources).
5. Redundancy, that is, the degree to which there exists a plurality of functionally effective options for achieving key outcomes for survival.

For the early medieval East Roman empire, I add a sixth key theme, namely the broader international context within which any political and cultural formation is inscribed and which co-determines certain aspects of its situation (e.g., strategic position and thus the nature and degree of external political and economic challenges). Together, these key elements are found within (1) the empire's geographical and geopolitical situation (including the nature and potential of the external political and military challenges it faced); (2) its climatic and environmental context, settlement geography, and demography; (3) the degree and forms of ideological cohesion and identity and the nature and forms of political authority and legitimacy; and (4) its administrative organization and infrastructure, which is to say, the systems of social, political, economic, and cultural command and control. The ways in which each of these intersected constitutes (5) the degrees of redundancy in achieving functional effectiveness in each element.

7.3 Context

Geopolitically the East Roman state at its height in the middle of the sixth century was overextended. With its political center at Constantinople, it stretched

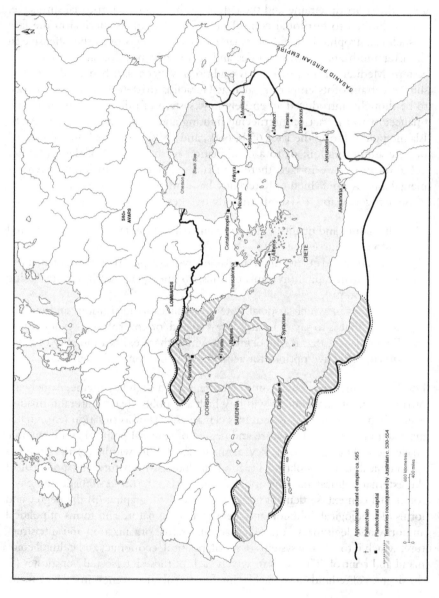

Figure 7.1 The Eastern Roman empire at its height ca. 560 CE

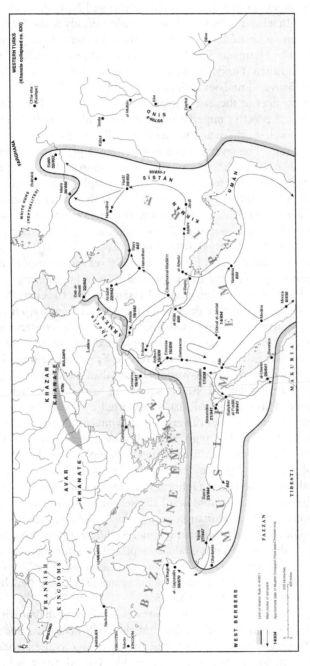

Figure 7.2 The rapid expansion of Islam ca. 632–690 CE.

as far west as the Balearic Islands, N. Africa as far as the straits of Gibraltar, most of Italy (with Sardinia, Corsica, and Sicily), and the Balkans; and in the east included Egypt and greater Syria (modern Syria and N. Iraq, much of Jordan, all of modern Israel and Lebanon). But beginning already in the 560s, this huge territory began to crumble (Whittow 2010; Cameron 2000; Whitby 2000; Maas 2005). The Germanic Lombards invaded and seized much of Italy from 568; Slavic and then Turkic invaders seized control of much of the Balkans between the 560s and mid-seventh century; and as noted the Arabs seized the wealthiest provinces in the east, Egypt, Syria, and N. Iraq between 634 and 642. This limited effective imperial authority and military control to the southern Balkan littoral, northern and western Anatolia and the central plateau, and the Aegean region. The seventh-century invasions deprived the government at Constantinople of its wealthiest tax-generating resources. But it also reduced it to a hard, defensible core, focused on Constantinople with its triple walls and sea defenses, protected by an Anatolian hinterland sheltered behind the Taurus and Anti-Taurus mountains in the south, penetration beyond which always eluded the Arabs, partly because of geographical, partly climatic conditions (Haldon 2016, 1997; Whittow 2010) (Figure 7.3).

The basic economic cycle of production of food and necessities was determined by this geography, the landscape, and its carrying capacity. Arable and pastoral land here was, with sub-regional variations, put to relatively intensive use during the sixth and first decades of the seventh century, characterized, in effect, by complexity, connectedness, and eventually conservatism. Both the palynological and the archaeological evidence indicate that much of the region was densely inhabited and characterized by mixed farming. But much of Anatolia experienced a rather wetter climate than hitherto during the sixth and up to the later seventh century, stretching in some areas into the early eighth century. This is a pattern that is supported by textual evidence, with a comparatively greater number of very severe winters and apparently unusually severe frosts and snows, but with relatively few events related to periods of aridity or drought and similar climate issues. It is also indicated by the paleoenvironmental evidence, especially pollens indicating changes or continuities in land use, and hence also demographics and settlement patterns. The pollen data show that beginning in the middle of the seventh century the intensive and relatively homogenous exploitation of land in Anatolia receded. There took place a simplification of the agrarian regime. At different rates according to the area, the established pattern was gradually replaced, by either natural vegetation or a more limited range of crops, with a particular emphasis on grain and livestock at the expense of viticulture and oleoculture (Table 7.1) (Izdebski 2013, 2012, 2011; Haldon et al. 2014: 132–150).

The onset of this simplification coincides partially with known political events, such as the impact of warfare and the Arab invasions, but not with any single "climate change" event; and the economic consequences of the warfare of the period were not all on one side. Indeed, there is pollen evidence for "rupture" in the rural economy on what becomes, from the 640s

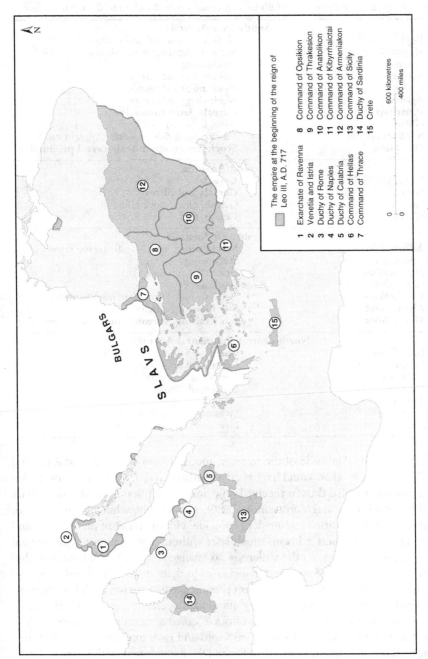

The empire at the beginning of the reign of
Leo III, A.D. 717

1 Exarchate of Ravenna
2 Venetia and Istria
3 Duchy of Rome
4 Duchy of Naples
5 Duchy of Calabria
6 Command of Hellas
7 Command of Thrace
8 Command of Opsikion
9 Command of Thrakesion
10 Command of Anatolikon
11 Command of Kibyrrhaiotai
12 Command of Armeniakon
13 Command of Sicily
14 Duchy of Sardinia
15 Crete

0   600 kilometres
0   400 miles

BULGARS

SLAVS

Figure 7.3 The core territories of the empire c. 717 showing military provinces and commands.

Table 7.1 Patterns of changing agrarian production from the seventh century CE in Anatolia as indicated from pollen data. Note: **Bold typeface** denotes the continuity of agriculture from the fifth to sixth century into the ninth to tenth century.

	South-west Anatolia
Beyşehir Gölü	Slight indication of stockraising
Hoyran Gölü	Some stockraising; + cereals from later 8th c.
Karamık Bataklığı	Stockraising
Bereket	Stockraising and cereals
Gravgaz	Stockraising and cereals
Ağlasun	Stockraising and cereals
Pinarbaşı	**Cereals, later stockraising**
Gölhisar	None indicated
Söğüt Gölü	**Stockraising 6th c. – 8th c., grain ca. 815 +**
Ova Gölü	**Stockraising, small-scale cereal production**

	West Anatolia
Köyceğiz Gölü	**Cereals**
Bafa Gölü	**Cereals and olives**
Gölçuk	Cereals, olives, stockraising
Alakilise	Cereals, fruit, livestock, olives, vines

	North-west Anatolia
Adliye valley	**Stockraising, small-scale arable farming**
Iznik Gölü	Stockraising
Manyas Gölü	Fruticulture until ca. 9th c.
Göksu river delta	Stockraising
Küçük Akgöl	Cereals, vines, fruit; olives from late 7th c.
Abant Gölü	**Stockraising, cereals, vines**
Melen Gölü	**Stockraising, cereals; vines from later 7th c.**

	North-central and central Anatolia
Ladik Gölü	Cereals and stockraising
Demiyurt Gölü	Cereals and stockraising
Çöl Gölü	Cereals and stockraising
Nar Gölü	None until 10th c.
Tuzla Gölü	None
Çadır Höyük	Livestock and some cereals
Pessinus	Livestock and some cereals

and 650s, the Arab side of the frontier, too, at Golbaşı (between Malatya and Diyarbakır), in what would have been a similarly challenged frontier zone: This is a subject that has thus far received only limited attention from historians so far (Eger 2014; Eger and Vorderstrasse 2020). Importantly, while in some areas of Anatolia the simplified regime does coincide with the onset of the more humid conditions, in others it begins much later without any obvious environmental stimulus; while in yet others there is no change at all. The conclusion is that while some farmers responded to a change in their environment, others did so only later and in response to different pressures, while yet others did not need to introduce any changes at all. A key question concerns the reasons for this shift.

The shift toward a grain and livestock-focused agrarian regime does seem to intensify during the Arab-Islamic invasions and raids into Anatolia, which had significant consequences for urban life and the demography of the region. There was a substantial demographic decline, although it was regionally nuanced and in some areas appears to have begun before the later sixth century Cassis et al.

2018); a ruralization of society more broadly as urban centers contracted and focused on defense rather than commerce and exchange (although these too continued unbroken in most cases, albeit on a reduced scale), and thus a loss of energy capture. It is here that the response of the eastern Roman state becomes especially relevant. One factor that played a role is that of the grain supply of the empire. The loss of Egypt in 618 to the Persians, and then permanently to the Arabs in 641, was a serious blow, because Egypt had been the breadbasket of the empire. New sources of grain for the capital were needed, while the presence of armies in Anatolia from the 640s and 650s onward also meant that the provinces had to feed substantial numbers of additional mouths, both human and animal. Documentary evidence for fiscal and resource management from the 660s into the first half of the eighth century suggests that the empire was able to reorientate its management of both the Constantinopolitan supply as well as the centers of grain production for its provincial armies (Haldon 2016: 215–282).

The simplification of agrarian output across Anatolia, and more especially the greater emphasis on cereal production and livestock, reflected a number of changes. First, farmers may have responded voluntarily to market demand for more grain. Second, however, given the intense pressure, it was under at this time, the state needed to generate the supplies needed to maintain its administrative apparatus and its armies—chiefly livestock and grain. Unaware as it would have been of the regional and relatively slow climatic shifts, increased fiscal demand for these products would nevertheless have directly impacted farmers' choices in production. The proxy data for the production of cereals and other crops necessary to livestock thus supports the hypothesis that the government at Constantinople re-orientated fiscal policy to increase its capture of this sort of resource, even if other causal factors, whether or not changing patterns of demand and market relations also contributed.

There were precedents. For example, the Roman government in fifth-century Italy seems likewise to have been able, through fiscal pressure, to encourage landlords and landowners to increase emphasis on grain production, so the response of the government in Constantinople during the later seventh century was neither without precedent nor was it an unknown planning strategy of the state (Haldon 2016: 281). We may thus suggest that it was the state, through its fiscal system, that contributed the key stimulus to this shift in the pattern of agrarian output. Evidence for a change in technical language in the tax system and in the military administration of the empire supports such a conclusion. Thus, paradoxically, conditions of climatic instability similar to those that provided the background and context for the gradual transformation of the Roman Empire in the course of the third-fifth centuries were precisely the conditions that—along with a range of other political, social, and economic factors—permitted the survival of the eastern Roman state in the seventh century. Here we see the consequences for a historical society of adaptation by individual farmers to both changing environmental and to changing fiscal pressure as well as shifting market and exchange circumstances. But this adaptation was a response or reaction that took place in part at least because the central government was itself responding flexibly to pressures placed upon its administrative, military, and fiscal arrangements resulting from demographic changes and warfare. Climate played a role, therefore, but it was a facilitating rather than a causal role.

These conditions alone, however, do not constitute a sufficient explanation for the empire's survival. Adaptation at one level only could hardly compensate for the existential challenge to the very fabric of state and society posed by the rise of Islam and the rapid expansion of the Arab-Islamic empire and the Umayyad caliphate. First, and crucially, there was an identity of vested interests between the court and the regional as well as central elites. The Anatolian elite identified its survival—physical survival, wealth and income, social status, and access to prestige and honors—with the imperial court. Its members perceived themselves as Roman and Christian, their fates bound together by common enemies and shared challenges to their future well-being. The contrasting fates of the empire's Italian territories and, more importantly, its North African provinces highlight the central importance for the court at Constantinople of keeping the elites on board. Where they failed—as they did in North Africa—they lost the provinces in question. That was by no means the only reason for the loss of North Africa, but it was an especially important one (Haldon 2016: 159–214; 2009).

Second, and especially relevant to the shared identity of court and elite, orthodox Christianity and Roman-ness represented two key ideological narratives through which the court and social elite in the capital and in the provinces reinforced the differentness (and the superiority) of the Romans as against those who attacked or threatened them. Christianity and its attendant institutions served also to bind the mass of the ordinary provincial and urban population of the empire to the traditional establishment (Haldon 2016: 79–119). Still other factors played a role as well. The empire inherited and maintained an extensive network of major roads across Anatolia and the Balkans, together with a tried-and-tested system of transportation that could move resources in both foodstuffs, solders, and war materiel around relatively efficiently both on land and by sea. Equipped with this substantial advantage and within the reduced strategic-geographical context of the later seventh century, imperial defenses were more readily organized around limited resources, a situation that worked to the advantage of the emperors both politically as well as militarily, since they were also able to control and monitor the provinces and their elites more effectively. This also enhanced the ability of the state to maintain a relatively flexible but remarkably effective fiscal-administrative apparatus and governmental infrastructure that permitted optimization of resource extraction, distribution, and consumption (see Figure 7.4). In respect of urban life, the civic culture of the Roman empire at its height had already during the sixth century CE begun to transition to a differently configured form of urbanism. The reasons for this are complex, but the changes essentially reflect evolving socio-cultural and socio-economic factors. In Anatolia, therefore, the warfare and economic dislocation of the later seventh and eighth centuries merely hastened an ongoing process along.

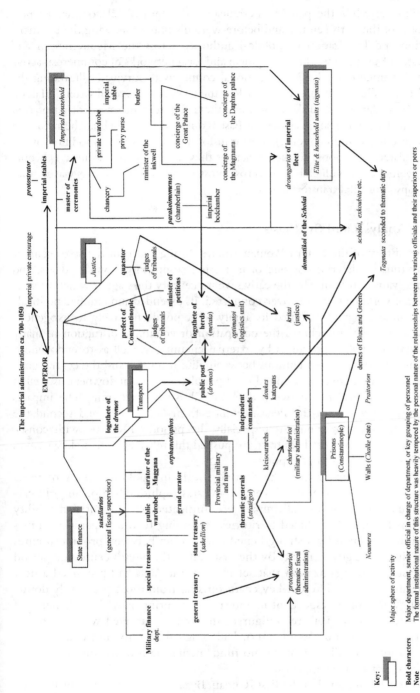

Figure 7.4 Schematic representation of the imperial administrative system.

Finally, while the pan-Mediterranean and international commercial networks of the sixth century and before were disrupted following the fragmentation and localization of political authority across the Mediterranean and western European world, the regional and local networks of commercial activity that underpinned this international connectivity survived, illustrating the relative resilience of sub-systems below the level of the overall system (Haldon 2012; Koder 2012). Taken together, these different processes of adaptation meant that, while some aspects of East Roman society (such as the nature of urban culture and economy) were transformed, others were modified or rearticulated in response to the challenges they faced. There was no synchronic convergence of vulnerabilities across most or all systems: There was neither collapse nor total transformation.

7.4 Analysis and Synthesis

The history of the eastern Roman empire during much of the sixth century may thus be described as one of increasing complexity, connectedness, and conservatism, reaching by the early seventh century the stage at which its various networks had become over-connected. Its extended and ramified political-economic geography limited its ability to respond effectively to exogenous challenges, which included the occupation or economic disruption of many Balkan and Italian provinces by external enemies; as well as to endogenous points of stress, such as tensions between elite magnates and the central government, and between exploited rural populations and landowners; as well as major ideological rifts between different Christian confessions. The impacts of first the war with the Persian empire from 602 to 626 and second the early Arab-Islamic conquests (especially the period 640s–670s, with consequent massive territorial contraction) pushed this relatively inflexible system as a whole beyond its tipping point.

But while the dramatic territorial, fiscal, and political losses of these decades represented at one level a near-catastrophic reduction in political-military reach, the overall impact was mitigated by substantial flexibility within the greatly reduced territories remaining to the imperial administration, as well as by a strengthened relationship between provincial elites and the court/government. By the first half of the eighth century, a period of systemic reorganization that set in from the 660s had produced a new equilibrium with different key characteristics from those previously dominant. While many aspects of its internal structuring as well as elements of its external form were reconfigured, the empire survived with no loss of system identity, no loss of internal ideological identity and content, and adaptation and adjustment but no fundamental transformation of its fiscal, military, or judicial apparatus.

The natural capital of the East Roman/Byzantine state was relatively modest in total area although extended across a considerable distance: While Anatolia became its heartland for over 200 years, it still retained outposts in

Sicily, Italy, and throughout the Aegean, and it held on to N. Africa until the last decades of the seventh century. These territories were connected by an exposed and frequently threatened but never broken maritime communications network that also retained a substantial commercial and exchange dynamic. Regarding population, we possess little demographic data, although the paleoenvironmental evidence suggests a fairly sharp demographic decline in the course of the seventh century (Roberts et al. 2018; also Cassis et al. 2018). We have good, if geographically patchy, data on landscape, land use, water resources, and agrarian production. We have a fairly good idea of the quality and nature of both physical and human capital, as well as about the degree of role specialization, the degree of institutional, socio-economic, and cultural differentiation and hierarchization, the nature and extent of differential access to resources and power, and the degree of multi-level functional organization in respect of political, economic, and cultural life (Brandes 2002; Haldon 1997; Hendy 1985).

The empire's resilience during this transformative period in its history can be explained through its relatively high degree of adaptive capacity: In the geographical and geopolitical advantages that accrued from its territorial reduction; in a series of broader climatic/environmental factors that—quite co-incidentally—contributed to its requirements for grain and livestock during the later seventh and eighth centuries; in its substantial organizational advantages (an effective military road infrastructure, logistical, and fiscal resource-management arrangements); in the relatively tight control the court and government at Constantinople was able to maintain over the Anatolian, Balkan and Italian/Sicilian elites who ran the financial and administrative affairs of the state and controlled local tax-paying populations (contrast with Syria, N. Africa); and in the degree of ideological cohesion and identity that was maintained and that served to reinforce state policies. In other words, system identity survived and was reinforced, while systemic complexity was retained at all levels: See Figure 7.5. In each of these instances, there existed also a degree of functional redundancy, so that damage—demographic, economic, or institutional—was compensated rapidly, enabling the system as a whole to continue to function. And this general situation was helped by the structural problems faced by its challenger in the east, the Umayyad caliphate.

At only one level, that of spatial extent, did there take place what was in effect a "simplification." As we have seen, even though imperial territory continued to be widely dispersed across the central and east Mediterranean basin, the empire was very considerably reduced in both total area and the quality of the lands remaining to it. This reduction in territory reduced to a degree also the extent—and costs—of the state's apparatus, thus in effect reducing overall costs and administrative-institutional complexity by a certain degree. It is very clear from the sources that this loss of territory in fact contributed to increased central command and control over both resources and people, thus also to sustainability and resilience; and that it was compensated by resilient fiscal strategies that permitted the state to maintain an effective political and

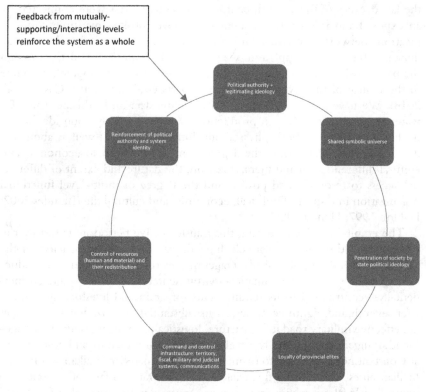

Feedback from mutually-supporting/interacting levels reinforce the system as a whole

Political authority + legitimating ideology

Shared symbolic universe

Penetration of society by state political ideology

Loyalty of provincial elites

Command and control infrastructure: territory, fiscal, military and judicial systems, communications

Control of resources (human and material) and their redistribution

Reinforcement of political authority and system identity

Figure 7.5 Interdependencies: A resilient system in which all elements connect and mutually reinforce one another (the eastern Roman/Byzantine state in the seventh to eighth century CE).

military reach, thus bearing out points made by Joseph Tainter (Tainter 2006, 1998). The result was that the state survived with an unchallenged system identity and infrastructure that was well able to respond flexibly to substantial existential challenges.

This contrasts very clearly with the fate of the western Roman empire in the course of the fifth century. The reasons for its breakdown and fragmentation are complex and have been the subject of intensive study. But briefly summarized, the western Roman state—with its political center in Italy—faced loss of territorial integrity, loss of resources and fiscal income, the alienation of regional elites in Gaul, Spain, and N. Africa, and to a degree in Britain, further exacerbating the reduced access to resources. As a consequence, it also faced a loss of political legitimacy, thus of command and control. The vested interests of key elements of the different regional elites no longer chimed with those of the center, and substantial numbers of those elites survived by collaborating with the new political-military powers, in many cases merging with the

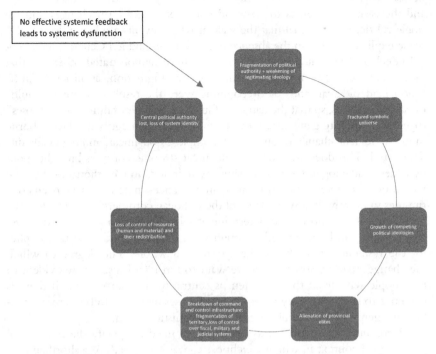

Figure 7.6 Interdependencies: systemic breakdown, elements disconnected, systemic identity lost (the western Roman state in the fifth century CE).

conquerors or occupiers and thus establishing an important degree of social and cultural continuity: See Figure 7.6.

But the political system of empire disappeared and was replaced by a cluster of so-called "successor kingdoms." While Italy and N. Africa were reconquered (for a while) under the eastern emperor Justinian in the period 530–550, the remaining provinces henceforth went their own way. The last vestige of the western Roman state was, in fact, the papacy at Rome which, along with the eastern empire with its capital at Constantinople, remained foci of cultural authority and legitimacy throughout western Europe for another two centuries (Wickham 2009).

7.5 Concluding Remarks

Three key points arise from this brief survey. First, "collapse" needs to be historicized and contextualized: What is the chronology and geographical impact of a "collapse"—at what scale of social process are we deploying the word and to what end? Looking from the perspective of geological time, societal transformations that occur over several centuries can appear to be sudden, rapid, and catastrophic, and there is some utility in using the term in that sense at that level of discourse. But given that the more remote the period, the less data we have, and the easier it becomes to write off complex longer-term changes under a single rubric, it is essential that the scale at which events are being described is made explicit. Finally, in the absence of an SCE—a Sudden Catastrophic Event (Mordechai 2018)—it should be axiomatic until demonstrated otherwise that fundamental changes in system identity and configuration, at all levels, institutional, ideological, and socio-economic were the result of complex multi-causal associations, so that the dangers of lumping a series of different "collapses" together in order to generalize about systemic societal integrity need to be borne in mind. Societal change is multicausal, complex, non-linear, and regionally differentiated. This does not exclude sudden catastrophic collapses brought about by widespread exogenous factors—vulcanism, inundation, earthquake—because we should also note that even in such circumstances there may have been continuities in lifeways below the level of the political, commercial, or ideological.

Second, it is important to determine at what levels of a socio-cultural system collapse can be identified, through what evidence, and what that implies for the resilience or frailty of the system as a whole. The degree to which the changes that constitute what we want to term "collapse" were evident to the people who lived through them is central to such an inquiry. If there is evidence to show that they were, their responses need also to be factored in—human agents are not simple cogs in a mechanistic system.

Third, and with these points in mind, we need to specify the intellectual and political context in which we choose to use "collapse." As a shorthand for large-scale transformations that often took place over a century or longer, the term serves a purpose, but if it elides different types and chronologies of change, and/or imposes collapse on transformative processes that were not collapses at all when examined in greater detail, it can be very misleading and generate entirely false conclusions. Comparisons between the fate of the Roman empire and any modern "imperial" system—most recently comparison with the current situation of the USA (see USA and the Roman Empire; Washington Post 09-23-202), or between pre-modern Chinese states and empires and the situation of the contemporary PRC (CCP rule and the collapse of China)—are often flawed for exactly these reasons. Such comparisons can be valid, at some levels, but these should be very carefully specified—and generalized notions of "collapse" really do not have any role to play here.

References

Anderies, J.M. 2006. 'Robustness, institutions, and large-scale change in social-ecological systems: The Hohokam of the Phoenix Basin', *Journal of Institutional Economics* 2(2): 133–155.

Ando, C. 2008. 'Decline, fall and transformation', *Journal of Late Antiquity* 1(1): 31–60.

Bell, C. 2006. *The Evolution of Long-distance Trading Relationships Across the LBA/Iron Age Transition on the Northern Levantine Coast: Crisis, Continuity and Change*. British Archaeological Reports, International Series 1574. Archaeopress, Oxford.

Berkes, F. and Ross, H. 2016. 'Panarchy and community resilience: Sustainability science and policy implications', *Environmental Science and Policy* 61: 185–193.

Bowes, K. and Loseby, S. 2005. 'Rethinking the later Roman landscape', *Journal of Roman Archaeology* 18: 405–413.

Brandes, W. 2002. *Finanzverwaltung in Krisenzeiten.* Loewenklau, Frankfurt.

Cameron, Av. 2000. 'Justin I and Justinian', in Cameron, Av., Ward-Perkins, B. and Whitby, M. (eds.), *The Cambridge Ancient History, XIV. Late Antiquity: Empires and Successors, A.D. 425–600.* CUP, Cambridge: 63–85.

Caruth, C. 1996. *Unclaimed Experience: Trauma, Narrative and History.* Johns Hopkins UP, Baltimore, MD.

Caseldine, C. 2012. 'Conceptions of time in (paleo)climate science and some implications', *WIREs Climate Change* 3: 329–338.

Cassis, M., Doonan, O., Elton, H. and Newhard, J. 2018. 'Evaluating archaeological evidence for demographics, abandonment, and recovery in late antique and Byzantine Anatolia', *Human Ecology* 46(3): 381–398.

Cumming, G.S. and Peterson, G.D. 2017. 'Unifying research on social–ecological resilience and collapse', *Trends in Ecology and Evolution* 32(9): 695–713.

Dark, K. 2016. *The Waves of Time: Long-Term Change and International Relations.* Bloomsbury, London and New York. Eger, A. 2014. *The Islamic-Byzantine Frontier: Interaction and Exchange Among Muslim and Christian Communities.* I.B. Tauris, London.Eger, A. and Vorderstrasse, T. 2020. 'Gaps or transitions? North Syrian/South Anatolian ceramics in the Early, Middle, and Late Islamic Periods', *HEROM. Journal on Hellenistic and Roman Material Culture* 9: 381–420.

Fussell, P. 1975. *The Great War and Modern Memory.* OUP, Oxford and New York.

Goldstone, J. and Haldon, J.F. 2009. 'Ancient states, empires and exploitation: Problems and perspectives', in Morris, I. and Scheidel, W. (eds.), *The Dynamics of Ancient Empires: State Power from Assyria to Byzantium.* OUP, Oxford: 3–29.

Gunderson, L.H. and Holling, C.S. (eds.). 2002. *Panarchy: Understanding Transformations in Human and Natural Systems.* Island Press, Washington, DC.

Gunderson, L.H. and Pritchard, L. (eds.). 2002. *Resilience and the Behavior of Large Scale Systems.* Island Press, Washington, DC.

Haldon, J.F. 1997. *Byzantium in the Seventh Century: The Transformation of a Culture.* CUP, Cambridge.

Haldon, J.F. 2007. '"Cappadocia will be given over to ruin and become a desert": Environmental evidence for historically-attested events in the 7th–10th centuries', in *Mediterranea. Festschrift Johannes Koder.* Austrian Academy, Vienna: 215–230.

Haldon, J.F. 2009. 'Social élites, wealth and power', in Haldon, J.F. (ed.), *The Social History of Byzantium.* Blackwell, Oxford: 168–211.

Haldon, J.F. 2012. 'Commerce and exchange in the seventh and eighth centuries: Regional trade and the movement of goods', in Morrisson, C. (ed.), *Trade and Markets in Byzantium.* Dumbarton Oaks and Harvard UP, Washington, DC: 99–122.

Haldon, J.F., Roberts, N., Izdebski, A., Fleitmann, D., McCormick, M., Cassis, M., Doonan, O., Eastwood, W., Elton, H., Ladstätter, S., Manning, S., Newhard, J., Nichol, K., Telelis, I. and Xoplaki, E. 2014.'The Climate and Environment of Byzantine Anatolia: Integrating Science, History, and Archaeology', *Journal of Interdisciplinary History* 45/2 (2014), 113–161 https://doi.org/10.1162/JINH_a_00682

Haldon, J.F. 2016. *The Empire That Would Not Die: The Paradox of Eastern Roman Survival, 640–740.* Harvard University Press, Cambridge, MA.

Haldon, J.F., Binois-Roman, A., Eisenberg, M., Izdebski, A., Mordechai, L., Newfield, T., Slavin, P., White, S. and Wnęk, K. 2021. 'Between resilience and adaptation: A historical framework for understanding stability and transformation of societies to shocks and stress', in Linkov, I., Trump, B.D. and Keenan, J.M., *COVID-19: Systemic Risk and Resilience*. Springer Nature, Dordrecht 2021: 235–268 https://doi.org/10.1007/978-3-030-71587-8_14.

Haldon, J.F., Chase, A.F., Eastwood, W., Medina-Elizalde, M., Izdebski, A., Ludlow, F., Middleton, G., Mordechai, L., Nesbitt, J. and Turner, B.L. 2020. 'Demystifying collapse: Climate, environment, and social agency in pre-modern societies', *Millennium* 17(1): 1–33. https://doi.org/10.1515/mill-2020-0002.

Haldon, J.F. and Rosen, A.M. 2018. 'Society and environment in the East Mediterranean ca 300–1800 CE. Problems of resilience, adaptation and transformation', *Human Ecology* 46/3: 275–290. https://doi.org/10.1007/s10745-018-9972-3.

Hendy, M.F. 1985. *The Byzantine Monetary Economy c. 300–1450*. CUP, Cambridge.

Holling, C.S. 2001. 'Understanding the complexity of economic, ecological, and social systems', *Ecosystems* 4(5): 390–405.

Izdebski, A. 2011. 'Why did agriculture flourish in the late antique east? The role of climate fluctuations in the development and contraction of agriculture in Asia Minor and the Middle East from the 4th till the 7th c. AD', *Millenium* 8: 291–312.

Izdebski, A. 2012. 'The changing landscapes of Byzantine Northern Anatolia', *Archaeologia Bulgarica* 16(1): 47–66.

Izdebski, A. 2013. 'The economic expansion of the Anatolian countryside in late antiquity: The coast versus inland regions', in Lavan, L. (ed.), *Local Economies? Production and Exchange of Inland Regions in Late Antiquity*. Brill, Boston, MA and Leiden: 343–376.

Izdebski, A., Holmgren, K., Weiberg, E., Stocker, S.R., Büntgen, U., Florenzano, A., Gogou, A., Leroy, S.A.G., Luterbacher, J., Martrat, B., Masi, A., Mercuri, A.M., Montagna, P., Sadori, L., Schneider, A., Sicre, M.-A., Triantaphyllou, M. and Xoplaki, E. 2016. 'Realising consilience: How better communication between archaeologists, historians and natural scientists can transform the study of past climate change in the Mediterranean', *Quaternary Science Reviews* 136: 5–22.

Kaplan, E.A. 2005. *Trauma Culture: The Politics of Terror and Loss in Media and Literature*. Rutgers UP, New Brunswick, NJ.

Koder, J. 2012. 'Regional networks in Asia Minor during the middle Byzantine period, seventh-eleventh centuries: An approach', in Morrisson, C. (ed.), *Trade and Markets in Byzantium*. Dumbarton Oaks and Harvard UP, Washington, DC: 147–175.

Levin, S.A. et al. 2013. 'Social-economic systems as complex adaptive systems: Modelling and policy implications', *Environment and Development Economics* 18(2): 111–132.

Lewit, T. 2009. 'Pigs, presses and pastoralism: Farming in the fifth to sixth centuries A.D.', *Early Medieval Europe* 17(1): 77–91.

Maas, M. (ed.). 2005. *The Cambridge Companion to the Age of Justinian*. CUP, Cambridge.

Mordechai, L. 2018. 'Short-term cataclysmic events in premodern complex societies', *Human Ecology* 46(3): 323–333. https://doi.org/10.1007/s10745-018-9971-4.

Odorico, P. 2018. 'Le temps de l'empire', in Saranti, E.G., Dellaporta, Ai and Kollyropoulou, Th. (eds.), *Opseis tou Vyzantinou Chronou*. Deltapress Demopoulos, Athens: 30–41.

Roberts, N., Cassis, M., Doonan, O., Eastwood, W., Elton, H., Haldon, J., Izdebski, A. and Newhard, J. 2018. 'Not the end of the world? Post-classical decline and recovery in rural Anatolia', *Human Ecology* 46(3): 305–322. https://doi.org/10.1007/s10745-018-9973-2.

Rosen, A.M. 2007. *Civilizing Climate: Social Responses to Climate Change in the Ancient Near East*. Rowman Altamira, Lanham, MD.

Scheffer, M. 2009. *Critical Transitions in Nature and Society*. Princeton University Press, Princeton, NJ.

Sewell, W. 1996. 'Historical events as transformations of structures: Inventing revolution at the Bastille', *Theory and Society* 25(6): 841–881.

Sherrat, S. 2003. 'The Mediterranean economy: 'Globalization' at the end of the second millennium B.C.E.', in Dever, W.G. and Gitin, S. (eds.), Symbiosis, Symbolism and the Power of the Past: Canaan, Ancient Israel, and Their Neighbors from the Late Bronze Sage through Roman Palaestina. Proceedings of the Centennial Symposium W.F. Albright Institute of Archaeological Research and American Schools of Oriental Research, Jerusalem, May 29–31, 2000. Eisenbrauns, Winona Lake, IN.

Tainter, J.A. 1988. *The Collapse of Complex Societies*. CUP, Cambridge.

Tainter, J.A. 2000. 'Problem solving: Complexity, history and sustainability'. *Population and Environment: A Journal of Interdisciplinary Studies* 22: 3–41.

Tainter, J.A. 2006. 'Archaeology of overshoot and collapse', *Annual Review of Anthropology* 35: 59–74.

Walker, B., Holling, C.S., Carpenter, S.R. and Kinzig, A. 2004. 'Resilience, adaptability and transformability in social–ecological systems', *Ecology and Society* 9(2): 5–13.

Whitby, M. 2000. 'The successors of Justinian', in Cameron, Av., Ward-Perkins, B. and Whitby, M. (eds.), *The Cambridge Ancient History, XIV. Late Antiquity: Empires and Successors, A.D. 425–600*. CUP, Cambridge: 86–111.

Whittow, M. 2010. 'The late Roman/early Byzantine Near East', in Robinson, C. (ed.), *The New Cambridge History of Islam, 1: The Formation of the Islamic World, Sixth to Eleventh Centuries*. CUP, Cambridge: 72–97.

Wickham, C. 2009. *The Inheritance of Rome: A History of Europe from 400 to 1000*. Allen Lane, London.

8 *Fluctuat Nec Mergitur*

Seven Centuries of Pueblo Crisis and Resilience

Timothy A. Kohler, R. Kyle Bocinsky,
and Darcy Bird

8.1 Introduction

Perhaps one-quarter of the world's people—mostly in Latin America and Africa—support themselves as small-holder (subsistence) farmers (Rapsomanikis 2015). The directed climate change of the Anthropocene, unless mitigated, will cause many of the areas they currently inhabit to be hotter in 50 years than almost any area on the surface of the planet today (Xu et al. 2020). If their farms fail, will there be massive demand for immigration into the temperate, developed world? It is helpful to have some knowledge about how past episodes of climate change—even if not driven by human-generated greenhouse gases—affected small-scale farmers in the past. Because of its high temporal resolution and depth of study, the prehispanic history of the Upland US Southwest (UUSS, as defined in Bocinsky et al. 2016) provides a key case for understanding how pre-Anthropocene climatic variability affected small-scale farming societies in semi-arid environments,[1] and how such variability interacted with social dynamics to produce outcomes that varied from resilience, to collapse.

Previous work (especially in the heavily researched central Mesa Verde region) has clearly demonstrated that climate variability affected production of dry-farmed maize (corn) in this area in the two millennia prior to the sixteenth-century Spanish conquest and colonization (Van West and Dean 2000). Until about 1300,[2] most agriculture in the UUSS was rain fed, and in addition to topographic variability that entrains orographic differences in precipitation, there is considerable variability from year to year in the amount of precipitation falling in any single area. Already by the first millennium BCE, maize constituted the main staple, and that increased to the point where it was providing up to 90% of the calories by the 1200s (Matson 2016). The landraces grown by the Puebloan peoples in the UUSS were selections derived from ancestors growing in tropical subhumid portions of south-central Mexico (Buckler and Stevens 2006), suggesting that both temperature and precipitation may have been limiting in the UUSS. Prehispanic dry farmers selected fairly narrow elevational subsets of the available region, also suggesting their crops were susceptible to variability in precipitation and temperature. Production levels

DOI: 10.4324/9781003331384-11

of maize affected local Puebloan population size through both birth rates and mobility, including habitat tracking (Schwindt et al. 2016).

The northern portion of the UUSS is sometimes called the "Four Corners" since Colorado, New Mexico, Arizona, and Utah meet in this portion of the Colorado Plateau. We will alternately consider the UUSS (our largest context) and three subsets of it: the Four Corners, the central Mesa Verde (CMV) region it contains, and the northern Rio Grande (NRG) region, slightly off the Colorado Plateau and southeast of the CMV (Figure 8.1). Andrew E. Douglas (1929) suggested that drought limiting or precluding successful farming in the late 1200s provoked the famous departure of all farmers from the northern US Southwest toward the NRG and other areas to the south. The main goal of this chapter is to review the status of that hypothesis—much debated and refined over the last three decades.

For almost two decades, the Village Ecodynamics Project (VEP) has examined how climate, landscape, and people co-produced the northern Pueblo societies in the centuries prior to the appearance of the Spanish (Kohler and Varien 2012). The VEP concentrated on two study areas, VEPIIN (in the CMV) and VEPIIS (in the NRG) (Figure 8.1). Here we rely on our findings from that project, in addition to other research, to paint a general picture (in

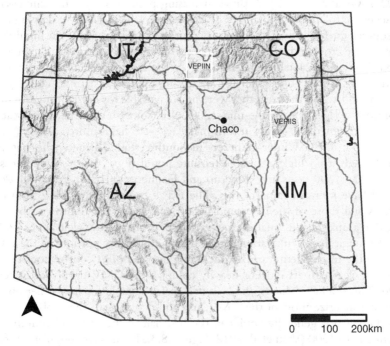

Figure 8.1 The four states containing the Upland US Southwest (UUSS, black box), the VEPII study areas (white boxes), and Chaco Canyon.

Background) which we dissect and discuss in the third section. In the end we will be interested not just in the single collapse episode of the late 1200s, but in weaving a much longer account of the relationships of climate and social dynamics in this time and place. In the end, determining cause and effect requires lots of data subjected to statistical modeling and detailed temporal analyses and replication. Archaeology cannot do this as convincingly as any experimental science, but this particular case allows us to go further down this path than is typical for archaeology. Much of the relevant work is done here by citation, given length restrictions. We try to concentrate first on establishing the big picture, and second, on identifying the main internal (social) and external (climate, non–Pueblo peoples) factors driving the dynamics of interest to this volume.

8.2 Background

Maize is a main actor in our story, like Shiva both as creator and destroyer. Though animal protein, beans, and a wide diversity of other foods of course supplemented the diet, the remarkable population growth typifying much of the two millennia before the arrival of the Spanish was largely made possible by maize (Kohler and Reese 2014). By the late 1900s, maize farmers were colonizing large portions of the central and northern portions of Utah (Richards 2022). On the other hand, these increasing populations became increasingly susceptible to climatic variability by depressing various slowly renewing biotic resources for food, fuel, and construction, locking in reliance on highly variable maize crops and entraining competitive violence contributing to aggregation (Kohler 2012a: table 15.1). By early in the second millennium, population had grown to the point where an increasing number of farmers could not be accommodated in the areas that were most favorable for dry farming. Living in compact villages that by the mid-1200s were sometimes perched in locations that were difficult to access in turn made access to fields more costly.

Of course, the hunter-gatherers in Southwestern Mexico who began to select seeds from highly variable teosinte populations, maize's wild ancestor, more than 7500 years ago (Piperno and Flannery 2001; Piperno et al. 2009) could have foreseen none of this. The maize eventually resulting from their efforts and those of their descendants arrived in the US Southwest by 2100 BCE as a small-eared, small-kernel variety of probably low yield (Diehl 2005).

Although maize cultivation spread throughout many portions of the UUSS during the first millennium BC, including into the NRG, for reasons that are not yet clear farmers did not heavily colonize the CMV until shortly before 600. This might be due to the lack of a maize suitable for the cooler uplands that characterize most of the CMV, in conjunction with the probability that the UUSS was generally cooler in the first half of the first millennium, than from 600 to 1300 (Viau et al. 2012: Figure. 8.3). In any case, populations grew rapidly throughout the Southwest, though slightly more slowly in lowland desert areas where water management was required to grow maize. In the

Southwest as a whole, the *rate* of population increase likely peaked between 500 and 1000. Population *size* in the prehispanic Southwest likely peaked in the twelfth or thirteenth century (Dean et al. 1985; Hill et al. 2004; Kohler and Reese 2014).

By the mid-1920s, archaeologists had conducted enough research to propose a Southwest-wide stage taxonomy (Kidder 1927). Today this is applied only to the northern upland ("Pueblo") portions of the Southwest, which does not include the irrigated desert areas where the Hohokam tradition developed, or the areas south of the Pueblo tradition surrounding those deserts where the Mogollon tradition developed. This taxonomy—known as the Pecos periods since this scheme was hammered together at what is today Pecos National Historical Park—recognized three Basketmaker periods, BMI–III (the first of which is no longer used), and five Pueblo periods (PI–V, where PV postdates contact with the Spanish). These were defined on the basis of relatively internally coherent "diagnostic culture traits" including ceramics, lithics, architecture, and settlement size and layout. In 1927 these periods could already be put into their correct relative sequence, but it would be two years before Douglass and his colleagues were able to cross-date beams permitting an absolute chronology back to 700 (today of course extending much earlier).

At a very high-level overview from BMII to PIV, long-term trends in the Pueblo area can be identified for increasing aggregation, leading to larger settlements. This aggregation, in conjunction with the pattern of dwelling placement, likely signals a gradual reduction in autonomy for households, as first corporate kin groups and later, larger social groupings took on more prominence (Lipe and Hegmon 1989; Rohn 1977; Steward 1937). Household activities came increasingly under the influence of wider social demands that were at once religious/ceremonial, political, and economic in nature (see, e.g., Gumerman and Gell-Mann 1994).

From a closer perspective though various discontinuities become prominent. These include, in the PI period, an early episode of village growth and collapse from the late 700s to the early 900s in the northern Southwest (Wilshusen et al. 2012; Kohler and Reed 2011). These exploited a full Neolithic package of well-adapted domesticates, Colorado Plateau-appropriate farming and building technologies, and increasingly complex forms of supra-household organization needed for larger sedentary communities. In late PI, an unpromising-looking canyon in northwestern New Mexico hosted the rise of the Chaco regional system which in PII, from about 1030 to 1140, spread its distinctive Great House architecture and settlement pattern throughout much of the northern and eastern Southwest (Lekson 2006). This system partially collapsed amid drought in the mid-1100s, but elements of its operation continued from more northerly centers near the San Juan River, close to the present border between Colorado and New Mexico (Reed 2008). Interpretations of how Chaco worked vary widely, but the present authors, and perhaps most other southwesternists, consider it to have been underlain by the most politically and religiously hierarchical society in the prehispanic Southwest. Not surprisingly these features were coupled with the most pronounced degree of wealth inequality seen in the Pueblo Southwest (Ellyson et al. 2019).

Other than the catastrophe of Spanish colonization beginning in the late 1500s, though, the most spectacular discontinuity in the Pueblo area is the late PIII (mid/late 1200s) depopulation of large portions of the upland Southwest. This included the Four Corners, encompassing the CMV. By 1285 there were no farmers left in the northern Southwest, even though 40 years earlier more than 25,000 people lived in the VEPIIN area alone (Schwindt et al. 2016). As the northern Southwest was depopulated, population grew commensurately in the NRG (Ortman 2014). Destinations for farmers leaving more westerly portions of the northern Southwest included locations near the present Pueblo of Hopi in northeastern Arizona (Dean 2010; Clark et al. 2019).

Life in the post-1300s Southwest, especially in the NRG, was dramatically different than it had been in the north. Water-managed farming became more common, mitigating some of the variability in maize production that had previously contributed to conflict (Kohler et al. 2014). Towns take over from villages as the largest settlements, forming around spacious plazas serving various social activities presumably including dances, other ceremonies, and probably periodic markets (Kohler et al. 2004) fueled by increasingly productive specialization and interethnic exchange (Ortman 2019). Ortman and Lobo (2020) argue that agglomeration effects markedly improved material living standards in NRG towns compared with earlier villages in the same area. It must also be noted though that across the Southwest after 1300, life expectancies at 15 years of age and crude birth rates were both in steep decline (Kohler and Reese 2014), possibly reflecting unsolved public health issues in these settlements (Phillips et al. 2018) and limited options for excess offspring to colonize new areas that had typified much of the previous millennium. Post-1300 towns in the NRG were an order of magnitude larger than the largest pre-1300 villages in the CMV (which topped out at about 100 households or 500 people) though the total area occupied by post-1300 Pueblo peoples was dramatically smaller than in the PII period.

Archaeologists agree that the causes for the depopulation of the northern Southwest include climate variability negatively affecting maize production. There is little agreement though as to whether this was itself sufficient to have caused such a massive rupture, which not only moved thousands of families but caused the loss of a large number of distinctive artifact and structure types, architectural practices, and settlement and community patterns (Lipe 2010). Other contributing factors can easily be adduced, but it is difficult to assign them a relative weight. Mark Varien (2010) notes that in addition to climatic variability, human impact on the environment, warfare, and disease have long been invoked as causal factors. These other factors may indeed have played important roles, though at present there is no hard evidence for disease as a factor in the depopulation. Katherine Spielmann and colleagues (2016) note that the depopulation of the CMV was preceded by the appearance and spread of new forms of ceremonial structures that they interpret as evidence for factionalism (following Glowacki 2015). In the next section we suggest an approach to help distinguish between social crises precipitated by such internal factors, versus those more connected to external drivers such as climatic variability. First though it is useful to put the 1200s in the northern Southwest into a larger climatic context that includes temperature as well as precipitation.

Even though analyses of tree-ring widths (or in a few cases, wood-density measurements) provide the best high-frequency paleoclimatic reconstructions for the UUSS (Van West and Dean 2000), such reconstructions may underestimate long-term trends in temperature (Cook et al. 1995). Pollen analysis on the other hand is useful for understanding low-frequency changes in climate that cause spatial shifts in the abundance of plants and the amount of pollen they produce. In Southwest Colorado, ratios of spruce pollen to ponderosa pine pollen were in decline after about 1150, falling below the long-term mean from about 1220 until 1390. Wright (2010) interprets this ratio as a temperature proxy, though Benson and colleagues (2013) point out that increases in spruce may alternatively reflect increased precipitation. More recent analyses of pollen frequencies, using the Modern Analog Technique which escapes the potential weaknesses of reconstructions based on ratios of two species from one or a small number of sites, demonstrate decreased mean temperature of the warmest month between about 1100 and 1600 for a large "Desert" region that includes the UUSS (Viau et al. 2012). High-frequency temperature reconstructions for the Four Corners area summarized by Wright (2010: fig. 14.3) suggest that the first two decades of the 1200s were especially cold. A recent tree-ring-based spatial reconstruction of temperature in the northern hemisphere shows temperatures were below the long-term mean from 1262 to 1351 for the UUSS, with the completion of the 1285 depopulation corresponding to a nadir (Figure 8.2C) (Anchukaitis et al. 2017).

8.3 Analysis and Synthesis

In the early 1980s archaeologist Michael Berry noticed that the accumulated population of tree-ring samples from archaeological sites throughout the Southwest (i.e., the UUSS as used here) contained several prominent frequency peaks in cutting activity that roughly corresponded to the middle portions of periods BMIII–PIV (Berry 1982). He attributed these construction peaks to wetter periods in which farmers in this semi-arid landscape would be thriving, growing in numbers, and building, though the independent measure of drought he was able to muster did not clearly establish this correlation (Berry 1982: fig. 13).

While suspicions linger that these distributions of tree-ring-dated samples contain sampling biases (Nash 2021), more recent analyses with larger databases, augmented by cultural resource management (CRM) work in which investigator bias is less likely, largely show the same pattern noted by Berry. Using the then-current version of these data, Bocinsky and colleagues (2016)

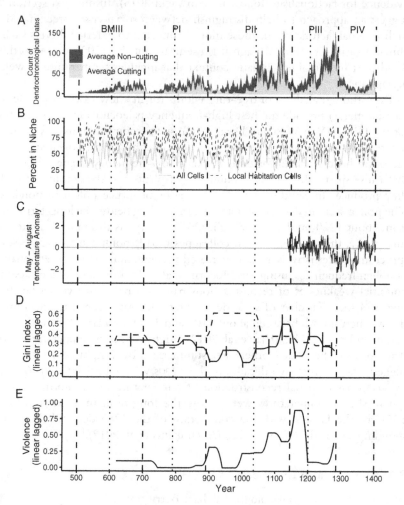

Figure 8.2 Changes in tree-cutting, availability of productive dry-farming plots, history of summer temperatures, wealth inequality, and violence in the UUSS or its subsets. Panels A–C use a 4-year linear smooth plotted on the 4th year; panels D–E use a 21-year linear smooth plotted on the 21st year. A: Stacked histogram of cutting dates + near cutting dates, and non-cutting dates, after Bocinsky et al. (2016: fig. 8.2a); spatial scope, UUSS. B: Percent of cells in dry-farming niche; "All cells" represent the entire UUSS; "Local Habitation cells" are only those with a tree-ring date in the plotted year or any of the previous 3 years, and were therefore demonstrably occupied during the plotted years; after Bocinsky et al. (2016: fig. 8.2c); spatial scope, UUSS. C: Temperature-field reconstruction applicable to the northern portions of the UUSS (Anchukaitis et al. 2017); D: Gini index; spatial scope, dashed line, northern portions of UUSS (see text), after Ellyson et al. (2019): table 2; solid line, CMV, with 80% confidence interval shown with vertical lines. E: Proportion of skeletal remains exhibiting violent trauma, after (Cole 2012); spatial scope, CMV, and adjacent areas to the west. Periods of Exploration and Exploitation after Bocinsky et al. (2016).

proposed that the prehispanic macrohistory of the UUSS between 500 and 1285 can be interpreted as containing four periods of "Exploration" averaging 98 years in length, each followed by a period of "Exploitation" averaging 99 years in length. Exploration periods contain relatively few tree-ring dates overall (Fig. 8.2A), and these come from relatively small, dispersed clusters of sites and contain relatively high proportions of non-cutting dates among the tree-ring samples. Exploitation periods on the other hand contain more dates overall, more cutting dates among those, and the sites from which they were obtained show strong and significant spatial clustering.

The really intriguing thing about this way of looking at the UUSS, though, is that the ends of these periods of Exploitation happen to coincide with the ends of the BMIII, PI, PII, and PIII periods devised almost a century ago to mark internally cohesive patterns of architecture and artifacts. It's important to re-emphasize that the definition of the boundaries for the periods of Exploration/Exploitation was based solely on characteristics of the types, frequencies, and spatial distributions of the archaeological tree-ring records, so this coincidence needs some explaining. We think the periods of Exploitation emerged when combinations of locations, growing conditions, and organization (including local and regional political and religious leadership) successfully converged to allow populations and settlements to grow and thrive (Kohler and Bocinsky 2017). Broadly shared understandings and common purposes must have underlain these episodes. As these periods came to a close (for reasons we'll be exploring), populations tended to disaggregate, explore new settlement locations, and build less (or at least produced fewer tree-ring dates overall, including fewer cutting dates). These were the periods of Exploration. The dotted lines in Figure 8.2E separate the Pecos periods into subperiods of Exploration and Exploitation.

Bocinsky and Kohler (2014) devised an estimator for the spatial and temporal distribution of the maize dry-farming niche based on 205 tree-ring chronologies developed for paleoclimatic research. This estimator determines whether any plot of land in the UUSS got enough precipitation, and was warm enough, to produce a maize crop in any year. These estimates are spatialized at a scale of a little under 1 km², created separately for each of 691,200 such cells within the UUSS. When summed and averaged across space for each year, they show, *contra* Berry (1982), that on average the periods of Exploitation were no better for maize production than were the periods of Exploration, at least in terms of the size of the maize dry-farming niche. The periods of Exploitation though do typically *end* in or near times when the maize niche was significantly constricted (Figure 8.2B).

These terminations, around 700, 890, 1145, and 1285, also seem to be points of social crisis. First, the VEPIIN area suffers population declines ca. 890 and 1145 and was completely depopulated by 1285 (Schwindt et al. 2016: fig. 3). Temporal resolution is insufficient to resolve whether there was also a decline ca. 700.

Second, another very direct measure of crisis is interpersonal violence. Figure 8.2E displays the incidence of skeletal remains bearing signs of violent trauma through time (Cole 2012). Sarah Cole derived this series from published and gray literature reporting excavations in and around the VEPIIN (CMV) area. As Fig. 8.2E shows, at least the last three of the four terminations of periods of Exploitation also coincide with peaks in violence.[3]

Third, another possible indicator of crisis is the history of wealth inequality. Walter Scheidel (2017) has argued that "normally functioning" societies tend to exhibit stable or slowly increasing degrees of wealth inequality, and that only major crises such as widespread conflict or pandemics have the power to decrease wealth inequality. We estimate wealth inequality using a Gini coefficient based on house-size distributions as explained by Kohler and Higgins (2016). Figure 8.2D, derived from recent work by Laura Ellyson and colleagues (2019),[4] shows two series. That for just the CMV can be plotted at a higher temporal resolution, and indeed shows the expected declines at the three later crisis points noted above. As with violence, lower temporal resolution early in this series makes it unclear whether there was also a decline ca. 700.

In a recent paper that focused exclusively on the VEPIIN area, Kohler and colleagues (2020) examined the statistical relationships among wealth inequality, violence, degree of aggregation, momentary population size, maize production per capita, and several other relevant variables.[5] This was motivated in part by frustration in seeing archaeologists assert the existence of relationships between climatic variability and social transformations with no statistical proof (Kohler and Rockman 2020). Another motivation was the difficulty of finding statistical support for particular episodes of crisis considered individually. Keith Kintigh and Scott Ingram (2018) examined 11 transitions of various types throughout the Southwest, including the depopulation of the CMV between 1250 and 1300. They used a sophisticated procedure to evaluate whether each transition could be directly connected with drought (or in some cases, decrease in the size of the maize farming niche). They showed that *not one* of the cases examined could be significantly associated with drought using their approach, even though they admit that there are highly plausible arguments that some of these transitions were in fact related to climatic variability.

To go beyond these sorts of problems with "one-shot hypotheses" Kohler and colleagues (2020) examined the *entire series* (not just one episode) from VEPIIN, starting in the 600s up to 1280, dividing it into 25 temporal snapshots taken every 25 years. Some of the statistically significant conclusions we drew relevant to the problems here are that violence goes up as climatically controlled average production per capita goes down across time slices. Low production per capita also leads to high violence in the next time slice. Moreover, high wealth inequality in one time slice leads to high violence in the next time slice. Somewhat oddly the inverse is also true: high violence in one time slice leads to high wealth inequality in the next time slice. This relationship—it's not quite a contradiction—seems to arise because, through time, this sequence tends to exhibit alternating periods of high wealth inequality, and high violence (compare the solid line in Figure 8.2D with 8.2E).

To summarize then, it might seem that climate variability decreasing the size of the maize niche, or reducing maize production, has a clear role in causing several classic indicators of crisis: population decline, increases in violence, and declines in wealth inequality.[6] While we believe this to be true, a close inspection of the relationship between the Exploitation terminations and the maize-niche size history in Figure 8.2B reveals that although each of these terminations *does* coincide with a niche constriction, there are other constrictions that *do not* cause terminations. For example, the end of PII (and its Exploitation period) in 1145 was clearly a time of very poor production, but not markedly worse than the downturn ca. 1100 that did not seem to have had widespread or long-lasting effects. So the relationship between niche constriction and period termination is imperfect, statistically speaking.

Why do some roughly equivalent climatic crises cause major upheavals (including steep declines in construction, decreases in wealth inequality, and violence) while others do not? Marten Scheffer and colleagues (2021) address this question through an analysis of the database of archaeological tree rings from the UUSS, drawing on theory developed in Scheffer et al. (2012) and elsewhere. One symptom of a social system that is losing resilience is a phenomenon called "critical slowing down," commonly thought to be an early warning signal of impending system collapse. Imagine a ball in a two-dimensional valley that readily returns to its lowest point on perturbation.[7] This is the image of a resilient system. But if the hills on either side of the valley were to decrease in slope, the ball would take longer to return to the low point. A probe that tracked the location of the ball at high frequency would find that there is a stronger temporal autocorrelation in the ball's location in the second system than in the first. This is the phenomenon of critical slowing down. Essentially the system has a stable state, or status quo, in which it operates, and perturbations knock the system from this status quo. As a system experiences increased fragility over time, it will take longer to recover from these perturbations, and this increasingly delayed recovery period is known as critical slowing down.

Scheffer et al. (2021) identify increased critical slowing down in the time series of cutting dates over the duration of each of the BMIII, PI, PII, and early PIII periods using the mounting lag-1 temporal autocorrelation of tree-cutting activity that they demonstrate in each of these periods. But late PIII is different: it begins with very poor maize-growing conditions and a dramatic decrease in construction activity, which is followed by a temporary climate amelioration followed by full-scale emigration from the area as conditions again worsen. Notably, late PIII did not experience increased temporal autocorrelation or variance (another symptom of decreased resilience) in the detrended time series, unlike the four earlier periods, suggesting that this termination was highly anomalous.

What might cause this critical slowing down in the sorts of societies in question? The most likely candidate is some process that slowly mounts on time scales of decades, but is brought to a head by a climatic downturn. A leading possibility we believe is that growing inequality over the course of the periods of Exploitation, as villages grew in size, led to mounting dissatisfaction which eventually resulted in loss of legitimacy for leadership when a crisis did develop, precipitating departures from existing villages and the collapse of their local and regional systems. Although it is sometimes assumed that the balanced recipro-cal relationships that likely structured exchanges among non-kin in such socie-ties (Sahlins 1972) result in fairly equal distributions of wealth, in fact there is no reason that the comparative advantages of more productive farming plots, held within lineages in stable sedentary systems by the founders of a village, would not result in differences in lineage size over just a couple generations. Such labor advantages would further multiply productive differences between first and later arrivers, leading to substantial material and embodied wealth differences among lineages such as those driving patron–client relationships (Smith and Choi 2007) unless other leveling mechanisms were in place. Other processes could also mount on the scale of decades as the villages that typify periods of Exploitation grew in size, including depletion of slowly renewing resources such as fuelwood and large game, and increasing distance to fields. We suggest that such material inconveniences in the context of mounting inequalities contributed to social frictions and increasing dissatisfaction with the status quo, needing only a proximate crisis to light the fuse.

There is an old argument in Southwestern archaeology about whether the periodic crises that confronted Pueblo societies were fundamentally social (endogenous) or climatic/environmental (exogenous). What we are suggesting is that slow processes—both material and social in nature if we are correct—repeatedly set up pre-1300s Pueblo societies for transformations that were then *triggered* by climatic events. So we think the correct answer to this old question is, "both."

What are we to make of the fact that the most radical transformation of all, the late PIII depopulation, came to its dramatic climax with no signs of mounting social fragility in the autocorrelation metric developed through con-struction activity? The clear implication is that this crisis was unique in being fundamentally exogenous in nature. This elevates the prime suspect to be del-eterious climate change, quite possibly in conjunction with turmoil caused by (or exacerbated by) the infiltration of hunting-gathering people into the north-ern Pueblo area. We know from a large body of perishable materials from the Promontory Caves firmly (and recently) dated to the 1250–1290 interval, with numerous items that can be unambiguously linked to the Dene (Diné), that these populations were no further than a few hundred miles to the north (and quite possibly closer) by the time the depopulation was commencing ca. 1250 (Ives 2020). These highly mobile peoples were likely armed with recurved bows which were much more powerful than the self-bows of the contempo-rary Pueblo peoples.

The demographic dimensions of the quasicycles we have documented above have not gotten the attention they deserve. Figure 8.3 is made by differencing the two lines shown in Figure 8.2B. In that panel, the bottom

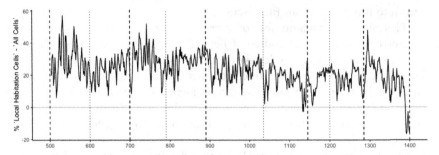

Figure 8.3 Declining freedom in the choice of farmable plots through time, UUSS. This line is made by subtracting the percentage of all cells in the dry-farming niche from the percentage of inhabited cells that are in the dry-farming niche. Decreasing percentages suggest mounting constraints on the ability to find unclaimed farmable land.

line ("All cells") represents the percent of cells in the entire UUSS that are within the maize-growing niche in the current year or any of the previous three years. The line for the "Local Habitation cells" plots the percent of cells having a tree-ring date in the plotted year or any of the previous three years that are in the maize-growing niche. These are therefore demonstrably occupied. Early on, through most of the 500s–700s, the difference between these two lines is quite large, indicating that people were almost always able to select a location within the maize niche, even when the "average cell" in the population of cells is not within that niche. However there is a long-term trend beginning in the mid-700s for the difference between these two lines to decrease.

To be clear, these percentages have different denominators, so when the line in Figure 8.3 is at zero that does not mean, in any straightforward way, that farmers could not find any locations in the niche. The line in Figure 8.3 responds to four main signals. First, there's a strong climatic signal of course, that is mostly purely recorded in the "All Cells" line in Figure 8.2B. Second, growth in population could claim most or all the cells in the niche, constraining marginal populations to settle for locations outside the niche, lowering the line. Third, the process of aggregation could allow choices of places to live that were not necessarily in the niche, even though fields accessible from the village were in the niche. Finally, increased use of water management through time could free farmers from having to live where precipitation made dry farming possible, though adequate temperatures would still be required.

This last factor likely contributes to the extremely low values that Figure 8.3 reveals for the late 1300s (though this was also a period of niche constriction). But the declines prior to the 1300s have to be explained, mainly, by some mixture of the first three processes. We suspect that most of this signal is due to the joint effects of climatic variability and population growth. If this is true, it helps explain why the crises at ca. 700, 890, 1145, and 1285 were increasingly severe: they scaled with the sizes of the contemporaneous population. We'll return to this point in our final section.

This analysis raises a number of interesting culture-historical questions that cannot be systematically addressed here. A leading puzzle is why the largest scale of analysis we undertake in this paper has any coherence whatsoever. The UUSS is a very large area that contains many subareas that are traditionally treated separately by archaeologists. It is certain that there were considerable ethnolinguistic barriers within this area. Yet we see patterns in tree-cutting activity that seem to speak to some homogeneity in behaviors throughout this area.

One possible explanation might be that the tree-cutting record is severely biased—say for example, mostly made up of samples from the CMV. In fact there is a bias in that direction, but even so, the CMV samples make up only about 35% of the total population, so by themselves they cannot form these patterns. Archaeologists over the past several decades have spent a great deal of time looking for and explaining variability. In the Southwest it now seems that maybe we need to work harder on explaining long-distance similarity. We suspect that the synchrony we see is entrained by large-scale climatic variability, but this suggestion warrants further localized analyses.

One other similarity throughout the UUSS that doesn't get the attention it deserves is that it is not just the northern Southwest that loses Pueblo peoples in the late 1200s and 1300s. Large tracts further south were also depopulated as farmers concentrated in the areas surrounding the currently occupied Pueblos of Hopi, Zuni, Acoma, Laguna, and along the Northern and Middle Rio Grande. We suspect that this poorly understood phenomenon is connected with the cold temperatures and increasing presence of Dene peoples that, we suggest, also contributed to the depopulation of the northern regions in the late 1200s.

8.4 Governance and Mitigation

Until the rise of the Chaco system beginning in the mid-800s and spreading across large portions of the UUSS after about 1030, the dominant political organization throughout our area would have been provided by villages and clans structured at relatively local levels, as described by Johnson and Earle (2000:101–206). For various spatial scales but centered on the CMV, Crabtree and colleagues (2017) analyze a variety of simulated and empirical data to argue for the existence of village-spanning polities (regional systems) beginning in some areas as early as 890, centered on Chaco, expanding to include nearly all the northern UUSS until 1145. Thereafter, at least in the CMV, village-spanning polities probably continued in some form but at smaller spatial scales until the depopulation ca. 1280.

An interesting analysis (not yet done to our knowledge) would be to ask whether, within the domain of the Chaco regional system, there is evidence that this system prevented local collapses under climatic conditions that would have caused local collapses were the system *not* present. This would provide some insight into how Chaco actually functioned. What we can say is the period under which the lag-1 temporal autocorrelation of tree-cutting activity slowly rises, indicating increasing social fragility, takes longer in the PII (245 years) than in any other period (BMIII, 183 years; PI, 166 years; Early PIII, 58 years) (Scheffer et al. 2021). Assuming that these periods suffer climatic challenges at approximately the same rate, this seems to be a provisional measure of Chaco's robustness, suggesting that it did provide services within its domain that increased the survivability of the system as a whole.

Once again, these analyses raise interesting culture-historical points that cannot be pursued in detail here. The much lower degree of inequality in the CMV from the late 800s to the mid-1000s than among societies just to the south (Figure 8.2D) is rather startling. This has a possible connection to an argument that PI village and ceremonial life in the Dolores Archaeological Project area (a subset of the CMV) may have tended to level social differences and reinforce equality (Kohler and Higgins 2016). It can also be connected to the observation that burials in the heartlands of the Chaco regional system (Chaco in the 1000s, and Aztec in the 1200s) were female-biased whereas they were male-biased in those same periods in the CMV. This has been read as evidence that Chaco periodically raided the CMV for its women (Kohler and Turner 2006). Finally, it has been noted that in the CMV the incidence of violence can be nicely predicted from (lagged) population size until the late 900s and early 1000s, when there is an anomalous spike in violence that precedes the expansion of the Chaco regional system into the CMV by about two generations. We have suggested that this represents an early and ultimately futile resistance to Chaco expansion (Kohler et al. 2009). Put together it seems reasonable to suggest that most local communities in the CMV tended to embrace egalitarianism during PI and for the next century, successfully resisting the advances of the hierarchical Chacoan system even as (and perhaps partly because) they were targets for raiding as Chaco began to expand in the early 1000s.

8.5 Insights, Relevance, and Applicability

The societies of the Upland US Southwest in the last half of the first millennium CE and the first three centuries of the second were inordinately sensitive to climatic fluctuations affecting agricultural productivity. Downturns in production tended to increase violence and decrease local population, and construction activity, and spoil the prospects of emergent elites.

These climate effects though were filtered through societies that—we suggest—were more or less capable of shrugging off downturns so long as the participants had confidence in their leadership and felt that they were part of a shared enterprise. Over the course of each of the periods examined here—except the very final one, late PIII—these feelings seem to slowly erode. We have suggested that this erosion was partly due to expanding internal social differences, including mounting wealth inequality, that were connected with living in villages that were typically founded near the outset of periods of Exploitation. Village-spanning polities (most obviously the Chaco regional system) seem to slow this erosion, perhaps by moving food around when and where it was needed—a suggestion needing further research through isotopic compositions of food remains. Eventually though in each case a climatic crisis also causes a social crisis, bringing an end to one of the periods of Exploitation.

Following the final crisis in the northern Southwest of the mid-late 1200s and the reorganization of the early 1300s, the relationship between climate, production, violence, and inequality changed fundamentally (see contributions to Adams and Duff 2004). After that time, climatic downturns seem to no longer precipitate violence or disaggregation (Kohler et al. 2014) though the record of inequality has so far resisted analysis. There is a hopeful message for contemporary society in the eventual ability of prehispanic Pueblo societies to overcome the boom-and-bust cycles with their periodic violence that we describe above, but the costs as well have to be tallied. These included the hardships during the very difficult years of the 1200s, but also there was the transition to a very slow-growth demography (and eventually even a con-traction) as post-1300 sedentary farmers learned to live in compact territories under pressure from hostile, mobile raiders.

Less hopeful perhaps for people today is the positive relationship between the severity of the Puebloan crises from 600 to 1300 and their population sizes through time. In a world approaching 8 billion people that is facing the prob-ability of massive population displacement due to warming, a rational manager would either stop population increase or mitigate climate change, or a little of both. We also need to worry about how our population size in tandem with our extreme connectedness has the potential to allow local or regional crises to rapidly cascade into global disasters (Kemp et al. 2022).

Happily, the Pueblo peoples persist today despite all that we have recounted here—storm-tossed but never sunk—and despite the later insults by Spanish and Euro-American colonists. Perhaps that persistence provides the greatest measure of hope for societies today.

Acknowledgment

We thank Miguel Centeno and Peter Callahan of Princeton for the kind offer to participate in their symposium and this volume. This research could not have been done without our many VEP colleagues over the years, as well as a large number of other archaeologists and tree-ring scientists who for many years have contributed to the records analyzed here. We are also grateful for the insightful comments by Richard Wilshusen and Christina Grozinger on earlier drafts. We dedicate this chapter to Eric Grimm, whose contributions to comparative palynology are not as widely appreciated as they deserve.

Notes

1 Much of our study area, most of which lies on the Colorado Plateau, is classified today as having a cold semi-arid climate (BSk in the Köppen-Geiger classification) (Beck et al. 2018). We analyze construction activity in the UUSS through the frequency of tree-ring dates, most of which reflect construction activity. These dates are rare at sites below about 6,000'. Even though the UUSS as defined by the rectangle on Figure 8.1 contains large areas below that elevation, sites in these areas fall outside our analyses here.

2 All dates herein are either tree-ring or calibrated ^{14}C dates and are CE unless otherwise specified.

3 The first termination, ca. 700, falls within the long first period of the VEP chronology which extends from 600–725, so it's unclear if there's also a peak in violence ca. 700. Skeletal remains and Gini indices are dated only to VEP periods, which average 49 years in length. The series in Figure 8.2D and E are therefore much smoother than the series plotted in Figure 8.2A–C, which are derived from annual values with a linear four-year smooth plotted on its final year.

4 The "All" series in Figure 8.2D pools data from sites in the central Mesa Verde, Chaco Canyon, Middle San Juan, and the Chuskas, so they emphasize the northern portions of the UUSS. See Ellyson et al. (2019: fig. 1). The "CMV" series is included in the "All" data but when presented by itself it can be plotted at the higher temporal resolution provided by the VEP periods, rather than the "Explore/Exploit" boundaries used for "All."

5 For statistical details, see Kohler et al. (2020). In that paper, we used estimates of the absolute amount of maize production as explained in Kohler (2012b), rather than the sizes of the dry-farming maize niche used here. We truncated the long first period to its final portion, so the average period length became 43 years. These series were then smoothed with a 21-year linear filter plotted on its final year. Therefore, the value in 810 for example represents the average over the previous 20 years, including signals from the 725–800 period, and from the 800–840 period.

6 The relationship between production and population asserted here is by visual inspection of histograms presented in Kohler and colleagues (2020). In that paper we created the variable "production per capita" (i.e., potential production / momentary population) to assess its relationship with violence and inequality, and did not statistically assess the relationship of production and population through time.

7 This intuition is formalized in a simple mathematical model in Scheffer et al. (2021). This process is also described in the "bifurcation-tipping" scenario by Timothy M. Lenton in this volume (2023: Fig. 13.2D). where some slow process causes a progressive shallowing of the adaptive valley until a given perturbation is able to dislodge the system from its current equilibrium and move it to a new one.

References

Adams, E. Charles, and Andrew Ian Duff (editors). 2004. *The Protohistoric Pueblo World, A.D. 1275–1600.* University of Arizona Press, Tucson.

Anchukaitis, Kevin J., Rob Wilson, Keith R. Briffa, Ulf Büntgen, Edward R. Cook, Rosanne D'Arrigo, Nicole Davi, Jan Esper, David Frank, Björn E. Gunnarson, Gabi Hegerl, Samuli Helama, Stefan Klesse, Paul J. Krusic, Hans W. Linderholm, Vladimir Myglan, Timothy J. Osborn, Peng Zhang, Milos Rydval, Lea Schneider, Andrew Schurer, Greg Wiles, and Eduardo Zorita. 2017. Last millennium Northern Hemisphere summer temperatures from tree rings: Part II, spatially resolved reconstructions. *Quaternary Science Reviews* 163:1–22.

Beck, Hylke E., Niklaus E. Zimmermann, Tim R. McVicar, Noemi Vergopolan, Alexis Berg, and Eric F. Wood. 2018. Present and future Köppen-Geiger climate classification maps at 1-km resolution. *Scientific Data* 5:180214. https://doi.org/10.1038/sdata.2018 .214.

Benson, Larry V., Douglas K. Ramsey, David W. Stahle, and Kenneth L. Petersen. 2013. Some thoughts on the factors that controlled prehistoric maize production in the American Southwest with application to southwestern Colorado. *Journal of Archaeological Science* 40(7):2869–2880.

Berry, M. S. 1982. *Time, Space and Transition in Anasazi Prehistory*. University of Utah Press, Salt Lake City.

Bocinsky, R. Kyle, and Timothy A. Kohler. 2014. A 2,000-year reconstruction of the rain-fed maize agricultural niche in the US Southwest. *Nature Communications* 5:5618.

Bocinsky, R. Kyle, Johnathan Rush, Keith W. Kintigh, and Timothy A. Kohler. 2016. Exploration and exploitation in the Macrohistory of the pre-Hispanic Pueblo Southwest. *Science Advances* 2(4):e1501532. https://doi.org/10.1126/sciadv.1501532.

Buckler, Edward S., and Natalie M. Stevens. 2006. Maize origins, domestication, and selection. In *Darwin's Harvest: New Approaches to the Origins, Evolution, and Conservation of Crops*, edited by Timothy M. Motley, Nyree Zerega, and Hugh Cross, pp. 67–90. Columbia University Press, New York.

Clark, Jeffery J., Jennifer A. Birch, Michelle Hegmon, Barbara J. Mills, Donna M. Glowacki, Scott G. Ortman, Jeffrey S. Dean, Rory Gauthier, Patrick D. Lyons, Matthew A. Peeples, Lewis Borck, and John A. Ware. 2019. Resolving the migrant paradox: Two pathways to coalescence in the late precontact U.S. Southwest. *Journal of Anthropological Archaeology* 53:262–287. https://doi.org/10.1016/j.jaa.2018.09.004.

Cole, Sarah M. 2012. Population dynamics and warfare in the central Mesa Verde region. In *Emergence and Collapse of Early Villages: Models of Central Mesa Verde Archaeology*, edited by Timothy A. Kohler, and Mark D. Varien, pp. 197–218. University of California Press, Berkeley.

Cook, Edward R., Keith R. Briffa, David M. Meko, Donald A. Graybill, and Gary Funkhouser. 1995. The 'segment length curse' in long tree-ring chronology development for palaeoclimatic studies. *Holocene* 5(2):229–237.

Crabtree, Stefani A., R. Kyle Bocinsky, Paul L. Hooper, Susan C. Ryan, and Timothy A. Kohler. 2017. How to make a polity (in the central Mesa Verde region). *American Antiquity* 82(1):71–95.

Dean, Jeffery S. 2010. The environmental, demographic, and behavioral context of the thirteenth-century depopulation of the northern Southwest. In *Leaving Mesa Verde: Peril and Change in the Thirteenth-Century Southwest*, edited by Timothy A. Kohler, Mark D. Varien, and Aaron M. Wright, pp. 324–345. The University of Arizona Press, Tucson.

Dean, Jeffrey S., Robert C. Euler, George J. Gumerman, Fred Plog, Richard H. Hevly, and Thor N. V. Karlstrom. 1985. Human behavior, demography, and paleoenvironment on the Colorado Plateaus. *American Antiquity* 50(3):537–554. https://doi.org/10.2307 /280320.

Diehl, Michael W. 2005. Morphological observations on recently recovered early agricultural period maize cob fragments from Southern Arizona. *American Antiquity* 70(2):361–375. https://doi.org/10.2307/40035708.

Douglass, Andrew Ellicott. 1929. The secret of the Southwest solved by talkative tree rings. *National Geographic* 54:737–770.

Ellyson, Laura J., Timothy A. Kohler, and Catherine M. Cameron. 2019. How far from Chaco to Orayvi? Quantifying inequality among Pueblo households. *Journal of Anthropological Archaeology* 55:101073. https://doi.org/10.1016/j.jaa.2019.101073.

Glowacki, Donna M. 2015. *Living and Leaving: A Social History of Regional Depopulation in Thirteenth-Century Mesa Verde.* University of Arizona Press, Tucson.

Gumerman, George J., and Murray Gell-Mann. 1994. Cultural evolution in the prehistoric Southwest. In *Themes in Southwest Prehistory*, edited by George J. Gumerman, pp. 11–32. School of American Research Press, Santa Fe.

Hill, J. Brett, Jeffery J. Clark, William H. Doelle, and Patrick D. Lyons. 2004. Prehistoric demography in the Southwest: Migration, coalescence, and Hohokam population decline. *American Antiquity* 69(4):689–716. https://doi.org/10.2307/4128444.

Ives, John (Jack) W. 2020. The view from Promontory Point. In *Spirit Lands of the Eagle and Bear: Numic Archaeology and Ethnohistory in the Rocky Mountains and Borderlands*, edited by Robert H. Brunswig, pp. 90–117. University Press of Colorado, Boulder.

Johnson, A. W., and T. K. Earle (editors). 2000. *The Evolution of Human Societies: From Foraging Group to Agrarian State.* Stanford University Press, Stanford.

Kemp, Luke, Chi Xu, Joanna Depledge, Kristie L. Ebi, Goodwin Gibbins, Timothy A. Kohler, Johan Rockström, Marten Scheffer, Hans Joachim Schellnhuber, Will Steffen, and Timothy M. Lenton. 2022 Climate Endgame: Exploring catastrophic climate change scenarios. *Proceedings of the National Academy of Sciences of the United States of America* 119(34):e2108146119. https://doi.org/10.1073/pnas.2108146119

Kidder, A. 1927. Southwestern archeological conference. *Science* 66(1716):489–491.

Kintigh, Keith W., and Scott E. Ingram. 2018. Was the drought really responsible? Assessing statistical relationships between climate extremes and cultural transitions. *Journal of Archaeological Science* 89:25–31. https://doi.org/10.1016/j.jas.2017.09.006.

Kohler, Timothy A. 2012a. The rise and collapse of villages in the central Mesa Verde region. In *Emergence and Collapse of Early Villages: Models of Central Mesa Verde Archaeology*, edited by Timothy A. Kohler, and Mark D. Varien, pp. 247–262. University of California Press, Berkeley.

———. 2012b. Modeling agricultural productivity and farming effort. In *Emergence and Collapse of Early Villages: Models of Central Mesa Verde Archaeology*, edited by Timothy A. Kohler, and Mark D. Varien, pp. 85–112. University of California Press, Berkeley.

Kohler, and R. Kyle Bocinsky. 2017. Crises as opportunities for culture change. In *Crisis to Collapse: The Archaeology of Social Breakdown*, edited by Tim Cunningham, and Jan Driessen, 11: pp. 263–273. AEGIS Actes de Colloques. UCL Presses Universitaires de Louvain. Louvain, Belgium.

Kohler, Timothy A., Sarah Cole, and Stanca Ciupe. 2009. Population and warfare: A test of the Turchin model in Puebloan societies. In *Pattern and Process in Cultural Evolution*, edited by Stephen Shennan, pp. 297–295. Origins of Human Behavior and Culture. University of California Press, Berkeley.

Kohler, Timothy A., Laura J. Ellyson, and R. Kyle Bocinsky. 2020. Beyond one-shot hypotheses: Explaining three increasingly large collapses in the northern Pueblo Southwest. In *Going Forward by Looking Back: Archaeological Perspectives on Socio-Ecological Crisis, Response and Collapse*, edited by Felix Reide, and Payson Sheets, pp. 304–332. Berghahn Books, New York.

Kohler, Timothy A., Katie Grundtisch, Scott G. Ortman, Carly Fitzpatrick, and Sarah M. Cole. 2014. The better angels of their nature: Declining conflict through time among prehispanic farmers of the Pueblo Southwest. *American Antiquity* 79:444–464.

Kohler, Timothy A., Sarah Herr, and Matthew J. Root. 2004. The rise and fall of towns on the Pajarito (A.D. 1375–1600). In *Archaeology of Bandelier National Monument: Village Formation on the Pajarito Plateau, New Mexico*, edited by Timothy A. Kohler, pp. 215–264. University of New Mexico Press, Albuquerque.

Kohler, Timothy A., and Rebecca Higgins. 2016. Quantifying household inequality in early pueblo villages. *Current Anthropology* 57(5):690–697. https://doi.org/10.1086/687982.

Kohler, Timothy A., and Charles Reed. 2011. Explaining the structure and timing of formation of Pueblo I villages in the northern US Southwest. In *Sustainable Lifeways: Cultural Persistence in an Ever-Changing Environment*, edited by Naomi F. Miller, Katherine M. Moore, and Kathleen Ryan, pp. 150–179. Penn Museum International Research Conferences. University of Pennsylvania Museum of Archaeology and Anthropology, Philadelphia.

Kohler, Timothy A., and Kelsey M. Reese. 2014. Long and spatially variable Neolithic demographic transition in the North American Southwest. *Proceedings of the National Academy of Sciences* 111(28):10101–10106.

Kohler, Timothy A., and Marcy Rockman. 2020. The IPCC: A primer for archaeologists. *American Antiquity* 85(4):627–651. https://doi.org/10.1017/aaq.2020.68, accessed November 13, 2020.

Kohler, Timothy A., and Kathryn Kramer Turner. 2006. Raiding for women in the pre-Hispanic northern Pueblo Southwest? A pilot examination. *Current Anthropology* 47(6):1035–1045.

Kohler, Timothy A., and Mark D. Varien. 2012. Emergence and collapse of early villages in the central Mesa Verde. In *Emergence and Collapse of Early Villages: Models of Central Mesa Verde Archaeology*, edited by Timothy A. Kohler, and Mark D. Varien, pp. 1–14. University of California Press, Berkeley.

Lekson, Stephen H. (editor). 2006. *The Archaeology of Chaco Canyon, an Eleventh-Century Pueblo Regional Center*. School of American Research Press, Santa Fe.

Lenton, Timothy M. 2023. Climate change and tipping points in historical collapse. In *How Worlds Collapse: What History, Systems, and Complexity Can Teach Us about Our Modern World and Fragile Future*. Routledge, New York.

Lipe, William D. 2010. Lost in transit: The central Mesa Verde archaeological complex. In *Leaving Mesa Verde: Peril and Change in the Thirteenth-Century Southwest*, edited by Timothy A. Kohler, Mark D. Varien, and Aaron M. Wright, pp. 262–284. University of Arizona Press, Tucson.

Lipe, William D., and Michelle Hegmon. 1989. Historical and analytical perspectives on architecture and social integration in the prehistoric pueblos. In *The Architecture of Social Integration in Prehistoric Pueblos*, edited by William D. Lipe, and Michelle Hegmon, 1: pp. 15–34. Occasional Papers. Crow Canyon Archaeological Center, Cortez.

Matson, R. G. 2016. The nutritional context of the Pueblo III depopulation of the northern San Juan: Too much maize? *Journal of Archaeological Science: Reports* 5:622–631. https://doi.org/10.1016/j.jasrep.2015.08.032.

Nash, Stephen E. 2023. The promise and peril of seductively large tree-ring date distributions. In *Pushing Boundaries: Proceedings of the 2018 Southwest Symposium*, edited by Stephen E. Nash and Erin L. Baxter, pp. 53-73. University Press of Colorado, Boulder.

Ortman, Scott G. 2014. Uniform probability density analysis and population history in the northern Rio Grande. *Journal of Archaeological Method and Theory* 23(1):95–126. https://doi.org/10.1007/s10816-014-9227-6, accessed April 26, 2016.

Ortman, Scott G. (editor). 2019. *Reframing the northern Rio Grande pueblo economy*. Vol. 80. Anthropological Papers of the University of Arizona. University of Arizona, Tucson.

Ortman, Scott, and José Lobo. 2020. Smithian growth in a nonindustrial society. *Science Advances* 6(25):eaba5694. https://doi.org/10.1126/sciadv.aba5694.

Phillips, David A., Jr, Helen J. Wearing, and Jeffery J. Clark. 2018. Village growth, emerging infectious disease, and the end of the Neolithic Demographic Transition in the Southwest United States and Northwest Mexico. *American Antiquity* 83(2):263.

Piperno, Dolores R., Anthony J. Ranere, Irene Holst, Jose Iriarte, and Ruth Dickau. 2009. Starch grain and phytolith evidence for early ninth millennium BP maize from the Central Balsas River Valley, Mexico. *Proceedings of the National Academy of Sciences* 106(13):5019–5024.

Piperno, D. R., and K. V. Flannery. 2001. The earliest archaeological maize (*Zea mays* L.) from highland Mexico: New accelerator mass spectrometry dates and their implications. *Proceedings of the National Academy of Sciences of the United States of America* 98(4):2101–2103. https://doi.org/10.1073/pnas.98.4.2101.

Rapsomanikis, George. 2015. *The Economic Lives of Smallholder Farmers: An Analysis Based on Household Data from Nine Countries*. Food and Agriculture Organization of the United Nations, Rome.

Reed, Paul F. (editor). 2008. *Chaco's Northern Prodigies: Salmon, Aztec, and the Ascendancy of the Middle San Juan Region After AD 1100*. University of Utah Press, Salt Lake City.

Richards, Katie K. 2022 The Fremont Frontier: A Multi-Scalar Approach to Understanding the Late Fremont Period through Painted Ceramic Production and Exchange. Unpublished Ph.D. Dissertation, Department of Anthropology, Washington State University, Pullman.

Rohn, Arthur H. 1977. *Cultural Change and Continuity on Chapin Mesa*. University Press of Kansas, Lawrence.

Sahlins, Marshall. 1972. *Stone Age Economics*. Aldine, Atherton.

Scheffer, Marten, Stephen R. Carpenter, Timothy M. Lenton, Jordi Bascompte, William Brock, Vasilis Dakos, Johan van de Koppel, Ingrid A. van de Leemput, Simon A. Levin, Egbert H. van Nes, Mercedes Pascual, and John Vandermeer. 2012. Anticipating critical transitions. *Science* 338(6105):344–348. https://doi.org/10.1126/science.1225244.

Scheffer, Marten, Egbert H. van Nes, Darcy Bird, R. Kyle Bocinsky, and Timothy A. Kohler. 2021. Loss of resilience preceded transformation of prehispanic Pueblo societies. *Proceedings of the National Academy of Sciences* 118 (18) e2024397118.

Scheidel, Walter. 2017. *The Great Leveler: Violence and the History of Inequality from the Stone Age to the Twenty-First Century*. Princeton University Press, Princeton.

Schwindt, Dylan M., R. Kyle Bocinsky, Scott G. Ortman, Donna M. Glowacki, Mark D. Varien, and Timothy A. Kohler. 2016. The social consequences of climate change in the central Mesa Verde region. *American Antiquity* 81(1):74–96. https://doi.org/10.7183/0002-7316.81.1.74.

Smith, Eric Alden, and Jung-Kyoo Choi. 2007. The emergence of inequality in small-scale societies: Simple scenarios and agent-based simulations. In *The Model-Based Archaeology of Socionatural Systems*, edited by Timothy A. Kohler, and Sander van der Leeuw, pp. 105–120. School for Advanced Research Press, Santa Fe.

Spielmann, Katherine A., Matthew A. Peeples, Donna M. Glowacki, and Andrew Dugmore. 2016. Early warning signals of social transformation: A case study from the US Southwest. *PLOS ONE* 11(10):e0163685. https://doi.org/10.1371/journal.pone.0163685.

Steward, Julian H. 1937. Ecological aspects of Southwestern society. *Anthropos* 32:87–104.

Van West, Carla R., and Jeffrey S. Dean. 2000. Environmental characteristics of the AD 900–1300 period in the central Mesa Verde region. *The Kiva* 66(1):19–44.

Varien, Mark D. 2010. Depopulation of the northern San Juan region: Historical review and archaeological context. In *Leaving Mesa Verde: Peril and Change in the Thirteenth-Century Southwest*, edited by T. Kohler, M. Varien, and A. Wright, pp. 1–33. The Amerind Foundation and University of Arizona Press, Tucson.

Viau, A. E., M. Ladd, and K. Gajewski. 2012. The climate of North America during the past 2000 years reconstructed from pollen data. *Global and Planetary Change* 84–85:75–83. https://doi.org/10.1016/j.gloplacha.2011.09.010.

Wilshusen, Richard H., Gregson Schachner, and James R. Allison (editors). 2012. *Crucible of Pueblos: The Early Pueblo Period in the Northern Southwest.* Cotsen Institute of Archaeology Press, University of California, Los Angeles.

Wright, Aaron M. 2010. The climate of the depopulation of the northern Southwest. In *Leaving Mesa Verde: Peril and Change in the Thirteenth-Century Southwest*, edited by T. Kohler, M. Varien, and A. Wright, pp. 75–101. The Amerind Foundation and University of Arizona Press, Tucson.

Xu, Chi, Timothy A. Kohler, Timothy M. Lenton, Jens-Christian Svenning, and Marten Scheffer. 2020. Future of the human climate niche. *Proceedings of the National Academy of Sciences of the United States of America* 117(21):11350–11355. https://doi.org/10.1073/pnas.1910114117.

9 Episodes of the Feathered Serpent

Aztec Imperialism and Collapse

Deborah L. Nichols and Ryan H. Collins

The Triple Alliance, or Aztec empire, as it is more widely called, represented the largest state in the history of prehispanic Mexico and Central America. It encompassed approximately 200,000 km^2 extending from Mexico's Central highland plateau to the Gulf and Pacific coasts and the southern highlands of Mexico (Figures 9.1 and 9.2). The Triple Alliance's homeland, the Basin of Mexico, was the heartland for the development of a series of large and influential cities and states interspersed with episodes of political fragmentation. Mexico City, the capital of the modern nation-state, overlies the remains of the imperial Aztec capital, Tenochtitlan. First contact between the indigenous societies of the Americas and the states of Eurasia was undeniably world-changing, making the collapse of the Triple Alliance an especially instructive and timely case to examine.

Understanding the collapse of the Triple Alliance has undergone significant revisions in recent decades from early views that were based on the narrative accounts of Spanish conquistadores (Carballo 2020; Hassig 2006; Matthews and Oudijk 2007; Oudijk and Castañeda de la Paz 2017; Restall 2018). The role of indigenous politics, along with disease, warfare and invasion, ecology, and Spanish colonialism has received much more attention. Theories of ancient, pre-modern state collapse in recent decades have focused on environmental degradation, over-intensification, climate or environmental changes, and class conflict (Tainter 1988, 2016). These factors were important triggers in other cases (Middleton 2017) and have been invoked in the collapses of Teotihuacan and Toltec Tula that preceded the Triple Alliance empire. Another significant theoretical shift is in recognizing that collapse, entailing a decrease in social complexity or fragmentation of a polity, is as much part of the evolutionary process as is the increase of social complexity and polity expansion (Tainter 2016). In the case of Mexica imperialism, recent scholarship counters popular narratives of Aztec conquest and collapse, pushing us to understand a more complex intersection of indigenous and European politics—emphasizing that Aztec imperialism had internal fissures, factions, and distinct worldviews, and local and inter-continental ecologies. Therefore, it is crucial

DOI: 10.4324/9781003331384-12

Figure 9.1 Basin of Mexico Map Aztec City-States.

to recognize the role of multiple indigenous and foreign actors and examine coupled social and environmental systems involving epidemic disease, plants and animals, the so-called Columbian exchange, demography, and their sociopolitical context.

While scholarship is extensive on the Aztecs, the Triple Alliance (and its antecedents), along with the conquest and Spanish settler colonialism, we will

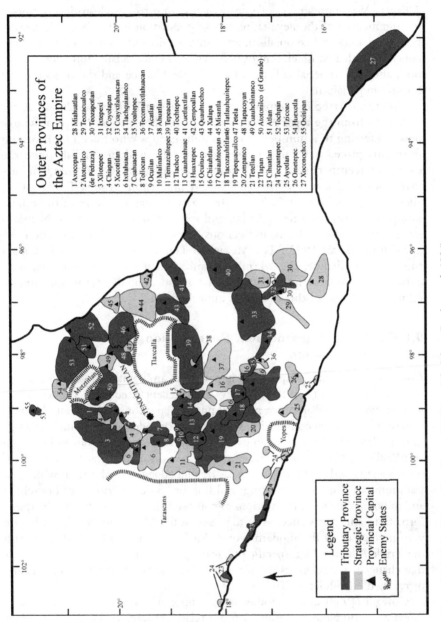

Outer Provinces of the Aztec Empire

1 Axocopan
2 Atotonilco (de Pedraza)
3 Xilotepec
4 Chiapan
5 Xocotitlan
6 Ixtlahuaca
7 Cuahuacan
8 Tollocan
9 Ocuilan
10 Malinalco
11 Temazcaltepec
12 Tlachco
13 Cuauhnahuac
14 Huaxtepec
15 Ocuituco
16 Chiauhtlan
17 Quiauhteopan
18 Tlacozauhtitlan
19 Tepequacuilco
20 Zompanco
21 Tetellan
22 Tlapan
23 Cihuatlan
24 Teepantepec
25 Ayotlan
26 Ometepec
27 Xoconochco
28 Miahuatlan
29 Teozacualco
30 Teozapotlan
31 Ixtepexi
32 Coyolapan
33 Coayxtlahuacan
34 Tlachquiauhco
35 Yoaltepec
36 Tecomaixtlahuacan
37 Acatlan
38 Ahuatlan
39 Tepeacan
40 Tochtepec
41 Cuetlaxtlan
42 Cempoallan
43 Quauhtochco
44 Xalapa
45 Misantla
46 Tlatlauhquitepec
47 Tetela
48 Tlapacoyan
49 Cuauhchinanco
50 Atotonilco (el Grande)
51 Atlan
52 Tochpan
53 Tzicoac
54 Huexotla
55 Oxitipan

Legend

■ Tributary Province
■ Strategic Province
▲ Provincial Capital
〰 Enemy States

Figure 9.2 Triple Alliance Empire ca. 1519 (modified from Berdan et al. 1996).

only touch on major recent themes here (see Carballo 2020). We begin with a consideration of collapse and then discuss state formation in Central Mexico and episodes of centralization and fragmentation that underlay the Triple Alliance. We consider its collapse with attention to new historical revisions, the significance of the devastating loss of population in the sixteenth century from epidemics and colonialism, and what we do and do not know. We also conclude with a consideration of Nahua's persistence, adaptation, and innovation, after the imperial collapse of the Triple Alliance and the imposition of Spanish imperialism.

The term Aztec is complicated and controversial (Berdan 2014). Aztec is derived from the term Aztlan, "place of the herons" or "place of whiteness," referring to a number of indigenous groups who traced their origins from this place. Aztec has been most widely used in English since the early nineteenth century. The term Aztec Empire is not found in primary sources, nor was it employed by any indigenous groups (Rodgríquez-Alegría and Nichols 2017: 2–3). Mexica is the name of one of the ethnic groups who migrated from Aztlan and spoke Nahuatl. The term Nahua is sometimes used to refer to indigenous people in Central Mexico after the Spanish (Lockhart 1992). The Mexica of Tenochtitlan dominated a tripartite military alliance, the "Triple Alliance," that led to an imperial state expansion incorporating other city-states and confederations and diverse ethnicities. None of these terms is unproblematic.

9.1 Collapse, Fragmentation, Regeneration, and Termination

Controversies about collapse stem in part from ambiguities about the concept itself, as Middleton (2017: 11) reviews in his recent discussion. Tainter (1988: 4–5) emphasizes collapse as a political phenomenon, involving a rapid reduction in sociopolitical complexity. Diamond (2005) adds to this to include a significant demographic reduction over a large area. Cowgill (1988) and Cowgill and Yoffee (1988) highlight the importance of distinguishing the concepts of state, society, and civilization, as states are embedded in civilizations with great traditions, arts, literature, writing, and folk or "little traditions" of household and quotidian lifeways. Invocations of collapsed civilizations obscure the transformations and persistence, as in the cases of the Maya and Pueblos, who are very much part of the modern world (McAnany and Yoffee 2010). As with the Triple Alliance, "it is specific political regimes that collapsed, social systems that changed, and religious and ideological systems that were transformed and/or rejected" (Middleton 2017: 12).

Cowgill (1988) draws another set of important distinctions, between terminations, complete cessations that are relatively rare, versus fragmentations of regional states, hegemonic city-states, and empires that were common, and between episodes and cycles. Recurrent phases of centralization-fragmentat ion-regeneration are part of state formation processes often discussed as political cycling (Faulseit 2016: 12–13; Marcus 1992; Schwartz 2016; Schwartz and Nichols 2006). Cowgill (1988, 2012) argues that these are more accurately characterized as episodes because the duration is variable, sometimes long, other times short, but rarely intervals of equal length and the variability in duration is significant. (Schwartz and Nichols 2006). The first states in Mesoamerica developed in a milieu of competitive pre-state or peer polities, as was the case for the earliest states, Cuicuilco and Teotihuacan, in the Basin of Mexico (Charlton and Nichols 1997).

The end of Teotihuacan, the first political unification of the Basin of Mexico and adjacent regions, involved fragmentations and regeneration and the establishment of a city-state system (Cowgill 2015; Nichols 2016). The city-state was the dominant polity in Postclassic Mesoamerica. Episodically, one city-state among its peers grew through alliances and by subjugating others, added outlying less powerful provinces, and centralized regional power to become a hegemon. But Postclassic city-states in Central Mexico, like their counterparts elsewhere, resisted long-term political unification, and hegemonic city-states fragmented until a new episode of unification would begin as a former province became the new regional power (Marcus 1992; Trigger 2003). Relatively large pre-modern states rarely persisted for more than a few centuries before fragmenting into smaller polities (Trigger 2003). This state cycling certainly captures the broad outlines of prehispanic state political dynamics out of which the Triple Alliance or Aztec empire formed in the early fifteenth century. But Cowgill (2012) points out that pre-modern state formation is not just self-propelled cycling. Why did episodes of fragmentation, centralization, and regeneration vary in duration? Why did centralization under some states such as Teotihuacan last much longer, while others were short-lived?

Trigger (2003: 93) emphasized that much of this variation could be explained by differences between city-state and territorial state organization. He disagreed that city-states and territorial states are not necessarily successive stages of development. In this model, the strength of city-states to resist political unification meant that fragmentation was the norm among pre-modern states, with territorial states much rarer.

Blanton, Kowalewski, and Fargher (2020) examine state cycling from the perspective of collective action to ask to what degree do collective action and governments that provide collective benefits create states that are more enduring, and less prone to collapse than more autocratic states? Their analysis found collective action was not necessarily associated with greater state endurance. More authoritarian pre-modern states were associated with minor declines vs. states high in good governance experienced major collapses, perhaps because of greater integration. Thus, degrees of collective action might account for some differences in state cycling and magnitudes of collapse.

Below, we review episodes of collapse in the Basin of Mexico, as the Triple Alliance did not develop in a historical vacuum but was built on a substrate of statecraft while innovating new strategies in their expansion until it abruptly stopped in 1519–1521. But unlike prior episodes of "collapse," the Triple Alliance empire to quote, historian Matthew Restall (2017: 12), "did not fade away nor collapse through over-extension, nor implode in a revolutionary uprising or independence movement, but rather was terminated by an outside invasion" supported by longstanding enemies and even some recent allies. In other words, both internal Mesoamerican political dynamics of alliances, networks, and conflicts among city-states and confederations and external invaders were involved in the collapse of the Aztec empire and the creation of "New Spain."

9.2 Modeling Collapse

There have been various recent synthetic discussions and modeling of collapse, including the works of Joseph Tainter (1988, 2006) and Jared Diamond (2005). Middleton (2017) provides a good recent synthesis. Climatic change and anthropogenic degradation have drawn much recent attention as triggers. Butzer (2012: 3633), however, observes that the focus on environmentalism needs to "more effectively address coupled systems that include a great tapestry of variables." Butzer attempts to overcome simplistic explanations by probing historical examples from the Middle East, Old Kingdom, and New Kingdom Egypt, and Islamic Mesopotamia to construct a conceptual model of historical collapse (Figure 9.3).

From this analysis, Butzer draws several generalizations: (1) The most common attribute at the early stage of every breakdown was institutional failure, *viz.* incompetence, loss of economic networks, corruption, or dynastic crises; (2) civil war or invasion was as critical as any climatic force; (3) environmental degradation, such as soil erosion, was only documented for Axum and the

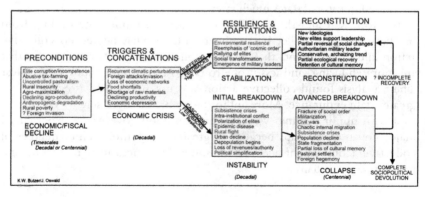

Figure 9.3 Butzer's (2012:3636) conceptual model of historical collapse.

Black Death. In contrast, climatic perturbations helped trigger breakdowns in Old and New Kingdom Egypt, the Fayum, or Mesopotamia on the eve of the Islamic conquest; (4) demographic retraction was prevalent during or after collapse, linked with pestilence. The Black Death is a classic example of pathogen–driven, catastrophic depopulation; and (5) ideological shifts accompanied collapse in part overlapping with foreign intrusion or ethnic change. Butzer sees poor leadership, administrative dysfunction, and ideological ambivalence as "endemic to the process of collapse" with war or climatic perturbations as triggers and demographic decline as a coagent or consequence. His "triggers and concatenations" are examples of the more general "income problem" that pre-modern states faced (Cowgill 1988).

In broad strokes, Butzer's model seems especially applicable to the Triple Alliance empire because it considers warfare and invasion, demography, and epidemic disease, among other elements, and offers a starting point to place the Aztec case in a broader context.

9.3 Basin of Mexico: Antecedents

The Triple Alliance did not form de novo but was the last and largest of a series of states centered on the Basin of Mexico that is now home to Mexico City (Table 9.1). Here we will briefly overview the episodes of state formation in

Table 9.1 Archaeological Chronology of the Basin of Mexico

General Chronology	Teotihuacan Valley	Years
Early Colonial	Aztec IV	1521–1600 CE
Late Postclassic	Late Aztec	
	Aztec III-IV	ca. ?1450–1521
	Aztec III	1350/1400–1450
Middle Postclassic	Early Aztec	1150–1350
	Aztec II	1150/1200–1350
Early Postclassic	Aztec I	900/1000–1150
	Atlatongo-Tollan	1000–1150/1200
	Mazapan	900–1000?
Epiclassic	Coyotlatelco	650-900
	Early Epiclassic/Oxtotipac	?600-700 CE
Classic	Metepec	550–650 CE
	Late Xolalpan	450–550 CE
	Early Xolalpan	350–450 CE
	Late Tlamimilolpa	250–350 CE
	Early Tlamimilolpa	150–250 CE
	Miccaotli	100–150 CE
Terminal Formative	Tzacualli	1–100 CE
	Patlachique	100-1 BCE
	Tezoyuca	200-100 BCE
Late Formative	Late Cuanalan	c. 600–200 BCE
	Early Cuanalan	650–600 BCE
Middle Formative	Chiconautla	900-650 BCE
Early-Middle Formative	Altica	?1050-900 BCE

the Basin of Mexico that preceded the Triple Alliance. By doing so, we will broadly illustrate the episodic processes for formation, centralization, fragmentation, and regeneration – where the earliest states developed from a milieu of competitive hierarchical peer polities during Late Formative, or Preclassic, from which formed the earliest kingdoms and regional states of the Classic period, and whose fragmentations and perhaps terminations created Postclassic city-state systems.

9.4 First City

The period archaeologists call the Late Formative (600–200 BCE) in the Basin of Mexico and elsewhere in Mexico was among the most politically dynamic of any time span with the development of the first cities and states. First founded as a village or series of small villages by 400 BCE, Cuicuilco in the southwestern corner of the Basin had grown to a city of four km^2 with an estimated population of ca. 20,000 people (Sanders et al. 1979: 99, 193). We know few details about the growth of Cuicuilco because lava flows and modern constructions cover most of the remains. Cuicuilco must have dominated the southwestern Basin of Mexico but how far its direct control reached is unclear (Sanders 1979 et al.: 172, 174). Elsewhere in the Basin of Mexico, six other regional centers were the foci of small hierarchical polities (Sanders et al. 1979: 97). Ash deposits and lava from an eruption of the Ixtle volcano covered most of the remains of Cuicuilco, and the conventional interpretation was that they caused the city's abandonment. However, it now appears that many of the buildings were already in disuse prior to the Xitle ash and lava flow, now dated between 200 and 350 CE *after* most of Cuicuilco was abandoned (Cowgill 2015; Nichols 2016).

However, an earlier eruption in the mid-first century of a different volcano, Popocatepetl, in Puebla southeast of the Basin of Mexico, might have blocked one of Cuicuilco's important trade routes and, thus, contributed to the city's decline as it vied with the settlement of Teotihuacan in the northeast Basin of Mexico (Plunket and Uruñuela 2012: 33). People fleeing ash-covered villages and farmlands in Puebla augmented Teotihuacan's rapid growth. Although a natural disaster contributed to the Basin of Mexico's first urban and state termination, perhaps altering regional political competition, the same catastrophe also helped fuel the explosive growth of its rival Teotihuacan, which became the largest city and most influential state in Mesoamerica until ca. 550 CE (Cowgill 2015: 42–50).

9.5 Teotihuacan

Teotihuacan's rapid growth involved a radical restructuring of the region, as most settlements in the Basin of Mexico were abandoned, and 85 percent of the regional population resided in the city. The Teotihuacan state's core heartland included about 25,000 km^2, including the Basin of Mexico, southern Hidalgo, northeastern Guerrero, adjoining portions of Puebla-Tlaxcala, and eastern Morelos (Nichols 2020; Millon 1988: 113). It represents the first political unification of the Basin of Mexico. However, relations with its immediate hinterlands ranged from direct involving settlements by people from Teotihuacan or closely affiliated to more indirect relations (Nichols 2020, 2016). Teotihuacan's foreign relations reached both the Pacific and Gulf Coasts, the southern Mexican highlands, and extended to the Maya lowlands. Smith and Montiel argue that Teotihuacan was Mesoamerica's first empire (2001). Others see it as a regional hegemon (Cowgill 2015). As a first-generation state, Teotihuacan's dominance was unusually long-lived, lasting from ca 100 BCE to CE 550 as it had no immediate rivals during its early hegemony.

Teotihuacan's foreign relations began to contract ca. 450/500 CE at the start of the Metepec phase (450–550 CE). It also began to experience increasing political and economic retractions in its outer hinterlands, and inner hinterlands of the Basin of Mexico, and the area under its direct political control began to shrink (Nichols 2020; Cowgill 2015). As provincial elites and intermediate elites within the city established their authority and basis of power, it seems likely they were able to divert resources and disrupt or realign provisioning networks creating an economic crisis or strains as in Butzer's (2012) model (Healan 2012; Nichols 2016: 29–30, 2020). Teotihuacan is often considered the exemplar of corporate governance among Mesoamerican states, inequalities and tensions also increased in the city (Storey 2006).

The fiery destruction of public buildings and monuments along the city's main avenue ca. 550 CE marked the termination of Teotihuacan's regional dominance (Cowgill 2015). Millon (1988: 156) thinks the destruction was done by people in the city, but Cowgill (2015) and López Luján (2006: 32) suspect the hand of neighboring polities allied with urban dissidents. Whoever was directly involved annihilated Teotihuacan's rulership, ritually terminated their cosmic, sacred power, and rejected symbols and practices associated with the city. The multi-family Teotihuacan apartment compound, for example, that had been the standard residence in the city and regional centers disappeared. Despite Teotihuacan's strategic location straddling the only low pass out of the Basin of Mexico, the city could not flourish without a reliable flow of migrants, food, and other resources that its hinterlands and interregional relations and networks once provided.

Park et al. (2018) point to oxygen isotope data from sediments in lakes in the Bajío, indicating drought conditions from 600 to 700 CE due to frequent El Niño-like conditions and sunspot activity – invoking drought as causing or contributing to Teotihuacan's collapse. However, it appears that Teotihuacan's hinterland retraction and troubles began prior to the droughts, although drought could have exacerbated difficulties provisioning the city, there is no clear evidence from Teotihuacan itself (McClung 2012). Teotihuacan's collapse, as Blanton et al. (2020) found among other corporate states precipitated a major regional restructuring, demographic, economic, social, political, and ideological (Cowgill 2015; Crider 2013). The city lost a substantial population as people moved to its hinterlands, new centers were established, and other minor centers grew. City-states became the dominant state form, along with confederations in the wake of Teotihuacan's collapse and also other Classic-period regional states. Political fragmentation marked Teotihuacan's end, along with a demographic reduction in the city and regeneration in the form of the Postclassic city-state system.

9.6 Fragmentation and the Toltec Regeneration

The fragmentation of the Teotihuacan state system and a dramatic reduction in the urban population provided an opening for some provincial centers to grow, new centers to be founded, and the establishment of the Postclassic city-state system. For at least the next three centuries, 650–950 CE, the Basin of Mexico was divided into a series of city-states and confederations, but none dominated. The Toltec center of Tula in Teotihuacan's former hinterland northwest of the Basin of Mexico grew into a regional power ca 950 CE that extended its domain into the northern and eastern Basin of Mexico. This episode of centralization lasted at most two centuries, and, as is characteristic of city-states systems, by 1150 CE, the Toltec state fragmented, and its capital city, Tula, lost much of its population (Healan 2012). The "demise, destruction and depopulation at Tula" (Healan 2012: 94) initiated a new episode of regeneration with the development of the Aztec city-state system involving population movements, ethnic asserta-tions, dynastic struggles, warfare, and militaristic tributary city-states, alliances, and confederations, but also increased market integration (Berdan et al. 2017; Charlton and Nichols 1997; Healan 2012; Nichols 2017). The *altepetl* or city-state continued as the building block of Middle and Late Postclassic Aztec politics (Berdan 2014; Charlton and Nichols 1997; Hodge 1997). After two centuries, two confederations or fragile imperial alliances, the Acolhua in the eastern Basin of Mexico and Tepaneca in the western Basin of Mexico, began to consolidate political control. This consolidation by the early 1400s laid the basis for a military alliance between the Mexica of Tenochtitlan, the small city-state of Tlacopan in the western Basin of Mexico, and the more powerful Acolhua confederation of the eastern Basin of Mexico. Their defeat of the Tepaneca capital of Azcapotzalco launched the Triple Alliance empire dominated by the Mexica of Tenochtitlan.

9.7 Triple Alliance

The Triple Alliance empire consolidated control of the Basin of Mexico (Table 9.1). It expanded through conquests and alliances south in the high-lands and west into the cacao-growing Pacific Coast and east to the Gulf Coast. By the early sixteenth century, the empire with a population of five to six million had expanded to the Gulf and Pacific coasts and had begun send-ing ambassadors to highland Guatemala, often the prelude to military action and annexation. The Mexica and their allies employed a hegemonic, tributary city-state model to integrate city-states. *Altepetl,* city-state, remained important as semi-autonomous administrative units and rulers retained much autonomy over internal affairs as long as tribute payments were met and they were loyal to the Triple Alliance (Berdan et al. 1996; Hassig 1985, 1988). The region experienced rapid demographic growth and also climatic perturbations but serious droughts and famines, agriculture intensified, market integration increased, and both urban and rural populations reached their greatest size and density in the Basin of Mexico under the Triple Alliance (Evans 2008).

9.8 Spain

In his recent book, David Carballo (2020) reviews the complex political history of the Iberian Peninsula. As a key link between the Mediterranean and Atlantic, it had been invaded and conquered multiple times. Its deep geopolitical history shaped Spain's unification following the Reconquista and its subsequent Atlantic expansion with interesting parallels and contrasts to the Aztecs (Carballo 2020). Even prior to its Atlantic expansion, Spain's interaction sphere was already more expansive and intercontinental than any state in prehispanic Mesoamerica. Spanish colonialism in the Atlantic began in 1492 in the Caribbean as they sought gold, trade routes, and souls for Christianity; both fame and fortune in the Americas depended on indigenous labor (Wolf 1982: 182–183). The decimation of indigenous Caribbean people from maltreatment, hardships, and introduced diseases as well as the end of the gold supply prompted both the beginnings of African slavery in the Americas and explorations of the Mesoamerican mainland that lead to the third expedition captained by Hernán Cortés, who departed from Cuba on 10 February 1519.

9.9 Spanish-Mexica War and Aztec Collapse

Cortés, with 11 ships and 450 soldiers, landed on the Yucatan coast and then sailed along the coast relying on local supplies to Totonac lands of the central Veracruz coast that were part of the Triple Alliance domain and where they met emissaries of Moctezuma (Hassig 2006). The ensuing Spanish-Mexica war has been detailed in many books, including by Spanish conquistadors and most recently in English by David Carballo (2020) and Matthew Restall (2018). The collapse of the Triple Alliance empire has undergone significant revision in recent decades, undermining the conventional triumphant Spanish narrative. The "new conquest" history grew out of archival research drawing on new sources to consider the role of indigenous conquerors, not only Spanish, with their city-state/confederation politics and alliance systems seeking to advance their positions toward multiple ends, not just autonomy from Mexica imperialism (Oudijk 2012: 426; Restall 2018).

Horses offered an initial tactical advantage in battles with the Maya (Carballo 2020; Hassig 2006), but also important was alliance making and indigenous armies. Facilitating alliance making between Mesoamericans and Spanish were the translation skills of Geronimo de Aguilar, a shipwrecked Spanish sailor who learned to speak Maya in captivity, and the better-known Marina, or La Malinche, a Nahua woman "gifted" to Cortés who spoke Classical Nahuatl and Chontal Maya (Hassig 2006). Totonac allies from the Gulf Coast and the alliance with Tlaxcalteca of the highlands, a powerful enemy confederation who, although surrounded by the Triple Alliance, remained independent, proved crucial; together, they provided 10,000 forces for the initial march to Tenochtitlan (Carballo 2020: 184).

Contrary to debates about Moctezuma's leadership (Diamond 1997, 2007, but c.f. Hassig 2006), Restall (2018: 341) argues that the actual collapse of the Aztec empire did not happen when Cortés and his men first entered the capital, Tenochtitlan, in 1519. The Triple Alliance collapsed in the second half of the war after the Spanish were driven out of Tenochtitlan and then returned with even more allies, 200,000 (Hassig 2006). Restall challenges the role of Moctezuma as a weak leader (Diamond 2007). He argues that Moctezuma brought the Spanish into Tenochtitlan to observe and hunt them. The reversed outcome and subsequent defeat of Tenochtitlan and collapse of the Triple Alliance was ultimately tied to infectious disease and politics and shifting alliances deeply rooted in prehispanic Mexico. Although the powerful confederation of Tlaxcala was a key ally for the Spanish, the decision of Texcoco and Acolhua, originally part of the Triple Alliance, to break with the Mexica and ally with the Spanish and Tlaxcala in the second half of the war was actually more important in the siege and defeat of Tenochtitlan. It removed the Mexica's most powerful ally with a large army and provided a strategic location from which to launch the siege of Tenochtitlan (Carballo 2020: 220). The fierce resistance of the Mexica during the siege of Tenochtitlan, even while cut off from water, food, and allies, and while dying from disease, contradicts the notion of fatalism contributing to the collapse. Conquests by Spanish and indigenous allies in Mesoamerica continued long after the defeat of Tenochtitlan. Spanish imperialism in Mexico and Central America itself was a protracted process, neither neatly nor quickly completed (Carballo 2020: 227–228).

If the Conquest was "not primarily a conflict between Mexico and Spain but between Mesoamerican groups supporting Cortés. The clash was centered on issues internal to Mesoamerica" (Hassig 2006). Indigenous allies saw the breakup and overthrow of the Triple Alliance and Mexica hegemony as a benefit for themselves, at least in the short term. For them, the political restructuring following the collapse of a hegemon was a change in hierarchy, not seen initially as a fundamental change in the political system of Mesoamerican states (Hassig 2006). Unlike prior episodes of state cycling, fragmentation, and regeneration, this collapse was different as indigenous city-states never again were politically autonomous.

Contrary to the current emphasis on overshoot and anthropogenic change in explanations of pre-modern and historical state collapse, Central Mexico experienced its most significant environmental degradation after the end of the collapse of Mexica imperialism and the massive demographic decline of the sixteenth century (Gibson 1964; Melville 1994; Sanders et al. 1979). Massive sheet and gully erosion of hillsides followed the "Columbian exchange" and Spanish introduction of grazing animals, forced relocations, and abandonment of indigenous lands and terrace systems. The massive decline in population and demand for Indian labor, not overpopulation and lack of Spanish understanding of the Mexica's hydraulic management of lake waters and chinampas caused erosion, deposition, and destruction of productive land use systems (Luna Golya 2014). The New Conquest History points to invasion and conquest linked with Mesoamerica state politics and alliance networks, infectious disease, demographic decline and depression, and colonialism as the critical factors in the Aztec collapse.

9.10 Epidemics

Had the sixteenth-century epidemics not occurred, then the question is not would the Spanish Conquest of Mesoamerica have happened, but rather, what would the character of colonial rule have looked like in early New Spain, and would the occupation have been as long (Carballo 2020: 247)? The spread of epidemic disease was a significant factor in the Aztec Empire's collapse—but it was not singularly decisive. Rather, epidemic disease contributed to the large-scale and long-term demographic decline in the Basin of Mexico, exacerbating a multitude of social and political factors resulting from warfare, conquest, and colonization. Nonetheless, understanding the epidemics of the sixteenth century will enable us to better explore the collapse of the Aztec Empire and the subsequent demographic decline of the Basin of Mexico.

The evidence of epidemics in the sixteenth century comes by way of Spanish and Aztec accounts and the archaeological record—though each line of evidence has its limitation. By April or May of 1520, the first wave of smallpox had reached the Basin of Mexico on the eve of conquest (McCaa 2000; Prem 1992). Likewise, smallpox was subsequently followed by waves of other deadly infectious diseases, including measles, typhus, bubonic plague, and influenza (Alchon 2003: 68). Though, unlike the fourteenth-century Great Mortality, better known as the Black Death, in Europe, several epidemic diseases swept through the Basin of Mexico in three major waves over the sixteenth century. While European populations rebounded by the end of the fourteenth century, indigenous populations in the Basin of Mexico would not begin to recover until the seventeenth century, while it would be longer still in other areas of Mexico. However, as will be discussed below, the epidemics alone are insufficient to explain the sustained population loss. Nonetheless, it is important to understand the epidemic waves, which diseases were transmitted when, population loss, and related factors that accounted for them.

There is little doubt that the first major epidemic wave, occurring between 1520 and 1531 CE, was largely related to smallpox, which came to be known as *Zahuatl* in Nahuatl. The earliest confirmed occurrences of smallpox in Tenochtitlan took place in 1520, on the eve of conquest. After Montezuma's death, Cuitlahuac, his successor, was among the first casualties of the epidemic—undoubtedly contributing to the multitude of political and social disruptions faced by the Triple Alliance (León-Portilla 2006: 92). The first accounts of smallpox emerged between 1520 and 1521 CE, while the Spanish were in Tlaxcala after fleeing Tenochtitlan. According to León-Portilla, the initial outbreak of smallpox lasted for seventy days and impacted nearly the whole city (2006: 92, 132). While smallpox killed many at this time, so too did hunger, which resulted from a largely incapacitated workforce (León-Portilla 2006: 93). Even though there were survivors, the initial outbreak of smallpox was worsened by the specter of the looming invasion of Tenochtitlan. Making matters worse, the Spanish cut off external food supplies and water from Tenochtitlan on the eve of the invasion.

Smallpox continued to ravage the Basin of Mexico throughout the 1520s, and measles also appeared by the early 1530s. With ongoing conquest, warfare, and colonization, the population loss in the Basin of Mexico in the decade following the siege of Tenochtitlan was the most dramatic of the three major sixteenth-century demographic declines (Whitmore 1991: 478). Whitmore's modeling suggests a loss of indigenous life of approximately 700,000 or roughly 40% of the estimated population in the Basin of Mexico by the early 1530s (1991: 478).

The second major epidemic wave occurred between 1545 and 1548 CE, and the collective diseases responsible for this even came to be known as *Cocoliztli*, or "pest" in Nahuatl. For centuries, historians and scholars of this period assumed that epidemic was a resurgence of smallpox. However, a close look at historical sources and descriptions of the symptoms suggests otherwise, minimally, that Cocoliztli was not smallpox alone. Symptoms such as strong headaches, mouth dryness, dizziness, abdominal pain, and hemorrhages, as well as death within four or five days of symptoms, are distinct from smallpox (Marr and Kiracofe 2000; Puente and Calva 2017: 1). Based on symptoms, Typhus, hemorrhagic fever, and Pneumonic Plague were proposed as potential diseases responsible for the epidemic (Whitmore 1991: 471). Concrete evidence in the archaeological record of a particular disease responsible for the great mortality in any of these epidemic episodes is incredibly difficult to detect, as the diseases will often kill an individual before leaving discernable marks on a host's body. Still, paleopathology is a growing field that is rapidly offering new insights into ancient pathogens.

Recently, Vågene and colleagues proposed that S. Paratyphi C (2018), a form of salmonella, be considered a candidate for one of the diseases contributing to the 1545 CE Cocoliztli. The data contributing to these findings come from investigators at the site of Teposcolula-Yucundaa, in the Mixteca Alta of Oaxaca, who identified this strain of salmonella in 10 out of 11 individuals from dental pulp genomic reconstruction (Puente and Calva 2017: 2). The 11 individuals sampled were buried in a cemetery associated with the 1545 Cocoliztli (Vågene et al. 2018).

This salmonella species is known to be transmitted by the fecal–oral route and would have been facilitated by poor sanitary conditions. As such, salmonella could have been a contributing cause for the CE 1545 Cocoliztli. As Vågene and colleagues argue (2018), the spread of salmonella would relate more to climate change, periods of drought, and infrastructural issues related to colonization—particularly with the flooding of Lake Texcoco. However, it remains possible that S. Paratyphi C could have been spread by asymptomatic carriers (Puente and Calva 2017: 2). Furthermore, the identification of S. Paratyphi C does not rule out the possibility of other diseases being involved or, in fact, confirm that the bacterium was responsible for the 1545 CE Cocoliztli. Puente and Calva argue that the presence of S. Paratyphi C suggests "mixed infections," or syndemics, were possible.

Yet, it remains unclear if S. Paratyphi C was the deciding factor, even at Teposcolula-Yucundaa. While S. Paratyphi C was present in the dental pulp of 10 out of a total of 11 individuals from the Grand Plaza burials at Teposcolula-Yucundaa, the sample size remains small for the overall region. Whether Teposcolula-Yucundaa is representative of other burials in the Basin of Mexico during this period needs to be further tested. Likewise, while suggestive, the presence of S. Paratyphi C is not definitive as the cause of death. Seven of the ten individuals with evidence of S. Paratyphi C were considered weak positives (Vågene et al. 2018: 522), showing variation in the degree of infection. At least some of the sampled individuals might have suffered from and survived S. Paratyphi C during their lives.

On the advent of the third significant epidemic wave in the Basin of Mexico, Whitmore's demographic modeling suggests that by 1569 CE, the indigenous population of the Basin of Mexico had been reduced to but 21.5% of its estimated 1519 CE zenith. The third major epidemic referred to as *Matlazahuatl* in Nahuatl spanned from 1575 to about 1581 CE. Like the 1545 CE cocoliztli, the 1575 epidemic has been challenging to identify. Historical records suggest symptoms such as "netlike eruptions on the skin," which counter assumptions of smallpox alone (Alchon 2003: 55). Typhus, hemorrhagic fever, and Pneumonic Plague have been proposed for this third major epidemic (Morfin and Storey 2017: 8; Whitmore 1991: 471). However, 1576 also sees the end of a great drought, coinciding with Lake Texcoco's severe flooding (Marr and Kiracofe 2000: 354). The severity of the flooding spurs desires to abandon Mexico City (formerly Tenochtitlan), culminating in the lake's large-scale draining beginning in the seventeenth century.

Acuña-Soto and colleagues propose that the great mortality during this third epidemic wave in the Basin of Mexico to disease and environmental degradation, related famine, and unsanitary city conditions (2004). During this time, Acuña-Soto and colleagues suggest the significant epidemic disease could have been indigenous hemorrhagic fevers transmitted by rodent hosts and aggravated by extreme drought conditions (2002). If their interpretations are correct, then the demographic devastation of this third epidemic episode did not result from new exposure to a "virgin soil" epidemic. Instead, the devastation of infectious disease was compounded by social and environmental factors.

9.11 Demography

The role of "virgin soil" epidemics introduced by the Spanish has long been acknowledged as a critical factor in the Triple Alliance's demographic collapse. However, despite the uniqueness of several new infectious diseases in three particularly devastating epidemic episodes, the sustained loss of population cannot be attributed to one disease or even "new" diseases alone (Livi Bacci 2008). Even Whitmore acknowledges that the sustained rise in morbidity, with decreased birth rates, famine, and environmental changes would contribute to the great population loss in the sixteenth century (1991: 479). As Livi-Bacci (2008) calculates, if virgin soil epidemics were the sole factor, then indigenous populations in Latin America should have recovered in several generations. This recognition alludes to two critical questions explored by Rebecca Storey (2012). First, what was the population in the Basin of Mexico before European colonization? Second, why was the demographic loss in the Basin of Mexico so severe if epidemics cannot solely explain it? As we will see, the "social chaos" created by escalating warfare and conquest, subsequent colonization, rising rates of malnutrition, overcrowding, and falling birth rates with new waves of infectious disease created the conditions that kept birth rates low and prevented the indigenous population from rebounding (Alchon 2003: 144; Jones 2003: 708).

Population estimates in the Basin of Mexico varied throughout the twentieth century. While there is a generally accepted estimate, or "happy" medium, today—true accuracy depends on further studies of archaeological settlements, more historical documentation, and further modeling. Because of these factors, the scale and population which succumbed to the sixteenth-century epidemics remain somewhat contested. A precise measure of the population in the Basin of Mexico in 1520 remains the subject of debate as no census or demographic data are known from this period. Population estimates tend to vary with opinions on how complex Mesoamerican societies were, as well as with opinions on the devastation of the sixteenth-century epidemics (Morfín and Storey 2017: 5). Borah and Cook (1963) famously created a population estimate for pre-contact Mexico using Aztec Tributary lists—with relatively high numbers ca. 25 million for Mexico and ca. 3 million for the Basin of Mexico. However, correlations between tribute, households, and population are loose, drawing criticism (Morfín and Storey 2017).

Using a mix of documentary and archaeological evidence, William T. Sanders (1976) established an estimate in the range of ca. 1–1.2 million people for the Basin of Mexico. Sander's model seems relatively close to that proposed by Whitmore (1991). In establishing his model, Sanders had to wrestle with several problems. It was impossible to survey most of the large nucleated Late Postclassic towns and cities, such as Azcapotzalco, Tenochtitlan-Tlatelolco, Texcoco, among others because Colonial and modern constructions cover them (Sanders et al. 1979). Sanders also had to address estimating rates of "the severest and most protracted human mortality ever to occur" in the Americas following European expansion and reaching Central Mexico during 1519–1521 (Cook and Lovell 1992). The earliest reliable census available for the Basin of Mexico puts the population between 404,000 and 407,000 in 1568 (Sanders 1976: 130).

No one disputes that a population decline had already occurred by the mid-sixteenth century. The debate is over the magnitude. Sanders (1976) critiqued the "Berkeley School" estimates showing why they are too high, although his estimate of 1.0–1.2 million for the population of the Basin of Mexico is generally considered conservative (Cook and Lovell 1992; Morfin and Storey 2017; Prem 1992; Whitmore 1991). The dramatic population decline from disease and colonialism reshaped both ecology and society in the Basin of Mexico and throughout the Americas (Alchon 2003).

Based on archaeological and historical data run through simulation, Whitmore's estimate suggests around 1.59 million people were living in the Basin of Mexico in 1520 at its apogee with a sum Mexican population of around 16 million (Whitmore 1991: 483). By Whitmore's widely accepted modeling, the native population was reduced by 80–90 percent of its 1520 apogee over the sixteenth century (Whitmore 1991: 464). By 1569 the population had declined to only 21.5 percent of its 1519 zenith, a reduction estimated at 343,000 (Whitmore 1991: 478). By 1607, the number of indigenous peoples living in the Basin of Mexico was reduced to roughly 180,000—roughly a 90 percent decrease from the estimated 1519 zenith (Whitmore 1991: 477).

More recently, scholars have viewed Whitmore's numbers as being somewhat inflated, gravitating toward a smaller population estimate for Tenochtitlan and the Basin of Mexico (Restall 2018: 314). Regardless of the population estimates' accuracy, whether high or low, the subsequent Great Dying in the Basin of Mexico resulted in a population loss that took centuries from which to recover. But the looming question pertains to the severity and role of epidemics, potentially as a principal cause, in this demographic collapse of ancient states—in opposition to/accounting for colonization, violence, slavery, Spanish cruelty, and reduced fertility (Whitmore 1991: 465).

Along these lines, Alchon makes two important points about demographic decline and depression. First, indigenous people's response to new infectious pathogens is not very different from how populations reacted elsewhere in the world during epidemics. But there were two significant differences. Unlike the Black Death in Europe, where populations recovered by the end of the thirteenth century relatively quickly, there was no single epidemic event in the Basin of Mexico (Alchon 2003: 143–144). As such, the length of mortality due to epidemics was extended for a far greater period. At no other point in history did populations experience multiple (at least three waves), highly infectious, new pathogens in a very short period. But even this does not account for the decline and long demographic depression.

Epidemics impact the health and well-being of the population and interfere with everyday agricultural production and resource distribution (Whitmore 1991: 474). As Alchon suggests, the sustained disruptions to everyday life

Table 9.2 Matthew Restall's (2003) Myths of the Spanish Conquest

1. Myth of Exceptional Men
2. Myth of the King's Army
3. Myth of the White Conquistador
4. Myth of Completion
5. Myth of (Mis) Communication
6. Myth of Native Desolation
7. Myth of Superiority

resulting from European colonization over decades exacerbated the indigenous mortality of epidemics and undermined social, economic, and political institutions (2003: 144). Under colonial rule, the forced changes to indigenous ideologies, slavery, abusive labor practices, land loss, forced migration, and environmental degradation all severely impacted population recovery (Lockhart 1992; Livi Bacci 2008; Newson 1993: 262). For Jones, the poverty, malnutrition, environmental stress, geographic dislocation, and social disparity exacerbated by colonization were the critical and complex factors that made the sixteenth-century epidemics in the Basin of Mexico so devastating—not immunologic, genetic determinism (2003: 742). As Restall makes clear, if the population estimates for Tenochtitlan and Mexico are lower than once thought, and epidemics, therefore, play a lesser role than once thought, then, coupled with ongoing local warfare, "outright slaughter, starvation, and enslavement accounted for more casualties at all stages of the war than has been recognized" (2018: 315).

9.12 Resilience and Change

After the defeat of Tenochtitlan in 1521, the New Conquest history has shown that many indigenous people did not view themselves as conquered by the Spanish (Oudijk and Castañeda 2017; Restall 2003; Rodríguez-Alegría and Nichols 2017). They saw themselves as agents of the Mexica defeat and collapse of the Triple Alliance; their role and that of Africans in the long and unfinished conquest of Mesoamerica has gained greater recent recognition. Both archaeology and documentary studies show a significant continuity in Nahua daily life, especially in rural regions, and in economics and politics in the first decades of Spanish rule. Spanish colonialism initially depended significantly on Nahua corporate organization, social relations, and economy (Carballo 2020; Johnson 2017; Lockhart (1992).

No indigenous state ever again was politically autonomous in Mexico and Central America but the altepetl remained important, especially in the early sixteenth century. Lockhart (1992) used language as an index of changes in Nahua society, culture, and ideology (Table 9.4). Nahua continuities and changes, transformations, adaptations, syncretism, and hybridity are the subjects of many scholarships. Johnson (2017) has shown how *Tlaxilacalli* corporate

Table 9.3 1519–1595 Population Reduction, Adapted from McCaa (2000)

Source	1519 population (millions)	1595 population (millions)	Percent decline
Mexico			
Rosenblat	4.5	3.5	22
Aguirre-Beltrán	4.5	2.0	56
Zambardino	5–10	1.1–1.7	64–89
Mendizabal	8.2	2.4	71
Cook and Simpson	10.5	2.1–3.0	71–80
Cook and Borah	18–30	1.4	78–95
Central Mexican Symbiotic Region			
Sanders	2.6–3.1	O.4	85–87
Basin of Mexico			
Whitmore	1.3–2.7	0.1–1.4	69–96
Gibson	2.6–3.1	0.2	87

Table 9.4 Lockhart's (1992) Three-Stage Model of Nahuatl Change

Stage	Description
1. 1521–1545	Resilience, limited change in Nahua sub-imperial organization, technology, or concepts; altepetl, tlaxilacalli
2. 1550–1650	Nahua organization continued, but discrete additions of Spanish culture in all arenas. Massive addition of Spanish nouns, grammar, syntax little change
3. 1650–1810	Amalgamation, hybridity, Nahua incorporate Spanish elements into organizational structure, large-scale bilingualism, fragmentation of indigenous corporations

networks below the altepetl that were present long before the Triple Alliance proved especially resilient after the collapse. Tlaxilacalli were key to both collective action and state politics that anchored and "metabolized" imperial rule as mediators between households and regional alliances. Tlaxilacalli's importance manifested both in the material and spiritual worlds – making New Spain Roman Catholic was a complex transformation. Tlaxilacalli religious specialists persisted into the first generation of Spanish rule, but Tlaxilacalli also organized labor to destroy temples and build local chapels and churches making church building part of collective identities (Burkhart 2017; Johnson 2017: 125).

Just as the rapid increase in population during the fifteenth century shaped the Aztec world, so too did the massive demographic decline and depression impact Nahuas. As in the current COVID-19 pandemic, class and ethnicity impacted disease spread, mortality, and fertility (Johnson 2017: 80). The loss of population became a kind of "intensifier" of colonialism. Acute labor shortages impacted the environment and society and set up intense exploitation and competition for Indian labor, lands, and souls as the Hispanic world took form, as most "local hierarchies crumbled, populations evaporated, and ecosystems deranged, the tlaxilacalli remained a rare bastion of order and autonomy" (Johnson 2017: 88) This competition between indigenous elites, the Spanish crown, the Catholic Church, and Criollos continued for three centuries, even after revolution, independence from Spain, and the development of the modern nation-state (Lockhart 1992; Sanders et al. 2001; Wolf 1982).

The recovery of the indigenous population begins in 1620–1640, but the demographic revolution in Mexico did not really get underway until late in the Colonial period and increased dramatically in the twentieth century (Livia Bacci 2008: 228; McCaa 2000). Demography and colonialism also were intertwined in the collapse of New Spain. Coupled natural and social systems (Butzer 2012) along with history, and agency collapsed both Aztec and Spanish imperialism whose legacies continue to shape the modern world.

References

Acuña-Soto, Rodolfo, David W. Stahle, Malcolm K. Cleaveland, and Matthew D. Therrell. 2002. Megadrought and Megadeath in 16th Century Mexico. *Emerging Infectious Diseases* 8(4): 360–362.

Acuña-Soto, Rodolfo, David W. Stahle, Matthew D. Therrell, Richard D. Griffin, and Malcolm K. Cleaveland. 2004. When Half of the Population Died: The Epidemic of Hemorrhagic Fevers of 1576 in Mexico. *FEMS Microbiology Letters* 240(1): 1–5.

Alchon, Suzanne Austin. 2003. *A Pest in the Land: New World Epidemics in a Global Perspective*. University of New Mexico Press, Albuquerque.

Berdan, Frances F. 2014. *Aztec Archaeology and Ethnohistory*. Cambridge University Press, Cambridge.

Berdan, Frances F., Richard E. Blanton, Elizabeth Hill Boone, Mary G. Hodge, Michael E. Smith, and Emily Umberger. 1996. *Aztec Imperial Strategies*. Harvard University Press, Cambridge.

Berdan, Frances F., Kenneth G. Hirth, Deborah L. Nichols, and Michael E. Smith. 2017. Introduction: Aztec Economy and Empire Through the Lens of Objects. In *Rethinking the Aztec Economy*, edited by Deborah L. Nichols, Frances F. Berdan, and Michael E. Smith, pp. 3–18. University of Arizona Press, Tucson.

Blanton, Richard E., Gary M. Feinman, Stephen A. Kowalewski, and Lane F. Fargher. 2020. Moral Collapse and State Failure: A View from the Past. *Frontiers in Political Science* 2: 568704.

Borah, Woodrow W., and Sherburne F. Cook. 1963. *The Aboriginal Population of Central Mexico on the Eve of the Spanish Conquest*. University of California Press, Berkeley.

Burkhart, Louise M. 2017. The Aztecs and the Catholic Church. In *The Oxford Handbook of the Aztecs*, edited by Deborah L. Nichols and Enrique Rodríguez-Alegría, pp. 675–688. Oxford University Press, Oxford.

Butzer, Karl W. 2012. Collapse, Environment, and Society. *PNAS* 109(10): 3632–3639.

Butzer, Karl W., and Georgina H. Endfield. 2012. Critical Perspectives on Historical Collapse. *PNAS* 109(10): 3628–3631.

Carballo, David M. 2020. *Collision of Worlds: A Deep History of the Fall of Aztec Mexico and the Forging of New Spain*. Oxford University Press, New York.

Charlton, Thomas H., and Deborah L. Nichols. 1997. Diachronic Studies of City-States: Permutations on a Theme—Central Mexico from 1700 B.C. to A.D 1600. In *The*

Archaeology of City-States: Cross-Cultural Approaches, edited by Deborah L. Nichols and Thomas H. Charlton, pp. 169–207. Smithsonian Institution Press, Washington, DC.

Crider, Destiny L. 2013. Shifting Alliances: Epiclassic and Early Postclassic Interactions at Cerro Portezuelo. *Ancient Mesoamerica* 24(1): 107–130.

Cook, Noble David, and W. George Lovell. 1992. Unraveling the Web of Disease. In *"Secret Judgments of God": Old World Disease in Colonial Spanish America*, edited by Noble David Cook and W. George Lovell, pp. 213–242. University of Oklahoma Press, Norman.

Cowgill, George L. 1988. Onward and Upward with Collapse. In *The Collapse of Ancient States and Civilizations*, edited by Norman Yoffee and George L. Cowgill, pp. 244–276. University of Arizona Press, Tucson.

———. 2012. Concepts of Collapse and Regeneration in Human History. In *The Oxford Handbook of Mesoamerican Archaeology*, edited by Deborah L. Nichols and Christopher A. Pool, pp. 301–308. Oxford University Press, New York.

———. 2015. *Ancient Teotihuacan: Early Urbanism in Central Mexico*. Cambridge University Press, New York.

Diamond, Jared. 1997. *Guns, Germs, and Steel: The Fates of Human Societies*. W. W. Norton, New York.

———. 2005. *Collapse: How Societies Choose to Fail or Succeed*. Penguin, New York.

Evans, Susan T. 2008. *Ancient Mexico & Central America: The Archaeology and Culture History of Mesoamerica*. Thames & Hudson, New York.

Faulseit, Ronald K. 2016. Collapse, Resilience, and Transformation in Complex Societies: Modeling Trends and Understanding Diversity. In *Beyond Collapse: Archaeological Perspectives on Resilience, Revitalization, and Transformation in Complex Societies*, edited by Ronald K. Faulseit, pp. 3–26. Center for Archaeological Investigations Occasional Paper No. 42. Southern Illinois University, Carbondale.

Gibson, Charles. 1964. *The Aztecs Under Spanish Rule: A History of the Indians of the Valley of Mexico, 1519–1810*. Stanford University Press, Stanford.

Hassig, Ross. 1985. *Trade, Tribute, and Transportation: The Sixteenth-Century Political Economy of the Valley of Mexico*. University of Oklahoma Press, Norman.

———. 1988. *Aztec Warfare: Imperial Expansion and Political Control*. University of Oklahoma Press, Norman.

———. 2006. *Mexico and the Spanish Conquest*, 2nd edition (1st edition 1994). University of Oklahoma Press, Norman.

Healan, Dan M. 2012. The Archaeology of Tula, Hidalgo, Mexico. *Journal of Archaeological Research*, 20(1): 53–115.

Hodge, Mary G. 1997. When Is a City-State?: Archaeological Measures of Aztec City-States and Aztec City-State Systems. In *The Archaeology of City-States: Cross-Cultural Approaches*, edited by Deborah L. Nichols and Thomas H. Charlton, pp. 209–227. Smithsonian Institution Press, Washington, DC.

Johnson, Benjamin D. 2017. *Pueblos within Pueblos: Tlaxilacalli Communities in Acolhuacan, Mexico, ca. 1272–1692*. University Press of Colorado, Boulder.

Jones, David S. 2003. Virgin Soils Revisited. *The William and Mary Quarterly* 60(4): 703–742.

Lachniet, Matthew S., and Juan Pablo Bernal-Uruchurtu. 2017. AD 550–600 Collapse at Teotihuacan: Testing Climatic Forcing from a 2400-Year Mesoamerican Rainfall Reconstruction. In *Megadrought and Collapse: From Early Agriculture to Angkor*, edited by Harvey Weiss, pp. 183–204. Oxford University Press, New York.

Livi Bacci, Massimo. 2008. *Conquest: The Destruction of the American Indios*. Translated by Carl Ipsen. Polity Press, Malden.

Lockhart, James. 1992. *The Nahuas After the Conquest: A Social and Cultural History of the Indians of Central Mexico, Sixteenth Through Eighteenth Centuries.* Stanford University Press, Stanford.

León-Portilla, Miguel. 2006. *The Broken Spears: The Aztec Account of the Spanish Conquest of Mexico.* Beacon Press, Boston.

Luna Golya, Gregory G. 2014. Modeling the Aztec Agricultural Waterscape of Lake Xochimilco: A GIS Analysis of Lakebed Chinampas and Settlement. PhD dissertation, Dept. of Anthropology, Pennsylvania State University, University Park.

Marcus, Joyce. 1992. Political Fluctuations in Mesoamerica. *National Geographic Research & Exploration* 8(4): 392–341.

Marr, John S., and James B. Kiracofe. 2000. Was the *Huey Cocoliztli* a Haemorrhagic Fever? *Medical History* 44(3): 341–362.

Mathew, Laura E, and Michel R. Oudijk (editors). 2007. *Indian Conquistadors: Indigenous Allies in the Conquest of Mesoamerica.* University of Oklahoma Press, Norman.

McAnany, Patricia A., and Norman Yoffee. 2010. Why We Question Collapse and Study Human Resilience, Ecological Vulnerability, and the Aftermath of Empire. In *Questioning Collapse: Human Resilience, Ecological Vulnerability, and the Aftermath of Empire,* edited by Patricia A. McAnany and Norman Yoffee, pp. 1–20. Cambridge University Press, Cambridge.

McCaa, Robert. 2000. The Peopling of Mexico from Origins to Revolution. In *The Population History of North America,* edited by Michael R. Haines and Richard H. Steckel, pp. 241–304. Cambridge University Press, Cambridge.

McClung de Tapia, E., 2012. Silent Hazards, Invisible Risks: Prehispanic Erosion in the Teotihuacan Valley, Central Mexico. In *Surviving Sudden Environmental Change: Answers From Archaeology,* edited by Jago Cooper and Payson Sheets. University Press of Colorado, Boulder, pp.143–165.

Melville, Elinor G. K. 1994. *A Plague of Sheep: Environmental Consequences of the Conquest of Mexico.* Cambridge University Press, Cambridge.

Middleton, Guy D. 2017. *Understanding Collapse: Ancient History and Modern Myths.* Cambridge University Press, Cambridge.

Millon, René. 1988. The last years of Teotihuacan Dominance. In *The Collapse of Ancient States and Civilizations,* edited by Norman Yoffee and George L. Cowgill, pp. 102–164. University of Arizona Press, Tucson.

Morfín, Lourdes M., and Rebecca Storey. 2017. Population History in Precolumbian and Colonial Times. In *The Oxford Handbook of the Aztecs,* edited by Deborah L. Nichols and Enrique Rodríguez-Alegría, pp. 189–200. Oxford University Press, New York.

Newson, Linda A. 1993. The Demographic Collapse of Native Peoples of the Americas, 1492–1650. In *The Meeting of Two Worlds: Europe and the Americas, 1492–1650,* edited by Warwick Bray, pp. 247–288. Oxford University Press, Oxford.

Nichols, Deborah L. 2016. Teotihuacan. *Journal of Archaeological Research* 24(1): 1–74.

———. 2017. Farm to Market in the Aztec Imperial Economy. In *Rethinking the Aztec Economy,* edited by Deborah L. Nichols, Frances F. Berdan, and Michael E. Smith, pp. 19–43. University of Arizona Press, Tucson.

———. 2020. City, State, and Hinterlands: Teotihuacan and Central Mexico. In *Teotihuacan: The World Beyond the City,* edited by Kenneth G. Hirth, David M. Carballo, and Bárbara Arroyo, pp. 227–276. Harvard University Press, Cambridge.

Oudjik, Michel R. 2012. The Conquest of Mexico. In *The Oxford Handbook of Mesoamerican Archaeology,* edited by Deborah L. Nichols and Christopher A. Pool, pp. 459–470. Oxford University Press, New York.

Oudjik, Michel R., and María Castañeda de la Paz. 2017. Nahua Thought and the Conquest. In *The Oxford Handbook of the Aztecs*, edited by Deborah L. Nichols and Enrique Rodríguez-Alegría, pp. 161–171. Oxford University Press, New York.

Park, Junjae, Roger Byrnee, and Harald Böhnel. 2018. Late Holocene Climate Change in Central Mexico and the Decline of Teotihuacan. *Annals of the American Association of Geographers* 109(1): 104–120.

Plunket, Patricia, and Gabriela Uruñuela. 2012. Where East Meets West: The Formative in Mexico's Central Highlands. *Journal of Archaeological Research* 20(1): 1–51.

Prem, Hanns J. 1992. Disease Outbreaks in Central Mexico during the Sixteenth Century. In *"Secret Judgments of God": Old World Disease in Colonial Spanish America*, edited by Noble David Cook and W. George Lovell, pp. 3–19. University of Oklahoma Press, Norman.

Puente, José Luis, and Edmundo Calva. 2017. The One Health Concept – The Aztec Empire and Beyond. *Pathogens and Disease* 75(6): 1–2.

Restall, Matthew. 2003. *Seven Myths of the Spanish Conquest*. Oxford University Press, New York.

———. 2017. The Aztec Empire: A Surprise Ending? *The Historian* 134: 12–17.

———. 2018. *When Montezuma Met Cortés: The True Story of the Meeting That Changed History*. Harper Collins, New York.

Rodgríquez-Alegría, Enrique, and Deborah L. Nichols. 2017. Introduction – Aztec Studies: Trends and Themes. In *The Oxford Handbook of the Aztecs*, edited by Deborah L. Nichols and Enrique Rodgríquez-Alegría, pp. 1–17. Oxford University Press, New York.

Sanders, William T. 1976. The Population of the Central Mexican Symbiotic Region, the Basin of Mexico and the Teotihuacan Valley in the Sixteenth Century. In *The Native Population of the Americas in 1492*, edited by William M. Denevan, pp. 85–151. University of Wisconsin Press, Madison.

Sanders, William T., Susan T. Evans, and Thomas H. Charlton. 2001. Colonial Period Cultural Geography of the Teotihuacan Valley and Temascalapa Region. In *The Aztec Period Occupation of the Valley Part 3 – Synthesis and General Bibliography*, edited by William T. Sanders and Susan T. Evans, pp. 889–930. Occasional Papers in Anthropology No. 27. Department of Anthropology, Pennsylvania State University, University Park.

Sanders, William T., Jeffrey R. Parsons, and Robert S. Santley. 1979. *The Basin of Mexico: The Ecological Processes in the Evolution of a Civilization*. Academic Press, New York.

Schwartz, Glenn M. 2006. From Collapse to Regeneration. In *After Collapse: The Regeneration of Complex Societies*, edited by Glenn M. Schwartz and John J. Nichols, pp. 3–18. University of Arizona Press, Tucson.

Smith, Michael E., and Lisa Montiel. 2001. The Archaeological Study of Empires and Imperialism in Pre-Hispanic Central Mexico. *Journal of Anthropological Archaeology* 20(3): 245–284.

Storey, Rebecca. 2006. Mortality through Time in an Impoverished Residence of the Precolumbian City of Teotihuacan: A Paleodemographic View. In *Urbanism in the Preindustrial World: Cross-Cultural Approaches*, edited by Glenn R. Storey, pp. 277–294. University of Alabama Press, Tuscaloosa.

———. 2012. Population Decline during and after Conquest. In *The Oxford Handbook of Mesoamerican Archaeology*, edited by Deborah L. Nichols and Christopher A. Pool, pp. 908–915. Oxford University Press, New York.

Tainter, Joseph A. 1988. *The Collapse of Complex Societies*. Cambridge University Press, Cambridge.

————. 2006. Archaeology of Overshoot and Collapse. *Annual Review of Anthropology* 35: 59–74.

————. 2016. Why Collapse Is So Difficult to Understand. In *Beyond Collapse: Archaeological Perspectives on Resilience, Revitalization, and Transformation in Complex Societies*, edited by Ronald K. Faulseit, pp. 27–39. Center for Archaeological Investigations Occasional Paper No. 42. Southern Illinois University, Carbondale.

Trigger, Bruce G. 2003. *Understanding Early Civilizations*. Cambridge University Press, Cambridge.

Vågene, Åshild J., Alexander Herbig, Michael G. Campana, Nelly M. Robles García, Christina Warinner, Susanna Sabin, Maria A. Spyrou, Aida Andrades Valtueña, Daniel Huson, Noreen Tuross, Kirsten I. Bos, and Johannes Krause. 2018. *Salmonella enterica* Genomes from Victims of a Major Sixteenth-Century Epidemic in Mexico. *Nature Ecology & Evolution* 2: 520–528.

Whitmore, Thomas M. 1991. A Simulation of the Sixteenth-Century Population Collapse in the Basin of Mexico. *Annals of the Association of American Geographers* 81(3): 464–487.

Wolf, Eric R. 1982. *Europe and the People Without History*. University of California Press, Berkeley.

Yoffee, Norman. 1988. Orienting Collapse. In *The Collapse of Ancient States and Civilizations*, edited by Norman Yoffee and George L. Cowgill, pp. 1–19. University of Arizona Press, Tucson.

10 The Black Death

Collapse, Resilience, and Transformation

Samuel K. Cohn, Jr.

The Black Death constitutes one of Western Civilization's best examples of a reversal of fates from an event's initial explosive devastations and horrendous human responses to its longer-term consequences. I was asked to contribute to the Princeton seminars on collapse because of the Black Death's fundamental reputation as a monumental mortality collapse that occurred in a brief period of four to six months in any given place. The demographic evidence across Europe and the Middle East has been gathered and debated for several generations and now is beginning to be more broadly investigated for Northern Africa and parts of Asia, where few, if any, documents or archaeological evidence survive from this devastation. This history awaits analysis with new tools of DNA, genome sequencing, and phylogenetic extrapolations.

The Princeton Institute for International and Regional Studies' Global Systemic Risk (PIIRS GSR) Princeton workshops on collapse had an accurate reading of the historiography of the Black Death, which for the last several decades has emphasized the bright side of life for its survivors: That the catastrophe did not spell long-term disillusionment, decline, or collapse of civilizations, at least in Europe, but instilled remarkable resilience. One of the foremost historians to emphasize this bright side quantitatively was David Herlihy (1930–1991) who was my mentor.[1] In this chapter, I will not overturn this presently dominant picture that extends from 1348 through most of the fifteenth century. I will, however, argue that the picture is not as simple or straightforward as is sometimes illustrated. Over the wide sweep of the Black Death's near-global coverage of the Old-World hemispheres, differences in the timing of changes were profound and not always what we might have expected. Beginning with collapse, I will then argue that the Black Death's consequences were of transformation rather than ones merely of resilience or a return to the status quo.

10.1 Population as a Sign of Collapse?

Immediately questions arise about plague mortality rates and population stagnation or recovery when confronting the Black Death and its long-term impact. The first problem regards population estimates before the Black Death and

DOI: 10.4324/9781003331384-13

the paucity of quantitative records such as tax surveys. To take one example: Historical consensus places Paris as Western Europe's largest city before 1348 and through the Middle Ages. Estimates of its peak pre-plague population, however, range from fewer than 50,000 to over 300,000.[2] Few places possess trustworthy figures of population before the Black Death. Afterward, the number, frequency, and quality of fiscal and demographic records increase and improve across most of Europe, fundamentally because of a shift in consciousness spawned by the Black Death. Almost immediately, contemporaries realized communities had not suffered equally, and direct taxation based on previous community population estimates was no longer viable. Here, the metaphors of the Florentine chronicler Matteo Villani, who continued his brother's chronicle in the year of the Black Death, were perspicacious: "it struck in the way of a hailstorm, leaving one area intact while destroying another." With the plague's second major assault in 1362, he changed his metaphor but delivered the same message: Its "effect" was "similar to early thin clouds through which rays of sunlight appear, casting light here but not there."[3] In the 1930s, English historians began seeing the same patterns from manorial rolls recording vacant holdings because of the death of tenants. In parts of Cambridgeshire, these mortality figures varied between 5 and 76 percent of the pre-plague populations.[4] Historians later found similar results for France's Massif Central, near St-Flour.[5]

One of Europe's largest cities before the Black Death—Florence—possesses a unique statistical report on the city's economy and demography for a single year before the Black Death in 1338. It was not a tax survey with the usual problems of tax exemptions for nobles and clergy and serious underreporting of the poor. Instead, it was an annual report compiled by Florence's statistically minded chronicler and banker Giovanni Villani and comprised figures on the consumption of cereals, wool production, numbers of infants baptized, children attending grammar schools, and abled-bodied Florentine men, 15–70 years old, allowed to carry arms. Furthermore, he supplied an estimate of Florence's population of around 1338 of 90,000, excluding foreigners, visitors, soldiers, and members of religious communities.[6] Despite questions about these statistics, David Herlihy and Christiane Klapisch-Zuber argued that they bear a careful internal consistency (except for slight deviations in baptisms and consumption). Yet our estimates of Florence's population on the eve of the Black Death continue to hover between 94,000 and 120,000 inhabitants.[7]

Moreover, Florence is blessed with a second series of statistics compiled almost immediately after the plague of 1348, in 1352 and again in 1355. These were rare tax surveys of Florence (the city as opposed to its countryside) that counted and taxed directly the urban population. In 1352, less than 10,000 households remained in the city. By estimating the numbers of household members from later tax records and especially from the city's new tax system of 1427, Herlihy and Klapisch calculated that Florence circa 1352 possessed around 25,000.[8] By this figure, the Black Death would have stripped at least 75 percent of Florence's urban population, far more than the usual

European-wide estimates of 30 to 50 percent, based largely on chroniclers' conjectures, and which some scholars have claimed are grossly exaggerated.[9] However, the decline measured by the post-plague fiscal records has not subtracted the mass migration from the countryside into Florence that would have ensued immediately after the Black Death with peasants seeking charitable assistance or better-paying jobs in the city.[10] On the other hand, given exemptions and under-counting those without taxable property, these fiscal records certainly underestimated Florence's population in 1352 and 1355. More serious are questions estimating Florence's demographic dynamics between 1338 and 1348 with a mysterious plague in the spring of 1340 that according to Villani, killed 15,000[11] and famine conditions in 1347 that probably lowered population levels in the city but could have instead increased them with destitute peasants pouring into the city.[12] Nonetheless, the Black Death's devastation exceeds the usual estimates across Europe, even at the upper limits of 50 percent of population felled.

Any argument for the Black Death engendering collapse or severe decline is best made for the long-term demographic trends. In the medium term to perhaps as late as the plague of 1400, major urban populations across Europe made strides to regain their Black Death losses, despite severe transregional plagues in 1361–1363, 1374–1375, and 1383. Again, let's view one of the best-documented cities, Florence. Through chronicle estimates and quantifiable records, its population from around 25,000 rebounded to about 42,000, before Florence was struck by a second plague in 1363, and, on the eve of its sixth plague in 1400, it had reached 60,000, through increased fertility and immigration from its hinterland (contado) and smaller towns.[13] Afterward, the urban population stabilized at just over 40,000 until the 1470s. Then the Florentine population began to increase but only gradually through the early modern period, despite no future plague within Tuscany ever approximating the plague mortalities from 1363 to 1400.[14] In fact, even after industrialization and the beginnings of international tourism, Florence had not recovered its pre–Black Death population of 100,000 until the 1860s. Moreover, market towns in its hinterland, such as Impruneta, or even previous centers of commerce and banking as with San Gimignano have yet to recover their pre-plague populations.[15] Almost as impressive is England's slow pace of demographic recovery, which regained its pre-1348 numbers only in the eighteenth century.[16] However, far from being a disadvantage, economic historians have credited this demographic sluggishness as the key element in England sustaining higher real wages for laborers and artisans than any country in Europe, enabling the English economy to grow through the early modern period and take off in the eighteenth century.[17] Closer in time to the Black Death, demographic stagnation can be seen aiding prosperity and economic growth in the mountain villages of the Alpi fiorentine on the northern borders of the Florentine state. Even after the Black Death, this region counted several of the largest villages in the Florentine contado, such as Mangona, with populations well over a thousand but was one of the poorest regions measured by taxable wealth anywhere in the Florentine state. However, after 1400, population growth in these regions became one of the slowest within the Florentine state, while their prosperity climbed seven-fold to the 1470s, bringing these communities from the brink of starvation to become among the richest of Florentine peasants:[18] So much for the Malthusian theory that after a catastrophe, resources increase arithmetically, while population normally increases exponentially, leading inevitably to a cyclical pattern of crises. Here, factors other than the availability of land and resources figured. Politics were critical. Led by war and peasant uprisings in 1402, these mountaineers forced Florence to change its fiscal system that had taxed distant mountain villages more heavily and disproportionately than anywhere within the Florentine state.[19]

Another surprising demographic twist concerns the disappearance of villages. Despite colossal population losses, evidence of "lost villages" after the Black Death was much less significant than historians and archaeologists before World War II had assumed. It did not even equal losses during other moments in medieval history without evidence of climatic or disease-related catastrophes. As the field archaeologist Maurice Beresford discovered in the early 1950s, the plague years had not hastened "the retreat of villages," and those to disappear had already been in steep decline before the Black Death. Beresford charged that historians had given the Black Death "too much credit."[20] Christopher Dyer later followed in Beresford's footsteps but went further. On lost villages, "the Black Death seems to have had only a limited impact," and those that disappeared soon after the Black Death should be taken as signs of opportunities, not collapse. As Dyer suggests, lords and big farmers were not the only ones "who could make profit-seeking decisions." Through migration, the Black Death opened new avenues for peasants to do the same, despite England's severe price and wage legislation bent on stifling mobility.[21]

10.2 Initial Perceptions and Realities of Collapse

Chronicles, which survive across European and into the Middle East in the hundreds for the Black Death, are our best indicators of general opinions across social classes, and in 1348, they signal fear and despair of a world in collapse. Apocalyptic visions of the origins of the Black Death in little-known distant lands fill the chronicles' Black Death entries. Such was the chronicle of a Dominican friar from Ferrara, who described massive rains of worms and serpents in parts of China (*Catajo*), which "devoured large numbers of people. Fire rained from heaven in the form of snow that burnt mountains and fires of pestilential smoke killed all who smelt it within twelve hours."[22] These preternatural events could, however, be imagined closer to Europe as with an anonymous chronicler of Pistoia. In 1348, he reported a dragon at Jerusalem like the one slain by Saint George, which devoured all who crossed its path. In the region of a Tana, a city of forty thousand called Lucco was totally demolished by "the fall from heaven of a great quantity of worms, big as a fist with eight legs, which killed all by their stench and poisonous vapors."[23] Such visions could even be claimed for major European cities. The Augustinian canon of Leicester Henry Knighton imagined:

> an earthquake and tempest destroyed the whole city of Naples. The earth opened suddenly as though a stone was thrown into water, and everyone perished with the friar who was preaching, except another friar, who fled and escaped into a garden outside the town.[24]

More disturbing than these visions of total collapse with chroniclers anticipating similar fates soon to befall their own towns were realities happening across large swaths of German-speaking regions and parts of the Low Counties, Spain, and France. These were the processions of flagellants and, worse, the extermination of Jews and, in places, priests, Catalans, and beggars. In at least 235 communities in German regions, entire Jewish populations—men, women, and children—were massacred. The atrocities were not, however, universal across Europe.[25] They were unknown in Italy, the British Isles (because no Jews were left after Edward I's expulsions in 1290), and most regions of France and the Low Countries. Nor did they arise anywhere in the Middle East. Instead, the events to horrify chroniclers the most across Western and Eastern Europe were abandonment by clergy, notaries, and doctors of the sick and dying and, worse still, flight by family members from their own kin that included parents abandoning their children. For chroniclers and commentators such as Giovanni Boccaccio, this behavior threatened the end of Christian civilization.[26] The Florentine chronicler, Matteo Villani called such "cruelty" the "habits of the barbarians" that began with the infidel.[27] For the Florentine poet Antonio Pucci, it was worse: "Not even Saracens, Jews, or traitors deserve such treatment!"[28]

For decades, historians have commented on these horrors and human responses to impending collapse, often exaggerating the universality of the burning of Jews and belittling the cries of abandonment as *topoi*, copied from one chronicle to another (despite the improbability of such copying in a matter of months across long distances from Eastern Europe to Ireland and across contrasting cultural registers from isolated monastic scribes to merchant chroniclers and nobles attached to princely courts). Historians have, however, yet to reflect on just how short-lived these perceptions and human responses of 1348 were. With numerous future waves of this bubonic pestilence, which could still level cities by half as with Naples, Genoa, and Milan in plagues of the seventeenth century, the apocalyptic visions of pestilential origins were no longer imagined; massacres of Jews accused of poisoning streams and foodstuffs associated with plague were no longer repeated;[29] and descriptions of abandonment by clergy, doctors, and kinsmen of their own families surfaced only rarely.[30] Perhaps most telling of these abrupt reversals was the re-appearance of the next flagellant movement to accompany a plague since the Black Death. In 1400, after half a century of plague deaths on the decline, mortalities in cities such as Pistoia jumped to heights not seen since 1348. In contrast to the flagellants of

1348–1351, who marched from Hungary as far west as London, creating division, violence, and sparking riots in cities such as Tournai,[31] the flagellants of 1400, called the Bianchi, because of their cheap white linen dress, were a peace movement. Instead of division, they unified followers across social class, gender, city, and countryside and strove to end conflict from everyday litigation among neighbors to aristocratic clan violence and interregional warfare then raging between Milan and Florence.[32] From its origins as a force of brutal divisiveness, plague had become a cry for solidarity and compassion.

10.3 Resiliency vs Transformation

If not collapse, were the post-Black Death changes matters of resilience? For a tale of late medieval resilience, we need to turn to a climatic story that affected chiefly northern Europe a generation before the Black Death. This was the Great Famine of 1314–1317, triggered by unusually cold and damp summers, which was repeated for three consecutive years, leading to ruined harvests with crops rotting in water-logged fields for four years. Beyond starvation, these years spawned human diseases, probably the usual ones arising from famine—typhoid fever, dysentery, and diarrhea—along with ergotism.[33] Yet William Chester Jordan, Christopher Dyer, Nigel Saul, H. E. Hallam, and John Hatcher have argued that the extraordinary conditions of 1314–1317 produced a severe but only brief moment, with recovery in the 1320s.[34] Despite regions in England and the Low Countries losing upwards of 15 percent of their populations,[35] crop yields recovered rapidly along with human populations. But the recovery shows no evidence of transformation in land settlement, introduction of new crops, new systems of crop rotations, increases in crop yields, changes in land exchange, land distribution, tenure, or new technologies.[36] Instead, the only long-term consequence of the famine argued by some historians and bioarchaeologists was its prelude to the Black Death. The survivors of the Great Famine comprised fragile populations that a generation later fueled the Black Death's super mortalities.[37] However, as William Chester Jordan has recently argued, no studies have yet to demonstrate any geographic correlations between the severity of the Great Famine and Black Death levels of mortality.[38] As noted above, Florence's moralities were as high as any city in Europe, but the Great Famine had not afflicted this city or the rest of Mediterranean Europe.[39]

10.4 Transformation: The Land

The Black Death tells another story. A rich historiography going back at least to the 1960s sketches post-Black Death transformations in land holdings, tenancies, labor relations, and settlement patterns for various parts of Western Europe. However, these changes did not all take hold immediately with the Black Death. For a generation afterward and in places as late as the fifteenth century, resilience, more than transformation, was the Black Death's upshot.

In his famous *thèse d'état* of 1966 on the peasants of Languedoc (southern France), Emmanuel Le Roy Ladurie described in detail transformations as far as the agrarian world was concerned. These included the growth of share-cropping (*métayage*), switches to greater concentration on animal husbandry, and changes in arable agriculture principally from cereals to what he called "promiscuous agriculture," where in plains and hills cereals, vineyards, and olive groves were interspersed.[40] Yet these changes became widespread only during the fifteenth century. At the same time, David Herlihy was finding similar transformations, again beginning at the end of the fourteenth and early fifteenth century. His regional analysis of Pistoia showed the growth of share cropping (the *mezzadria* system) coupled with increased investment in the land from urban patricians but (as I later found in regions close to Florence's city walls[41]) also included artisans and shopkeepers. These transformed relations between capital and labor, and the initiatives did not stem only top down. As the chronicle Matteo Villani attested, Tuscan peasants would no longer accept a lease unless the landlord supplied the oxen and seed.[42] In addition, peasant migration in search of more productive plots changed settlement patterns: Peasants left marginal hillsides for alluvial plains closer to urban markets, while more distant mountain communities remained stable because of increased demand for meat and wool.[43] Later, Herlihy and Christiane Klapisch-Zuber expanded this analysis to include Florence's territorial state in its entirety.[44] These patterns of agriculture, land tenure, and the "paesaggio" (or organization of the countryside)[45] were of long duration, persisting until national laws in 1974 abolished the *mezzadria* and industrialized vertical plowing for viniculture, which took off in the 1980s. These late-fourteenth-century transformations also had consequences for caloric intake, diet, and the health of peasants and urban artisans alike, bringing more meat, fish, ale, cider, and wine to their tables, along with new luxury items and better housing as Guy Bois has shown for Normandy during the fifteenth century[46] and Christopher Dyer and others for England and Wales at the same time.[47] However, the precise dating of these post-Black Death transformations for cities and the countryside remains unclear, and historians have only begun to analyze them: Did they start within four or five years of the great dislocations provoked by the Black Death, or lag at least a generation until the 1370s, as appears with the rise of artisans' real wages in England,[48] or later into the fifteenth century as in Bruges and Ghent?[49]

10.5 The Timings of Transformations

Certainly, the timing and character of these transformations were not everywhere the same, even within the same regions of northern or Mediterranean Europe. In England, reaching back to George Holmes's study of the higher nobility, agrarian laborers employing their new advantage in the labor market to force landlords to relax servile conditions and erode landlords' income did not begin until the 1370s or later. Holmes, however, was brief and somewhat uncertain about the mechanisms by which landlords maintained their position for at least a generation in the face of the new Black Death market forces.[50] Rodney Hilton later went further, arguing that it was "a feudal reaction," similar to transformations in parts of Eastern Europe that would continue in places such as Russia until the mid-nineteenth century.[51] The sudden dramatic shift in the supply of labor, wrought by the Black Death, had failed to free laborers in England to gain better working conditions and higher real wages. Instead, landlords and especially monastic ones, assisted by the crown, could turn the clock backward, by imposing harsher forms of body serfdom and measures to constrain peasant mobility.[52] Evidence of the collaboration between the English nobility and the crown is not difficult to find: The English price and labor ordinances of 1349 and statutes of 1351 exacted harsher conditions than similar post-plague labor laws anywhere in Europe.[53] Unlike ones imposed by the Kingdom of Provence, the Ile-de-France, or Florence, and other city-states such as Orvieto, Siena, and Milan, which either vanished quickly or changed fundamentally after several years or even months, the English laws persisted into the fifteenth century with increasingly severe punishments, such as branding the foreheads of violators and adding whippings to their fines.[54] Moreover, the English laws were the only ones to provoke popular insurrections, and these lasted until 1356.[55] Secondly, monastic lords of boroughs, such as St Albans and Bury St Edmunds, continued imposing feudal monopolies over grinding grain in their mills and baking bread in their ovens even after the English Uprising of 1381. In these towns, international merchants were legally classified as serfs. Thirdly, key demands of the English Uprising centered on the abolition of serfdom.

However, recently, Mark Bailey has challenged the timing of this transformation. From a sample of 38 manors across different species of landlords and regions of England, he argues that no "feudal reaction" ensued for the first generation following the Black Death. Instead, almost immediately, servile labor duties began "to decay on all types of manors."[56] The Black Death of 1348–1349 was the turning point. The shift in labor supply alone pressured landlords into negotiating with their laborers and instituting fundamentally new labor conditions. Nevertheless, whether the transition occurred around 1355 or 1375, the Black Death was pivotal, not as a return to the *status quo ante* but for systemic transformation.

10.6 Demography: Marriage and Fertility

As suggested above from the mountains of Tuscany, demographic behavior constitutes another systemic transformation wrought by the Black Death and its successive plagues. The Malthusian interdependency between resources and rates of fertility loosened, or, as Herlihy has put it: "the Malthusian trap" became "unlocked."[57] Population decline no longer resulted exclusively from collapses in foodstuffs or other material resources. Lower rates of fertility, later ages of marriage,[58] and out-migration to cities for better job opportunities, especially for women,[59] meant that men who stayed at home prospered.[60] The tipping point of this transformation from low population levels and starvation to prosperity did not, however, emerge until the early fifteenth century.

More broadly, E. A. Wrigley and Roger Schofield's study of the population of England, which begins with the appearance of parish vital statistics in 1541, demonstrates a longer-term demographic transformation from Malthusian "positive" checks—famine, war, and plague—to "preventive" ones—later ages of marriage, higher rates of celibacy, lower rates of fertility, and out-migration. By their starting point, they argued that this demographic transformation was already on course.[61] As Herlihy concluded more broadly: "Out of the havoc of plague, Europe adopted what can well be called the modern Western mode of demographic behavior."[62]

10.7 Equality

Recently, Guido Alfani and his équipe at the Bocconi University, Milan, have discovered the longest period that can presently be calculated from records on wealth or income when the gap between rich and poor narrowed.[63] This period followed the Black Death either immediately or, as seen with several other shifts above, a generation or later. This transformation appears universally across Europe and also has been discovered in the Middle East.[64] However, unlike settlement patterns and land usage in Tuscany or southern France, the decline of serfdom and demesne farming in England, or changes in demographic regimes explored above, this transformation lasted only a century or less. Around 1450 in some places, the 1470s in others, and for a few as late as the early sixteenth century, inequality rose again and persisted with only a few brief intermissions until the First World War. Historians, however, have yet to concentrate on this post-Black Death century of economic equality: (1) To explore its differences in timing and (2) to consider the consequences for nonelites in other spheres as with a paradoxical decline in artisans' social and political rights at the same time.[65]

10.8 Attitudes

The Black Death also spurred fundamental changes in thought and attitudes, concerning childhood, education, popular revolt, medicine, and public health. In the remaining space, I will explore only one area where attitudes and institutional change were interlinked—popular piety, charity, and notions of the afterlife. Across cities and regions in Europe, a source can be tapped that unveils attitudes and behavior, not only of elites, but of middling sorts, peasants, poor widows, and even workers without rights of citizenship. These are last wills and testaments, which, despite populations dwindling, increase sharply after the Black Death. Through quantitative analysis, changes emerge, which again suggest transformations originating with the Black Death or shortly thereafter. One is a change in strategies for the afterlife from what I have called "mendicant piety" to a "new attachment to things." Across central and northern Italy and probably more widely, even hard-headed merchants and shopkeepers on their deathbeds employed their testaments to decry "ill-gotten gains," achieved through usury and exploiting the poor. Further, they renounced their worldly gains by instructing their executors to sell off their properties and then to splinter the proceeds into amounts as tiny as several pennies to be bequeathed to numerous ecclesiastic and charitable causes.

Not in 1348, but with the next plague pandemic across Europe from 1361 to 1363 (depending on the region), a distinct structural change in giving began. Instead of obliterating one's lasting memory by disintegrating possessions into small monetized amounts, testators strove to preserve their earthly remembrance beyond the grave by offering fewer but larger bequests, such as commissioning paintings or other sacred works to stand on or beside their graves. Furthermore, artisan testators, widows without family names, and occasionally peasants, demanded that their images along with those of their ancestors be painted "in their very likeness (ad simultudinem)" at the feet of their chosen patron saints.[66] In addition, testamentary contingency clauses spread from testaments of nobles to commoners, stipulating that certain prized pieces of property were to remain in the family to be passed down through generations and never to be alienated. If an heir violated the clause, the executors were to intervene and pass the property to another recipient. For poorer artisans or peasants, these clauses encumbered strips of land, even humble items of clothing. By the last decades of the fourteenth and increasingly through the fifteenth and sixteenth centuries, wills in Italy and other regions[67] had been transformed into legal instruments to orchestrate desires from the grave with precise timings of perpetual masses and instructions for future transmissions of property, now holding beneficiaries accountable to preserve and celebrate the remembrances of testators' earthly lives.

These changes in attitudes also demonstrate transformations in poor relief. Until the 1360s, its principal form seen in testaments was indiscriminate handouts of pennies or scraps of bread to the poor. By the late fourteenth century, such offerings to "the poor of Christ" had disappeared. In their place, new dowry funds grew in number and value, which were neither indiscriminate nor one-off injections of aid. Now testators instructed their executors or specific churches to select small numbers of deserving girls of "buon costume" to be granted dowries that would initiate and support new families over a lifetime and from which further families could proliferate.[68]

10.9 Epilogue

Had the Black Death occurred without successive waves of plague at 10–12-year intervals and descending levels of mortality, its consequences for thought and action would have been different. As the stabs at population recovery following plague outbreaks from 1348 to 1400 suggest, the Black Death might have led to resilience but not to transformation. Circa 1400, pre-Black Death population numbers could have even been totally recovered in places, but with it, much the same practices that had buttressed medieval economies and societies from the early fourteenth century with their more sluggish, episodic dynamics of change would have persisted. Instead, after the first decades of the fifteenth century, signs of collapse or resilience alone are hard to find in Western Europe.

However, as Stuart Borsch's comparative study on landholding between England and Egypt demonstrates, the Black Death did not spell everywhere the same long-term consequences. Long-term increases in wealth for English peasants after the Black Death contrasted sharply with the impoverishment of Egyptian peasants.[69] Within Western Europe, the Black Death consequences could also differ, as with transformations favorable to agrarian laborers. In places they sprang immediately after the Black Death, while for others, they lagged for a generation or more. Furthermore, some of these transformations, such as the prosperity of mountain people in Tuscany or Europe-wide trends in economic equality lasted a century, while settlement patterns or the *paesaggio* of the countryside endured into the twentieth century. If we wish to image the experiences of those who survived the Black Death along with their children, the timing of these switches from poverty to prosperity is crucial. In places, Black Death survivors would have never experienced or envisaged the plagues' eventual silver linings. Young Tuscan mountaineers who survived the Black Death, for instance, would have seen their livelihoods and family prospects spiraling downwards, imperiled by further plagues, wars, and increasingly disproportionate taxation. No matter what the eventual fortunes of their distant progeny, these survivors' worlds were neither of resilience nor transformation; rather, they were ones of severe decline or collapse. They would have been left unaware of changes on the horizons that came into focus only during the second decade of the fifteenth century.

Here, reflections on post-Black Death trajectories might assist in imaging our present pandemic predicament. Thus far, no pandemic in history has shown the kaleidoscopic differences in health consequences from one country to the next, even among neighboring nations with comparable social, ecological, and economic profiles. Extraordinary contrasts in COVID-19 case numbers and mortalities have arisen, for instance, between Norway and Sweden; Ireland and England; Uruguay and Brazil; and Canada and the USA. As with the early fifteenth-century Tuscan mountaineer, so too for us today, it remains difficult to envisage the futures that await our children or how governments' handling or mishandling of the pandemic will affect these countries' subsequent prominence.

Notes & References

1 See especially his *Medieval and Renaissance Pistoia: The Social History of an Italian Town* (New Haven: Yale University Press, 1967) and, posthumously, his *The Black Death and the Transformation of the West*, ed. Cohn (Cambridge: Harvard University Press, 1997). On the origins of a Black Death silver lining with I. F. C. Hecker's *Der schwarze Tod im vier-*

sehnten Jahrhundert, published in 1832; see Gaye Getz, "Black Death and the Silver Lining: Meaning, Continuity, and Revolutionary Change in Histories of Medieval Plague," *Journal of the History of Biology* 24 (1991): 265–289.

2 David Herlihy, *Opera Mulierbria: Women and Work in Medieval Europe* (New York: McGraw-Hill, 1990), 128.

3 Matteo Villani, *Cronica con la continuazione di Filippo Villani*, ed. Giuseppe Porta, 2 vols (Parma: Fondazione Pietro Bembo, 1995), I, 301 and II, 585–586.

4 F. M. Page, *The Estates of Crowland Abbey* (Cambridge: Cambridge University Press, 1934), 120–125; and Ada Elizabeth Levett, *Studies in Manorial History*, ed. H. M. Cam, M. Coate, and L. S. Sutherland (Oxford: Oxford University Press, 1938), 249–250 and 253.

5 Henri Dubois, "La dépression: XIVe et XVe siècles," in *Histoire de la population française*: I. *Des origines à la Renaissance*, 4 vols, ed. Jacques Dupâquier (Paris: P.U.F., 1988), 313–366, 321.

6 Giovanni Villani, *Nuova cronica*, ed. Giuseppe Porta, 3 vols (Parma: Fondazione Pietro Bembo, 1990–1991), III, book XII, chapter XCIV.

7 The earliest work to analyze these statistics is Niccolò Rodolico. *La Democrazia fiorentina nel suo tramonto (1378–1382)* (Bologna: Zanichelli, 1905), 18–21. Enrico Fiumi, "La demografia fiorentina nelle pagine di Giovanni Villani," *Archivio Storico Italiano*, CVIII (1950): 78–158, questioned Villani's statistics. See more recently W. R. Day, Jr., "The Population of Florence before the Black Death: Survey and Synthesis," *Journal of Medieval History* 28 (2002): 93–129. David Herlihy and Christiane Klapisch-Zuber, *Les Toscans et leurs familles: Une étude du Catasto de 1427* (Paris: Presse del foundation nationale des sciences politiques, 1978), 173–177, have provided the most thorough analysis of these figures and the population trajectories of the Florentine state into the modern period.

8 Herlihy and Klapisch-Zuber, *Les Toscans*, 177.

9 See for instance, J. F. D. Shrewsbury, *A History of Bubonic Plague in the British Isles* (Cambridge: Cambridge University Press, 1970), 24, 36, 40, 77, 104, who claimed that the Black Death mortality in England could not have exceeded 1 in 20 (123).

10 On immigration into Florence immediately after the Black Death, see Charles M. de La Roncière, *Prix et salaires à Florence au XIVe siècle (1280–1380)* (Rome: École française de Rome, 1982), 661–678.

11 Giovanni Villani, *Cronaca*, II, Libr XI, cap. CXIII, 232–235.

12 Day, Jr., "The Population of Florence," does not attempt any estimates of the city's demographic decline between 1338 and 1348, except to say that it declined (108).

13 See Herlihy and Klapisch, *Les Toscans*, 177.

14 On Florence's population trends through the sixteenth century, see Herlihy and Klapisch, *Les Toscans*, 181–188.

15 Enrico Fiumi, "Fioritura e decadenza dell'economia fiorentine," *Archivio Storico Italiano* 117 (1959): 447–502.

16 Şevket Pamuk, "The Black Death and the origins of the 'Great Divergence' across Europe, 1300–1600," *European Review of Economic History* 11 (2007): 289–317, 293–294.

17 Ibid., and Robert C. Allen, "The Great Divergence in European Wages and Prices from the Middle Ages to the First World War," *Explorations in Economic History* 38 (2001): 411–447, 434–444.

18 Samuel Cohn, Jr, *Creating the Florentine State: Peasants and Rebellion, 1348–1434* (Cambridge: Cambridge University Press, 1999), 92.

19 Ibid., 109 and pt. 2.

20 Maurice Beresford, *The Lost Villages of England* (London: Lutterworth Press, 1954), 157 and 159.

21 Christopher Dyer, "Villages in crisis: social dislocation and desertion, 1370–1520," in *Deserted Villages Revisited*, ed. Dyer and Richard Jones (Hatfield: University of Hertfordshire Press, 2010), 28–45, 45.

22 *Polyhistoria fratris Bartholomæi Ferrariensis ordinis Prædicatorum ab an. MCCLXXXVII usque ad MCCCLXVII called Libro del Polistore*, in *Rerum Italicarum Scriptores* [hereafter, *RIS*], ed. Lodovico Muratori (Milan: Societatis Palatinae, 1738), XXIV, 806.

23 *Storie Pistoresi [MCCC-MCCCXLVIII]*, ed. Silvio Adrasto Barbi, *RIS*, XI/5 (Città di Castello: Lapi, 1907–1927), 236.

24 *Knighton's Chronicle 1337–1396*, ed. and trans. G. H. Martin (Oxford: Oxford University Press, 1995), 96–97.

25 Nico Voigtländer and Hans-Joachim Voth, "Persecution Perpetuated: The Medieval origins of Anti-Semitic Violence in Nazi Germany," *The Quarterly Journal of Economics* 127 (2012): 1339–1392; for a higher estimate, see Cohn, "The Black Death and the Burning of Jews," *Past & Present* 196 (2007): 3–36.

26 Giovanni Boccaccio, *Decameron*, ed. Vittore Branca (Milan: Mandadori, 1976), 13–15.

27 Matteo Villani, *Cronica*, I, 11.

28 Antonio Pucci, "Come in questo quadro delle crudeltà della pestilenza," in *Storia Letteraria d'Italia*, ed. Natalino Sapegno (Milan: Villardi, 1948), 413.

29 Trials of supposed plague spreaders arose in the 1530s into the early eighteenth century. These, however, were few and scattered. In the most infamous of these, Milan's trials during the plague of 1630, around ten suspects were executed, not the thousands burnt in 1348; see Cohn, *Epidemics: Hate & Compassion from the Plague of Athens to AIDS* (Oxford: Oxford University Press, 2018), ch. 6.

30 For the geographic coverage and trends in abandonment, see ibid., ch. 3.

31 *Chronicon Aegidii Li Muisis, abbatis Sancti-Martini Tornacensis alterum*, in Corpus Chronicorum Flandriae, ed. J.-J. de Smet, 4 vols. (Brussels: Commission royale d'Histoire, 1837–65), iii, 341–342.

32 See Cohn, *Epidemics: Hate & Compassion*, ch. 3, and Daniel Bornstein, *The Bianchi of 1399: Popular Devotion in Late Medieval Italy* (Ithaca: Cornell University Press, 1993).

33 Philip Slavin, *Experiencing Famine in Fourteenth-Century Britain* (Torhout: Brepols, 2019), 258, who does not mention ergotism, which historians such as Le Roy Laduire, Neithard Bulst, and others have argued may have been this famine's principal disease.

34 For these arguments and references, see Jordan, *The Great Famine: Northern Europe in the Early Fourteenth Century* (Princeton: Princeton University Press, 1996), 184–185. Slavin, *Experiencing famine*, 358, emphasizes the important consequences of the bovine pestilence of 1319–1320 and subsequent food shortages in the 1320s, thereby claiming that signs of recovery do not begin until the 1330s. Bruce Campbell, *The Great Transition: Climate, Disease and Society in the Late-Medieval World* (Cambridge: Cambridge University Press, 2016), 52, 198, argues that longer-term climatic catastrophes triggered by falling global temperatures and determined by "diminished solar irradiance and low or zero sunspot activity," were the underlying causes of this and other famines and pestilences of the early fourteenth century.

35 Slavin, *Experiencing famine*, 5 and 288, suggests that in England, it was higher, 20% and 17%, respectively, but admits it is an "educated guess" (288).

36 Campbell and Mark Overton, "A New Perspective on Medieval and Early Modern Agriculture: Six Centuries of Norfolk Farming c. 1250-c.1850," *Past & Present* (1993), 38–105; more generally Campbell, "Population-Pressure, Inheritance and the Land Market in a Fourteenth-Century Peasant Community," in *Land, Kinship and Life-Cycle*, ed. Richard Smith (Cambridge: Cambridge University Press, 1984), 87–135, 107; and for Jordan and others cited above, see Jordan, *The Great Famine*, 184–185.

37 On these arguments, see Slavin, *Experiencing Famine*, 358–363.

38 William C. Jordan "The Great Famine: 1315–1322 Revisited," in *Ecologies and Economies in Medieval and Early Modern Europe: Studies in Environmental History for Richard C. Hoffmann*, ed. Scott G. Bruce (Leiden: Brill, 2010), 45–62, 60.

39 Food shortages were severe in Rome, Siena, and Florence in the late 1320s, but, unlike the north of Europe in 1314–1317, municipal interventions with subsided shipments of grain and rationing caused these crises to be short-lived; see Cohn, *Lust for Liberty: The*

Politics of Social Revolt in Medieval Europe, 1200–1425 (Cambridge: Harvard University Press, 2006), 71. According to La Roncière, *Prix et salaires*, 758, during Florence's worst food shortage in 1329, the price of wheat had increased by a factor of 6, but in Flanders in 1316, the increase was by 24 times.

40 Le Roy Ladurie, *Les paysans de Languedoc*, 2 vols (Paris: De Gruyter Mouton, 1966).

41 Cohn, Creating the Florentine State, 18, 40, 102–103.

42 Matteo Villani, *Cronica*, I, 93; and Herlihy, *The Black Death*, 49.

43 Herlihy, *Medieval and Renaissance Pistoia.*

44 Herlihy and Klapisch, *Les Toscans et leurs familles.*

45 Emilio Sereni, *Storia del paesaggio agrario italiano* (Bari: Laterza, 1961).

46 Guy Bois, *Crise du féodalisme: économie rurale et démographie en Normandie orientale du débute du 14e siècle au milieu du 16e siècle* (Paris: Presses de la Fondation Nationale des Sciences Politiques, 1976), ch. 4.

47 Dyer, *Standards of Living in the Later Middle Ages: Social Change in England c.1200–1520* (Cambridge: Cambridge University Press, 1989); idem, *Making a Living in the Middle Ages: The People of Britain 850–1520* (New Haven:Yale University Press, 2002); and A. R. Bridbury, *Economic Growth: England in the Later Middle Ages* (Brighton: Harvester Press, 1975).

48 J. A. F. Thomson, *The Transformation of Medieval England, 1370–1529* (London: Longman, 1983), 13.

49 Jan Dumolyn, Wouter Ryckbosch, Mathijs Speecke, "Cycles of Urban Revolt in Medieval Flanders: The Economics of Political Conflict," in *La mobilita sociale nel medioevo italiano. 4. Cambiamento economic dinamiche sociali (secoli XI-XV)* (Rome: Viella, 2019), 329–348, 326; and J. H. Munro, "Wage-Stickiness, Monetary Changes, and Real Incomes in Late-Medieval England and the Low Countries, 1300–1500: Did Money Matter?," *Research in Economic History* 21 (2003): 185–297, 219.

50 George Holmes, *The Estates of the Higher Nobility in Fourteenth-Century England* (Cambridge: Cambridge University Press, 1957), 88, 90, 113–119.

51 Hilton, *Bond Men Made Free: Medieval Peasant Movements and the English Rising of 1381* (London: Temple Smith, 1973), part II. For discussions of a second serfdom in East of the Elbe, see among other places, *The Brenner Debate: Agrarian Class Structure and Economic Development in Pre-Industrial Europe*, ed. T. H. Aston and C. H. E. Philpin (Cambridge: Cambridge University Press, 1985).

52 Also see A. R. Bridbury, *The English Economy from Bede to the Reformation* (Woodbridge: The Boydell & Brewer, 1992), 210, and others to mark the shift to lords leasing out their demesnes only by the last quarter of the fourteenth century.

53 See Cohn, "After the Black Death: Labour Legislation and Attitudes Towards Labour in Late-Medieval Western Europe," *Economic History Review* 60 (2007): 457–485.

54 Chris Given-Wilson, "The Problem of Labour in the Context of English Government, c.1350–1450," in *The Problem of Labour in Fourteenth-Century England* (Woodbridge: Boydell & Brewer, 2000), 85–100, 88–89; Cohn, "After the Black Death," 476–477.

55 Cohn, *Popular Protest in Late Medieval English Towns* (Cambridge: Cambridge University Press, 2013), 127–128, 305.

56 Mark Bailey, *The Decline of Serfdom in Late Medieval England: From Bondage to Freedom* (Woodbridge: Boydell & Brewer, 2014), esp., 285–306, cit. on 287.

57 Herlihy, *The Black Death*, 52–53.

58 On the systemic change in marriage patterns, see John Hajnal, "Age at Marriage and Proportions Marrying," *Population Studies* 7 (1953): 111–136.

59 Christiane Klapisch-Zuber, "Women Servants in Florence during the Fourteenth and Fifteenth Centuries," in *Women and Work in Preindustrial Europe*, ed. Barbara A. Hanawalt (Bloomington: Indiana University Press, 1986), 56–80, on rising salaries of domestic servants and nurse-maids (*balie*) in fifteenth-century Florence.

60 Cohn, *Creating the Florentine State*, ch. 3.

61 Wrigley and Schofield, *The Population History of England: A Reconstruction* (London: Edward Arnold, 1981); and Herlihy, *Black Death*, 53.

62 Herlihy, *The Black Death*, 57.

63 For longer periods of inequality not expanding but based on combinations of sources and estimates taken from archaeological remains, see Walter Scheidel, *The Great Leveller: Violence and the Global History of Inequality from the Stone Age to the Present* (Oxford: Oxford University Press, 2017); and Scheidel and Steven J. Friesen, "The Size of the Economy and the Distribution of Income in the Roman Empire," *The Journal of Roman Studies* 99 (2009): 61–91. As they admit: "Our reconstruction is in its entirety a matter of controlled conjecture: undeniably conjecture, given the paucity of 'hard' data" (63).

64 With various participants stemming from his European Research Council project on inequality, Alfani has written over twenty working papers and essays in journals such as *Economic History Review*. For a summary of these and the project's major conclusions, see his "Economic inequality in preindustrial times: Europe and beyond," *Journal of Economic Literature* 59, 2021): 3–44. For the Middle East, see Pamuk, "The Black Death and the origins of the 'Great Divergence' across Europe, 1300–1600" ; and idem and Maya Shatzmiller, "Plagues, Wages, and Economic Change in the Islamic Middle East 700–1500," *Journal of Economic History* 74, 1 (2014): 196–229.

65 See Cohn, "Rich and Poor in Western Europe, c. 1375–1475: The Political Paradox of Material Well-Being," in *Approaches to Poverty in Medieval Europe: Complexities, Contradictions, Transformations, c. 1100–1500*, ed. Sharon Farmer (Turnhout: Brepols, 2016), 145–173. On the changing character of equality after the Black Death from an equality grounded in poverty across class divides to one propelled by rising real wages of nonelites, see Cohn, *Paradoxes of Equality in Renaissance Italy* (Cambridge University Press), ch. 1. On equality as grounding in poverty, also see Scheidel, *The Great Leveller*, 78–79; and Scheidel and Friesen, "The Size of the Economy and the Distribution of Income in the Roman Empire."

66 Cohn, "Piété et commande d'oeuvres d'art après la Peste Noire," *Annales: Histoire, Sciences Sociales* 51 (1996): 551–573, idem, "Renaissance Attachment to Things: Material Culture in Last Wills and Testaments," *Economic History Review* 65 (2012): 984–1004.

67 Cohn, "The Place of the Dead in Flanders and Tuscany: Towards a Comparative History of the Black Death," in *The Place of the Dead: Death and Remembrance in Late Medieval and Early Modern Europe*, ed. Bruce Gordon and Peter Marshall (Cambridge: Cambridge University Press, 2000), 17–43.

68 In addition to the above, see Cohn, *The Cult of Remembrance and the Black Death: Six Renaissance Cities in Central Italy* (Baltimore: Johns Hopkins University Press, 1992).

69 Stuart J. Borsch, *The Black Death in Egypt and England: A Comparative Study* (Austin: University of Texas Press, 2005).

11 The Cases of Novgorod and Muscovy

Using Systems Thinking to Understand Historical Civilizational Response to Exogenous Threats

Miriam Pollock, Benjamin D. Trump, and Igor Linkov

11.1 Introduction to Resilience and Systems Thinking

The study of complex systems is a growing field of scholarship driven by the desire to understand how various societal, infrastructural, and economic interconnections collectively influence actions and outcomes. Such systems thinking usually seeks to understand modern society's susceptibility to extreme events or shocks, focusing on the increasing reliance of modern complex societies upon interconnected digital systems that facilitate functionality. Though this sort of scholarship is certainly helpful in building resilience for modern society against a variety of uncertain and complex disruptive events, its emphasis on exploring modern systems to the exclusion of the past ignores a promising avenue of inquiry—the ability to explain and understand why certain historical civilizations or institutions were able to survive and recover from significant disruptions of their own, and why others collapsed or withered into a reduced form for extended periods of time. In addition to providing a unique approach to historical analysis, insights gleaned from applying systems thinking to past societies can be used in constructing more resilient societies for the future.

Systems theory and resilience are philosophies and analytical strategies that can help explain how internal system structure and characteristics (or "endogeneities") influence the capacity of systems to prevent, mitigate, and recover from external shocks and stresses of a systemic nature (or "exogeneities"). Systemic threats are those with consequences or outcomes that can reverberate throughout various elements of society, such as an epidemic that has the capacity to disrupt local economies or governance procedures. States with rigid, maladaptive, or brittle institutional, political, and economic systems are prone to lasting disruption and even collapse. On the other hand, those with the capacity for recovery and adaptation in the face of systemic exogenous shocks are far more likely to survive and even thrive in the aftermath of such disruptions.

DOI: 10.4324/9781003331384-14

A key characteristic here includes a civilization or state's *resilience*, or its capacity to plan and prepare for, absorb and withstand, recover from, and adapt to adverse events and systemic disruptions. Within such a notion, a series of complex and interconnected systems (e.g., trade, defense, environment, infrastructure, society) influence the characteristics and function of a given civilization, where nested dependencies between such systems often generate cascading effects (e.g., a reduction in commerce can result in fewer resources to spend on military power).[1]

A civilization with high resilience is one that is better able to overcome disruptions of a systemic nature, while one with low resilience would require considerable time and resources to recover from a systemic disruption—if recovery were even possible. History is rife with examples of systemic threats that had large impacts on states, such as the Black Death, which caused the broad collapse of fourteenth-century western economies. Within such examples, an exogenous shock leverages a brittle component of a societal system—be it internal civil strife, an underprepared military, environmental, or agricultural calamity, or any number of other disruptions that a civilization may face—resulting in the society's collapse. Often, multiple such stressors co-occur and influence one another in a vicious feedback loop. Conversely, resilient societies are able to absorb, recover from, and adapt to the stressor at hand, enabling their survival despite losses.

Systemic resilience provides a theoretical explanation of why certain civilizations, states, organizations, or groups are able to prevent, withstand, recover from, and/or adapt to crises and disruptions—as well as why others are susceptible to failure and even collapse. Exogenous events are commonly touted as responsible for collapses, such as the decline and fall of the Western Roman Empire due to barbarian invasion or the extensive collapse of much of Eastern Europe and Asia due to an unstoppable Mongol Horde. Such explanations are tempting—they offer relatively neat and simple explanations to traumatic turning points in history—yet they often diminish the importance of *why* a given nation or tribe was susceptible to such exogenous attacks in the first place. Systemic resilience requires us to consider the endogenous principles and system interdependencies that make a nation vulnerable to decline or collapse on the one hand or swift recovery and adaptation toward an even more successful future on the other. This includes an understanding of how core societal systems are developed and strengthened both in isolation and through feedback loops (e.g., a robust economy enabling a civilization to backstop military expenses to ward off invaders). Some of the core systems that inform civilizational resilience against systemic threats include economic, social, religious, cultural, military, and governance/institutional systems.

One pivotal period in history where an understanding of systemic resilience can provide a better understanding of civilizational response to extreme exogenous shock is that of Mongol invasion and conquest of the Kievan Rus'. Beginning in the early thirteenth century, an expanding Mongol Empire came into contact with the loose confederation of principalities comprising Kievan Rus', destroying most of them. Interestingly, however, certain principalities were able to persist and even thrive despite the Mongol disruption. Using the language of the resilience of complex systems, we can make sense of why specific polities were able to recover from and adapt to the considerable military, societal, and economic disruption wrought by the Mongols and their successor states.

This chapter is organized as follows. First, brief background on Kievan Rus', Novgorod, Muscovy, and the Mongols is provided. Then, the characteristics which contributed to Novgorod's resilience are explored. Next, Muscovy's resilience is assessed in a similar fashion. The chapter concludes by proposing that resilience and systems theory can enhance our understanding of historical civilizations and events and have potentially broader applications than typically assumed.

11.2 Applying Resilience and Systems Theory to Kievan Rus' and Muscovy: The Cases of Novgorod (Early Thirteenth Century) and Muscovy (Fourteenth and Fifteenth Centuries)

Kievan Rus' was a confederation of principalities founded in the late ninth century by Scandinavian chieftains, called the Riurikids, who soon became Slavicized. The Rus' lands stretched over much of what is now modern-day Belarus, Ukraine, and Western Russia. The Rus' throne was at Kiev, and the grand prince of Kiev was officially ruler of all Rus'. In practice, however, the grand prince executed minimal power and control over the various principalities that constituted his realm. The other princes were free to contest the throne at Kiev, and each principality had a significant degree of autonomy (Thompson and Ward, 2018).

The major cities, and consequently principalities, were Kiev, Chernigov, Polotsk, Smolensk, Pskov, Rostov, Suzdal, Vladimir, Ryazan, and Novgorod. Together, along with rural settlements and unpopulated or sparsely populated lands, they constituted Kievan Rus'. These territories were surrounded by different tribes, at times friendly and at times threatening.

At its height, the population of Kievan Rus' has been estimated at between seven and eight million. Of this maximum population, fewer than one million lived in towns and cities. In most of these towns the population was fewer than 5,000 people; in the largest, like Kiev, there lived probably between 20,000 and 50,000 people (Thompson and Ward, 2018).

While the eleventh century was a Golden Age for Kievan Rus', with the state reaching its geographic height and flourishing economically, over the next century things began to fall apart. The Byzantine Empire, formerly an important and powerful trading partner to Kievan Rus', declined in importance, with Constantinople eventually sacked in 1204. New trade routes not involving Rus' or Byzantium rose in prominence. Meanwhile, a series of weak rulers in Kiev led to internal conflict, with the federation itself becoming brittle. As Thompson and Ward (2018) explain, by the late twelfth century the principalities of Rus' were spending "more time fighting each other than their common external enemies." The grand princes of Kiev had little chance of curtailing such inter-principality warfare, leading to the gradual waning of both military power and period is missing here after cohesion.[2] This, in turn, left them more vulnerable to external invaders.

By the time of the first Mongol incursion into the region, the principalities varied in size, power, and influence. During 1237–1240, the Mongols conquered all the territories of Kievan Rus', save Novgorod. Over the course of the next several centuries, a new power center would arise from the old Kievan Rus' territories: Muscovy[3]. Under the leadership of the Daniilovich princes, Muscovy emerged to challenge and eventually overthrow the Golden Horde (the principal Mongol successor state).

Why were these two polities, Novgorod and Muscovy, able to recover and adapt, when other larger, more spiritually/politically important, or more military-inclined polities were swept aside? For Novgorod, several answers have been put forth, mostly based on the geography of the region. Halperin holds that Novgorod was not sacked merely because of its "far away" location (1985). Vaissman and Yarygin (2017), Gabriel (2004), May (2016), and Silfen (1974), among others, agree that a "timely spring thaw" (May, 2016) stopped the Mongol invasion "only by chance" (Vaissman and Yarygin, 2017), as the thaw rendered the area around Novgorod a muddy swampland through which the Mongol horsemen could not easily travel.

For Muscovy, additional importance is given to Moscow's location (Klyuchevsky, 1908-1916; Blum, 1961; Pitts, 1978; Martin, 2007; Crummey, 2013). In particular, the Moscow River, which flows through Moscow, connected Muscovy with both the Oka and Volga Rivers, the two main river systems of European Russia, making it an important trade center; three major overland trade routes also went through Moscow. Likewise, Moscow's location far north of the steppe and to the west of the border with the Mongols gave it some degree of natural protection (Crummey, 2013). This may have led refugees to flee to Moscow from Kiev, Vladimir, Rostov, and other power centers hit harder by the Mongol invasion (Klyushevsky, 1908-1916; Pitts, 1978; Crummey, 2013). In turn, the thinking goes, this increased population led to an enlarged tax base and thus an enriched Moscow (Klyuchevsky, 1908-1916). As is the case with the traditional analysis of Novgorod's success, however, such explanations are somewhat reductionist in their analysis of the broader Muscovite system and tend to underemphasize the significant economic, military, societal, and governmental innovations that characterized a resurgent Muscovite state.

What links the cases of both polities together is in fact their fundamental capacity for resilience. The resiliency of Kievan Rus' in general and Novgorod and Muscovy in particular can be assessed along four parameters: economy, governance, military (structure and power), and social cohesion and religion.

These characteristics are crucial for understanding the systems at play in Kievan Rus'; moreover, they provide us a structure for identifying and cataloging the ways in which Novgorod and Muscovy were unique.

Both polities struggled under the Mongols, yet both had some endogenous ability to recover and adapt their core systems and strategies to persist and eventually overcome Mongol domination. Rather than by good fortune or a happy accident of geography or battlefield timeliness, both polities had a capacity for resilience that ultimately framed their recovery and adaptation to external stress. Using the logic of systems theory and resilience, we review both cases below.

11.3 Kievan Rus', Novgorod, and the Initial Mongol Invasion

The sources that exist for this period in Kievan Rus' can be divided into roughly two categories: Contemporaneous written material and archaeological finds. In the first category are included a number of chronicles, primarily written and compiled by monks. The most detailed of these is *The Primary Chronicle*, which covers the history of Kievan Rus' from its apocryphal founding up until 1113. Unfortunately, ample logical and chronological inconsistencies have given scholars doubts as to the reliability of *The Primary Chronicle* (Isoaho, 2018; Karamzin, 2012; Likhachov, 2007; Duczko, 2004). Also significant is the *First Novgorod Chronicle*, which spans the period from 1016 to 1471 (*Chronicle of Novgorod*, 1914). Additional primary sources include the chronicles of peoples who interacted with the Rus', as well as legal documents, notably the *Russkaya Pravda*, or Rus' legal code, which dates from the early twelfth century. In the second category are remnants of material culture that can provide clues into the lifestyle, economies, trade networks, and governmental institutions of the residents of medieval Rus'. These include coins, official seals, household goods, pottery, jewelry, clothing and textiles, tools, weapons (especially swords), and remnants of fortresses and wooden houses. The condition of archaeological remains in Novgorod is especially good, enabling us to know more about Novgorodian society than many other contemporaneous societies (Herszenhorn, 2014; Yanin, 1990; Dolgikh and Aleksandrovskii, 2010).

The Mongol Empire represented a major threat to Rus'. In 1237, the Mongols launched a full-scale invasion of the then-weakened principalities of Kievan Rus'. The Mongol fighting style was different from that of the European powers of the time. The Mongols relied on swift, flexible, "highly-mobile" cavalry units that could deliver a crippling blow to an enemy and then retreat before the enemy had time to organize (Ostrowski, 1990).

The Mongol leader Batu Khan (grandson of Genghis Khan) founded the Golden Horde in 1242. At its height, the Golden Horde ruled over vast swathes of Eastern Europe and Asia, aided by an innovative, well-organized administrative system.

For instance, the highly developed postal system operated efficiently despite the Mongol's vast holdings (Halperin, 2000), enabling the collection of numerous taxes. This, in turn, contributed to a robust economy (Halperin, 2000). Another unique feature of Mongol governance was the *qarachi bey* system. Four *qarachi beys* (noble chieftains) performed a councilor duty, advising the khan (Woodworth, 2009). Their approval was necessary for most internal policy decisions, and they also tended to be present in most key foreign policy meetings and signings of agreements (Ostrowski, 2000).

The flexible Mongol administrative system was linked with the Mongols' economic success:

> Mongol institutions and bureaucratic practices were all directed toward increasing revenues and encouraging trade and commercial activity which could serve as the backbone of a nomadic economy with access to all of Eurasia.
>
> (Kalra, 2018)

The Mongols invested in infrastructure on the Silk Road, including fresh horses and safe lodging which were made available to travelers and traders (Kalra, 2018). This ensured a steady flow of commerce and trade, which contributed significantly to the economic prosperity of the Mongol Empire (Kalra, 2018).

11.3.1 Novgorod: Last Principality Standing

11.3.1.1 Economy

Novgorod began as a large town; shortly after its founding, in the late ninth or early tenth centuries, the *First Novgorod Chronicle* tells us it was already paying the substantial tribute tax of 300 *grivny* to Kiev (*Chronicle of Novgorod*, 1914). Birnbaum (1981) notes that this was a substantial sum at the time, indicating Novgorod was already a "community of some size and wealth." Novgorod's location was excellent for trade: It was on the main waterway from Scandinavia to Byzantium, and also linked Central and Eastern Europe with the Middle East via the Volga Bulgars. As a result, "Novgorod early became one of the chief points of distribution and trans-shipment in an international network of trade routes" (Birnbaum, 1981). As well as serving as a distribution center, Novgorod traded its own goods, primarily furs, honey, wax, and timber (Thompson and Ward, 2018). It also arose as a manufacturing center, a "thriving commercial" town that quickly accumulated wealth (Martin, 2007). Novgorod's merchants were so successful that—atypically for the time and region—they sometimes sponsored the construction of new churches (Martin, 2007). This indicates that wealth in the city was high enough that not just the aristocracy but also merchants had some degree of discretionary income. By the end of the eleventh century, Novgorod, having extended its dominion over resource-rich lands to the north and northeast, had "economic advantages unique among the Rus' principalities" (Martin, 2007). Feldbrugge calls

Novgorod the "wealthiest ... of all medieval Russian polities" (2018); Majeska is more equivocal but still holds that by the thirteenth century, Novgorod was likely the wealthiest of the principalities of Kievan Rus' (2016).

Its closest rival economically was likely Kiev. From the ninth to the middle of the eleventh century, Kiev was the biggest city in Rus' both in terms of area and population. While neither geographic size nor population is direct evidence for the economic strength of a city, a correlation is generally assumed (Mezentsev, 1989). Accordingly, by evaluating the archaeological evidence Mezentsev can conclude that:

> [T]here can be no doubt that Kiev underwent a period of intensive socio-economic, political, and cultural expansion in the ninth to eleventh centuries. Various sources indicate that in this period Kiev attracted population from all of Rus' and neighboring lands.
>
> (Mezentsev, 1989)

The relative power and prosperity of Kiev in the twelfth and thirteenth centuries has been a matter of scholarly debate (Mezentsev, 1989). Some scholars believe that despite increasing internecine conflicts and the dissolution of Rus' into independent principalities, Kiev maintained its status as the wealthiest and most powerful of the cities of Rus' through the twelfth and thirteenth centuries. However, the archaeological and textual evidence indicates that building, population growth, and territorial growth all stagnated during this period (Mezentsev, 1989). Accordingly, it seems far more likely that even if cultural and political life were vibrant in Kiev during this period, the city saw a decline in economic power. Kiev "reached its maximum extent" in the 1060s; after that time, while it "continued to be one of the greatest cities in Rus'," it had "lost primacy" (Mezentsev, 1989)—with Novgorod attaining economic superiority.

The economic picture for most of the other principalities is much murkier. Miller's 1989 study of monumental buildings in Kievan Rus' provides an invaluable way of comparing the economies of the smaller cities of Rus'. Miller notes that—across centuries and countries—monumental building (building with stone or brick) is strongly correlated with economic prosperity, whereas a lack of building is correlated with economic downturns (1989). Therefore, monumental building can be used as a metric for the economic health of a region or town. Miller only studied the period from 1138 to 1462; still, this includes the century before the Mongol invasion and accordingly is useful for our purposes. Miller has found that Ryazan and Suzdal, in the north, had a "stable and strong" building trend throughout the pre-Mongol period. Additionally, he notes that:

> [B]uilding in the northern lands of Novgorod [including Pskov], Suzdalia [including Vladimir and Rostov], and Riazan' increased not only over time but also as a percentage of total building in Rus'. The increase was

significant, from 41 percent during 1138-1162 to 63 percent during 1213-1237. … It appears likely that northern Rus' was growing in wealth and possibly in population more rapidly than Rus' as a whole before the Mongol invasion.

(Miller, 1989)

Miller's assertion about the relative wealth of northern Rus', of which Novgorod constituted a major part, reinforces the textual and archaeological evidence cited above regarding Novgorod's wealth. In contrast, construction in other regions, such as Polotsk and Smolensk, dropped off almost completely decades *before* the Mongol incursions into Rus'. Thus, while these regions may at one point have enjoyed prosperity, they saw an economic decline that was not triggered by the Mongols and, in fact, preceded the Mongol invasion.

In summary, then, based on the limited sources available, it appears that Kiev was the wealthiest region from the formation of Kievan Rus' until the 1060s. After that time, Kiev seems to have mostly stopped growing, while the principalities of northern Rus' grew bigger and richer. Among these, a strong case can be made that Novgorod was economically preeminent, in large part due to its critical location on the path of several major trade routes, as well as the talent and prolificacy of its artisans and its access to highly sought-after fur pelts. Critically, diverse and growing trade routes into Novgorod also afforded the city's leadership a window into how other polities governed their territories and addressed critical challenges of the day—providing not only resilient commerce systems not dependent upon a single trade partner but also inspiration and foresight into how to improve state governance and economics to overcome disruptions and limitations posed by a variety of endogenous and exogenous stressors (Hynes et al. 2022).

On the eve of the Mongol invasion, Novgorod was one of the wealthiest principalities in all of Rus'—and likely the wealthiest. This gave it the resources to both pay tribute to invading Mongol forces and reposition and outfit its geopolitical and military capacities to address other threats (e.g., the Teutonic Order via the Battle of the Ice—April 1242).

11.3.1.2 Governance

The principalities of Kievan Rus' can be organized, following Vladimirsky-Budanov (1909/2005) and Thompson and Ward (2018, p. 24), into three geographical regions, each with its own predominating form of government. In the Southwest, comprising Volynia and Galicia, the boyars ruled. In the Northwest, including Novgorod and its satellite city of Pskov, rule was by the *veche*; Thompson and Ward (2018) characterize this as "democratic/oligarchic." The Northeast, with Suzdal and Moscow, was monarchic, with rule by a prince.

Much has been written about the Novgorodian system of governance, and the extent to which it resembled a democratic system. It is beyond the scope of this chapter to do a deep dive into the various arguments; in brief, we can definitively say that Novgorod had a *more* democratic system of government than did most of its contemporaries. Most of the city officials of Novgorod were elected by something called the *veche*,[4] a congregation of all the free men of the city.[5] After 1136, the *veche* was also responsible for inviting princes to rule—and for ordering them to leave. While some scholars argue that this system was "illusory democracy" (Yanin, 1962),[6] with the people of Novgorod "not really masters of their own destiny" (Paul, 2008), the general scholarly consensus is that the *veche* was, if not democratic, at least proto-democratic or republican and that the people of Novgorod had far more control over their governance than did the peoples of the other principalities (Thompson and Ward, 2018). As neither women nor slaves had a voice in the *veche*, Novgorod of course cannot be said to have been perfectly republican; nevertheless, it was clearly *more* democratic than its peers.

The *veche* elected *posadniki* (mayors), *tysiatskie* (government/military officials[7]), from 1136 princes, and from 1156 even archbishops (though these still had to be confirmed by the metropolitan of Kiev) (Paul, 2007, Platanov, 1965). Thus Podvigina is able to conclude that Novgorod was a state "very much *sui generis*, sharply differing in its political system from all the other ancient Russian lands" (1976). Democratic governments generally perform better—more resiliently—than other forms of government (Mandelbaum, 2007). Also unlike all the other principalities of Rus', Novgorod "never became consistently associated with a single branch of the [Riurikid] dynasty" (Martin, 2007, p. 44). Whether this was the cause or consequence of the relative lack of power of the prince in Novgorod, it was the people of Novgorod who had the ultimate say over who would rule them.

Different dynasties, stemming from the various sons of the early rulers of Rus', eventually managed to establish themselves in various principalities of Rus'. This was not the case in Novgorod, which was able to select its prince from among the most powerful and capable men of different dynasties (Paul, 2008). To be sure, the people did not always choose the best possible ruler to be the prince. But the unique powers of the *veche* of Novgorod ensured that if a lackluster candidate was installed, the mistake could be quickly rectified, with the bad prince expelled and a new one invited to rule instead.

Given this proto-democratic style of addressing disruption, Novgorodian leaders relied less upon a mandate of power and spirituality (as did, for instance, Kiev, Vladimir, and Chernigov) and more on pragmatism and survival—affording Novgorod the capacity to adapt to nominal Mongol suzerainty through tribute without losing legitimacy amongst the public.

Meanwhile, as the complicated *rota* succession system broke down in the mid-twelfth century, near-constant internecine infighting and squabbling rendered Kiev mostly impotent (Kollmann, 1990). Indeed, from 1235 to 1240 no fewer than seven princes ruled in Kiev (Birnbaum, 1984). Thus on the eve of the Mongol invasion, the governance of Kiev was quite brittle.

11.3.1.3 Military (Structure and Power)

Each prince of Kievan Rus' had a *druzhina*, or retinue, which consisted of between hundreds of men and a few thousand men, depending on the prince's needs, financial resources, and desires. According to Bushkovitch, the use of the term in the chronicles varies, meaning anything from "whole body of warriors at the disposal of any one Riurikovich prince" to "the private armed followers of the prince" (1980). Regardless of the narrowness or broadness of the definition, it is clear that each prince had a certain stable retinue of warriors. From the upper ranks of the *druzhina* were formed the boyars, or aristocratic class.

By the end of the eleventh century, many boyars in turn had their own *druzhinas* (Bushkovitch, 1980). In addition to these "very effective ... highly mobile corps of able-bodied, well-armed, and well-trained horsemen," each city could also call on a militia in times of emergency. The militia consisted of virtually all able-bodied men of fighting age; it was the prince's duty to provide these men with weapons and horses (Vladimirsky-Budanov, 1909/2005; Vernadsky, 1973). Often he did so by requisitioning supplies. Food would also be requisitioned or simply looted, as the military supply lines were not well-developed (Vladimirsky-Budanov, 1909/2005; Vernadsky, 1973). Members of the militia also ordinarily received a salary (the members of the *druzhina* were compensated through land and other non-monetary gifts) (Stefanovich, 2011).

Accordingly, it stands to reason that the princes of the richest lands could field the most well-fed, well-equipped, largest armies. Additionally, as each army was directly dependent upon the population size of the city from which it was drawn (Vernadsky, 1973), the largest cities could field the largest armies. As shown above, on the eve of the Mongol invasion Novgorod was probably the wealthiest principality of all Rus'. Additionally, while Kiev, with an estimated population of 50,000, was likely the biggest, Novgorod was still among the largest cities in Kievan Rus' (and all of Europe) at the time, with a population of around 30,000 (Hamm, 1993; Thompson and Ward, 2018). Therefore, we can conclude that Novgorod would have been able to field a remarkably robust, well-equipped, strong, and large fighting force financed by a diverse and wealthy economic system. Likewise, Novgorod was best positioned to overcome potential losses of equipment or manpower in the battlefield. There was a positive feedback loop among a flourishing economy, a large population, and a strong military. Each enabled and encouraged the other, and Novgorod grew in strength—and resilience.

Novgorod's unique system of governance also contributed to the resilience of its military. The pattern of princes being intermittently summoned and sent away provides further evidence for the claim that Novgorod's military was uniquely capable. As the people chose the prince directly, and as the prince was generally in charge of military matters, the people tended to select militarily competent princes. If a prince was not, he could—and would—be expelled.

The Novgorod Chronicle provides numerous cases of a prince being expelled or rejected by the *veche* (*Chronicle of Novgorod*, 1914). While in most cases the Chronicle does not note the exact reason that the people disliked the prince, the struggles of 1136, after which the *veche* would choose the prince, are illustrative. In this instance, the first in which the Novgorodians forcibly expelled a prince, the Chronicle cites three reasons the people gave for not wanting Vsevolod to remain prince. Notably, one reason is his military incompetence (*Chronicle of Novgorod*, 1914). It is also useful to remark on an important check on the ambitions of the prince at Novgorod. He was legally bound "not to plot a war without the word of Novgorod" (Vladimirsky-Budanov, 1909/2005). While Vladimirsky-Budanov (1909/2005) notes that this principle was operative in other principalities as well, only at Novgorod was it codified into law. The competent governance of Novgorod directly contributed to its adept military.

Novgorod was probably the wealthiest city of Kievan Rus', one of the largest, and the only one to elect a prince and, consequently, military commander. Both because of its enviable economic position and unique form of governance, Novgorod had an especially powerful and competent military that fostered a meritocratic system of military leadership and strategy. And a powerful and competent military, well-supplied and trained and with an experienced and talented commander at the helm, is a resilient military. The smaller principalities were unable to field large or well-supplied forces nor were other principalities able to reject poor commanders and select the best ones. As such, Novgorod had one of the most resilient militaries of all the principalities of Kievan Rus'. At the same time, the Novgorodian prince had the wisdom, as well as the approval of his constituents, not to engage the Mongols under Subutai or Batu Khan. Due to this, the Novgorodians were able to recover from tribute demands yet still field capable forces to ward off other attackers (e.g., at the Battle of the Ice).

11.3.1.4 Social Cohesion and Religion

Socially, Novgorod was cohesive, with disagreements among the townspeople on political matters mitigated by the strong Novgorodian identity. This identity was encapsulated by the peoples' name for their town: "Lord Novgorod the Great." The anthropomorphization of Novgorod indicates the intensity and robustness of its identity. Even sovereignty did not belong to an individual (such as the prince or the archbishop) but to the city itself, with the mayors, religious elite, and boyars acting "as a collective in formulating and executing policies" (Paul, 2007).

As with other spheres, the unique religious and spiritual life within Novgorod gave it a degree of flexibility in facing disruptions such as an external invading force. Compromise, rather than outright military resistance, was acceptable to the social mores of the Novgorodian public and leadership, whereas such willing tribute and subjugation was unthinkable in other Rus' principalities. In this way, the resilient religious system within Novgorod was fundamentally rooted in pragmatism—survival at all costs. Novgorod's Church spread its houses of worship more or less evenly throughout the city while keeping its own unchallenged center inside the Detinets (Kremlin), namely, at St. Sophia Cathedral and the adjoining episcopal palace, known as the House of St. Sophia. Throughout the twelfth century, the number of churches in Novgorod increased significantly. This construction contributed to social integration and cohesion by physically uniting the different districts, creating a unified and coherent city (Paul, 2003). Perhaps even more importantly, the Church established a chain of largely fortified monasteries in the immediate environs of the city, thus providing it if not with a formidable outer defense system then at least with an "early warning system" (Birnbaum, 1981).

Novgorod's Church was uniquely powerful in Rus': Novgorod was the only archbishopric in the Russian Church through the late fourteenth century, and only Kiev's metropolitan outranked Novgorod's archbishop (Paul, 2007). Additionally, the archbishop tended to have more power in secular affairs than his fellow bishops in other regions of Rus' (Paul, 2007). Another unique aspect was that Novgorod's archbishop was usually chosen by lots by the *veche*, rather than appointed by the metropolitan or grand prince (as were other bishops in Rus') (Paul, 2007). Taken together, these factors point to a strong, resilient, and cohesive Church that both reflected and contributed to the social cohesion of Novgorod.

11.3.2 Assessing Novgorodian Resilience Amid Mongol Invasion

The theory that Novgorod's distant and tree-riddled geography helped it escape pillaging at the hands of the Mongols is rather unsatisfactory. By the time the Mongols reached the borderlands of the principality of Novgorod, they were more than 5500 km from the Mongol capital at Kharkhorin and a mere 35 km from Novgorod (*Chronicle of Novgorod*, 1914). The Mongol Empire would come to be the largest contiguous empire in history, and exhibited great prowess at defeating massive armies on all manner of terrain. The Mongols had adequate logistics, supplies, and military strategy to contest Novgorod—evidenced by their swift conquest of most other principalities. As nomads, they were used to riding long distances on horseback in adverse weather conditions. The Mongol *yam*, or postal service, enabled everything from messages to fresh fruits from across the vast Mongol Empire to be delivered to the Khan in a speedy and reliable manner (Lane, 2004). The efficiency of this system attests to the logistical capabilities of the Mongols, which surely translated to their military supply chains as well.

Even if mud and flooding may have temporarily halted the Mongols, there is no reason they could not have waited out the spring for the mud to dry. Indeed, "It was the habit of the Mongols to stop fighting in the spring and let their horses go free to water and graze, and to multiply so that they would be ready for war in the autumn" (Sinor, 1999). It would not have been difficult or unusual for the Mongols to simply return to Novgorod in better weather conditions, i.e. fall or winter. Novgorod was a wealthy and powerful region, and its conquest would have been sure to enrich the Horde.

We argue that more than Novgorod's swamp-like spring conditions or northerly location, it was its resilience that enabled it to resist destruction by the Mongols. Internal characteristics, rather than externalities, can best explain Novgorod's escape from ruin. The other principalities of Kievan Rus' lacked resilience: Political strife, weakening trade routes, limited or mostly adversarial contact with neighbors, poor social cohesion, lack of a strong identity, and disorganized military units, among other issues, rendered the majority of the principalities of Kievan Rus' in the decades before the Mongol invasion quite susceptible to exogenous threats. In other words, they were vulnerable, rigid, and brittle, poorly equipped to face an unexpected and unprecedented attack.

Novgorod, on the other hand, was quite resilient. Its economy was strong—perhaps the strongest in all of Kievan Rus'—and diversified. Its people essentially elected their prince, making internecine conflict rare and governance competent and pragmatic. The people of Novgorod had a strong identity, a large degree of social cohesion, and secure religious beliefs. We can view Novgorod as a system, with all these elements operating in combination to ensure the system of Novgorod was particularly capable of preparing for and withstanding the Mongol attack. Essentially, it was not because of the strategic decisions of the Mongols or because of spring "only by chance" arriving in the nick of time that Novgorod did not fall, but because of Novgorod itself: Its ability to prepare for and withstand adverse and unexpected events, or in other words, its inherent resilience.

11.4 1263–1480: Muscovy—Rising from the Ashes of Kievan Rus'

Why was it Moscow, and not any of the other important cities or towns of Kievan Rus', like Tver, Kiev, or Novgorod, which rose to preeminence in the centuries after the Mongol Conquest? The theories of historians tend to center around individual factors: Perhaps it was Moscow's geographic location, or else the political acumen or dynastic status of its princes, or its adept courting and bribing of the khans of the Golden Horde, or its adoption of primogeniture. We generally agree with these assessments, but argue that it was not any of these factors on its own which explains Moscow's success. Rather, the key to Moscow's ascendancy was its resilience, with each of the named factors above contributing to building resiliency through positive feedback loops.

The question of Moscow's relationship with the Golden Horde is a complicated and important one. Halperin (1985) lays out the historiography of the issue, highlighting two schools of thought. One, originating with the work of the nineteenth-century conservative scholar Karamzin, holds that "Moscow's ascendance was the direct result of its alliance with the Horde and the political and military support that came with it" (Halperin, 1985). The other, based on the thesis of Soloviev—another nineteenth-century conservative historian—asserts that Moscow leveraged *opposition* to the Mongols in order to increase its legitimacy and power (Soloviev, 1851-1879; Halperin, 1985). This latter view builds on the fact that the Horde's policy was explicitly designed to limit the power of any one principality in Rus', playing them off against one another so that none would become dominant enough to threaten the Horde. However, as part of this policy the Golden Horde spent much of the first half of the fourteenth century propping up Moscow as a counterbalance to Tver. As such, the Soloviev view cannot be completely correct: For much of its rise, Moscow in fact allied itself with the Horde and benefited from its largesse. But neither does Karamzin's view fully accord with the facts, as many times throughout the period of Mongol rule the Mongols threw their weight behind Tver or other principalities and not Moscow. In fact, it was Moscow's adaptability to the changing tides of Mongol favor, or in other words its resilience, which empowered it to succeed.

11.4.1 Economy

In economic matters, Moscow quickly adapted Mongol taxation methods in order to enhance its own wealth.

The principality started from a fairly advantaged position. Its location at the confluence of several major rivers and overland routes would have been beneficial for trade. Pitts (1965) cleverly applied graph theory to the towns of early Rus', using a shortest path algorithm to determine which town had the best connections to the others. He found that Moscow was the second-most well-connected settlement (Pitts, 1965). In other words, it was quite easy to get from Moscow to all the other towns and cities of Rus'. This would have made it a natural commercial center.

Miller (1989) found that, while still less wealthy than Novgorod, Moscow began building increasing wealth in the fourteenth century (Miller, 1989). Moscow's first stone building, evidence of a stronger economy, was erected in 1326 jointly by Grand Prince Ivan Kalita (aptly nicknamed "moneybag") and Metropolitan Peter. From that point forward, "Moscow's record of masonry construction in each time period was greater than the combined total for all other principalities in Suzdalia" (Miller, 1989). Vladimir, for example, while nominally the capital of Rus' until 1360, built just one small chapel after 1237: It never really recovered from the Mongol invasion (Miller, 1989). And while Tver's wealth also rose in the fourteenth century, this was to a lesser extent, with a decreased ability to quickly recover from attacks (Miller, 1989). For instance, from the year 1353 to 1394, Tver "was unable to afford to build at all ... as (losing) wars devastated its economy numerous times" (Miller, 1989). Moscow's economy was resilient enough to recover from such attacks.

Moscow was able to afford more than three times as many laborers as most other European cities at the time. Ostrowski (1998) asserts that by the second half of the fourteenth century, northeastern Rus' was wealthier than it had been at any point in its history. Furthermore, Ostrowski (1998) finds that this region alone "may have been more prosperous than the whole of Rus'" had ever been. The richest of the principalities within this region was, by the middle of the fourteenth century, Moscow.

Moscow generated much of its wealth through trade, given that (as discussed above) it was well-situated for commerce. Additionally, under the Mongols—the initial economic downturn notwithstanding—trade with the east was revitalized, and in such a way that benefited Moscow (Halperin, 1985; Crummey, 2013). The new hub of trade became the Golden Horde's capital at Sarai, well connected via the Volga River to Moscow. And the Mongols patrolled the main trade routes, preventing what had previously been frequent and devastating raids from nomads (Crummey, 2013). It was in the interest of the Mongols, after all, to ensure the Rus' lands would generate wealth. Moscow managed to gain more from this policy than any other principality.

The Mongol exacted a heavy series of tribute payments on all the principalities of Rus' in their control. However, Moscow was even able to turn this burdensome taxation regime into a benefit. Moscow adapted Mongol taxation methods and processes, "subvert[ing] the Mongol tribute to suit Muscovite needs" (Langer, 2007).

The Mongols ceded the duty of collecting and handing over the tribute to Rus' officials, enabling Moscow to learn and borrow the Mongol system of assessment, administration, and collection (Halperin, 1985). By the reign of Ivan I (1325–1341), the grand princes, inspired by the Mongol system, imposed additional taxes on commercial activity in both the urban center and surrounding rural lands (Langer, 2007). It is likely that the revenue generated was at first shared between the Muscovite princes and the khans of the Golden Horde; however, it seems that eventually the revenue from the commercial tax, at least, went entirely to Moscow (Kashtanov, 1982; Langer, 2007). Indeed, even after Moscow stopped paying tribute to the Mongols, it still levied the full tribute on the Rus' people, simply keeping it for its own coffers (Halperin 1985). In addition to taxes to be paid to the Golden Horde, the people were also obligated to pay certain taxes to the Muscovite prince.

Dmitrii Donskoy and Vasily I, notes Langer (2007), showed even "greater confidence in appropriating and transforming such tributary practices [of the Mongols] to their own ends." Beyond just imposing additional taxes on their own people, the Muscovite princes arrived at another clever way to leverage the Mongol tribute requirement. As Halperin (1985) explains, they "manipulated the allocation of the tax burden" by forcing the appanage territories to pay the entirety of the tribute owed to the Golde Horde and releasing the crown lands from paying any tribute at all. This resulted in "massive" profits while being equally acceptable to the Mongols, as they were still receiving the same amount (Halperin, 1985).

In sum, by adapting the Mongol taxation system to their own ends, and merging its most exploitative elements with the pre-existing taxation system, Moscow was able to generate more revenue than ever before (Halperin, 1985). Even though it faced some of the most frequent and brutal further attacks of any Rus' principality, Moscow was able to adapt to the Mongol tribute system, becoming the richest principality in northern Rus', and eventually surpassing even Novgorod in wealth. In quickly adapting to and adopting Mongol taxation methods, Moscow demonstrated its resilience to Mongol suzerainty. It turned its suzerainty into a benefit, rather than a curse.

11.4.2 Governance

In organizing their administration, the Muscovite princes borrowed heavily from the best elements of the Mongol model, which, employed to rule over an empire of 2 million square miles, was particularly effective. Indeed, the Mongol administrative system has been cited as "one of the most significant Mongol contributions to the rise of Moscow" (Halperin, 1985). Frequent trips to Sarai, some of which lasted for years, enabled the Muscovite princes to develop an in-depth understanding of Mongol institutions and governance (Halperin, 1985; Ostrowski, 2000). Then, they engaged in what Ostrowski (2000) significantly describes as "intelligent adaptation," modifying the Mongol administrative apparatus to suit their smaller, sedentary population.

Elements of the Mongol system borrowed by Moscow likely included the postal system, the currency, the allocation of fiscal and judicial immunities, the treasury, certain legal practices and punishments, the preservation of documents for posterity, and, as mentioned above, the taxation regime (Halperin, 2000). Additionally, one of the key aspects of the Mongol administration was the Khan's reliance on a group of councilors, the *qarachi beys* (Woodworth, 2009). This, too, the Muscovites appropriated and adapted to suit their own ends. According to Woodworth (2009), Moscow actually managed to implement this councilor system more successfully than the Mongols themselves had, engaging the boyars in questions of governance. As a result, the organization of the Muscovite political system has been described as key to Moscow's success by a number of scholars (e.g. Keenan, 1986; Bogatyrev, 2000).

The responsibilities of the boyars were greater than those of most other councils of state at the time (Ostrowski, 2000), and as such they served as an important check on the power of the grand prince—much as the *veche* had served as a check on the princes of Novgorod. On the other hand, the boyars were in many ways beholden to the grand prince, relying on him for land and wealth (Alef, 1959; Langer, 1976; Bogatyrev, 2000). Thus, they generally served him and his interests loyally, rather than compete to destabilize him. The balance of power between the boyars and the grand prince at this stage was relatively stable, enabling a competent, resilient system of governance.

The high degree of trust and unity among Daniilovich princes led successive princes to maintain the inherited advisers of their predecessors (Martin, 2007). As a consequence, explains Martin (1995), "the core of families that achieved elite status at the Muscovite court remained relatively stable and formed strong bonds of mutual dependency and loyalty with the House of Daniil." The empowered and devoted boyars then intervened in disputes over who would be the next grand prince in favor of the Muscovite candidate. For example, they were mainly responsible for a young Dmitry Donskoy gaining the grand princely crown after Moscow had lost it for several years to a different principality (Martin, 2007).

Martin describes the characteristics of the Daniilovich court that made it, and in turn Moscow, so resilient:

> The character of the Daniilovich court, small enough to function on the basis of personal relationships, flexible enough to absorb selected new arrivals into its highest ranks, and unhampered by division among its princes, became an essential component in the growth and development of Muscovy.
>
> (Martin, 2007)

This flexibility is a key element in resilience. Indeed, an examination of the relationships between the Daniilovichi and rival princes indicates that when faced with intradynastic (intra-Riurikid) obstacles, the Muscovite princes were more resilient than their foes. While the support of the Golden Horde was key to power in Rus' (more on this in the next section), that power could not be secured without some degree of military might (Martin, 2007). To this end, the Daniilovichi focused on conquering lands—both those near Moscow which could enlarge their power base and those that had traditionally belonged to the grand principality—and on forming alliances with other branches of the Riurikid dynasty (Martin, 2007).

Each element in this strategy informed and contributed to the others. A larger power base meant a greater population, which meant more income from taxes and more fighting men. This, in turn, paved the way for taking over more land. As Muscovy gained in size and power, its rulers were more likely to find willing partners to form alliances, with these alliances further enriching its military capabilities.

Utilizing these strategies—a combination of appealing to the Horde, acquiring land through political and military methods, and making savvy marriage alliances—by 1533 the Daniilovichi had succeeded in annexing all formerly autonomous principalities, including Rostov, Beloozero, Iaroslavl', Nizhny Novgorod, Vologda, Tver, Pskov, Ryazan, Smolensk, and Novgorod.

11.4.3 Military (Structure and Power)

During the years between 1317 and 1380, while Moscow waited for an exploitable weakness in the Horde, it strengthened its economy and gained political legitimacy and power while also working to develop its military. Spare funds, rather than enriching the rulers, often went toward advancing the military. This advancement consisted of augmenting Moscow's forces as well as improving strategy, techniques, defenses, and weapons technology.

As was the case with its administrative system, Muscovy borrowed much from the Mongols in building its military (Halperin, 1985; Ostrowski, 1990; Halperin, 2000; Crummey, 2013). In style, tactics, structure, strategy, weaponry, and other elements, the Muscovite military was modeled in large part on that of the Mongols (Halperin, 1985; Ostrowski, 1990; Halperin, 2000). Ostrowski (1990) even goes so far as to say that "the entire military and cavalry system of Muscovy was based directly on the Mongol system." After all, it was necessary to study and adapt Mongol tactics and strategies "if only to survive by countering them in battle" (Halperin, 2000). Moreover, the Daniilovichi noted the unprecedented successes of the Mongols in battle and realized that in utilizing the Mongol military apparatus, they could hope to see some of the same success—even if not on the same scale—against both the Mongols and other enemies.

Tactically, the Muscovite force relied on both "light and heavy cavalry," an innovation borrowed from the Mongols (Ostrowski, 1990). Structurally, Moscow used a "highly mobile five-unit formation" (Ostrowski, 1990). This also came from the Mongols. Indeed, for the steppe fighters of the Golden Horde, speed was prized above all else. The Muscovites adopted this same emphasis on flexibility and quickness. Rather than wear the heavy chain mail of their Western European counterparts, Muscovites fought wearing light chain mail and carrying light weaponry, "like mounted raiders" (Crummey, 2013). The element of surprise was important as well, with contemporary observers noting that Muscovite forces would suddenly and wildly charge the enemy (Fletcher, 1591). If retreat was necessary, this was also swift, with the Muscovites firing both backward and forward as they galloped away (Fletcher, 1591). The flexibility and mobility of Moscow's fighting forces helped constitute a resilient military.

The Muscovite army was able to develop into a "highly effective" force by studying and adopting the practices of the Mongols (Crummey, 2013). This was a resilient approach to being subjugated; rather than try to avoid anything Mongol, the Muscovites recognized that adopting the same military system that enforced their vassalage was their best hope to one day overcome it.

Another major innovation was in ending the "right of departure." This right had permitted princes, nobles, and their men to choose whether or not to participate in a given campaign. But as Moscow grew in size and power, the "position and rights of noble warriors changed dramatically," such that those under Moscow's dominion were to arrive for muster when ordered (Crummey, 2013). No longer could they depart at will; they now served at the behest of the Daniilovich prince. Of course, the institution of a more formalized military process, with warriors required to serve and fight when so ordered by the grand prince, improved Moscow's military in a number of ways. It was now larger and thus stronger, and additionally, its leaders could plan and strategize more effectively, secure in the knowledge that a number of troops would not suddenly depart without warning, or decide not to fight.

In terms of weaponry, Moscow borrowed the best technology of the day from other nations, both friend and foe. In addition to Mongol weapons, Muscovites used armaments from the Turks, Arabs, and Western Europeans. A typical light horseman serving in the Muscovite force, for example, would carry with him a *saadak*, a set of quivers, bows, arrows, and bow case; this came from the Turks (Esper, 1969; Fletcher, 1591). The bow itself, meanwhile, closely resembled Arab bows, though it was produced in Muscovy (Esper, 1969).

The Daniilovichi also concentrated on building artillery, though this tended to be more useful against the more heavily armed Poles and Lithuanians than the Mongols (Fletcher, 1591; Esper, 1969). In 1475, Ivan III, presaging an approach masterfully used by Peter the Great a little over two centuries later, imported workers from the technologically superior West. These foreign workers (most notably Rodolfo Fioraventi, a Bolognese polymath who had worked for the Medicis) taught the Muscovites how to manufacture bronze cannon (Esper, 1969).

The homegrown industry evidently flourished, for by 1591 the English traveler Giles Fletcher could remark:

> It is thought that no prince of Christendom hath better store of munition than the Russe emperor. And it may partly appear by the artillery house at Moscow where are of all sorts of great ordnance, all brass pieces, very fair, to an exceeding great number.
>
> (Fletcher, 1591)

In addition to weaponry, the Muscovite princes also invested in high-quality defenses. Dmitry Donskoy, for instance, built the only stone fortress in the northeastern region, thus creating for himself and his descendants "an important military advantage" over their enemies (Miller, 1989). In addition, Donskoy built walled monasteries in several towns on the Moscow and Oka rivers, thus fortifying the border (Martin, 2000).

All these advancements—in tactics, structure, organization, weaponry, and fortifications—enabled Moscow's rise. Savvy political moves also played a part in Muscovy's acquisition of new territory, but fundamentally, it was Muscovy's military might which allowed it to steadily conquer and annex territories. From 1301 to 1304, the principality's territory increased threefold, with the acquisition of all the land between the towns of Kolomna (110 km to the southeast of Moscow) and Mozhaisk (110 km to the southwest of Moscow), as well as Pereyaslavl (Crummey, 2013). Ivan Kalita was credited with "aggressively" expanding Moscow through marriage alliances and the purchase of territory (Martin, 2000). Through a combination of these factors, by the middle of the fourteenth century, Moscow was "the ascendant principality in northeastern Rus'" (Martin, 2007).

In the second half of the fourteenth century, Ivan Kalita's grandson Dmitry Donskoy consolidated control over these purchases (Beloozero, Uglich, and Galich) (Martin, 2000) and also took over Kostroma and the Starodub area east of Suzdal (Martin, 2000; Crummey, 2013). Donskoy is most well-known, though, for the victory at Kulikovo Pole.[8]

After a few skirmishes, Mamai, commander of the Golden Horde,[9] decided to mount a full-fledged attack on Moscow. He secured the support of powerful allies and mustered his forces, including many mercenary troops (Skrynnikov, 1985; *Tverskaya letopis'*, p. 57). This worried Donskoy, who in turn set about confirming and establishing alliances of his own and gathering troops (Skrynnikov, 1985; Crummey, 2013). Donskoy and his forces moved southeast toward the steppe, fording the Oka river to meet Mamai and his troops (Halperin, 2013). The two armies converged at Kulikovo Pole, near the mouth of the Don river,[10] on September 8, 1380.

Halperin (2013) believes that the Rus' chose the location of the battle as Kulikovo Pole due to their "awareness of the Mongols' style of fighting"; this choice enabled Donskoy and his men to be positioned well for the Mongol's "favorite flanking maneuver" (Halperin, 2013). This decision was evidence of the Rus' resilience, in particular their ability to adapt to the enemy. In the end, while the Rus' suffered very high casualties, they won the battle (*Skazanie o Mamaevom Poboishche*; Halperin, 2013; Crummey, 2013). Mamai and his troops fled in chaos. It was the first major defeat of the Mongols since they had looted and conquered Rus' some 140 years earlier (Halperin, 1985).

Historians are divided on the battle's significance. After all, it would be another 100 years before Mongol rule in Rus' was ended, and the victory at Kulikovo had a minor impact on the military strength and power of the Mongols. It did, however, destroy Mamai's career. Weakened, his forces defected to Khan Tokhtamysh, who was able to take control of the Horde and, in 1382, sacked Moscow as punishment for its insubordination (Halperin, 2013; Crummey, 2013).[11] Thus was the Horde's authority over Rus' reestablished "in no uncertain terms" (Crummey, 2013).

Still, the importance of symbolic victories in building Moscow's resilience, namely through the construction and reinforcement of national identity, should not be underestimated: Kulikovo was and would remain hugely important in this sense. After Kulikovo, "no other branch of Riurikids ever again challenged the seniority of the Muscovite line" (Martin, 2000). Indeed, from that point the office of grand prince would belong only to the Daniilovichi (Crummey, 2013). They no longer were reliant on the Mongols for legitimacy (Martin, 2000). Dmitry Donskoy's victory had provided Moscow with a credible claim to be the leader of Rus', one that was based not on the support of an external occupying force but on Moscow's own inherent political and military abilities. And Kulikovo "implanted the vision" in the minds of the Rus' that, one day, the Mongols could be defeated (Crummey, 2013).

Donskoy's successor and son, Vasily I, annexed more territories, including Nizhny Novgorod, Murom, and Vologda. By the end of Vasily's reign in 1425, Moscow was the largest and most powerful principality in northeastern Rus' (Martin, 2007). While Vasily I's successor, Vasily II, one of the main parties in the Muscovite Civil War, was generally too preoccupied with either holding or retaking his throne to amass much territory, he did manage to consolidate control over the territories he had been bequeathed (Backus, 1954).

Vasily II's heir, Ivan III, thus inherited a "homogeneous and firmly controlled area of about fifteen thousand square miles" upon his ascension in 1462 (Backus, 1954). Throughout his rule, Ivan III incorporated large swaths of territory into Moscow, most significantly conquering Rostov, the formerly rich and independent Novgorod, and Moscow's once-great rival Tver. Next, Vasily III added Pskov, Smolensk, and Ryazan to Moscow's land. In sum, from the beginning of Ivan III's rule to the end of Vasily III's rule (1462–1533), the Muscovite territory was increased by about 25,000 square miles (Backus, 1954). By the end of this period, it included virtually all the lands of Rus' (Zlotnik, 1979). No longer would Moscow's rivals be other principalities, but rather the great states of Northern and Eastern Europe: Poland, Lithuania, and Sweden.

Moscow's military power was due in large part to its structure, flexible and adaptable—resilient—by design. It also benefited from a strong economy and decisive leadership, with these elements forming a positive feedback loop: The strong economy enabled a larger, better-equipped military, which helped secure economic gains and provide political legitimacy to the Daniilovichi, whose leadership then further enhanced Moscow's military might. This is characteristic of how modern resilient systems work, with each element or subsystem in the broader system interacting with the others in a positive feedback loop.

11.4.4 Social Cohesion and Religion

Assessing the social cohesiveness of Moscow under the Mongols is difficult. To be sure, determining social cohesiveness is a murky task even when examining modern-day societies, about which there is no shortage of evidence. Overall, the well-developed identity of the Muscovites (about which more later) certainly indicates a degree of social cohesion. Among the peasants, there was a "tradition of mutual responsibility and solidarity," strong enough that the government was able to successfully institute a policy of collective taxation of the communes (Crummey, 2013).

Muscovy's cosmopolitan nature probably also improved social cohesion. This is not immediately obvious: The existence in the same place of many different people, from different backgrounds, with different religions and ethnicities, would seem likely to lead to tension and clashes. But this is not what happened. In fact, Moscow readily integrated new immigrants (Rakhimzyanov, 2010). The Muscovite princes tended to ally with non-Christians against their supposed compatriots in other principalities like Tver, Novgorod, and Ryazan (Rakhimzyanov, 2010). In addition to pragmatism playing a role in these alliances, the grand princes "exhibited ... a relative lack of religious or cultural prejudice" (Rakhimzyanov, 2010). This lack of prejudice and acceptance of heterogeneous peoples, so long as they were loyal, probably played a role in Moscow's rise. It also indicated the development of an independent Muscovite culture and identity, apart from religion or ethnicity, with Muscovites feeling connected to their society and displaying solidarity among different groups. While we cannot say to what extent, it seems clear that a shared set of attitudes and norms, including a sense of belonging, were present in early Moscow, and probably to a larger degree than in other, less cosmopolitan principalities. With the probable exception of Novgorod, then, in terms of social cohesiveness, Moscow likely outperformed its competitors.

The Muscovites came to develop a strong identity centered around several core foundational beliefs and concepts. These included the grand prince as sovereign, Moscow as savior and ruler of "all the Russian lands," and Moscow as the inheritor of the great Kievan and Mongol states and of the Roman and Byzantine churches (the "Third Rome" concept). Some of these aspects of identity arose naturally, but for the most part they were constructed. Still, that did not make the identity any less salient, and it played an important role in enhancing the resilience of Moscow.

The grand prince began to be described as sovereign (*ospodar'/gosudar'*) during the reign of Vasily II, a change that further solidified Moscow's identity and social unity.

What did "sovereign" represent or signify that "grand prince" did not? Filyushkin writes, "sovereign proved to be at a height which was unobtainable for the remainder of the aristocracy. There could not be more than one sovereign"[12] (Filyushkin, 2006). That is, in naming themselves sovereigns, the Muscovite princes were asserting their preeminence among all the princes of Rus'.

This transition, from "grand prince" to "sovereign," heralded another major shift, which would come in 1547, when the Russian sovereigns adopted the title of tsar. (Alef, 1959; Filyushkin, 2006). The movement to increasingly elevated titles along this spectrum both reflected and helped construct Moscow's identity as the absolute ruler of the Rus' people and the center of a nascent empire.[13] As Filyushkin puts it, the "very adoption of ... the title of sovereign became a turning point in the formation of national statehood"[14] (Filyushkin, 2006).

In parallel, an important phrase began to gain currency in fourteenth century Moscow: The "Russian land" (Halperin, 1980). As Halperin (1980) has demonstrated, the transition from describing Moscow as located in the "Suzdalian land" to the "Russian land" was of great ideological importance. Kievan Rus' had employed the term as one of its "central political myth[s]" (Halperin, 1980), and so it was not an unfamiliar phrase in the Rus' context. But its adaptation by Moscow was neither immediate nor expected. Rather, this adaptation contributed to enhancing the status and (national) identity of Moscow.

Another powerful unifying force came from Moscow purposefully constructing and strengthening its relationship with the Orthodox Church.[15] Reciprocally, the Church utilized its relationship with the Principality of Moscow in order to enhance its own position. This enabled both institutions to achieve hegemony in their respective domains.

By the fourteenth century, the Church was already championing unity (Martin, 2000). This made sense: From the Church's perspective, a strong, centralized state was seen as critical to the "creation and protection of the ecclesiastical unity of the see" (Martin, 2000). Alef adds that "past experience" had demonstrated that a powerful Church "could be achieved only through secular consolidation under a single power that could settle differences" (Alef, 1959). That is, the centralization of the state around Moscow went hand-in-hand with the centralization of the Church around Moscow.

As the centers of power for both institutions coalesced around Moscow, they both increasingly served as "sources of cohesion" for the Rus' people (Crummey, 2013). Even the Mongols, recognizing the unifying and pacifying potential of the Church, supported it (Crummey, 2013). Indeed, under the protection of the Mongols the Church's wealth expanded significantly (Halperin, 1985). Eventually the Church's power would eclipse that of the Mongols, and it would be the support of the metropolitan, not of the khan, which was necessary to hold the grand princely title (Martin, 2000). This support was an important factor in legitimizing the Daniilovichi rule, which had always been an issue given their usurpation of the traditional laws of inheritance.

Thus, in the sphere of religion and the Church, there was another series of positive feedback loops which contributed to the resilience of the system of Moscow. In this case, a powerful Church legitimized and incentivized a powerful government, which in turn was able to protect and strengthen the Church.

In the late fifteenth and early sixteenth centuries, Muscovite religious and cultural elites began formulating the idea of Muscovy as the "Third Rome."[16] This idea was built on the Byzantine self-conception of Constantinople as a Second Rome, carrying on the rightful legacy of Christian Rome after its conquest by barbarians (Strémooukhoff, 1953). Now, the thinking went, in acceding to the demands of the heretical Catholic Church at the Council of Florence, Constantinople had betrayed Orthodoxy (Strémooukhoff, 1953). The new heir was Moscow.

Perhaps paradoxically, Moscow also asserted ownership of Mongol inheritance. Finding it difficult to "extricate itself from the political legacy of the Golden Horde" after the Horde had broken up, Moscow instead claimed to be one of its successors (Khodarkovsky, 1999). This enabled it to "justify its expansion southward and eastward," in the areas that had formerly been the domain of the Golden Horde (Khodarkovsky, 1999). However, it is important to note that it was "Muscovite reality, as opposed to ideology" that was Mongol in nature (Halperin, 2010). In other words, while Moscow had borrowed much of its political tradition from the Golden Horde and acknowledged itself as a successor to the Horde, it did not claim direct descent as it did from Kiev. Moscow saw itself as taking over after the Horde, not as being a continuation of it. In this way its identity vis-à-vis the Horde was different from its identity vis-à-vis Kiev.

11.4.5 Assessing Muscovite System Capacity for Resilience

Thinking in terms of complex and interconnected societal systems, scholars point to Moscow's administrative, economic, military, and societal effectiveness as the sources of its success (Halperin, 1985; Bogatyrev, 2000). The princes of Moscow managed an increasingly large territory quite well, utilizing many techniques borrowed from the Mongols (Halperin, 1985). After all, the Mongols were experts at administering a large area effectively, and the Muscovite princes, given their close ties with the Khans of the Golden Horde and exposure to its practices, were able to adopt and adapt these practices for themselves. Halperin (1985) touches on the core reason for Moscow's preeminence:

> Moscow triumphed over its rivals because it took better advantage of the Mongol presence and used Mongol administrative techniques more effectively than other power centers such as Tver'.
>
> (Halperin, 1985)

In other words, Moscow was better at *adapting* to Mongol rule: It utilized this new reality as a learning experience, carefully observing Mongol customs and then adapting them to fit the Muscovite world. Keenan (1986), while he does not focus on this point or use the language and toolbox of resilience, also arrives at the key idea:

> how did so successful and durable a political system—embodied in an enormous and vigorous state—emerge at all under such seemingly adverse conditions? And how, in particular, did a single tiny group—the Muscovite dynasty and its boyar relatives—maintain military control in a territory so vast, where fortifications were minimal, major troop concentrations unusual and crushingly expensive, and all but the most fortunate towns vulnerable to siege by a few hundred men? ... Indeed when one considers the tasks and conditions that faced the early Muscovite political system, he must wonder that any effective state was organized on this territory at all, least of all a great empire ... Such an accomplishment, it appears, was made possible by a form of *adaption to circumstances*.
>
> (Keenan, 1986; emphasis added)

It is important to note that the military, economic, political, social, and religious aspects of Moscow were all linked and interconnected. A strong economy, for instance, enabled a larger, better-equipped military. A close relation with the Church inspired greater social cohesion and the strong "Third Rome" identity. A more powerful military provided legitimacy and muscle in the political sphere. A strong, closely allied metropolitan intervened in military affairs on Moscow's behalf. Political allies fought on Moscow's behalf, bolstering its military. Openness to the outside enabled the adoption of superior military technologies. Examples of such linkages are everywhere. This illustrates the significance of systems theory in analyzing Moscow's rise. All the components of the system worked together in order to enhance Moscow's resilience and thus enable its ascendancy.

11.5 Conclusion: Endogenous Resilience as a Predictor of Civilizational Response to Exogenous Shock

Kievan Rus' and the Mongol invasion represent only one example of how an improved understanding of endogenous system principles can explain why some nations are able to prevent and plan for (i.e., Novgorod), or recover from and adapt to (i.e., Moscow), adverse events. Even in the same time period, a lack of endogenous resilience played a significant role in leaving various kingdoms and empires ripe for Mongol Conquest, such as the Xi Xia, Jin, Sung, Kara Khitai, Khwarezm, and Abbasid states. Likewise, the capacity for system resilience enabled specific polities (initially Novgorod, later Muscovy) to recover, survive, and adapt—while many others were far less fortunate.

Why do some states succeed where others fail? Do great and unique individuals make history, or do the contextual circumstances of the times place societies on a path-dependent trajectory? Or is it all down to chance? What are the fundamental processes at work that cause historical change? Of course, there are many potential answers to these questions. One possible contribution to many of these questions centers upon systems theory and resilience—understanding societies as webs of nested, interdependent, and complex systems and subsystems that mutually reinforce positive and negative feedback loops (Haldon et al., 2022; Jackson et al. 2022). This represents a novel approach to these fundamental questions about the nature of history and societies.

Systems theory, as well as the science of resilience, can help shape our understanding of historical societies and their relative capability in overcoming challenges and disruption in various forms (Linkov & Trump 2019). For some societies, such as Muscovy and Novgorod, resilient economic, governmental, military, religious, and social practices enabled their survival and longer-term success. For others, like many other principalities of Kievan Rus', brittle trade lines, ineffective governance, societal disorder, and poorly led and improperly equipped military forces made them susceptible to collapse. Upon the arrival of the Mongols, who themselves were a highly adaptive and resilient polity, especially militarily, those principalities lacking in key areas of societal resilience were quickly overcome.

Notes

1 "For more on systems theory and panarchy, see Gunderson and Holling, 2002."
2 As Thompson and Ward (2018, p. 20) note, "between 1139 and 1169, the throne changed hands seventeen times."

3 Hereafter used interchangeably with "Moscow."
4 See Sevastyanova, O. (2010). In Quest of the Key Democratic Institution of Medieval Rus':
   Was the "Veche" an Institution that Represented Novgorod as a City and a Republic?
   Jahrbücher Für Geschichte Osteuropas, 58(1), neue folge, 1–23 for a good overview of the historiographical interpretations of the *veche*.
5 The only requirement for free men being in the *veche* was owning 1 square meter of property
   (Platonov, 1965); thus, it was not merely an oligarchy consisting of the wealthy merchants and
   boyars.
6 Yanin, one of the pre-eminent scholars of medieval Novgorod, was perhaps overly influenced
   by Marxist and Soviet ideas and ideals. He characterizes Novgorod as rife with class struggle, seeing the *veche* not as a democratic instrument but instead as yet another means for the
   upper-class boyars to control and oppress the lower classes of Novgorod. However, even he
   admits that "the veche system, as compared to the form of government in the [other] principalities, was actually notable for visible characteristics of democracy in their medieval forms"
   (1962).
7 The tysiatskie were "originally commander of the town militia but gradually developed into
   a government official who oversaw, among other things, the commercial courts" (Paul, 2007).
8 Most of our information about Kulikovo comes from the so-called Kulikovo cycle of literary
   works: Historical recordings in the Russian chronicles, in particular the Trinity Chronicle, the
   epic *Zadonshchina* ("beyond the Don"), and the *Skazanie o Mamaevom Poboishche* ("Narration
   of the Battle with Mamai"). The sources face numerous problems, including unresolved questions of textual transmission and integrity and uncertain dating (Skrynnikov, 1985; Halperin,
   2013). As such, it is difficult to determine precisely how the battle at Kulikovo unfolded.
9 Because he was not a descendent of Chingis Khan, he was prohibited from serving as khan;
   rather, figurehead rulers served as khans in his stead (Crummey, 2013).
10 It was this location that gave Dmitry the epithet "Donskoy," or "of the Don," illustrating
   the historical significance of the battle.
11 Mamai himself fled to Kaffa, where he was killed by the Genoese (Crummey, 2013).
12 Государь же оказывался на высоте недостижимой для остальной аристократии.
   Более одного государя быть не могло.
13 Another element of this new, more powerful identity was the change in formal style. In
   emulation of the ecclesiastical title "Metropolitan of Kiev and of all Russia," the Muscovite
   princes began to be styled as grand prince or sovereign "of all Russia" rather than merely
   "of Vladimir" or "of Moscow" (Alef, 1959). The phrase "of all Russia" had started to be used,
   sparingly, in the fourteenth century. By the fifteenth century—as Moscow grew in power—it
   had become more prominent, appearing in coinage, documents, and seals (Alef, 1959). This
   phrase, as Alef notes, "reflected the aspirations of the Muscovite princes to impose their
   hegemony over the neighboring de facto independent principalities" (Alef, 1959).
14 Принятие же … титула государя стало поворотной точкой в становлении
   отечественной государственности.
15 Hereafter "the Church" refers to the Christian Orthodox Church with its episcopal see at
   Vladimir from 1299 to 1325 and at Moscow from 1325 on.
16 See Strémooukhoff (1953) for more on the origins, sources, and expressions of this idea.

Disclaimer

The views and opinions expressed herein are the authors' views and opinions alone and not
necessarily those of their host institutions.

References

Alef, G. (1959). The Political Significance of the Inscriptions on Muscovite Coinage in the
   Reign of Vasili II. *Speculum 34*(1): 1–19. https://doi.org/10.2307/2847975.

Backus, O. P., III. (1954). Was Muscovite Russia Imperialistic? *American Slavic and East European Review 13*(4): 522–534. https://doi.org/10.2307/2491639.

Birnbaum, H. (1981). *Lord Novgorod the Great: Essays in the History and Culture of a Medieval City-State.* Columbus, Ohio: Slavica.

Birnbaum, H. (1984). The Subcultures of Medieval Russia: Chronology, Regional Distribution, Internal Links, and External Influences. *Viator 15*: 181–236. https://doi.org/10.1484/j.viator.2.301440.

Blum, J. (1961). *Lord and Peasant in Russia: From the Ninth to the Nineteenth Century.* Princeton, NJ: Princeton University Press.

Bogatyrev, S. (2000). *The Sovereign and His Counsellors: Ritualised Consultations in Muscovite Political Culture, 1350s-1570s.* Helsinki: Gummerus Printing.

Bushkovitch, P. (1980). Towns and Castles in Kievan Rus': Boiar Residence and Landownership in the Eleventh and Twelfth Centuries. *Russian History 7*(3): 251–264. Retrieved from http://www.jstor.org/stable/24652413.

Crummey, R. O. (2013). *The Formation of Muscovy 1304–1613.* New York: Routledge.

Chronicle of Novgorod, 1016–1471, The. (1914). London: Royal Historical Society.

Dolgikh, A. V., and Aleksandrovskii, A. L. (2010). Soils and Cultural Layers in Velikii Novgorod. *Eurasian Soil Science 43*(5): 477–487. https://doi.org/10.1134/s1064229310050017.

Duczko, W. (2004). *Viking Rus: Studies on the Presence of Scandinavians in Eastern Europe.* Leiden: Brill.

Esper, T. (1969). Military Self-Sufficiency and Weapons Technology in Muscovite Russia. *Slavic Review 28*(2): 185–208. https://doi.org/10.2307/2493223.

Filyushkin, A. I. (2006). *Tituli russkikh gosudarei* [*Titles of the Russian Sovereigns*]. St. Petersburg: Alliance-Archeo.

Fletcher, G. (1591). Of the Russe Common Wealth. Or, Maner of Gouernement of the Russe Emperour, (Commonly Called the Emperour of Moskouia) with the Manners, and Fashions of the People of That Countrey. Retrieved from https://quod.lib.umich.edu/e/eebo/A00947.0001.001?view=toc.

Gabriel, R. A. (2004). *Subotai the Valiant: Genghis Khan's Greatest General.* Westport, CT: Praeger.

Gunderson, L. H., and Holling, C. S. (2002). *Panarchy: Understanding Transformations in Human and Natural Systems.* Washington, D.C.: Island Press.

Halperin, C. (1980). Kiev and Moscow: An Aspect of Early Muscovite Thought. *Russian History 7*(1): 312–321. https://doi.org/10.1163/187633180X00229.

Halperin, C. (1985). *Russia and the Golden Horde: The Mongol Impact on Medieval Russian History.* Bloomington, IN: Indiana University Press.

Halperin, C. (2000). Muscovite Political Institutions in the 14th Century. *Kritika: Explorations in Russian and EurAsian History 1*(2): 237–257. https://doi.org/10.1353/kri.2008.0033.

Halperin, C. (2010). National Identity in Premodern Rus'. *Russian History 37*(3): 275–294. https://doi.org/10.1163/187633110X510446.

Halperin, C. (2013). The Battle of Kulikovo Field (1380) in History and Historical Memory. *Kritika: Explorations in Russian and EurAsian History 14*(4): 853–864. https://doi.org/10.1353/kri.2013.0061.

Hamm, M. (1993). *Kiev: A Portrait, 1800–1917.* Princeton, NJ: Princeton University Press.

Herszenhorn, D. M. (2014, October 18). Where Mud Is Archaeological Gold, Russian History Grew on Trees. *The New York Times.* Retrieved from https://www.nytimes.com/2014/10/19/world/europe/where-mud-is-archaeological-gold-russian-history-grew-on-trees.html.

Isoaho, M. (2018). Shakhmatov's Legacy and the Chronicles of Kievan Rus'. *Kritika* 19(3): 637–648.

Kalra, P. (2018). *The Silk Road and the Political Economy of the Mongol Empire.* Abingdon, Oxon: Routledge.

Karamzin, N. M. (2012). *Istoriâ gosudarstva Rossijskogo v. I, chapter II.* Moscow: OLMA Media Group.

Kashtanov, S. M. (1982). Finansovoye Ustroistvo Moskovskogo Kniazhestva v Seredine XIV Veka Po Dannim Dukhovnikh Gramot [The Financial Structure of the Moscow Principality in the Middle of the XIV Century According to Ecclesiastical Certificates]. In *Issledovania po Istorii i istoriografii feodalizma* [*Studies in the History and Historiography of Feudalism*] (Ed. B. D. Grekov), 173–189. Moscow: Nauka.

Keenan, E. (1986). Muscovite Political Folkways. *Russian Review* 45(2): 115–181. https://doi.org/10.2307/130423.

Khodarkovsky, M. (1999). Taming the "Wild Steppe": Muscovy's Southern Frontier, 1480–1600. *Russian History* 26(3): 241–297. https://doi.org/10.1163/187633199X 00094.

Klyuchevsky, V. O. (1908–1916). Kurs Russkoy Istorii [*The Course of Russian History*]. The State Public Scientific Technological Library of the Siberian Branch of the Russian Academy of Sciences. http://www.spsl.nsc.ru/history/kluch/kluchlec.htm.

Kollmann, N. (1990). Collateral Succession in Kievan Rus'. *Harvard Ukrainian Studies* 14(3/4): 377–387.

Lane, G. (2004). *Genghis Khan and Mongol Rule.* Westport, CT: Greenwood Press.

Langer, L. (1976). Plague and the Russian Countryside: Monastic Estates in the Late Fourteenth and Fifteenth Centuries. *Canadian-American Slavic Studies* 10(3): 351–368. https://doi.org/10.1163/221023976X00963.

Langer, L. (2007). Muscovite Taxation and the Problem of Mongol Rule in Rus'. *Russian History* 34(1/4): 101–129. https://doi.org/10.1163/187633107X00077.

Likhachov, D. (2007). *Velikoe nasledie: Klassicheskie proizvedenija literatury Drevnej Rusi. Zametki o Russkom* [*The Great Heritage: Classical Works of the Literature of Ancient Rus. Notes about Russian*]. Moscow: Logos.

Majeska, G. P. (2016). Politics and Hierarchy in the Early Rus' Church: Antonii, a 13th-Century Archbishop of Novgorod. In *Tapestry of Russian Christianity: Studies in History and Culture* (Eds. N. Lupinin, D. Ostrowski, and J. B. Spock), 23–38. Columbus, OH: Department of Slavic and East European Languages and Cultures and the Resource Center for Medieval Slavic Studies, The Ohio State University.

Mandelbaum, M. (2007). *Democracy's Good Name: The Rise and Risks of the World's Most Popular Form of Government.* New York: Public Affairs.

Martin, J. (2000). From Kiev to Muscovy: The Beginnings to 1450. In *Russia: A History* (Ed. G. L. Freeze), 1–26. New York: Oxford University Press.

Martin, J. (2007). *Medieval Russia, 980–1584.* New York: Cambridge University Press.

May, T. M. (2016). *The Mongol Art of War.* Barnsley, UK: Pen & Sword Books Ltd.

Mezentsev, V. I. (1989). The Territorial and Demographic Development of Medieval Kiev and Other Major Cities of Rus: A Comparative Analysis Based on Recent Archaeological Research. *Russian Review* 48(2): 145–170. https://doi.org/10.2307/130324.

Miller, D. B. (1989). Monumental Building as an Indicator of Economic Trends in Northern Rus' in the Late Kievan and Mongol Periods, 1138–1462. *The American Historical Review* 94(2): 360–390. https://doi.org/10.2307/1866831.

Ostrowski, D. (1990). The Mongol Origins of Muscovite Political Institutions. *Slavic Review* 49(4): 525–542. https://doi.org/10.2307/2500544.

Ostrowski, D. (1998). *Muscovy and the Mongols: Cross-Cultural Influences on the Steppe Frontier, 1304–1589*. New York: Cambridge University Press.

Ostrowski, D. (2000). Muscovite Adaptation of Steppe Political Institutions: A Reply to Halperin's Objections. *Kritika: Explorations in Russian and EurAsian History* 1(2): 267–304. https://doi.org/10.1353/kri.2008.0117.

Paul, M. (2003). Episcopal Election in Novgorod, Russia 1156–1478. *Church History* 72(2): 251–275.

Paul, M. (2007). Secular Power and the Archbishops of Novgorod before the Muscovite Conquest. *Kritika: Explorations in Russian and EurAsian History* 8(2): 231–270. https://doi.org/10.1353/kri.2007.0020.

Paul, M. (2008). Was the Prince of Novgorod a "Third-Rate Bureaucrat" after 1136? *Jahrbücher für Geschichte Osteuropas 56*(1), neue folge: 72–113.

Pitts, F. R. (1965). A Graph Theoretic Approach to Historical Geography. *The Professional Geographer* 17(5): 15–20. https://doi.org/10.1111/j.0033-0124.1965.015_m.x.

Pitts, F. R. (1978). The Medieval River Trade Network of Russia Revisited. *Social Networks* 1(3): 285–292. https://doi.org/10.1016/0378-8733(78)90025-4.

Platonov, S. F. (1965). Smutnoe Vremia [*The Time of Troubles*]. The Hague: Europe Printing.

Podvigina, N. L. (1976). *Ocherki sotsial'no-ekonomicheskoi i Politicheskoi Istorii Novgoroda Velikogo v XII–XIII vv* [*Essays in the Social, Economic, and Political History of Novgorod the Great in the 12th–13th Centuries*]. Moscow: Vysshaia Shkola.

Rakhimzyanov, B. (2010). Muslim Iurts of Muscovy: Religious Tolerance of the Steppe in the XV-XVI Centuries. In *Religion und Integration im Moskauer Russland: Konzepte und Praktiken, Potentiale und Grenzen 14.-17. Jahrhundert* (Ed. L. Steindorff), 181–200. Berlin: Otto Harrassowitz Verlag.

Sevastyanova, O. (2010). In Quest of the Key Democratic Institution of Medieval Rus': Was the "Veche" an Institution That Represented Novgorod as a City and a Republic? *Jahrbücher für Geschichte Osteuropas 58*(1), neue folge: 1–23.

Silfen, P. H. (1974). *The Influence of the Mongols on Russia: A Dimensional History*. Hicksville, NY: Exposition Press.

Sinor, D. (1999). The Mongols in the West. *Journal of Asian History 33*(1): 1–44.

Skazanie o Mamaevom Poboishche [Narration of the Battle with Mamai]. (V. V. Kolesov, Trans). In *Voinskiye povesti Drevnei Rusi* [*Military Stories of Ancient Rus'*] (Ed. N. Ponyrko). 1985. Leningrad: Lenizdat. http://www.vostlit.info/Texts/rus8/Mamaj/text.phtml?id=895.

Skrynnikov, R. G. (1985). The Battle at Kulikovo Field. *Soviet Studies in History: a Quarterly Journal of Translations 24*(1–2): 11–44. https://doi.org/10.2753/RSH1061-198324010211.

Soloviev, S. M. (1851–1879). Istoria Rossii s drevneishikh vremen [The History of Russia from Ancient Times]. The State Public Scientific Technological Library of the Siberian Branch of the Russian Academy of Sciences. Retrieved from http://www.spsl.nsc.ru/history/solov/main/solovlec.htm.

Stefanovich, P. S. (2011). The Great Squad (druzhina) of Ancient Rus'. Rossiiskaia Istoria, 5: 78–90.

Strémooukhoff, D. (1953). Moscow the Third Rome: Sources of the Doctrine. *Speculum 28*(1): 84–101. https://doi.org/10.2307/2847182.

Thompson, J. M. and Ward, C. J. (2018). *Russia: A Historical Introduction from Kievan Rus' to the Present*. New York: Routledge.

Tverskaya letopis' [*Tver Chronicle*]. In Polnoe Sobranie Russkikh Letopisei [*Complete Collection of Russian Chronicles*], 15(1). Retrieved from http://psrl.csu.ru/toms/Tom_15.shtml.

Vaissman, M., and Yarygin, A. A. (2017). Mongoly v XIII-XIV Vekakh i mongol'skoye Nashestviye na Rus' [The Mongols in the XIII-XIV centuries and the Mongol invasion of Rus']. *Vestnik Mariyskogo gosudarstvennogo universiteta*, 3(11): 61–72.

Vernadsky, G. (1973). *Kievan Russia*. New Haven, CT: Yale University Press.

Vladimirsky-Budanov, M. F. (2005). Obzor Istorii Russkogo Prava [Survey of the History of Russian Law]. Moscow: Izdatel'skii Dom "Territoriya budushchego." (Original Work Published 1909).

Woodworth, C. (2009). The Birth of the Captive Autocracy: Moscow, 1432. *Journal of Early Modern History* 13(1): 49–69. https://doi.org/10.1163/157006509X462276.

Yanin, V. L. (1962). *Novgorodskie posadniki* [*Novgorod Mayors*]. Moscow: Izdatel'stvo Moskovskogo Universiteta.

Yanin, V. L. (1990). The Archaeology of Novgorod. *Scientific American* 262(2): 84–91. https://doi.org/10.1038/scientificamerican0290-84.

Zlotnik, M. D. (1979). Muscovite Fiscal Policy: 1462–1584. *Russian History* 6(1): 243–258. https://doi.org/10.1163/187633179X00113.

Linkov, I., & Trump, B. D. (2019). *The science and practice of resilience*. Cham: Springer International Publishing.

Haldon, J., Izdebski, A., Kemp, L., Mordechai, L., & Trump, B. (2022). SDG 13: How societies succeeded or failed to respond to environmental disruption. In *Before the UN sustainable development goals: A historical companion*. Oxford Scholarship Online.

Jackson, R., Hartman, S., Trump, B., Crumley, C., McGovern, T., Linkov, I., & Ogilvie, A. E. J. (2022). Disjunctures of Practice and the Problems of Collapse. In *Perspectives on Public Policy in Societal-Environmental Crises* (pp. 75–108). Springer, Cham.

Hynes, W., Trump, B. D., Kirman, A., Haldane, A., & Linkov, I. (2022). Systemic resilience in economics. *Nature Physics*, 18(4), 381–384.

12 Resilience of the Simple?

Lessons from the Blockade of Leningrad

Jeffrey K. Hass

12.1 Accidental Resilience: Lessons from the Blockade of Leningrad

If discussions of collapse often (but not always) look at longer periods of time and at complex relations of structures and environment, we can also learn about collapse and resilience from an examination of meso- and micro-levels under duress. In this chapter, I attempt just this, proposing that one city can give us some insights into the causes and patterns of collapse and resilience (or both simultaneously). The city in question was in the midst of a brutal war, with no clear end or victory in sight, and tensions of uncertainty and institutional strain were clearly felt. The winter was brutally cold, food was increasingly scarce, and civilians were blaming not only the enemy but also their own officials for growing deprivation taking its toll on patriotism and collective sacrifice. Soldiers in the city, whether wounded or for whatever other reason, spoke of how their officers were unprepared for war and that they themselves were not so well provisioned. And desperate civilians were breaking rules and norms—rules against theft, norms against cannibalism—to survive. The social order was under assault from various directions.

This could be 1917 Petrograd, where deprivations and stresses of war sparked the collapse of authority and order and set in motion a chain reaction throughout the Russian empire. Instead, our case is the Blockade of Leningrad (1941–1944), which for all its tragedy and death had a fine balance between decay and resilience (by its fingertips) of institutions and collective practices underpinning the political and social order. If some components of revolution were absent (e.g. an organized opposition and military and police defecting from the regime), the ingredients for decay were not. Dissent might not have been widespread, but morale among civilians and soldiers remained a worry.[1] Shadow markets of stolen food, sold to desperate civilians at speculative prices, were a threat to regime efficacy and even legitimacy: Stolen food sold in black markets was food the state could not use for dependency and obedience, and a black market that aided civilian survival created a competitor for loyalty. Inequality in food access was clear to all; that some workers received higher

DOI: 10.4324/9781003331384-15

rations than others and that food store clerks did not seem so emaciated were noticed by average (starving) Leningraders.[2]

Yet somehow, not only did more Leningraders survive than die—the institutional order and authority persisted, without recourse to significant repression. Resilience was unplanned but not without fundamental foundations. First, facets of Soviet institutions designed for control did not perform so well, and instead, other dynamics—usually seen as pathological—buttressed the social and institutional order and contributed to innovations that aided survival and resilience. Second, dynamics of empathy, social distance, and relations to anchors of valence grounded individuals into smaller collectives themselves linked into institutions. These anchors of valence anchored Leningraders into a social order that buttressed institutions. My discussion will focus on institutions and practices and take for granted the natural world and technology; survival practices reflected the first and shaped the use of the second. Instead, I will explore how micro-practices concatenated into resilience and order.

In the Blockade, *food* was key. Food was scarce, and the state had a difficult time supplying enough food for civilians (after feeding soldiers). Deprivation and its shift in incentives combined with institutional forces to undermine institutional efficacy and order—deprivation raised the threat of "bank runs" on institutions for food. In this context, we might expect *either* expanded draconian order (Stalin's hierarchical, repressive system) *or* collapse, if we take seriously Pitirim Sorokin's claims of how hunger degrades norms and order (a claim seconded by Sergei Iarov).[3] Yet order did not all part. It turned out that lower-level dynamics can simultaneously sap the strength of institutions *and* buttress their bare-bones operation, maintaining enough semblance of order to keep overall relations from disaggregating into myriad, perhaps competing, communities (a war of all against all). Drawing on the Blockade, I make the following arguments of order and disorder. First, *interests and incentives* contributed to institutional weakness and simultaneously maintained institutions. Dependency can create a basis for opportunism or defection, and critical attitudes to authority and order. Second, social and symbolic distance could facilitate transgressions of laws and norms *and* support them. Closer social relations engendered empathy, which increased perceived costs of violating rules and norms *if such violations might bring harm to the Other of empathy.* Distance (e.g. being out of sight), on the other hand, meant a possible victim of opportunism (e.g. theft) was out of mind. Empathy was strongest when it was local, and this could act as a counterweight to some forms of opportunistic behavior that could rip apart social relations and the social order. Third, actors' identities, interests, and practices were coupled to broader fields through *anchors*, entities that actors invest with identity and emotional relations (empathy, usually sympathy) that tie their senses of self to the external world and order.

This story of order and disorder, change and continuity, endogenous and exogenous shocks, and responses to them—what we do when our backs are against the wall—is a core theme of my scholarship, from post-socialist economic change to wartime survival.[4] I offer the Blockade of Leningrad as a micro-study of resilience versus collapse, drawing our attention to meso- and micro-level forces that can buttress or hinder the capacity of people to hold together. Most contributions to this volume explore resilience and collapse via two perspectives "from above": Macrohistorical (*longue durée*) or macrostructural (broad relations and rules that are emergent properties of collective practices), or some combination of both (sometimes using comparisons of cases). Those studies set out to pinpoint tipping points, dynamics of transformation and broad disaggregation, and other measures and forces that break up complex systems. My goal is to complement my colleagues' work by diving deep into the micro-level of practices and responses of individuals and local relations—a dive into the "quantum mechanics" or resilience and reproduction, disaggregation and decay, and transformation. This case study of the Blockade, a moment of extreme duress in which order was on a knife edge, might provide some insights into forces at lower structural levels, and how they contribute to resilience and to decay. My contribution is not meant to replace rigorous cognitive psychology of duress (true social quantum mechanics), and I make no claims (yet) about specifics of concatenation and emergence from local to broader relations. As environments and constellations of institutions and structures shift, contradict, and rupture, what happens "below" might be of supreme importance to resilience, adaptation, and survival.[5] Let us see what Leningrad can offer for this discussion.

12.1.1 The Context of Order or Collapse: War, Blockade, and Starvation

The Blockade was an urban famine created by a Nazi siege.[6] On June 22, 1941, the Germans launched Operation Barbarossa, and by late August the Wehrmacht had torn through western Soviet territory, taking cities and Red Army soldiers on the way to the Caucasus, Moscow, and Leningrad. By September 8, the Germans had reached Lake Ladoga, to the southeast of the city. With the Finnish army to the north of Leningrad, the Axis had created a near-complete blockade. Hitler ordered Army Group North to destroy the city through air raids and artillery bombardments and to starve the inhabitants—victory meant wiping the city's infrastructure and people off the map. Thus began 872 days of horrors of death from above, starvation and ensuing suffering, and stresses and terror of war brought home to a peaceful civilian population.

The usual story of the Blockade focuses on the first winter, among the coldest in the twentieth century (temperatures reached as low as −25°C, and constant warmth did not arrive until late May). Because of botched civilian evacuations, there were 3.4 million people in and around Leningrad: 2,544,000 civilians in the city proper, 343,000 people in suburban areas, 500,000 soldiers, and 82,795 refugees from the west. In the first winter, the bread ration fell to 250 grams daily for workers for military production, and 125 grams for all others. By November hunger had taken hold; by December there were reports of cannibalism, and a massive wave of death began to crash over the city. Starvation death was no longer hypothetical: It stared people in the face, on streets and in homes, and from 800,000 to 1.2 million civilians ultimately died, most from starvation. No small part of the problem was policy failures, as Leningrad's political elite—which I dub "Smolny" (the former girls' school from which Lenin and company launched their October 1917 *coup d'état*)—did not take seriously an invasion by a German war machine that had terrorized the rest of Europe. Evacuations and food security seemed to be afterthoughts. Soviet trade minister A. V. Liubimov advised Leningrad leader Andrei Zhdanov to begin rationing at the earliest moment, in light of the experience of the Russo-Finnish War.[7] Yet Zhdanov waited until the deadline of July 18 to institute rationing, and initially civilians received more food than they usually bought before the war. Civilians could also obtain several days of food at once to create stocks of food (of dubious legality). Only by the end of August, as the Wehrmacht approached the city, did Smolny realize how quickly the city was using food.[8] The authorities began to reduce civilian rations[9] and additionally ordered scientific institutes to create ersatz food and organized transporting additional food across Lake Ladoga. Despite these efforts, by November 20, category I rations (the highest ration category) for bread fell to 250 grams per day; everyone else received 125 grams.[10] Mass death and mass desperation were about to begin. Over 50,000 civilians died in December 1941;[11] the death rate exceeded 100,000 for each of January and February 1942.[12] The Soviets reported a grand total of 632,253 civilian deaths from starvation or related causes and 16,747 from bombs and artillery shells for the Nuremberg trials,[13] but other scholars claim this was an undercount.[14]

Perhaps the most powerful sign of the decay of institutions and norms was the appearance of cannibalism. While exact data are impossible to come by, the most frequent observation was flesh cut from corpses frozen in the street: Some Leningraders wrote in diaries that of walking past a particular corpse on the street every day and noticing more and more flesh missing. While civilians did not want to write about this topic,[15] ignoring the phenomenon became impossible as the number of mutilated corpses increased and became increasingly visible.[16] Meanwhile, police reports make for gruesome reading about the discovery of cannibals in action—from desperate civilians robbing the dead from graveyards for their own sustenance[17] to the (mercifully) few who killed civilians to sell their flesh in meat pies.[18] In all these accounts, one thing was clear: With cannibalism becoming part of the city's material and symbolic landscape, Leningraders were at risk of crossing a Rubicon, from order into disorder.

12.2 Near Collapse and Accidental Resilience from Above: Institutions

Soviet institutions have long been criticized for inefficiencies and various forms of shadow activity often labeled as "corruption." Soviet institutions were formally hierarchical, shadowed by an equally hierarchical Party structure. In theory, this should have been a system ready for the challenges of war: Orders from above (Stalin) would filter down through the chain of command and facilitate rapid adaptation, from conversion to military production to implementing civilian evacuations and rationing systems. In the first months of the war, this system was further streamlined. The State Defense Committee was set up in Moscow as the supreme decision-making body, and similar bodies were created in locales near the front. Political operations, from industrial policy to mobilizing and feeding civilians to directing the war effort, would follow one hierarchy, into which the rest fed. For example, the Military Council of the Leningrad Front was set up to coordinate civilian and military structures and avoid contradictions in the lines of authority. Some decisions were carried out with admirable capacity: For example, evacuations of industrial technology and (some) personnel from the western part of the country to the east of the Urals was carried out quickly and saved some industrial production from German capture or destruction. While the military–industrial complex was impressive, conversion from civilian to military output and mobilizing the civilian population to produce for the war effort was impressive as well.

Yet just as there were victories, there were also setbacks that threatened not only victory but especially survival. Stalin's problematic decisions before and early in the war are well known. Rather, our question is how existing institutions and procedures threatened to undercut any resilience and bring the whole edifice crashing down. One institutional legacy of the Soviet command economy was a curse of interdependency. In the structure of command economy, enterprises were dependent on inputs from other enterprises that might not be nearby—even if there was a perfect substitute in closer proximity. (This would persist until the collapse of the USSR and would contribute to economic woes after the USSR broke up into 15 sovereign countries.) Once the Blockade set in, Leningrad factories, including those in food preparation, were on their own and had to readjust supply lines, sometimes making up for what the rest of the country could no longer supply. As flour supplies became increasingly tenuous, local research institutes created ersatz ingredients: Pine needle extract, cellulose, and soy were among the more famous new ingredients for Blockade bread and other foodstuffs. This lag in developing replacement ingredients meant a drop in food availability—although this was a case where scientific know-how did manage to adjust quickly enough to provide some aid for the starving.

Such successes would be few and far between (besides the Red Army stabilizing the Leningrad Front) until 1942. While the regime announced that the bread ration would rise on December 25, 1941—ending the trend of declining rations—the reality was that stores did not have that extra bread. Mass death and institutional decay had begun.

12.2.1 Bureaucratic Failure and Institutional Compromise

The flip side is that hierarchy and concentration of authority in nodes along the way also threatened information and decision overload—too much to coordinate too quickly, perhaps by the wrong people—such that elites faced a new quantity and quality of challenges that they could not handle. Friedrich Hayek warned that Soviet-style systems risk bureaucratic failure because of information inefficiencies; in contrast, market signaling by autonomous actors is better at filtering and transmitting information about needs and desires than bureaucratic hierarchy.[19] Hayek was not entirely wrong: The Soviet command economy was notorious for information problems, from uneven reporting to outright lying by managers and officials desperate to game the Plan-oriented system. In the context of war and Blockade, information inefficiencies were combined with information overload: The wartime context was one of uncertainty, with constantly shifting challenges from the Germans, desperation inside the city, and rules and procedures from above (Moscow and Party headquarters in Leningrad) for coping with the situation. Institutional routines reinforce habits and skills for interpreting and responding. Sudden shocks, like war, can present institutional actors (elites and cadres) with unfamiliar situations, such that they cannot rely on routines (collective memory) and their own routines (individual memory) to cope effectively, at least in the short run. Such was the case in Leningrad. Many lower-level officials joined the Red Army, leaving their previous offices understaffed and now bereft of experienced personnel.[20] Routines and discipline suffered as a result.[21] Cadres were often moved from position to position and task to task, despite the fact that their experience and skills might not have a match for what they were supposed to do—and all of this in the middle of significant wartime uncertainty. (This was true even in the security services.)[22] In addition to the problematic fit between challenges, skills, and routines, many officials were too hungry to perform tasks properly,[23] and limited heat and electricity hindered various official duties, especially propaganda.[24]

These organizational challenges stemmed from a mismatch between institutional structures and routines, on the one hand, and new circumstances: The institutional design was not up to the context at the start. At the same time, the Soviet command economy already had created other obstacles to capacity that existed before the war and were only exacerbated by new desperation. One such manifestation of preexisting bureaucratic failure was *insider opportunism and competing nodes of dependency*. Institutions can be compromised internally when structures create opportunities and temptations within a system with too little and/or overburdened monitoring and sanction. This might be particularly problematic when control or distribution of food or similar resources is centralized and in only a few institutions (e.g. state-run or oligopoly), such that a few actors have access to those resources. This sounds counterintuitive—a few nodes should mean easier monitoring and authority—but the lack of competition creates the temptation to use access for opportunistic use. In other words, a centralized, hierarchical structure with too many links in the chain can increase the likelihood of opportunism and, as a result, a *de facto* "urge" to disaggregate—the essence of shadow economies everywhere.[25] Food stolen from the state can be sold in shadow markets, creating a competing node vis-à-vis the state.

This is just what happened in Leningrad. The command economy of the 1930s was already riddled with informal relations of favors and exchange that would later grow and be labeled the "shadow economy" (*tenevaia ekonomika*)—sometimes for private gain, other times to ensure that production ran more smoothly than it otherwise might have. Given that shadow practices already existed, and given that shadow exchange occurs in various other economies and societies at war, we would be surprised if exactly this did *not* happen in Leningrad. The scarcity of food meant that those with access to food faced a powerful temptation to steal some of that food, not only to eat better them-selves but also to resell that stolen food for speculative profit. And there were different ways to engage in such opportunistic behavior. One strategy involved ration cards (*prodovolstvennye kartochki*) and ration coupons (*talony*). Ration cards were distributed by local state agencies for set amounts of meat, bread, sugar, and other foodstuffs. This was one institutional site for opportunism: In return for kickbacks, cadres handing out ration cards might give some civil-ians more ration coupons (i.e. a higher ration category) than they deserved or give replacements for lost ration cards that actually had not been lost.[26] Various administrators sometimes took extra rations for their own use or to trade.[27] Another node for ration card abuse was at the point of exchange: bakeries, food stores, and canteens. Clerks at these places were supposed to take the proper number of ration coupons from civilians (no more than required), and they were supposed to glue used coupons to a blank sheet and mark them as used—in this way they could not be reused. Apparently, not all staff were doing this, quite possibly so that they could reuse them.[28] Another form of opportunistic food theft was illegal surpluses (*izlishki*). Employees at canteens and food stores were supposed to give civilians a carefully measured amount of food equal to the ration coupons exchanged, especially using scales to weigh precise amounts. This created another chance for opportunism: Food employ-ees could recalibrate scales so that they gave employees slightly less food than they deserved, and the employees could set aside the different. Some food managers were ambitious enough to steal food from their stores or depots.[29]

Those who stole food did not always consume it—there were profits to be made by selling that stolen food at higher speculative prices to starving civilians. One important site where supply and demand for this shadow exchange could meet was the *rynok*, collective farmers' markets.[30] The *rynok* ultimately consti-tuted an alternative node of relations and practices for obtaining food, and ulti-mately it existed partly in the shadows of institutions and as an institution in its own right. As a rule, "*rynok*" usually meant a few major sites in key population centers where significant market trade was carried out. (There were also "flea markets" on street corners that were shorter-lived and involved fewer people.) As Boris Mikhailov noted when recounting his Blockade youth, hungry civil-ians brought books, gold watches, and perhaps something stolen from work (such as glycerin); the sellers would come with food, usually bread.[31] Laws of supply and demand dominated: For example, by January 1, 1942, a kilogram of bread sold for 600 rubles, an astonishing sum (and ten times the price in

November 1941).[32] While the regime did investigate and arrest some of those internal opportunists supplying such shadow trade,[33] overall the regime could do little, and did do little, to suppress *rynok* speculation and trade.[34]

If civilians might be angry at such speculation and profit from desperation, they also saw this shadow trade in stolen food as a possible difference between life and death. This informal, lower-level privatization of food trade provoked angry letters from civilians to Leningrad chief Andrei Zhdanov, and many civilian diaries mention the signs of such corruption (e.g. food store managers and clerks looking better fed than average civilians).[35] Insider opportunism and shadow trade—made possible by centralized, hierarchical institutions, problematic monitoring, and preexisting opportunistic habits of the Soviet shadow economy—grew in importance and threatened the state's dependency power and perhaps even its right to rule. And it certainly threatened the state's capacity to maintain order and provide for the entire population.

12.2.2 Elite Coherence and Paradoxes of Parasitism

Order in Leningrad was hanging on by its fingertips as the distinct possibility of a Hobbesian war of all against all—Primo Levi's Law of the Lager, "eat your own bread, and if you can, that of your neighbor"[36]—hung like a shadow over the city. Yet Leningrad did hang on, and not entirely thanks to rules and structures designed by Stalin et al. in the 1930s or as invoked by Soviet historians and others since. Resilience and survival came from other quarters: Institutional accidents, innovations in the heat of the moment, and lower-level dynamics of general human behavior that the Soviet project was supposed to override but that, in the end, survived Stalin's politics and ultimately helped save the city. Formal governance structures both created possibilities for bureaucratic failure and facilitated opportunistic shadow practices that undercut state's capacity and authority, creating dangers to the survival of institutions and civilian life. But those governance structures also had unintended by-products that provided accidental resilience. The Prisoners' Dilemma was a real possibility, but an individually rational but collectively irrational outcome can also lead to *compelled opportunism and innovation* facilitating survival as well as collapse.

First, the hierarchical nature of the Soviet system created weaknesses, but it also did allow a coherent elite to mobilize and punish as a counterweight to disorder. In particular, if forces of repression still identify with the elite and institutions, then there is one more buttress to holding the system together just enough. For a modern example, if the internet goes out but cops on the beat have guns and orders to control key points in a city, then it might be possible to muddle through (or at least create new order). Stalin's elite remained coherent enough—although just why still requires more research—allowing them to punish or devolve as need be. This was a strategic disaggregation of picking and choosing what to hold together and what to allow to disaggregate. In Leningrad, Aleksei Kuznetsov, the second most authoritative person after Andrei Zhdanov, exhibited iron will and was willing to threaten disciplinary actions (the military tribunal and firing squad) to cajole or threaten subordinates to do their jobs. Additionally, the lack of competition allowed for some institutional inertia. There were no competing organizations formally or underground, as in 1917, thus averting disaggregation from turning into multiple sovereignty. Further, Leningraders did not imagine radically different political practices and political economy.[37] While they could, and did, imagine more responsive bureaucrats and maybe some loosening of politics and economics, for the most part they accepted the *status quo* as what they were defending, along with the city, the country, and their people. While civilians did not know how well their elites lived—those stories would come out decades later—they heard some of their leaders on the radio regularly, and Kuznetsov and the rest of the elite were constantly active and working together in the face of challenge after challenge. The ferocity of the German assault, paradoxically, created greater solidarity in the upper reaches of Leningrad's political institutions.

The second dynamic of adaptation and survival was, also paradoxically, market opportunism. Just as shadow theft and trade was draining the state of resources and reducing its capacity to maintain order through dependency relations, opportunists also contributed to reproducing order because, while they operated *parasitically* vis-à-vis the state, they did not act *competitively*. Shadow practices required those very institutions and rules holding Leningrad's political economy together: Given the absence of property rights (or, better, the state monopoly on property rights), speculators relied on this very economic order to keep them in business. And in fact, the evidence suggests that assistant managers, storage depot guards, accountants (covering the tracks of stolen food), drivers (taking food to the *rynok*), and others did not challenge the existing structure of food distribution and control. Insider opportunists wanted to maintain their benefits—inside positions and broader networks facilitating trade and theft—but they did not want the responsibility of investing in those structures, so they did not set up further shadow networks beyond the necessary, which could have further threatened institutional coherence. As an important comparative point, this more harmful alternative is what happened to Mikhail Gorbachev: *Perestroika* ultimately encouraged a radical increase in shadow practices and the transfer of wealth from the state sector to a legitimated private sector.

The shadow economy had other effects as well. First, it challenged state elites and officials to improve the formal provision for the civilian population. For example, in 1942 the state restructured feeding: Provision and content of meals were rationalized with a focus on workplace cafeterias, so that Leningraders could eat at work and worry less about hunting for food around the city. This also improved the relation between the state-run workplace and civilians, reducing uncertainty and increasing the state's dependency power. At one point in the middle of 1942, Zhdanov et al. considered competing with shadow trade directly, by providing civilians with the opportunity to trade personal belongings to the state in return for food vouchers—a legal form of quasi-market exchange. For reasons not entirely clear, however, this idea never went beyond the planning stage. Finally, while the state provided a basic amount of food, civilians were also allowed to settle their own accounts for survival. That is, the state was passing on some autonomy and responsibility for survival to people—reducing stress on already overburdened cadres—while also maintaining a modicum of order and provision to maintain legitimacy.

That the state could not stop insider opportunism and shadow trade could work to the benefit of resilience and survival. With hindsight, these challenges to the survival of institutions and lives were predictable: The Soviet system was Weberian bureaucracy on steroids, complete with the pathologies that scholars afterward noted: Information costs and information overload; bureaucratic failure; mismatches of skills and procedures in the context of a new and rapidly changing environment; and institutional shadows parasitically draining the state of the capacity to enforce order, in this case through dependency. Yet paradoxically, some of these traits would also create centripetal forces that buttressed institutions and order. Further, the decline in state's capacity and beginning of institutional decay revealed lower-level, local social forces and practices that did hold Leningrad together—forces often under the radar in analyses of macro-level phenomena and *longue durée*.

12.3 Resilience from Below: Anchors and Valences

While the story from above was a fine balance of decay and resilience, it was also a story of some disaggregation to lower levels of social organization. What happened "below" is no less crucial to our story of resilience under duress. Among families and small collectives of neighbors and fellow employees, local relations were not in perfect harmony. There were cases of theft, apartment robberies, and murders, but at the same time, Leningraders also maintained a semblance of social order as they braved hunger and cold to visit each other, share food, and hang on to a sense of "civilized" identities and local norms of everyday practice. Arguably, this was the crucial level of order, just as it was the crucial level of suffering. But what held this lower level of the order together? "Interests" is one possible candidate: Supporting existing norms and relations would benefit all. Yet the shadow of the Prisoners' Dilemma—especially the cell of individual interest and collective cost—hung over the city. Stealing food from others (including from one's own family) might contribute to collective decay, but it could get one to another day. Cooperation could not and did not depend on interests aligning on their own.

Something else was in play—and that something was *empathy*. The capacity to identify with others' pain and suffering made social relations that much more powerful and brought them into Leningraders' conscious strategies and practices. Yet empathy (especially in its positive form, sympathy) requires a direct object, and the fuzzier the target of empathy, the more likely such empathy has shallow roots. And empathy in the Blockade (as elsewhere) was not free-floating and chaotic. Rather, relations of empathy could be particularly acute and embedded in relations to *anchors*, entities of valence with which actors significantly identified emotionally and personally and into which they invested significant senses of self.[38] This concept comes from several different sources. First, in economic theory, actors "anchor" expectations about the future in current economic circumstances: Expectations and predictions are not free-floating but are grounded in what we know here and now.[39] A second source for this idea is attachment theory,[40] according to which human cognition and behavior are oriented initially to those who are close (e.g. parents for babies), which provides a sense of stability and security that allows us then to tackle the unknown parameters of our environments. In other words, we don't venture forth unless we start from a safe harbor—we anchor ourselves in known commodities. The third source for his idea is Bruno Latour's concept of "mediators"—animate, inanimate, or virtual entities we imbue with meaning via social relations.[41]

I suggest that we pin down Latour and others and ask just *in what* we anchor expectations and meanings. I suggest we think of *anchors* as entities into which we invest our identities, emotions, and interests so that these entities resonate senses of self. We define ourselves in terms of other entities, but anchors are particularly salient and central to those self-definitions (e.g. "child" to "parent"); anchors also structure the distribution and intensity of our senses of empathy (sympathy *and* antipathy).[42] As such, anchors link us into social contexts because those anchors are also embedded in relation to other actors, groups, and entities. We can think of this relationship as *self ⟺ anchor ⟺ social*. (I cannot yet comment on whether we can predict anchors *a priori*; maybe they are ultimately contingent.) The upshot of this concept of anchors is this: Because these anchors were linked to other social relations, they anchored individual Leningraders more firmly to families, local communities (neighborhoods and even workplaces), and the broader city community. Such relations also constrained strategies, for example reducing perceived gains or acceptability of instrumentally rational action, and they compelled other actions, such as defending these anchors or the general norms of behavior that affected them. Additionally, work in cognitive psychology has revealed that we are risk-averse: We tend to weigh risks over rewards when calculating different strategies and choices.[43] However, when we avoid risk, the next question is: Risk to what or whom? An obvious answer is risk to ourselves, but we are not atomized individuals; we are embedded in social relations. My suggestion is that one powerful set of such relations is vis-à-vis anchors of valence. Because they contribute to our senses of (persona and emotional) self, the risk to anchors becomes part of our calculation of risk and reward. A risk to an anchor (mate, child, close comrade, close collective) becomes something to avoid; conversely, their well-being is to be preserved. Defending anchors might then also mean defending a modicum of the norms and practices in which those anchors are embedded.

One received a bit of wisdom that soldiers fight first for comrades, then for families, and only then for king and country. This is no surprise: The first two construct the individual's identity through personal and emotional valence.

This suggests that the survival of individuals and the city in the Blockade was an example of *resilience of the simple*, grounded in empathy directed at specific Others, and this in turn linked Leningraders into wider fields of relations and institutions. As they were defending themselves, they were defending their own, and from there they were defending the broader community. To flesh out this argument and this facet of survival and resilience in the Blockade, I use two quick examples of anchors at work: Gender and food.

12.3.1 Positive Valences and Order: Gender

Gender relations and identities in the USSR were not so different from those elsewhere in the modern world. As elsewhere, women were compelled to identify themselves vis-à-vis an intimate Other,[44] mates and children in particular. As well, the compulsion to perform the second shift—carrying out such domestic tasks and economically finding and preparing food for kith and kin and caring in general—bequeathed women skills that, if manifestations of inequality before 1941, were now crucial for survival. While Leningrad women were not unaware of gender inequities of Soviet institutions and practices, they accepted them as the way things were—and in the Blockade, they soon realized that (1) these gendered skills were crucial for the survival of the whole city, and (2) they gained new status from helping husbands, fathers, and children survive. Just as they took over men's positions in factories, they also became the true breadwinners as well as caregivers of their families.

And women did so less out of a sense of gain or interest, than out of this sense of gendered identity. For women, mates and children were anchors of valence, and so they channeled their remaining energies into everyday prewar practices of caregiving. Varvara Vraskaia's husband, a professor of the city *intelligentsia*, would not deign to trade family belongings at markets for extra food. In contrast, Vraskaia was more willing to do so to save herself, her husband, and their daughter Irina (whose growing hunger she noticed long before her husband did). In late 1941, her husband died, and Vraskaia traded away the family goods for food and money that she used to keep herself and Irina alive and then survive the long evacuation trek to Tbilisi.[45] Ultimately, breadseeking and pragmatism saved herself and her daughter; her husband's less pragmatic attitude led to his death. Had he taken his wife's concerns and suggestions seriously, he might have survived. Even more revealing of the importance of women's efforts and unquestioning dedication to families came from men themselves. Mikhail Pelevin wrote that he and his father were too weak to leave their beds. Each day his mother would come to see each of them after work—father and son lived in separate places—and always bringing food. The eldest daughter of a neighbor's family, according to Pelevin, went throughout the city seeking food to keep her family alive.[46] Worker Lev Kogan repeatedly noted his wife's comings and goings, always for food or tobacco. Without her selfless efforts, he admitted, he would not have survived.[47]

This sense of women anchored in relation to key Others—anchors of valence—was further reinforced by women's sense of improved status and even superiority in comparison with men. Women clearly observed that men succumbed to hunger and weakness more quickly, and they deduced that this was because men more readily gave up and stopped being active—activity, they surmised, was the key to remaining alive.[48] Women both explained their greater energy and judged men to be weaker simultaneously, through this anchor relation. That they accepted caregiving became a foundation for their narrative of wartime heroism. Commenting on how much other women did, artist Anna Ostroumova-Lebedeva admitted,

> the impression that men are many times weaker than women in the struggle for life and resistance to death … The majority of men, if their wives are evacuated and they [men] remained alone (if they had not taken different wives!), very weakly resist difficulties of our life and die faster than women.[49]

According to Antonina Liubimova, women

> never were so helpless, never were such psychological dystrophics, as men. I never saw women begging for bread or ration cards. Men always begged for something, although rarely did anyone give them anything; those who did not leave for the front or evacuate and had not yet died had a look of complete idiotism.[50]

Mates, parents, children, and close friends were one set of anchors whom women defended as part of their sense of self and employing caregiving skills and dispositions imparted by everyday experience and demands of the second shift. Another wider anchor was the city itself—a city made up of other families like theirs and defended by soldiers who were women's sons, brothers, and husbands. And so Leningrad itself was a second-order personal anchor of valence for many women. The Red Army was staffed mostly by men, and so women ended up taking their places in factories producing munitions or other important output. While there was a material incentive to do so—women could earn better wages and, more importantly, higher category rations—women also generally embraced this as a "patriotic" duty, with patriotism refracted through real, concrete soldiers whom they knew at the front.[51] While women had worked in industry before the war, more often than not they were lower-status and lower-paying waged in textile and similar factories. Their new male bosses often did not think these women were up to the task of physically demanding and skilled labor, but the women quickly adapted and showed that they were men's equals—often to the surprise, and satisfaction, of these male bosses.[52] The foreman at one textile factory relayed his surprise that women could move from lower-skilled to high-skilled work so quickly in late 1941: "As a man, I must say that never in my life could I have thought that women workers could have that much strength in the winter of 1941-1942."[53] Some women—such as Sofia Akselrod, Party secretary for the Vena factory— were not surprised that women were up to the task.[54]

In one case, women's devotion to anchors of valence—in this case, children—set them at odds with the authorities. This issue was the evacuation of children in summer 1941. With the Wehrmacht on the move, Leningrad's authorities decided to try to evacuate children to summer camps outside the city. Mothers were not always keen on the idea of letting go of their children in wartime, and it took a great effort by Party activists to get to them agree to do so.[55] This would soon appear to be a grave mistake, as reports came in that some trainloads of children had been sent toward the German army.[56] Mothers were not inclined to let their children go before; now, many mothers set out to bring their children home.[57] This was no easy task: The railways were already strained by the logistics and load of transporting Red Army soldiers to various destinations, requiring women to be creative and persevering.[58] Yet mothers put up with the trials and tribulations to bring their children out of one harm's way and, tragically, back into another.

These are only a few of many stories, told from the points of view of husbands, children, and women themselves about how Leningrad women rose to the challenge of defending the city on several fronts. They did not do so out of any calculation for improving their lives in the future—a tit-for-tat, I-saved-you-now-you-respect-me agreement. Rather, women did this because this was what women were supposed to do—not simply care for individuals, families, and collectives but do so out of a sense of self linked to important Others. Key to our topic is that women were the bedrock of Blockade survival, and women did so out of a sense of gendered duty toward positive anchors of valence. When the state could not provide sufficient food and other needs for survival, women stepped up, and not out of interest or emotion alone. Rather, the construction of identities and senses of self involved close Others whose well-being was crucial to many (although not all) women. If defending family and bravado led men to volunteer for fighting at the front, gendered anchors of valence and relations of caregiving facilitated resilience at primordial levels of social relations—family and intimate peers. Without this, the state might have organized sufficient *military* defense of the city—but what would have been left to defend without women and gendered anchors is too tragic a thought to contemplate.

12.3.2 Negative Valences and Order: Innovations of "Food"

In this previous case, women felt compelled to take on the burdens of caregiving and military work to defend close Others. This was an example of positive anchors' compelling action that would protect the well-being of positive Others. However, there were anchors of negative valence—repulsive Others that might have been unavoidable, but whose negative traits compelled Leningraders to defend general norms and a sense of "civilization" lest such negative Others reshape Soviet society for the worse. In other words, just as some anchors compelled defense, others were compelled to keep up the fight to retain some semblance of humanity's dignity, even if this put at risk otherwise rational strategies for survival.

This sense of negative anchors and defense of a dignified social order was more relevant to the *moral order* rather than the institutional order. Violating institutional systems—for example, breaking the law to trade in the shadow economy—might have raised some distaste, but for the most part such practices were coded as necessary for survival. Many civilians did not find it moral and desirable that they had to pay high prices for food at the *rynok*, but they accepted this as a means to survival because they were purchasing traditional "food." However, if survival strategies and adaptations required rethinking "food," even in the context of mass starvation, then symbolic and moral revulsion might hinder using such strategies, at least initially. And when bread and other "normal" food became too scarce in the first Blockade winter, Leningraders had to use unorthodox sources: aspic made with glue, boiled leather belts, and pressed seed husks, among other things. Leningraders had no problem mentioning such non-traditional "food" in a casual manner in their diaries, without much deep or troubling reflection on this deviation from traditional consumption. Some diarists even referred to glue aspic as tasty; one could, after all, add bay leaf and salt to the concoction.

However, desperate hunger and no clear end to the siege drove starving civilians to expand the boundaries of the consumable, and this began to create trepidation and put Leningraders in a bind: Was there anything *not* edible? If anything could be reclassified as "food," what might this do to the entire moral and social order that soldiers were defending at the front and that civilians were defending with their sacrifices and suffering patience? When anything could become "food," then survival was ultimately a Hobbesian nightmare, threatening lower-level solidarity that was providing resilience and robustness for the city. This slippery slope began as hungry Leningraders turned to animate sources of food beyond the traditional. Eating meat from chickens and cows had long been accepted, and even eating horse meat was not entirely out of the question; when a German artillery shell would kill a horse, civilians on hand might run up to it to collect whatever meat they could. However, transforming other animals into food demonstrated to civilians not only how desperate they were but also the moral and personal costs of survival. Cats, dogs, and birds could provide sustenance and survival—but these animals had a domestic meaning to them (even when wild), unlike beasts of burden or normal consumption. As such, they usually enjoyed human empathy and were not entirely "objects" that could be used as one desired. This led to increasing foreboding: Along with fear of hunger and rising death rates (visible through the growing number of corpses on the street toward the end of 1941), Leningraders began to fear the death of civilization. In diaries and recollections, Leningraders drew attention to the disappearance of cats and dogs in more than a perfunctory manner (unlike blasé references to glue jelly). In particular, discussions about eating cats were laced with normative judgments (this was immoral) and that this was a bad omen for human nature.

However, such negative reflection on eating cats—whether a response to stories of consuming cats, or actually eating cat meat—ended up being something else besides surrendering to fatalism. Rather, Leningraders' negative reflections on eating cats reinforced a sense of boundaries that should not be crossed, or at least not crossed except in dire straits and by accident. In other words, eating cats enhanced a sense of *necessary boundaries* not to be crossed, and when crossed, resurrected as quickly as possible. Glafira Korneeva wrote, "[One acquaintance] and I hated these cat-eaters as our personal enemies. Let them die, I have little pity."[59] Despite being extremely hungry, Serafima Evdokimova refused her aunt's soup because she suspected it was made with cat meat.[60] Olga Mikhailova recalled that one friend committed suicide after her mother ate her cat, because this was a horrible Rubicon: If one ate cats, what came next?[61]

"What came next" was often too horrifying for Leningraders to write about initially. If anything, cannibalism revealed limits to what many Leningraders claimed they would do for survival. Diary narratives and judgments about the news of cannibalism reveal a fear that their civilization was truly falling apart: Even more than eating cats, consuming human flesh suggested that people really were no different from animals, in which case human civilization (Soviet or otherwise) was illusory. This threatened resilience from below: Why suffer and sacrifice for something so superficial in the first place? Writing about the subject almost seemed to normalize it, and so many Blockade diarists mentioned cannibalism only briefly—and clearly with difficulty—once the signs of cannibalism began to appear.[62] However, as stories spread of corpses in the streets missing flesh or the police arresting people for killing children and selling their flesh in meat pies,[63] diarists wrote down more detail. And they did so not in a dispassionate manner. Instead, they used tones of disgust and terror, stressing the abnormality and even criminality of such a practice. (It was the rare Leningrader who discussed cannibalism as normal in such extreme circumstances.) This was a further extension of the logic of what could be consumed: Glue was allowable, and eating dogs and cats was bad enough but was justified by extreme hunger. Eating human flesh, even if taken from a corpse, was a bridge too far. While data on the extent of cannibalism are sketchy at best, what is surprising is that available data suggest that cannibalism was far rarer than one might expect for such a large number of starving and dying people. What is also informative is that stories of cannibalism in Leningraders' diaries often enough linked the practice to *children* and the *market*: Cannibals were not desperate civilians but instead were predators preying on the most innocent and helpless civilians (children), and they were using the flesh of children to sell meat pies at the marketplace (*rynok*) for profit. In this way, civilians used the signs of clear desperation (corpses missing flesh) to construct narratives of extreme abnormality that had to be combated—at the least in one's own diary and in one's head. In this way, civilians used cannibalism not to bewail the end of that illusory civilization but rather to rally themselves to defend it. Rather than driving the degeneration of social solidarity and norms, cannibalism contributed to local will and efforts at resilience.

For women, a sense of gendered relations to positive anchors compelled extra efforts aimed at others' survival. On the other hand, negative anchors—in this case, non-traditional food and especially cannibalism—served as warnings that everyday norms, not to mention formal laws, were in danger of collapsing altogether. A "rational" defense of eating cats and dogs was treated with the implied caveat that this was abnormal practice for a highly abnormal situation; while Leningraders could bounce back if the food supply improved, this was still a dangerous adaptation. Eating human flesh, however, was for many a bridge too far. By describing cannibalism in a negative vein, rather than as one more rational adaptation against starvation, Leningraders used cannibalism as a symbolic border between civilized and uncivilized. While revulsion against cannibalism did not maintain order by itself, it contributed to the compulsion to defend norms and a sense of collective order. Like gendered Others and gendered duty, cannibalism paradoxically aided resilience at this lower level of social organization.

12.4 Insights from Leningrad's Tragedy and Triumph

World War I broke social order in Petrograd and then in the rest of the Russian Empire. World War II turned out differently, although resilience and then victory were not preordained by any stretch. For our story of resilience, Stalinist fields of power—which we still do not understand well enough—did not collapse, but neither did they escape the catastrophe unscathed. The war triggered a new search for identities and narratives[64] and briefly held the possibility of some degree of change, albeit on the margins and not directly threatening the Communist Party's monopoly of power.[65] Most importantly, despite the massive loss of human life and even more massive amount of suffering that civilians endured, Leningrad survived. Resilience was not entirely thanks to the Red Army: Had the city not endured, soldiers would have been dying in vain with nothing to defend.

Are there broader lessons about resilience and collapse that we can extract from the Blockade experience?[66] At the "macro"-level—a higher-order level of social organization, the aggregate of institutions and especially those of the state—complexity and shocks can create overload or mismatches between institutional skills and routines and new needs. This can trigger disaggregation, which in some cases threatens decay (Leningrad) or eruption (Petrograd). Centralization and hierarchy can provide some degree of order and coordination, but they can also provide possibilities and temptations for opportunism and thus decay of order. At the same time, such opportunism can reproduce the template of basic order parasitically; when this buttresses the institutional order (Leningrad 1941) or leads to further decay (Leningrad and the USSR under Gorbachev), there remains a question that requires much more comparative research.

A bigger insight of the Blockade is that there are fundamental forces at lower levels of social order that can provide a backstop to disaggregation and a basis for resilience. Empathy, anchors of valence, and dignity ultimately might be centripetal forces that can mediate against centrifugal forces of bureaucratic failure and opportunism. As broader systems disaggregate, there might be something below providing a foundation for concatenation once again. It might be that bigger "civilizations" do decay or collapse under the weight of external challenges and internal contradictions—but we could think of this as disaggregation to lower levels of order less dependent on those bigger formal institutions. In such a case, "collapse" becomes a relative term, although disaggregation means losing some economies of scale and scope. The overall story of the Soviet political economy (at war and in peacetime) demonstrated the drawbacks of centralization and hierarchy and the advantages of devolution and local knowledge; arguably, the USSR is a case study of bureaucratic failure. This does not mean we automatically condemn bigger structures, for these also provide capacities for mobilization at a grand scale, whether for classic industrial production or a rapid shift to a needed green economy.

One interesting lesson from the Blockade experience might point to a general dynamic of resilience at lower levels of social organization. If my analysis is correct, shocks and duress such as war can facilitate or even compel new thinking and innovations that threaten the existing order and challenge resilience. Opportunistic shadow exchange in the Blockade was one such example; a more extreme example is revolution.[67] However, this suggests a linear dynamic: More shocks and duress lead to more weakness in existing structures and institutions, and thus greater autonomous or opportunistic behavior—and the whole thing comes crashing down. But maybe this is not entirely true; maybe there are limits to disaggregation. Perhaps instead we should think of an *inverted U-shaped curve*: Degree of shock and increasing disorder and uncertainty along the x-axis; degree of opportunism or autonomy (disaggregation) along the y-axis. Institutions and structures hold together when there is no real shock; power and habit persist unless something hinders them. However, at some point, *the assault on order becomes too great*. In these cases, the threat of disorder—real or predicted—becomes great enough that people pull back from taking advantage of autonomy and avoid a war of all against all. In other words, if disaggregation seems to be turning into an institutional avalanche, enough actors might think consciously about *defending* existing order and relations, because however costly these might be, the alternative is that Hobbesian state of nature. If anchors of valence do matter, then people might defend the basic norms and rules of order not only to save themselves but also to save those close Others. (This is especially true if we are risk-averse at heart.) If uncertainty becomes too great, innovation or opportunism can contribute to a sense of increasing threat that will reduce urges or incentives to innovate or to be opportunistic as a rule.

Despite incredible strains and suffering, institutional contradictions and opportunism, and incentives to guard one's back, Leningraders were resilient. In 2020, COVID-19 tested institutional resilience, revealing weaknesses in decision-making abilities and health care policies (but not personnel), and exacerbating preexisting political polarization and contentious politics (e.g. supporters of strict measures on the Left versus libertarians rejecting the danger of COVID-19 and instead noting dangers to the economy). However, the experience of shared threat—and one visible in illness and deaths of real people—has often enough created senses of compassion and solidarity. Resilience in the face of the novel coronavirus might come not only from states with the right balance of centralization and devolution but also from people taking small actions not only to save their own lives but also to save those of others whose empathy and identity compel care and attention.

Notes & References

1 Nikita Lomagin, "Soldiers at War: German Propaganda and Soviet Army Morale During the Battle of Leningrad, 1941-44," *The Carl Beck Papers in Russian and East European Studies*, #1306 (Pittsburgh: University of Pittsburgh, 1998).

2 Jeffrey K. Hass, *Wartime Suffering and Survival: The Human Condition under Siege in the Blockade of Leningrad, 1941-1944* (New York: Oxford University Press, 2021), chapters 2, 5, and 7.

3 Pitirim Sorokin, *Hunger as a Factor in Human Affairs* (Gainesville, FL: University of Florida Press, 1975); Sergei Iarov, *Blokadnaia etika: Predstavleniia o morale v Leningrade v 1941-1942 gg* (St. Petersburg: Nestor-Istoriia, 2011).

4 Jeffrey K. Hass, *Power, Culture, and Economic Change in Russia 1988-2008:To the Undiscovered Country of Post-Socialism* (New York and Abingdon: Routledge, 2011); *Rethinking the Post-Soviet Experience. Markets, Moral Economies, and Cultural Contradictions of Post-Socialist Russia* (New York and Basingstoke: Palgrave Macmillan, 2012); *Wartime Suffering and Survival;* "Anchors, *Habitus*, and Practices Besieged by War: Women and Gender in the Blockade of Leningrad," *Sociological Forum* 32/2 (2017), pp. 253–276; "War, Fields, and Competing Economies of Death. Lessons from the Blockade of Leningrad," *Poetics* 48 (2015), pp. 55–68; "Norms and Survival in the Heat of War: Normative versus Instrumental Rationalities and Survival Tactics in the Blockade of Leningrad," *Sociological Forum* 26/4 (2011), pp. 921–949.

5 I cannot address all facets of this story of survival. For example, in this chapter I have to elide a discussion of "tragic agency" and how anchors (defined below) reshape dynamics and notions of "power." I discuss these more at length in my book, but even then there remains more to explain regarding power and resilience (and collapse) that go beyond the usual treatments of power and order in much social science (e.g. literature on revolutions). For one take on power not so different from my own (but not the same, either), see Lucia A. Seybert and Peter J. Kazenstein, "Protean Power and Control Power: Conceptual Analysis," in Peter J. Kazenstein and Lucia A. Seybert (eds.), *Protean Power: Exploring the Uncertain and Unexpected in World Politics* (New York: Cornell University Press, 2018), pp. 3–26.

6 The Soviet government sent materials about the Blockade to the Nuremberg trials as evidence of Nazi crimes against humanity.

7 A.V. Liubimov, *Torgovlia i snabzhenie v SSSR v gody Velikoi Otechestvennoi voiny* (Moscow: Ekonomika, 1969), pp. 20–22.

8 TsGAIPD SPb (Central State Archive of Historical-Political Documents, St. Petersburg) f. 25, op. 15, d. 143, l. 75–78.

9 TsGAIPD SPb f. 4000, op. 20, d. 9, l. 2; Pavlov, *Leningrad v blokade*, p. 89, 112; TsGAIPD SPb f. 4000, op. 20, d. 4, l. 11.

10 A. R. Dzeniskevich, *Leningrad v osade. Sbornik dokumentov o geroicheskoi oborone Leningrada v gody Velikoi Otechestvennoi voiny 1941-1944* (St. Petersburg: Liki Rossii, 1995), pp. 199, 203–208.

11 TsGA SPb (Central State Historical Archive, St. Petersburg) f. 4965, op. 3, d. 45, l. 3.

12 TsGAIPD SPb f. 24, op. 2b, d. 1322, l. 51, in Dzeniskevich, *Leningrad v osade*, p. 298.

13 TsGA SPb f. 8557, op. 6, d. 1109, l. 1, in Dzeniskevich, *Leningrad v osade*, p. 562.

14 V. M. Kovalchuk, and G. L. Sobolev, "Leningradskii rekviem (o zhertvakh naseleniia v Leningrade v gody voiny i blokady)," *Voprosy istorii* #12 (1965), pp. 191–194; Nadezhda Cherepenina, "Golod i smert v blokirovannom gorode," in John Barber and Arkadii Dzeniskevich (eds.), *Zhizn i smert v blokirovannom Lenignrade* (St. Petersburg: Dmitrii Bulanin, 2001), pp. 35–80.

15 For example, RNB OR (Russian National Library, Manuscripts Division) f. 1015, d. 57, l. 160, 171.

16 For example, RNB OR f. 1015, d. 57, l. 177, 178.

17 TsGA SPb f. 7179, op. 53, d. 57, l. 1, 2, 28.

18 E.g. TsGAIPD SPb f. 4000, op. 10, d. 484, l. 5; TsGAIPD SPb f. 4000, op. 11, d. 57, l. 17; Tatiana Maksimova, *Vospominaniia o Leningradskoi blockade* (St. Petersburg: Zhurnal "Neva," 2002), p. 19. For a broader discussion of cannibalism, see Hass, *Wartime Suffering and Survival*, chapter 3.

19 Friedrich Hayek, "The Use of Knowledge in Society," *American Economic Review* 34/4 (1945): 519–530; also *The Road to Serfdom* (Chicago: University of Chicago Press, 1944).

20 TsGAIPD SPb f. 24, op. 2v, d. 5766, l. 35; TsGAIPD SPb f. 411, op. 2, d. 11, l. 14–15.

21 TsGAIPD SPb f. 411, op. 2, d. 11, l. 17–18, 21; TsGAIPD SPb f. 4000, op. 10, d. 363, l. 4–6; TsGAIPD SPb f. 4000, op. 10, d. 1173, l. 1.

22 TsGAIPD SPb f. 24, op. 2v, d. 5766, l. 44–51.

23 TsGAIPD SPb f. 25, op. 10, d. 330, l. 19; TsGAIPD SPb f. 4000, op. 20, d. 17, l. 1, 25; TsGAIPD SPb f. 4000, op. 20, d. 57, l. 50; TsGA SPb f. 7384, op. 4, d. 60, l. 186; TsGA SPb f. 7384, op. 4, d. 69, l. 16; Lomagin, *Neizvestnaia blokada*, vol. 1, pp. 154, 156; Lomagin, *Leningrad v blokade*, pp. 342–343;

24 TsGAIPD SPb f. 25, op. 10, d. 330, l. 2, 11, 17, 19.

25 As Elena Osokina pointed out in her study of Soviet rationing in the 1930s and "hierarchies of consumption," American wartime rationing allowed civilians to choose what rationed goods they needed more than others. This led to the more efficient distribution of rationed goods. Soviet wartime rationing followed the prewar model: Strict and uniform ration rules for the entire country, with ration amounts linked to the utility for the regime (and the war effort after 1941). Granted, food shortages in the USSR were far worse than in the USA.

26 Dzeniskevich, *Leningrad v osade*, pp. 224–225; TsGA SPb f. 7384, op. 4, d. 88, l. 198–199.

27 TsGA SPb f. 7384, op. 4, d. 88, l. 200–202.

28 TsGA SPb f. 7384, op. 4, d. 88, l. 143.

29 TsGAIPD SPb f. 411, op. 2, d. 44, l. 3; TsGAIPD SPb f. 25, op. 2, d. 4448, l. 34.

30 On the Blockade *rynok* system, see V. L. Piankevich, "Rynok v osazhdennom Leningrade," in B. P. Belozerov (ed.), *Zhizn' i byt blokirovannogo Leningrada* (St. Petersburg: Nestor-Istoriia, 2010), pp. 122–163; Hass, *Wartime Suffering and Survival*, chapters 2 and 5. On the pre-war *rynok* system in Leningrad, see Elena Tverdiukova, "Kolkhoznaia torgovlia Leningrada 1930-kh godov," *Vestnik St.-Peterburgskogo universiteta, Seriia 2: Istoriia*, #4 (2007), pp. 126–134.

31 Boris Mikhailov, *Na dne blokady i voiny* (St. Petersburg: VSEGEI, 2000), p. 58.

32 TsGAIPD SPb f. 4000, op. 11, d. 54, l. 9.

33 For example, see TsGAIPD SPb f. 4000, op. 20, d. 57, l. 1–3; TsGAIPD SPb f. 24, op. 2v, d. 990, l. 80–86; f. 4000, op. 10, d. 372, l. 5–6.

256   *Jeffrey K. Hass*

34 TsGA SPb f. 7384, op. 4, d. 67, l. 62–84.
35 For example, see I. A. Vladimirov, *"Pamiatka o velikoi otechestvennoi voine."* Blokadnye *zametki 1941-1944 gg* (St. Petersburg: Dmitrii Bulanin, 2009), pp. 79–82; Dmitrii I. Kargin, *Velikoe i tragichnoe. Leningrad 1941-1942* (St. Petersburg: Nauka, 2000), p. 38, 42–43; G. A. Kniazev, *Dni velikikh ispytanii. Dnevniki 1941-1945* (St. Petersburg: Nauka, 2009), pp. 564–565.
36 Primo Levi, *Survival in Auschwitz and the Reawakening* (New York: Summit, 1985), p. 160.
37 Hass, *Wartime Suffering and Survival*, chapter 7.
38 Hass, *Wartime Suffering and Survival*, chapters 1 and 4.
39 Refet Gürkaynak, Andrew Levin, Andrew Marder, and Eric Swanson, "Inflation Targeting and the Anchoring of Inflation Expectations in the Western Hemisphere," *Economic Review*, Federal Reserve Bank of San Francisco 2007 (2007), pp. 25–47; Fritz Strack and Thomas Mussweiler, "Explaining the Enigmatic Anchoring Effect: Mechanisms of Selective Accessibility," *Journal of Personality and Social Psychology* 73 (1997), pp. 437–446; Adrian Furnham and Hua Chu Boo, "A Literature Review of the Anchoring Effect," *Journal of Socio-Economics* 40 (2011), pp. 35–42.
40 Mario Mikulincer, Philip R. Shaver, and Dana Pereg, "Attachment Theory and Affect Regulation: The Dynamics, Development, and Cognitive Consequences of Attachment-Related Strategies," *Motivation and Emotion* 27, #2 (2003), pp. 77–102; John Bowlby, *Attachment and Loss: Vol. 1 Attachment*, 2nd edition (New York: Basic Books, 1982), *Attachment and Loss: Vol. 2. Separation: Anxiety and Anger* (New York: Basic Books, 1973); Nyla R. Cranscombe, Naomi Ellemers, Russell Spears, and Bertjan Doosje, "The Context and Content of Social Identity Threat," in Russell Spears (ed.), *Social Identity: Context, Commitment, Content* (Oxford: Blackwell, 1999), pp. 35–58.
41 Bruno Latour, *Reassembling the Social: An Introduction to Actor-Network Theory* (New York: Oxford University Press, 2005).
42 While I will focus primarily on anchors with positive valence, negative valences— anchors that define us by actively repelling us—are also possible. I briefly discuss negative anchors toward the end of this chapter.
43 Daniel Kahneman and Amos Tversky, "Prospect Theory: An Analysis of Decision under Risk," *Econometrica* 47, #2 (1979), pp. 263–291; Amos Tversky and Daniel Kahneman, "Advances in Prospect Theory: Cumulative Representation of Uncertainty," *Journal of Risk and Uncertainty* 5, #4 (1992), pp. 297–323.
44 Cf. Simone de Beauvoir, *The Second Sex* (New York: Alfred A. Knopf, 1952).
45 RNB OR f. 1273, d. 13, l. 31–38.
46 RNB OR f. 1273, d. 49, l. 4–5, 27–32.
47 RNB OR f. 1035, d. 1, l. 1, 3, 6, 17.
48 Cf. TsGAIPD SPb 4000/11/34-35, 39, 74–77.
49 RNB OR f. 1015, d. 59, l. 71.
50 TsGALI SPb (Central State Archive of Literature and the Arts, St. Petersburg) f. 114, op. 1, d. 5, l. 35.
51 Sometimes women used this fact when complaining to the authorities: Namely, that they deserved more food or better treatment, otherwise their soldier husbands might become angry. This was in a city where soldiers rebelled during a war and sparked a revolution. Cf. Hass, *Wartime Suffering and Survival*, chapter 4.
52 For example: TsGAIPD SPb f. 4000, op. 10, d. 839, l. 2–4; f. 4000, op. 10, d. 565, l. 11; f. 4000, op. 10, d. 628, l. 1–2.
53 TsGAIPD SPb f. 4000, op. 10, d. 327, l. 47.
54 TSGAIPD SPb f. 4000, op. 10, d. 484, l. 3.
55 TsGAIPD SPb f. 4000, op. 12, d. 859, l. 10.
56 TsGAIPD SPb f. 4000, op. 10, d. 496, l. 1–3.
57 TsGAIPD SPb f. 5, op. 3, d. 35, l. 21; TsGALI SPb f. 522, op. 1, d. 39, l. 29.
58 RNB OR f. 1273, d. 13, l. 5–7.
59 TsGAIPD SPb f. 4000, op. 11, d. 51, l. 21.

60 Dmitrii Oberderfer, *Blokada Leningrada glazami ochevidtsa (po vospominaniiam uchastnitsy oborony Leningrada)* (Omsk: OmGPU, 2000), p. 38.
61 TsGALI SPb f. 107, op. 3, d. 336, l. 18–19.
62 For example, RNB OR f. 1015, d. 57, l. 160 (diary of Anna Ostroumova-Lebedeva); S. K. Bernev and C. V. Chernov (eds.), *Blokadnye dnevniki i dokumenty* (St. Petersburg: Evropeiskii Dom, 2004), p. 69.
63 For example, TsGALI SPb f. 107, op. 3, d. 374, l. 11–12; f. 107, op. 3, d. 423, l. 92–93.
64 Amir Weiner, *Making Sense of War* (Princeton: Princeton University Press, 2001).
65 Julie Hessler, "A Postwar Perestroika? Toward a History of Private Enterprise in the USSR," *Slavic Review* 57 (1998), pp. 526–543; A. Z. Vakser, *Leningrad poslevoennyi 1945–1982* (St. Petersburg: Ostrov, 2005).
66 While I have discussed resilience and summarized a few lessons, the Blockade also speaks to the story of *transformation*—including in this case *possible* transformations (embryonic and underway) later suddenly denied when repression returned in the Leningrad Affair and high Stalinism. That discussion is too complex (and that next part of this larger project on duress, institutions, and survival), and I leave it aside for now, except to note that these experiences of wartime survival were compelling a more fundamental shift in the nature of Soviet institutions and authority that could have resulted in more pragmatic Soviet political culture.
67 Theda Skocpol, *States and Social Revolutions* (New York: Cambridge University Press, 1979).

Section 3

Systemic Collapse Insights from Ecology, Climate, and the Environment

The studies of systemic risk, resilience, collapse, and transformation have benefited greatly from the work of scholars in the environmental sciences. Seeking to make sense of complex socio-ecological systems where flora, fauna, and the environment interact across multiple temporal and spatial scales, environmental science scholars have worked to develop frameworks and methodologies that can be applied to the study of systems more generally. The chapters in this section draw from and build upon diverse literature from the environmental sciences to provide rich and multidisciplinary perspectives on historical collapse, mechanisms of resilience, and systemic collapse more generally.

This section begins with a chapter by Timothy Lenton in which he identifies an array of concepts and methodologies from environmental science that are well suited to the study of historical collapse. Concepts like resilience, positive and negative feedback loops, tipping points, system identities, stable states, and ball in valley (or ball in basin) models are applied critically to the study of human societies. Linking some historical collapses to past climate events and conditions, Lenton also works to dispel the myth that recorded human history has been characterized mostly by a stable and predictable climate. Instead, he shows how past civilizations had to overcome turbulent climatic challenges during the Holocene and that, paradoxically, climate stressors have served as catalysts for both the origin and downfall of complex societies. Looking to the future, Lenton advocates for more thorough study of the feedback dynamics present in historical collapse cases and argues that more rigorous modeling of these feedback mechanisms could unlock insights relevant to our modern challenges.

Next, John Anderies and Simon Levin also discuss the importance of studying feedback loops to understanding collapse, writing that these mechanisms are "extraordinarily powerful," critical for creating and maintaining a system's structure and dynamics, and that their regulation is "ubiquitous in biological and social systems." With the criticality of these mechanisms in mind, the authors discuss the potential usefulness of the "Coupled Infrastructure Systems" (CIS) framework, which highlights how feedback loops within the biophysical world of natural resources and the built environment are linked to those within the political and economic realms of decisionmakers. This link between

DOI: 10.4324/9781003331384-16

loops creates a "feedback network" that can become complex and opaque, and begin to hide fragilities within a system. Seeing civilization through a biological lens, the authors discuss how these networks function in complex societies. They introduce the notion of "hard robustness limits," show how regulatory feedbacks contribute to robustness tradeoffs, and pose the question: Is societal collapse inevitable?

Finally, Christina Grozinger and Harland Patch round out this section with a concrete case study from the natural world. Looking at bee colonies, Grozinger and Patch examine the feedback loops, species characteristics, and resilience strategies that make these insects both vulnerable and resilient to colony collapse. As generalists with unique abilities to alter the makeup of their population, honey bees are well suited to manage shocks to their ecosystem. These characteristics, however, prove unsustainable in situations of chronic stress and make colonies vulnerable to collapse if they approach certain temporal thresholds or tipping points. An understanding of the resilience strategies used by other species, along with an awareness of how they interact with broader systemic characteristics, could prove invaluable to our discussion on collapse as we work to model and develop strategies to overcome fragilities in our human systems.

13 Climate Change and Tipping Points in Historical Collapse

Timothy M. Lenton

13.1 Introduction

In a world beset by rising inequality, widespread ecological degradation, and escalating climate change, the prospect of triggering "tipping points" of societal collapse is of growing concern. Climate change looms particularly large as a threat, in at least part of the popular consciousness, because climate sets the boundary conditions for life—including growing food and providing water—and global warming is the biggest impact humans are having on the planet (at least in mass terms, as its most important driver, CO_2, is our most abundant pollutant). Contemporary concerns in turn tend to shape the way we interpret the past.

There is a popular narrative that the Holocene—the present interglacial period that began 11,700 years ago (11.7 ka)—represents a kind of climatic "promised land," with a remarkably stable climate that was conducive to the development of complex societies (Rockström et al. 2009). As we leave this promised land, we leave the "safe operating space for humanity"—at our peril (Rockström et al. 2009). However, the Holocene climate was not that stable, and there is burgeoning literature postulating links between past (Holocene) climate changes and historical collapse (briefly summarized herein). What these perspectives from Earth system science have in common is the assumption that complex societies are fragile to climate change.

But, as archaeologists, anthropologists, and historians point out, complex societies are "problem-solving organizations," and as numerous examples attest, "dealing with adverse environmental conditions may be one of the things that complex societies do best" (Tainter 1988). Clearly "no society can maintain complexity when its resource base is depleted beyond a certain point" (Tainter 1988). Hence there could be a role for particularly detrimental climate changes in some historical collapses—and contemporary climate change is already exceeding Holocene variability (Steffen et al. 2018). But in general, to understand collapse, we need to take a complex system view (Tainter 1988). Complex societies are subject to both internal evolution and multiple external factors, of which climate change is but one, interacting with the internal dynamics of a society, and the network dynamics of interconnected societies.

DOI: 10.4324/9781003331384-17

Embracing this evolutionary and complex system view of collapse (Tainter 1988), I focus here on how historical collapses may be characterized as due to "tipping points" in the internal and networked dynamics of a complex society (Janssen, Kohler, and Scheffer 2003), and the different ways climate change could conceivably trigger tipping. This includes the possible role of tipping points in the climate or environmental conditions (Lenton et al. 2008; Lenton 2013). Resolving what, if any, role climate change played in historical collapse should be a matter of testing hypotheses—and I offer some steps toward that.

By considering the interplay of climate change and historical collapses, we may gain some generic insights relevant to the threat that climate change poses to contemporary civilization. Or we may conclude that the situation is so different now that there is little transferability of knowledge. Either way the ride should be interesting—if a little unsettling.

13.2 Background

Here I briefly review what we know about Holocene climate changes to get a handle on what complex societies have experienced. I adopt an evolutionary position on the nature and origin of complex societies. Then I briefly review postulated links between climate change and historical collapse, and recent broader insights into influences of climate on society.

13.2.1 The Nature of Holocene Climate Changes

While the Holocene climate was more stable than the ice age, there were multiple changes within it. Here I progress from longer to shorter timescales, with a particular focus on the last ~8000 years in which complex societies rose and fell.

In the early Holocene, the Earth was still warming from the last ice age, ice sheets were still melting away, and sea level and atmospheric CO_2 were still rising. Variations in the Earth's orbital parameters represent the longest-term forcing of Holocene climate change. Northern hemisphere (NH) summer coincided with the nearest approach to the Sun (perihelion) ~9 ka, under relatively high obliquity (axial tilt) of 24°, giving ~40 W m^{-2} extra NH summer heating (compared to today). This shifted the inter-tropical convergence zone of rainfall (ITCZ) and associated NH summer monsoons—in Africa, Asia, and the Americas—northward (relative to today). It also made the planet slightly warmer, but ongoing recovery from the ice age meant that peak warmth—the Holocene climatic optimum—was delayed until ~8 ka. Since then, declining NH summer insolation has tended to move the ITCZ and monsoons southward and generate a slight (~0.5°C) cooling of the planet (until anthropogenic climate change reversed it). Within this slow orbital change, there were faster changes in monsoon systems—notably a "browning of the Sahara" ~6 ka to ~4 ka. This was "time transgressive" (Shanahan et al. 2015)—occurring at different times in different places—but was nevertheless more rapid than the orbital forcing.

Overlaid on the orbital forcing are a series of "Bond events" (Bond et al. 1997; Bond et al. 2001)—cold events of drift ice in the North Atlantic, including at ~8.2 ka, ~5.9 ka, ~4.2 ka, ~2.8 ka, ~1.4 ka (Late Antique Little Ice Age), and ~0.5 ka (Little Ice Age). These North Atlantic cold events of centennial duration correlate with associated drying events in NH monsoon regions—sometimes labeled "megadroughts." The events at ~8.2 ka and ~4.2 ka were sufficiently global in their climate effects that stratigraphers now use them to divide the Holocene into three stages (Walker et al. 2019). Multiple possible causes are recognized for the events (Wanner et al. 2011). Bond argued from correlation with fluctuations in cosmogenic nuclides for a solar driver (Bond et al. 2001). The ~8.2 ka event is convincingly associated with a large meltwater input from the final collapse of the Laurentide ice sheet (Alley and Ágústsdóttir 2005). Explosive volcanic eruptions may have triggered some of the events. The Atlantic ocean's overturning circulation has its own centennial internal variability, so an external causal trigger may not be required. Whatever the cause, there is some consensus that weakening of the Atlantic overturning circulation amplified and prolonged the events and connected cooling in the North Atlantic region to the southward shift of the ITCZ and weakening of NH monsoons.

A key source of climate variability in this context is the passing of tipping points, whereby feedbacks within climate dynamics propel abrupt change (Lenton et al. 2008). Two are particularly pertinent. First, the North Atlantic contains an inherent instability whereby the subpolar gyre can abruptly weaken (shutting off deep convection in the Labrador Sea), sea ice extends, and cooling ensues (Levermann and Born 2007). This is implicated in the 8.2 ka event (Born and Levermann 2010), and the Little Ice Age (Moreno-Chamarro et al. 2017), and could be a more general characteristic of Holocene cooling events. Second, monsoon systems contain an inherent strong positive feedback where moist air drawn in from the ocean rises and releases the latent heat of condensation, propelling the overall monsoon circulation (Levermann et al. 2009). This can give rise to alternative stable states of monsoon strength and is implicated in abrupt monsoon weakening events during the Holocene—particularly in Asia (Wang et al. 2005). Whether the browning of the Sahara involved monsoon tipping points continues to be debated.

The Bond events were originally thought to represent periodic ~1500-year "cycles" and other studies argue for ~1000-year, ~500-year, or ~210-year cyclic variability in Holocene climate records linked to solar variability. Claims of *periodicity* should be viewed with caution, but even if irregular, centennial-millennial timescale variability of Holocene climate is real—and often correlated across large spatial scales. On shorter timescales, multi-decadal climate variability in both the Atlantic ("Atlantic Multidecadal Oscillation") and Pacific ("Pacific Decadal Oscillation") domains extends back through the Holocene (Kirby et al. 2010; Knudsen et al. 2011). So does the stronger, shorter timescale

El Niño Southern Oscillation (ENSO) variability (Cobb et al. 2013), and the North Atlantic Oscillation (Goslin et al. 2018).

In summary, the climate has been changing on a wide range of timescales, through a multitude of causes, throughout the Holocene.

13.2.2 The Nature of Complex Societies

Having established that the Holocene climate was not that stable, the idea that climate stability might help complex societies persist (Rockström et al. 2009) remains reasonable (if moot). However, any intimation that stability triggered the development of complex societies lacks a clear mechanism and thus might be dismissed as a "mystical" explanation (Tainter 1988). Instead, the multiple independent origins of complex societies appear to demand an evolutionary explanation.

I adopt the view that the origin of states was an evolutionary transition to a new level of organizational complexity (distinct from e.g., chiefdoms) (Powers, Schaik, and Lehmann 2016). Typically, such evolutionary transitions carry benefits and drawbacks that are unevenly distributed. Often it is the case that the components of a new level of organization pay some "fitness" penalty to participation—e.g., taxes—but the new entity can be more successful at spreading (across space) or persisting (through time) relative to simpler units of social organization (Lenton et al. 2021). Correspondingly, major evolutionary transitions to new levels of organization are vulnerable (at least initially) to reversal to a (preceding) lower level of organization (Maynard Smith and Szathmáry 1995). Hence, unusual conditions may need to be invoked to account for their origin. Interestingly, major evolutionary transitions tend to be associated with environmental *in*stability (Lenton and Watson 2011), not with stability. Indeed, extreme environmental conditions that favor the cooperative pooling of resources and isolate cooperative groups from invasion by "cheats" can provide selective conditions for increased complexity (Boyle, Lenton, and Williams 2007).

In this I follow the "integrationist" school of thought—that complexity arose out of the needs of society, and specifically as a solution to a problem (or problems) (Tainter 1988). One potentially important problem to solve is that of thriving in a marginal climate, and possibly a deteriorating one. Social complexity carries clear benefits of pooling and controlling precious resources. Well-established theories are that complexity arose to manage scarce water resources (Wittfogel 1955) or that climatic and geographic constraints ("environmental circumscription") triggered conflict, resource concentration, and associated social complexity (Carneiro 1970). Particularly pertinent is evidence that climate deterioration appears correlated with increasing social complexity in several historical cases (Brooks 2006). The evolutionary hypothesis is that climate deterioration provided selection pressure for more complex social organization.

Consistent with this, there are occasional proposals that climate improvement, alleviating a stress factor, has caused societal collapse—although examples seem restricted to simpler societies (Tainter 1988). This reasoning potentially extends to the instability of the earliest experiments in state formation in Mesopotamia (Scott 2017), as environmental conditions fluctuated. However, the collapse literature is dominated by hypotheses that climate deterioration triggered historical collapse. This poses the obvious puzzle: If climate deterioration is a credible trigger for the origin of complex societies, then how can it also be a trigger of their demise? Clearly, some additional, contingent evolutionary dynamics would need to be at play—such as an endogenous trend toward increasing vulnerability of a complex society over time—e.g., due to diminishing marginal returns on complexity (Tainter 1988). I return to this in Section 13.3.

13.2.3 Effects of Climate Change on Societies and Collapse

Parking this puzzle for now, there are several mediating mechanisms through which climate changes could conceivably have contributed to historical collapse. The most obvious is that climate affects the availability of key resources, notably food and water, but also fuelwood. Consistent with this, current climate change hypotheses for historical collapse (Table 13.1) largely sit within this "resource depletion" theme (Tainter 1988).

A brief and non-comprehensive review of hypotheses in the literature (Table 13.1) suggests an overriding focus on the deleterious effects of anomalous droughts on agriculture and food supply as a postulated cause of collapse. This makes some sense given that early complex societies were predominantly centered in already dry parts of the sub-tropics, and prolonged droughts in those regions are one of the clearest Holocene climate changes. Where water management was a key part of social complexity (Wittfogel 1955), the inference must be that system became unable to cope. For example, the 4.2 ka event has been linked to the collapse of the Akkadian empire (Weiss et al. 1993; Cullen et al. 2000), but others contest this (Butzer 2012). Dependence of agriculture on Nile floods apparently made Old Kingdom and New Kingdom Egypt vulnerable to drought (Butzer 2012).

Droughts may also play a role in a more networked view of collapse. The Late Bronze Age Eastern Mediterranean collapse is fascinating as trade between civilizations apparently helped buffer against collapse as the Hittites received "food aid" from New Kingdom Egypt (Cline 2014). But later, as drought hit multiple civilizations in the network (Kaniewski et al. 2013; Kaniewski, Guiot, and Van Campo 2015), including Nile failures in Egypt (Butzer 2012), the buffering trade network broke down (Cline 2014). Some even speculate that the mysterious "Sea Peoples" might have been provoked to invade because drought forced out-migration from wherever they came from—but if their aim was to find greener pastures they headed in the wrong direction! Drought elsewhere provoking out-migration has also been linked to invasions associated with the decline and fall of the Western Roman Empire (Drake 2017).

Table 13.1 Example Postulated Links Between Climate Change and Collapse. A Non-comprehensive List, Noting that Almost All Climate Hypotheses Are Contested and That Other Drivers Are Recognized for Most Instances of Collapse (and in Some Cases Are Clearly More Important)

Complex society(s)	Approximate timing of collapse	Postulated climate change(s)	Proximate factors/features	Example source(s) for climate hypothesis
Late Uruk	5.2 ka (3200 BCE)	Drought		Weiss and Bradley 2001; Clarke et al. 2016
Akkadian empire	4.2 ka (~2200 BCE)	Aridification	Urban abandonment, political collapse	Weiss et al. 1993; Butzer 2012
Old Kingdom Egypt	4.2 ka (2180–2160 BCE)	Aridification, Nile failures	Famine, civil war	Butzer 2012
Late Bronze Age Eastern Mediterranean	3.2 ka (~1200 BCE)	Aridification	Famine, invasion, loss of trade network	Kaniewski, Guiot and Van Campo 2015
New Kingdom Egypt	3.2 ka (1187–1064 BCE)	Aridification, Nile failures	Subsistence crises, loss of royal power	Butzer 2012
Western Roman Empire	1.6 ka (200–476 CE)	North Atlantic Oscillation shifts, drought elsewhere	In-migration events	Drake 2017
Moche IV–V, Peru	1.4 ka (~600 CE)	Aridification	Irrigation failure, abandonment	Shimada et al. 1991; deMenocal 2001
Lowland Classic Maya	1.2 ka (790–890 CE)	Aridification		Hodell, Curtis, and Brenner 1995 deMenocal 2001
Tiwanaku	0.9 ka (~1100 CE)	Aridification	Abandonment	deMenocal 2001
"Anasazi" / Pueblo	0.7 ka (~1300 CE)	The 1280s' "Great Drought"	Abandonment	Bocinsky et al. 2016
Black Death in Europe	0.65 ka (1347–1353 CE)	Good conditions in Asian source regions	Pandemic	Schmid et al. 2015
Angkor, Khmer empire	0.6 ka (1431 CE)	Fluctuation between drought and floods	Cascading infrastructure failure	Buckley et al. 2010; Penny et al. 2018
Ming Dynasty Collapse	0.35 ka (1644 CE)	Drought (1638–1641)		Cook et al. 2010; Zheng et al. 2014

Too much water causing destructive flooding of water infrastructure has also been implicated in at least one collapse—that of Angkor (1431 CE) (Buckley et al. 2010; Penny et al. 2018).

Beyond droughts and floods, there are several ways that climate can affect societies. Regional changes in temperature could have affected past societies. Climate affects the physiological function of humans and domesticated animals. Warming above ~20°C reduces human labor productivity (Hsiang 2010), and in the extreme, the combination of high temperature and high humidity (wet bulb temperature 35°C or above) threatens mammal life (Sherwood and Huber 2010). From observational data, warming is correlated with increased conflict at scales from the individual to modern civil wars (Hsiang, Burke, and Miguel 2013). Analyses of the last millennium suggest correlations between temperature changes, population declines, and war (Zhang et al. 2007, 2011a, 2011b)—although sometimes cooling is implicated and sometimes warming, depending on the climate zone (Zhang et al. 2011b). One factor that could have mediated population decline is climatic effects on the prevalence of pathogens—whether on people, domesticated animals, or crops. Most strikingly, the Black Death and subsequent reintroductions of the plague bacterium (*Yersinia pestis*), via fleas, to Europe have been linked to anomalous climate intervals in the source regions of Asia (Schmid et al. 2015).

13.2.4 The (Apparent) Human Climate Niche

These considerations naturally lead to the question: Is there a human climate niche? That is, a set of temperature and precipitation conditions where human population density is maximized. We recently deduced such a niche from a mixture of contemporary climate and population data and from past climate and population reconstructions (Xu et al. 2020).

The contemporary climate niche (Figure 13.1) shows a peak of human population density centered on ~13°C and a secondary peak centered on ~25°C (mostly corresponding to people in the South Asian monsoon region). There is also a peak at ~1000 mm mean annual precipitation, a steep drop-off at lower precipitation, and a weaker drop-off at higher precipitation. These features are also reflected in human crop production, livestock distribution, and GDP. The latter supports an earlier independent analysis that economic productivity is maximized at ~14°C mean annual temperature (Burke, Hsiang, and Miguel 2015). It should be noted that the climate distribution of available land space is very different from the distribution of people (i.e., the niche) (Xu et al. 2020).

The niche is surprisingly conserved going back to times of much lower overall population (Xu et al. 2020). One possible explanation is that the HYDE dataset of past population distribution is biased toward their present locations. Hence, we independently reconstructed population distribution ~6 ka BP from the ArchaeGLOBE dataset and assumed population densities for particular modes of life. While this evens out the distribution of population with respect to temperature somewhat, the two main peaks remain, albeit with the

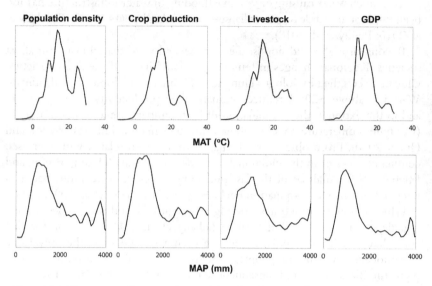

Figure 13.1 The apparent human climate niche. Contemporary human population density (2015), crop production (2000), livestock (2006), and GDP (2015), as a function of mean annual temperature (MAT) and mean annual precipitation (MAP). Analysis from Xu et al. (2020).

main peak shifted to somewhat lower temperatures (relative to today and to HYDE for 6 ka).

It is natural to then ask: Where did complex societies rise and fall with respect to the apparent climate niche? It should come as no surprise that the centers of ancient civilizations were heavily biased toward the dry side of the human climate niche (with some notable exceptions). This is consistent with the arguments that complexity arose to manage scarce water resources (Wittfogel 1955) and may have been triggered by climate drying (Brooks 2006). Drier places and monsoon regions were in turn challenging places to be because of the instability in the (sub)tropical hydrological cycle and monsoon systems in the Holocene. They experienced the greatest hydrological variability, repeatedly posing problems for complex societies to solve.

As larger empires developed, they began to span the climate niche. The Roman Empire, centered at ~16°C and ~800 mm near the optima of the niche, at its greatest extent (117 CE) spanned arid (<250 mm) to wetter (>1000 mm) climates and a mean annual temperature range ~10°C to ~30°C that covers much of the temperature niche. One might infer that the Roman Empire should have been resilient to climate change, at least compared to earlier civilizations centered at the dry edge of the niche, but it would have been least so at its peripheries.

13.3 Analysis and Synthesis

Having reviewed current thinking on climate change and historical collapse, the aim here is to conceptualize collapse as a tipping point, broaden consideration of the ways climate change could be involved in collapse, and offer some steps toward testing hypotheses.

13.3.1 Characterizing Collapse as a Tipping Point

A simple conceptualization of collapse is as a switch between alternative (stable) states of a system (Janssen, Kohler, and Scheffer 2003). An encompassing definition for social–ecological systems describes collapse as a change in *identity* of a system that is fast, persistent, and involves loss of capital (Cumming and Peterson 2017). Both avoid notions of hierarchical structure—but for the specific context here, I adopt the narrower definition that historical collapse is associated with loss of level(s) of social complexity (Tainter 1988).

The recognition of *levels* of complexity suggests complexity is a discrete (rather than continuous) variable, consistent with the wide use of terms such as "chiefdom" or "state." Presumably, there are many such levels of social complexity. The crucial point is that to be persistent and thus recognizable, specific levels of organizational complexity must have some characteristic features including self-damping (mathematically negative) feedbacks that stabilize their identity. These negative feedbacks give each level of complexity some resilience—i.e., the ability to counteract perturbations. This invites a mathematical characterization of different levels of social complexity as different *attractors*, and for visualization purposes, we can simplify this down to alternative *stable states* (i.e., fixed-point attractors) (Figure 13.2A).

Collapse occurs when resilience is lost—i.e., damping negative feedbacks are overwhelmed or disappear—and self-amplifying (mathematically positive) feedbacks take over and propel a transition between different states of a system. A "tipping point" describes the point at which this occurs and even a small perturbation can produce a qualitative change in the identity of a system. Tipping points and the associated transitions can go in either direction—"creation" or collapse.

Collapse is associated with cascading causal interactions that remove complexity (Butzer 2012). It is often assumed that collapse must be rapid from a human perspective. However, in complex systems, the pace of a tipping point transition is determined by the natural timescale of the *internal* dynamics (including the feedbacks) at work. In the case of social systems those dynamics can be very fast—e.g., involving escalating violent conflict—but they can also be slower—e.g., involving downward-spiraling loss of revenues and of political authority (Butzer 2012). Crucially, even if the dynamics appear slow—e.g., because there is a large reservoir of capital in the system that takes time to drain—they should be difficult to reverse, because self-amplifying (positive) feedbacks are dominating the dynamics.

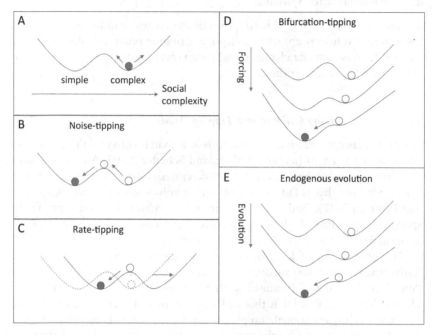

Figure 13.2 Collapse through different types of tipping points. (A) Conceptualizing levels of complexity as alternative attractors. (B) Noise-induced tipping. (C) Rate-dependent tipping. (D) Bifurcation tipping. (E) Endogenous evolution to a bifurcation tipping point.

For those keen on a conceptualization of collapse that captures aspects of societal structure using network theory—in terms of "nodes" and their interactions—the concept of a tipping point remains valid. Tipping points can occur in two ways in networks—either a tipping point in the state of nodes on a network, which maintains its structure, or a tipping point in the structure of the network itself. Typically, a more connected and homogeneous network is more prone to a "global" (network-scale) collapse, whereas a more heterogeneous and less connected network is less prone to overall collapse (Scheffer et al. 2012). The modularity of networks—i.e., distinct subsystems—can also beget stability. For present purposes, I will keep things simple.

13.3.2 Types of Tipping Point Collapse

To visualize collapse as a tipping point between alternative stable states, I use the "ball in valleys" diagram (Figure 13.2A). Valleys represent attractors—stable states of a system, here on a deliberately vaguely defined axis of "social complexity." Let us consider just two levels of social complexity, intuitively labeled "simple" and "complex" (no value judgement is intended), with "collapse" corresponding to the transition from "complex" to "simple" society. The ball represents the actual state of the system (in terms of social complexity), and it may be subject to short-term external perturbations (nudges), e.g., from the weather or short-term climate variability such as ENSO. "External" here just means outside of the causal influence of whatever we have defined as our system. Self-damping negative feedbacks are what maintain the valleys—the stronger they are, the deeper the valley, and the more resilient a system is to perturbation—you push the ball, and it rolls back faster. The hill between valleys represents an unstable (steady) state. From this starting point, several types of tipping point collapse are possible.

Sometimes a system can take a short-term hit that is large enough to push it to the top of the hill and over—from one stable state (valley) to the other (Figure 13.2B)—mathematically this is called a "noise-induced transition" and can occur without forewarning. Many people would intuitively describe the top of the hill (the unstable steady state) as a type of "tipping point"—like the one reached when you lean back on a chair—because a perturbation one way or the other gives a very different outcome. The term "noise-induced tipping" ("N-tipping") describes situations where the ball is pushed over the hill by a short-term fluctuation.

Another possibility is that a system is forced hard in one direction faster than its internal feedbacks can respond. This is akin to shoving the whole set of valleys firmly in one direction and the ball responds underneath it (Figure 13.2C). The ball may get pushed over the hilltop if the shove is hard enough. This is called "rate-induced tipping" ("R-tipping"). It could correspond to passing a climate tipping point that is faster than the internal processes of societal collapse.

Most important to understand are tipping points where the initial state of a system loses its stability—i.e., the valley gets progressively shallower until it disappears—and then the system inevitably transitions into a different state (the ball rolls off into a different valley) (Figure 13.2D). This can happen when a system is subject to a slow external forcing in one direction, which destabilizes the initial state—i.e., weakens negative feedbacks (and/or strengthens positive feedbacks). "External" forcing of past societies could include e.g., persistent changes in climate, or a progressive invasion of outsiders. "Bifurcation tipping" ("B-tipping") describes this type of collapse, which belongs to "catastrophe theory." Implicit here is that the forcing changes slower than the timescale of collapse.

What about endogenous, evolutionary social change? Here we start to sidestep the mathematical formalism, which has thus far considered autonomous systems (where the form of the dynamical equations does not change over time), because now we are considering evolution that changes dynamical relationships over time (a non-autonomous system). Nevertheless, I retain the same visual representation for the sake of simplicity. Now internal evolution alters the stability landscape, and may involve new feedbacks being introduced, and/or existing ones being removed (deliberately or otherwise). This could go in either direction: Internal evolution may increase or decrease the stability of the complex state. Where it decreases stability, collapse is once again cartooned as reaching a bifurcation tipping point where self-propelling positive feedbacks take over from self-damping negative ones (Figure 13.2E).

13.3.3 Ways Climate Change Could Be Involved in the Creation or Collapse of Complexity

We can use this simple framework to conceptualize different ways that climate change could be involved in the "creation" or collapse of complexity. Setting aside for now proposals of an "early Anthropocene" (Ruddiman 2003, 2007), we can treat climate changes as an "external" factor for past societies, as they were not influenced by a society's activities (with a few possible exceptions)—a situation which has changed profoundly now.

Let us start by considering "creation" and a snapshot in time, where a society is in a "simple" state, but an alternative more "complex" state could also exist. Perhaps it is ~5500 BCE (~7.5 ka) in Mesopotamia. Environmental conditions are good for simplicity—resources are abundant for foraging—and early farming is an undesirable drag (Scott 2017). The "simple" state is more stable than the "complex" one (Figure 13.3A), but there may be "experiments" going on with the latter, which soon fall apart. Conceivably an extreme weather event that reduces wild food populations for foraging could act like a perturbation toward the more complex farming state, noise-tipping some groups into that state. But a more modest good weather event (opposite perturbation) could readily noise-tip things back to simplicity—a mild case of collapse. Apparently, such flip-flopping was common in Mesopotamia at the time (Scott 2017).

A more persistent climate forcing (Figure 13.3B)—e.g., drying, associated loss of marshland, and wild food populations—could act to increase the stability of the more complex farming-with-irrigation state and reduce the stability of the foraging state—shifting the overall distribution of the population toward the complex state (although the drying of North Africa concentrating people in the Nile Valley is a more persuasive example [Brooks 2006]).

As "dealing with adverse environmental conditions may be one of the things that complex societies do best" (Tainter 1988), the "complex" social state can be interpreted as resilient with respect to detrimental climate perturbations. But what could have made it resilient to improvements in climate and reversion to a simpler foraging state? Here we need to consider endogenous social evolution creating social "policing" mechanisms that deterred people from reverting to a simpler foraging lifestyle (Scott 2017). Such developments are a generic feature of evolutionary transitions to new levels of organization (Maynard Smith and Szathmáry 1995). This amounts to "raising the hill" between the complex and simple states and steepening the landscape (Figure 13.3C). Now the "complex" social state has considerable stability—both against climate perturbations and rebellion from within—but it is not invulnerable. The flipside of introducing internal policing (negative feedback) mechanisms to maintain the complex

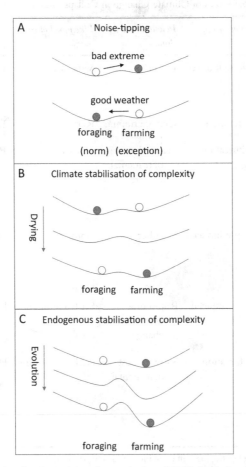

Figure 13.3 Scenarios for the origin of complexity. (A) Noise-induced tipping between simple (foraging) and more complex (farming) social states. (B) Climate forcing (drying) stabilizes the complex (farming-with-irrigation) state. (C) Endogenous evolution of policing mechanisms further stabilizes the complex state against climate improvement.

state is that if they break, collapse will be more dramatic. Complexity brings its own jeopardy.

Climate could now play several possible roles in collapse (Table 13.2, "resilient" complexity case). A particularly extreme short-term climate/weather event could still conceivably cause (noise-induced) collapse (Figure 13.2B)—but this would (by definition) be a rare event. It would also be hard to spot in paleoclimate archives, likely depending on written records. Equally, an abrupt, large, and persistent change in climate could conceivably cause (rate-induced) collapse (Figure 13.2C). Such climate tipping points are much easier to spot in paleoclimate records but are still fairly rare. Alternatively, a steady change in

Table 13.2 Possible Roles of Climate Change in Collapse and Their Testability

Stability of complexity	Type of tipping	Potential role for climate	Likelihood of event/ change	Prospects for detection of climate contribution
High (resilient)	Noise induced	Extreme weather event	Very rare	Low—needs written record of extreme event
	Rate induced	Climate tipping point	Rare	Easy to spot climate tipping point
	Bifurcation	Large, slow detrimental change	Unclear	Easy to detect climate change, hard to associate with collapse, look for early warning signals
Low (fragile)	Noise induced	Weather	Common	Hard to detect weather, hard to associate frequent events with collapse
	Rate induced	Rapid modest detrimental change	Fairly common	Possibly detectable event, but hard to associate with the collapse
	Bifurcation	Slow modest detrimental change	Fairly common	Hard to detect modest change, hard to associate with collapse, look for early warning signals

Note: The likelihood of tipping will combine the likelihood of the societal state and the likelihood of the (hypothetical) climate trigger. Resilient complexity is expected to be the norm (i.e., likely), fragile complexity the exception, which may develop endogenously over time (Tainter 1988).

climate could conceivably progressively reduce a resource base and hence the stability of the "complex" state to a bifurcation tipping point, where its own internal dynamics propel collapse (Figure 13.2D). Perhaps the complex society stores grain and is dependent on generating an agricultural surplus to maintain an army as well as internal policing mechanisms. A steady deterioration of climate reduces agricultural production removing the surplus and emptying the grain stores, triggering internal breakdown. Such cases are interesting because the proximate causes of collapse will appear to be internal, and the ultimate climate cause may be hard to spot. Slow change in climate may be detected in paleoclimate records but would not be readily associated with collapse unless there was a correlated record of the resource base dwindling to a critical point.

Now let us add in endogenous social evolution that reduces stability of the complex state (Figure 13.2E), such as diminishing marginal returns on complexity over time (Tainter 1988) (Table 13.2, "fragile" complexity case). Now it does not require a change in climate or any other external factor to bring about collapse. But when the complex social system has brought itself to a fragile state, it is likely to get tipped by some external factor before the internal dynamics remove all stability. Modest weather extremes or modest abrupt or smooth changes in climate could conceivably trigger collapse. Internal evolution would be the ultimate cause (Tainter 1988), and climate a possible proximate cause of collapse. Spotting the role of climate could be difficult, as now weather events or climate changes that the society had previously ridden out repeatedly could be fatal.

13.3.4 How to Advance Scientifically?

To advance a research agenda requires some hypotheses that link specific examples of collapse to cases in this typology and means of testing/falsifying those hypotheses. I am not (yet) in a position to align cases. However, some general testability considerations can be summarized from the above (Table 13.2). Overall, the prospects for testing climate hypotheses do not look great and it is perhaps easy to see why climate researchers have focused on finding abrupt climate change events and trying to temporally associate them with collapses—as these are easiest to spot. But that in no way means they are the most likely relationship between climate and collapse. They also raise more general concerns about how to test for temporal correlation in data that do not share a common stratigraphy and/or carry age errors. The legitimacy of making spatial inferences when a paleoclimate record is not in the same place as the site of collapse has also been raised in the literature, although there is a characteristically large synoptic ~1000 km scale of weather that reduces this concern, particularly in the extra-tropics.

Interestingly, there is an additional way of testing whether a particular case of collapse is due to a bifurcation tipping point in a society's internal dynamics—regardless of whether the steady forcing involves climate change—because bifurcation tipping carries early warning signals, as negative feedbacks are weakened. Notably, the system becomes slower at recovering from perturbations before the tipping point occurs (as the valley gets shallower), exhibiting increased temporal autocorrelation (self-similarity in time) and increased variance (Lenton et al. 2008; Scheffer et al. 2009). This signal can be looked for in time-series data if an appropriate system variable is sampled frequently enough, i.e., more frequently than the timescale of the dynamics that govern collapse. As to what is an appropriate variable to sample, for climate hypotheses, a critical resource would be ideal (e.g., grain harvest or storage level), whereas for dwindling economic returns on complexity (Tainter 1988), an economic metric (e.g., currency value) seems apt. These variables may already directly signal collapse, but here the aim is to try and deduce the nature of the dynamics preceding collapse—if the signal of "critical slowing down" can be statistically robustly demonstrated, this would provide support for a slow-forcing-to-bifurcation scenario of collapse.

To complement such a purely data-derived approach, developing simple systems models of specific case studies should help narrow down the hypothesis space. The first thing a complexity scientist usually does to try to understand a system is to draw out feedback loops of causal interactions, as a step toward developing a model. Yet despite increasing enthusiasm for a complex systems' approach to historical collapse, and frequent mention of "feedbacks" in the literature, (e.g., Butzer 2012), it is rare to see these visualized in a feedback diagram. It should help progress in the field to make such drawings—because it makes the processes at play explicit, and closed loops of causality often lead to non-intuitive as well as non-linear behavior. Hence, we need to develop models of them to retrain our intuition and gain understanding.

13.4 Insights, Relevance, and Applicability

Historically climate change and extreme weather were viewed as an act of god(s) with little or no agency to control it—save making ritualistic sacrifices or similar that have no causal effect on climate but might change social dynamics to being more or less resilient. There was however governance of resources affected by climate—notably water, food, fuelwood—and interventions could affect the resilience of these resources, even if climate could not be changed. Nowadays we would call this *adaptation* to climate change.

We find ourselves in a very different situation now: We are collectively causing global climate change (some of us more than others), and that climate change is already exceeding anything experienced during the Holocene (Steffen et al. 2018). Global temperature is ~1.2°C above pre-industrial levels and ~0.7°C above the early Holocene. Climate tipping points may already have been crossed and more are to be expected (Lenton et al. 2019). We have the capacity to *mitigate* climate change by tackling its underlying causes—primarily the burning of fossil fuels, followed by land-use practices—but thus far only modest mitigation efforts are visible in some long-industrialized regions. Globally, anthropogenic greenhouse gas emissions are still accelerating as industrialization continues to spread across the world. Even if governments were to follow through on their (non-binding) commitments to the 2015 Paris Agreement on climate change, we are still heading for ~3°C global warming later this century.

Combined with projected population growth, principally in sub-Saharan Africa, this will put around 3 billion people—notably in India, the Sahel, and Brazil—outside of the "apparent human climate niche" (Figure 13.1) on the hot side, experiencing mean annual temperatures at or above what only nomads in the Sahara and the rich, air-conditioned citizens of Mecca experience today (Xu et al. 2020). Life-threatening humid heat extremes that are already occurring in some localities will become more widespread and prolonged (Raymond, Matthews, and Horton 2020). The locations that are best for agriculture and GDP will move large distances (Xu et al. 2020). It seems hard not to conclude that there will be massive, climate-driven migration of people.

Yet, despite industrialization, we are still overwhelmingly based in sedentary societies dependent on sedentary agriculture, and our current political world has generally limited tolerance of migrants. In some historical cases, trading food successfully increased resilience, because detrimental climate changes were localized (Cline 2014). Now we have a somewhat globalized marketplace, which should help resilience, but for food the economy has never been fully globalized. Furthermore, we are subject to global climate change that can impact food-producing regions simultaneously. When trouble hits, we have seen recent cases of localization—notably in summer 2010, when Russia suffered a severe heatwave and shut off wheat exports, and other grain-producing regions were also hit by climate extremes, causing the food price index to skyrocket, fueling the political revolutions of the "Arab Spring."

Are there any causes for optimism (outside the quasi-religion of neoliberal economics)? Well, we live among the most complex societies yet seen, which suggests they should have the greatest experience of problem solving, and potentially the greatest capacity for it—although diminishing marginal returns on complexity were already apparent over 30 years ago (Tainter 1988). In my view we are now looking at transformational societal change to avoid future collapse: Either radical adaptation involving a profound spatial reorganization of the human world, or radical mitigation to transform the sources of energy and the relationship with resources that underpin complex societies. A "middle road" of modest mitigation and adaptation may simply not be available. Either transformative path will require extraordinary innovation in many realms of human affairs. To that end, I am joining others in mapping out transformative mitigation pathways utilizing the same principles of complex systems and tipping points applied herein (Lenton 2020; Sharpe and Lenton 2021)—because I'd rather tackle the underlying drivers of climate change than the symptoms. What is also needed is a society-wide burst of problem-solving innovation that bucks the trends previously identified (Tainter 1988).

Acknowledgment

I thank Marten Scheffer for ongoing collaboration on the topics herein—especially the scenario for the creation of social complexity in Figure 13.3. I thank Xi Chu, Tim Kohler, Jens-Christian Svenning, and Marten Scheffer for their collaboration on the human climate niche.

References

Alley, R. B. and A. M. Ágústsdóttir (2005). "The 8k event: Cause and consequences of a major Holocene abrupt climate change." *Quaternary Science Reviews* 24(10): 1123–1149.

Bocinsky, R. K., J. Rush, K. W. Kintigh and T. A. Kohler (2016). "Exploration and exploitation in the macrohistory of the pre-Hispanic Pueblo Southwest." *Science Advances* 2(4): e1501532.

Bond, G., B. Kromer, J. Beer, R. Muscheler, M. N. Evans, W. Showers, S. Hoffmann, R. Lotti-Bond, I. Hajdas and G. Bonani (2001). "Persistent solar influence on North Atlantic climate during the Holocene." *Science* 294(5549): 2130–2136.

Bond, G., W. Showers, M. Cheseby, R. Lotti, P. Almasi, P. deMenocal, P. Priore, H. Cullen, I. Hajdas and G. Bonani (1997). "A pervasive millennial-scale cycle in North Atlantic Holocene and glacial climates." *Science* 278(5341): 1257–1266.

Born, A. and A. Levermann (2010). "The 8.2 ka event: Abrupt transition of the subpolar gyre toward a modern North Atlantic circulation." *Geochemistry, Geophysics, Geosystems* 11(6): Q06011.

Boyle, R. A., T. M. Lenton and H. T. P. Williams (2007). "Neoproterozoic "snowball Earth" glaciations and the evolution of altruism." *Geobiology* 5(4): 337–349.

Brooks, N. (2006). "Cultural responses to aridity in the Middle Holocene and increased social complexity." *Quaternary International* 151(1): 29–49.

Buckley, B. M., K. J. Anchukaitis, D. Penny, R. Fletcher, E. R. Cook, M. Sano, L. C. Nam, A. Wichienkeeo, T. T. Minh and T. M. Hong (2010). "Climate as a contributing factor in the demise of Angkor, Cambodia." *Proceedings of the National Academy of Sciences* 107(15): 6748–6752.

Burke, M., S. M. Hsiang and E. Miguel (2015). "Global non-linear effect of temperature on economic production." *Nature* 527(7577): 235–239.

Butzer, K. W. (2012). "Collapse, environment, and society." *Proceedings of the National Academy of Sciences* 109(10): 3632–3639.

Carneiro, R. L. (1970). A theory of the origin of the state: Traditional theories of state origins are considered and rejected in favor of a new ecological hypothesis. *Science* 169(3947): 733–738.

Clarke, J., N. Brooks, E. B. Banning, M. Bar-Matthews, S. Campbell, L. Clare, M. Cremaschi, S. di Lernia, N. Drake, M. Gallinaro, S. Manning, K. Nicoll, G. Philip, S. Rosen, U.-D. Schoop, M. A. Tafuri, B. Weninger and A. Zerboni (2016). "Climatic changes and social transformations in the Near East and North Africa during the "long" 4th millennium BC: A comparative study of environmental and archaeological evidence." *Quaternary Science Reviews* 136: 96–121.

Cline, E. H. (2014). *1177 B.C.: The Year Civilization Collapsed*. Princeton, NJ: Princeton University Press.

Cobb, K. M., N. Westphal, H. R. Sayani, J. T. Watson, E. Di Lorenzo, H. Cheng, R. L. Edwards and C. D. Charles (2013). "Highly variable El Niño–southern oscillation Throughout the Holocene." *Science* 339(6115): 67–70.

Cook, E. R., K. J. Anchukaitis, B. M. Buckley, R. D. D'Arrigo, G. C. Jacoby and W. E. Wright (2010). "Asian monsoon failure and megadrought during the last millennium." *Science* 328(5977): 486–489.

Cullen, H. M., P. B. deMenocal, S. Hemming, G. Hemming, F. H. Brown, T. Guilderson and F. Sirocco (2000). "Climate change and the collapse of the Akkadian empire: Evidence from the deep sea." *Geology* 28(4): 379–382.

Cumming, G. S. and G. D. Peterson (2017). "Unifying research on social–ecological resilience and collapse." *Trends in Ecology and Evolution* 32(9): 695–713.

deMenocal, P. B. (2001). "Cultural responses to climate change during the Late Holocene." *Science* 292(5517): 667–673.

Drake, B. L. (2017). "Changes in North Atlantic Oscillation drove Population Migrations and the Collapse of the Western Roman Empire." *Scientific Reports* 7(1): 1227.

Goslin, J., M. Fruergaard, L. Sander, M. Gałka, L. Menviel, J. Monkenbusch, N. Thibault and L. B. Clemmensen (2018). "Holocene centennial to millennial shifts in North-Atlantic storminess and ocean dynamics." *Scientific Reports* 8(1): 12778.

Hodell, D. A., J. H. Curtis and M. Brenner (1995). "Possible role of climate in the collapse of Classic Maya civilization." *Nature* 375(6530): 391–394.

Hsiang, S. M. (2010). "Temperatures and cyclones strongly associated with economic production in the Caribbean and Central America." *Proceedings of the National Academy of Sciences of the United States of America* 107(35): 15367–15372.

Hsiang, S. M., M. Burke and E. Miguel (2013). "Quantifying the influence of climate on human conflict." *Science* 341(6151): 1235367.

Janssen, M. A., T. A. Kohler and M. Scheffer (2003). "Sunk-cost effects and vulnerability to collapse in ancient societies." *Current Anthropology* 44(5): 722–728.

Kaniewski, D., J. Guiot and E. Van Campo (2015). "Drought and societal collapse 3200 years ago in the eastern Mediterranean: A review." *WIREs Climate Change* 6(4): 369–382.

Kaniewski, D., E. Van Campo, J. Guiot, S. Le Burel, T. Otto and C. Baeteman (2013). "Environmental roots of the late Bronze Age crisis." *PLOS ONE* 8(8): e71004.

Kirby, M. E., S. P. Lund, W. P. Patterson, M. A. Anderson, B. W. Bird, L. Ivanovici, P. Monarrez and S. Nielsen (2010). "A Holocene record of Pacific Decadal Oscillation (PDO)-related hydrologic variability in Southern California (Lake Elsinore, CA)." *Journal of Paleolimnology* 44(3): 819–839.

Knudsen, M. F., M.-S. Seidenkrantz, B. H. Jacobsen and A. Kuijpers (2011). "Tracking the Atlantic Multidecadal Oscillation through the last 8,000 years." *Nature Communications* 2(1): 178.

Lenton, T. M. (2013). "Environmental tipping points." *Annual Review of Environment and Resources* 38(1): 1–29.

Lenton, T. M. (2020). "Tipping positive change." *Philosophical Transactions of the Royal Society B: Biological Sciences* 375(1794): 20190123.

Lenton, T. M., H. Held, E. Kriegler, J. Hall, W. Lucht, S. Rahmstorf and H. J. Schellnhuber (2008). "Tipping elements in the Earth's climate system." *Proceedings of the National Academy of Sciences* 105(6): 1786–1793.

Lenton, T. M., T. A. Kohler, P. A. Marquet, R. A. Boyle, M. Crucifix, D. M. Wilkinson and M. Scheffer (2021). "Survival of the systems." *Trends in Ecology and Evolution* 36(4): 333–344.

Lenton, T. M., J. Rockstrom, O. Gaffney, S. Rahmstorf, K. Richardson, W. Steffen and H. J. Schellnhuber (2019). "Climate tipping points - Too risky to bet against." *Nature* 575(7784): 592–595.

Lenton, T. M. and A. J. Watson (2011). *Revolutions That Made the Earth.* Oxford: Oxford University Press.

Levermann, A. and A. Born (2007). "Bistability of the Atlantic subpolar gyre in a coarse-resolution climate model." *Geophysical Research Letters* 34(24): L24605.

Levermann, A., J. Schewe, V. Petoukhov and H. Held (2009). "Basic mechanism for abrupt monsoon transitions." *PNAS* 106(49): 20572–20577.

Maynard Smith, J. and E. Szathmáry (1995). *The Major Transitions in Evolution.* Oxford: Freeman.

Moreno-Chamarro, E., D. Zanchettin, K. Lohmann, J. Luterbacher and J. H. Jungclaus (2017). "Winter amplification of the European Little Ice Age cooling by the subpolar gyre." *Scientific Reports* 7(1): 9981.

Penny, D., C. Zachreson, R. Fletcher, D. Lau, J. T. Lizier, N. Fischer, D. Evans, C. Pottier and M. Prokopenko (2018). "The demise of Angkor: Systemic vulnerability of urban infrastructure to climatic variations." *Science Advances* 4(10): eaau4029.

Powers, S. T., C. P. V. Schaik and L. Lehmann (2016). "How institutions shaped the last major evolutionary transition to large-scale human societies." *Philosophical Transactions of the Royal Society B: Biological Sciences* 371(1687): 20150098.

Raymond, C., T. Matthews and R. M. Horton (2020). "The emergence of heat and humidity too severe for human tolerance." *Science Advances* 6(19): eaaw1838.

Rockström, J., W. Steffen, K. Noone, A. Persson, F. S. Chapin, E. F. Lambin, T. M. Lenton, M. Scheffer, C. Folke, H. J. Schellnhuber, B. Nykvist, C. A. de Wit, T. Hughes, S. van der Leeuw, H. Rodhe, S. Sorlin, P. K. Snyder, R. Costanza, U. Svedin, M. Falkenmark, L. Karlberg, R. W. Corell, V. J. Fabry, J. Hansen, B. Walker, D. Liverman, K. Richardson, P. Crutzen and J. A. Foley (2009). "A safe operating space for humanity." *Nature* 461(7263): 472–475.

Rockström, J., W. Steffen, K. Noone, Å. Persson, I. F. S. Chapin, E. Lambin, T. M. Lenton, M. Scheffer, C. Folke, H. Schellnhuber, B. Nykvist, C. A. D. Wit, T. Hughes, S. v. d. Leeuw, H. Rodhe, S. Sörlin, P. K. Snyder, R. Costanza, U. Svedin, M. Falkenmark, L. Karlberg, R. W. Corell, V. J. Fabry, J. Hansen, B. Walker, D. Liverman, K. Richardson, P. Crutzen and J. Foley (2009). "Planetary boundaries: Exploring the safe operating space for humanity." *Ecology and Society* 14(2): 32.

Ruddiman, W. F. (2003). "The anthropogenic greenhouse era began thousands of years ago." *Climatic Change* 61(3): 261–293.

Ruddiman, W. F. (2007). "The early anthropogenic hypothesis: Challenges and responses." *Reviews of Geophysics* 45(4): RG4001.

Scheffer, M., J. Bacompte, W. A. Brock, V. Brovkin, S. R. Carpenter, V. Dakos, H. Held, E. H. van Nes, M. Rietkerk and G. Sugihara (2009). "Early warning signals for critical transitions." *Nature* 461(7260): 53–59.

Scheffer, M., S. R. Carpenter, T. M. Lenton, J. Bascompte, W. Brock, V. Dakos, J. van de Koppel, I. A. van de Leemput, S. A. Levin, E. H. van Nes, M. Pascual and J. Vandermeer (2012). "Anticipating critical transitions." *Science* 338(6105): 344–348.

Schmid, B. V., U. Büntgen, W. R. Easterday, C. Ginzler, L. Walløe, B. Bramanti and N. C. Stenseth (2015). "Climate-driven introduction of the Black Death and successive plague reintroductions into Europe." *Proceedings of the National Academy of Sciences* 112(10): 3020–3025.

Scott, J. C. (2017). *Against the Grain: A Deep History of the Earliest States*. New Haven, CT and London: Yale University Press.

Shanahan, T. M., N. P. McKay, K. A. Hughen, J. T. Overpeck, B. Otto-Bliesner, C. W. Heil, J. King, C. A. Scholz and J. Peck (2015). "The time-transgressive termination of the African humid period." *Nature Geoscience* 8(2): 140–144.

Sharpe, S. and T. M. Lenton (2021). "Upward-scaling tipping cascades to meet climate goals: Plausible grounds for hope." *Climate Policy* 21(4): 421–433.

Sherwood, S. C. and M. Huber (2010). "An adaptability limit to climate change due to heat stress." *Proceedings of the National Academy of Sciences* 107(21): 9552–9555.

Shimada, I., C. B. Schaaf, L. G. Thompson and E. Mosley-Thompson (1991). "Cultural impacts of severe droughts in the prehistoric Andes: Application of a 1,500-year ice core precipitation record." *World Archaeology* 22(3): 247–270.

Steffen, W., J. Rockström, K. Richardson, T. M. Lenton, C. Folke, D. Liverman, C. P. Summerhayes, A. D. Barnosky, S. E. Cornell, M. Crucifix, J. F. Donges, I. Fetzer, S. J. Lade, M. Scheffer, R. Winkelmann and H. J. Schellnhuber (2018). "Trajectories of the earth system in the Anthropocene." *Proceedings of the National Academy of Sciences* 115(33): 8252–8259.

Tainter, J. A. (1988). *The Collapse of Complex Societies*. Cambridge: Cambridge University Press.

Walker, M., M. J. Head, J. Lowe, M. Berkelhammer, S. BjÖrck, H. Cheng, L. C. Cwynar, D. Fisher, V. Gkinis, A. Long, R. Newnham, S. O. Rasmussen and H. Weiss (2019).

"Subdividing the Holocene Series/Epoch: Formalization of stages/ages and subseries/ subepochs, and designation of GSSPs and auxiliary stratotypes." *Journal of Quaternary Science* 34(3): 173–186.

Wang, Y., H. Cheng, R. L. Edwards, Y. He, X. Kong, Z. An, J. Wu, M. J. Kelly, C. A. Dykoski and X. Li (2005). "The Holocene Asian monsoon: Links to solar changes and North Atlantic climate." *Science* 308(5723): 854–857.

Wanner, H., O. Solomina, M. Grosjean, S. P. Ritz and M. Jetel (2011). "Structure and origin of Holocene cold events." *Quaternary Science Reviews* 30(21): 3109–3123.

Weiss, H. and R. S. Bradley (2001). "What drives societal collapse?" *Science* 291(5504): 609–610.

Weiss, H., M.-A. Courty, W. Wetterstrom, F. Guichard, L. Senior, R. Meadow and A. Curnow (1993). "The genesis and collapse of third millennium north Mesopotamian civilization." *Science* 261(5124): 995–1004.

Wittfogel, K. (1955). Developmental aspects of hydraulic societies. In J. H. Steward (Ed.), *Irrigation Civilizations: A Comparative Study*. Washington, DC: Pan American Union, 43–57.

Xu, C., T. A. Kohler, T. M. Lenton, J.-C. Svenning and M. Scheffer (2020). "Future of the human climate niche." *Proceedings of the National Academy of Sciences* 117(21): 11350–11355.

Zhang, D. D., P. Brecke, H. F. Lee, Y.-Q. He and J. Zhang (2007). "Global climate change, war, and population decline in recent human history." *Proceedings of the National Academy of Sciences USA* 104(49): 19214–19219.

Zhang, D. D., H. F. Lee, C. Wang, B. Li, Q. Pei, J. Zhang and Y. An (2011a). "The causality analysis of climate change and large-scale human crisis." *Proceedings of the National Academy of Sciences* 108(42): 17296–17301.

Zhang, D. D., H. F. Lee, C. Wang, B. Li, J. Zhang, Q. Pei and J. Chen (2011b). "Climate change and large-scale human population collapses in the pre-industrial era." *Global Ecology and Biogeography* 20(4): 520–531.

Zheng, J., L. Xiao, X. Fang, Z. Hao, Q. Ge and B. Li (2014). "How climate change impacted the collapse of the Ming dynasty." *Climatic Change* 127(2): 169–182.

14 Conservation of Fragility and the Collapse of Social Orders

John M. Anderies and Simon A. Levin

14.1 Introduction

The collapse of societies, as this volume attests, has long been of great interest to scholars. Since Malthus' (1798) concern with the fact that the human population grows geometrically while arable land to support them grows at best linearly, studies have incorporated Boserupian (1965) technological change that relieves resource constraints and institutional innovation that addresses collective action problems that are the root drivers of overpopulation and resource degradation. The dynamics of population growth, economic development, natural resource regeneration, technological change, and institutional responses can be studied using formal mathematical models parameterized by empirical understanding derived from macroeconomic, demographic, archaeological, and historiographical data (e.g., Anderies, 2003; Galor and Weil, 2000; Steger, 2000; Beltratti, 1997; Cass and Mitra, 1991; Brander and Taylor, 1998).

While such models provide an experimental sandbox to explore the relative importance of economic, social, and ecological processes on the long-term dynamics of social orders, they commonly translate sets of empirically based model assumptions into a rather limited set of qualitative outcomes. Specifically, though more complicated dynamics may result, there are three main outcomes: (1) Monotonic convergence to an equilibrium (stable population, stable resource base, stable infrastructure), (2) oscillatory approach and eventual convergence to an equilibrium, or (3) convergence to oscillatory dynamics that are periodic, quasiperiodic, or "strange attractors" characteristic of chaotic dynamics. These potential qualitative long-run behaviors are called attractors or attractor sets, and models may exhibit multiple attractors. In models with multiple attractors, initial conditions determine which qualitative long-run behavior is exhibited. In the presence of stochastic influences, solutions may bounce around within or among "basins of attraction."

An unstable equilibrium, in the classical sense, does not imply system collapse; indeed, variation about an equilibrium may confer robustness on a broader scale (Holling, 1973). The simplest models of systems are "autonomous," meaning that the dynamics do not depend on outside influences or temporal variations in parameters. Exogenous factors, from gradual change

DOI: 10.4324/9781003331384-18

(e.g. due to climate or nutrient loading) or major perturbations (e.g. warfare, earthquake) can lead to collapse, depending on how robust the intrinsic dynamics of the system are; such influences can be treated as shocks, or incorporated into the model description. Depending on the circumstances, the models may now be "non-autonomous," but that is not necessarily the case. In particular, many systems are characterized by "fast" variables, usually changing on the scale of interest, and "slow" variables, whose dynamics modify the dynamical descriptions on the fast time scales. For example, in a banking system, the increasing interconnectedness of a network over time may gradually erode the robustness of the system, just as the loss of biological diversity may be a slow variable eroding ecosystem robustness. Such models, like the shallow lakes that have received much attention (Scheffer, 1990; Carpenter et al., 1999), may admit multiple attracting regimes, and loss of robustness may lead to regime shifts (Steele, 1998). In such models, sequences and/or combinations of small events (see e.g. Frank et al., 2014, on femtorisks) can move the system across a boundary between one basin of attraction (e.g. a desirable one) to another basin (e.g. an undesirable one). The crossing of this boundary may be hardly noticed by agents within the system and may, in fact, have been crossed due to a well-intentioned adaptive response to an outside shock (e.g. Anderies, 2006). Nonetheless, once in the new basin, the system is inexorably drawn toward the limiting set that defines the basin. This attractor set can characterize a degraded landscape and population decline and the movement toward it is often not abrupt and "collapse-like" on time scales relevant to human perception (minutes to decades) but, rather, characterized by centuries of slow decline (Abbott, 2003).

Many of the formal models used to study collapse in "social–ecological systems" come directly from theoretical ecology where humans act as the predator and the resource base is the prey (e.g. Brander and Taylor, 1998; Anderies, 1998) or bioeconomics where instead of fishers harvesting fish, people extract resources from the environment (harvest) (e.g. Brander and Taylor, 1998; Pezzey and Anderies, 2003) or a combination of economic growth and bioeconomic models in which people invest in hard infrastructures (capital) that increase their capacity to extract resources (e.g. Anderies, 2003; Clark et al., 1979). None of these models tend to focus on the intrinsic properties of feedback systems themselves that are central to feedback control theory (Doyle et al., 2013) and, more precisely, robust control theory (Zhou and Doyle, 1998). In the design of real-world control mechanisms, designers face fundamental constraints in the capacity of feedback systems to cope with variability. There is the familiar robustness–performance trade-off (e.g. risk–rate of return), the efficiency–robustness trade-off (e.g. efficient supply chains that minimize redundancy lose robustness to specific shocks), and the much less well-known robustness–fragility trade-off. Robustness–fragility trade-offs are critical in the design of electrical circuits (signal processing and amplifier design) in which this "conservation of fragility" was first discovered (Bode, 1945). Feedback regulation is ubiquitous in biological and social systems, and tools and ideas from robust control theory are making their way out of electrical engineering and into biology (e.g. Csete and Doyle, 2002; Doyle and Csete, 2011; Kitano et al., 2004; Csete and Doyle, 2004; Stelling et al., 2004; Carlson and Doyle, 2002), economics, and the interdisciplinary science of social–ecological systems (e.g. Anderies et al., 2007; Janssen and Anderies, 2007). Societies are, in fact, social–ecological systems (they all rely on natural resources that come from human-managed ecosystems) and are composed of networks of regulatory feedbacks within social and ecological systems and, most often with the help of human-made infrastructure (technology), across these systems. These regulatory networks are foundational to maintaining stable patterns, i.e. the distribution of species that underlie ecosystems and the distribution of infrastructures, processes, and ideas of the underlying social and technological orders. As a result, the "robustness trade-offs" framework can be a useful lens through which to study how societal collapse can result from emerging fragilities in these regulatory feedback networks.

14.2 Feedback, Information Processing, and Intrinsic Fragility

All realistic models from population biology, theoretical ecology, and resource economics involve feedback mechanisms, e.g. auto-catalytic positive feedback in population growth or capital accumulation and negative feedback due to resource depletion, crowding, predation, or entropic decay. In the case of resource economics, there is an explicit, designed feedback (an "environmental policy loop") added to control the system via a fictitious benevolent social planner whose aim is to optimize system performance in some way. The intrinsic features of feedback systems discussed above are seldom considered in the analysis of collapse. Specifically, feedback is extraordinarily powerful—it provides us with the capacity to drive a system to a long-run attractor and hold it there (i.e. the socially optimal stock size in a fishery). However, it can also be dangerous. For feedback systems to work well, the "controller" (e.g. polity, governance system) must have excellent *information processing* capacity. That is, the controller must have access to accurate information and an excellent internal model of the underlying system that information represents. The internal model allows the controller to translate information inputs into actions through which the system is driven to desired attractors (long-run stable patterns). Such an idealized situation is shown in Figure 14.1A.

Output from the system (right block) is perfectly measured, fed back into the system, and compared to the welfare goal. The result of the comparison (the "error") is fed into the decision-making system (left block) and translated into an action (effort and asset allocations) which is fed into the natural resource system completing one cycle. Such "error-detection-error-correction" loops are extremely effective in creating and maintaining patterns. The capacity of the controller (or planner) to maintain whatever long-run pattern sustains the welfare goal is limited only by the intrinsic dynamics of the natural

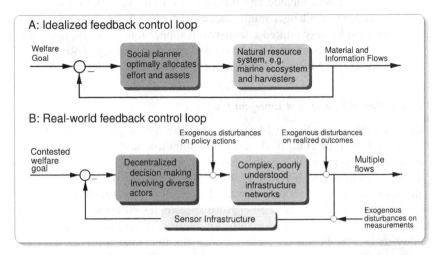

Figure 14.1 Block diagram showing examples of general feedback loops. (A) Idealized loop with perfect information, perfect measurement, and a planner/policy actor with a perfect internal model of the system being controlled. (B) Real-world loop with imperfect information and exogenous shocks, imperfect measurement with decentralized actors with very limited models of the system being controlled.

system, technology, and limits of the actors. Because the controller has perfect information (is aware of all possible system variations) and has a perfect internal model (can exactly predict outcomes of their actions), the planner can avoid intrinsic tipping points (if any) in the natural system making "collapse" impossible (or it is inevitable, and the social planner has taken this into account, as in the famous cake-eating problem where you can't have your cake and eat it too). Another possibility is that the controller is not trying to maintain a system at equilibrium but to control the system trajectory in a way that leads to effective exploration of options (Ott et al., 1990).

In practical applications in the real world, both the information about the state of the controlled system in real time and the understanding of its dynamics can be quite limited, especially in the case of social–ecological systems. Figure 14.1B illustrates this situation. First, measurement of the system is limited by sensor technology and is thus always imperfect. Second, the system being "controlled"—a collection of organisms and technologies—is complex and the internal model of the "controller" is approximate at best. Third, the controller has a limited capacity to effectively translate information into action. On top of these structural imperfections, information and material flows may experience exogenous disturbances as indicated in Figure 14.1B. Examples of exogenous disturbances to policy actions include errors in or misapplication of directives transmitted from the decision-making entity to actors in the controlled system. Exogenous disturbances on realized outcomes include fires, pest outbreaks, or invaders that destroy forests or standing crops. Exogenous disturbances on measurements might include any number of interferences (noise) on signals. These numerous challenges might suggest that the effectiveness of feedback control would be very limited in real-world applications. The surprising thing is that *robust* feedback control can be used to effectively manage systems in such circumstances (within some bounds), but this robustness comes at a cost.

14.2.1 Robust Control and Emergent Fragilities

Consider the case in Figure 14.1B in which the system components (decision block, system to be controlled, and sensor infrastructure) are reasonably well-understood and reasonably well-behaved. In this case, a robust control law can be designed to maintain system performance in the face of exogenous shocks and some uncertainty about the internal dynamics of the system components. Of course, there are robustness-performance trade-offs associated with such control laws and, more importantly for the discussion here, robustness-fragility trade-offs. This latter trade-off takes the following form: Control laws designed to reduce sensitivity (robustness) to one class of disturbances (e.g. of a given frequency, or occurring in certain system components) will necessarily increase sensitivity (fragility) to disturbances of other frequencies or occurring in other system components. These ideas have been applied to the standard bioeconomic model for natural resource management (Clark, 2010) where it has been shown, for example, that increasing robustness to uncertainty in the biological system (e.g. growth rate, carrying capacity) increases sensitivity to uncertainty in the economic system (e.g. prices, discount rate, opportunity costs) (Rodriguez et al., 2011; Anderies et al., 2007). Thus, not only can general robustness not be achieved, efforts to increase robustness to perceived threats necessarily generate fragilities that are the seeds of a potential collapse of social orders.

These same ideas from robust control theory have been used to argue that evolution drives biological systems toward "hard robustness limits," i.e. to a Pareto frontier defining trade-offs between robustness to different types of variability and uncertainty. For example, Kitano et al. (2004) argue that metabolic syndromes result from basic processes of our physiological systems that ensure robustness against unstable food supply and pathogenic infections. An unfortunate byproduct of these processes is that they generate chronic inflammation that leads to cardiovascular disease. That is, heart disease may result from a hard robustness trade-off. Csete and Doyle (2002) argue that elaborate hierarchies of protocols and layers of feedback regulation driven by demand for robustness that generate biological complexity entrain fragilities that may lead to catastrophic cascading failures such as autoimmune diseases and cancer. On the other hand, elaborate regulatory networks that increase the capacity of a system to exploit an environment characterized by disturbances within a specific frequency range (typically on shorter time scales) block the capacity of that system to reorganize to explore new system architectures for novel problems. Mutation, recombination, apoptosis, and organismal death are, in a sense, evolved fragilities. They may produce catastrophic failures on short time scales but allow systems to explore new solutions for novel environments on long time scales. These considerations beg the question of what fragilities are entrained in social orders that are driven by the demand for robustness to variation in resources (food, water, and shelter) and human behavior (violence). To what extent are social orders prone to cascading, catastrophic failures observed in biological systems? Perhaps these failures or, perhaps more aptly named, "critical reorganization events" akin to Schumpeter's (1942) notion of creative destruction are the only mechanisms by which social orders may adapt to rare novel environments.

14.2.2 Efficiency, Architectures, and Fragilities

In the cases described above, the controller and the system being controlled are assumed to be constant. To take the argument one step further, consider a case in which a drive for efficiency translates into internal feedbacks that change the structure of these systems. An obvious example is land system change toward large-scale agriculture that homogenizes species with the goal of improving solar-energy biomass conversion through simplified food webs. Another is the creation of hierarchical networks that increase the efficiency of information processing in organizations. Both are examples of simplified networks in which most network connections pass through a few dominant nodes generating a so-called bow-tie or hourglass architecture. Fragilities associated with these architectures in metabolic pathways may manifest in disease (Csete and Doyle, 2004). The central nodes in these architectures are protocols that connect various layers of organizational forms and provide hints to where we might look for fragilities that may have emerged in cases of historical collapse and how to design architectures to avoid future collapses. It is interesting to note that regulatory feedback networks often function so well as to produce what we might call magic (you reading this sentence). As a result, their fragilities remain largely hidden.

One potential example of bow–tie-like architectures of interest to readers of this volume is the collapse of nine civilizations in the eastern Mediterranean in the Late Bronze Age. Of the typical candidate causes of drought, famine, earthquakes, rebellions, migrations (invasions), and collapse of trade routes, there is no evidence of a single shock that precipitated the collapse. Rather, Cline (2021) suggests that the collapse was related to inherent fragilities in the globalized system consisting of the polities and the trade network that connected them. That these fragilities were largely hidden from those in the system is evidenced in texts from various houses and archives at Ugarit that suggested it was business as usual with normally functioning trade routes until the very last possible moment before collapse (Cline, 2021). If all network nodes had been fully connected to all other nodes, it would have been difficult for such unawareness to persist. This suggests that the trade network may have had some characteristics of a bow-tie architecture. The specialization that drives trade often leads to networks composed of subnetworks connected through "bow-tie knot" nodes that provide key protocols (technology for producing bronze) that link them to critical raw material "precursors." In the case of the bronze age, this critical precursor was tin. The analogue for tin in our modern globalized context is, of course, oil.

Each of the local economies in this trade network certainly had its own particular fragilities. The trade network no doubt increased the robustness of each by smoothing the spatial–temporal variation in resources across the landscape spanned by the network. This local robustness comes at the cost of at least two fragilities beyond the critical dependence on tin: One local, and the other global. First, the well-functioning trade network by its very nature masked local fragilities (e.g. sensitivity of food production systems), thus weakening incentives for local investment in response mechanisms. Second, in the bow-tie architecture typical of trade systems, the knot hides (or delays) information about the fragilities of nodes on the bows on either side of the knot. For example, local fragilities in some nodes exposed by stresses beyond the response capacity of the trade network may cause cascading failures in a subnetwork on one side of the bow tie. Information about these failures may be delayed for subnetworks on the other side of the bow tie, reducing their ability to effect timely responses. This trade-off between the capacity of networks to build local robustness on short time scales at the cost of global fragility on longer time scales seems to be a basic feature of human organizational forms whether the nodes are polities or banks (May et al., 2008). It might be a stretch of the imagination to suggest that there are necessarily hidden fragilities in our modern social and economic orders that are characterized by spiraling complexity, but given the time between the collapse of the eastern Mediterranean global system in 1200 BCE and the Western Roman Empire in 476, in the grand scheme of things two millennia is not long to wait to see one exposed.

14.3 A Formal Model of the Stability of Social Orders

It is extraordinarily difficult to model and analyze systems characterized by complex regulatory feedback networks. We can, however, attempt to capture some key processes and uncover themes that may guide future research.

To illustrate robustness-fragility trade-offs for systems relevant to historical collapse where there is a particular structure for the decision-making block, we can represent a minimal set of relevant feedbacks using the Coupled Infrastructure Systems (CIS) Framework (Anderies et al., 2016). The CIS Framework (Figure 14.2) breaks the biophysical block in Figure 14.1A into natural and built infrastructures. The controller block is broken into two groups: Non-elites/citizens, and political elites who allocate shared resources (taxes collected along links 6 and 3) to infrastructure through link 3. The biophysical system to be "controlled" (to which governance policies are to be applied) consists of a natural infrastructure system and a human-made infrastructure system. These infrastructures are typically shared (at least partially

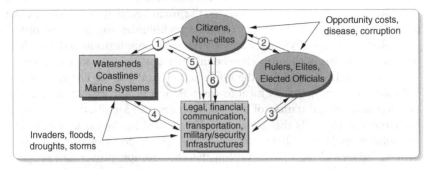

Figure 14.2 Coupled Infrastructure Systems (CIS) Framework illustrating a generalized conceptual model of a social order with elites, non-elites, natural, and built infrastructures. The loops on the left and right loops illustrate management and political feedback loops that are integrated through shared infrastructures.

in the sense that property rights are not completely specified over all potential uses of and flow from the infrastructure). The shared human-made infrastructure provides capacity for action to citizens (non-elites) in various ways depending on the system in question in the form of security (capacity to conduct warfare against shared enemies) or property rights of some sort through link 6. It may also provide public order and capacity for coordination through a system or regulations (institutions) again through link 6. This security and clarity of rights enables citizens to direct efforts toward exploiting the resource and extracting resources through link 1. The shared infrastructure may directly alter the landscape with structures such as roads, dams, canals, dykes, and aqueducts to enhance the productive capacity of the citizens through link 4. It may also monitor the state of the natural infrastructure through link 4 to provide information to other actors in the system through links 3 and 6 or use it to set regulations imposed through links 5 and 6.

Of course, there are many details concerning what flows and interactions occur along these links (see Anderies et al., 2019, for a taxonomy) for any given social order. These are of less interest to us here than the general observation that this structure gives rise to two sets of feedbacks: The *management* loops on the left and the *political economy* loops on the right. These feedback loops are coupled through the public infrastructure (institutions, organizations) to create a regulatory feedback network. This network can create and support persistent complex structures (nation states, empires, etc.) but comes with the challenges described above. At the risk of being too simplistic, at a minimum, a balance must be achieved between the loops on the left and those on the right. With a little imagination, it is not difficult to see the many ways this can go wrong.

Two examples of recent work have highlighted the delicate balance between these loops in quite general terms. Piketty (2020) explores the basic function of this system across two main types of social orders: The ternary social order and the ownership social order. In the ternary social order the elites are split into the warrior/noble class and the clerical class which, with the addition of the non-elites, creates the main social groups. The nobles provide security while the clerics create and administer an "imagined order" or "collective imaginary" that enables large-scale coordination and mobilization of individuals in the non-elite/commoner class. In such societies, almost all property rights are held by the noble and clerical classes. The commoners hold almost no property. Critical to the function of ternary systems was the creation and administration of imagined orders, i.e. a collection of powerful narratives, to justify this gross inequality backed by the capacity of nobles to mobilize violence. These narratives and capacity for violence maintain a delicate balance along link 2. Within the elite groups, power and property are negotiated through inter-marriage and other alliances that make for great stories of greed, depravity, and violence as the two groups fight for power. It is not hard to imagine breakdowns in the link 2-3-6 and 6-3-2 feedback loops where the capacity of elites to provide basic public services and the clergy to maintain the status of the narratives they curate fails. Social collapse soon follows.

These sorts of intrinsic instabilities created by the very unequal distribution of property rights and the resource-intensive arms races and power struggles they create are obvious sources for candidate mechanisms of historical collapse. Piketty argues that a natural successor to such collapse is the emergence of the "ownership" society where the main role of the state is to enforce the property rights of a much larger number of non-elites. This may serve to re-legitimize inequalities in the distribution of property, wealth, and income by recasting it as a result of differences in personal capacities rather than of cosmic or divine order, but ownership societies have their own instabilities. Now, rather than balancing the legitimacy of stories with the maximum tolerable misery of non-elites in ternary societies (which is actually reasonably "controllable"), the balancing act is between the rate of return on capital (e.g. land and machines), and the growth rate of the economy (output per worker plus population growth). If the former is greater than the latter, inequality will grow endogenously, without bound, until it again threatens social stability. The second example of recent work mentioned above relates to the notion of the "narrow corridor" which Acemoglu and Robinson (2020) use to refer to the delicate balance between the power of the state and the power of society. The stability of social order is then achieved through link 2 as society "shackles the leviathan."

In every case, the stability of a given social order is maintained through the balance of dynamic tensions maintained by regulatory feedback. Figure 14.2 provides a simple structural view of various possible feedback networks. These feedbacks emerge to stabilize intrinsic instabilities present in the biophysical system of interest. The "social order" can then be viewed as an emergent feature of this evolutionary process. Robust control theory tells us that all such systems will exhibit fragilities when the environment in which they were "tuned" changes. As the system becomes more highly optimized to its embedding environment, ever smaller changes may lead to cascading failures for which there is no easy mechanistic explanation. We can, however, make this process easier to visualize with the help of formal mathematical models.

In a series of two manuscripts, Muneepeerakul and Anderies (2018, 2020) develop a simple, general bioeconomic model for all the elements and links in the CIS Framework. The elements of the model are:

- Link 1: Resource users (citizens) exert effort, to harvest resources. The harvest depends on the level of shared infrastructure provided by the public infrastructure providers (state).
- Resource system: The resource system resembles a watershed—there is a natural inflow and outflow of water that generates a water stock available at a given time (the water in a river).
- Shared infrastructure (canals, dams, institutions for resource access) increases access to the resource through link 4.
- Public infrastructure providers extract a tax through link 2, extract rent for themselves, and invest the remainder in the creation and maintenance of shared infrastructure.
- Resource users choose between remaining in the system or migrating out to better opportunities (or protesting and being killed or otherwise removed from the system).
- Public infrastructure providers will leave the system if it is less productive than other options as in the "roving bandit" of Olson (1993).

The model thus represents a dynamic game between "society" (the resource users) and "the state." See Muneepeerakul and Anderies (2018) for the mathematical details. The analysis of the model provides a succinct picture (Figure 14.3) of the endogenous fragilities discussed above. The shaded region in Figure 14.3 Panel (a) shows the "viable" strategy space for the public infrastructure providers. Any point in this region will sustain the infrastructure at some level and support some level of resource use (there will be some resource users in the system). The curves in Figure 14.3 Panel (a) labeled "partially functioning PI" and "fully functioning PI" define the boundaries of the region where the shared infrastructure is positive (solid) and maximum (dashed). The black curve specifies combinations of tax rate and investment levels that maximize total system output. The white star represents the tax rate (quite high) and proportion of tax invested in maintenance (quite low) that maximizes the income for the public infrastructure providers. In this case, the infrastructure is maintained at an intermediate level with a few resource users (20% of the population) in the system. The few who remain have access to an abundance of natural resources and thus can tolerate high taxes. But participation is low and the relative productivity is low (about 60% of maximum) (Figure 14.3 Panel (c)). The key is that the white star is in an unstable region where the system oscillates (participation and productivity oscillate as a result of a Hopf bifurcation in which the stabilizing fluctuations about an equilibrium have grown larger and larger until they are no longer stabilizing) at the top boundary of the hatched region. Such oscillatory behavior could, for example, generate social unrest.

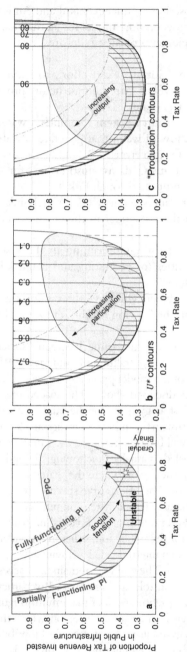

Figure 14.3 The strategy space of public infrastructure providers. Panel (a) Boundaries of the viable strategy space. Dark black curve specifies combinations of tax rate and investment levels that maximize total system output. Different points on this curve represent different distributions of revenue between resource users (citizens) and public infrastructure providers (the state). Panel (b) Participation contours. Panel (c) Production contours. Adapted from Muneepeerakul and Anderies (2018).

This is a clear example of how strategies of self-interested state actors can destabilize a system by not understanding the underlying dynamics of the resource and infrastructure systems. Redistributive policies, i.e. increasing state investment in public services that move the system up and to the left along the curve that runs through the white star in Figure 14.3 Panel (a), which increases participation (Figure 14.3 Panel (b)) and total output from the resource system (Figure 14.3 Panel (c)) can re-stabilize the system. This does, however, put more pressure on the resource base. That is, fragility can be transferred from the built environment and political system to the resource system but cannot be removed. Although such mathematical analysis loses much of the richness of specific case studies, it may help triangulate groupings of cases that exhibit similar "collapse-like" dynamics.

14.4 Conclusions

The aim of this chapter has been to emphasize the fundamental importance of regulatory feedback networks in creating and maintaining persistent patterns. In the context of historical collapse, these persistent patterns include organizational forms, institutional structures, modes of production, and cultural forms that constitute complex societies. Leveraging the notion of robustness-fragility trade-offs or, more succinctly, the conservation of fragility, we have illustrated how the feedback networks that are essential to create and maintain complex societies also contain the seeds for their potential collapse. Drawing on analogies from biology, we may speculate that as societies create ever more regulatory feedbacks to cope with exogenous disturbances and endogenous instabilities, they may evolve toward hard robustness limits characterized by spiraling complexity, increasingly tight regulation prone to oscillation, and the potential for cascading failures when faced with novel disturbances. These stylized facts may be too coarse to understand the details of a particular historical collapse event, but they may be used to triangulate similar cases and map dominant feedback architectures, information flows, and modes of action in societies to detect recurrent themes across cases. Given the notion of hard robustness limits, we might conclude that all societies must eventually collapse, just as all species will eventually go extinct. However, as complex social–ecological structures undergo a cascading failure process, sub-units of functional infrastructure may persist that provide a basis for reorganization. So rather than predicting that all societies must collapse, conservation of fragility may predict an essential frequency of social reorganization for various classes of societies.

References

Abbott, D. R., editor. (2003). *Centuries of Decline during the Hohokam Classic Period at Pueblo Grande*. Tucson, AZ: University of Arizona Press.

Acemoglu, D., and Robinson, J. A. (2020). *The Narrow Corridor: States, Societies, and the Fate of Liberty*. New York : Penguin Books.

Anderies, J. M. (1998). Culture and human agro-ecosystem dynamics: The Tsembaga of New Guinea. *Journal of Theoretical Biology*, 192(4):515–530.

———, (2003). Economic development, demographics, and renewable resources: A dynamical systems approach. *Environment and Development Economics*, 8(2):219–246.

———, (2006). Robustness, institutions, and large-scale change in social-ecological systems: The Hohokam of the Phoenix Basin. *Journal of Institutional Economics*, 2(2):133–155.

Anderies, J. M., Barreteau, O., and Brady, U. (2019). Refining the robustness of social-ecological systems framework for comparative analysis of coastal system adaptation to global change. *Regional Environmental Change*, 19(7):1891–1908.

Anderies, J. M., Janssen, M. A., and Schlager, E. (2016). Institutions and the performance of coupled infrastructure systems. *International Journal of the Commons*, 10(2):495–516.

Anderies, J. M., Rodriguez, A., Janssen, M., and Cifdaloz, O. (2007). Panaceas, uncertainty, and the robust control framework in sustainability science. *Proceedings of the National Academy of Sciences of the United States of America*, 104(39):15194–15199.

Beltratti, A. (1997). Growth with natural and environmental resources. In Carraro, C., and Siniscalcoa, D., editors. *New Directions in the Economic Theory of the Environment*. Cambridge: Cambridge University Press:7–42.

Bode, H. W. (1945). *Network Analysis and Feedback Amplifier Design*. Princeton, NJ: D. Van Nostrand.

Boserup, E. (1965). *The Conditions of Agricultural Growth: The Economics of Agriculture under Population Pressure*. London: George Allen & Unwin Ltd.

Brander, J. A., and Taylor, M. S. (1998). The simple economics of Easter Island: A Ricardo-Malthus model of renewable resource use. *American Economic Review*, 88(1):119–138.

Carlson, J., and Doyle, J. (2002). Complexity and robustness. *Proceedings of the National Academy of Science*, 99(Suppl. 1):2538–2545.

Carpenter, S. A., Ludwig, D., and Brock, W. A. (1999). Management of eutrophication for lakes subject to potentially irreversible change. *Ecological Applications*, 9(3):751–771.

Cass, D., and Mitra, T. (1991). Indefinitely sustained consumption despite exhaustible resources. *Economic Theory*, 1(2):119–146.

Clark, C. W. (2010). *Mathematical Bioeconomics: The Mathematics of Conservation* (Vol. 91). Hoboken : John Wiley & Sons.

Clark, C. W., Clarke, F. H., and Munro, G. R. (1979). The optimal exploitation of renewable resource stocks: Problems of irreversible investment. *Econometrica*, 47(1):25–47.

Cline, E. H. (2021). *1177 B.C.: The Year Civilization Collapsed: Revised and Updated*. Princeton, NJ: Princeton University Press.

Csete, M., and Doyle, J. (2004). Bow ties, metabolism and disease. *Trends in Biotechnology*, 22(9):446–450.

Csete, M. E., and Doyle, J. C. (2002). Reverse engineering of biological complexity. *Science*, 295(5560):1664–1669.

Doyle, J. C., and Csete, M. (2011). Architecture, constraints, and behavior. *Proceedings of the National Academy of Sciences*, 108(Suppl. 3):15624–15630.

Doyle, J. C., Francis, B. A., and Tannenbaum, A. R. (1992). *Feedback Control Theory*. New York : Macmillan Publishing Co.

Frank, A. B., Collins, M. G., Levin, S. A., Lo, A. W., Ramo, J., Dieckmann, U., Kremenyuk, V., Kryazhimskiy, A., Linnerooth-Bayer, J., Ramalingam, B., et al. (2014). Dealing with femtorisks in international relations. *Proceedings of the National Academy of Sciences of the United States of America*, 111(49):17356–17362.

Galor, O., and Weil, D. (2000). Population, technology, and growth: From Malthusian stagnation to the demographic transition and beyond. *American Economic Review*, 90(4):806–828.

Holling, C. (1973). Resilience and stability of ecological systems. *Annual Review of Ecology, and Systematics*, 4:2–23.

Janssen, M., and Anderies, J. (2007). Robustness trade-offs in social-ecological systems. *International Journal of the Commons*, 1(1):43–66.

Kitano, H., Oda, K., Kimura, T., Matsuoka, Y., Csete, M., Doyle, J., and Muramatsu, M. (2004). Metabolic syndrome and robustness tradeoffs. *Diabetes*, 53(Suppl. 3):S6–S15.

Malthus, T. R. (1798). *An Essay on the Principle of Population, as It Affects the Future Improvement of Society, with Remarks on the Speculations of Mr. Godwin, Mr. Condorcet, and Other Writers*. London: J. Johnson.

May, R. M., Levin, S. A., and Sugihara, G. (2008). Ecology for bankers. *Nature*, 451(7181):893–894.

Muneepeerakul, R., and Anderies, J. M. (2018). Strategic behaviors and governance challenges in social-ecological systems. *Earth's Future*, 5(8):865–876.

Muneepeerakul, R., and Anderies, J. M. (2020). The emergence and resilience of self-organized governance in coupled infrastructure systems. *Proceedings of the National Academy of Sciences of the United States of America*, 117(9):4617–4622.

Olson, M. (1993). Dictatorship, democracy, and development. *American Political Science Review*, 87(3):567–576.

Ott, E., Grebogi, C., and Yorke, J. A. (1990). Controlling chaos. *Physical Review Letters*, 64(11):1196.

Pezzey, J., and Anderies, J. M. (2003). The effect of subsistence on collapse and institutional adaptation in population-resource societies. *Journal of Development Economics*, 72(1):299–320.

Piketty, T. (2020). *Capital and Ideology*. Cambridge, MA: Harvard University Press.

Rodriguez, A. A., Cifdaloz, O., Anderies, J. M., Janssen, M. A., and Dickeson, J. (2011). Confronting management challenges in highly uncertain natural resource systems: A robustness–vulnerability trade-off approach. *Environmental Modeling and Assessment*, 16(1):15–36.

Scheffer, M. (1990). Multiplicity of stable states in freshwater systems. Ramesh D. Gulati, Eddy H. R. R. Lammens, Marie-Louise Meijer, Ellen Donk, In *Biomanipulation Tool for Water Management*. Amsterdam: Springer, 475–486.

Schumpeter, J. A. (1942) *Capitalism, Socialism, and Democracy*. 1st edition. New York: Harper & Brothers.

Steele, J. H. (1998). Regime shifts in marine ecosystems. *Ecological Applications*, 8(sp1):S33–S36.

Steger, T. M. (2000). Economic growth with subsistence consumption. *Journal of Development Economics*, 62(2):343–361.

Stelling, J., Sauer, U., Szallasi, Z., Doyle III, F. J., and Doyle, J. (2004). Robustness of cellular functions. *Cell*, 118(6):675–685.

Zhou, K., and Doyle, J. (1998). *Essentials of Robust Control*. Upper Saddle River, N.J. : Prentice Hall.

15 Resilience and Collapse in Bee Societies and Communities

Christina M. Grozinger and Harland M. Patch

15.1 Introduction

The co-evolved mutualism of flowering plants and bees forms the basis of terrestrial ecosystems (Bascompte & Jordano, 2007). Nearly 90% of flowering plant species benefit from bees and other pollinators transporting their pollen, to support seed set and fruit production (Ollerton, Winfree, & Tarrant, 2011), which both support plant reproduction and serve as a base of ecological food webs. Pollinators, in turn, obtain nutritional resources from flowering plants in the form of nectar and pollen (Willmer, 2011). Bees are especially efficient pollinators, as they evolved to collect pollen from flowers and transport it back to their nests to feed their larval offspring: Pollen is their sole source of protein and fats (Danforth, Minckley, & Neff, 2019). Over 20,000 bee species have been described, but one of the best-studied and most important for human agricultural systems is the honey bee (*Apis mellifera*). This species evolved a eusocial lifestyle, resulting in large colonies consisting of tens of thousands of sterile female worker bees and a single reproductive female queen (Tautz, 2008). Honey bees originally evolved in tropical regions (it is debated if they evolved in Africa or Asia) and subsequently colonized Europe, and ultimately were transported to all continents except Antarctica by humans (Dogantzis & Zayed, 2019). Honey bees were initially managed by humans primarily for honey production, but with the rise of large-scale agriculture they have become vital pollinators of agricultural crops, due to their large colony sizes and portability (Delaplane & Mayer, 2000; Kritsky, 2017).

The structure and organization of honey bee colonies and plant–pollinator communities make them uniquely resilient and sensitive to collapse (reviewed in Bascompte & Jordano, 2007; Lever, van Nes, Scheffer, & Bascompte, 2014 and Barron, 2015). The organization of honey bee colonies is the result of decentralized, local interactions, where an individual's physiology and behavior are influenced by social interactions and vice versa. Multiple feedback loops ensure a stable distribution and allocation of individual bees to different colony tasks. Thus, the colony can recover readily even if a seemingly large portion of the population is lost. However, once the population drops below a certain number, a tipping point is reached where the colony cannot recover, and the

DOI: 10.4324/9781003331384-19

same feedback loops that create resilience can lead to collapse. Similarly, plant–pollinator communities are organized as networks, where individual pollinator species will visit one or more plant species, and individual plant species will be visited by one or more pollinator species. They are often described as mutualistic networks in which species exist in a relationship that benefits each partner by increasing reproductive output. Because of their particular architecture, plant–pollinator communities are resilient to perturbation, but they are prone to sudden collapse after critical transition points.

Honey bee colonies and plant–pollinator networks represent outstanding systems to understand the intrinsic and extrinsic drivers of resilience and collapse. Because of their importance for food security and ecosystem function, there is considerable interest in developing models and methods for conserving, restoring, expanding, and managing these systems. However, significant declines in populations of both wild and managed bee species (and insect species in general) have been reported across the world (Wagner, Grames, Forister, Berenbaum, & Stopak, 2021). To some extent, our food systems can be buffered to declines in bee populations and their associated pollination services by changes in agricultural production systems, such as shifting to self-pollinating crop cultivars, including transgenic crops, or bringing more land into agricultural production (Aizen et al., 2019; Aizen & Harder, 2009). However, a major goal to conserve terrestrial biodiversity, and its associated ecosystem services, is to develop agricultural practices which require fewer inputs (including reduced use of managed honey bee colonies) and less land (Kok et al., 2020). Similarly, diversified cropping systems provide greater ecosystem benefits and are more resilient, nutritious, and accessible for growers and consumers (Kremen & Merenlender, 2018). Since the primary stressors that honey bee colonies and plant–pollinator networks experience are due to human activities (habitat loss, environmental toxins, and climate change), an understanding of the socioeconomic factors contributing to these activities is necessary for developing sustainable solutions.

15.2 Background

In the winter of 2006–2007, beekeepers in the United States reported unexpected and substantial mortality of their honey bee colonies, in a phenomenon later termed "colony collapse disorder" (van Engelsdorp et al., 2009). These losses caused considerable concern among beekeepers, farmers, the scientific community, and the public, because the pollination services provided by honey bees are critical for food production and security. During the same period, the National Academy of Sciences published a groundbreaking report "The Status of Pollinators in North America," which highlighted the importance of pollinators for creating productive and healthy agricultural and natural ecosystems, summarized reports of population declines and losses in multiple species and geographic regions, and evaluated the ongoing and emerging threats to these populations (National Research Council, 2006). Finally, in October 2006, the honey bee genome was published, ushering in a new era in which genomic tools and resources could be used to investigate bee behavior and health at a heretofore unprecedented scale (Weinstock et al., 2006).

In the years since these events, it has been established that both managed and wild bee populations are showing significant declines, including local extinctions, across the globe (Potts et al., 2010). In the United States, annual surveys of beekeepers have found that ~30% of beekeepers' colonies die each year (Bruckner et al., 2020). In the years since the winter of 2006, beekeepers typically attribute this mortality to factors other than "colony collapse disorder," which had specific symptoms, including rapid loss of adult bee population, with the queen, young workers, and developing larvae remaining in the colony (van Engelsdorp et al., 2009). There are many factors and mechanisms by which a colony can collapse which do not exhibit the same symptoms as "colony collapse disorder" (discussed below). Notably, despite these high annual losses, the total number of colonies in the United States has been relatively stable in recent years because beekeepers are able to generate new colonies during the growing season. Indeed, a large industry has grown around producing bee colonies in southern states for sale to northern states. However, since 1960 the number of acres of pollinator-dependent crops planted across the world has increased at a rate far greater than the number of managed honey bee colonies, raising concerns about inadequate pollination services limiting crop yields (Aizen & Harder, 2009). Wild bees and other pollinators can provide pollination services that can replace or complement those of managed honey bees. However, studies have documented dramatic declines of wild bumble bee species in the United States (Cameron et al., 2011), butterfly species in the United States (Wepprich, Adrion, Ries, Wiedmann, & Haddad, 2019), wild bee species in the Netherlands and the United Kingdom (Biesmeijer et al., 2006), among others (Wagner et al., 2021).

Declines in honey bee colony survival and species diversity and abundance of wild bee communities are driven by multiple interacting factors (Potts et al., 2010). These factors include land use changes, which reduce nesting habitat for wild bees (which nest in the ground, in stems, or in above- or below-ground cavities) and the abundance and diversity of flowering plants that bees depend on to meet their nutritional needs. Increasing exposure to insecticides can kill bees outright or reduce their ability to make nests, forage, or reproduce. Bees weakened by reduced nutrition or increased insecticide exposure are more sensitive to pathogens and parasites. Furthermore, new pathogens and parasites have been introduced to bee populations through the human-mediated movement of bees and/or their pathogens/parasites. Finally, climate change can negatively influence both flowering plants and bees (reviewed in Forrest, 2016; Rafferty, 2017; Scaven & Rafferty, 2013). Exposure to altered weather conditions can shift the timing and duration of plant flowering, as well as the quantity and quality of the nectar and pollen produced by plants; for example, an increase of 1-3°C resulted in a 90% decrease in nectar production in studies of a key plant species used for honey production in the Tibetan plateau (Mu et al., 2015). Changes in weather patterns can also limit bees' ability to forage (bees cannot forage when it is rainy, too cool, or too hot), which can reduce the number of offspring successfully reared. Finally, bees have strategies for surviving hot summer conditions and cold winter conditions (including entering a quiescent phase called diapause), but survival can be negatively affected by the length and severity of these conditions. In recent analyses evaluating the effects of forage resource availability, insecticide use patterns, landscape composition, and climate on managed honey bee winter survival and the abundance and diversity of bee species in the eastern United States, weather and climate factors were found to be the major drivers of declines (Calovi, Grozinger, Miller, & Goslee, 2021; Kammerer, Goslee, Douglas, Tooker, & Grozinger, 2021).

The accumulating evidence of bee declines and increased awareness of the causes have led to changes in the behavior of individuals as well as at the federal level. The extent to which these changes have influenced bee declines remains to be determined. For example, studies of consumer preferences have demonstrated that people will pay more money for plants labeled as "pollinator friendly" from garden supply stores (Campbell, Khachatryan, & Rihn, 2017). The US federal government released a Pollinator Partnership Action Plan in 2016 (Pollinator Health Task Force, 2016) which sought to increase funding and coordination efforts to achieve three main goals: (1) Reduce honey bee overwintering colony losses to no more than 15% within 10 years, (2) increase the Eastern population of the monarch butterfly to cover approximately 15 acres in the overwintering grounds in Mexico, and (3) restore or enhance 7 million acres of land for pollinators over the next 5 years. In Europe, concerns about the role of neonicotinoids (a class of insecticides) in driving pollinator declines led to a ban on the use of three of these insecticides on field crops in 2018 (Bass & Field, 2018). Because the drivers of bee declines include factors linked to core human activities (land use changes due to agriculture and urbanization, climate change due to rising CO_2 levels), changing these conditions at a large scale requires a substantial reorganization in how we approach these activities. However, because of the visibility, charisma, and importance of bees, they are both outstanding indicators of ecosystem health and ambassadors for change.

15.3 Analysis and Synthesis

15.3.1 Factors Contributing to Resilience and Collapse of Honey Bee Colonies

15.3.1.1 Resilience of Honey Bee Colonies

The physiology, behavior, and social structure of honey bee colonies make them both resilient to external stressors and also susceptible to sudden collapse (reviewed in Page, 2020). Honey bee colonies are often described as "superorganisms," because the tasks in the colony are divided up between different individuals, and the activity of hundreds or thousands of individuals is needed for the colony to properly function. Honey bees have a reproductive division of labor, where a single female (the queen) can mate and lays all the eggs in the colony, and the other females (workers) are facultatively sterile and perform the other colony tasks. The workers also exhibit a division of labor which is based on worker age (termed behavioral maturation or temporal polyethism). Young workers (the nurse bees) feed developing brood, by consuming nectar and pollen and converting it to a nutritionally rich secretion (using glands found in their heads) which is deposited in honeycomb cells containing developing larvae. Middle-age workers perform other in-hive tasks, such as building honeycombs, storing food, removing dead bees (undertaking), or guarding the colony entrance. The oldest bees in the colony are foragers, leaving the colony and searching the surrounding landscape for flowers producing nectar and pollen, which they collect and bring back to the hive. Foragers can fly several kilometers on their trips, and communicate the location of food resources to other foragers in the hive through a symbolic dance language, thereby allowing honey bee colonies to rapidly take advantage of floral resources available in the landscape. Foraging is physiologically challenging, and the transition to foraging is associated with a reduced lifespan: Workers can survive in the colony for months as nurses if they do not transition to foraging.

While worker division of labor is correlated with worker age, the rate of behavioral maturation can be altered, or even reversed, by social cues from the colony (reviewed in Robinson, 2002). If all the forager bees in a colony are removed, some of the young nurse bees will accelerate their maturation so that they become foragers at an unusually young age. These "precocious foragers" are not as efficient at collecting food and take fewer trips and return to the hive with less food per trip (Perry, Sovik, Myerscough, & Barron, 2015). They also will not live as long as typical foragers. If the brood is removed from the colony so that there are no new young bees emerging to take the place of the nurses, the nurses will remain in the nursing state longer: These "over-aged nurses" can survive for months. If nurses are removed from the colony, some of the foragers will revert back to performing nursing behavior. These behaviors are regulated by pheromones: Foragers release a pheromone which inhibits the behavioral maturation of young bees (Leoncini et al., 2004), while brood releases a pheromone which can inhibit or accelerate the maturation of young bees (Le Conte & Hefetz, 2008). It has also been hypothesized that the spatial organization of the hive contributes to this variation in behavior, with nurse bees staying on the interior of the hive, over the brood nest, but ultimately being forced to the edges of this area—and distant from the brood pheromone—by the emergence of new adult bees (Johnson, 2010).

15.3.1.2 Collapse of Honey Bee Colonies

The social structure of the colony can increase resilience to stressors, but it can also lead to sudden collapse (reviewed in Barron, 2015, see Figure 15.1). If a subset of workers is lost due to acute, short-term stress (such as a disease

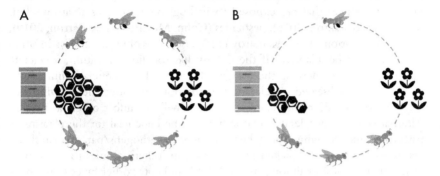

Figure 15.1 Chronic stress can unbalance the honey bee colony structure and lead to colony collapse. In honey bee colonies (A), young bees work as nurses and convert nectar and pollen to glandular secretions, which are fed to developing larvae (brood). As they mature, they become foragers collecting nectar and pollen from flowers. Once a bee becomes a forager, she usually only lives a short time. When colonies are stressed (B), young bees accelerate their maturation to become foragers earlier. These precocious foragers are not as effective at foraging and bring back less pollen and nectar to the colony. These precocious foragers also have a higher mortality rate. The reduced number of foragers leads to accelerated maturation of the young bees to replace them. The reduced workforce of nurses and reduced amount of food brought back to the hive reduce the amount of brood that can be reared, leading to further reductions in the workforce. Ultimately this can lead to colony collapse.

outbreak or insecticide exposure), the task allocation of the remaining workers can be adjusted to compensate, thereby ensuring that all the colony tasks continue to be performed. If the stress is chronic (Figure 15.1B), it can unbalance the colony demographic structure and result in too few nurses to care for developing brood, or too few foragers to bring food back to the colony, and thus the colony will not be able to rear enough workers to keep the colony above the population threshold needed to function. If forager mortality rates increase, it will cause young bees to become precocious foragers. As noted above, these precocious foragers have a higher mortality rate, and low efficiency of foraging (Perry et al., 2015). Thus, if this process continues for an extended period of time, too little food is being returned to the colony to rear new workers to compensate for the increased mortality of the foragers, and the colony collapses (see models in Khoury, Barron, & Myerscough, 2013; Khoury, Myerscough, & Barron, 2011). This "tipping point" has been modeled in other social bee species, such as bumble bees, which are more sensitive to stressors due to the overall smaller colony size (bumble bee colonies consist of a few hundred workers, while honey bee colonies consist of tens of thousands of workers; Bryden, Gill, Mitton, Raine, & Jansen, 2013).

Individual worker bees have common physiological and behavioral responses to different stressors: They accelerate their behavioral maturation to become foragers earlier. This accelerated behavioral maturation response has been documented for bees that are exposed to pathogens or parasites (Natsopoulou, McMahon, & Paxton, 2016), pesticides (Colin, Meikle, Wu, & Barron, 2019), and poor nutrition (Toth, Kantarovich, Meisel, & Robinson, 2005). In some cases, this can be adaptive: If the colony has too little nutrition, accelerating maturation to increase the foraging force can be beneficial. Similarly, if an individual is diseased, acceleration maturation can move the individual to the edge or outside of the colony, where it will not infect others as readily. Alternatively, the accelerated maturation can be beneficial for the parasite or pathogen, since foraging honey bees can deposit pathogens/parasites on flowers, where they can be picked up by bees from other colonies (or even bees from other species) or ill foragers can "drift" and enter other hives (Grozinger & Flenniken, 2019). Regardless, if too many bees within the colony accelerate their maturation, it can unbalance the colony structure and lead to collapse.

15.3.2 Factors Contributing to Collapse and Resilience of Plant–Pollinator Communities

15.3.2.1 Network Architecture

High degrees of nestedness are a hallmark of plant–pollinator communities (see Figure 15.2B, discussed in Olesen, Bascompte, Dupont, and Jordano, 2007). A nested community structure is best understood by accounting for the identity and activities of the interacting species within a community. While specialist pollinators may only visit one or a few plant species in a network, those plant species typically are generalists and tend to be visited by other pollinators, that themselves visit many plant species. In essence, this core group of generalists (honey bees being the most generalist of bee species) has functional redundancy that creates community stability over time as species populations naturally fluctuate. If these interactions are represented in a grid format, it resembles nested Chinese boxes where the set of animals or plants is nested inside the larger set of the next most generalized animal or plant species (Bascompte & Jordano, 2007; Bascompte, Jordano, Melian, & Olesen, 2003) (Figure 2B). This architecture has a number of important consequences for community interaction and stability. Nested communities minimize temporal resource competition and increase specialization dynamically with resource availability. They also increase the number of coexisting species (Bastolla et al., 2009) and are more robust to random extinctions (Burgos et al., 2007; Memmott, Waser, & Price, 2004) and habitat loss (Fortuna & Bascompte, 2006).

Modularity is a property of most complex networks (Figure 15.2C). Instead of equally distributed interactions of species in a homogeneous network, large plant–pollinator communities are made up of subsets of species that have fewer and shorter connections within the group and relatively fewer interactions with species in other subsets (Olesen et al., 2007). Depending on the defining characteristics, modules can be multiple and

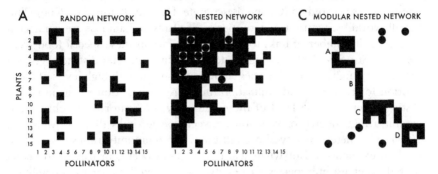

Figure 15.2 Structure and dynamics of plant–pollinator community networks. Blocks indicate interaction links between a plant species, numbered 1–15, and a pollinator species, numbered 1–15. Circles indicate hub interactions that interconnect modules. (A) A hypothetical randomly organized plant–pollinator network where most species have few interactions. *In silico* simulations show that such networks are susceptible to rapid extinction. (B) Real-world nested matrix network with plant species and pollinator species sorted from the upper-left corner according to descending species degree. Plant 1 is the most generalized plant in this network since it is visited by the most pollinators. Plants 13–15 are more specialized with only two or three pollinator species visiting. Similarly pollinators 14 and 15 only visit one plant species. While nested communities are more resilient to perturbation these specialists are the first species to go extinct in a declining community. Plants generally persist longer in communities exhibiting declines. (C) Modular matrix version of the same network as in B. Here the species are sorted according to their modular affinity. Circle cells are species links that connect modules A–D together. After Oelson et al 2007.

overlapping in terms of participants. Within modules, species can have convergent morphological traits (coevolved units) and these can form the mutualistic building blocks of the nested network. An illustrative example is the flower–bee community studied by studied by Kantsa et al. (2017) on the Mediterranean Island of Lesvos. The 41 bee-pollinated plants in this community exhibited mosaic modules for both flower color and odor volatile phenotypes, suggesting pollinator-mediating facilitation or fitness benefits to co-flowering. More broadly, modularity for biotic species decreases time scales, when compared to the whole community, and is the source of dynamic change from phenotypes to community composition (Bascompte & Olesen, 2015). Modules can also have hubs (Figure 15.2C), or highly connected species within the module, and also super generalists that connect modules, large bees and some flies being most prominent in this functional group (Olesen et al., 2007). Further research into the relative role of these species is needed. It should also be noted that for mutualistic networks, modularity under certain conditions decreases the persistence of the network, even as nestedness increases its resilience (Thebault & Fontaine, 2010).

Species in pollinator networks are more closely linked than in any biotic communities yet studied (Olesen, Bascompte, Dupont, & Jordano, 2006). This "small-world" structure is where species of plants and animals are connected with a small number of links to any other species in these special food webs (Watts & Strogatz, 1998). A higher density of links, shorter distance between species, and higher level of species clustering result in both high levels of competition for resources and pollination, but here competition results in mutualistic resilience at the level of the community. Pollinator communities also exhibit a high degree of variation between species links (Sole & Montoya, 2001). This heterogeneity also contributes to community robustness against random extinctions. But when selective declines occur, of particularly connected generalist hub species, these networks can exhibit degrees of fragility.

15.3.2.2 System Collapse

The magnitude and direction of ecosystem change, including plant–pollinator networks, are determined by the strength and interaction of positive and negative community–environment feedback loops (Lever et al., 2020). These feedback mechanisms can be identified in many systems and empirically measured. For pollinator communities, negative immediate interactions such as intraspecific competition can have stabilizing effects. Positive interactions like large plant population size can drive the growth of pollinator populations by increasing food resources, which in turn will set more seeds for more plants. These "reinforcing" feedbacks are destabilizing and are the basis of the alternative stable states (Guoze, 1998; Lever et al., 2020; Snoussi, 1998; Thomas, 1981). Stable states are characterized by different species composition and numbers and relatively high immediate negative feedback loops. A transition between the states occurs when the positive feedback interactions become stronger relative to the negative stabilizing interactions often as a result of strong changes in environmental conditions. An illustrative example of this would be that a decline in pollinator abundance (potentially from stressors such as climate change or pesticide use) would negatively impact seed production in plants which would itself feedback into fewer flowering resources for pollinators. *In silico* models of declining pollinator networks give us insight into the dynamics of these communities under abstract generalized stressors (Lever et al., 2014).

Tipping points, where systems move from one equilibrium state to another, are preceded in many systems by a critical slowing-down period (Scheffer et al., 2009; Wissel, 1984). This period is marked by increased variance and correlation and a concomitant loss of system resilience. In mechanistic terms if indicators of these slowing-down periods can be identified, tipping points for community network rewiring and collapse can be anticipated. Environmental stress response models based on empirical descriptions of plant–pollinator communities provide invaluable insight into the dynamics of decline (Dakos & Bascompte, 2014). A decline in mutualistic interactions resulted in a decrease in overall biomass. Every species declined in all 79 *in silico* simulations until the first species extinction, which marked the community tipping point. These simulations also yield insight into the best indicator species for the onset of the critical slowing-down period. Specialists pollinators were the first to collapse, and because of their low level of interaction with other species, they tend to give a clear signal of their decline. In addition, specialist species commonly showed greater variance in abundance (measured as the coefficient of variation). These results suggest that in real communities the loss of species with high variance in abundance, particularly specialists, could be an indication of the onset of a community tipping point.

Lever et al 2020 proposed a novel class of indicators to detect how species are affected by stressors as they approach the critical transition. Particularly, they were interested in modeling the systems' increased sensitivity to small disturbances and identifying indicators of transitions (van Nes & Scheffer, 2007; Wissel, 1984). These studies found that the system has a characteristic set of parameters as the transition point is neared, which characterized transition states generally, but the particulars of these parameters indicate the abundance of species after the transition. Model simulations of mutualistic networks approaching transitions showed that as interspecific competition decreased, instability increased and at least one species became extinct. Other species in the network either showed asymmetric increase or decrease in abundance depending on community-specific interactions and how they are affected by environmental conditions. The direction of change is manifest at the beginning of the transition. Over time the abundance of asymmetries increases as the network loses resilience and transitions to another equilibrium state or collapses entirely. Interestingly, when competition between species is absent, full network collapse becomes common. After a transition, small perturbations are highly influential and can result in any number of future states.

15.3.2.3 Collapse and Recovery

Under stress, nested communities show higher levels of stability, a linear decline in the abundance of pollinators, and only one point of community extinction. Furthermore, these communities collapse when a generic driver of decline, a "general reduction of pollinator growth rates or increase mortality rates," reaches a critical value (see Lever et al., 2014 for model details). This is in contrast to randomly organized non-nested communities with low levels of connectance (Figure 15.2A). These communities have low levels of stability and typically experience several partial collapses each with some degree of pollinator abundance increase, before a comparatively early community extinction. Both random (Figure 15.2A) and nested (Figure 15.2B) communities with low pollinator abundance collapsed earlier than communities with high abundance.

Lever et al. (2014) ran both of these community topologies in "reverse" by decreasing the generic driver of declines and increasing pollinator growth rates, to model the dynamics of community recovery. Randomly organized

community topologies showed multiple points of recovery in 92% of communities. In nested pollinator communities only 21% of communities recovered.
The large difference between collapse and recovery in these high-connectance
mutualistic communities suggests a need to disproportionally reduce drivers
of declines to restore real-world plant–pollinator communities. In short it is
not sufficient to return to conditions prior to transition, but larger changes are
needed until the system returns to a primary state—some form of a co-evolved
species-rich community.

There is considerable evidence suggesting anthropomorphically driven
declines of insects including pollinators in several regions across the world
(Wagner, 2020). Insects broadly play a profound role in global ecosystems,
and plant–pollinator communities are disproportionally important for much of
terrestrial biodiversity including human food systems. Although the architecture of plant–pollinator networks confers resilience under changing ecological
conditions when stressors increase beyond a critical point, these networks are
increasingly susceptible to collapse and species are susceptible to local extinction. Early indicators of communities reaching critical transition points are loss
of specialist species and loss of other species that show a great deal of variance
in abundance. Once these nested communities collapse, recovery may require
more inputs to attain former levels of stability and diversity, suggesting an
important role for strategies for plant–pollinator community conservation.

15.4 Conclusions

Insect-mediated pollination of flowering plant species is a critical but unappreciated element of our food systems, which impacts the economic well-being and
health of human societies. Insect-mediated pollination services contributed $34
billion to the US economy based on food production and values from the 2012
US Department of Agriculture Census (Jordan, Patch, Grozinger, & Khanna,
2021), and over $350 billion worldwide (based on 2009 values, see Lautenbach,
Seppelt, Liebscher, & Dormann, 2012). There is a substantial economic value
derived from the production and collection of pollinator-dependent crops in up-
and downstream industrial sectors that broadly contribute to economic growth
(Chopra, Bakshi, & Khanna, 2015). Furthermore, pollinated crops are a major
source of micronutrients in human diets (Eilers, Kremen, Smith Greenleaf,
Garber, & Klein, 2011), and regions where populations experience high micronutrient deficiencies also grow micronutrient-providing crops with high pollinator dependencies (Chaplin-Kramer et al., 2014). The amount of land used for
pollinator-dependent (versus independent) crops has increased globally (Aizen
& Harder, 2009), as have the prices for these crops (Lautenbach et al., 2012).
Thus, overall, our dependence on pollinators for food production is increasing, but there is clear evidence for local or regional declines in populations of
both managed and wild pollinators, and many examples of species extinctions
(Wagner, 2020). It could be possible to mitigate the impact of declines on our
food systems through increased production of managed pollinators (as is the

case in honey bees, where localized producers sell and ship "packages" of bees nationally across the United States), bringing more land into agricultural production or increasing other inputs, such as fertilizers, to improve yield for crops that are only partially dependent on pollinators (Tamburini, Bommarco, Kleijn, van der Putten, & Marini, 2019), transitioning to crop varieties, including through transgenic methods, that can self-pollinate and do not need the services of animals, or developing artificial, mechanical pollination systems. However, all of these scenarios require greater input and management into the food production system and reduced diversity of crops, pollinators, and landscapes, which reduces the accessibility and stability of these systems.

For managed honey bees and wild bee communities, the organization and structure of the systems provide resilience to acute stressors but can facilitate rapid collapse under conditions of chronic stress. Many anthropogenic factors generate chronic stress in both these systems, including changing land use patterns, environmental pollution (particularly from pesticides applied to agricultural crops), and climate change. While it is well-recognized that multiple, interacting factors contribute to bee declines, it has not been properly acknowledged that these factors work at relatively large scales. Thus, most of the focus on strategies to mitigate bee declines has been on localized changes, on the management strategies used on individual farms or gardens, for example, and not at the large, landscape scale needed to provide the stable resources or microclimate conditions needed to support a sufficiently large and genetically diverse population of bees. Furthermore, conservation of wild bees has focused primarily on individual species that are endangered or threatened, but it is clear that robust plant–pollinator networks and communities need to be supported and preserved. Such a holistic approach to the health of managed and wild bee communities requires coordinated efforts among beekeepers, conservationists, landowners, and policymakers, and a full accounting of the private and public costs and benefits of supporting pollinators and pollination services (Lonsdorf, Koh, & Ricketts, 2020).

Acknowledgment

We are grateful to Princeton Institute for International and Regional Studies Global Systemic Risk program and organizers and participants of the 2019 and 2020 Workshop on Historical Systemic Collapse for giving us the opportunity to reflect on and synthesize these concepts and data. Grozinger and Patch are supported by funding from the US Department of Agriculture-National Institute of Food Agriculture, National Science Foundation, Penn State Huck Institutes of the Life Sciences, and Penn State College of Agricultural Sciences.

References

Aizen, M. A., Aguiar, S., Biesmeijer, J. C., Garibaldi, L. A., Inouye, D. W., Jung, C., ... Seymour, C. L. (2019). Global agricultural productivity is threatened by increasing pollinator dependence without a parallel increase in crop diversification. *Glob Chang Biol*, *25*(10), 3516–3527. doi:10.1111/gcb.14736.

Aizen, M. A., & Harder, L. D. (2009). The global stock of domesticated honey bees is growing slower than agricultural demand for pollination. *Curr Biol*, *19*(11), 915–918. doi:10.1016/j.cub.2009.03.071.

Barron, A. B. (2015). Death of the bee hive: Understanding the failure of an insect society. *Curr Opin Insect Sci*, *10*, 45–50. doi:10.1016/j.cois.2015.04.004.

Bascompte, J., & Jordano, P. (2007). Plant–animal mutualistic networks: The architecture of biodiversity. *Annu Rev Ecol Evol Syst*, *38*(1), 567–593.

Bascompte, J., Jordano, P., Melian, C. J., & Olesen, J. M. (2003). The nested assembly of plant-animal mutualistic networks. *Proc Natl Acad Sci U S A*, *100*(16), 9383–9387. doi:10.1073/pnas.1633576100.

Bascompte, J., & Olesen, J. M. (2015). Mutualistic networks. In J. L. Bronstein (Ed.), *Mutualism* (pp. 203–220). Oxford University Press.

Bass, C., & Field, L. M. (2018). Neonicotinoids. *Curr Biol*, *28*(14), R772–R773. doi:10.1016/j.cub.2018.05.061.

Bastolla, U., Fortuna, M. A., Pascual-Garcia, A., Ferrera, A., Luque, B., & Bascompte, J. (2009). The architecture of mutualistic networks minimizes competition and increases biodiversity. *Nature*, *458*(7241), 1018–1020. doi:10.1038/nature07950.

Biesmeijer, J. C., Roberts, S. P., Reemer, M., Ohlemuller, R., Edwards, M., Peeters, T., … Kunin, W. E. (2006). Parallel declines in pollinators and insect-pollinated plants in Britain and the Netherlands. *Science*, *313*(5785), 351–354. doi:10.1126/science.1127863.

Bruckner, S., Steinhauer, N., Engelsma, J., Fauvel, A. M., Kulhanek, K., Malcolm, E., … Williams, G. (2020). 2019–2020 Honey Bee colony losses in the United States: Preliminary results https://beeinformed.org/citizen-science/loss-and-management-survey/.

Bryden, J., Gill, R. J., Mitton, R. A., Raine, N. E., & Jansen, V. A. (2013). Chronic sublethal stress causes bee colony failure. *Ecol Lett*, *16*(12), 1463–1469. doi:10.1111/ele.12188.

Burgos, E., Ceva, H., Perazzo, R. P., Devoto, M., Medan, D., Zimmermann, M., & Maria Delbue, A. (2007). Why nestedness in mutualistic networks? *J Theor Biol*, *249*(2), 307–313. doi:10.1016/j.jtbi.2007.07.030.

Calovi, M., Grozinger, C. M., Miller, D. A., & Goslee, S. C. (2021). Summer weather conditions influence winter survival of honey bees (Apis mellifera) in the northeastern United States. *Sci Rep*, *11*(1), 1553. doi:10.1038/s41598-021-81051-8.

Cameron, S. A., Lozier, J. D., Strange, J. P., Koch, J. B., Cordes, N., Solter, L. F., & Griswold, T. L. (2011). Patterns of widespread decline in North American bumble bees. *Proc Natl Acad Sci U S A*, *108*(2), 662–667. doi:10.1073/pnas.1014743108.

Campbell, B., Khachatryan, H., & Rihn, A. (2017). Pollinator-friendly plants: Reasons for and barriers to purchase. *HortTechnology*, *27*(6), 831–839.

Chaplin-Kramer, R., Dombeck, E., Gerber, J., Knuth, K. A., Mueller, N. D., Mueller, M., … Klein, A. M. (2014). Global malnutrition overlaps with pollinator-dependent micronutrient production. *Proc Biol Sci*, *281*(1794), 20141799. doi:10.1098/rspb.2014.1799.

Chopra, S. S., Bakshi, B. R., & Khanna, V. (2015). Economic dependence of U.S. Industrial sectors on animal-mediated pollination service. *Environ Sci Technol*, *49*(24), 14441–14451. doi:10.1021/acs.est.5b03788.

Colin, T., Meikle, W. G., Wu, X., & Barron, A. B. (2019). Traces of a neonicotinoid induce precocious foraging and reduce foraging performance in honey bees. *Environ Sci Technol*, *53*(14), 8252–8261. doi:10.1021/acs.est.9b02452.

Dakos, V., & Bascompte, J. (2014). Critical slowing down as early warning for the onset of collapse in mutualistic communities. *Proc Natl Acad Sci U S A, 111*(49), 17546–17551. doi:10.1073/pnas.1406326111.

Danforth, B. N., Minckley, R. L., & Neff, J. L. (2019). *The Solitary Bees: Biology, Evolution Conservation.* Princeton University Press.

Delaplane, K. S., & Mayer, D. F. (2000). *Crop Pollination by Bees.* CABI.

Dogantzis, K. A., & Zayed, A. (2019). Recent advances in population and quantitative genomics of honey bees. *Curr Opin Insect Sci, 31*, 93–98. doi:10.1016/j.cois.2018.11.010.

Eilers, E. J., Kremen, C., Smith Greenleaf, S., Garber, A. K., & Klein, A. M. (2011). Contribution of pollinator-mediated crops to nutrients in the human food supply. *PLOS ONE, 6*(6), e21363. doi:10.1371/journal.pone.0021363.

Forrest, J. R. (2016). Complex responses of insect phenology to climate change. *Curr Opin Insect Sci, 17*, 49–54. doi:10.1016/j.cois.2016.07.002.

Fortuna, M. A., & Bascompte, J. (2006). Habitat loss and the structure of plant-animal mutualistic networks. *Ecol Lett, 9*(3), 281–286. doi:10.1111/j.1461-0248.2005.00868.x.

Grozinger, C. M., & Flenniken, M. L. (2019). Bee viruses: Ecology, pathogenicity, and impacts. *Annu Rev Entomol, 64*, 205–226. doi:10.1146/annurev-ento-011118-111942.

Guoze, J. L. (1998). Positive and negative circuits in dynamical systems. *Journal Biol Syst, 6*(1), 11–15.

Johnson, B. R. (2010). Division of labor in honeybees: Form, function, and proximate mechanisms. *Behav Ecol Sociobiol, 64*(3), 305–316.

Jordan, A., Patch, H. M., Grozinger, C. M., & Khanna, V. (2021). Economic dependence and vulnerability of United States agricultural sector on insect-mediated pollination service. *Environ Sci Technol.* doi:10.1021/acs.est.0c04786.

Kammerer, M., Goslee, S. C., Douglas, M. R., Tooker, J. F., & Grozinger, C. M. (2021). Wild bees as winners and losers: Relative impacts of landscape composition, quality, and climate. *Glob Chang Biol.* doi:10.1111/gcb.15485.

Kantsa, A., Raguso, R. A., Dyer, A. G., Sgardelis, S. P., Olesen, J. M., & Petanidou, T. (2017). Community-wide integration of floral colour and scent in a Mediterranean scrubland. *Nat Ecol Evol, 1*(10), 1502–1510. doi:10.1038/s41559-017-0298-0.

Khoury, D. S., Barron, A. B., & Myerscough, M. R. (2013). Modelling food and population dynamics in honey bee colonies. *PLOS ONE, 8*(5), e59084. doi:10.1371/journal. pone.0059084.

Khoury, D. S., Myerscough, M. R., & Barron, A. B. (2011). A quantitative model of honey bee colony population dynamics. *PLOS ONE, 6*(4), e18491. doi:10.1371/journal. pone.0018491.

Kok, M. T. J., Meijer, J. R., van Zeist, W.-J., Hilbers, J. P., Immovilli, M., Janse, J. H., ... Alkemade, R. (2020). Assessing ambitious nature conservation strategies within a 2 degree warmer and food-secure world. *bioRxiv* https://www.biorxiv.org/content/10 .1101/2020.08.04.236489v1.abstract.

Kremen, C., & Merenlender, A. M. (2018). Landscapes that work for biodiversity and people. *Science, 362*(6412). doi:10.1126/science.aau6020.

Kritsky, G. (2017). Beekeeping from antiquity through the middle ages. *Annu Rev Entomol, 62*, 249–264. doi:10.1146/annurev-ento-031616-035115.

Lautenbach, S., Seppelt, R., Liebscher, J., & Dormann, C. F. (2012). Spatial and temporal trends of global pollination benefit. *PLOS ONE, 7*(4), e35954. doi:10.1371/journal. pone.0035954.

Le Conte, Y., & Hefetz, A. (2008). Primer pheromones in social Hymenoptera. *Annu Rev Entomol, 53*, 523–542.

Leoncini, I., Le Conte, Y., Costagliola, G., Plettner, E., Toth, A. L., Wang, M., … Robinson, G. E. (2004). Regulation of behavioral maturation by a primer pheromone produced by adult worker honey bees. *Proc Natl Acad Sci U S A, 101*(50), 17559–17564.

Lever, J. J., van de Leemput, I. A., Weinans, E., Quax, R., Dakos, V., van Nes, E. H., … Scheffer, M. (2020). Foreseeing the future of mutualistic communities beyond collapse. *Ecol Lett, 23*(1), 2–15. doi:10.1111/ele.13401.

Lever, J. J., van Nes, E. H., Scheffer, M., & Bascompte, J. (2014). The sudden collapse of pollinator communities. *Ecol Lett, 17*(3), 350–359. doi:10.1111/ele.12236.

Lonsdorf, E. V., Koh, I., & Ricketts, T. H. (2020). Partitioning private and external benefits of crop pollination services. *People Nat, 2*(3), 811–820.

Memmott, J., Waser, N. M., & Price, M. V. (2004). Tolerance of pollination networks to species extinctions. *Proc Biol Sci, 271*(1557), 2605–2611. doi:10.1098/rspb.2004.2909.

Mu, J., Peng, Y., Xi, X., Wu, X., Li, G., Niklas, K. J., & Sun, S. (2015). Artificial asymmetric warming reduces nectar yield in a Tibetan alpine species of Asteraceae. *Ann Bot, 116*(6), 899–906. doi:10.1093/aob/mcv042.

National Research Council. (2006). Status of Pollinators in North America. Retrieved from Washington, DC https://nap.nationalacademies.org/catalog/11761/status-of -pollinators-in-north-america .

Natsopoulou, M., McMahon, D. P., & Paxton, R. P. (2016). Parasites modulate within-colony activity and accelerate the temporal polyethism schedule of a social insect, the honey bee. *Behav Ecol Sociobiol, 70*, 1019–1031.

Olesen, J. M., Bascompte, J., Dupont, Y. L., & Jordano, P. (2006). The smallest of all worlds: Pollination networks. *J Theor Biol, 240*(2), 270–276. doi:10.1016/j.jtbi.2005.09.014.

Olesen, J. M., Bascompte, J., Dupont, Y. L., & Jordano, P. (2007). The modularity of pollination networks. *Proc Natl Acad Sci U S A, 104*(50), 19891–19896. doi:10.1073/pnas.0706375104.

Ollerton, J., Winfree, R., & Tarrant, S. (2011). How many flowering plants are pollinated by animals? *Oikos, 120*(3), 321–326.

Page, R. E. (2020). *The Art of the Bee: Shaping the Environment from Landscapes to Societies.* Oxford University Press.

Perry, C. J., Sovik, E., Myerscough, M. R., & Barron, A. B. (2015). Rapid behavioral maturation accelerates failure of stressed honey bee colonies. *Proc Natl Acad Sci U S A, 112*(11), 3427–3432. doi:10.1073/pnas.1422089112.

Pollinator Health Task Force. (2016). Pollinator Partnership Action Plan. Retrieved from Washington, DC https://obamawhitehouse.archives.gov/sites/whitehouse.gov/files/ images/Blog/PPAP_2016.pdf .

Potts, S. G., Biesmeijer, J. C., Kremen, C., Neumann, P., Schweiger, O., & Kunin, W. E. (2010). Global pollinator declines: Trends, impacts and drivers. *Trends Ecol Evol, 25*(6), 345–353. doi:10.1016/j.tree.2010.01.007.

Rafferty, N. E. (2017). Effects of global change on insect pollinators: Multiple drivers lead to novel communities. *Curr Opin Insect Sci, 23*, 22–27. doi:10.1016/j.cois.2017.06.009.

Robinson, G. E. (2002). Genomics and integrative analyses of division of labor in honeybee colonies. *Am Nat, 160*, S160–S172.

Scaven, V. L., & Rafferty, N. E. (2013). Physiological effects of climate warming on flowering plants and insect pollinators and potential consequences for their interactions. *Curr Zool, 59*(3), 418–426. doi:10.1093/czoolo/59.3.418.

Scheffer, M., Bascompte, J., Brock, W. A., Brovkin, V., Carpenter, S. R., Dakos, V., … Sugihara, G. (2009). Early-warning signals for critical transitions. *Nature, 461*(7260), 53–59. doi:10.1038/nature08227.

Snoussi, E. H. (1998). Necessary conditions for multistationarity and stable periodicity. *J Biol Syst*, *6*(1), 3–9.

Sole, R. V., & Montoya, J. M. (2001). Complexity and fragility in ecological networks. *Proc Biol Sci*, *268*(1480), 2039–2045. doi:10.1098/rspb.2001.1767.

Tamburini, G., Bommarco, R., Kleijn, D., van der Putten, W. H., & Marini, L. (2019). Pollination contribution to crop yield is often context-dependent: A review of experimental evidence. *Agric Ecosyst Environ*, *280*, 16–23. doi:10.1016/j.agee.2019.04.022.

Tautz, J. (2008). *The Buzz about Bees: Biology of a Superorganism*. Springer.

Thebault, E., & Fontaine, C. (2010). Stability of ecological communities and the architecture of mutualistic and trophic networks. *Science*, *329*(5993), 853–856. doi:10.1126/science.1188321.

Thomas, R. (1981). On the relation between the logical structure of systems and their ability to generate multiple steady states or sustained oscillations. In Della Dora, J., Demongeot, J., Lacolle, B. *Numerical Methods in the Study of Critical Phenomena* (pp. 180–193). Berlin, Heidelberg : Springer https://doi.org/10.1007/978-3-642-81703-8_24.

Toth, A. L., Kantarovich, S., Meisel, A. F., & Robinson, G. E. (2005). Nutritional status influences socially regulated foraging ontogeny in honey bees. *J Exp Biol*, *208*(24), 4641–4649. doi:10.1242/jeb.01956.

van Nes, E. H., & Scheffer, M. (2007). Slow recovery from perturbations as a generic indicator of a nearby catastrophic shift. *Am Nat*, *169*(6), 738–747.

Vanengelsdorp, D., Evans, J. D., Saegerman, C., Mullin, C., Haubruge, E., Nguyen, B. K., ... Pettis, J. S. (2009). Colony collapse disorder: A descriptive study. *PLOS ONE*, *4*(8), e6481. doi:10.1371/journal.pone.0006481.

Wagner, D. L. (2020). Insect declines in the Anthropocene. *Annu Rev Entomol*, *65*, 457–480. doi:10.1146/annurev-ento-011019-025151.

Wagner, D. L., Grames, E. M., Forister, M. L., Berenbaum, M. R., & Stopak, D. (2021). Insect decline in the Anthropocene: Death by a thousand cuts. *Proc Natl Acad Sci U S A*, *118*(2). doi:10.1073/pnas.2023989118.

Watts, D. J., & Strogatz, S. H. (1998). Collective dynamics of 'small-world' networks. *Nature*, *393*(6684), 440–442. doi:10.1038/30918.

Weinstock, G. M., Robinson, G. E., Gibbs, R. A., Worley, K. C., Evans, J. D., Maleszka, R., & Honeybee Genome Sequencing Consortium. (2006). Insights into social insects from the genome of the honeybee Apis mellifera. *Nature*, *443*(7114), 931–949. doi:10.1038/Nature05260.

Wepprich, T., Adrion, J. R., Ries, L., Wiedmann, J., & Haddad, N. M. (2019). Butterfly abundance declines over 20 years of systematic monitoring in Ohio, USA. *PLOS ONE*, *14*(7), e0216270. doi:10.1371/journal.pone.0216270.

Willmer, P. (2011). *Pollination and Floral Ecology*. Princeton University Press.

Wissel, C. (1984). A universal law of the characteristic return time near thresholds. *Oecologia*, *65*(1), 101–107. doi:10.1007/BF00384470.

Section 4

Future Systemic Collapse and Quantitative Modeling

A primary goal of this research collaboration on collapse has been to apply lessons from history, archaeology, the natural sciences, and systems science to our potentially fragile present and future. In this section, we present five chapters that work to model, understand, and ultimately avoid modern civilizational collapse. Using theoretical, methodological, and quantitative approaches to the study of systems and history, these authors investigate the causes and effects of system dynamics over time, looking to better understand the life of civilizations.

In the diverse studies of historical collapse presented in this volume, a common thread has been that each civilization lacked control over the precise timing and cause of collapse. In the first chapter of this section, Zia Mian and Benoît Pelopidas present an analysis of nuclear weapons as an "exterminist structure"—a discovery of modern science that gives humans the horrifying agency to instigate a civilizational collapse, potentially choosing the appointed hour. In motivating their analysis of nuclear collapse, Mian and Pelopidas provide a historical survey since the naissance of the nuclear age. They outline philosophical reasoning in the nuclear debate, the inexorable transformation of international relations, and the nuclear establishment's political–psychological goal of removing the apocalyptic possibility of nuclear collapse from popular imagination by making this threat effectively "invisible." They show that the inescapable planetary impact of a nuclear collapse on humanity and the environment is a compelling rationale for achieving greater public understanding of this threat.

Next, in his chapter, "From Wild West to Mad Max: Transition in Civilizations," Richard Bookstaber outlines many of the "grand answers" that historians have presented for the failures of ancient civilizations and counterposes these explanations with a modern systems theory approach. Analyzing collapse through the lens of complexity, he presents a framework that has the insightful benefit of explaining both the creative and destructive processes in the lifecycle of civilizations. During the rise of a civilization, network connections form through which interdependence emerges. Bookstaber compares this civilizational nascent stage to the "Wild West," where in an era of risk taking, danger, and reward, towns and trade routes evolved in the US western

DOI: 10.4324/9781003331384-20

territories of the 1800s. The downhill phase of civilization is the reversal of this process: Network connections break down and only the independent and self-reliant can survive. He characterizes this as "Mad Max," the dystopian vision of humans fighting to survive on the margins. Modeling civilizations as multilayer networks, Bookstaber simulates the random processes underlying the emergent aggregation and disintegration of societal network complexity to capture how civilizations can fall victim to the inherent uncertainty of complex systems.

In our theoretical and methodological investigation of the structure and dynamics of complex social systems, we have found it necessary to derive insights from both qualitative and quantitative approaches. Critical to the study of systemic risk is a scientific and mathematical understanding of complex dynamic systems. In this section, we include a scientific inquiry from George Hagstrom and Simon Levin comparing and contrasting critical transitions that occur in complex adaptive systems—such as the socio-ecological systems that characterize complex human societies—and phase transitions in physics. A key insight that may be applied to our understanding of the theory of collapse more broadly, is the presence of—and ability to recognize—early warning indicators signaling the potential or imminence of such a transition in the state of a system.

In the next chapter, Anders Sandberg brings his long-term perspective of human prospects from Oxford's Future of Humanity Institute and asks whether civilizational failure is an inevitability of "old age." Using databases of empires and civilizations, he fits these data to probability models to ascertain whether failure rate increases with age. He adds comparative insights to his analysis by presenting similar studies on whether aging occurs in complex systems such as firms, organizations, and software code, and explores the extinction timescale of individual biological species.

For the final chapter in this volume, we turn to Peter Turchin, a scholar of complexity science and historical collapse who has received renown for his prescient 2010 forecast in *Nature* of political instability in 2020. In his chapter here on "Multipath Forecasting: The Aftermath of the 2020 American Crisis," Turchin presents his novel transdisciplinary approach to modeling social break-down, recovery, and resilience. With the goal of reducing subjectivity in the analysis of social instability, Turchin has constructed rigorous quantitative time series data sets of historical crisis periods. He employs structural–demographic theory as a modeling framework that incorporates measures of income inequality, age distribution, and overproduction of elites, among other factors, as explanatory causal variables. He uses his results to first explain and then predict the dynamics of socio-political instability and finally to illustrate how such causal relationships can be used to explore the effects of policy interventions on future trajectories. He applies this analysis to instability in the US from 1810 to 1990 to create and calibrate his multipath forecasting model. Turchin concludes with a roadmap for future study in which he plans to apply this methodology to the analysis of other societies, and in particular, quantify the characteristics of historical collapses studied in this volume.

16 Producing Collapse

Nuclear Weapons as Preparation to End Civilization[1]

Zia Mian and Benoît Pelopidas

> Madmen govern our affairs in the name of order and security. The chief mad-men claim the names of general, admiral, senator, scientist, Secretary of State, even President. The fatal symptom of their madness is this: they have been carrying through a series of acts which will lead eventually to the destruction of mankind, under the solemn conviction that they are normal responsible people, living sane lives and working for reasonable ends.
>
> *Lewis Mumford[2]*

16.1 Introduction: On Living with Collapse

The possibility of an end of humankind has always existed, in fact and in the imagination.[3] We focus on what has changed over the last 75 years with the coming of nuclear and thermonuclear weapons, their structures of governance, and the contentious politics around them and over the human future. In short, the nuclear age will be the focus of this chapter. The civilizational feature that characterizes this age has been described by E. P. Thompson as an exterminist structure encompassing "the [nuclear] weapons system, and the entire economic, scientific, political, and ideological support system to that weapons system—the social system which researches it, 'chooses' it, produces it, polices it, justifies it, and maintains it in being."[4] This structure is geared around the ambitions of producing and deferring the sudden catastrophic ending of civilization—what Thompson calls the "thrust of exterminism."

From the beginning, those who set the world on the path to nuclear weapons understood this path led to and could end with catastrophe. In his memo of April 25, 1945, US Secretary of War Henry Stimson explained to President Harry Truman that the nearly completed atomic bomb would be "the most terrible weapon ever known in human history [...] modern civilization might be completely destroyed."[5] Stimson also shared his judgment that this weapon technology would be such a dominant political and moral structure as to overwhelm civilization itself, observing that "the world in its present state of moral advancement compared with its technical development would be eventually at the mercy of such a weapon." For his part, Truman came to a different understanding. He recorded in his diary, "We have discovered the most terrible

DOI: 10.4324/9781003331384-21

bomb in the history of the world. It may be the fire destruction prophesied in the Euphrates Valley Era, after Noah and his fabulous Ark."[6] A few months later, once the bomb had been built, tested in New Mexico, and used to destroy the Japanese city of Hiroshima, Truman wrote in his diary that the bomb was "the greatest thing in history."[7]

The exterminist structure now exists in nine states, who as of 2020 together hold roughly 13,400 nuclear weapons, with the United States and Russia holding just over 12,000 (90 percent) of these weapons.[8] A related shadow structure exists in those states allied to the United States who rely for their defense on the United States' use and threat of use of its nuclear weapons (Belgium, Germany, Italy, the Netherlands, and Turkey have US nuclear weapons stationed on their territory, unlike other US allies in Europe or elsewhere that are covered by US nuclear weapon use commitments). North Korea possesses an arsenal which is estimated currently to be the smallest in size of any of the nuclear-armed states, but its few tens of nuclear weapons are sufficient to devastate nations. In all these states, the existence of an exterminist structure should not be taken to mean that it is supported by a majority of the population. In fact, it is largely invisible.

In this chapter, we aim to outline the production of a planetary-scale nuclear destructive capacity over the last 75 years alongside the production of its invisibility. Our goal is to show how and why the dangers inherent in the nuclear age and its foreseen possible catastrophic ending have not been and still are not well understood.

16.2 Planning on Producing Nuclear Collapse at a Planetary Scale

The history of planning and preparing for nuclear war is the history of producing collapse and ending civilization. The early scientific efforts to understand the possibility of making a nuclear weapon included seeking to assess the possible consequences of the effects of such a weapon. A pioneering example is the secret Frisch–Peierls technical memorandum of 1940 "On the Construction of a 'Super-bomb' based on a Nuclear Chain Reaction in Uranium" to the British government. This inferred from basic physical principles what would be needed technically to build a simple atomic bomb and its effects: The destruction of a city by blast and the killing of a large number of civilians even miles away from the explosion by radioactive fallout.[9]

In 1942, as part of the secret US Manhattan Project to build the atomic bomb, which was inspired in part by the earlier British work in this direction, Edward Teller conjectured that the explosion from an atomic bomb might generate so much heat that it would trigger a runaway fusion reaction, igniting the earth's atmosphere. Robert Oppenheimer, who led the scientific work at Los Alamos on bomb design, was told of this and is reported to have "got quite excited" and declared "That's a terrible possibility."[10] This concern about quasi-instantaneous extinction was questioned by Hans Bethe, who led the

Theoretical Division at Los Alamos. In a later interview Bethe said he judged the prospect "incredibly unlikely," but noted that the concern clearly persisted since in July 1945, on the eve of the first nuclear weapon detonation, fellow Manhattan project physicist, and Nobel Laureate, Enrico Fermi offered to his colleagues: "let's make a bet whether the atmosphere will be set on fire by this test."[11] Some of the Manhattan Project scientists were willing to wager on this outcome. Uncertainty about triggering the end of the world did not stop scientists and military planners from moving forward with the project of developing such weapons.

The first nuclear test (Trinity, carried out in New Mexico) inspired a vision of the bomb as a threat not only to mankind but to all forms of life. Physicist I. I. Rabi who witnessed the explosion observed:

At first I was thrilled. It was a vision. Then a few minutes afterwards, I had gooseflesh all over me when I realized what this meant for the future of humanity. Up until then, humanity was, after all, a limited factor in the evolution and process of nature. The vast oceans, lakes and rivers, the atmosphere were not very much affected by the existence of mankind. The new powers represented a threat not only to mankind but to all forms of life: the seas and the air. One could foresee that nothing was immune from the tremendous power of these new forces.[12]

In the 1950s, the destructive capacity of nuclear arsenals in the United States and, to a lesser extent, the Soviet Union, increased massively with the creation of thermonuclear weapons (hydrogen bombs). The new weapons were orders of magnitude more destructive than the previous generation of weapons, with yields measured in thousands of kilotons (megatons), thousand times the yield of the simple atomic weapon in the Trinity test and those later used to destroy the cities of Hiroshima and Nagasaki. As before, some leading scientists imagined and shared their concerns about the pursuit and consequences of the destructive power being considered even before work started.[13]

The US government scientific committee that was set up in 1949 to consider the possibility of a hydrogen bomb included some of the physicists who had built the first atomic bomb, among them Robert Oppenheimer, Enrico Fermi, and I. I. Rabi. In its secret report the committee assessed that thermonuclear weapons could probably be built within five years, but strongly opposed it. The majority on the committee took the view that the proposed weapon would be a "weapon of genocide," and a minority on the committee went further, declaring "The fact that no limits exist to the destructiveness of this weapon makes its very existence and the knowledge of its construction a danger to humanity as a whole. It is necessarily an evil thing considered in any light."[14]

Focusing on the US arsenal only, Daniel Ellsberg dates the birth of a nuclear "doomsday machine" to the 1950s.[15] On March 16, 1958, General Robert Cutler, President Eisenhower's special assistant for national security affairs, wrote to the President that military requirements called for "all the nuclear weapons that could be produced and as rapidly as possible," while noting that a recent war game had involved seven million kilotons of nuclear explosives and that he worried that "the effect of any such exchange is quite incalculable. [...] It is possible that life on the planet may be extinguished."[16] As Cutler proposed, the US nuclear arsenal expanded quickly, growing from around 7000 weapons in 1958 to around 20,000 weapons in 1960, with a total yield exceeding 20 million kilotons (20,000 megatons), almost three times larger than what had been imagined as would be used in the nuclear wargame.[17] The "incalculable" and possibly life-ending consequences of such an arsenal appeared to offer no restraint.

A similar awareness that early nuclear war plans would produce collapse at least at the national level was shared among the few who studied the effects of nuclear warfare in Britain and France.[18] As early as 1954, a French journal on civilian protection stated that 15 thermonuclear weapons would suffice to annihilate France.[19] Similarly, in 1955, in Britain, the secret report on the implications of thermonuclear weapons by the Ministry of Defence's Strath Committee judged that:

> Something like ten "H" Bombs, each of a yield of about 10 megatons, delivered on the western half of the UK or in the waters close in off the Western seaboard, with the normal prevailing winds, would effectively disrupt the life of the country and make normal activity completely impossible.[20]

In 1955, the Soviet Union had a total of 200 nuclear weapons and by the end of the decade it would have over 1000 (the United States had over 12,000 nuclear weapons) and thermonuclear weapons were to become an increasing fraction of their arsenals, and at no point in time since then has the destructive capability of the global nuclear arsenal been lower.[21]

Military planners and political leaders prepared for nuclear war and believed they knew the consequences. In 1961, the US Joint Chiefs of Staff were asked by the White House to provide an assessment of the casualties expected from the current US nuclear war plan—Daniel Ellsberg wrote this question on behalf of President Kennedy. The answer: Anticipated casualties of 600 million deaths within six months, not including deaths of people in the United States from possible Soviet retaliation.[22] The arithmetic of mass destruction was explained by US Secretary of Defense Robert McNamara in 1964, when he offered his judgment of what it could take to kill a country: "the destruction of, say, 25 percent of its population and more than two thirds of industrial capacity would mean the destruction of the Soviet Union as a national society." McNamara estimated that it would require about 400 nuclear weapons of the kind the United States then had in its arsenal to wreak this level of devastation. Despite McNamara's analysis, the number of US warheads grew dramatically, reaching its peak of over 31,000 weapons in 1967.[23] That same year, Robert McNamara grimly noted:

> Technology has now circumscribed us all with a conceivable horizon of horror that could dwarf any catastrophe that has befallen man in his more

than a million years on earth. Man has lived now for more than twenty years in what we have come to call the Atomic Age. What we sometimes overlook is that every future age of man will be an atomic age. If, then, man is to have a future at all, it will have to be a future overshadowed with the permanent possibility of thermonuclear holocaust.[24]

Along with the expansion of violent destruction from city-killing to nation-killing, civilization-ending, and world-ending scales, and the extension of such a prospect into whatever was to be the future-time of humankind, the speed at which atomic collapse could actually be perpetrated changed dramatically. Intercontinental-range ballistic missiles, first introduced into service at the end of the 1950s, typically have a range on the order of 10,000 km and an average speed of around 25,000 km/hour, while long-range aircraft typically travel at less than 1000 km/hour, roughly 20 times slower. This makes protection and defense against nuclear weapons explosions and the associated collapse effectively impossible when such nuclear-armed missiles are available. In January 1977, Secretary of State Henry Kissinger remarked that "It is an incongruous situation for a country to plan for nuclear war and not to save its society."[25] The civil defense programs in the United States and the Soviet Union both reached the conclusion that saving their societies was an impossible goal in the nuclear age that they had helped create.[26] People, whole nations, were to be defended to death, even if that meant the end of civilization on a global scale.

While it is true that since the end of the Cold War, the number of nuclear warheads on the planet has massively decreased, from a peak of over 70,000 in the 1980s, over 13,000 nuclear weapons remain as of 2020, and current nuclear weapons postures and plans largely unchanged from the Cold War, still aim at producing collapse. A first-order simulation of a nuclear war between the United States and Russia in 2020, using current forces, postures, and doctrines, found that after only a few hours of conflict, immediate casualties and fatalities would exceed 90 million people, and expected deaths from nuclear fallout and long-term effects would certainly increase that estimate.[27] The destruction and casualties were based only on the effects of blasts and immediate heat and radiation rather than on what happens when cities are set on fire by nuclear weapons.

It is noteworthy that at least in the US case, the fire effects of nuclear explosions have not been included in damage assessments for weapons requirements and targeting purposes by military planners.[28] The military historically has believed that the prediction of fire effects should not be included in the consequence calculations of nuclear weapons use and therefore not in nuclear war planning, because it is more uncertain than the predictable effects of shockwaves from explosions. These shockwaves can be reproducibly measured, calibrated, and scaled. No one has ever deliberately set a whole city on fire to measure exactly the fire effects. The fire effects became salient in the nuclear winter studies of the 1980s.[29] Mandated by a United Nations

General Assembly resolution in 1985, a United Nations expert study concluded in 1989:

[A] major nuclear war would entail the high risk of a global environmental disruption. The risk would be greatest if large cities and industrial centres in the northern hemisphere were to be targeted in the summer months. In the opinion of the Group, residual scientific uncertainties are unlikely to invalidate this conclusion. The Group indicates that the depletion of food supplies that might result from severe effects on agricultural production could confront targeted and non-targeted nations with the prospect of widespread starvation. The socio-economic consequences would be grave … The socio-economic consequences in a world intimately interconnected economically, socially and environmentally would be grave. The functions of production, distribution and consumption in existing socio-economic systems would be completely disrupted … further global environmental consequences of a major nuclear exchange may yet be identified.[30]

More recent work using climate change models has shown that beyond the already catastrophic levels of death and destruction from blast, fire, and radiation at the target, the cities set ablaze by nuclear attacks would create soot that would self-loft into the stratosphere and have global environmental impacts lasting for more than a decade even for a conflict involving a few hundred modern nuclear weapons.[31] One of the environmental effects comes from the reduction in sunlight reaching the earth's surface, as a result the temperature goes down. A second effect is a reduction in precipitation. There also is destruction of atmospheric ozone, allowing more UV to come through to the ground. All three effects have potentially catastrophic effects on biological systems, whether agricultural systems or natural biosystems. Nuclear war involving even a few hundred weapons could destroy modern civilization and condemn billions to starvation and death.[32]

Levels of casualties which would be incompatible with any notion of proportionality are planned and communicated by so-called smaller nuclear-armed states, most of which have arsenals of the order of a few hundred nuclear weapons each. For instance, in a 2016 documentary produced by the communication agency of the French Ministry of Defense, the voice-over states: "No surgical nuclear strike is possible. This is precisely the dreadful character of this weapon."[33] A similar remark could be made about all other nuclear-armed states: Britain, China, Israel, India, Pakistan, and North Korea.[34] Even South Africa, which built a nuclear arsenal of half a dozen weapons, the smallest in the history of the nuclear age, had developed a nuclear strategy which relied on the possibility of its own collapse as a society.

There is a particular irony here in that at the heart of US and Soviet nuclear force sizing decisions has been the notion of reducing the damage one might suffer in case of nuclear war. This goal of nuclear planning as "damage limitation" may seem at first sight to run against the logic presented earlier of nuclear planning as being to produce collapse. The opposite is true. Trying to limit the scale of nuclear war through damage limitation logically required preparing to make it worse. A "damage-limiting" nuclear force structure relies on counterforce targeting, in which nuclear weapons target adversary nuclear weapons and related complexes to destroy them preemptively. If for no other reason than that conservative military planners assume it may take more than one of your weapons to reliably destroy one weapon of the adversary, the pursuit of a damage-limiting force structure was used to justify an expansion of the nuclear arsenal. It also led to investments in civil defense (later seen as futile). Both were claimed initially to contribute to the survivability of nuclear war.[35]

If nuclear weapons are treated as fully controllable instruments, and as solutions to problems of possibly excessive damage in a war-prone world in which adversaries' future intentions cannot be known for sure, and if it is wiser to plan for the worst, then reducing the vulnerability of your own weapons and increasing the vulnerability of the adversary's weapons may be the foremost concern. A diversification of the arsenal is then a net benefit and the only conceivable solution. In the United States, this argument was articulated by Albert Wohlstetter, an early nuclear strategist, who argued that even with the coming of nuclear weapons:

> The basic aims of warfare had not changed. The destruction of an opponent's fighting power remained the ultimate objective of any attempt to engage a predatory enemy. The best form of deterrence, then, would be to upgrade [...] "second strike" in favor of a war-winning strategy of "counterforce."[36]

For Wohlstetter, "the best defense would be a spending offense: an investment in technologically sophisticated nuclear arms that possessed both offensive and defensive capacities."[37] Independently from the influence of Albert Wohlstetter as an individual strategist, this logic of damage-limiting was one of the drivers of US nuclear weapons procurement.[38] While the Soviet Union did not explicitly use the concept of damage limitation, its nuclear war planning from the early 1960s was also based on the imperatives of producing a collapse of the enemy—hitting the adversary nation hard enough to knock it out of the war and be sure to destroy its nuclear forces to reduce its ability to strike back again.[39]

General Lee Butler, who served at the end of the Cold War as head of US Strategic Air Command and its successor body US Strategic Command, and had responsibility for all nuclear forces, looked back on his experience a decade later and concluded:

> "The Cold War lives on in the minds of those who cannot let go the fears, the beliefs and the enmities born of the nuclear age. They cling to deterrence, clutch its tattered promise to their breast, shake it wistfully

at bygone adversaries and balefully at new or imagined ones. They are gripped still by its awful willingness not simply to tempt the apocalypse but to prepare its way."[40]

In the two decades since Butler wrote these words, there is no evidence that this situation has changed.

16.3 Making the Possibility of Nuclear Collapse Invisible

Nuclear war and the consequent collapse of civilization could start in at least four ways: Deliberate, accidental, inadvertent, or unauthorized nuclear strike. As demonstrated above, large bureaucracies keep preparing and planning for it. In this section, we emphasize two mechanisms which have contributed to making these four possibilities invisible: A universal form of shortsightedness of our imagination which affects us all and situated commitments and beliefs on the part of nuclear weapons experts and officials which make them prone to produce and keep invisible the possibility of nuclear collapse.[41]

The first mechanism has been diagnosed by nuclear-age philosopher Günther Anders in the late 1950s to the early 1960s. Reflecting on Hiroshima, he identified it as "world-condition" marked by what he called a "Promethean discrepancy" between our ability to produce collapse and our ability to imagine it, represent it, and relate to it morally, which makes us "inverted utopians":

> We are incapable of mentally realizing the realities which we ourselves have produced. Therefore we might call ourselves "inverted utopians": while ordinary Utopians are actually unable to produce what they are able to visualize, we are unable to visualize what we are actually producing.[42]

Anders' insight is important because it reminds us that this Promethean discrepancy is not limited to a segment of the population. Elites in charge of those weapons are not immune. Indeed, it is not enough to say that nuclear-induced collapse is possible to believe that it is and to act accordingly. President Barack Obama's attitude on the matter seems to give a recent illustration of this problem. In 2016, on the first ever visit to Hiroshima by a US President, standing at the Hiroshima Peace Memorial, Obama declared: "Hiroshima teaches this truth. Technological progress without an equivalent progress in human institutions can doom us. The scientific revolution that led to the splitting of an atom requires a moral revolution, as well."[43] His reaction to the review of the US nuclear war plan (Single Integrated Operational Plan or SIOP) however illustrates both a sense of disbelief and a failure to translate it into actions anywhere near the "revolution" he was calling for. During one of the follow-up meetings of the National Security Council to lay out the nuclear weapons employment guidance (the principles and policies underlying decisions on nuclear arsenal size and structure, posture, and use of nuclear weapons), Obama grew impatient with the scenarios and calculations that were presented to him and said: "Let's stipulate that this is all insane" but left the numbers and the plan unchanged.[44]

Another indicator of the problem is how unwilling and unprepared people, including decision makers, are to think about nuclear war and the role they would play. Public attention to nuclear dangers historically has been at best episodic and linked to immediate crises, and the official and mainstream expert discourse on the matter has pictured more public involvement in the nuclear debate as ill-informed, unnecessary, and troublesome. As for leadership, the last US President who has been personally involved in a nuclear crisis simulation was Jimmy Carter, over four decades ago. A broad set of interacting psychological and behavioral factors has been offered as explanation for such shortsightedness in the nuclear age. No one, not even a President, has been adequately prepared to decide on the use of nuclear weapons because we have been psychologically desensitized through "psychic numbing, compassion collapse, tribalism, dehumanization of others, blaming of victims, attentional failures, and faulty decision-making processes, all of which work to destroy feelings and understanding that would normally stop us from planning, executing, and tolerating such inhumane acts."[45] In Anders' terms, we have become "lazy people of the apocalypse" in dire need of exercising our moral sense and imagination.[46]

The playing out of these behavioral factors is evident in a study of US nuclear war planners by sociologist Lynn Eden, who concluded that "planners strip out the human meaning of the consequences of the hypothetical actions they are planning." One self-reflective "government official working in strategic nuclear war planning" told Eden that it was:

[An] emotional burden to read the war plans. You begin to lose sight that you're talking about the end of civilization. You look at this and think you might actually have to employ one of these [plans] some day and it's just mind boggling. ... I thought, "My God, [it] isn't just an abstraction, it's real. This is what we intend to do in x, y, or z situation." So that was incredibly overwhelming and ... . It was actually hard to work during the first couple of weeks. Hard to take any of them seriously because I ... wanted to shake them and say, "Are you fucking kidding me? ... Are you out of your mind? How can you possibly consider an attack option that looks like that?" ... . I think that when you work long enough on targeting, you ... at a certain point [you] have to stop thinking about what executing one of those options really means. Because I don't know how you could live with yourself if you did.[47]

The second mechanism grows from what E. P. Thompson called the "scientific, political, and ideological support system" to the nuclear exterminist structure, "the social system which researches it, 'chooses' it, produces it, polices it, justifies it, and maintains it in being." This system is characterized by an unusual level of secrecy, technological complexity, and the privileging of specialized competence and access.[48] However, the positions and commitments of experts and officials in this system tend to make them largely incapable of shedding light on all forms of nuclear-induced collapse, which we will call material nuclear vulnerabilities. In other words, one cannot count on such experts to compensate for our failure to imagine the possibility of nuclear-induced collapse.

Officials and most experts in nuclear weapons states are caught in the double work, descriptive and performative, of the discourse of deterrence.[49] Their specialized competence and/or access to classified information make them go-to-people for a description of the workings of nuclear weapon systems. At the same time, their discourse about deterrence is aimed to convince several audiences of the adequacy and effectiveness of the policy of nuclear deterrence. This performative function of the expert discourse of deterrence in a context where even one nuclear explosion is intolerable creates specific constraints on what can be said. Those experts end up having to claim that the nuclear system as a system of control works perfectly, so that their audiences believe in the credibility of the pledge of nuclear retaliation and do not fear accidental explosions, escalation, or a nuclear first strike caused by a breach in the command-and-control protocol. This excessive display of control over the future is particularly visible in the United States in the production of government planning documents on managing nuclear war consequences by institutions as diverse as the Federal Emergency Management Agency or the US Postal service. The production of such "fantasy documents," as described by sociologist Lee Clarke, was part of a performance of control, predictability, and survivability even in the face of nuclear war.[50]

Beyond these discursive obstacles to an acknowledgment of all paths to nuclear-induced collapse, the institutional positions of the experts who would be consulted on these matters create a possible duty to hide or understate vulnerabilities and limits of control on this matter. Information can only be gathered from individuals who have pledged for some mix of professional and patriotic reasons to serve institutions which have an interest in not displaying the limits and weaknesses of the national nuclear weapon infrastructure. This interest is also part of their mandate. Even one unwarranted nuclear explosion would be so consequential, and deemed so intolerable, that nuclear weapon system controls are almost unique in the requirement of perfection imposed upon them. In a major assessment of the history of US nuclear weapon system accidents, Eric Schlosser has suggested that "had a single weapon been stolen or detonated, America's command-and-control system would still have attained a success rate of 99.99857 percent."[51] This is not uniquely American, however. The head of the French agency for nuclear weapons, the *Directeur des Applications Militaires* of the Atomic Energy Commission, presents a similar sense of the intolerability of any unwanted nuclear explosion.[52] More generally, it is worth noting that to date there have been no accidental or inadvertent nuclear weapon explosions reported by any of the ten states that so far have made nuclear weapons. But that does not mean that this outcome can be attributed to the perfect implementation of control practices.

In the United States, Sandia National Laboratory nuclear weapon safety engineers Robert L. Peurifoy and Gordon O. Moe have spoken on the difficulty of letting the upper management of a nuclear weapons laboratory acknowledge the limits of the institution's control over their nuclear weapons.[53] A similar attitude can be found in the memoirs of Admiral Jean Philippon, Chief of Staff to President de Gaulle, where he confessed never reporting to the President the case of a Mirage IV which took off with a nuclear weapon under its wing because of a technical failure, because this would have been assessed as a serious loss of control.[54] These incentives converge in overstating the level of control over nuclear weapons in the present or past cases of avoidance of unwanted nuclear weapons explosions.[55] For such institutions and their employees, acknowledging the limits of their control and knowledge of possibilities is admitting failure. So, in the best-case scenario, one can expect institutional and personal limits on what is actually said regarding the limits of control over nuclear-induced collapse, but in any case the picture of those limits will be far from complete.

Through a series of unproven assumptions, beliefs, and an ideology of "nuclear order," most nuclear weapons experts and officials have managed to act and speak as though they believed that nuclear war will never happen.[56] Such beliefs may be sincere or simply loyalty to the commitments made to institutions mandated to maintain the credibility of nuclear deterrence. Either way, the effect of denial of possibilities of nuclear-induced collapse is the same and gives an intellectual layer to Anders' diagnosis of the shortsightedness of the imagination. For strategists, the seduction of techno-strategic discourse makes nuclear war look impossible through an illusion of perfect control over a docile technology.[57] Anthropologist Hugh Gusterson has called this the "central axiom" present in most of his conversations with scientists at the Lawrence Livermore National Laboratory at the end of the 1990s.[58] It seems based on the belief that technology is inert and only depends on and responds to human demands—in effect an instrumentalist philosophy of technology—and that humankind (or least some part of it based on views about gender, race, class, education, and other social distinctions) is sufficiently rational to not use those weapons and so to conclude that nuclear war is impossible and will never happen. These baseless assumptions are enough to invisibilize the four possible origins of nuclear-induced collapse: An accidental explosion following a technological malfunction, a false alarm, an unauthorized launch, and a deliberate launch.

War gaming professionals, whose mission was to identify specific conditions under which a nuclear war could begin, were not better at this. Indeed, the most famous designers of those games from the beginning of the 1960s did not manage to get nuclear war started, which reveals how difficult it is to conceive of its possibility within the framework of classic strategic thought.[59] In a 1986 interview with PBS, former Secretary of Defense Robert

McNamara broadens this observation to the entirety of the Cold War.[60] And, this is not typically American. Similar assumptions can be found in a 1971 interview by one of the most respected French nuclear strategists, General André Beaufre.[61]

The inability to see and accept the possibility of nuclear-induced collapse is shared widely by the people of the nuclear weapon support system. The 2015 testimony of Lieutenant Kristin Nemish of the US Air Force, in charge of launching a set of ten nuclear-armed intercontinental ballistic missiles, reveals a direct expression of self-deluding faith in nuclear control. She can comfortably assert that: "Regardless of what happens at work, it always is fine when you walk through that door and see [the smiling faces of my children]."[62] She forgets that what could happen at work, and what justifies in large part her work, is the beginning of a nuclear war, in which—in all likelihood—her children would not survive, especially since they live in an area close to missile silos and an airbase that would certainly be nuclear targets.

The challenge of taking seriously the possibility of nuclear collapse therefore seems common, even among the professionals in charge of planning and unleashing it. Beyond the central axiom described above, "nuclear taboo" talk also contributes to perpetuating a sense of impossibility of one of the modes of nuclear-induced collapse, i.e., deliberate nuclear strike.[63] President Obama is said to have conducted his nuclear weapons policy as though he believed that a nuclear taboo existed and mattered.[64] The shared idea of a fundamental taboo allows strategic, political, and technical decision makers to take risks that open the door to nuclear weapon use by serving as a moral safety net of last resort for a death-defying performance. This allows the exterminist system to continue to operate as normal and be risk-tolerant, rather than have to bring to a crashing halt the planning and preparation for the threat and use of nuclear weapons. Nuclear-age historian Richard Rhodes has corroborated this insight:

> Despite several close calls, ... no one in authority believes the damned things will go off, and so everyone wants to play with them, like treasure hunters wallowing in a vault of golden coins laced with guardian scorpions, like children discovering the loaded gun their parents thoughtlessly neglected to lock away.[65]

A final word on the current situation can be given to General John Hyten, who was head of US Strategic Command from 2016 to the end of 2019. Hyten described in 2018 the annual Global Thunder command-and-control exercise run by his command:

> I just want you to ask in your own head, how do you think it ends? It ends the same way every time. It does. It ends bad. And the bad meaning it ends with global nuclear war. And guess what? We have to actually practice that every day. And we do. We practice it every day because we have to be good at it.[66]

16.4 Conclusion: The Future of Nuclear Collapse

The beginning of the nuclear weapons age, through the worldwide radioactive fallout traces left by atmospheric nuclear weapon testing, is one candidate for marking the shift of our planetary history into a new geological era, often called the "Anthropocene." In this era, humankind's intended and unintended but often foreseeable agency over the biosphere of the planet has been magnified—we and our actions are now a planet-shaping process.[67] If it is true that the nuclear age creates this new form of agency for the species, it is crucial that we become fully aware that this power is tied to a small number of deeply entrenched and powerful exterminist structures with the capability and willingness to produce planetary collapse through nuclear war. Out of the 193 member-states of the United Nations, only nine states have nuclear weapons today.

This chapter has tried to establish that for at least the past 75 years, there has been the technical possibility and a related political imagination to produce catastrophic nation-level collapse and possibly end civilization, with catastrophic consequences for human well-being worldwide. The planning and preparation of this collapse has been a central thrust of the nuclear weapons institutions and policies of the nuclear-armed states, and implicitly of their allies, who reproduce the claims that only nuclear weapons can produce national security.[68] There has been throughout these years individual and collective resistance and a determined continuous politics around the world aimed at confronting this set of exterminist systems and the threats it poses.[69] The two processes together have served as one factor binding humanity into a common global experience over this period. If we are a global civilization, in part it is because nuclear weapons create a world condition that we are compelled to share. All life and politics, even that aimed at the future, takes place within this condition because of the shadow of the catastrophe it embodies.

At the dawning of this age of exterminism, the newly founded Emergency Committee of Atomic Scientists, led by Albert Einstein, warned in 1947 of the danger and sought to chart a path to contending with the bomb:

> Through the release of atomic energy, our generation has brought into the world the most revolutionary force since prehistoric man's discovery of fire. This basic power of the universe cannot be fitted into the outmoded concept of narrow nationalisms. For there is no secret and there is no defense; there is no possibility of control except through the aroused understanding and insistence of the peoples of the world … In this lies our only security and our only hope—we believe that an informed citizenry will act for life and not death.

With so much of the burden of effort placed on trying to understand the nuclear danger and the possibility of control, a space is opened up to a temptation to seek reassurance, to want to believe the claims of leaders and experts that it is possible to live with the bomb safely, even though they do not know and cannot explain or control all the possibilities leading to nuclear war and the resulting collapse. We have yielded to this temptation over these many years. It took at least two forms: The Promethean discrepancy, identified by Günther Anders, that leads our ability to cause harm to overwhelm our ability to represent this harm and relate to it, and the inabilities of nuclear weapons professionals to want to search for and describe all paths to nuclear-induced collapse when their privileged position within the exterminist structure puts them in a unique place to do so. This epistemic vulnerability adds to the material vulnerability of the possibility of civilization collapse.

Proponents of national and international security based on nuclear weapons—the part of the exterminist system that "'chooses' it, produces it, polices it, justifies it, and maintains it in being"—ultimately claim that the continued possibility of producing collapse is a requirement to preventing it. Whereas the anti-systemic movement, seeking non-nuclear national and international security, claims that avoiding such collapse requires dismantling the weapons, facilities, institutions, and knowledge structures that produce the "thrust to exterminism." In ethical terms, the first camp would not give up the possibility to commit mass nuclear violence under any circumstance as a condition for its survival—a permanent present for nuclear states, their regimes, and institutions, serving to colonize and close off other possibly benign futures for humankind. The nuclear weapon-free world camp would not support, threaten, or commit nuclear violence anywhere, whatever the consequences—survival permits future politics and actions able eventually to realize and create new human possibilities. As the late Jonathan Schell recognized,

> The day that the last nuclear weapon on earth was destroyed would be a great day. It would be a day for celebrations. We would have given substance to our choice to create the human future. We would have dispelled once and for all the fatalism and lack of faith in man which, like some dark shadow of extinction itself, have crept over us.[70]

Those two political and ethical positions are radically incompatible. The entry into force in early 2021 of the United Nations Treaty on the Prohibition of Nuclear Weapons, supported by 122 countries but none of the nine nuclear-armed states, acts as a stark reminder of this incompatibility. Among other international legal obligations, the treaty commits states "never under any circumstances to: Develop, test, produce, manufacture, otherwise acquire, possess or stockpile nuclear weapons or other nuclear explosive devices ... use or threaten to use nuclear weapons or other nuclear explosive devices."

While the possibility of nuclear collapse still looms, it is deeply contested and likely to become more given the contradictions between the nuclear-armed states and the non-weapon states and between mobilized citizens and nuclear establishments within the nuclear-armed states, especially the ones with democratic political governance.[71] Choosing how one handles it as an individual, a collective, or a political community, requires first and foremost coming to terms with the existence of exterminist systems and the material and epistemic dimensions of the nuclear vulnerabilities they generate and we suffer.

Notes & References

1 This essay has been made possible by funding from the European Research Council (ERC) under the European Union's Horizon 2020 research and innovation programme (grant agreement no. 759707, NUCLEAR project).

2 Lewis Mumford, "Gentlemen, You are Mad!" *The Saturday Review of Literature*, March 2, Vol. XXIX, No. 9, 1946, pp. 5–7, p. 5.

3 Thomas Moynihan, *X-Risk: How Humanity Discovered its Own Extinction*. Boston, MA: MIT Press, 2020.

4 E. P. Thompson, "Notes on Exterminism, the Last Stage of Civilization," *New Left Review*, Issue 121, May/June 1980, p. 22.

5 Henry Stimson, "Memorandum Discussed with the President, April 25, 1945," https://nsarchive.gwu.edu/documents/atomic-bomb-end-world-war-ii/006b.pdf.

6 Harry S. Truman, Diary, July 25, 1945, http://www.dannen.com/decision/hst-jl25.html.

7 Martin Sherwin, *A World Destroyed: Hiroshima and the Origins of the Arms Race*. New York: Vintage Books, 1987, p. 221.

8 Hans M. Kristensen and Matt Korda, "Status of World Nuclear Forces Federation of American Scientists," https://fas.org/issues/nuclear-weapons/status-world-nuclear-forces. The arsenal estimates are for 2020.

9 Otto Frisch and Rudolf Peierls, "Memorandum on the Properties of a Radioactive Superbomb," reprinted in Lorna Arnold, "The History of Nuclear Weapons: The Frisch-Peierls Memorandum on the Possible Construction of Atomic Bombs of February 1940," *Cold War History*, 3, April 2003, pp. 111–126.

10 John Horgan, "Bethe, Teller, Trinity and the End of Earth—A leader of the Manhattan Project Recalls a Discussion of Whether the Trinity Test Would Ignite Earth's Atmosphere and Destroy the Planet," *Scientific American*, August 4, 2015, https://blogs.scientificamerican.com/cross-check/bethe-teller-trinity-and-the-end-of-earth.

11 Ibid.

12 Ferenc Morton Szasz, *The Day the Sun Rose Twice: The Story of the Trinity Site Nuclear Explosion, July 16, 1945*. Albuquerque, NM: University of New Mexico Press, 1984, p. 90.

13 Zia Mian, "Out of the Nuclear Shadow: Scientists and the Struggle against the Bomb," *Bulletin of the Atomic Scientists* 71(1), January 2015, pp. 59–69.

14 General Advisory Committee, United States Atomic Energy Commission, Report on the "Super," October 30, 1949. Reprinted in: Herbert F. York, *The Advisors: Oppenheimer, Teller, and the Superbomb*. Stanford, CA: Stanford University Press, pp. 160–161.

15 Daniel Ellsberg, *The Doomsday Machine*. New York: Bloomsbury, 2017.

16 Cited in Martin J. Sherwin, *Gambling with Armageddon*. New York: Alfred Knopf, 2020, p. 136.

17 Robert S. Norris and Hans M. Kristensen, "U.S. Nuclear Warheads, 1945–2009," *Bulletin of the Atomic Scientists*, 65(4), 2009, pp. 72–81.

18 For Britain, see the work of British physicist Patrick Maynard Stuart Blackett, *Fear, War and the Bomb: Military and Political Consequences of Atomic Energy*. New York: McGraw-Hill, 1949; *Atomic Weapons and East-West Relations*. Cambridge: Cambridge University Press, 1956; *Studies of War: Nuclear and Conventional*. New York: Hill and Wang, 1962.

19 Isabelle Miclot, "Guerre Nucléaire, Armes et … Parades?: Hypothèses Conflictuelles et Politique de Protection Civile en France Dans les Années 1950'–1960'," halshs-00816621, 2011, p. 10, note 29.

20 Jeff Hughes, "The Strath Report: Britain Confronts the H-Bomb, 1954–1955," *History and Technology*, 19(3), 2003, p. 263.

21 Robert S. Norris and Hans Kristensen, "Global Nuclear Weapons Inventories 1945–2013," *Bulletin of the Atomic Scientists*, 69(5), 2013, p. 78.

22   Ellsberg, *The Doomsday Machine*, p. 2.

23   Norris and Kristensen, "Global Nuclear Weapons Inventories 1945–2013".

24   Robert McNamara, "U.S. Nuclear Strategy," Remarks to United Press International Editors and Publishers, San Francisco, September 18, 1967. Published in *Bulletin of the Atomic Scientists*, 23(10), December 1967, pp. 26–31.

25   Memorandum of conversation, "Secretary's Meeting with the General Advisory Committee on Arms Control and Disarmament," January 6, 1977, Digital National Security Archive, available online at http://nsarchive.gwu.edu/nukevault/ebb521-Irans -Nuclear-Program-1975-vs-2015/07.pdf.

26   Edward Geist, *Armageddon Insurance: Civil Defence in the United States and the Soviet Union*. Chapel Hill, NC: University of North Carolina Press, 2018.

27   "Plan A: How a Nuclear War Could Progress," *Arms Control Today*, July/August 2020, pp. 23–36; video at https://youtu.be/2jy3JU-ORpo.

28   Lynn Eden, *Whole World on Fire: Organizations, Knowledge and Nuclear Weapons Devastation*. Cornell: Cornell University Press, 2004.

29   Richard P. Turco, Owen B. Toon, T. P. Ackerman, J. B. Pollack, and Carl Sagan, "Nuclear Winter: Global Consequences of Multiple Nuclear Explosions," *Science*, 222(4630), December 23, 1983, pp. 1283–1292; *The Cold and the Dark: The World after Nuclear War*, eds. Paul Ehrlich Carl Sagan, Donald Kennedy, and Walter Orr, New York: Norton, 1984.

30   Department for Disarmament Affairs, Report of the Secretary-General, *Study on the Climatic and Other Global Effects of Nuclear War*. New York: United Nations, 1989, pp. 6–7.

31   Owen B. Toon, Charles G. Bardeen, Alan Robock, Lili Xia, Hans Kristensen, Matthew McKinzie, R. J. Peterson, Cheryl Harrison, Nicole S. Lovenduski, and Richard P. Turco, "Rapid Expansion of Nuclear Arsenals by Pakistan and India Portends Regional and Global Catastrophe," *Science Advances*, 5(10), 2019, pp. 1–13.

32   Alan Robock et al., "A Regional Nuclear Conflict Would Compromise Global Food Security," *Proceedings of the National Academy of Sciences*, 117(13), March 31, 2020.

33   Voice over in Stéphane Gabet, *La France, le Président et la Bombe*, 2016, at 15'10s.

34   For South Asia, see, e.g., Zia Mian, "Kashmir, Climate Change, and Nuclear War," *Bulletin of the Atomic Scientists*, December 7, 2016, available online (last accessed November 26, 2022).

35   Gabriel Kolko, "Can Civil Defense Be Effective?" in Seymour Melman (ed.), *No Place to Hide: Fallout Shelters-Fact and Fiction*. New York: Grove Press, 1962, p. 131.

36   Ron Robin, *The Cold World They Made: The Strategic Legacy of Roberta and Albert Wohlstetter*. Cambridge, MA: Harvard University Press, 2016, p. 85.

37   Ibid., p. 86.

38   Lynn Eden, "The U.S. Nuclear Arsenal and Zero: Sizing and Planning for Use—Past, Present, and Future," dans Catherine Kelleher et Judith Reppy (eds.), *Getting to Zero: The Path to Nuclear Disarmament*, Stanford (Calif.), Stanford University Press, 2011, pp. 69–70; Ellsberg, *The Doomsday Machine*, pp. 120–123, 341, 344–345, 349.

39   David Holloway, "Racing Towards Armageddon? Soviet Views of Strategic Nuclear War 1955–1972," in John Ikenberry and Michael Gordin (eds.), *The Age of Hiroshima*. Princeton, NJ: Princeton University Press, 2020, pp. 76–77.

40   Lee Butler, "The False God of Nuclear Deterrence," *Global Dialogue*, Autumn 1999, pp. 74–81, p. 81.

41   For more sources of invisibilisation and empirical evidence for them, see Benoît Pelopidas, *Repenser les choix nucléaires. La seduction de l'impossible*. Paris, Presses de Sciences Po, 2022, pp. 183-216.

42   Günther Anders, "Theses for the Atomic Age," *Massachusetts Review*, 3(3), Spring 1962, pp. 496–497.

43   Remarks by President Obama at the Hiroshima Peace Memorial, Hiroshima, Japan, May 27, 2016, https://obamawhitehouse.archives.gov/the-press-office/2016/05/27/remarks -president-obama-and-prime-minister-abe-japan-hiroshima-peace.

44 Fred Kaplan, *The Bomb: Presidents, Generals and the Secret History of Nuclear War*. New York: Simon & Schuster, 2020, pp. 243–244.

45 Paul Slovic and Herbert S. Lin, "The Caveman and the Bomb in the Digital Age," in Harold Trinkunas (ed.), *Three Tweets from Midnight*. Stanford, CA: Hoover Press, 2020, p. 58 and Paul Slovic et Daniel Västfjäll, "The More Who Die, the Less We Care. Psychic Numbing and Genocide," in Scott Slovic et Paul Slovic (eds.), *Numbers and Nerves: Information, Emotion, and Meaning in a World of Data*. Corvallis (OR: Oregon State University Press, 2015, pp. 55–68.

46 Günther Anders, "L'Homme Sur le Pont," *Journal d'Hiroshima et de Nagasaki*, 1958 reprinted in Günther Anders, *Hiroshima est Partout*, p. 194. This should not be understood to mean that we are all *equally* responsible for this state of affairs. On the role of fiction as a way of moving beyond this defective condition, see Benoît Pelopidas, "Imaginer la Possibilité de la Guerre Nucléaire Pour y Faire Face," *Cultures et Conflits* 123-124 Fall/Winter 2021, pp. 173-212.

47 Lynn Eden, "U.S. Planning for Pandemics and Large-Scale Nuclear War Lynn," Working Paper presented to The 75th Anniversary Nagasaki Nuclear-Pandemic Nexus Scenario Project, October 31–November 1 and 14–15, 2020, http://nautilus.org/wp-content/uploads/2020/11/Eden_WP_Nagasaki_20201124_Final.pdf.

48 The planners of nuclear war frequently consider that their practices and discussions should not be made public. See for instance Former US Stratcom Commander Russell E. Dougherty states it explicitly in, "The Psychological Climate of Nuclear Command," in *Managing Nuclear Operations*. Washington, DC: Brookings Institution Press, 1987, p. 420.

49 Benoît Pelopidas, "Nuclear Weapons Scholarship as a Case of Self-Censorship in Security Studies," *Journal of Global Security Studies*, 1(4), November 2016, pp. 326-336.

50 Lee Clarke, *Mission Improbable: Using Fantasy Documents to Tame Disaster*. Chicago, IL: Chicago University Press, 1999, pp. 30–40.

51 Eric Schlosser, *Command and Control*. New York: Allen Lane, 2013, p. 480.

52 François Gezelnikoff in Stéphane Gabet, *La France, le Président et la Bombe*, 2016, at 27'.

53 Private archives of Robert L. Peurifoy, Kerrville, TX, USA, and Robert L. Peurifoy, "A Personal Account of Steps towards Achieving Safer Nuclear Weapons in the US Nuclear Arsenal," in George P. Shultz and Sidney D. Drell (eds.), *The Nuclear Enterprise: High-Consequence Accidents: How to Enhance Safety and Minimize Risks in Nuclear Weapons and Reactors*. Stanford, CA: Hoover Press, 2012, pp. 67–89. Interview of one of the authors with Gordon O. Moe, who submitted in July 1988 a study on the Grand Forks fire of September 1980. Kerrville, Texas, November 26, 2017.

54 Vice-Admiral Jean Armand Marc Philippon, *La Royale et Le Roi*. Paris: France Empire, 1982, p. 154.

55 For further analysis of how limits of control over and knowledge about nuclear weapons are underestimated, neglected, or treated inconsistently, see Benoît Pelopidas, "The Unbearable Lightness of Luck: Three Sources of Overconfidence in the Controllability of Nuclear Crises," *European Journal of International Security*, 2(2), 2017, pp. 245–248, "Power, Luck and Scholarly Responsibility at the End of the World(s)," *International Theory*, 12(3), 2020, pp. 459-470 and "Facing nuclear war. Luck, learning and the Cuban Missile Crisis" in Christian Reus-Smit et. al. (eds.), *Oxford Handbook in History and International Relations* (with Richard Ned Lebow), Oxford: Oxford University Press, 2023.

56 Steven Kull, *Minds at War: Nuclear Reality and the Inner Conflicts of Defense Policymakers*. New York: Basic Books, 1988; Kjølv Egeland, "The Ideology of Nuclear Order," *New Political Science* 43(2), 2021, pp. 208-230.

57 Carol Cohn, "Sex, Death and the Rational World of Defense Intellectuals," *Signs*, 12(4), 1987, pp. 687-718; Robert J. Lifton and Eric Markusen, *The Genocidal Mentality*. New York: Basic Books, 1990.

58 Hugh Gusterson, *Nuclear Rites: A Weapons Laboratory at the End of the Cold War*. Berkeley, CA: University of California Press, 1996, chap. 3.

59 Fred Kaplan, *The Wizards of Armageddon*. New York: Simon & Schuster, 1983, p. 302; Thomas Schelling, "Harvard Kennedy School Oral History:Thomas Schelling," minutes 39 and 40; Robert Dodge, *The Strategist: The Life and Times of Thomas Schelling*. New Hampshire, Hollis Pub. Co, 2006, pp. 82–83 and Marc Trachtenberg, "Strategic thought in America," *Political Science Quarterly*, 104(2), 1989, pp. 301–334 at 310.

60 Thomas Schelling's "disappointment" and "incomprehension" in the face of the self-explanatory ending of Dr. Strangelove is revealing of this blindness. He says, "*Strangelove* ending; you're not sure what the ending is because somebody goes down with a bomb and then the movie is over and then there are mushroom clouds all over the place and you don't know whether that's meaning 'and so war occurred' or this just emblematic and you don't know what the outcome is." Thomas Schelling, "Harvard Kennedy School Oral History:Thomas Schelling," minute 43. As Sharon Ghamari-Tabrizi wrote, "Strangelove's meaning was undeniable but not everyone could see it." *The Worlds of Herman Kahn; The Intuitive Science of Thermonuclear War*. Cambridge, Harvard University Press, 2005, p. 278.

61 Jean Offredo, "Interview avec André Beaufre et Gilles Martinet, "La guerre atomique est-elle possible?" in Jean Offredo (dir.), *Le Sens du Futur*. Paris: Éditions Universitaires, 1971, p. 110.

62 "BLUE Episode 4: A Nuclear Family," *Air Force TV*, April 20, 2015.

63 Nina Tannenwald, *The Nuclear Taboo: The United States and the Non-Use of Nuclear Weapons Since 1945*. Cambridge: Cambridge University Press, 2007, p. 16 and "The Legacy of the Nuclear Taboo in the Twenty-First Century," in Michael Gordin and G. John Ikenberry (eds.), *The Age of Hiroshima*. Princeton, NJ: Princeton University Press, 2020, p. 292. For critiques, see T.V. Paul, *The Tradition of Non-Use of Nuclear Weapons*. Stanford, CA: Stanford University Press, 2009; Lynn Eden, "The Contingent taboo," *Review of International Studies*, 36(4), 2010, pp. 831–837.

64 Kaplan, *The Bomb*, p. 230.

65 Richard Rhodes, "Absolute Power," *New York Times Sunday Book Review*, March 21, 2014.

66 General John Hyten, "The Mitchell Institute Triad Conference," US Strategic Command, July 17, 2018, http://www.stratcom.mil/Media/Speeches/Article/1577239/the-mitch-ell-institute-triad-conference.

67 Joseph Masco, "Terraforming Planet Earth," in Casper Sylvest and Rens van Munster (eds.), *The Politics of Globality Since 1945: Assembling the Planet*. London: Routledge, 2016; Matt Reynolds, "Welcome to the Anthropocene: Nuclear Testing and Pollution Have Pushed Earth into a New Epoch," *Wired UK*, August 30, 2016.

68 Benoît Pelopidas, "Renunciation, Reversal and Restraint," in Joseph Pilat and Nathan E. Busch (eds.), *Routledge Handbook of Nuclear Proliferation and Policy*. London: Routledge, 2015, pp. 337–348 and "The Nuclear Straightjacket: American Extended Deterrence and Nonproliferation," in Stéfanie von Hlatky and Andreas Wenger (eds.), *The Future of Extended Deterrence: NATO and Beyond*. Washington, DC: Georgetown University Press, 2015, pp. 73–106.

69 Lawrence S. Wittner, *A Short History of the World Nuclear Disarmament Movement*. Stanford, CA: Stanford University Press, 2009. See also the three-volume series *The Struggle Against the Bomb* detailing the history and impacts of the contentious politics for nuclear disarmament around the world since 1945: *One World or None: A History of the World Nuclear Disarmament Movement Through 1953*, Stanford, 1993; *Resisting the Bomb: A History of the World Nuclear Disarmament Movement, 1954–1970*, Stanford, 1997; *Toward Nuclear Abolition: A History of the World Nuclear Disarmament Movement, 1971–Present*, Stanford, 2003.

70 Jonathan Schell, *The Abolition*. New York: Knopf, 1984, p. 163.

71 Zia Mian, "After the Nuclear Weapons Ban Treaty: A New Disarmament Politics," *Bulletin of the Atomic Scientists*, July 7, 2017, available online (last accessed November 26, 2022).

17 From Wild West to Mad Max

Transition in Civilizations

Richard Bookstaber[1]

17.1 Introduction

What caused the fall of Rome? The German historian Alexander Demandt counted over 200 explanations by scholars, some creative, I-never-would-have-thought-of-that causes such as useless eaters, bathing, sadness, women's emancipation, and freedom in excess (Demandt 1984). Historians have covered all the bases, one arguing the opposite case of another: One lists slavery, another points to releasing of slaves; one points to militarism, another attributes the decline to pacifism; one to prosperity, another to poverty; one to the loss of central power, another to totalitarianism; one to laziness, another to striving.

What caused the end of the Late Bronze Age? The decline of Rome is fascinating and widely studied, but the Late Bronze Age is more similar to our current world, a global system of highly connected, interdependent civilizations. Anthropologist Eric Cline runs through the list of explanations that have been proposed for its collapse, albeit a list less ambitious than that for the fall of Rome, with scholars having argued for earthquakes, invaders and the Sea People, drought, famine, severed trade routes, forced migration, the undermining of the economy by private merchants, concentration of control in the Palace, and internal rebellion (Cline 2014).

The study of the fall of the Roman Empire or the Late Bronze Age would seem to mark the graveyard of broad theories of the failure of civilizations. If we cannot get a clear answer to these, how can we for civilizations in general? Nonetheless, scholars propose such theories. The quest has run through the last century, Arnold Toynbee in the 1930s, Joseph Tainter in the 1980s, and Jared Diamond in the 1990s, each with a hypothesis filtered through the concerns of the day. Toynbee's thesis of the cycle of challenge and response developed during a time of multifaceted global stress; the kernel of Tainter's thesis that a civilization collapses when its energy fails to keep up with its demands arose in the aftermath of the energy crisis; and Diamond's thesis of environmental failure occurred during the environmentally charged period of the 1990s (Toynbee 1934; Tainter 1988; Diamond 1997, 2004).

More recently, an alternative approach has emerged that responds to the failure of these grand answers. It is a systems approach that looks at collapse

DOI: 10.4324/9781003331384-22

through the lens of complexity theory. This has roots extending 40 years back to Colin Renfrew, who used chaos theory as his tool (Renfrew 1973, 1978). This approach begins by recognizing that a civilization is a complex system, and its failure is the result of interactions and dynamics. It turns the investigation of collapse from finding the cause to describing the process.

After treating the variety of causes that scholars have pointed to for the widespread failure of the interlocking civilizations that made up the Late Bronze Age, Cline concludes in *1177 B.C.: The Year Civilization Collapsed* that none of these individual factors would have been cataclysmic enough on their own to bring down even one of these civilizations, let alone all of them (Cline 2014). However, he argues they could have combined to produce a scenario where the repercussions of each factor were magnified, in what he calls a multiplier effect, resulting in a system collapse that led to the disintegration of one society after another. He writes, "It is possible that we need to turn to what is called complexity science, or, perhaps more accurately, complexity theory, in order to get a grasp of what may have led to the collapse of these civilizations."

Thus, rather than address *why* civilizations rise and fall, to search for "patient zero" as the prime mover, we can more successfully address the question of *how* they rise and fall. Look at the process, the dynamic. It is a systems approach. Connections fail in multiple directions: Sources of production and distribution, communication and control, and the social fabric woven through cultural connections. There is a cascade with feedback making instabilities worse, contagion from one part of the system to another, and emergent phenomenon where the aggregate result has complexity that is not apparent in the individual dislocations. The rise and fall are the building up and then the breaking down of connections and interrelationships, and the development and then the weaning off of dependence.

The systems approach and the complexity that it implies leads to characteristics for studying the rise and fall of the civilization that ultimately circumscribe limits to what we can discover in our historical enterprise. In a complex dynamic system, especially one with human interaction, transitions can occur in a seemingly random and certainly unpredictable way, with no particular antecedent, as what are called emergent phenomena. There might be no explanation at all. Each civilization is new. It is the product of the human invention. So, we ask what is common within these transitions even as we find a structurally determined limit to our knowledge.

17.2 From Wild West to Mad Max

The transitions in the rise and fall of civilizations are the outcome of complexity, marked by the ebb and flow of connections and dependence among societies. The connections include communication, trade, shared technology, and, over time, culture. Dependence emerges from the connections and includes economic connections related to consumption, the supply chain, and the joint production of goods relying on specialization; an integrated political system and military force to build and support common infrastructure and to tax for funding these enterprises; and social and cultural connections such as common religion and legends, shared language, literacy, diplomacy, and contracts.

The connections and dependence are causally integrated, with connections giving rise to dependence. This causality runs in two directions, leading to two simple propositions.

The first is the process leading from the building of connections to the rise in dependence:

- Dependence takes root only after connections such as communication and trade have been established.

The second is the process leading from the breaking of connections to the end of dependence:

- Connections break more quickly than a civilization can wean itself from dependence.

Communication and trade can end in a flash through war or natural calamities. However, even as connections fail, dependence remains because of the slow process of retooling toward self-sufficient production, reorienting consumption to no longer depend on materials acquired through trade, ending reliance on unmaintainable infrastructure, and establishing local rule and security. The period of dependence absent the trade and communication to support it is one of marked instability.

For example, Cline discusses the decline as beginning with a breaking of connections across the traditional elite class, centralized administrations, and interlinked centralized economies, followed by unstable conditions, repeated catastrophes, and migration. With the loss of these connections came a decline of the dependence among the civilizations which had allowed for refined culture and production. Mycenaean pottery gave way to coarser local styles. Metalwork became less intricate, and writing disappeared. Iron implements replaced bronze because the decline in trade affected the availability of tin. Craftsmen and artisans vanished. The population declined by 75 or more. Even areas peripheral to the devastation, such as Athens, suffered a political and social collapse. By 1050 BC Mycenaean Civilization disappeared, and the Greek Dark Ages began (Cline 2014).

The same dynamic occurred in post-Roman Britain. Even up to the sixth century, connections linked pottery as distant as Scottish Iona to a production site thousands of miles away in what is modern Tunisia. But Britain then moved into what Ward-Perkins calls the end of civilization (Ward-Perkins 2005). Whatever more favorable term might be used for this period, it nonetheless is one of broken connections and the loss of the tools and resources to meet the dependence that remained.

These two propositions are the transition phases of a cycle of civilization that runs through four periods marked by different relationships between connections and dependence:

- The rise of civilization, with emerging connections that set the stage for interdependence.
- The civilization itself, which is connected and dependent; where connections are more or less settled, and where progress comes more from increasing interdependence than the forging of new connections.
- The breakdown of the civilization, with dissolving connections but continuing dependence.
- The end of civilization, no longer connected or interdependent, with largely self-sufficient loosely linked villages—or wasteland.

I call the transitions, the first and third of these four periods, Wild West and Mad Max.[2] I choose these names because they are evocative of the nature of these transitional periods: unruly, helter-skelter, without structure or stability.

The Wild West is a time of growing connections, but it is not yet highly dependent. For the Wild West, we see discovery and conquest, fresh and shifting alliances; skirmishes and disputes for advantage; sharing technology and founding of trade routes; specialization of production, and integration of the religious and cultural with emerging shared legends and semiotics.

For Mad Max, whether it is attributed to war and revolution, famine, or pestilence, we see the connections forged by civilization breaking apart. However, even as connections fail, interdependence remains because of the slow pace of retooling toward self-sufficient production (think of the time needed to cultivate olive trees if the distant source of olive oil is lost). The population is left without the goods it has depended on that require the coordination of specialized activities and resources, and where it lacks the complement of materials, skills, and infrastructure to produce them locally.

The process is shown in Figure 17.1. This pear leaf shape shows the rise of connections that then move more toward increasing dependence. After a point, increasing dependence comes more as the offshoot of already existing dependence than as the result of the continued building of connections.

Toward the top right, we have the corpus of high civilization. Then there comes the point where connections begin to break in a cascade. But dependence remains nearly the same, until through retooling it reduces as well, leading at the bottom left to a self-sufficient and splintered society of low civilization.

As Figure 17.1 shows, Mad Max is not the Wild West in reverse. We do not merely trace back along the same line, the arrow pointing the other way. On the way up with Wild West, as connections are made, new sources of dependence only emerge after all the required precedents are in place. But on the way down logic does not define what is gone and what remains behind. In that respect, Wild West is graceful; dependence moves forward sensibly. Mad Max is not. Someone happening upon a Mad Max period might think, "This

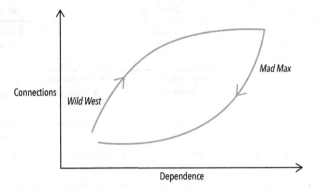

Figure 17.1 A "Pear leaf" view of the progression of a civilization from Wild West through Mad Max. High civilization is toward the top right, low civilization and possibly proto-civilization is at the bottom left. The figure has no time scale; there is no indication of the time spent at any point on the diagram.

makes no sense. Why are they stabling horses in villas? Why have they turned aqueducts into sewers? Why are they using swords for reaping?" Or, from of a satire of our current time, "why are they pulling a car with horses?"

There is lower literacy and less social and cultural integration and communication beyond villages. There is less economic interaction; less trading, joint production, and specialization. There is a breakdown of authority and central control, leading to a decline in the tax base. The resulting drop in government revenue and authority leads to the decay of infrastructure. The military is weakened because of the reduced revenue, and also because the breakdown in the social and cultural bonds reduces the willingness of the populace to take on foreign aggression. In the end there are small, disconnected go-it-alone states, often facing one another with ongoing strife and conflict.

Table 17.1 gives indicative examples of historical events and characteristics of the Wild West and Mad Max for ten civilizations, as well as the intervening periods of the civilization, as dependence grows and as connections break.

For an example of the Wild West, we can look at the period of the Warring States extending into the Qin dynasty. In 771 BC the last Western Zhou ruler was killed in battle and the capital city sacked. The Zhou then splintered into scores of small, autonomous states. These states heaved to and fro, forging and breaking alliances, engaging in wars, and annexing one another until the seven Warring States eventually emerged. One of the Warring States, the Qin, became increasingly powerful, and the other six states turned their focus toward contending with the Qin threat.

There were two approaches toward this conflict: One was called the "vertical alliance," where the states would ally with one another against the Qin; the other was the "horizontal alliance," where a state would join with the Qin to share in the spoils of its ascent. Neither the horizontal nor the vertical approach

Table 17.1 Examples of historical events for Wild West and Mad Max, as well as for the periods of rising dependence and breaking connections

Civilization	Wild West: Building Connections	Rising Dependence	Breaking Connections	Mad Max: Losing Support
Late Bronze Age	centralized states	developing aristocracy	sea peoples, declining trade	declining shipbuilding, tin
Roman	Horatius Cocles	patrician versus plebian	divided imperium	declining infrastructure
Han	common written language	public works, Great Canal	independent military command	Yellow Turban Rebellion
Byzantine I	Council of Nicaea	Justinian I, centralization	monophysitism	rise of Islam, conquests
Byzantine II	contact with West	centralized control of trade	depopulation of Constantinopolis	depleting natural resources
Song	reopening trade, diplomacy	rebuilding canals	bureaucratic infighting	Mongols, Siege of Kai-Feng
Western I	Mediterranean trade	early feudalism	Black Death	labor shortages
Western II	oceanic trade	slave trade		
Inca	creation myth	corvée labor, textile industry		
Polynesian	voyages of exploration	specialized trade	Māori Wars, declining trade	degrading environment

fared well. The vertical alliances broke down because of mutual suspicions among allied states, and the Qin exploited the horizontal strategy to defeat the states one by one.

In 221 BC, completing the gradual consolidation that began over three centuries, the Qin replaced the Zhou, and in the consummation of the Wild West period built a connected and unified empire with standards for the units of length, weight, and volume in trade; the widths of axles so that carts could run in the same ruts in the roads; and script for common written language.

For Mad Max, Ward-Perkins looks at post-Roman Britain, the inhabitants of countless rural microcosms of self-sufficient and isolated villages with their "drafty timber walls, rotting and leaking roofs, and dirty floors" (Ward-Perkins 2005, 110). The connections during the Roman period led their local skills and local networks to whither, so once the connections were severed, every building craft disappeared. In the fifth century Britain had no quarrying of building stone, preparation of mortar, or manufacturing of bricks and tiles. It took centuries to rebuild the connections, skills, and technology, even for something as simple as the pottery wheel.

Civil war became commonplace, society fragmented and common identity faded. Peter Brown in *The Rise of Western Christendom* notes that rather than seeking to integrate into Roman society and culture, there was a pull toward ethnicity for the ruling elite (Brown 2003). The common use of Latin gave way to mutually unintelligible dialects that formed the kernels of the Romance languages.

17.3 Civilization as a Multi-layer Network

On September 27, 2003, Rome hosted the White Night, a city-wide all-night carnival. Shops and bars, theaters, and art galleries stayed open into the wee hours of the morning. There were circus acts, music on the streets, a performance of Romeo and Juliet at the Globe Theatre, and a performance of Tosca near the town hall.

Then, at 3:27 AM, the lights went out. A blackout enveloped Italy. On any other day, a power outage at three in the morning would have had little impact, but on the White Night, 30,000 people were stranded on 110 trains, and others caught in the subways. And it was raining. A *New York Times* reporter covering the event described "a ghostly legion of wet and bedraggled nocturnal revelers found themselves stranded on the streets" (Povoledo 2003)

The outage began 26 minutes earlier when heavy winds created a flashover between a conductor cable and a tree on one of the main electric transmission lines, the Lukmanier line, that runs between Switzerland and Italy. After spending ten minutes unsuccessfully trying to restore the Lukmanier line, the Swiss network operator alerted his Italian counterpart to lighten the load on the San Bernardino line, because the physics of electrical flows dictated that the electricity would overload that transmission line. But this fail-safe maneuver was prevented by another line-to-ground fault at 3:25 AM that led to the San Bernardino line shutting down as well. There then followed sequential failures of other transmission lines in the border region, resulting in a catastrophic blackout throughout Italy at 3:27 AM (Bacher et al. 2003).

The propagation of grid failures generally occurs due to a cascade of overloads that triggers breakers from node to node in the network. The operators on the Swiss and Italian sides of the border were frantically dropping loads across lines and trying to restart, but the devices refused to switch and reopen the breakers. The operators did not know that the source of the Italian blackout was different from what their manual of emergency procedures had anticipated. In the Italian blackout, the problem came from the interaction between the electrical network and a second network, a communications network that controlled the power network's operation. That is, it was due to the interaction of a two-layer network.

When the node on the Lukmanier failed, it spanned to the communication network by disabling a nearby server. That server failure affected adjacent servers because they depended on one server as a part of their communication cluster. The power stations connected to these servers then shut down because of the loss of their controllers. This then affected the servers adjacent to that node. The failure propagated, hopscotching between one node on the power layer to one on the communication layer, from that node to other nodes on the communication layer, and then back to the power node through these servers. The communication network depended on the electric network for power, and the power network depended on the communication network for its instructions and coordination.

Multi-layer networks are evident in civilizations, with dynamics not dissimilar from those on the White Night. For example, even as far back as the Late Bronze Age, the global economy was tied to diplomatic, commercial, transportation, and communication networks. And in the collapse of the Late Bronze Age all of these networks were linked, from the breakdown of central units of administrations, to the collapse of the economy, to the erosion of the elite social class (Cline 2014).

I posit three general layers to represent the multi-layer structure: The government and military; the economic; and the social and cultural. This is illustrated in Figure 17.2.

These layers echo three general features proposed by Colin Renfrew in his model of the collapse of a dynamical system (Renfrew and Cooke 1979)[3]:

Collapse of central administrative organization of the early state: (a) Disappearance or reduction in a number of levels of central hierarchy. (b) fragmentation of military organization. (c) Abandonment of palaces and central storage facilities. (d) Eclipse of temples as major religious centers (often with their survival, modified, as local shrines). (e) Effective loss of literacy for secular and religious purposes. (f) Abandonment of public building works

Collapse of centralized economy: (a) Cessation of market exchange. (b) External trade very markedly reduced, and traditional trade routes disappear. (c) Cessation of craft-specialist manufacture. (d) Cessation of specialized or organized agricultural production, with agriculture instead on a local "homestead" basis.

Disappearance of the traditional elite class: (a) Abandonment of rich residences, or their reuse in impoverished style by "squatters." (b) Cessation in the use of costly assemblages of luxury goods, although individual items may survive.

The multi-layer network has implications for systemic risks that are qualitatively different from those for a single-layer network. Perhaps not unexpectedly, the mode of propagation of risk, the path a shock takes, and the value of integration versus segregation of the functions of various agents or nodes all have a different and richer nature as we move to a multi-layer view. In the Italian blackout, the flow of communication between servers and from servers to the station control units was different from that of the flow of power along the grid and into the servers. So, the links between layers lead to a different functional effect and lead to a transformation from one function to another.

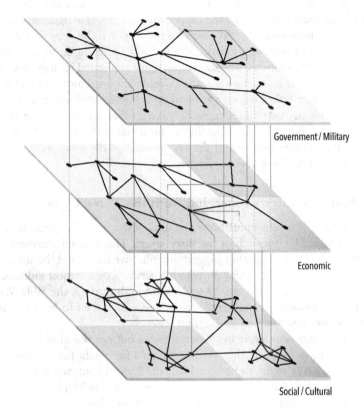

Government / Military

Economic

Social / Cultural

Figure 17.2 A three-layer network for civilization, showing networks within the Government/Military, Economic, and Social/Cultural layers, and links between each of these.

It is not surprising that the addition of these functional relationships and transformations in the types of flows that arise for interlayer connections creates vulnerabilities that do not exist in a plain vanilla, single-layer network. All three layers can lay claim to a role in the collapse of civilizations. Consider the attribution to these layers for the decline of the Late Bronze Age that is implicit in the systems approach: The collapse of the Palace, the central point of organization; the faltering of long-term trade that led to economic instability; and the breakdown of links between disparate social and cultural groups.

17.3.1 Network Types Within a Civilization

Each of the three layers has its own particular organizational features, leading to different network structures.

The government/military is a hierarchical or tree network. One agent reports to one other agent, in a child–parent structure, up to the top node, which is the ultimate authority, e.g., the king or emperor.

The economic layer of production and consumption does not have a clean structure because it is dictated by the happenstance of modes of transportation, natural resources, hubs for trade, and centers of production technology and artisans. It has what is called a random network. Because most agents engage in the economy as consumers and producers, the network is highly connected in high civilization.

The social/cultural structure is a small world network; clusters of highly connected villages are linked through a few of the agents to other villages.[4] In a small world network any two nodes might only have a few degrees of separation.

Figure 17.3 illustrates the tree/hierarchical network of the government/military, the random network of the economic, and the small world network of social/cultural. These also can be seen in Figure 17.2.

17.4 Systemic Effects Emerging from the Three Layers

In this section, I present simulations that look at the transition periods of Wild West and Mad Max for each of the three layers. The differing network structures from one layer to another suggest different dynamics, and the simulations for each of those can shed light on which layers will be the most vulnerable to a Mad Max decline, which are the quickest to push through the Wild West to form the foundation for high civilization, and which tend to be stable in the non-transition high and low civilization states.

I treat the different layers in this simulation, but not the links between the layers. That is, so to speak, the floor on which a fire might flare up the quickest, be most easily extinguished, or burn the longest, but not the likelihood it will jump from that floor to the next floor of the building. The approach I am using here borrows heavily from Monin and Bookstaber (Monin and Bookstaber 2017). I present it here without mathematical details and refer the reader to that paper for a more analytical treatment.

The civilization is comprised of agents. The agents can most easily be thought of as individuals or family units. All agents are treated identically so that the only differences in dynamics come from the structure of the layers of the civilization, as opposed to the nature of the agents themselves.

Each agent has a notion of satisfaction that is measured by k. There is a maximum potential satisfaction that can be attained within the civilization, k^*.

Each agent has a probability of death in any period. There is a baseline probability of death for any agent, and added to that there is a probability of death based on the distance between the agent's k and k^*. These are identical for all of the agents.

The objective for any agent is to have the distance between its k and k^* be as small as possible, because that will give it the highest probability of surviving to the next period. The agent's k is set based on a weighted average of the values of k for agents to which it is connected. The more connections an agent has, and the greater the age of those connections, the smaller the distance tends to be. The idea here is that the connections increase the dependence and specialization that improves the prospects within the civilization.

Tree/Hierarchy

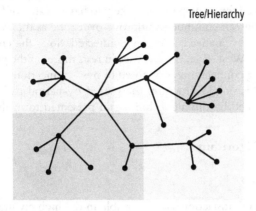

Random

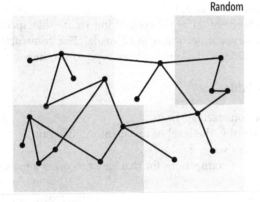

Small World

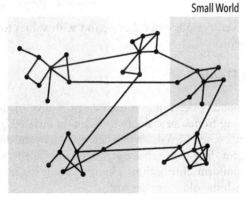

Figure 17.3 A stylized illustration of the networks for each of the layers. The Government/ Military layer is a hierarchical or tree network. There is a parent–child relationship between the nodes, reflecting the command structure. The Economic layer is a random network, where nodes and links depend on the happenstance of resources, transportation hubs, and population centers. The Social/Cultural layer is a small world network with highly connected villages sparsely linked.

Age is an indicator of the value of a particular connection, because an agent who has survived for many periods is likely to have a value of k close to k^*. The high civilization can continue to improve over time as the average age of the agents increases even after it is highly connected. So as the civilization moves out of the Wild West stage, the civilization rests more on the growing dependence of existing connections as opposed to new connections.

Based on this simple structure, the period-by-period path of the civilization is determined by this algorithm, again presented formally in Monin and Bookstaber:

Simulation Algorithm

Parameters

- Level of satisfaction that is possible in the high civilization, k^*
- Baseline death rate, b
- Probability of an agent connecting to another specific agent, given that a new connection is to be made. The construction of this probability differs from one network type to another.

State Variable

In each period, each agent has:
- A value of k, the level of the agent's satisfaction;
- The agent's age, a;
- The set of connections for that agent to other agents, M

Algorithm

- For a given period, enter that period with values for k, a, and M for each agent.

A1. Check Death

- Simultaneously determine if each agent is alive or dead. This is done by drawing from a probability distribution dictated by (1) the baseline death rate, b; and (2) a death rate determined by the distance of k and k^*.
- If an agent dies, then replace it with a new agent, whose k is drawn from a uniform distribution. The new agent has no connections—all those with the old agent are lost.
- If an agent survives, then increment its age by one period.

A2. Connect

- For each agent, find the set of agents with which it is not connected. If this set is non-empty, then:

- First determine if the agent is to make a new connection.
- If so, then make the connection based on the probability connecting with specific agents (which is part of the exogenous parameters, and will vary based on the network structure).
- For each agent, reset the set of agents with which the agent is not connected accordingly.

A3. Update

- Each agent updates their satisfaction based on a weighted average of the satisfaction of their connections weighted by the respective ages of those connections.
- Steps A1 through A3 determine new values for the state variables k, a, and M to apply in the algorithm for the next period of the simulation.

Figure 17.4 shows an example of one simulation running for 500,000 periods.[5] If a period is considered to be a day, this simulation extends for almost 1400 years. In this case the simulation is for the economic layer, and so is run on a random network. In this run there are four high civilizations bracketed by a Wild West on the left and a Mad Max on the right, one of which might be called stillborn

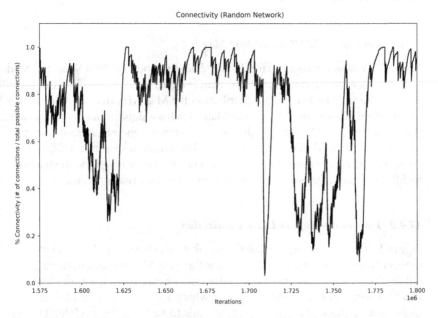

Figure 17.4 The connections over time as a civilization within a simulation segment passes from periods of high civilization to periods of low civilization. The Wild West transition is during periods of a notable rise in connections, and the Mad Max transition is during periods of notable decline. This figure shows five instances of high civilization, one occurring for a very short period.

because of its short time span.[6] The selection of the parameters leads to a cycle that more or less conforms with the time scale we see historically. Furthermore, it demonstrates the highly non-linear nature of the cycle of civilization.

Notably, this complex result comes from a model that is not only simple, but that draws its probabilities from standard distributions. And significantly, the complexity, the rises and falls, do not require any exogenous or special events. No shocks that might represent famines, earthquakes, or wars are introduced. The simulation moves forward based on the day-to-day variations imposed by the model. So we have two major points:

- A simple dynamic for civilization can lead to complex results.
- Rises and falls of civilizations need not be attributable to any one cause and indeed can occur without an apparent attribution to any combination of causes.

Figure 17.4 shows only 500,000 periods in order to be easier to read. For a fuller analysis, I have simulated for a longer number of periods—20 million for the tree and small world, 8 million for the random—in order to extract 82, 90, and 104 civilization cycles for the tree, random, and small world, respectively. This is about 600 years on average for each cycle for the tree and small world, and 200 years for the random.

17.4.1 Time for Wild West and Mad Max

Figure 17.5 shows histograms for the number of periods for Wild West and Mad Max for each civilization layer. The manifest characteristic in all of the layers is that there is a "fat tail" to the distribution for Mad Max that does not appear for the Wild West period. Note that Mad Max has a significant number of cases where the time for the fall is in the extreme left bin, whereas there are no cases in that bin for Wild West. This suggests that although sometimes falls can be "graceful," there are times the civilization crashes. The average and median time to fall is no shorter than the time to rise, but the crash risk is far greater.

17.4.2 Time in the High and Low Civilization

Figure 17.6 shows histograms for the number of periods a high and a low civilization lasted. Just as there is a fat tail for the Mad Max transition, there is a fat tail for the time spent in the high civilization. That is, there is a high likelihood of a "stillborn" high civilization, one of which appears in Figure 17.4. But not so for low civilizations. Once there, it tends to be there for a while. There is not much propensity for a bounce.

Once we take the stillborn civilizations out of the calculation, the average and median time in a high civilization is 200,000 periods, about 500 years if we take each period to be a day.

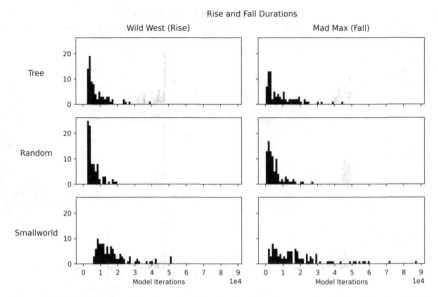

Figure 17.5 A histogram showing the distribution for the number of periods for Wild West and Mad Max transitions for the civilization layers over each of multiple simulations.

17.4.3 Distinctions for the Three Layers

There are clear differences in the effects between the three layers.

For Figure 17.5 on Wild West and Mad Max:
The random layer is the most "impatient" for both the rise and fall. So problems will propagate faster in the economic layer. This is because the economic network allows connections across everyone, and there are no rules or set structure for connections. The network embodies the phrase "It's just business"; connections are indifferent to rank, agent satisfaction, or social status.

Rise times and fall times are notably longer for the small world than the other two. With only a few channels for propagation, the social network takes longer to take hold and longer to dissipate.

There is less of a sudden crash risk for the small world. That is, not much mass in the extreme left tail for fall times. This is for the same reason – there not many channels for the fire to spread.

For Figure 17.6 on high and low civilizations:
As with the speed of the transition periods, the random network of the economic layer is less stable than the social and the government layers. For high times, the most stable is the government (tree), for low times it is the social (small world). In high times, the government network is fleshed out

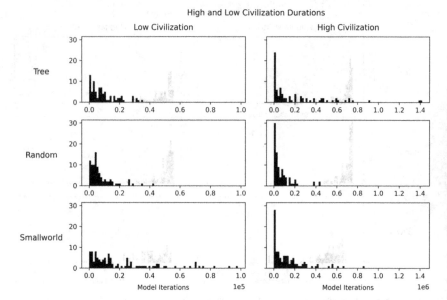

Figure 17.6 A histogram showing the distribution for the number of periods the high and low civilizations were maintained over each of multiple simulations based on each of the three layers.

and nodes can be replaced. But the villages start to have greater specialization and relationships and dependence. In low times, the village links continue independent of and largely unaffected by the rest of the world.

17.4.4 Putting It All Together in the Three-Layer System

In Figure 17.7, we combine the three layers together. We find a consistent change in the distribution when compared to each of the three-layer-specific distributions.

For both the rise and fall of civilizations, the three-layer system is both a tighter and more symmetric distribution than for any of the three layers. Consistent with this increased symmetry, the three-layer system has less weight in the left-hand tail and has an increase in weight given to the right-hand tail. That is, it has lower probability of a very swift rise or fall, and a higher probability of being on the extreme in terms of the time a rise or a fall takes.

For the time spent in the high civilization state, the three-layer system is tighter than any of the one-layer cases. It is more symmetric and thus has less weight on the left side and more on the right side. It also is much flatter.

For the time spent in the low civilization state, the three-layer system is both tighter and on average shorter than the one-layer distributions. That is, it is more likely to spend time in the low civilization state, and the time in that state is more predictable.

The interaction across layers leads to a more predictable system, and one that is less prone to short-term dynamics. This is true both for the rise and the

Distributions of Three-layer State Durations

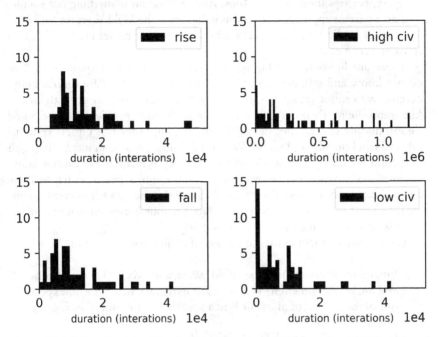

Figure 17.7 A histogram showing the distribution for the number of periods the high and low civilizations for the three-layer system. This can be compared to the results for each of the one-layer distributions.

fall of civilizations. When we look at the time spent in the low civilization compared with the high civilization, the former tends to have a shorter lifespan than for the one-layer distributions, whereas the latter has a longer lifespan. Thus, it appears that compared to the one-layer cases, connections begin to be generated more quickly and consistently, while the connections take longer to begin the downward cascade. There is more robustness for the high civilization and less robustness for the low civilization.

The reduction in the frequency of short-term changes is contrary to the general sense of what happens as we move from a one-layer to a multi-layer system, as was discussed above with the White Night. Indeed, having the three layers of government, economics, and cultural all linked together creates a less risky and more predictable structure for civilization. This might be because the layers each have different network types, and so do not have the same process and the same time frame for the propagation or breaking of connections.

17.5 Conclusion

History is not mechanistic. No area of social science is, although some—namely economics—at their peril have styled themselves to be. History is human and is subject to the sweep of invention, creativity, and adaptation. As is evident from Section 17.4, positing a civilization even within a simple system can lead to complex, perhaps inexplicable results. And civilization is anything but simple. Within a systems approach, transitions in history—the Wild West rise and Mad Max fall of civilization—can occur without a specific cause, even without an apparent set of causes.

There are limits to our knowledge; *maxim ignoramus et ignorabimus*, "we do not know and will not know." Limits related to logic: We cannot know because we cannot create a consistent, self-contained system of mathematics (the impossibility theorem); we cannot know because problems can be posed algorithmically that are not decidable (the halting problem). Others relate to processes and the physical world: We cannot know because in interacting with the world we change the world (the uncertainty principle); we cannot know because depicting the evolution of the system requires precision beyond any physical capability (chaos). For the problem of the rise and fall of civilizations, we have what I call the four horsemen. Not the four horsemen that precipitate collapse, but that constrain our study of collapse.[7]

We see two of them in the simulation of civilizations in Section 17.4:

1. Emergent phenomena. The Wild West and Mad Max transitions are emergent phenomenon, system-wide dynamics that arise unexpectedly out of the actions of individuals in a way that is not simply an aggregation of that behavior.

2. Computational irreducibility. There is a deeply held conviction that our world can reduce to models founded on the solid ground of axioms, plumbed by deductive logic into rigid, universal mathematical structures. Our behavior is so complex and our interactions so profound that there is no mathematical shortcut for determining how they will evolve. The only way to know the result of these interactions is to trace out their path over time; essentially, we must live our lives to see where they will go. We need simulations rather than mathematical models to attack computationally irreducible problems. And these problems are the norm for a dynamical system.[8]

   The two others are not part of our simple simulation but clearly envelope the whole of the study of history:

3. Non-ergodicity. An ergodic process is one that does not vary with time or experience. It follows the same probabilities today as it did in the distant past and will in the distant future. That works for physics. And for the game of roulette. But the richness of our experiences and the interplay between our experiences and interactions cannot be reduced to something like roulette. Our world changes; we learn and we discover. Our individual actions, even if based on established and deterministic rules, can lead to unexpected dynamics in the swirl of human interactions.

4. Radical uncertainty. During the war in Iraq, then Secretary of Defense Donald Rumsfeld referred, somewhat indecorously, to "unknown unknowns" when describing US operations (Rumsfeld 2002). In financial circles, the concept goes by the term "Knightian uncertainty" to

honor the economist who recognized it (Knight 1921). More broadly, it is called radical uncertainty (Kay and King 2020). It is meant to describe outcomes or events that are unanticipated, that cannot be put into a probability distribution because they are outside our list of things that might occur. History is replete with radical uncertainty, and of course this cannot be modeled; we cannot model things that we do not know exist.

These four horsemen have far-reaching implications for those undertaking the task of unraveling the mysteries of the rise and fall of civilizations. We wish every problem to have an answer. We wish our study of history to uncover the prime mover for the rise and fall of civilizations. But we cannot understand the dynamics of civilization's rise and fall unless we operate within the limits of these dynamics.

As Gaddis has remarked in *The Landscape of History*, this leaves historians "in the curious position of having come out on the cutting edge of a revolution by persisting in a thoroughly reactionary stance" (Gaddis 2002). Historians are in an enviable position, grappling with issues that are at the leading edge of scientific pursuit: dynamical systems and complexity theory.

Appendix: Matrices for Wild West and Mad Max for Ten Civilizations

Below are examples of events that relate to the Wild West and the Mad Max periods for ten civilizations:

Late Bronze Age
Roman
Han
Eastern Roman (Byzantine I)
Byzantine II
Song
Western I (with Mad Max in the fourteenth century)
Western II (Wild West only)
Polynesian
Inca (Wild West only)

These are set in a matrix with three rows and three columns that represent three layers that operate on their own and interact with the others, namely the political/military, economic, and social/cultural.

The historical events in these matrices reflect the links within and between the layers. The rows are the "from" and the columns at the "to." So, for example, for the Mad Max of Western Civilization I, the Hundred Years' War was a military event that affected the economic layer. As another example, the legend of Horatius Cocles and the Sublician Bridge, where Horatius and two companions held the bridge against the Etruscan army until it could be destroyed behind them, is a case of the political/military linking to the social/cultural (Table 17.2).

Table 17.2 Network Interaction for Wild West and Mad Max Events

Late Bronze Age Civilization(s)

Wild West

	Political/Military	Social/Cultural	Economic
Political/Military	Egyptian New Kingdom, Hittite Old Kingdom	defeat of Hyksos, centralization	Mycenaean Greece
Social/Cultural	nativism (Egypt)	Linear B, expansion of writing	Aristocracy
Economic	horses, chariots, precious metals	Reopening Eastern Mediterranean trade	Phoenician navigation, Syrian land routes

Mad Max

	Political/Military	Social/Cultural	Economic
Political/Military	Egyptian 20th dynasty, Hittite Collapse, rise of Assyria	collapse of Greek city-states	Trojan War
Social/Cultural	Sea Peoples, increasing priestly power in Egypt	literature disappears	Philistines, instability in Phoenicia
Economic	breakdown of Syrian trade routes, Egyptian famines	climate change	decline in shipbuilding, depletion of tin

Roman Civilization

Wild West

	Political/Military	Social/Cultural	Economic
Political/Military	Pyrrhic War, Samnite War, Second Punic War	Horatius Cocles and the Sublician Bridge, patrician vs. plebian	Roman roads, triumphs
Social/Cultural	Cincinnatus, secession(s) of the plebs, Etruscan influence	Twelve Tablets, *do ut des*	villa system, slavery
Economic	Ostia, Carthaginian trade routes	Greek tutors, spoils of war	Mediterranean agriculture, cornish tin

Mad Max

	Political/Military	Social/Cultural	Economic
Political/Military	divided imperium, Adrianople, Odoacer	Julian the Apostate, Sack of Rome, rapid succession of emperors	Germanic invasion, abandoning Britain
Social/Cultural	depopulation of Italy, nationalism	breakdown of patron/client, Alexandria burns, Hypatia	fleeing frontiers, hoarding money
Economic	economic collapse in the West, return of piracy	third-century cold snap, reduced public works	cutting currency, decreased shipbuilding

(*Continued*)

Table 17.2 (Continued)

Han Civilization

Wild West

	Political/Military	Social/Cultural	Economic
Political/Military	Ch'in expansion, centralization, *Kao-tzu*	*Shih Huang-Ti*, bureaucracy	forced public works
Social/Cultural	legalism, decreasing mysticism, *Ssu-ma Ch'ien*	Confucianism, Taoism, perfection of writing	peasant system
Economic	iron forging, improved food distribution	The Great Canal, agriculture on the North China Plain	sericulture

Mad Max

	Political/Military	Social/Cultural	Economic
Political/Military	child emperors, strong aristocracy	generals with independent commands	aristocratic monopolies
Social/Cultural	Yellow Turban Rebellions, imperial eunuchs	Taoist unrest, the massacre of eunuchs	North/South tension, repeated floods
Economic	loss of silk-producing regions	debased coinage, increasing use of silver	loss of the Tarim Basin

Eastern Roman Civilization

Wild West

	Political/Military	Social/Cultural	Economic
Political/Military	Constantine, *Foederati*, Armenia	Adrianople, Byzantine diplomacy	divided rule
Social/Cultural	Constantinopolis, St. Athanasius	Christian Empire, Hypatia, Council of Nicaea	closing borders, Greek nationalism
Economic	decline of the Western Empire, the Golden Horn	reduced demand for tin	short trade routes

Mad Max

	Political/Military	Social/Cultural	Economic
Political/Military	rise of Islam, Arab conquests, collapse of the Sasanian Empire	Heraclius (decline), Bulgarian Empire	depletion of manpower, corruption of officials
Social/Cultural	Plague of Justinian, early seventh-century emperors	Monophysitism, Pope Honorius I	extremes of faith (iconoclasm), decline of fleet strength
Economic	breakdown of taxation	overuse of diplomacy	loss of eastern trade routes

Byzantine Civilization

Wild West

	Political/Military	Social/Cultural	Economic
Political/Military	long siege of Constantinopolis, fall of the Umayyads, Constantine V	Empress Irene, iconoclasm	theme system

(Continued)

Table 17.2 (Continued)

Social/Cultural	cultural synthesis, third council of Constantinopolis	development of Eastern Orthodoxy, Mount Athos	development of Asia Minor
Economic	Byzantine traders, Eastern Mediterranean naval domination	agricultural improvements	restored contact with the West

Mad Max

	Political/Military	**Social/Cultural**	**Economic**
Political/Military	Kosovo and Varna, John Cantacuzenus, Constantine XI	Fourth Crusade, Ottoman foothold in Europe	Manzikert, increasing power of the nobility
Social/Cultural	depopulation of Constantinopolis, anti-Latin riots, early crusades	mystic revival, fourteenth-century cultural rebirth	tenant farmers
Economic	Genoa in Gelata	severe depletion of natural resources	Venetian trade domination

Song Civilization

Wild West

	Political/Military	**Social/Cultural**	**Economic**
Political/Military	imperial marriages, civil command, *T'ai-tzu*	less militarism, reunification in the South	separate financial administration
Social/Cultural	war weariness, civil service	Neo-Confucianism, ethnocentrism, flexible administration	improved peacetime agriculture
Economic	*Khitan* tribute, increased silver production	rebuilding canals	reopening trade, "trade diplomacy"

Mad Max

	Political/Military	**Social/Cultural**	**Economic**
Political/Military	Siege of *Kai-feng*, the Juchen Wars, Siege of *Lin-an*	the Mongols, the "Sea Suicide"	bureaucratic infighting
Social/Cultural	*Chu Hsi* school, loss of the West, cultural stability	Neo-Confucianism splinters, "Looking Back"	clerical abuses and bribery, labor-intensive solutions
Economic	debasing coinage, pleasure-loving emperors	technological decline	decreasing trade with Central Asia

Western Civilization, Part I

Wild West

	Political/Military	**Social/Cultural**	**Economic**
Political/Military	Charlemagne, early feudalism	Alfred the Great, division of the Carolingian Empire	invasions of the Northmen
Social/Cultural	"Pornocracy"	serfdom, continental monastic revival	increasing population

(*Continued*)

Table 17.2 (Continued)

Economic	stirrups, Venice	European warm period	revival of trade (Mediterranean)

Mad Max

	Political/Military	Social/Cultural	Economic
Political/Military	last Capetians, Edward II, Sicilian Vespers	John II the Good, devastation of France	Hundred Years' War
Social/Cultural	papal corruption, religious extremes, peasant revolts	Black Death, "Babylonian Captivity"	Great Famine, animal plagues
Economic	labor shortages	Little Ice Age, breakdown of spice trade	Italian trade wars

Western Civilization, Part II

Wild West

	Political/Military	Social/Cultural	Economic
Political/Military	Spanish unification, feudalism falls, Louis XIV	end of the Hundred Years' War, rise of Austria, Russia, Ottomans	colonialism, Thirty Years' War
Social/Cultural	gunpowder, English Civil War	de rerum natura, the Reformation, Renaissance Art	destruction of Aztec/Inca, Age of Sail
Economic	"Middle Class," new model army	slave trade, Spice Islands	oceanic trade

Mad Max

There is no Western Part II Mad Max yet.

Notes

1 Head of Risk and co-founder, Fabric RQ. I am indebted to Stephen Cornine for help in laying out the historical interrelationships in Table 17.1 and in the Appendix, and to Tejovan Parker for assistance with the model simulations in Section 17.4.

2 The term Mad Max comes from the film of the same name which depicts a world devolved into tribal gangs operating with vestiges of the technology of the recently destroyed industrial age, struggling as key components that keep the technology running become depleted.

3 A fourth feature, which Renfrew labels Settlement Shift and Population Decline, echoes components of Mad Max: (a) Abandonment of many settlements, (b) shift to dispersed patterns of smaller settlements, (c) "flight to the hills," and (d) marked reduction in population density (Renfrew and Cooke 1979, 482, 483).

4 See Watts on small world networks (Watts and Strogatz 1998; Watts 1999).

5 The specific parameters in the simulation are:

Number of agents = 25

$k^* = 0.6$

Exogenous/baseline Death Probability = $2e^{-5}$

Probability of connection = 0.005

For the small world network:

Tribal preference = 0.6, meaning anytime a node makes a connection, there is a 60% chance that connection will be with an agent in its tribe/village, or no connection will be made if all in-group connections have already been made. There is a 40% chance that connection will be with any random agent, which could still be with one of its village/ tribe agents.

Village size = 5, meaning there are five villages of five agents each.

For the tree network:

The number of reporter agents is 6, meaning 6 of the 25 agents only make a single in-connection (in-connections are the ones that affect the node's value of k).

6   We define the high civilization as the period where the connections are 90% or more of the maximum possible connections, and low civilization as where there are less than 40% of the maximum number of connections.

7   I have discussed these in *The End of Theory* within the context of the failure of neoclas-sical, mechanistic economics, where I call them the four horsemen of the econopolypse (Bookstaber 2017).

8   Even simpler ones, such as the three-body problem or Conway's "Game of Life" (Gardner 1970).

References

Bacher, Rainer, Urs Näf, Martin Renggli, Werner Bühlmann, and Hans Glavitsch. 2003. "Report on the Blackout in Italy on 28 September 2003." Berne: Reoprt Swiss Federal Office of Energy (SFOE). https://www.academia.edu/4736440/Swiss_Federal_Office _of_Energy_SFOE_.

Bookstaber, Richard. 2017. *The End of Theory: Financial Crises, the Failure of Economics, and the Sweep of Human Interaction*. Illustrated edition. Princeton, NJ: Princeton University Press.

Brown, Peter. 2003. *The Rise of Western Christendom: Triumph and Diversity, A.D. 200– 1000*. 2nd edition. The Making of Europe. Malden, MA: Blackwell Publishers.

Cline, Eric H. 2014. *1177 B.C.: The Year Civilization Collapsed*. Princeton, NJ: Princeton University Press.

Demandt, Alexander. 1984. *Der Fall Roms: Die Auflösung des römischen Reiches im Urteil der Nachwelt*. München: Beck.

Diamond, Jared M. 1997. *Guns, Germs, and Steel: The Fates of Human Societies*. New York : W. W. Norton & Company.

———. 2004. *Collapse: How Societies Choose to Fail or Succeed*. New York: Viking.

Gaddis, John Lewis. 2002. *The Landscape of History: How Historians Map the Past*. 1st edition. Oxford and New York: Oxford University Press.

Gardner, Martin. 1970. "Mathematical Games." *Scientific American* 223(4): 120–23.

Kay, John, and Mervyn King. 2020. *Radical Uncertainty: Decision-Making Beyond the Numbers*. 1st edition. New York: W. W. Norton & Company.

Knight, Frank H. 1921. *Risk, Uncertainty and Profit*. New York: Houghton Mifflin.

Monin, Phillip, and Richard M. Bookstaber. 2017. "Information Flows, the Accuracy of Opinions, and Crashes in a Dynamic Network." SSRN Scholarly Paper ID 3044458. Rochester, NY: Social Science Research Network. https://doi.org/10.2139/ssrn .3044458.

Povoledo, Elisabetta, and International Herald Tribune. 2003. "Massive Power Failure Sweeps Across Italy." *The New York Times*, September 28, 2003, sec. World. https://

www.nytimes.com/2003/09/28/international/europe/massive-power-failure-sweeps
-across-italy.html.

Renfrew, Colin. 1973. *Explanation of Culture Change: Models in Prehistory*. Pittsburgh, PA: University of Pittsburgh Press.

———. 1978. "Trajectory Discontinuity and Morphogenesis: The Implications of Catastrophe Theory for Archaeology." *American Antiquity* 43(2): 203–22. https://doi .org/10.2307/279245.

Renfrew, Colin, and Kenneth L. Cooke, eds. 1979. *Transformations: Mathematical Approaches to Culture Change*. 1st edition. New York: Academic Press.

Rumsfeld, Donald H. 2002. "DoD News Briefing - Secretary Rumsfeld and Gen. Myers, February 12, 2002." US Department of Defense News Transcript. https://archive.ph /20180320091111/http://archive.defense.gov/Transcripts/Transcript.aspx#selection -407.0-407.2.

Tainter, Joseph A. 1988. *The Collapse of Complex Societies*. New Studies in Archaeology. Cambridge, Cambridgeshire, and New York: Cambridge University Press. http://www .cambridge.org/us/academic/subjects/archaeology/archaeological-theory-and-methods /collapse-complex-societies.

Toynbee, Arnold J. 1934. *A Study of History*. Oxford: Oxford University Press.

Ward-Perkins, Bryan. 2005. *The Fall of Rome: And the End of Civilization*. Oxford and New York: Oxford University Press.

Watts, Duncan J. 1999. *Small Worlds*. Princeton, NJ: Princeton University Press.

Watts, Duncan J. and Steven H. Strogatz. 1998. "Collective Dynamics of 'Small-World' Networks." *Nature* 393(6684): 440–42. https://doi.org/10.1038/30918.

18 Phase Transitions and the Theory of Early Warning Indicators for Critical Transitions

George I. Hagstrom and Simon A. Levin

18.1 Introduction

Revolutions, economic collapses, and social collapses are among the most dramatic and impactful historical events. They can occur with breathtaking speed such as the fall of Socialist governments in Eastern Europe in 1989 [1] or the Black Monday 1929 stock market crash [2], and they often defy the expectations of both the general public and experts, who did not foresee such sudden changes [3]. Although exogenous shocks can play a role in triggering large-scale social or economic collapse, in many cases no such shock exists and internal dynamics instead play a dominant role [4]. Understanding how collective behavior manifests in regime shifts and identifying precursors to such shifts remain an elusive challenge in social science, economics, and other fields involving complex systems.

The term *critical transition* describes a phenomenon where a small-scale shift in the forces driving a complex system leads to a large-scale change in the state of that system [5].[1] Critical transitions commonly arise in complex systems across a number of different fields, from the social sciences and economics to ecology and geosciences. A simple dynamical system involving a ball rolling around a double-well potential (a landscape with two "valleys" or "basins" which correspond to the wells, divided or bifurcated by a peak that separates them) provides a simple illustration of critical transitions. A ball that is trapped in one of the valleys will remain there so long as any random perturbations do not have sufficient magnitude to push the ball above the peak between the two wells. However, if the shape of the landscape slowly changes so that the height difference between the well containing the ball and the peak disappears, the ball will suddenly escape from its well and roll to the other well, resulting in a transition to a different stable equilibrium. The resulting change in the system state is very large compared to the infinitesimal shift in the shape of the landscape preceding it. Furthermore, if the changes to the system reverse so that its landscape returns to the original double-well shape, the ball will remain trapped in the second well. This *hysteresis*—where a systemic transition, once triggered, may be difficult or even impossible to reverse—is a hallmark of many critical transitions, and has profound implications.

DOI: 10.4324/9781003331384-23

Critical transitions are an example of *emergent phenomena*, which arise in systems consisting of large numbers of small-scale components (people, biological organisms, firms, etc.) whose interactions give rise to system effects, patterns, and behaviors occurring on a larger, macroscopic scale, which have no direct explanation in terms of their small-scale components [6]. Physicists first developed a theory of emergence in the late 1800s, to understand how macroscopic, thermodynamic laws arise from the microscopic interactions of matter. This remarkable theory, known as statistical mechanics, shows that arrangements of extremely large numbers of atoms or molecules often behave much more simply than arrangements of just a few and that often most of the details of the intermolecular interactions disappear after the system has been coarse-grained. Statistical mechanics thus provides a prototype theory for the study of emergent phenomena within complex systems in disciplines such as ecology or the social sciences. Consequently, statistical physics found many such fruitful applications, spawning subfields such as econophysics and sociophysics [7].

Phase transitions in statistical physics—such as the boiling and freezing of water, the development of superconductivity or superfluidity at low temperatures, or the appearance of ferromagnetism in certain metals below their Curie points—are emergent phenomena that each fit the definition of a critical transition. Discontinuous (also referred to as first-order) phase transitions in particular exhibit the same abrupt shift in state and subsequent irreversibility and hysteresis as classical critical transitions caused by a saddle-node bifurcation—a phenomenon similar to the double—well potential that we address below. Because of the overlaps between phenomena, the theory of phase transitions could insight into critical transitions and in particular how they manifest from dynamics on small scales.

The magnitude and irreversibility of critical transitions—both potentially catastrophic consequences—have motivated attempts to identify transition precursors, quantities, or metrics that indicate an impending transition when they cross a threshold [8]. In the example with the ball on the landscape, as the well containing the ball merges with the peak separating the ball from the other valley, the curve of the landscape surrounding the ball flattens. This flattening reduces the magnitude of the restoring forces that confine the ball to its equilibrium state, with consequences for the movement of the ball under the natural stochastic perturbations present in the system. Time series measurements of the location of the ball show *critical slowing down*, a phenomenon in which the relaxation time required for the ball to return to its equilibrium state diverges approaching the transition. The relaxation time depends on the convexity of the landscape in the neighborhood of the equilibrium state, and as the landscape becomes flatter approaching the transition, the strength of the restoring force vanishes and the return time of the ball to equilibrium becomes infinite. With velocity measured as distance divided by time, the speed at which the ball returns to its steady state thus slows down.

In addition to critical slowing down, the system's movement toward the critical transition leads to increased variance, auto-correlation, and skewness in the time series data for the system (position in the case of the ball), and increases in these quantities may thus warn of an impending critical transition, as has been proposed in multiple studies. These time series-based early warning indicators have a rigorous mathematical basis in the theory of bifurcations and stochastic dynamical systems, where the *saddle-node* or equivalently *cusp* bifurcation provides a simple normal form that illustrates many of the key phenomena that happen in critical transitions [9].

Despite the simplicity of early warning indicators as tools for detecting saddle-node bifurcations in one-dimensional dynamical systems, their application to real-world systems has yet to live up to their initial promise [10]. The reasons for this include high false-positive rates due to the *prosecutor's fallacy* [11], a problem of selection bias that arises from developing summary statistics-based thresholds in systems already known to exhibit bifurcations, difficulties with statistical estimation, and the inconvenient fact that real systems may exhibit much more complexity than indicated by a simple one-dimensional bifurcation. Indeed, although using a simplified "toy model" of one-dimensional time series or dynamical systems to represent a much more complex system enables the use of early warning systems for any system where we can make crude measurements, using instead a more complex framework that embraces the high dimensional complexity of these systems may lead to more robust early warning signals and also leverage the growth in data gathering and analysis capabilities that has occurred in recent years.

Statistical physics, and phase transitions in particular, seems like it could provide a framework to extend early warning indicators beyond those derived from one-dimensional dynamical systems. However, an attempt to synthesize phase transitions with early warning indicators immediately encounters inconsistencies, and critical transitions exhibit a mixture of phenomena usually found in different types of phase transitions. Phase transitions naturally divide into two classes (described in more detail in Section 18.2): (1) *discontinuous* or *first-order* phase transitions involve an abrupt, discontinuous change in the state of the system, such as the boiling of liquid to gas or the melting of a solid into a liquid state; and (2) *continuous* or *second-order* phase transitions (technically continuous describes second and all higher order phase transitions), which involve the appearance of long-range correlations, diverging susceptibility to external forces, and sometimes a change in the symmetry properties of the state of a system, such as the appearance of spontaneous magnetization in a ferromagnetic material at the Curie point, or the onset of superconductivity or superfluidity. The phenomena that occur at continuous transitions are called *critical*, and continuous transitions are often called *critical points*. Early warning indicators for critical transitions, including critical slowing down, increasing variance, auto-correlation, and spatial correlations also appear in the approach to a continuous transition, but other aspects of the phenomenology of these continuous transitions are inconsistent with saddle-node bifurcations. For example, continuous transitions do not exhibit irreversibility, hysteresis, or generally a large-scale jump in the state of the system. Discontinuous transitions, as we alluded to earlier, do exhibit these characteristics: At a discontinuous phase transition, the state of the system jumps discontinuously, and reversing the parameters that trigger the transition does not immediately lead to a reversal of the transition. However, as we will explain in Section 18.2, in the formalism of statistical physics, discontinuous phase transitions do not exhibit precursory phenomena or have early warning indicators.

In this chapter, we have two goals: (1) propose a resolution to the inconsistency between phase transitions and critical transitions and (2) propose early warning indicators inspired directly by the theory of phase transitions that could portend critical transitions in economic and social systems that involve collective interactions. We will accomplish this by shifting to a non-equilibrium framing of phase transitions, one which bears a much closer resemblance to the way that critical transitions occur in the real world. In making this shift, we will see that the lack of precursors of discontinuous phase transitions comes from how discontinuous phase transitions occur in equilibrium statistical mechanics and that a related concept called a *spinodal instability* [12] properly bridges the disconnect between critical transitions and discontinuous phase transitions, applying in the non-equilibrium situations that interest us. Spinodal instabilities share many characteristics of continuous phase transitions, including critical phenomena like divergent susceptibilities, long-range correlations, and critical slowing down, allowing for the development of early warning indicators. This critical behavior has rarely been observed in physical systems and so has remained understudied, but its generalization to out-of-equilibrium, athermal, or complex systems appears much more commonly [13] and thus we argue that the spinodal instability is an ideal toy model or normal form for some critical transitions that takes into consideration the full complexity of those systems.

18.2 Equilibrium Phase Transitions and Precursors

Statistical mechanics shows how macroscopic behavior emerges in physical systems from microscopic laws when there are large numbers of interacting molecules or atoms. Statistical mechanics involves a transition of viewpoints, starting with Newton's laws of motion (or whatever is analogous to the given system), and then abandoning the tracking of the state and trajectory of every single particle in favor of a probabilistic description— which is achieved by integrating over microscopic dynamics and thus zooming out to macroscopic scales where stochastic dynamics and statistical convergence overtake the determinism of classical Newtonian mechanics. The Gibbs–Boltzmann distribution lies at the heart of this description: Statistical mechanics postulates the probability of a given configuration of particles exchanging heat or other thermodynamic quantities with an environment. The macroscopic laws governing the system, which fundamentally relate the moments of the Gibbs–Boltzmann distribution to the parameters of the system and to each other, emerge in the thermodynamic limit, which involves allowing the system size to go to infinity. In this limit, the central-limit theorem leads to the suppression of fluctuations in macroscopic quantities.

Before we take the thermodynamic limit, moments of the Gibbs–Boltzmann distribution are *analytic* functions (infinitely differentiable and equal to their Taylor series expansion in a neighborhood of each point) of the temperature and other system parameters, due to the analyticity of the probability distribution. Thus finite systems only have smooth changes with external parameters (such as the temperature or externally applied fields) in equilibrium statistical mechanics. However, this analyticity does not always survive taking the thermodynamic limit. At places where it loses smoothness, macroscopic thermodynamic variables can exhibit discontinuities or other types of non-smooth behavior. These manifest as sudden changes in the macroscopic properties of the system caused by infinitesimal changes in the parameter values and are called *phase transitions*.

The simplest way to illustrate phase transitions and their relationship to critical transitions makes use of the approximate Ginzburg–Landau theory [14], developed initially to describe superconductivity. Ginzburg–Landau theory is based on the *free energy* of a physical system, which can be derived using the Gibbs–Boltzmann distribution and describes the thermodynamics equilibria of the system (on a macroscopic scale). Ginzburg–Landau formulates the free energy as a function of an abstract order parameter, which we imagine to be the magnetization m, an external field h, and the relative temperature T. The Ginzburg–Landau free energy takes the following form:

$$F(m,T,h) = N\mu\left(-hm + aTm^2 + bm^4\right)$$

Here N stands for the system size (number of spins in a magnetic system), a and b are constants, and μ is another constant, in some applications the magnetic moment of a single spin. According to equilibrium thermodynamics, the system state occupies the minimum of this free energy function. Figure 18.1 shows a plot of the free energy for different values of T at $h = 0$. When $T \geq 0$, the free energy F has a single global minimum at $m = 0$ and no local maxima. If T decreases and crosses through zero, a pitchfork bifurcation occurs creating two new minima and converting the original minima at $m = 0$ into a local maxima, so that the full set of extrema are $m = 0$ and $m = \pm\sqrt{-at/4b}$. The two new minima have lower values of free energy than the unmagnetized state at $m = 0$, and so the system undergoes a phase transition at $T = 0$ to either the positive or negative magnetization state. The development of magnetization is an example of spontaneous symmetry breaking—the free energy is symmetric under the reversal of all the spins, yet the state with spontaneous magnetization either has a negative or positive magnetization. The point $T = 0$ and $m = 0$ is called a *critical point* (the origin of the name does not refer to the calculus concept), and it is characterized by several notable features, namely power law *scaling* of system features approaching the transition.

Continuous Phase Transition

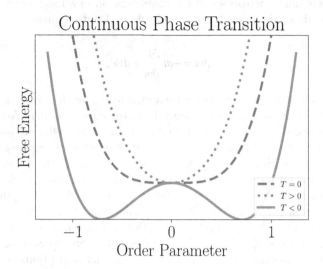

Discontinuous Phase Transition

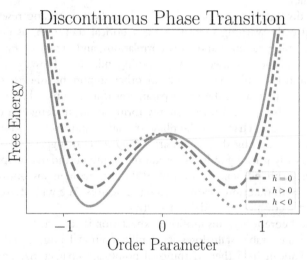

Figure 18.1 Phase transitions using the Ginzburg–Landau normal form. Figure (A) shows a continuous phase transition triggered by varying T while holding the external field parameter h constant at $h = 0$. With magnetization m as the order parameter, the free energy $F(m, T, h)$ undergoes a pitchfork bifurcation from a state at $m = 0$ to a state with spontaneous, non-zero magnetization m. At the critical temperature $T = 0$, the spatial and temporal correlations, the relaxation time, and the susceptibility to both temperature and the external field diverge. Figure (B), also with order parameter m, shows a discontinuous phase transition, driven by changing the external field parameter h, while T is held at a constant value $T < 0$. The transition occurs when the free energy levels of the two global minima are equal to each other. Unlike during the discontinuous transition, no significant change occurs in the local shape of the free energy at the transition point, and thus no critical phenomena occur.

First consider fluctuations of the magnetization in a Langevin framework. We write down the time-dependent Ginzburg–Landau equation:

$$dm = -dt \frac{\partial F}{\partial m} + dW,$$

where dW is noise. The restoring force that maintains the magnetization at a minimum of the free energy F depends on the curvature of F. Approaching the phase transition, the characteristic time for a return to the minimum scales as $t_{eq} \sim |T|^{-1}$. At the transition itself, the relaxation time diverges—a phenomenon known as critical slowing down. Also interesting are the susceptibility of the system to changes in either T or the external field h, both of which exhibit power law divergences at the critical point with the field following the following scalings: $m \sim |T|^{1/2}$ and $m \sim |h|^{1/3}$. One can consider the spatial variation in the system and study the correlation length as a function of T, deriving in the mean field context $\zeta \sim |T|^{-1/2}$, which shows that when approaching the critical point, the system becomes scale-free and spatial fluctuations occur on all length scales.

These divergences and power law scalings bear a striking resemblance to traditional early warning indicators for a critical transition, as critical slowing down, rising variance and auto-correlations, and diverging spatial correlations have all been proposed as early warning indicators. However, continuous phase transitions differ significantly in other important aspects from critical transitions. In particular, the order parameter (for example, the magnetization m in the Ginzburg–Landau free energy formulation) undergoes a continuous, rather than abrupt, change at the phase transition and the transition reverses if the parameters driving the system are reversed. This suggests two things: (1) traditional early warning indicators require careful use and may be produced by very different phenomena, and (2) we still must reconcile discontinuous phase transitions with traditional early warning indicators. We will attempt the latter in the next section on spinodal instabilities.

At least theoretically, this intuitive expectation is correct. We call the points where the metastable state loses its stability spinodal points, and within the context of mean field theory, spinodal points are characterized by much of the same phenomenology as critical points: They experience critical slowing down, they develop infinite susceptibility, and they develop power law spatial and temporal correlations. On this basis, we propose the spinodal instability as a potential candidate for connecting the theory of discontinuous phase transitions to critical transitions.

18.3 Discontinuous Phase Transitions and Spinodal Instabilities

Consider again the Ginzburg–Landau free energy introduced in the previous section, but now assume that $T < 0$ and that the external field parameter $h = 0$.

Figure 18.1B shows the free energy for several different values of the mag-netic field h. For the values shown, the free energy has two minima, one with positive and the other with negative magnetization. The magnitude of the applied field h determines which is the global minimum, and thus the state at equilibrium. If the field h varies from negative to positive, then there is a discontinuous phase transition where the system switches from a negative mag-netization to a positive one. The magnetization m jumps discontinuously at the transition. However, no special dynamical behavior occurs at the discontinuous phase transition point; relaxation times, correlation lengths, and susceptibilities remain finite. There is no sign of the impending phase transition because the shapes of the local minima do not change at the phase transition point.

The kinetics of discontinuous phase transitions depend on the particu-lar details of the system, and the transition requires time to occur. This time depends on the height of the free energy barrier and the relative temperature T of the system, which determines the rate of fluctuations large enough to push the system over the barrier into the global free energy minimum. Systems can remain trapped in these metastable states for significant—practically infinite—periods of time should the potential barrier be high enough. Diamonds provide the most famous example of such a metastable state—the graphite phase has a lower free energy at standard temperature and pressure but the activation energy barrier prevents the occurrence of the phase transition.

The spinodal instability provides a way for a system in a metastable state to transition to its thermodynamically stable equilibrium without requiring ther-mal fluctuation. Spinodal instabilities occur when the metastable state ceases to be a local minimum of the free energy, thus causing it to lose local thermody-namic stability. When the system reaches the spinodal point, the energy barrier disappears and the system spontaneously transitions to the equilibrium state. Figure 18.2 illustrates the spinodal instability of a system using the Ginzburg–Landau functional form. Here we continue increasing the external field, caus-ing the height difference between the two free energy minima to increase. Eventually the local minimum disappears as the local minimum and maximum collide in a saddle-node bifurcation, allowing the system to freely flow to the global free energy minimum.

Due to the vanishing of the second derivative of the free energy at the spinodal point, Ginzburg–Landau theory predicts critical or critical-like behav-ior. The relaxation time diverges as $t_{eq} \sim |h - h_0|^{-1}$, the heat capacity as $C \sim |h - h_0|^{-\frac{1}{2}}$, the magnetic susceptibility ($\xi = \partial m / \partial h$) as $\xi \sim |h - h_0|^{-1/2}$, and the correlation length as $\zeta \sim |h - h_0|^{-1/4}$. Thus, just like in the case of the critical point, a spinodal instability has a number of different precursors that could indicate the presence of an impending critical transition.

Spinodal instabilities are the natural analogs of critical transitions based on saddle-node bifurcations in the context of statistical physics. They exhibit a large-scale change in system state, hysteresis/irreversibility, and arise from the same saddle-node bifurcation within the context of time-dependent

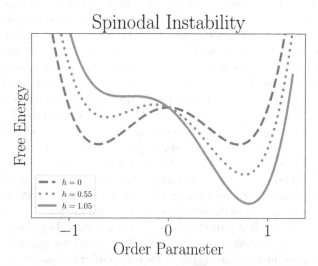

Figure 18.2 Spinodal instability triggered by changing external fields. With order parameter magnetization m, as the field parameter h increases, while temperature T is held at a constant value $T < 0$, the system undergoes a discontinuous phase transition but the system may remain trapped in a metastable state for a long period of time before reaching the other equilibrium state. At a certain critical value of the field parameter h, this metastable state loses stability and the system shifts rapidly to the lowest free energy state. Approaching the spinodal point, relaxation times, susceptibilities of the order parameter to external fields and temperature, and correlation functions may diverge, though with different critical exponents than during a continuous phase transition.

Ginzburg–Landau theory. Unlike discontinuous phase transitions, the loss of local stability leads to pronounced precursor phenomena through the critical exponents, which match our expectations derived from early warning indicators for critical transitions. However, continuous phase transitions have qualitatively similar precursors, and finding a way to distinguish between a spinodal instability and a critical point would be of enormous practical use. Table 18.1 summarizes the properties of critical transitions, discontinuous and continuous phase transitions, and spinodal instabilities.

18.4 Early Warning Signals in the Fiber Bundle Model

Critical phenomena occupy a special role in physics, and the universality of critical phenomena has captured the imagination of scientists in a variety of fields, from biology to economics to the social sciences. The concept known as *self-organized criticality* even posits that critical phenomena appear generically in complex systems, leading to the ubiquitous power law behavior observed in both natural and social systems. Spinodal criticality has drawn substantially less interest, and was discovered much more recently [13]. This relative lack of interest likely relates to the belief that spinodal criticality cannot be demonstrated in

Table 18.1 Comparison of phenomena accompanying critical transitions, continuous and discontinuous phase transitions, and spinodal instabilities

	Critical transitions	Discontinuous phase transitions	Continuous phase transitions	Spinodal instability
Domain	Complex systems	Physics	Physics	Physics
Example	Government collapse	Boiling water	Spontaneous magnetization of ferromagnets	Material failure under stress
Early warning	Yes	No	Yes	Yes
Abrupt shift	Yes	Yes	No	Yes
Hysteresis	Yes	Yes	No	Yes

real physical systems because thermal fluctuations will cause a phase transition before the system reaches the spinodal point. Although recent progress has been made demonstrating spinodal criticality in the superconducting Mott transition [15], spinodal instabilities arise regularly in a wide variety of non-equilibrium systems that have applications in the social sciences and other complex systems, in particular *athermal* systems with *quenched disorder*, and other non-equilibrium systems associated with damage phenomena. In these systems, temperature and thermal fluctuations play no role, and the system dynamics instead follow some deterministic rule—such as a spin in a magnet flipping when the local value of the magnetic field exceeds a certain threshold, a fiber in a material breaking when the stress reaches a certain level, or a farmer choosing to switch crops when conditions are suitable enough. Quenched disorder means that the system consists of heterogeneous elements—in our examples each spin, fiber, or farmer has a different threshold for changing its state. The probability distribution that describes the disorder of these elements plays the role of temperature in determining the properties of the system. These systems often evolve via *cascades* or *avalanches*, where the change in the state of a single element triggers other elements to change their state as well.

Spinodal criticality was first used to understand and predict impending transitions in geophysics. Earthquakes exhibit behavior characteristic of both discontinuous and continuous phase transitions, most famously the power law distribution of the earthquake frequency magnitude relation, known as the Gutenberg–Richter law [16]. Self-organized criticality offered a potential explanation, suggesting that the constant development of stresses in the Earth's crust continually drives the system to the critical point, with stress released through periodic earthquakes. However, the sudden drop in stress after an earthquake is much more characteristic of the discontinuous change at a discontinuous phase transition. Rundle et al. [16] developed a theory of earthquakes as a damage phenomenon described by a spinodal instability. Their theory predicted that a series of cascades (in this case *foreshocks*) characterized by critical exponents coming from the theory of spinodal instabilities precede large earthquakes, enabling their prediction.

Athermal systems with the quenched disorder also manifest avalanche cascades with such properties [13, 17]. A classic example is the phenomenon of Barkhausen noise, which are the avalanches of spin flips that occur in a magnet under an applied field. The zero-temperature Random Field Ising Model describes Barkhausen avalanches and has also been generalized to apply to a wide variety of sociological and economic phenomena, such as market crashes, spontaneous adoption of new technologies, or even political revolutions [18]. Here, however, we focus on an even simpler example of spinodal instability, the fiber bundle model (FBM).

The FBM provides a simple example of an exactly soluble, athermal model exhibiting spinodal criticality and large-scale failures. Originally invented to model the pattern of fiber failures and the eventual breakage of materials placed under increasing strain, the fiber bundle model has applications well beyond materials science, and it has been used to study fragility in food networks and other supply chains. It has also been applied to collective emergent social phenomena such as the sudden adoption of a behavior, for example, the formation of lines before boarding gates at airports or the cessation of applause following concerts. The fiber bundle model bears a close relationship to other important athermal systems which exhibit avalanche cascades and have been used to study social dynamics (including the Random Field Ising Model mentioned above). Here we select it to illustrate early warning indicators because of its relative simplicity and broad applicability.

In its materials science formulation, the fiber bundle model describes a material composed of a large number N of individual fibers. The ends of the material experience a tensile force pulling in the direction of the fibers, causing the fibers to elongate according to Hooke's law, which describes the force needed to elongate a coil spring. In the *democratic* fiber bundle model (DFBM), the strain in the material distributes equally among the fibers, so that the elongation relates simply to the number of fibers and the total strain:

$$\sigma = \frac{kx}{N}.$$

Here the spring constant k relates the strain σ to the elongation distance of the fibers x. Each fiber has a maximum elongation, beyond which it ruptures in a tensile or ductile failure. The elongation threshold length x_c for each fiber follows a probability distribution $p(x_c)$. Ruptured fibers do not bear any strain, and their breaking causes a redistribution of the load to the remaining fibers. Depending on the external strain σ, the material may come to a new equilibrium with some fraction of its fibers broken, but still be able to support the load. Conversely, if the load exceeds a certain critical threshold, all of the fibers will break and the material will fail catastrophically.

Consider a material experiencing a quasistatic increase in external stress. As the stress increases, fibers will begin to elongate beyond their thresholds and thus rupture. These ruptures will further increase the elongation, which may push other fibers across their thresholds and so on. The result is that as the stress slowly increases, a series of avalanches occur which slowly damage the material. Near the critical level of stress, one giant avalanche destroys a significant fraction of the fibers in the material, causing its failure. This catastrophic avalanche represents a spinodal instability—the stress-bearing state of the material is metastable, and at the failure point, the system transitions to the broken state. In the vicinity of this spinodal point, the avalanches exhibit spinodal criticality. The mean avalanche magnitude diverges at the spinodal point with a critical exponent of $-1/2$:

$$N_A \sim \left(\sigma_c - \sigma\right)^{-\frac{1}{2}}$$

Figure 18.3 illustrates an avalanche cascade in the DFBM with a uniform distribution of failure points. The power law scaling appears well before the actual spinodal point, suggesting the possibility of detecting the imminent collapse as proposed by Pradhan et al. [19] (and by Rundle et al. [16] in the specific context of earthquake prediction) who suggested using the power law behavior in a variety of complexity systems which exhibit either self-organized criticality or spinodal instability as precursors of large-scale disruptions or critical transitions.

Here we develop a system to predict the time of catastrophic failure in the DFBM from the time series of avalanches. Instead of using threshold or summary statistics-based approaches, which suffer from the difficulty of selecting an appropriate significance threshold, poor null models, low statistical power, and an inability to quantify uncertainty [10], we instead employ a Bayesian model-based system that fits the avalanche time series either to a distribution which has an explicit power law term to compute a posterior distribution of blow-up times and use information-criteria based model comparisons to compare with other possible null models.

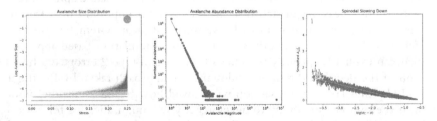

Figure 18.3 Avalanche behavior and critical exponents in the democratic fiber bundle model (DFBM): (Left) As stress increases, avalanche size increases, until a single avalanche many orders of magnitude greater in size than all preceding avalanches causes catastrophic failure of the entire bundle. (Center) The avalanche magnitude-abundance distribution shows a $-5/2$ power law scaling. (Right) The size of the mean avalanche increases approaching the spinodal point with a critical exponent of $-1/2$.

Specifically, given a time series of avalanche sizes N_t, we partition the time series into a large number of discrete windows and fit the avalanche distribution in each interval to a Borel distribution (avalanches at fixed strain follow a Borel distribution [20]) using maximum-likelihood methods. We then fit two alternative models to the resulting time series, a blow-up model that includes a term proportional to $\left(t_c - t\right)^{-1/2}$ and a null model that fits a parabolic function to the time series. The blow-up model takes the form:

$$\bar{N}_A(t) \sim C_0 + C_1 t + C_2 \left(t_c - t\right)^{-1/2} + \text{normal}(0, \epsilon)$$

while the null model obeys:

$$\bar{N}_A(t) \sim C_0 + C_1 t + C_2 t^2 + \text{normal}(0, \epsilon)$$

We similarly fit the parameters of each of these models to the time series using a Bayesian approach, implementing the models in the Stan probabilistic programming language [21, 22]. In the case of the blow-up model, we determined from partial time series in the lead-up to the catastrophe the posterior probability of each catastrophe time by marginalizing over the other parameters. We used the Widely Applicable Information Criterion (WAIC) [23] to compare the null model to the blow-up model, which we computed using leave-one-out cross-validation [24]. This allows for the comparison of models with different numbers of parameters. When the null model has a similar statistical weight to the blow-up model, we conclude that there does not exist sufficient evidence in the time series to predict a catastrophe.

Figure 18.4 shows how the posterior distribution of the failure time t_c evolves as the time series advances, and how the WAIC can quickly identify the correct model. Even a fair distance from the transition, the posterior begins to converge around the correct time, and all of the weight transfers to the blow-up model. Using the model based on the correct normal form for the bifurcation, we can provide early warning of catastrophic failure with robust measures of statistical uncertainty. An important next step in the development of such an early warning indicator system for use in a decision-theoretic framework is extending to a simulation-based approach that can explicitly quantify the rates of type 1 and type 2 errors as a function of the decision threshold, following the approach taken by Boettiger and Hastings [10]. In this section we showed how to use critical behavior near the spinodal instability to develop early warning indicators for critical transitions in complex systems. These early warning indicators were based on the statistics of failure cascades and could be applied to situations where elements of the system can change from one state to another after a threshold is crossed. This scenario commonly occurs in social science and economics, and our methods could help build an improved understanding of social and economic systems and collapses in particular.

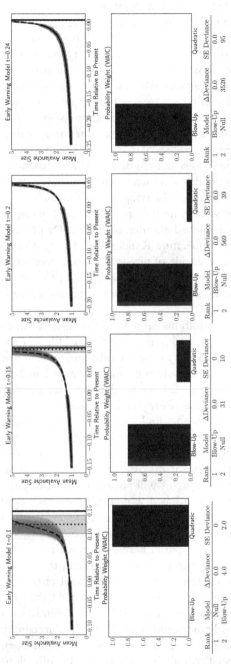

Figure 18.4 Prediction of catastrophic failure times in the democratic fiber bundle model from time series data. Each column of the top row shows draws from the posterior distribution of predictions of the mean avalanche size from a time series. Each time series originates from the same numerical simulation, but each (moving left-to-right across the chart) includes more data. Catastrophic failure occurs at time $t = 0.25009$, the first time series cuts off at $t = 0.1$, the second time series at $t = 0.15$, the third at $t = 0.2$, and the final at $t = 0.24$. The time value on each axis is relative to the point at which each time series stops. The solid trajectory is the mean of the posterior distribution. Trajectories from the avalanche data, and the dashed line at $t > 0$ corresponds to the mean forward projection of the posterior distribution. Trajectories from posterior draws are also plotted (light shaded curves near the dashed line), and the mean avalanche sizes from the RFIM data set are plotted using lightly shaded circles. The solid dotted line is the mean prediction for when failure occurs, the shaded rectangle surrounding it is a 95% credible interval of the failure time, and the solid black vertical line marks the actual failure location. The second and third rows of this figure show a model comparison between the blow-up and a quadratic (null) model, with row two comparing model weights computed using PSIS-LOO and posterior stacking, and row three showing the difference between model deviance as well as the standard error of that estimate. As the final point of the time series gets closer to failure, the predictive accuracy improves rapidly. For the first time series, the quadratic (null) model performs better than the blow-up model, but at all subsequent points the blow-up model becomes increasingly better.

18.5 Conclusions and Prospects

Critical transitions have always shared a close but imprecise connection with statistical physics and phase transitions. Here we propose making the analogy between the two concepts more direct, associating critical transitions in complex systems with the spinodal instability of statistical physics. This interpretation simplifies several seeming inconsistencies between the two concepts: The mismatch between the abrupt nature of critical transitions, which resemble discontinuous phase transitions, with the appearance of power laws and other precursor phenomena which normally occur only near critical points at continuous phase transitions. Spinodal instabilities, which occur when a metastable state loses stability, causing an abrupt transition to a thermodynamically stable state, simultaneously exhibit both characteristics of discontinuous and continuous phase transitions, though the criticality observed near spinodal points has received much less attention in the physics literature due to difficulties observing it experimentally.

However, it has been known for some time that spinodal criticality can be easily seen in athermal systems with quenched disorder, such as the Democratic Fiber Bundle Model and the Zero-Temperature Random Field Ising Model, models that have been widely applied outside of physics to social, economic, and ecological phenomena. In particular, the abrupt transitions that occur in these systems can model the large-scale collapse of complex social systems such as governments or trade networks.

Much of the research on critical transitions centers on the idea that they may exhibit precursory phenomena that enable their prediction. One of the strongest potential applications of the physics of the spinodal instability is that it provides a principled means of deriving early warning indicators based on the critical exponents near the spinodal point. Here we demonstrated the feasibility of this idea by building a model-based early warning indicator for the catastrophic failure of the fiber bundle model under increasing stress, which predicts a probability distribution for failure times and compares it with a null model that has no failure. Although the early warning indicator we proposed here is relatively simple, based on scaling of the avalanche size distribution near the spinodal point, more complex systems will possess a variety of critical exponents that can be simultaneously studied. Universality is a powerful phenomenon that causes seemingly different systems to have identical critical exponents, a tool that can be leveraged to extend knowledge between the collapses in different systems. Making a connection between critical transitions and phase transitions will help realize the tremendous promise in the theory of early warning indicators for critical transitions, but substantial challenges still remain. The ideas presented here relied heavily on mean field theories, which make for simpler analysis but can sometimes behave differently than low dimensional systems near spinodal points. Although the spinodal instability clearly arises in the special case exhibited here (and in other cases of interest), it is possible that some of the associated critical phenomena become difficult to observe in real-world systems. The power laws that we proposed to indicate an approaching spinodal instability can also indicate the presence of a regular critical point, which would not lead to an abrupt transition or an irreversible catastrophe. This study suggests several questions for further research. How easy is it to distinguish between spinodal instabilities and regular criticality? Lastly, the spinodal instability requires testing outside the context of systems from physics or materials science. Will social or economic systems provide enough data to fit models of the type that we proposed to use? Some promising work exists suggesting that it is possible to detect critical exponents indicative of a spinodal point in low-data systems such as the collapse of applause after a concert, and the dramatic increase in the availability of social and economic data in recent years gives us hope that we can find plenty of data-rich systems on which to test our hypotheses.

18.6 Acknowledgment

We would like to thank Pablo Debenedetti for helpful discussions on the physics of phase transitions and spinodal points. We would like to thank the editors of this volume, in particular Thayer Patterson, for helpful suggestions on the first draft of this manuscript. We also acknowledge gratefully support from the Army Research Office grant—W911NF-18-1-0325, the National Science Foundation Grants DMS 1951358, CCF1917819, and OCE1848576, the National Oceanic and Atmospheric Administration grant NA18OAR4320123, and DARPA Young Faculty Award number N66001-17-1-4038.

Note

1 The term *critical* appears in several contexts in the sciences, which unfortunately causes ambiguity in cross-disciplinary research such as complex systems. In dynamical systems, critical points refer to phenomena which occur when an important function has a critical point in the sense of calculus, or a point where the derivative of a function vanishes or does not exist. In a dynamical system that depends on a parameter p, $\dot{x} = f(x, p)$, when a critical point of f (for a multi-dimensional system, this means the Jacobian of f is singular) coincides with an equilibrium point, a *bifurcation* can occur, leading to a change in the number of equilibrium points. Alternatively, in a dynamical system defined by a gradient flow, $\dot{x} = \nabla \varphi(x)$, the critical points of φ are the equilibrium points of the dynamical system. Lastly, in thermodynamics, the term "critical point" (or critical temperature) was invented to describe a point where the gas and liquid phases of a substance become indistinguishable. The origin of the term "critical point" in thermodynamics does not reference the calculus critical point, but this phenomenon does coincide with critical points of some thermodynamic functions.

References

1. T. Kuran. The east European revolution of 1989: Is it surprising that we were surprised? *The American Economic Review*, 81(2):121–125, 1991.

2. D. Sornette. *Why Stock Markets Crash: Critical Events in Complex Financial Systems*, Volume 49. Princeton University Press, 2017.

3. T. Kuran. Sparks and prairie fires: A theory of unanticipated political revolution. *Public Choice*, 61(1):41–74, 1989.

4. N. S. Glance, and B. A. Huberman. The outbreak of cooperation. *Journal of Mathematical Sociology*, 17(4):281–302, 1993.

5. M. Scheffer. *Critical Transitions in Nature and Society*, Volume 16. Princeton University Press, 2020.

6. S. A. Levin. Ecosystems and the biosphere as complex adaptive systems. *Ecosystems*, 1(5):431–436, 1998.

7. S. N. Durlauf. How can statistical mechanics contribute to social science? *Proceedings of the National Academy of Sciences*, 96(19):10582–10584, 1999.

8. M. Scheffer, J. Bascompte, W. A. Brock, V. Brovkin, S. R. Carpenter, V. Dakos, H. Held, E. H. Van Nes, M. Rietkerk, and G. Sugihara. Early-warning signals for critical transitions. *Nature*, 461(7260):53–59, 2009.

9. C. Kuehn. A mathematical framework for critical transitions: Bifurcations, fast–slow systems and stochastic dynamics. *Physica D: Nonlinear Phenomena*, 240(12):1020–1035, 2011.

10. C. Boettiger, and A. Hastings. Quantifying limits to detection of early warning for critical transitions. *Journal of the Royal Society Interface*, 9(75):2527–2539, 2012.

11. C. Boettiger, and A. Hastings. Early warning signals and the prosecutor's fallacy. *Proceedings of the Royal Society B: Biological Sciences*, 279(1748):4734–4739, 2012.

12. P. G. Debenedetti. *Metastable Liquids: Concepts and Principles*, Volume 1. Princeton University Press, 1996.

13. S. G. Abaimov. *Statistical Physics of Non-Thermal Phase Transitions: From Foundations to Applications*. Springer, 2015.

14. V. L. Ginzburg, and L. D. Landau. On the theory of superconductivity. In *On Superconductivity and Superfluidity*. Springer, 2009, pp. 113–137.

15. S. Kundu, T. Bar, R. K. Nayak, and B. Bansal. Critical slowing down at the abrupt mott transition: When the first-order phase transition becomes zeroth order and looks like second order. *Physical Review Letters*, 124(9):095703, 2020.

16. J. B. Rundle, W. Klein, D. L. Turcotte, and B. D. Malamud. Precursory seismic activation and critical-point phenomena. In *Microscopic and Macroscopic Simulation: Towards Predictive Modelling of the Earthquake Process*. Springer, 2000, pp. 2165–2182.

17. S. Zapperi, P. Ray, H. E. Stanley, and A. Vespignani. First-order transition in the breakdown of disordered media. *Physical Review Letters*, 78(8):1408, 1997.

18. J.-P. Bouchaud. Crises and collective socio-economic phenomena: Simple models and challenges. *Journal of Statistical Physics*, 151(3–4):567–606, 2013.

19. S. Pradhan, and B. K. Chakrabarti. Precursors of catastrophe in the Bak-Tang-Wiesenfeld, Manna, and random-fiber-bundle models of failure. *Physical Review E*, 65(1):016113, 2001.

20. A. Hansen. The distribution of simultaneous fiber failures in fiber bundles. *Journal of Applied Mechanics*, 59(4):909, 1992.

21. Stan Development Team. Stan modeling language users guide and reference manual, v. 2.26. 2021.

22. B. Carpenter, A. Gelman, M. D. Hoffman, D. Lee, B. Goodrich, M. Betan-Court, M. Brubaker, J. Guo, P. Li, and A. Riddell. Stan: A probabilistic programming language. *Journal of Statistical Software*, 76(1), 2017.

23. S. Watanabe, and M. Opper. Asymptotic equivalence of Bayes cross validation and widely applicable information criterion in singular learning theory. *Journal of Machine Learning Research*, 11(12): 3571–3594, 2010.

24. A. Vehtari, A. Gelman, and J. Gabry. Practical Bayesian model evaluation using leave-one-out cross-validation and WAIC. *Statistics and Computing*, 27(5):1413–1432, 2017.

19 The Lifespan of Civilizations

Do Societies "Age," or Is Collapse Just Bad Luck?

Anders Sandberg

19.1 Introduction: The Course of Civilization

Do civilizations age? In many minds the archetype may be somewhat like Thomas Cole's series of paintings "The Course of Empire" (1833–1836) showing the same location over the ages: first a primitive savage state, then an Arcadian pastoral scene with emerging arts, then a grandiose classical city, then sack and destruction, and finally moonlit overgrown marble ruins. There is a clear life cycle.

We care about complex social organizations like states and civilizations for many reasons. They can allow the growth of human capital and well-being through economies of scale, as well as the accumulation of wealth and knowledge over time. They can maintain long-term projects, whether they are irrigation systems, the building of cathedrals, recording of astronomy and history, or various forms of moral, artistic, and scientific exploration. The coordinating power of complex societies may be necessary for averting local and global risks, and in the present and future reducing the threat of existential risks (Bostrom & Cirkovic 2011).

Conversely, their decline or fall induces significant losses of well-being, knowledge, and population—and may now induce existential risks. Had the Roman or Mongol empires possessed effective nuclear or biological weapons, the world might not have survived.

Even if the collapse is not the end of everything, it may well be the end of valuable long-term projects. In my own research on the very long-term future there are many potentially grand and valuable projects that take millennia or longer to succeed: Protecting the biosphere from the sun turning into a red giant, settling the stars, terraforming planets, building the infrastructure for life to survive beyond the stelliferous era. If there is an iron law that the societies or organizations involved will always collapse within a set timeframe, then it does not matter that these grand projects are physically and technically possible since a fact of social evolution—this iron law of inevitable civilizational mortality with maximum longevity—would preclude them if they take too long.

My interest is in social structures on the largest spatiotemporal scales, but the issue is the same for empires, states, societies, and (as we shall see) smaller social units. Are there reliable patterns limiting their longevity? In the following, I will briefly review macrohistorical theories on the limits of civilization

DOI: 10.4324/9781003331384-24

longevity, contrast them with empirical data from various forms of social organizations and systems, sketch a simple abstract model, and finish with a discussion about how to improve the longevity of civilizations.

19.2 Macrohistorical Theories

There is no shortage of macrohistorical theories on the limits of civilization and societal longevity. In many ways, this is *the* macrohistorical question: What is the overall shape of history? (Galtung & Inayatullah 1997).

How societies decline or collapse has been a popular subtopic. For a critical overview up to 1988, see Tainter (1988; Chapter 3). A rough categorization of macrohistorical theories may be (many of these overlap heavily):

- Cyclic theories
- Decadence
- Organic aging
- Entropy
- Internal power failure
- Unsustainable complexity
- Rising energy costs
- Environmental degradation
- Outside invasion
- Disasters, environmental shifts
- Multicausal processes

In cyclic theories, psychological, sociological, economic, or political factors conspire to produce situations that favor collapse. It may be loss of social cohesion (ibn Khaldun), each form of government having a form of instability (Polybius, Vico), or elite overproduction leading to conflicts (Turchin).

Decadence models argue that declines in civic virtues undermine necessary institutions leading to weakness and collapse (Gibbons), or other forms of biological or cultural degeneration set in due to civilized conditions.

Organic aging models liken a state or civilization to a person and describe it in terms of youth, maturity, senescence, and death (Rosseau, Mommsen). This is an essentially deterministic process resulting from "destiny," the fixed laws of internal development that govern the development of culture-organisms (Spengler).

Entropy models take the laws to be physical in nature, citing the universal applicability of thermodynamics. Typically, this consists of arguing that the second law of thermodynamics implies an overall inexorable inclination toward higher entropy—an increase in uncertainty, disorder, or chaos—and thus a decline of nature, humanity, and civilization (Adams) (Burich 1987). The main problem here is that Earth and humans are open systems that do not have to suffer entropy increase. Georgescu-Roegen invented alternative thermodynamical laws to get around it, but they are plainly contradicted by physics.

Toynbee argued that societies undergo challenges they have to respond to, requiring a proper interaction between the creative minority solving the problems and the majority implementing solutions. Eventually this symbiosis breaks and the minority merely becomes a ruling class, which then leads to further conflicts as it begins to construct a "universal state" social order that eventually collapses as the motivating religious or spiritual values weaken.

Unsustainable complexity takes the challenge-response model and builds an economic model where the past solutions to challenges have costs, but the return on investment declines as the society becomes too complex. Eventually it becomes unable to maintain itself and collapses (Tainter).

Rising energy costs frames the situation in terms of declining returns on investment (in agriculture or other sources of "energy") as the society grows, eventually becoming unsustainable (Homer-Dixon, Rifkin, Garrett).

Environmental debt or degradation can also make a society unsustainable, eventually undermining its basis (Diamond).

Finally, we have outside factors such as invasions, disasters, or environmental shifts. Relatively few macrohistorians appear to expect them in themselves to be a valid explanation of the collapse, but they may act as the triggering causal factor of a collapse of an already fragile system.

By its nature, collapse may nearly always be multicausal (Butzer 2012). In particular, as argued by Homer-Dixon et al. (2015), multiple stresses of a society can cause patterns of adaptation that increase the risk of far larger intersystemic cascades when a triggering crisis appears, including multiplicative effects when important systems fail synchronously. Collapse may be a form of normal accident (Perrow 2011) of the societal system: A large number of idiosyncratic small factors channeling together into an eventual disaster. The direct causes and particular events may be different, but there are systemic patterns to the course of disaster.

At this point one possible path is to dig deeper into the various macrohistorical and complexity models, attempting to find evidence for or against their validity in general or in particular. Another path, the one I will follow, is to move toward a more abstract yet loosely empirical approach: What kinds of explanations appear supported by data?

19.3 The Changing Hazard Rate

We can stylize the manifold details into a question of changing hazard rate[1]: How much does the risk of a society collapsing change over time, where risk is measured by the probability distribution of this age or length of time before failure? The actual risk for a particular society fluctuates year by year with climate, quality of rulers, and other factors, but here we are interested in the existence of a generic pattern.

Many of the models predict increasing risk over time. Models of decadence, organic aging, entropy, internal power failure, complexity growth, or environmental degradation all imply that at some rate (that may be unique to the society), the risk increases and eventually the hazard comes due. Optimistically, there may be opportunities to reset this risk, but these theories generally suggest there is a ratchet effect driving toward higher risk.

Outside factors represent a constant hazard rate. Cyclic theories have a cyclic hazard rate, where downturns correspond to increasing risk but do not necessarily imply the end. From afar, an ensemble of such societies may appear to have a constant hazard rate if their cycles do not align.

We can describe the probability distribution of how long a society in general survives using a survival curve, indicating the probability of finding it a certain number of years after formation. If the hazard rate is exactly constant, this curve will be an exponential decay curve with a half-life corresponding to the timescale where 50% of all societies have disappeared.

A commonplace example of increasing risk over time—as measured by the hazard rate—is human aging. After birth, in modern societies the annual risk of death is low. It rises among teenagers, and then it increases exponentially (Gompertz law) throughout life. The result is a "rectangular" survival curve where most deaths occur around 80–90 years of age. Similarly, if there is increased risk for societies over time, we should expect something similar: A life expectancy that is rarely exceeded by much.

There can also be declining risk: A high "infant mortality" followed by ever-lower risk, producing a survival curve that stretches toward old age with a slope flatter than the exponential decay. A population following this trend would have a fair number of early deaths but also a number of the very old.

There may also exist non-stationarities in the collapse risk: Maybe societies become more or less fragile over history as knowledge (warnings from history?), technology, and population grow.

19.4 Statistics of the Lifespan of Complex Systems: Is There Growing Risk?

One way of examining the lifespan of societies is to use the longevity of past societies as a (relatively) atheoretical guide. In particular, is there a sign that the likelihood of a society's ending as measured by the hazard rate increases with age? (Figure 19.1).

19.4.1 Statistical Method

A reasonable approach is to use a model that both includes the exponential case and some simple form of aging. One such distribution is the Weibull distribution, which has probability density function, where T represents the unknown time at which failure will occur:

$$f\left(t;k,\lambda\right) = \Pr\left(t < T < t+dt\right) / dt = \left(\frac{k}{\lambda}\right)\left(\frac{t}{\lambda}\right)^{k-1} e^{-\left(\frac{t}{\lambda}\right)^{k}}, \ t \geq 0$$

and cumulative density function:

$$F\left(t;k,\lambda\right) = \Pr\left(T < t\right) = 1 - e^{-\left(\frac{t}{\lambda}\right)^{k}}.$$

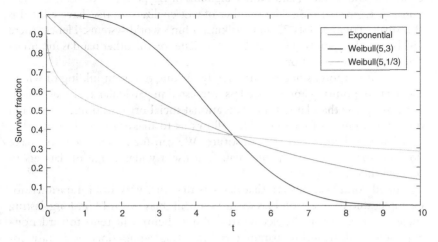

Figure 19.1 Plot of survival curves for Weibull-distributed longevities. The middle curve is a $k = 1$ exponential with constant risk per unit of time, the initially top curve $k = 3$ has increasing risk over time ("aging"), the initially lower curve $k = 1/3$ has decreasing risk: If one survives infancy, long-term prospects are fairly good.

λ corresponds to a scale parameter while k determines the shape. This distribution has hazard rate

$$H(t) = \frac{f(t)}{F(t)} \propto x^{k-1}.$$

Shape parameter $k = 1$ corresponds to a constant rate, while $k > 1$ indicates a risk that increases over time. This distribution is widely used for survival analysis since it is simple and robust.[2] I will use the Weibull distribution as a way of testing if there is noticeable aging in the data.

The simplest hypothesis, which I adopt as the null, is that there is no aging, in which case the risk as measured by the hazard rate would be constant, and we should expect an exponential decline in the number of survivors over time. Alternatively, it is entirely possible that there is a complex pattern of risk change representing some form of aging that will mainly show up as bad fits of survival curves to the curve $\bar{F}(t) = 1 - F(t; k, \lambda)$.

19.4.2 Data

An important problem is what things to measure. "Society" and "civilization" are ill-defined: The literature abounds with definitions and selects actual historical examples, hence becoming somewhat arbitrary. They also have fuzzy boundaries in time and space, making their longevities uncertain. Should we count the Old, Middle, and New Kingdoms of Egypt as one or three civilizations? (Taagepera 1978). The number of past civilizations that have existed is also small; Toynbee lists 23 and Wilkinson nine world systems. Hence, there will be few data points. The number of societies on the other hand is innumerable in the other direction.

For our purpose, since we are merely seeking to get an inkling of where the data are pointing and we are less interested in particular societies or civilizations *per se* than large transgenerational social organizations, we should use a wide range of datasets. This allows us to make use of data of other social system longevities as a substitute. We can (or rather, have to) make do with somewhat low-quality data and use a wider range of datasets to balance their limitations.

Added complications are that datasets that lack very brief durations (for example, due to selection bias or survivorship bias toward big, long-lasting societies with history books written about them) will tend toward non-exponential distribution parameters indicating aging since it is rare for exponentially distributed data to lack very low values; but the more general Weibull distribution can easily accommodate this pattern. Conversely, one can of course argue that the inclusion of spurious, very short-term lifespans can hide an actual aging effect. One must also take care with censoring, the fact that some societies have not yet collapsed. For this, at least standard methods are available.

19.4.3 Empires

Taagepera studied empires 3000–600 BC (Taagepera 1978), 600 BC–600 AD (Taagepera 1979), and 600 AD onward (Taagepera 1997). His definition of empire is "any relatively large sovereign political entity whose components are not sovereign." He defines duration as time from adulthood[3] (when the empire reaches 80% of its maximum stable size) to the final date; however, one may also add the rise time (from emergence to adulthood) to get a more expansive measure.

Using the data from the first two Taagepera papers, Arbesman argued that empire duration was distributed as an exponential random variable with a mean imperial lifetime of ≈ 220 years (Arbesman 2011). However, Arbesman settled on the exponential model by comparing the likelihood to fits to normal, lognormal, geometric, and gamma distributions, which is somewhat arbitrary and includes distributions with non-monotonic hazard rates (Figure 19.2).

Fitting a Weibull distribution to the Taagepera data leads to $\lambda = 188.1137$ years and $k = 1.0217$. The 95% confidence interval for k is [0.8101, 1.2887], containing $k = 1$: There is no evidence for aging. Indeed, an exponential distribution with $\lambda = 186.3659$ years is a good fit to the data. This corresponds to a median duration of 129.1790 years. Taagepera also notes that the median duration of polities to 130 years has no trends over time (Taagepera 1997) Fitting all data (excluding empires with only one data point) and instead using

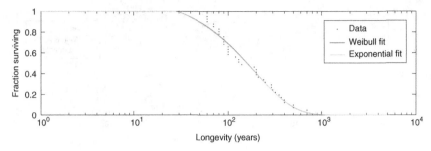

Figure 19.2 Survival curve of Taagepera empire data (dots) fitted with a Weibull and exponential fit. The empires show close to constant overall hazard rates.

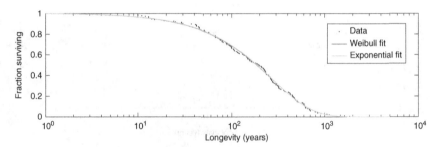

Figure 19.3 Survival curve based on Wikipedia's "list of empires."

the time from the first to the last date to denote duration gives $\lambda = 348.3815$ and $k = 0.9205$ (confidence interval [0.7869, 1.0768]).

19.4.4 Online Lists

We can compare these results to two convenience samples found online. If we use Wikipedia's list of "empires"[4] as a stand-in for large, organized structures, the result is very similar. The scale parameter is $\lambda = 270.9173$ years and the shape parameter $k = 0.9986$ (with 95% confidence interval [0.8951, 1.1141]). Again, we have no reason to reject the non-aging hypothesis.

The estimates by Larry Freeman on his blog of the durations of ancient civilizations[5] produce a weak rejection of the hypothesis; they lead to $\lambda = 381.8091$ and $k = 1.2500$ with a 95% confidence interval [1.0294, 1.5177]: Here there is a mild aging effect (Figures 19.3 and 19.4) (Freeman 2022).

19.4.5 World Systems

A very different list is the world systems approach that does not focus on sovereign states but rather on systems of inter-regional and transnational trade and coordination. Taking the nine past civilizations/world systems listed by

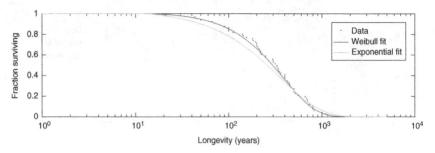

Figure 19.4 Survival curve based on Freeman's list of empires.

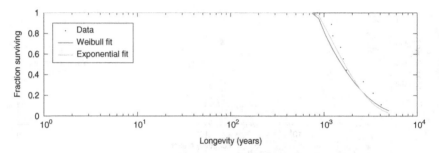

Figure 19.5 Survival curve based on Wilkinson's list of world systems.

Wilkinson (2009), the Weibull fit is $\lambda = 1080.7$ years (they persist far longer than their individual component empires) and $k = 0.8083$, confidence interval [0.4611, 1.4169]. Again, no support for the aging hypothesis, although the weak fit and minuscule data set should not be taken too seriously (Figure 19.5).

19.4.6 European States

On the other hand, looking at European states that had at least one city since the Middle Ages (Schönholzer & Weese 2018), gives $\lambda = 136.6277$ years and $k = 0.8604$ with 95% confidence interval [0.7950, 0.9312] (Figure 19.6).

This takes duration as the total time a state had a city; using the time from the first and last appearance produces a similar pattern. Here there is evidence for mild "infant mortality" in young states, although the effect is modest. Estimating a hazard rate by fitting a line to the empirical cumulative hazard function (which is fairly close to a piecewise linear function) gives 0.70% risk of failure per year for $t < 100$ and 0.54% risk per year for $t > 100$ years.

19.4.7 Conclusions on the lifespan of complex systems

The main conclusion from this exploration of the data is that aging does *not* appear to be a strong and clear force for social structures such as countries,

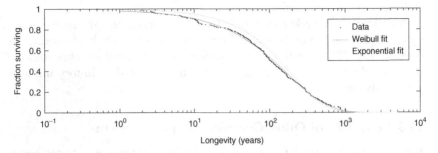

Figure 19.6 Survival curve of European states.

empires, and civilizations. It is also worth noticing the short duration of imperial social structures: Few last more than a millennium and most are gone within 300 years. This is still many human generations, but worrisome from an institutional longevity perspective. Individual states appear to have a noticeable childhood mortality and last even shorter (the median in the Schönholzer and Weese data is just 91 years). The fits to the Weibull distributions are also decent: There is little sign of complex changes in risk over time. In short, these data appear to weaken the case for models of collapse predicting a risk increasing with time.

What could explain this lack of aging?

Could a mixture of shape parameters, with different societies aging at different rates, make the overall population appear non-aging? It turns out that mixtures of Weibull distributions do not easily fake an exponential distribution since it is not possible to cancel early "infant mortality" with some aging cases and still get an approximately exponential curve. Uncertainties in duration would smear out a time-varying hazard rate, but it appears unlikely that the uncertainty is so large that it becomes comparable to the variation between cases.

A simple possibility may be that the resiliency of all units of analysis (whether civilizations or empires) remains constant and there is a constant rate and intensity of disturbances across history. This may be a too glib answer: Surely the early expanding era of any empire or civilization is going to be more fragile than when it has had time to establish itself? The inside and outside threats change in character (the Romans had to retreat many times in their quarreling with neighboring Latin tribes, yet eventually became a well-organized global military force that was only threatened by certain kinds of enemies; early Roman society had none of the economies of scale and market instabilities the fully developed society had, and so on).

One possibility is observer selection effects weeding out vulnerable structures before they become known, leaving only stable structures with a more limited range of disturbances. This is somewhat supported by the state-level data: Many mini-states are brief, and presumably, we are missing many would-be empires that fail before they get larger than a small kingdom and the ambitious dreams of its ruler.

A slightly more subtle theory is that as the threats change, the society scales up resiliency proportionally so that the net result is constant risk. However, this does not explain why they are well-matched. Why do some societies not scale up their stability far more than needed at some point in their history and then get a vastly extended history?

19.5 Longevity of Other Complex Adaptive Systems

It is illustrative to look at other complex adaptive systems (CAS). States, societies, and civilizations are all CAS. Among many researchers, there is a common background assumption (or more properly a fond hope) that maybe there are joint rules for large classes of CAS. Just like for history, the existence of macro patterns may be too much to ask for: Possibly, there are just individual cases that do not generalize. Still, the question of what kinds of CAS show limited lifespans is worth asking.

There are some categories of CAS for which we lack good data, like the longevity of cities, religious institutions, and universities. In these cases, the reason may be that they do not age, or age so slowly, such that the mortality rate is hard to measure: We do not have large databases of defunct cities, churches, and universities. Generally, there are enough examples of multimillennia or multicentury survival to show that it is possible (Jericho dates back at least 9,000 BC, the University of Ancient Taxila lasted from ca. fifth century BC to fifth century AD, the Orthodox Christian Church of Jerusalem has been around since 33 AD). We can at least conclude that there is evidence that institutions smaller than states can maintain themselves at millennial timescales, although they may be rare.

19.5.1 Firms

Firms have a largely age-independent mortality rate, with the typical half-life of publicly traded US companies around a decade after entering the public market, regardless of business sector (Daepp et al. 2015). This finding has been replicated in international data, with a constant rate for mature firms and (in some countries) a higher rate for new firms (Ishikawa et al. 2017). While the liabilities in bankruptcies are power law distributed, the lifespan of the involved firms follows a memoryless exponential distribution (Fujiwara 2004).

It is worth noting that companies often "die" by merging with other companies rather than bankruptcy and often emerge as splits and spin-offs from other companies. The evolutionary dynamics are clearly very different from organisms, and we have no reason to believe human or biological analogies would apply. While the mortality rate is often high, there are also examples of firms persisting for centuries. There is a degree of "liability of newness" and "liability of adolescence" where recently formed organizations have a higher risk due to a lack of resources, contacts, and market share, as well as the end of the initial honeymoon with investors. Theories of "liability of senescence" where internal ossification—the accumulation of rules, internal vested interests, etc.—predict that there should be an aging process, while theories of "liability of obsolescence" suggest mortality should increase since the external fit to the market may decline as the product or structure of the company becomes less aligned. Evidence seems particularly good for the liabilities of newness and adolescence that mostly affect companies below 5–7 years of age. Beyond this point, risk appears to level out (Coad 2018).

Geoffrey West suggests that one explanation for the constant rate is that for many companies, sales and expenses are closely balanced, and hence they are vulnerable to fluctuations (West 2017). They may also scale sublinearly, unlike cities that have superlinear returns to scale (and do not appear to age). Maybe cities, having many forms of bottom-up innovation, innovate more than top-down controlled companies do.

Kongō Gumi is a Japanese construction company founded in 578 AD that remained independent until 2006 (a span of 1,428 years) when it became a subsidiary of a larger company. Other extant (as of the time of writing) companies include the Japanese inns Nishiyama Onsen Keiunka, Koman, and Hōshi Ryokan (founded in 705, 717, and 718 AD respectively). Other extremely long-lived companies are active in fields such as restaurants, wine, religious goods, and brewing. Taking the tail-end of the age distribution and fitting a Weibull distribution to it suggests that even here k may be essentially 1 ($k = 0.9731$, 95% confidence interval [0.8521, 1.1114]).[6] In this case the estimated $\lambda = 168.2076$ years is significantly longer than the decade timescale for typical companies. A possible explanation for the longevity of these companies is that they are typically in businesses naturally tied to a location or regional agricultural production: They have a fixed, stable niche. Many are also family-owned, creating incentives for remaining in business rather than maximizing profit. It has been argued that they have the right balance of adaptivity and strong identity (de Geus 2002), although it is unclear what makes that balance stable over a long time horizon in these cases.

19.5.2 Organizations

Mette Eilstrup-Sangiovanni (2020) examined international governmental organizations (IGOs), finding that more than a third of IGOs created since 1815 have disappeared. In her dataset, the hazard rate is found to be high during the first 30 years, then leveling off to what appears to be a constant risk beyond 50 years of age.[7] She suggests that besides accumulating expertise, stakeholders will have invested more in long-lived organizations, and they may be better "environmentally embedded." Having a broad and diverse membership appears to help organizational endurance, as does focus on less contentious technical topics than more politically turbulent security issues.

Organizations can also go into a "coma" or minimally active "zombie state" rather than formally disbanding. As noted by Julia Gray, 38% of 70 international economic organizations extant during 1948–2013 were inactive (Gray 2018). From a practical perspective, they were gone. One reason for this possibility is that unlike societies or firms, such organizations do not have to be productive to persist. They can just parasitize existing countries and economies or persist in name only (like the Holy Roman Empire). Many end up in such states because they cannot compete with other organizations for skilled people. However, the actual factors determining the vitality and survival of such organizations remain relatively understudied (Grat 2018; Dijkstra 2019).

19.5.3 Species

In biology, constant extinction rates of species over time have been widely observed, with constant rates within the same taxa (but different rates between different ecological niches). Sometimes this is called the "law of constant extinction" (Van Valen 1973) or "Van Valen's law." As Van Valen wrote:

> The probability of extinction of a taxon is then effectively independent of its age. This suggests a randomly acting process. But the probability is strongly related to adaptive zones [roughly, the ecological niche]. This shows that a randomly acting process cannot be operating uniformly. How can it be that extinction occurs randomly with respect to age but nonrandomly with respect to ecology?

This has been attributed to "the Red Queen hypothesis"[8]: Species go extinct due to the competition from other coevolving species that make their ecological niche worse over time (plus rare speciation/disaster events) rather than any intrinsic property. A version of this might be imagined to apply to empires: They are brought down by the emergence of temporarily stronger competitors (whether other empires or "barbarians"). The problem with applying this idea to the collapse of civilizations is that many of the causes like environmental depletion and long-range invasion (e.g., Spain vs. the Incas) do not appear to have this coevolutionary nature.

Another conundrum is that the lifetimes of larger taxa, such as genera and families, appear to follow power law distributions. This might be due to statistical effects of bundling together many smaller populations and does not have to be due to species interactions (Pigolotti et al. 2005).

One modification of the Red Queen hypothesis is that both the biotic competition and the abiotic random environmental risks play a role but in different phases of a species' lifespan. Competition plays a larger role in determining how widespread and populous a species becomes and when it wanes toward smaller populations, while other factors determine the actual extinction rate (Žliobaitė, Fortelius, & Stenseth 2017).

This may hint at a multifactorial model of the histories of empires and civilizations. Competitive factors determine their eventual size and prosperity, while other factors play a role in their emergence and downfall. This may also dovetail nicely with smaller states behaving differently from empires and civilizations. The lesser entities exist in a different competitive ecology than the larger entities. The distance between decline and extinction is far smaller for a state with a handful of cities than for an empire or civilization where a loss of a region does not change the fundamental structure and viability of the whole.

19.5.4 Biological Aging

Senescence, a reduction in function, is common in multicellular organisms. The most popular explanation is that it is rarely if ever an issue in the wild since most organisms succumb to predation or environmental conditions at a high rate (indeed, often showing exponential survival curves after infancy). As long as the probability of surviving until reproduction is high enough, there is a lack of evolutionary pressure to remove genetic variants that cause late-life loss of function (Kirkwood & Austad 2000).

Certain species do not show aging (e.g., no functional reduction over time) as far as currently known (Archer & Hosken 2016). They include diverse species like perennial angiosperms, Blanding's turtle, olm, eastern box turtle, red sea urchin, rougheye rockfish, ocean quahog clam, bristlecone pine, and perhaps the Greenland shark.[9] Invertebrate animals can reverse their developmental stages but this may be more a matter of regeneration than lack of senescence. It is also worth noting that ecosystems and perhaps the biosphere as a whole do not show signs of increasing weakness.

These facts show that there are closely related CAS that exhibit either increasing or constant risk over time. At least in biology, the risk of individual collapse can change nature relatively easily, undermining claims that it must be due to some profound principle.

19.5.5 Software

It is well known in software engineering that software has a "lifecyle" where the initial system keeps on functionally evolving but structurally is deteriorating, eventually making it necessary to replace it. Other causes of software mortality are changing hardware or operating environment, changing user requirements, or just declining usage (Tamai & Torimitsu 1992).

In a 1992 survey of Japanese companies across several sectors, software longevity was found to be about 10 years, with a significant spread (Tamai & Torimitsu 1992). Large programs tended to survive longer, perhaps because of the cost of replacement. Fitting a Weibull distribution to their data gives $\lambda = 11.3745$ and $k = 1.7353$ (95% confidence interval [1.4924, 2.0177]), which does support a model where older software has a growing mortality.

Meir Lehman first described this process of structural deterioration in the 1970s as "a general upward trend in the size, complexity, and cost of the system and the maintenance process." His observations led him to propose a number of laws of software evolution (Belady & Lehman 1976; Lehman 1980).

The reason for these laws is the ongoing feedback between software and the surrounding organizations, users, and developers. While the laws were formulated in an old-fashioned mainframe environment, many of them appear relevant today. Software metrics measuring a literal entropy in terms of the probability that different parts are impacted by changes to other parts do show growth over time (Bianchi et al. 2001).

A particular problem is that many software systems depend on other systems, including commercial off-the-shelf software and packages maintained by other entities. This helps speed up development, avoids "reinventing the wheel," and allows many forms of flexibility. Unfortunately, over time the external systems change in uncontrollable ways breaking the functionality and requiring rewriting the code. As time goes by the volatility of outside code makes maintenance costly, either causing decay of the software or requiring re-engineering to make it maintainable. While there is some evidence for improvements in software lifespans over time, it might be that this software aging is an attractor state due to the economics of coding.

This CAS has many similarities with Tainter's complexity overshoot model (Tainter 1988).

19.5.6 Summary: Aging of CAS

CAS in general do not show aging in the sense of increasing risk of ending. They do show change over time, and a surprising range of systems has nearly constant risk, with possible infant mortality for young systems.

These examples also show that increased risk to a CAS over time can be caused by evolution—producing aging because of genetic drift—and through growth and unmitigated complexity. If competition caused aging, we should expect it to happen for firms and species. Instead, the story appears to be that the kind of niche a system exists in affects whether risk increases over time. The risk conditions may also change as the system grows and changes.

19.6 A Simple Model of Constant Risk

Resiliency against disturbances is a key factor for longevity. There is always some magnitude of disturbance generated on the inside or outside of a system that can overcome the defenses and cause an eventual collapse (Figure 19.7).

19.6.1 A Statistical Toy Model

A simple model assumes disturbances randomly occurring at some fixed rate λ, each with a random magnitude X drawn from a probability distribution. We will use the complementary cumulative distribution function $\bar{F}(x) = \Pr[X > x]$ to explore how likely they are to cause a crash. Societies have a threshold defensive strength, resilience, or coping ability θ and will persist until they

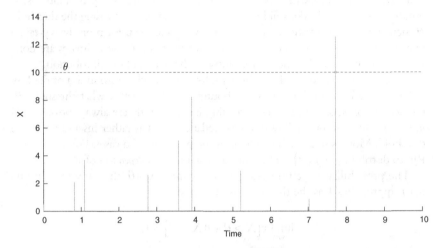

Figure 19.7 Visualization of the statistical toy model. The vertical lines represent shocks to the society arriving randomly over time and with random magnitude. The society collapses when the shock exceeds its threshold capacity θ.

encounter a disturbance larger than their strength. This will happen after a number of disturbances N, which is geometrically distributed[10] with parameter $\bar{F}(\theta)$, with expected time of survival (i.e., expected time of failure):

$$\tau_{survival} = \frac{1}{\lambda \bar{F}(\theta)}.$$

This only bounds the *expected* survival time, not the *actual* survival time, since the society may be unlucky on the very first trial. But it does give a sense of how longevity is affected by a society's resiliency.[11]

Because of the Markov inequality $\bar{F}(x) \leq E[X]/x$ (assuming the disturbance distribution has finite expectation), this gives the bound:

$$\tau_{survival} \geq \frac{\theta}{\lambda E[X]}.$$

Using the one-sided Chebyshev inequality $\bar{F}(x - E[X]) \leq \sigma^2/(\sigma^2 + x^2)$, where σ^2 is the variance of disturbances, we can get:

$$\tau_{survival} \geq \frac{\sigma^2 + (\theta + E[X])^2}{\lambda \sigma^2} = \frac{1}{\lambda}\left(1 + \frac{(\theta + E[X])^2}{\sigma^2}\right).$$

This also requires the existence of finite variance, restricting us to probability distributions with thin tails. For mild disturbance distributions, increasing the threshold θ hence gains a quadratic increase in longevity, and even for more heavy-tailed ones with divergent variance, there is a linear relation. These estimates are conservative in the sense that they ignore most of the details of the distribution.

For the most heavy-tailed distributions, like the Cauchy distribution or the low index power-law distributions, these bounds fail. No matter what threshold θ the civilization sets, disturbances exceeding it significantly are always possible and indeed likely. The probability of an exceedance event is rather insensitive to the threshold: More is not much better, as in the previous mild cases. For an extreme Pareto distribution ($f(x) \sim 1/x$) the survival time is *independent* of θ.

The probability of getting a larger exceedance $X - \theta$ than any fixed number t approaches 1 as the threshold is increased:

$$\lim_{\theta \to \infty} \Pr\left[X > \theta + t \mid X > \theta\right] = 1.$$

This occurs since $\bar{F}(x+t) \sim \bar{F}(x)$ as $x \to \infty$ (the long tail property). One can say that in this case, "if it is worse than you thought, then it is likely to be *much* worse." This would correspond to environments where arbitrarily large disasters can occur.

This case is unfortunately not implausible at all, given the tendency for disasters to have heavy tails. Heavy tails are common in natural disaster fatalities (earthquakes, volcanos, floods, tsunamis, etc.),[12] in Richardson's law of war fatalities (Clauset 2020), and appear likely for pandemic outbreak sizes (Chatterjee & Chakrabarti 2017; Cirillo & Taleb 2020). Complex societies also generate endogenous heavy-tailed events, for example, power grid blackout sizes (Hines, Balasubramaniam & Sanchez 2009), bankruptcies (Fujiwara 2004), and stock market crashes (Sornette 2017). If combining several factors, the most extreme tail dominates the size distribution. Furthermore, systemic factors can then trigger cascading event chains (Perrow 2011; Homer-Dixon et al., 2015).

19.6.2 Could One Improve Defense Indefinitely?

The survival time could diverge if resilience threshold θ were to increase enough over time, there was a continuing change to milder disturbances, distributions with less heavy tails, or even a sufficiently rapidly declining λ.[13] This may happen if there is a finite upper limit to the magnitude of disturbances, corresponding to a safe state for civilizations with sufficiently large θ. The real question is hence if/why the defenses weaken over time or do not grow fast enough to give a divergent survival time, something that theories of inevitable civilization collapse would argue to be endogenous and universal rather than exogenous and just bad luck.

Costs of increasing θ likely play a role. If the cost of increasing θ is significant, the utility or even feasibility of improvement may vanish. Consider a situation where $\tau_{survival} \propto \theta$ but the cost of achieving it is a fraction

ce^{θ} of the budget of the society where $0 < c < 1$. If the utility is measured in the remaining budget multiplied by the survival time, it will be $U(\theta) \propto \tau_{survival}(\theta)(1 - ce^{\theta})$, with a maximum for some value $0 < \theta_* < \ln(1/c)$. If utility is just survival, then all of the budgets will be used and $\theta_* = \ln(1/c)$.

Hence, another hypothesis of societal mortality is that either the cost of indefinite safety will always be prohibitive, or over time will increase so that defenses become insufficient. Competitive pressures (cost, alternative costs, competition) lead to finite θ since there will not be enough free resources. However, one should expect the threshold to grow proportional to the scale of the society and this will move the risk in the direction of nearly constant over time. Young societies have not yet protected themselves well and thus have higher infant mortality.

19.7 Synthesis: Collapse as Combined Bad Luck

We have seen that the survival time of complex social structures, whether firms, countries, empires, or civilizations, appear to be exponentially distributed. This should weaken our belief in explanations for collapse due to unavoidable processes that make these structures increasingly fragile: There is no "aging" here.

The debates about why firms, species, software, and institutions decline show that there may well be much else going on behind the scenes. Competitive pressures may in some cases lead to adaptation in such a way that the structure becomes marginal. External "designing" forces like evolution or software markets can produce aging behavior because they maximize something different from survival. As a structure grows, the threat profile may change in important ways. Certain "niches" may be protective or risky.

My tentative conclusion is that the simplest possible explanation for the observations is that often a social structure is subject to both external and internal challenges. These can be manageable, or they might be severe enough to disrupt the system. The disruption does not have to cause instant dissolution but could be a start of a series of normal accidents or Allee-like effects that gradually bring down the system. The challenges tend to have heavy-tailed distributions: Precautionary planning can only handle some of them, and the cost of maintaining constant readiness against everything is prohibitive. Hence at a certain rate, almost no matter what we do, some challenges will get through the defenses.

19.7.1 Can We Beat the House?

While ruling out unavoidable decline may be positive news, unavoidable random disasters may be worse. If it is correct that Lady Luck will get us no matter how much we prepare, we get a time horizon set by the rate and severity of challenges that are hard to budge and just as limiting for longtermist proposals as an iron law of decline.

One idea that has emerged from the world systems school of thought is the "Central World System." World systems gradually tend to coalesce with each other as communications improve. This may be through direct conquest, or just increased trade merging their worlds (Wilkinson 2004). The result after 5,500 years is a global civilization:

The present technical civilization of the planet Earth can be traced from Mesopotamia to Southeastern Europe, to Western and Central Europe, and then to Eastern Europe and North America.

(Shklovsky & Sagan 1966, p. 412)

On this vast scale, there has never been any real collapse: The Bronze Age collapse is a mere footnote since what matters is a vast cultural and causal continuity. To see the Central World System fall would probably require either global extinction or a long return to hunter-gatherer life. Unfortunately, this is entirely possible (Bostrom & Cirkovic 2011)—and worth protecting against.

One reason for the resilience of the Central World System is that most of the time it has not been one cohesive society but a network of societies. When one failed, other parts could pick up the cultural continuity and re-settle the now abandoned or disorganized region. This is similar to a metapopulation in ecology: A group of separated populations that weakly interact, so typically a local extinction is followed by migration from other populations. The overall resiliency of the metapopulation is far higher than the resiliency of the individual populations to uncorrelated threats.

Today that may mean a need to decouple parts of global civilization. This is hard to do on Earth: Economies of scale, the logic of trade, a shared global environment, and a communication network couple humanity together ever stronger on the planet. While nationalism, survivalism, and cold wars may work against integration, they are unlikely to decouple things strongly. It may hence be necessary in the long run to become a multiplanetary species in order to achieve the necessary decoupling through the distancing nature of light-speed limitations and space itself. In the meantime, we had better improve our resiliency (Cotton-Barratt, Daniel & Sandberg 2020).

The Central World System has been around for 5,500 years. We have rebuilt ever higher. Nevertheless, having off-site backups sound like a good idea.

Acknowledgment

I wish to thank Robin Hanson for asking the provocative question of why most systems age that led to this research. I thank Schönholzer and Weese for making their data available to me. This work was done on the European Research Council (ERC) Advanced grant "UNPrEDICT: Uncertainty and Precaution—Ethical Decisions Involving Catastrophic Threats."

Notes

1 Hazard rates are often used to study the probability distribution for the age or time of failure (or death) of a system, technological device, or living organism. For example, the

length of the lifetime before a lightbulb burns out can be characterized by a hazard rate function. Mathematically, the hazard rate function, or hazard function, is a probability density function (pdf) for the conditional failure rate, or conditional probability of failure at a time t (or in a small time interval around time t), provided the condition that the system is still alive, and therefore has already survived up until time t. Intuitively and practically, it can be thought of as: You are given the information that a system is still alive at time t; ignoring the beginning part of the pdf $f(t)$ that occurred before time t, of the 100% chance that the system will fail between that particular time t and infinity, what is the probability that it will fail at a time t?

If the time of failure (i.e., duration, lifetime, length of life, or age at failure) is a random variable T and is randomly distributed, the *unconditional* pdf of the lifetime, $f(t)$, provides $P(T = t)$, where time t is the support of the pdf from $0 < t < \infty$. The cumulative distribution function (cdf) for the failure time, $F(t)$, provides $P(T < t)$, which computes the probability that the system will fail (or will have failed) in the time elapsed *before* time t. For a living organism, this is the probability that death will occur before time t. The survival function $S(t)$ is $P(T \geq t)$, the *a priori* probability that the system will fail *after* time t, calculated as $S(t) = \bar{F}(t) = 1 - F(t)$ (the complement of the cdf, or $1 -$ cdf). In other words, the survival function provides the cumulative probability mass remaining in the life of the system at time t. To convert the portion of probability $f(t)$ to the right of t into a conditional probability, the area remaining in the pdf beyond time t must integrate to 1. In order to achieve this, it must be normalized by dividing by the remaining area beyond time t, which is given by $S(t) = \int_t^\infty f(t)$, thereby recalibrating the *remaining* probability mass in the pdf so that $f(t)$ over $(T \geq t)$ integrates to 1, and therefore represents a probability measure. The hazard rate $H(t) = f(t)/S(t)$, thus normalizes the pdf $f(t)$ over the remaining time $T \geq t$, dividing it by the survival function $S(t)$: As t increases approaching the right tail of the pdf, the probability $S(t)$ that the system has survived to that point in time approaches 0; this diminishing denominator $S(t)$ increasingly scales up the numerator, $f(t)$. The hazard rate, $H(t)$, therefore represents the conditional probability of failure at time t (or during a time interval around t), given that the system has lived or survived up until time t.

2 There is a deeper reason to consider this distribution: It is max-stable. Since the end of a society occurs when all parts of a society have disappeared, we should expect it to happen at the time $t_{max} = \max\left(t_1, t_2, \ldots, t_n\right)$ here the times represent the time of disappearance of its parts (that may well have their own parts). The well-known central limit theorem states that the sum (or average) of independent, identically distributed random variables with finite variance will approach the Gaussian distribution as the number of variables approach infinity. The distribution is called sum-stable. This is why the distribution is so ubiquitous, even gaining the unfortunate moniker "the normal distribution." If, instead, we select the maximum of a number of independent random variables (that are sufficiently well-behaved to allow convergence), we get attraction toward one of the max-stable distributions. The Fisher–Tippett–Gnedenko theorem states that depending on the type of random variables, the result will be either a Gumbel, Fréchet, or Weibull distribution. The Weibull distribution shows up when the input variables have heavy tails (including when part disappearance times t_i are themselves close to Weibull distribution).

3 He points out that no biological metaphor is intended. It is just convenient to use words like growth, maturity, and adulthood to describe the process rather than invent new terminology. This is also why this chapter uses biological terms like aging and longevity.

4 Wikipedia list of empires includes over 250 empires. https://en .wikipedia .org /wiki / List of empires

5 In his analyis, Freeman examines the lifespan of 55 ancient civilizations.

6 Note that these are current lifespans beyond 618 years (only companies founded before 1400 AD were considered). Previous fits were concluded lifespans; this one deals with ongoing lifespans.

7 This infant mortality applies to terrorist groups too, where a large fraction (25–74%) do not survive the first year but survivors tend to persist longer (Phillips 2017).

8 The name has over time also become attached to the more general idea that competition and coevolution forces all species to constantly evolve or go extinct, which is a somewhat different meaning from Van Valen's original use.

9 Data from the Animal Aging and Longevity Database http://genomics.senescence.info/species/nonaging.php.

10 The geometric distribution has cumulative density function $Pr(N < k) = 1 - (1 - p)^k$, probability mass function $Pr(N = k) = (1 - p)^{k-1}p$, with expected value $E(N) = 1/p$.

11 This model assumes a single kind of disturbance and a single kind of threshold. Clearly, reality is far more complex. However, if we were to model multiple kinds of disturbances and coping mechanisms, the result would still be a probability per disturbance that it causes the end modulated by the amount of coping ability. Unless there are strong anticorrelations between different kinds of coping, (e.g., having a high resiliency against risk 1 makes one vulnerable to risk 2, and vice versa) it makes more sense to assume a loosely defined single kind of resiliency against generic risks. Another complication may be that some risks cause a weakening of resiliency, making closely timed disturbances more dangerous (something that is observed in ecology, where synchrony and noise distribution affect extinction rates). Again, this can be handled by coarse-graining the model.

12 For many categories of natural disasters, fatalities have an upper bound due to the spatial cohesiveness of the disaster: A flood can only directly kill people in low-lying regions. Since human settlement is concentrated in a heavy-tailed way, this strengthens the heavy tail of the disasters.

13 For example, if $\lambda(t) \propto e^{-kt}$ for $k > 0$, then almost surely there will only be a finite number of challenges.

References

Arbesman, S. (2011). The life-spans of empires. *Historical Methods: A Journal of Quantitative and Interdisciplinary History*, 44(3), 127–129.

Archer, C. R., & Hosken, D. J. (2016). Evolution: Escaping the inevitability of ageing. *Current Biology*, 26(5), R202–R204.

Belady, L. A., & Lehman, M. M. (1976). A model of large program development. *IBM Systems Journal*, 15(3), 225–252.

Bianchi, A., Caivano, D., Lanubile, F., & Visaggio, G. (2001, April). Evaluating software degradation through entropy. In Proceedings Seventh International Software Metrics Symposium (pp. 210–219). IEEE.

Bostrom, N., & Cirkovic, M. M. (Eds.). (2011). *Global Catastrophic Risks*. Oxford University Press.

Burich, K. R. (1987). Henry Adams, the second law of thermodynamics, and the course of history. *Journal of the History of Ideas*, 48(3), 467–482.

Butzer, K. W. (2012). Collapse, environment, and society. *Proceedings of the National Academy of Sciences*, 109(10), 3632–3639.

Chatterjee, A., & Chakrabarti, B. K. (2017). Fat tailed distributions for deaths in conflicts and disasters. *Reports in Advances of Physical Sciences*, 1(1), 1740007.

Cirillo, P., & Taleb, N. N. (2020). Tail risk of contagious diseases. *Nature Physics*, 16(6) 1–8.

Clauset, A. (2020). On the frequency and severity of interstate wars. In *Lewis Fry Richardson: His Intellectual Legacy and Influence in the Social Sciences*. Gleditsch, N.P. (Ed.) Springer (Vol. 113). 113–127.

Coad, A. (2018). Firm age: A survey. *Journal of Evolutionary Economics, 28*(1), 13–43.

Cotton-Barratt, O., Daniel, M., & Sandberg, A. (2020). Defence in depth against human extinction: Prevention, response, resilience, and why they all matter. *Global Policy, 11*(3), 271–282.

Daepp, M. I., Hamilton, M. J., West, G. B., & Bettencourt, L. M. (2015). The mortality of companies. *Journal of the Royal Society. Interface, 12*(106), 20150120.

Dijkstra, H. (2019). Who gets to live forever? An institutional theory on the life and death of international organizations. *ECPR Joint Sessions, Mons,* 8–12.

Eilstrup-Sangiovanni, M. (2020). Death of international organizations: The organizational ecology of intergovernmental organizations, 1815–2015. *The Review of International Organizations, 15*(2), 339–370.

Freeman, L. (2022). How long did the civilizations of ancient empires last? In *Owlcation* blog. Accessed Jan 8, 2023. https://owlcation .com /humanities /How -long -do -empires -last

Fujiwara, Y. (2004). Zipf law in firms bankruptcy. *Physica A: Statistical Mechanics and its Applications, 337*(1–2), 219–230.

Galtung, J., & Inayatullah, S. (Eds.) (1997). *Macrohistory and Macrohistorians: Perspectives on Individual, Social, and Civilizational Change.* Praeger.

de Geus, A. (2002). *The Living Company.* Harvard Business Press.

Gray, J. (2018). Life, death, or zombie? The vitality of international organizations. *International Studies Quarterly, 62*(1), 1–13.

Hines, P., Balasubramaniam, K., & Sanchez, E. C. (2009). Cascading failures in power grids. *IEEE Potentials, 28*(5), 24–30.

Homer-Dixon, T., Walker, B., Biggs, R., Crépin, A. S., Folke, C., Lambin, E. F., … Troell, M. (2015). Synchronous failure: The emerging causal architecture of global crisis. *Ecology and Society,* 20(3): 6

Ishikawa, A., Fujimoto, S., Mizuno, T., & Watanabe, T. (2017). Dependence of the decay rate of firm activities on firm age. *Evolutionary and Institutional Economics Review, 14*(2), 351–362.

Kirkwood, T. B., & Austad, S. N. (2000). Why do we age? *Nature, 408*(6809), 233–238.

Lehman, M. M. (1980). Programs, life cycles, and laws of software evolution. *Proceedings of the IEEE, 68*(9), 1060–1076.

Perrow, C. (2011). *Normal Accidents: Living with High Risk Technologies-Updated Edition.* Princeton University Press.

Phillips, B. J. (2017). Do 90 percent of terrorist groups last less than a year? Updating the conventional wisdom. *Terrorism and Political Violence.* 31(6), 1255–1265.

Pigolotti, S., Flammini, A., Marsili, M., & Maritan, A. (2005). Species lifetime distribution for simple models of ecologies. *Proceedings of the National Academy of Sciences of the United States of America, 102*(44), 15747–15751.

Schönholzer, D., & Weese, E. (2018). *Creative Destruction in the European State System: 1000–1850.* Mimeo.

Shklovsky, I. S., & Sagan, C. (1966). *Intelligent Life in the Universe.* New York: Delta.

Sornette, D. (2017). *Why Stock Markets Crash: Critical Events in Complex Financial Systems* (Vol. 49). Princeton University Press.

Taagepera, R. (1978). Size and duration of empires growth-decline curves, 3000 to 600 BC. *Social Science Research, 7*(2), 180–196.

Taagepera, R. (1979). Size and duration of empires: Growth-decline curves, 600 BC to 600 AD. *Social Science History, 3*(3/4), 115–138.

Taagepera, R. (1997). Expansion and contraction patterns of large polities: Context for Russia. *International Studies Quarterly, 41*(3), 475–504.

Tainter, J. (1988). *The Collapse of Complex Societies.* Cambridge University Press.

Tamai, T., & Torimitsu, Y. (1992, November). Software lifetime and its evolution process over generations. In *Proceedings of the Conference on Software Maintenance – 1992*, Orlando, FL, USA, 9–12 November 1992; IEEE Computer Society Press: Washington, DC. pp. 63–69.

van Valen, L. (1973). A new evolutionary law. *Evolutionary Theory, 1,* 1–30.

West, G. B. (2017). *Scale: The Universal Laws of Growth, Innovation, Sustainability, and the Pace of Life in Organisms, Cities, Economies, and Companies.* Penguin.

Wilkinson, D. (2004). The power configuration sequence of the central world system, 1500–700 BC. *Journal of World-Systems Research,* X(3) Fall 2004, 655–720.

Wilkinson, D. (2009). States systems and universal empires. In Modelski, G. & Denemark, R.A. (Eds.), *World System History: Volume I.* EOLSS Publications. pp. 105–128.

Žliobaitė, I., Fortelius, M., & Stenseth, N. C. (2017). Reconciling taxon senescence with the Red Queen's hypothesis. *Nature, 552*(7683), 92–95.

20 Multipath Forecasting

The Aftermath of the 2020 American Crisis

Peter Turchin

20.1 Introduction

Collapse of historical states, empires, and whole civilizations is the subject of an enormous body of literature (for reviews see Tainter 1988, 1995; Diamond 2004; Butzer and Endfield 2012; Casti 2012; Cumming and Peterson 2017). *Collapse* is defined in various ways by different authors and disciplines (Cumming and Peterson 2017). Its various dimensions include rapid loss of social complexity (Tainter 1988), loss of centralized administration (Renfrew 1984), a drastic decrease in human population numbers (Diamond 2004), and even regional abandonment (Weiss and Bradley 2001).

Collapse, however defined, is a possible end result of social systems entering periods of falling resilience and heightened sociopolitical instability (collapse can also happen as a result of exogenous forces, such as a devastating invasion or a pandemic, but the focus of this article is on the internal causes). Historical analysis indicates that all complex societies organized as states experience such recurrent instability periods, or "Ages of Discord" (Turchin 2016). However, while entry into an Age of Discord is fairly stereotypical (see next section), exiting it can result in a broad fan of possibilities, ranging from deep collapse, at one extreme, to mild instability resolved by the elites and population pulling together to adopt the necessary reforms, at the opposite extreme.

There is now (as of February 2021, when this article was written) a broad acceptance by all parties that the United States has entered an Age of Discord. I analyzed the structural trends and social forces for instability that are currently spiking in a book published five years ago (Turchin 2016). Now that we are in crisis, the main question becomes, which route will our society take, and where will it fall in the fan of possibilities?

This article builds on previous collaborative research with Sergey Gavrilets, James Bennett, Daniel Hoyer, and the Vienna workshop on Social Complexity and Collapse (Turchin et al. 2018). I describe a computational model for projecting forward the dynamics of sociopolitical instability in the United States beyond 2020 under various scenarios. Because I am interested in exploring how various interventions can affect future trajectories, I will call this model

DOI: 10.4324/9781003331384-25

the "MPF engine," where MPF stands for *MultiPath Forecasting* (Turchin et al. 2018).

The proposed MPF engine is a lightly modified version of the model that I had previously used to make the prediction that the United States would experience an instability spike during the 2020s. This prediction was published in February 2010 (Turchin 2010), and the model details were elaborated in subsequent publications (Turchin 2013, 2016). As a caveat, the current version of the MPF engine is not a fully developed product, but merely a "prototype" that I use to illustrate the promise of the MPF approach.

This article is organized as follows. First, I give an overview of the structural-demographic theory, which provides the theoretical framework for the MPF model. Next, I review the data patterns that are most relevant to developing a predictive approach. The following section describes the computational model underlying the MPF engine. Next, I apply the model to the period of American history from the beginning of the nineteenth to the end of the twentieth century, with the goal of parameterizing the model and testing it against data. The final section (before the Conclusion) uses the parameterized model to forecast the dynamics of instability in the United States beyond 2020 and illustrates how MPF can be used to explore the effects of policy interventions.

20.2 Structural-Demographic Theory as the Modeling Framework

Historical research indicates that the dynamics of sociopolitical instability in complex societies organized as states are not purely random (Turchin et al. 2018). History is not just "one damned thing after another," as Arnold Toynbee famously said in response to another historian (Toynbee 1957: 267). There is a regular, albeit dynamically complex, pattern involving at least two cycles superimposed on each other (plus exogenous stochasticity on top of that). First, there are long-term waves of political instability periods with durations of a century or more (these are Ages of Discord) that are interspersed with relatively stable periods. Second, there is a shorter oscillation with an average period of c. 50 years.

Structural-demographic theory (SDT) offers an integrative framework for investigating the multiple interacting forces shaping the long-term social pressures that lead to revolutions, civil wars, and other major outbreaks of sociopolitical instability (Goldstone 1991; Turchin 2003; Korotayev and Khaltourina 2006; Turchin and Nefedov 2009). Furthermore, SDT can be, and has been, formulated as an explicit computational model capable of forecasting future quantitative dynamics of social unrest and political violence in specific social systems (Turchin 2010, 2013, 2016).

According to SDT, the causes of revolutions and major rebellions are in many ways similar to the processes that cause earthquakes (Goldstone 1991: 35). In the study of both revolutions and earthquakes, it is useful to distinguish "pressures" (structural conditions, which build up slowly) from "triggers" (sudden releasing events, which immediately precede a social or geological eruption). Specific triggers of political upheavals, like the self-immolation of Mohamed Bouazizi, which sparked the Arab Spring, are difficult, perhaps even impossible, to predict. On the other hand, structural pressures build up slowly and more predictably and are amenable to analysis and forecasting. Further, many triggering events themselves are ultimately caused by pent-up social pressures that seek an outlet—in other words, by structural factors. More importantly, the consequences of the triggering event are heavily mediated through the underlying context, namely these structural conditions. The self-immolation of Norman Morrison protesting US involvement in the Vietnam War, for instance, had a very different impact from that of Mohamed Bouazizi due to the divergent structural conditions.

The main focus of SDT is on the structural pressures undermining social resilience. The theory represents complex human societies as systems with three main compartments (the general population, the elites, and the state) interacting with each other and with sociopolitical instability via a web of non-linear feedbacks (see Turchin 2013, 2016). Over the past four decades, SDT has proven adept not only at explaining the dynamics of crisis, resilience, and recovery in a number of historical cases ranging from ancient empires to early modern states and nineteenth-century revolutions and civil wars (Goldstone 1991; Nefedov 2002; Turchin 2003; Turchin and Nefedov 2009; Korotayev and Khaltourina 2006, 2011) but also at predicting upcoming waves of violence and instability. In 2010 I used SDT to make the following forecast: "The next decade is likely to be a period of growing instability in the United States and western Europe" (Turchin 2010). This prediction was not simply a projection of the contemporary (in 2010) trend of social instability into the future—instability in Western countries had been, in fact, declining prior to 2010 (Figure 20.1). Rather, the basis for this forecast was a model that quantified structural drivers for sociopolitical instability, such as stagnating/declining real wages, a growing gap between rich and poor, overproduction of young graduates with advanced degrees, increasing public debt, and declining confidence in state institutions. This model highlighted 2020 as the year of spiking instability, a prediction that has unfortunately proven devastatingly accurate.

20.3 Data Patterns

The goal of the MPF approach is to first explain and then forecast the dynamics of sociopolitical instability (which is, therefore, the *response variable*). The computational model uses a variety of inputs to enable such forecasting (these inputs are, thus, *predictor variables*). In this section, I review the various proxies that allow us to quantify both responses and predictors.

20.3.1 Response Variable: Sociopolitical Instability

Political instability is violent group-level conflict within a state. It occupies the middle ground between interstate warfare and individual violence/crime.

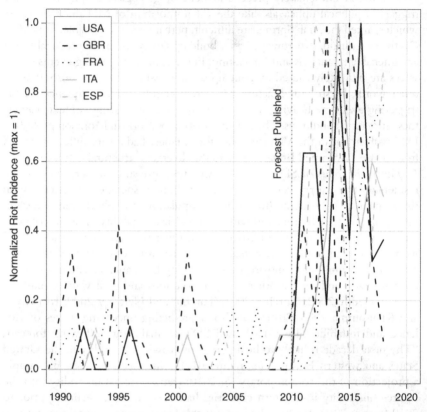

Figure 20.1 Temporal trends of violent riot incidence in five Western countries (Turchin and Korotayev 2020).

Instability events vary in scale from an intense and prolonged Civil War claiming thousands (sometimes even millions) of human lives to a one-day urban riot with a handful of deaths, or even a violent demonstration with none. However, when studying instability in past and contemporary societies, our primary focus is on *lethal* events, those that have caused loss of life. Such a conservative approach, while excluding a number of legitimate instability events, has two advantages. First, it clearly demarcates political violence from peaceful demonstrations and non-violent labor strikes. Second, and even more important, events that involve loss of life are much more likely to be reported in the media. Thus, focusing on lethal events reduces the effect of various reporting biases and allows us more faithfully to reconstruct the temporal dynamics of political violence.

Turchin (2012) describes a computerized database on the dynamics of sociopolitical instability in the United States between 1780 and 2010. This US Political Violence (USPV) database includes 1,590 political violence events such as riots, lynchings, and terrorism. Incidents of political violence in USPV database are classified by whether both opposing sides are substantial groups of people (specifically, more than 12 individuals), or whether one side is a group, and the other is one or few (under 12) individuals. The boundary of 12 between "few" and "many" is arbitrary: It simply follows the precedent established by Gilje (1996).

The generic term for group-on-group violence used both in the scientific literature (Gilje 1996; Grimstead 1998) and in American newspaper reports is *riot*. Gilje defines a riot as "any group of 12 or more people attempting to assert their will immediately through the use of force outside the normal bounds of law" (Gilje 1996: 4). Turchin (2012) modified this basic definition by distinguishing between group-on-group violence (proper riots) and group-on-individual violence (termed lynchings). If a riot is a conflict between groups of people, a *lynching* is lethal violence perpetrated by many on one or a few individuals. Violence perpetrated by one/few on many includes, first, terrorism, which is generally directed against some social or political institution, or society as a whole. A second important class is *assassination*, that is, when an individual is targeted not as a private person, but as a representative or an embodiment of some social group or political institution. The third category is *indiscriminate mass murder*, in America most often taking the form of shooting rampages. This is a relatively new type of violence that has become common in the United States only in the past three or four decades. Although they give the appearance of senseless, random violence because the great majority of shooting rampages do not target specific individuals, I treat indiscriminate mass murder as a form of terrorism—*suicide terrorism*—because the only difference between a rampage shooter and a suicide bomber is in the weapon used to inflict damage (in fact, indiscriminate mass murderers use not only guns, but knives, vehicles, and explosives). Both aim not at individual people but at groups, social or political institutions, or entire societies.

As the USPV database shows, the incidence of political violence fluctuated dramatically in the United States between 1780 and 2010 (Figure 20.2). The dynamical pattern revealed by the instability data was a secular wave with 50-year (bi-generational) cycles superimposed on it. The complete secular cycle began with a trough in 1820 and ended with another trough in 1950. In addition to this secular wave, the dynamics of instability exhibited shorter-term peaks, recurring with a period of approximately 50 years around 1870, 1920, 1970—and now 2020.

20.3.2 Predictor Variables: Structural-Demographic Instability Drivers

The fundamental structural-demographic driver for instability is *relative wage* or, alternatively, *relative income*. Relative wage is defined as the wage of a "typical" worker (ideally, the median wage; but where such data are unavailable, I use other proxies) divided by the GDP per capita. Relative income is defined

Figure 20.2 Temporal dynamics of sociopolitical instability in the United States. Data source (Turchin 2012); model prediction: PSI from Figure 20.6.

analogously, as the median household income divided by the average household income.

To approximate the wage of a typical worker, I use two time series constructed by Officer and Williamson (2013b) and updated yearly: For unskilled labor and manufacturing workers. Following the approach in Turchin (2016), I index both wages to 1 in 1860, average them, and then divide the mean by GDPpc, also obtained from MeasuringWorth (Officer and Williamson 2013a). All data are in nominal US dollars.

There are two secular waves evident in these data (Figure 20.3). The first one peaks in 1830 and ends with a trough in 1910. The second wave has a broad peak in 1940–1960 and then declines smoothly to the present (2020).

Data on median household incomes are available only from 1945. Fortunately, there is a linear relationship between relative incomes and relative wages (Figure 20.4). However, the amplitude of RelIncome is smaller: It varies between 0.75 and 0.91, whereas RelWage varies between 0.69 and 1.21 (for the same period). This effect is probably due to more members of the household joining the labor force when wages declined, as happened after 1970 in the United States.

Declining wages/household incomes are correlated with decreases in other measures of well-being, including biological (life expectancy, average stature) and social (age of marriage) indicators (Turchin 2016: Chapter 3). Decreasing well-being or, equivalently, growing *immiseration* contributes to the *mass mobilization*

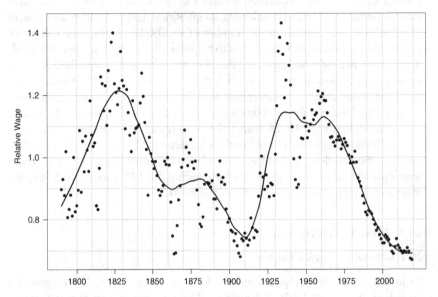

Figure 20.3 Temporal dynamics of relative wage in the United States, 1780–2019. The smoothed trend was obtained by LOESS.

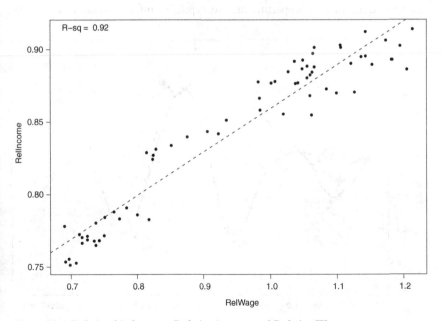

Figure 20.4 Relationship between Relative Income and Relative Wage.

potential (MMP) of the population (Goldstone 1991), which is one of the three most important SDT factors explaining sociopolitical unrest. Another component of MMP is a rapid growth in the number of youths. Unusually large cohorts of youths, also known as *youth bulges* tend to be politically destabilizing, because a sudden increase in new workers joining the labor force tends to depress their employment prospects and wages (Easterlin 1980; Macunovich 2002). Furthermore, young adults are particularly susceptible to radicalization and risk-taking. One way of capturing this driver for instability is to calculate the annual change in the relative size of the cohort aged 15–24 years (relative to the total population). These data (Figure 20.4) indicate that a huge youth bulge developed in the United States during the 1960s, resulting from a large "baby boomer" cohort coming of age. There were two additional youth bulges peaking during the 1920s and early 2000s, but these were much smaller in magnitude (Figure 20.5).

20.4 Model Description

20.4.1 Social Contagion Module

As noted above, the computational model at the core of the MPF engine was described in Turchin (2016: Chapter 2). The first component of it is a simple age-structured model of social contagion, inspired by the theoretical framework used in epidemiology, known as the SIR models (May and Anderson 1991). The SIR refers to the representation of the modeled population as composed of three compartments: **S**usceptible, **I**nfectious, and **R**ecovered

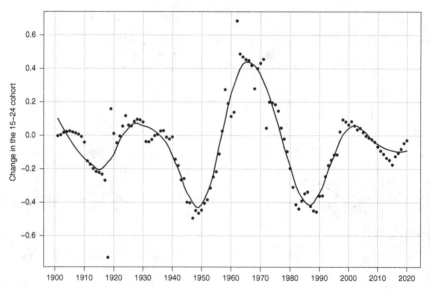

Figure 20.5 "Youth bulges" in the United States between 1900 and 2020. The units of change along the y-axis are percentage points (that is, the annual change in the percentage of the total population who are aged 15–24 years).

individuals. The mathematical theory of epidemics offers a natural framework for modeling the dynamics of such cultural traits as social attitudes and norms, because individuals learn them socially, from others—just as epidemics spread as a result of people infecting each other with germs.

There are three kinds of individuals in the model. The first is the "naïve" type, corresponding to the susceptibles in the epidemiological framework. This is the class into which individuals are put when they become adults (the model tracks only individuals who are active adults; so, children and the elderly beyond retirement age are not modeled and have no effect on the dynamics). Naïve individuals can become "radicalized" by being exposed to individuals of the radical type (corresponding to infectious individuals in the SIR framework). The process of radicalization can occur as a result of encountering radicals and becoming converted to their ideology. This process of social contagion is the central feature of the module.

My primary goal here is to understand the dynamics of sociopolitical instability. The proportion of radicals in the total population is thus the key variable that we need to track. When a high proportion of the population is radicalized, sociopolitical instability should be high. Under such conditions, riots are easily triggered and readily spread, terrorist and revolutionary groups thrive and receive support from many sympathizers, and society is highly vulnerable to an outbreak of Civil War. Thus, the proportion of radicals in the population is positively related to sociopolitical instability. Note, however, that there is likely to be a nonlinear relationship between these two variables, because as the proportion of radicals in the population grows, it becomes increasingly easy for them to link up and organize, potentially leading to an accelerating effect on the levels of political violence. For reasons of parsimony, the current model does not incorporate this realistic mechanism.

A naïve individual can also become radicalized by being exposed to violence resulting from radical activities. Note that all radicals will usually not belong to a single "Radical Party." During periods of high political instability, there are typically many issues dividing the population and the elites. Thus, there are many factions of radicals, warring with each other. Some become left-wing extremists, others join right-wing organizations.

The model does not track different factions of radicals, only their numbers (as a proportion of the overall population). The more radicals there are, the more likely it is that a naïve individual will be exposed to political violence and become radicalized as a result. For example, someone whose relative or friend has been killed in a terrorist act perpetrated by right-wing extremists might join a left-wing revolutionary group. This second route to radicalization is also a kind of social contagion (but mediated by violence, instead of radical ideology). Both routes result in similar dynamics, so I model them with one general functional form.

The third type of individual in the model is the "moderate" (corresponding to "recovered" in the SIR framework). This group comprises former radicals who have become disenchanted with radicalism and internecine warfare, and have come to the conclusion that society needs to pull together and overcome its differences. The moderates differ from the naïves in that they value peace and order above all, and work actively to bring it about. In other words, naïve individuals don't have an active political program, radicals work actively to increase instability, and moderates work actively to dampen it out.

Dynamical equations describing how the rates at which individuals pass into and out of the three compartments are:

$$S_{a+1,t+1} = (1 - \sigma_t)S_{a,t}$$

$$I_{a+1,t+1} = (1 - \rho_t)I_{a,t} + \sigma_t S_{a,t}$$

$$R_{a+1,t+1} = R_{a,t} + \rho_t I_{a,t}$$

The state variables are the proportions of naïve individuals in the population (S), of radicals (I), and of moderates (R; following the SIR convention of susceptibles–infected–recovered). Subscripts refer to age (a) and time (t); thus, $a = 1, \dots T$ where T is the maximum age (and the number of age classes). For example, $R_{25,1951}$, is the proportion of moderates in the age class 25 in the year 1951. "Age class 25," however, does not mean that individuals within it are 25 years old. The actual age depends on when "adulthood" starts. So, if the model begins to track individuals when they turn 21, age class 25 will correspond to individuals who are 45 years old.

This system of equations is simply an accounting device, keeping track of flows between different compartments. Thus, all individuals leaving the naïve compartment (at the rate σ_t) must be added to the radicalized compartment (keeping track of their age class). Similarly, all individuals leaving the radicalized compartment (at the rate ρ_t) are added to the moderate compartment. All the action is in the two coefficients, which are modeled as follows:

$$\sigma_t = \sigma_0 + \left(\alpha - \gamma \sum_a R_{a,t}\right)\sum_a I_{a,t} \quad 0 \leq \sigma_t \leq 1$$

$$\rho_t = \delta \sum_a I_{a,t-\tau} \quad 0 \leq \rho_t \leq 1$$

The first equation says that the social contagion rate, σ_t, increases together with the total number of radicals ($\Sigma I_{a,t}$, summing over all age classes). In other words, the more radicals there are, the more likely that a naïve individual becomes radicalized. However, there is an additional effect of the moderate presence: "Infection" by radicalism declines as moderates increase in numbers and exert their moderating, instability-suppressing influence to reduce the probability that a naïve will become radicalized. Finally, a small fraction of naïve individuals become radicals "spontaneously," without needing to be radicalized (at the rate σ_0).

The second equation models the effect of the level of political violence on the probability of a radical becoming disgusted with radicalism and turning into a moderate. Because I proxy instability by the number of radicals, the equation for ρ_t includes the sum of radicals in all age classes. However, note that there is a time delay, τ. This parameter reflects the observation that high levels of political violence do not instantly translate into the social mood of revulsion against violence and desire for internal peace. Violence acts in a cumulative fashion; many years of high instability, or even outright Civil War have to pass before the majority of the population begins to yearn for order earnestly.

In addition to the equations defining the rates of change, we also need boundary conditions. At every time step, a constant fraction is added to the first age class in the naïve compartment, $S_{1,t} = 1/T$, where T is the number of age classes (this ensures that the proportions of all age classes in all compartments always add up to 1). At the other end, individuals moving into age class $T + 1$ are simply eliminated (they die off or retire from active political life).

Parameter α indicates the likelihood that an encounter between a radical and a naïve will result in the naïve becoming radicalized, while γ measures the suppressive effect of moderates on the radicalization rate. Parameter δ translates the intensity of radicalism into the rate at which radicals turn into moderates. Parameter τ measures the time scale at which exposure to violent acts causes the backlash against it, and T is the period of adult activity.

20.4.2 Political Stress Index Module

The second component of the model links the social contagion dynamics to the dynamics of structural-demographic drivers for instability. We assume that α, propensity to radicalize, is positively related to Ψ, the Political Stress Index (PSI). When structural-demographic conditions result in high social pressure for instability, radical ideas should fall on fertile soil and readily take root and Ψ is high. Conversely, when pressures for instability wane, Ψ declines. The various structural-demographic factors that influence PSI are reviewed in Turchin (2016: Chapter 2). In the current implementation of the MPF engine, for reasons of parsimony, we use a stripped-down version of PSI, which tracks only three factors: Immiseration (inverse relative income), age structure of the population (focusing on youth bulges), and intra-elite overproduction/overcompetition (the numbers of elites in relation to the total population). The last factor assumes that the demand for elite positions is proportional to the elite numbers. The supply of such positions will grow in proportion to the total population. Thus, elite numbers relative to the total population are a measure of intra-elite competition for a limited number of positions. The equation for $\alpha(t)$ is given below (*Parameterizing the Model*).

20.4.3 Elite Dynamics Module

While immiseration and age effects are exogenous inputs into the model (this will be discussed in the next section), relative elite numbers are modeled endogenously. The calculations in this section can focus on either elite individuals and dividing them by the total population, or on counting elite households and dividing them by the total number of households. I will focus on household numbers and incomes.

Elite household numbers, E, can change as a result of two processes: endogenous population growth (the balance between births and deaths) and social mobility from and to the general population (with N being the total number of households). Accordingly, the equation for E is:

$$\dot{E} = rE + \mu N$$

where r is per capita rate of population growth and μ is the coefficient capturing the balance of upward and downward social mobility between the general population compartment and the elite compartment of the model.

The rate of net social mobility, μ, should be *inversely* related to the relative income, because if household incomes do not keep up with economic growth, the elites dispose of an increasingly large amount of surplus. A favorable economic conjuncture for employers, thus, creates greater upward mobility opportunities for entrepreneurial commoners. I assume that

$$\mu = \mu_0 \left(\frac{w_0}{w} - 1 \right)$$

where w is the relative income and μ_0 and w_0 are scaling parameters. Parameter μ_0 modulates the magnitude of response in social mobility to the availability of surplus. Parameter w_0 is the level at which there is no net upward mobility (when $w = w_0$, $\mu = 0$). The more w falls below that level, the more positive the term on the right-hand side will be, and the more vigorous upward social mobility. Conversely, when w increases above w_0, upward social mobility is choked off, and the net mobility is downwards (out of the elite compartment into the general population).

Combining these two equations, we have the following model for the dynamics of elite households:

$$\dot{E} = rE + \mu_0 \left(\frac{w_0 - w}{w} \right) N$$

If the demographic rate of elite increase is the same as that characterizing the general population, then this equation can be simplified by focusing on *relative elite numbers*, $e = E/N$. After some algebra we have

$$\dot{e} = \mu_0 \frac{w_0 - w}{w}$$

In other words, if the elites do not differ in their demography from commoners, the rate of change of relative elite numbers is simply the net rate of social mobility.

It is also useful to add to the model a calculation of how the average elite income changes with time. I will assume that the elites divide among themselves the amount of surplus produced by the economy. This surplus is $G - WN$, where G is the total GDP, W is the (commoner) household income (not scaled by GDPpc), and N is the number of households.

Dividing this quantity by the elite numbers (E) we obtain the average surplus per elite. Finally, we scale the average surplus per elite by the GDP per household ($g = G/N$), or *relative elite income*:

$$\varepsilon = \frac{1}{g} \frac{G - WN}{E}$$

which simplifies to

$$\varepsilon = \frac{1 - w}{e}$$

where w is the relative commoner income and e is relative elite numbers (elites as a proportion of the total population).

So far, the elite module has focused on upward social mobility—processes resulting in the expansion of the elite numbers. However, expansion cannot go on forever. Analysis of historical secular cycles (Turchin and Nefedov 2009; Turchin 2016) indicates that periods of downward social mobility from the elites into the commoner class are strongly associated with disintegrative phases, or "Ages of Discord." Political instability and internal warfare prune elite numbers in a variety of ways. Some elite individuals are simply killed in civil wars or as a result of assassination. Others may be dispossessed of their elite status by their faction losing in Civil War. Finally, general conditions of violence and lack of success discourage many of the "surplus" elite aspirants from continuing to pursue elite status, as a result of which they accept downward mobility.

A parsimonious way to model this process is by adding another term to the elite equation as follows:

$$\dot{e} = \mu_0 \frac{w_0 - w}{w} - (e_t - e_0)R$$

Here $(e_t - e_0)$ are the surplus elites (elite exceeding the level for whom elite positions are available e_0) and R is the proportion of the population that has converted from radicals to moderates. In other words, the assumption here is that surplus elites are first radicalized and then make the transition from radicals to moderates, in the process accepting non-elite status.

20.4.4 Parameterizing the Model

The fundamental driver of the dynamics in the model is the trajectory of relative income, $w(t)$. As we saw above, w varies between 0.91 and 0.75. I will assume that the level at which upward social mobility is zero, $w_0 = 0.9$, near the upper limit of observed w values. This assumption implies that when the social system is in equilibrium (that is, relative elite numbers are neither increasing nor decreasing), 90% of GDP goes to commoner households and 10% goes to elite households. Further assuming a conventional level for the relative elite numbers at this equilibrium, e_0, as 0.01 (the proverbial 1%), we have the mean elite income as $0.1/0.01 = 10$, or an order of magnitude greater than w_0. Note, however, that once the social system leaves the equilibrium, both relative elite numbers and their average incomes will change dynamically.

When relative incomes decline below w_0, elite numbers start increasing. The rate of increase is governed by the parameter μ, which I set to 0.3 because it results in 2–3-fold increase in elite numbers over 30 years, which is what happened both in the run up to Civil War (Turchin 2016: Table 8.1) and between 1980 and 2010 (Turchin 2016: Table 13.1).

Parameters of the social contagion module were the same as used previously (Turchin 2016: Caption of Figure 2.3): $\gamma = 1$, $\delta = 0.5$, $\tau = 10$, and $T = 35$. The key link between the social contagion and structural-demographic models is the parameter α (propensity to radicalize). As stated above, the model tracks three factors: Immiseration (inverse relative income), age structure of the population (with the focus on youth bulges), and intra-elite overproduction/overcompetition (the numbers of elites in relation to the total population). I used the following formula:

$$\alpha(t) = \alpha_0 + \alpha_w(w_0 - w) + \alpha_e(e - e_0) + A_{20}$$

where $\alpha_0 = 0.1$ is the base level, $\alpha_w = 1$ is the weight given immiseration, and $\alpha_e = 0.5$ is the weight given elite overproduction. The elite component weight is lower than that for immiseration because whereas the immiseration factor changed between 0 and 0.25, the elite factor changes with a greater amplitude, between 0 and 1. The youth bulge effect, A_{20}, was modeled as a single perturbation using a Gaussian functional form centered on 1965 with a standard deviation of 10 years and a peak value of 0.2.

20.5 Testing the MPF Engine with Historical Data

This section describes model dynamics for the period between 1810 and 1990. Because model parameters were selected based on historical data and to match model behavior with instability data during this time period, this is not a formal test of model accuracy. Rather, it is a test of whether the model is capable of generating historically observed dynamics for plausible values of parameters. We can think of the period 1810–1990 as the "training set" for the model, and the subsequent period (see the next section) as the "prediction set" (especially the period after 2010, which constitutes a formal test of model predictions published in 2010).

As Figure 20.3 shows, relative wage decreased between 1830 and 1860. Using the relationship between relative wages and relative incomes (Figure 20.4), we can assume that relative income, w, decreased from the equilibrium value of 0.9 to roughly 0.75. The first scenario that we examine is the effect

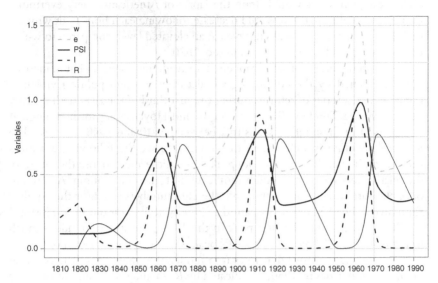

Figure 20.6 Model-generated dynamics assuming a single decline in *w* between 1830 and 1860.

of this decrease on the model-generated dynamics (Figure 20.6). Using the dynamics of *I* (proportion of the population that is radicalized, summing over all age classes, dashed curve in the figure) as a proxy for sociopolitical instability, we observe that the decline in *w* generates a rapid increase in *e* (relative elite numbers). Decline in *w* and increase in *e* translate into higher PSI and, therefore, growing propensity to radicalize (PSI, thick black curve). This is followed by a spike in *I* that peaks during the early 1860s (corresponding to the American Civil War). However, high *I* and associated political turbulence results in increasing *R* (the proportion of moderates), which eventually suppresses the violence wave. At the same time, violence reduces the elite numbers. Historically, this was a result of two processes. First, a high proportion of the Antebellum ruling class (slave-owning southerners) was killed in the Civil War battles. Second, and quantitatively even more important, was the freeing of the slaves, which destroyed the wealth of the Antebellum southern elites and eliminated them as national elites for decades to come. They were replaced by a northern elite, whose wealth was based on free labor and industrialization.

However, the release of social pressures resulting from the destruction of the Antebellum elites was short-lived. Because relative incomes stayed at a low level, the pump transferring wealth from workers to employers continued to operate and by the early 1900s elite overproduction reached and exceeded the 1860 level. In the absence of action that would stop the pump, the model predicts, the United States was doomed to experience a series of increasingly violent crises during the 1910s, then 1960s, and beyond, recurring at roughly 50-year intervals. As indicated by increasing peaks in PSI (black thick curve), each subsequent crisis would strain the fabric of American society evermore. Furthermore, although PSI would decrease following each bout of downward mobility, even between peaks it stayed at an elevated level, compared to where it was during the Era of Good Feelings c. 1820.

Fortunately, this is not what happened. Instead, the American elites, increasingly frightened by the continuing social turbulence and political violence, implemented a series of reforms during the first third of the twentieth century (for details, see Turchin 2016: Chapter 10 and Hoyer et al., forthcoming). A major result of these reforms was that between 1910 and 1940 w returned to w_0. Implementing this change in the model, we see the following dynamics (Figure 20.7). The 1910s instability peak is very little affected, but the return of the relative income to the equilibrium level shuts down the pump. As a result, once the surplus elites are eliminated, the elite numbers stay near the equilibrium levels. The PSI declines to another low by 1950, as it did in real history.

There is still a radicalization peak in the 1970s, but its magnitude is much lower than the 1910s peak. The 1970s peak is due to a combination of factors: first, the fathers–and–sons dynamics (the moderating memory of the previous instability peak fades by 1950, as indicated by R reaching zero) and, second, the effect of the 1960s youth bulge.

20.6 Using the MPF Engine for Forecasting Future Trajectories

I now use the MPF engine to investigate the possible trajectories that the American social system could take beyond 2020. The only parameter

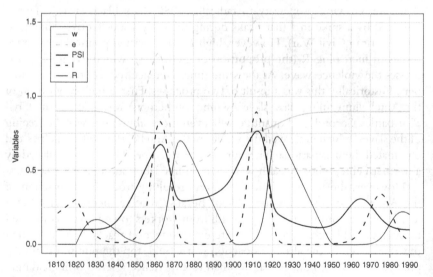

Figure 20.7 Model-generated dynamics assuming that a decline in w between 1830 and 1860 is followed by an increase between 1910 and 1940.

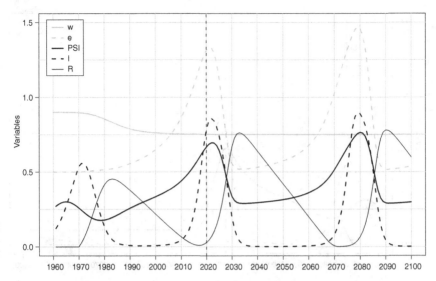

Figure 20.8 Model-generated dynamics assuming that a single decline in *w* between 1970 and 2000.

change I introduce is an increase in *T* (the length of active adult life) from 35 to 45. Whereas for the past (and especially for the nineteenth century) it made sense to assume that adults are active between 20 and 55 years of age, increased life expectancy today suggests that this period should be lengthened to 20–65.

As in the previous section, I start with a single transition, this time taking place between 1970 and 2000 (Figure 20.8). As before, the decline in *w* turns on the pump, and elite numbers begin to increase in an accelerating manner. The moderating effect of the previous (mild) peak of instability in the 1970s fades away by the early 2000s (the black curve). This releases a spike of radicalization, which should peak during the 2020s. Note that all dynamics have been well set before the 2010 forecast of future instability. In fact, the dynamics are set as soon as *w* finishes its transition. If nothing is done to bring *w* back up to its equilibrium level, we will see a temporary lull, with PSI declining somewhat (but not to its equilibrium level). As the pump would continue operating, another spike of violence would inevitably come, peaking in the late 2070s. In other words, we will have a repeat of the 1860s–1920s Age of Discord with two spikes about 50 years apart.

Let us now see what happens if action is taken to bring *w* back to *w₀*. Assuming (somewhat unrealistically) the most favorable scenario, *w* is brought up between 2020 and 2025 (Figure 20.9). This intervention will not eliminate, or even have much of an effect on the 2020s peak—there is too much inertia in the social system. Furthermore, it will result in a significant negative effect on the average elite incomes. Such relative impoverishment of the elites is

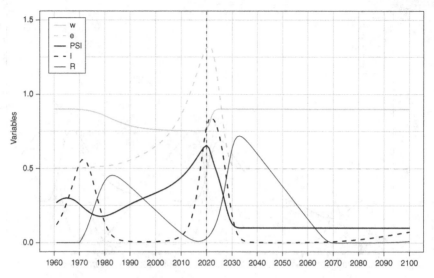

Figure 20.9 Model-generated dynamics in which a decline in *w* between 1970 and 2000 is followed by a rapid increase in the 2020s.

likely to exacerbate the crisis. However, after a painful and violent decade of the 2020s, the system will rapidly achieve its equilibrium. PSI will reach its minimum, the proportion of the population that is radicalized will fall, and the surplus elites will be eliminated. The only memory of the Troubles of the 2020s will be in a high proportion of moderates, who will gradually fade away toward 2070. The end result will be a "sharp short-term pain—long-term gain" outcome.

20.7 Conclusion

The ability of the "prototype" MPF model to reproduce the key aspects of the historical instability trajectory in the United States between 1810 and 1990 and, especially, the success of the 2010 forecast for 2020, are encouraging and support the overall feasibility of building a fuller version. However, I emphasize that this is an MPF prototype, not a fully developed product. Most importantly, we have not yet built in the prototype the ability for *ensemble forecasts*, in which the model is run repeatedly while affected by different sequences of stochastic perturbations. This feature will enable us to see how much uncertainty is associated with the model predictions. Furthermore, MPF is a nonlinear dynamic model, and thus it is likely that in some parts of the phase space the prediction will be affected by rapid trajectory divergence, while in others by slower divergence or even convergence.

Second, the MPF forecasts in the prototype assume that parameter values are fixed, whereas in reality they are always estimated with some error. We need to translate this source of uncertainty into predictions.

Third, and at a more general level, we need to investigate how including (or not) different mechanisms in the model affects its predicted dynamics. Related to this, a single success, as we saw with the 2020 prediction, could always be due simply to chance. It is imperative to replicate this case study for many more societies entering crisis and exiting from it. Such an effort is currently underway by the Seshat project, which is building a CrisisDB that will include several hundreds of past societies sliding into crises and then out of it. In particular, we are going to quantify the characteristics of several collapses discussed in this volume.

Overall, we are just starting on the road that would eventually yield a usable MPF engine. But it is already clear that this is a highly fruitful avenue of future research with potentially huge consequences for keeping our complex societies from collapsing.

Acknowledgment

I thank the participants of the working group at the Complexity Science Hub on Social Complexity and Collapse: Nina Witoszek, Stefan Thurner, David Garcia, Roger Griffin, Daniel Hoyer, Atle Midttun, James Bennett, Knut Myrum Næss, and Sergey Gavrilets. Daniel Hoyer provided helpful comments on a draft of this article. This research has been supported by Complexity Science Hub (CSH) Vienna and V. Kann Rasmussen Foundation.

References

Butzer, K. W., and G. H. Endfield. 2012. Critical Perspectives on Historical Collapse. *PNAS* 109(10):3628–3631.

Casti, J. L. 2012. *X-Events: Complexity Overload and the Collapse of Everything.* William Morrow, New York.

Cumming, G. S., and G. D. Peterson. 2017. Unifying Research on Social–Ecological Resilience and Collapse. *Trends in Ecology & Evolution* 32(9):695–713.

Diamond, J. 2004. *Collapse: How Societies Choose to Fail or Succeed.* Viking, New York.

Easterlin, R. 1980. *Birth and Fortune.* Basic Books, New York.

Gilje, P. A. 1996. *Rioting in America.* Indiana University Press, Bloomington, IN.

Goldstone, J. A. 1991. *Revolution and Rebellion in the Early Modern World.* University of California Press, Berkeley, CA.

Grimstead, D. 1998. *American Mobbing, 1828–1861: Towards Civil War.* Oxford University Press, New York.

Korotayev, A., and D. Khaltourina. 2006. *Introduction to Social Macrodynamics: Secular Cycles and Millennial Trends in Africa.* URSS, Moscow.

Korotayev, A., J. Zinkina, S. Kobzeva, J. Bozhevolnov, D. Khaltourina, A. Malkov, and S. Malkov. 2011. A Trap at the Escape from the Trap? Demographic-Structural Factors of Political Instability in Modern Africa and West Asia. *Cliodynamics* 2(2):276–303.

Macunovich, D. J. 2002. *Birth Quake: The Baby Boom and Its Aftershocks.* Universtiy of Chicago Press, Chicago, IL.

May, R. M., and R. M. Anderson. 1991. *Infectious Diseases of Humans: Dynamics and Control.* Oxford University Press, Oxford.

Nefedov, S. 2002. On the Theory of Demographic Cycles (in Russian). *Ekonomicheskaya istoriya* 8:116–121.

Nefedov, S. A. 2005. Нефедов С. А. Демографически-структурный анализ социально-экономической истории России. Екатеринбург 2005. 540

Officer, L. H., and S. H. Williamson. 2013a. The Annual Consumer Price Index for the United States, 1774–2012. MeasuringWorth. URL: http://www.measuringworth.com/uscpi/.

Officer, L. H., and S. H. Williamson. 2013b. Annual Wages in the United States, 1774–Present. MeasuringWorth. URL: http://www.measuringworth.com/uswages/.

Renfrew, C. 1984. *Approaches to Social Archaeology*. Cambridge University Press, Cambridge, MA.

Tainter, J. A. 1988. *The Collapse of Complex Societies*. Cambridge University Press, Cambridge.

Tainter, J. A. 1995. Sustainability of Complex Societies. *Futures* 27(4):397–407.

Toynbee, A. J. 1957. *A Study of History: Volume II*. Oxford University Press, London.

Turchin, P. 2003. *Historical Dynamics: Why States Rise and Fall*. Princeton University Press, Princeton, NJ.

Turchin, P. 2010. 2020: Political Instability May Play a Role. *Nature* 463(7281):608.

Turchin, P. 2012. Dynamics of Political Instability in the United States, 1780–2010. *Journal of Peace Research* 4(4):577–591.

Turchin, P. 2013. Modeling Social Pressures Toward Political Instability. *Cliodynamics* 4(2):241–280.

Turchin, P. 2016. *Ages of Discord: A Structural-Demographic Analysis of American History*. Beresta Books, Chaplin, CT.

Turchin, P., and A. Korotayev. 2020. The 2010 Structural-Demographic Forecast for the 2010–2020 Decade: A Retrospective Assessment. *PLOS ONE* 15(8):e0237458.

Turchin, P., and S. Nefedov. 2009. *Secular Cycles*. Princeton University Press, Princeton, NJ.

Turchin, P., N. Witoszek, S. Thurner, D. Garcia, R. Griffin, D. Hoyer, A. Midttun, J. Bennett, K. Myrum Næss, and S. Gavrilets. 2018. A History of Possible Futures: Multipath Forecasting of Social Breakdown, Recovery, and Resilience. *Cliodynamics* 9:124–139.

Weiss, H., and R. S. Bradley. 2001. What Drives Societal Collapse? *Science* 291(5504):609–610.

Index

Page numbers in **bold** denote tables, those in *italic* denote figures.

Abbasid Caliphate 31, 48
Acemoglu, D. 290
Acuna-Soto, R. 181
adaptive cycle 16, 104, 126
aging 314, 378–383, 387–388, 391;
  behavior 391; biological 387; evolution-
  producing 388; human 378; hypothesis
  382; lack of 383; non- 381, 383;
  noticeable 379; organic 376–377;
  process 385
agnotology 44
agrarian 39, 44, 46–47; laborers 201;
  output 135; production *134*, 139;
  regime 132, 134; resources 129; societies
  65, 81; world 197
Akkad 30–31; Empire 52, 265, **266**; Sargon
  of 26
Alchon, S. A. 183
Alef, G. 228
Alfani, G. 199
Amazonia 43
Anders, G. 322–323, 325, 328
Angkor **31**, 43, **266**, 267
apocalyptic 322–323; futures 5; movies
  1; possibility of nuclear collapse 313;
  visions 194–195
Arab 110, 132, 135, 224; conquests **338**,
  353; frontier 134; invasions 132; –
  Islamic conquests 138; –Islamic empire
  129, 136; –Islamic invasions 134; –
  Islamic polity 129; Spring 277, 399;
  translations 71
Arbesman, S. 380
archaeology 25, 61, 94–95, 128, 148, 156,
  184, 313; ancient 42; classical 98
artificial intelligence (AI) 65–66, 75, 78–79
Atomic Energy Commission 324

Aztec 159, 168, 170, 173, 177, 179,
  182; city-state 176; collapse 177, 179;
  conquest 167; destruction of **355**; empire
  94, 167, 170–172, 178–179; imperialism
  167, 186; politics 176; world 185

Bailey, M. 198
Basin of Mexico 167, *168*, 171, 173–177,
  179–184, **185**
basins of attraction 282
battle of Qadesh 99
bee: ability to forage 299; behavior 298;
  bumble 298, 301; colonies 260, 298–300;
  decline 299, 307; flower 303; forager
  300; health 298; honey 260, 296–302,
  307; human-mediated movement
  298; keepers 297–298, 307; nurse 300;
  populations 297–298, 307; species
  296–299, 301–302; strategies for survival
  299; wild 298, 307; worker 296, 301
Benson, L. V. 151
Beresford, M. 194
Berry, M. S. 151, 153
Bethe, H. 316–317
bias 3, 5, 94, 151, 158, 267–268; cognitive
  9; female- 159; investigator 151; male
  159; reporting 400; selection 360, 380;
  severe 158; survivorship 380
bifurcation **274**, 360, 362, 370; cusp
  360; Hopf 291; one-dimensional 360;
  pitchfork *363*; saddle-node 359–360,
  365; slow-forcing-to- 275; theory of
  360; tipping *270*, 271–272, **274**–275
biodiversity: loss 72; terrestrial 297, 306
biology 62, 94, 284, 293, 366, 386–387;
  population 284; synthetic 65
Birnbaum, H. 211

birth rates 147, 150, 182
Black Death 94, 125, 173, 179, 183,
     191–201, 207, **266**, 267, **338, 355**
black swan 93, 103
Blanton, R. E. 171, 175
Blockade of Leningrad 95, 236–237
Boak, A. E. 28
Boccaccio, G. 195
Bocinsky, R. K. 151, *152*, 153, **266**
Boettiger, C. 370
Bond, G. 263
Borah, W. W. 182
Boserup, E. 282
Brown, P. 339
Browning, I. 30
Buckley, B. M. **266**
Burj Khalifa 6–7
Bury, J. B. 29
Bushkovitch, P. 215
Butler, L. 321–322
Butzer, K. W. 172–173, 175, **266**
Byzantium 124, 208, 211; collapse of 93

Cahokia 31, **46**; collapse 30
cannibalism 236, 238–239, 251–252
Carballo, D. M. 177
cascades 15, 18, 160, 334, 336, 340,
     367–368; avalanche 368–369; downward
     349; failure. 370; intersystemic 377
Caudwell, C. 28
causality 335; closed loops of 276; collapse
     3–4; exogenous 11; stochastic 95
central Mesa Verde (CMV) 146–148, 150,
     152, 154, 158–159
centralization 39–40, 42, 64, 67, 118, 170–
     171, 174, 176, 228, 252–254, **338, 352**;
     bureaucratic 45; overt 120; power 65
Chaco Canyon 30–31, **46**, *147*
Chinese Civil War 78
civilization: ancient 18, 30, 268, 313, 381;
     breakdown 336; cage of 45; Christian
     195; collapse 1–2, 4–5, 9, 32, 63, *67*,
     105, 170, 191, 313, 316, 322, 328,
     333–334, 341, 386, 390; conquered 11;
     contemporary 262; cycles 16, 336, 346;
     death of 250; doomed 1, 8; dynamics
     of 351; early 52; Eastern Roman
     Civilization **353**; emergence of 32; end
     of 61, 315, 319, 323, 327, 335–336;
     established 11; failure 2, 5, 95, 314, 333;
     fall of 11, 334, 348–351; global 62–64;
     327, 392; Han **353**; historical 2, 11, 206,
     208; history 10; human 61, 65, 251;
     illusory 252; Indus 42; interdependent

333; interlocking 334; late Bronze
     Age **352**; lifecycle 313; limits of 376;
     longevity 375–376; modern 1, 18, 95,
     313–315, 320; mortality 375; past 259,
     381; resilience 207; response 207, 230;
     rise of 313, 334, 336, 348–351; Roman
     352; sense of 249; Song **354**; technical
     392; transformations 124; Western
     354–355
Clarke, J. **266**
Clarke, L. 324
climate: amelioration 155; benign-
     temperature 73; change 27, 29–32, 37,
     43–44, **46**, 50, 52–54, 65–68, 75, 79,
     93, 99–101, 114, 122, 132, 146, 151,
     156, 160, 167, 181, 260–262, 265, **266**,
     268–269, 271–272, **274**, 275–277, 297–
     299, 304, 307, 320, **352**; deterioration
     264–265, 274; distribution 267; -driven
     migration 276; drying 268; dynamics
     263; effects 94, 159, 263; events 259;
     extremes 277; factors 299; forcing 272;
     Holocene 261–265; hospitable 73;
     humanity's effect on 73; hypotheses 275;
     improvement 264; -induced constriction
     94; influences of 262; intervals 267;
     issues 132; marginal 264; micro- 307;
     niche 267–268, 276; paleo- 273–275;
     perturbations 272; predictable 259;
     science 94; shifts 11, 28; shocks 94;
     stability 264; stable 259, 261; stressors
     259; systems 16; tipping point 271, 273,
     274, 276; variability 146, 150, 155, 263,
     271; zone 267
Cline, E. H. 105, 287, 333–335
Cold War 32, 69, 81, 319, 321, 326
colonialism 52, 170, 179, 183, 185–186;
     settler 168; Spanish 167, 177, 184
complex adaptive systems (CAS) 3, 7, 11,
     18, 62, 79, 126, 314, 384, 387–388
concatenation of events 31–32, 119
conflict 27, 52, 65, 111–112, 117, 150,
     172, 178, 196, 264, 267, 319–320, 337,
     376–377, 401; armed 113; class 25,
     32, 167; diminishing 71; dynastic 116;
     external 30–31; factional 120; frontiers
     of 47; global 15; group-level 399;
     intensified 113; internal 50, 110–111,
     113, 117, 209; internecine 212, 218;
     intra-societal 31; military 109, 118;
     post- 69–70; recurrent 113; social 50;
     societal 31; theories 44; violent 269;
     widespread 154
Confucianism 115, **353**; neo- **354**

conquest 5, 11, 47, 50, **51**, 54, 76, 109,
168, 176–180, 182, 184, 207, 217–218,
228, 336, **338**; Arab **353**; Aztec 167;
benefits of 53; diminishing returns on
38, 46–47, 52; direct 53, 392; early 54;
Islamic 138, 172; Mongol 218, 230;
Spanish 146, 178–179, **184**; universal 47
contagion 11, 14–15, 18, 76, 334;
beneficial 15; mechanism of 15; social
404–407, 410
Cook, E. R. **266**
corruption 4, 12, 38, 45, 47–54, 114, 172,
239, 243, *289*, **353**, **355**
Coupled Infrastructure Systems (CIS)
Framework 259, 288, *289*, 291
COVID-19 1, 5, 7, 14, 65, 185, 201, 254
Cowgill, G. L. 170–171, 175
Crabtree, S. A. 158
Csete, M. E. 286
Cumming, G. S. 98
Cutler, R. 317–318
cyclicality 11, 17

dark ages 25, 29, 102, 335
decadence 31, 376–377
Demandt, A. 11, 333
deMenocal, P. B. **266**
democratization 76–78, 81
demographics 132; structural 49
deus ex machina 3, 32
Diamond, J. 170, 172, 333
Dill, Samuel. 28
diminishing returns on extraction (DROE)
38, 47–48, 51–54, 114
disaggregation 9–10, 38, 64, 67, 97, 160,
238, 244–245, 252–253; imperial 54;
political 63; strategic 243
disease 37, **46**, 53–54, 66, 71, 118, 150,
167, 177–183, 287, *289*, 300, 302;
autoimmune 286; cardiovascular 286;
collective 180; common 71; epidemic
168, 173, 179, 181; ethnicity impacted
185; events 114; germ theory of 71;
heart 286; human 196; infectious 178–
179, 181–182; potential 180; -related
catastrophes 194
dislocation 121, 197; economic 138;
geographic 184; individual 334; trade
route 93
Dolores Archaeological Project 159
Douglass, A. E. 149
Drake, B. L. **266**
drought 12, 16, 30, 50, 98–100, 105, 132,
147, 149, 151, 154, 175, 177, 181, 265,

266, 267, 287, *289*, 333; anomalous 265;
effects of 101; extreme 181; mega- 99–
100, 263; multi-decadal 125; prolonged
265; short-term 125; situation 103;
-tolerant crops 50
Dyer, C. 194, 196–197

Early Warning Signs (EWS) 104–105
earthquakes 11–12, 30–31, 66, 93, 99–101,
105, 125, 142, 195, 283, 287, 333, 346,
367–369, 398
ecological: conditions 306; degradation
261; deterioration 48; exploitation 41;
food webs 296; niche 386; phenomena
10, 372; processes 282; profiles 201;
regime shifts 80; socio- 259, 269,
283–285, 293, 314; systems 10, 12, 14,
16, 284; tipping points 65
ecology 2, 17, 41, 94, 167, 183, 358–359,
386, 392; competitive 387; theoretical
283–284
economics 184, 213, 244, 284, 349, 358,
367, 370; bio- 283; of coding 388; of
complexity 31; neoliberal 277; resource
284
economy 138, 184, 192–193, 209, 211,
218–219, 222, 254, 277, 290, 306, 333,
342, 409; centralized 340; collapse 340;
command 240–242; flourishing 215;
good 27; green 253; industrialized 72;
no-carbon 72; nomadic 211; political
46, 244, 253, 289; robust 207, 211; rural
132; shadow 242–244, 250; strong 226,
229
Eden, L. 323
efficiency 7, 287; cost of 18; drive for 287;
energy 43; of foraging 301; increasing
17; of information processing 287;
overemphasis on 12, 17; -robustness 283
Egyptian First Intermediate Period 30–31
Eilstrup-Sangiovanni, M. 385
Einstein, A. 327
El Niño 175; Southern Oscillation (ENSO)
264, 271
Ellsberg, D. 317–318
Ellyson, Laura J. 154
Emergency Committee of Atomic
Scientists 327
empire: Akkadian 52, 265, **266**; Aztec 94,
167, 170–171, 178–179; Bulgarian **353**;
Byzantine 54, 126, 208; Carolingian
354; Christian **353**; collapse 11, 114;
colonial 10; decline of 26; demise 50;
Eastern Roman 25, 110, 112, 120, 124,

126, 128–129, *130*; fall of 8, 27, **31**,
127; Han 93, 108–115, 118–121; High
Roman 48; Hittite 105; Holy Roman
386; Iranian 109; Islamic 129, 136; Jin
108–109, 112, 114, 121; Khmer **266**;
lifespan of 54; loss of 93; Macedonian
45; modern 47, 53; Mongol 207, 210–
211, 217, 375; Mughal 48; Ottoman
50; pan-Mediterranean 109; peak 108;
Persian 138; Qin 110; Roman 5, 11, 26,
93, 100, 108–110, 112–116, 118–120,
128, 135–136, 138, 142, 268; Russian
236, 252, 375; Sasanian 129, **353**;
survival of 128, 136, 138; Taagepera
381; Tang 121; Triple Alliance 167,
169, 171, 173, 176–177; Western
Roman 9, 25, 30–31, 41, 45–47, 50, 53,
61, 65, 93, 108–110, 112, 114–115, 117,
120–121, 140, 207, 265, **266**, 288, 333
energy 3, 7, 43, 45, 49, 55, 248; atomic
327; barrier 365; capital 41; capture 41,
46, 50, 64, 69, 126, 135; cliff 38, 50;
consumption 4; costs 376–377; crisis
333; demand 43; diminishing return
on 47; efficiency 43; extraction 41,
50, 52, 54; free 362, *363*, 364–365,
366; infrastructure 15; investment 44;
renewable 50; returned on energy
invested (EROEI) 72; return on
investment (EROI) 4, 38, 49, **51**, 114;
solar 50, 287; sources 54, 277, 377;
trophic chain of 49; use 39–41, 43;
wall 50
entropy 8, 376–377, 388
environmental: aspects 129; asymmetries
125; calamity 207; challenges 122;
change 11, 50, 124, 167, 182;
circumscription 264; concerns 29;
conditions 261–262, 264–265, 272,
304–305, 387; consequences 320;
context 129; damage 27, 79; debt 377;
degradation 32, 48, 50, 167, 172, 178,
181, 184, **338**, 376–377; depletion
386; deterioration 31, 50; dimensions
of social life 28; disruption 320; effects
320; extraction **51**, 53, 55; factors 65,
100–101, 114, 139, 181; failure 11, 333;
focus 29; hazards 6, 67; impacts 320;
inputs 48; instability 264; movement
32; overshoot 48; paloe- 132, 139;
policy 50, 284; pollution 307; problems
75; resources 27; returns 53; risks
125, 386; science 259; shifts 376–377;
shock 12; stimulus 134; stress 124, 127,

184, 304; systems 16, 168; toxins 297;
variations 28
epidemic 31, 94, 117, 170, 179–184, 206,
405; disease 168, 173, 179, 181; episodes
180–182; major 181; mortality due to
183–184; outbreaks 114; severity of
183; theory of 405; virgin soil 181–182;
waves 179–181
equilibrium 13–14, 138, 282, 285, 291,
359, 361, 365, 368, 410, 412, 414;
current 14; dis- 126; levels 412–413;
maintaining 51; non- 361, 367;
out-of- 361; of peace and prosperity
14; phase transitions 361; stable 358,
365; state 304–305, 359, 365, *366*;
statistical mechanics 362; structure 13;
thermodynamics 362; unstable 282
erosion 17, 116, 159–160, 179, 340; of
central governance 116; fiscal 117; sheet
and gully 179; soil 172
exploitation 41, 45, 52, 118, 132, 153–156,
160, 185
extinction 63, 67, 69, 73–77, 79, 81,
328, 386–387; community 305;
constant 386; global 392; human 4,
62; instantaneous 316; local 298, 306,
392; mass 10, 65, 80; outright 79;
probability of 69, 386; random 302,
304; rapid *303*; rates 386; risk 73;
species 305–306, 314

failure: admitting 325; of ancient
civilizations 313; attentional 323; brief
17; bureaucratic 240–241, 243, 253;
cascading 15, 117, 119, 121, **266**,
286–288, 290, 293, 370; catastrophic
287, 368–370, **371**; civilizational 2, 95,
314, 333; clustering of 15; of crops 27;
culpability for 12; endogenous 12, 18;
environmental 11, 333; of imagination
7; institutional 172; interaction of 16;
internal power 376–377; irrigation
266; isolated 6, 16; large-scale 368; of
leadership 27; localized 15; magnitude
of 15; managerial 18, 103; mitigation 6;
multiple 16; neighboring 15; Nile 265,
266; pathways to 13; points 369; policy
239; of prevention 120; prevention of
17; rate 314; recovery from 3; of rulers
26; sequential 339; simultaneous 16;
societal 4, 11–12; of the state 37, 49,
64–65, 67, 69; structural 103; susceptible
to 207; synchronous 15–16, 18;
synergistic interaction 15; of the system

80; systemic 1, 6–9, 12, 17–18; technical 325; vulnerability to 11; widespread 8
famine 26, 66, 74, 99, 101–102, 105, 117, 177, 181–182, 193, 196, 199, **266**, 287, 333, 336, 346; Egyptian **352**; Great (1314–1317) 196, **355**; urban 238
Federal Emergency Management Agency 324
feedback loops 13–15, 18, 39, 49, 65, 94, 117, 207, 259–260, 276, *285*, 289–290, 297; characteristic 14; community– environment 304; identification of 14; multiple 296; negative 14, 230, 259, 304; positive 14, 215, 218, 226, 228; social 14; vicious 207
Ferdinand, F. 15
Fermi, E. 317
fiber bundle model (FBM) 366–368, *369*, *371*, 372; Democratic 369, 372
Filyushkin, A. I. 227
financial 3, 12l administration **354**; affairs 139; circles 350; fragility 44; resources 215; system 10, 18
Five Pecks of Rice Rebellion 111
Fletcher, G. 224
food: access to 242; aid 265; alternative 81; availability 240; collapse 198; collection 300; depletion of supplies 320; deprived of 16; distribution 244, **353**; diversity of 148; employees 242; exporter 69; external supplies 180; global system 68; inequality in 236; innovations of 249; networks 368; non-traditional 250, 252; preparation 240; price index 277; production 68, 132, 277, 288, 297, 306–307; resilient 68; resources 136, 148, 300, 304; scarcity of 236–237, 242; security 239, 297; sources of 250; stolen 236, 241–245; stores 68, 242–243, 300; systems 297, 306; theft 242; trade 243, 277; traditional 250; unstable supply 286; vouchers 244; webs 287, 296, 304; wild 272
Forbidden City 44
Four Corners 147, 150–151
fragility 3, 5, 38, 52, 70, 95, 104, 286, 293, 368; conservation of 283, 293; degrees of 304; endogenous 12; financial 44; global 288; increasing 3; intrinsic 284; level of 126; precipitation of 2; robustness trade-off 51, 283, 286, 288, 293; social 156, 159; societal 49; state 48; systemic 1, 17; trajectory of 1
fragmentation 10, 47, 53, 67, 93, 97, 138, 140, 170–171, 174, 176, 178;

competitive 115; degree of 112; episodes of 170–171; of indigenous corporations **185**; lasting 109; of military organization 340; political 167, 176; of a polity 167; societal 10, 12
Frank, T. 28
Frisch, O. 316

Gabriel, R. A. 209
Gaddis, J. L. 351
Genuine Progress Indicator 64
Gibbon, E. 5, 11, 25, 27, 32
Gibson, C. **185**
Gilje, P. A. 401
Ginzburg, V. L. 362, *363*, 364–366
global: actors 5; capital stocks 70; catastrophe 73, 79; civilization 62–64, 327, 392; climate change 276–277; collaborative network 1; collapse 68–70, 73, 81, 270; complexity 1, 8; conflict 15; cooling period 93; disasters 160; economy 340; ecosystems 306; environment 392; environmental consequences 320; environmental disruption 320; environmental impacts 320; experience 327; extinction 392; financial crisis 1; food system 68; fragility 288; free energy minimum 365; impact 1; industrial society 73, 77; inequality 75; level 65; military force 383; order 10; population 45, 68; process of disaggregation 64; risks 375; scale 65, 319; shock 94; society 7, 64, 66–68, 73–77, 80–81; stress 333; system 6–7, 288, 333; systemic risk 8; systemic shocks 5; system-of-systems 7; systems 1, 3, 8; technical recovery 70; temperature 276; warming 32, 100, 261, 276; *see also* governance
Global Catastrophic Risk Institute 62
Global Financial Crisis (2008) 5, 10
globalization 3, 5–7, 14, 18, 68; present 18; retreat from 5; risks of 18; structure of 6; system of 8
Golden Horde 209–210, 218–220, 222–223, 225, 228–229
Goody, J. 43
Gorbachev, M. 76, 244, 253
Gothic War 54
governance 6, **51**, 102, 119, 158, 207, 209– 210, 213–214, 218, 221; architecture of 115; corporate 175; erosion of central 116; formal 243; fragmented global 65; global 65–66; good 171; higher-end

119; imperial 108, 117; ineffective 230; of Kiev 214; Mongol 211; Novgorodian 213, 215–216; policies 288; political 328; procedures 206; questions of 221; of resources 276; Roman 110, 119; routine 109; state 213; strategies 18; structures 243, 315; system 221, 284; urban 42
Gray, J. 386
Great Famine (1314–1317) 196, **355**
gross world product (GWP) 64
Gusterson, H. 325

habitat loss 297, 302
Halperin, C. 209, 218, 220, 225, 227, 229
Harappans 30–31
Hayek, F. 241
Hellenistic states 45
hemorrhagic fever 180–181
Heraclius 129, **353**
Herlihy, D. 191–192, 197–199
hierarchy 38–43, 45, 51–52, 178, 240, 252–253; administrative 120; breakdown of 108; bureaucratic 241; central 340; centralized 42; evidence of 42; extractive 47; problems of 47; state 39–40, 42
Hilton, S. 198
Hiroshima 316–317, 322
Hitler, A. 74–75, 78, 238
Hittites 30–31, 97–99, 101–105, 265, **338**; Neo- 103; Syro- 103
Hobson, J. A. 53
Hodell, D. A. **266**
Holling, C. S. 26
Holmes, G. 197
Homer-Dixon, T. F. 377
Human Development Index (HDI) 64
hunter-gatherers 39, 64, 148
Huntington, E. 30
Hussein, S. 75

ice age 262–263, **355**
immiseration 402, 407, 410
imperial: administration *137*, 138; alliances 176; aristocracy 109; authorities 111, 132; capitals 112, 119, 167; center 110, 113, 115–117; collapse 112, 170; core 53, 111; court 111, 115, 119, 136; decay 54; defenses 136; disaggregation 54; domains 117; dynasties 48; edifice 113; expansion 53; governance structure 117; heartland 53; household 109; immolation **51**, 53–54; institutions 108, 111; lifetime 380; marrriages **354**; order 118; overreach 54; overstretch

47; polities 118; power 108, 117; rule 111, 119, 185; social structures 383; state 109–110, 170; systems 122, 142; territory 139; unity 111, 115, 117, 120; unraveling 115
imperialism 53; Aztec 167, 186; British 53; Mexica 167, 177–178; new 53; Spanish 170, 178, 186
indigenous: actors 167; allies 178; armies 177; cities 186; city-states 178; conquerors 177; corporations **185**; groups 170; hemorrhagic fevers 181; ideologies 184; labor 177; lands 179; life 180; mortality of epidemics 184; peoples 94, 170, 177, 183–184; politics 167; populations 179, 181–182, 186; societies 167; state 184
Industrial Revolution 65, 70–72, 77
inequality 4, 32, 38–40, 44, **46**, 47–52, 54, 65, 78, 114, 159–160, 199, 236, 290; Chebyshev 389; economic 49; global 75; gross 290; growing 156; high 117; income 314; level of 49, 52; manifestations of 247; Markov 389; rampant 54; record of 160; rising 119, 122, 261; unsustainable 12; wealth 49, 150, *152*, 154–155, 160
infant mortality 378, 382–383, 388, 391
information processing 38–39, 41, 43, 64, 69, 284, 287
integration 43, 171, 336, 392; cultural 337; dis- 314, 334; market 176–177; social 217; value of 340
international organizations (IGOs) 81, 385
inter-tropical convergence zone (ITCZ) 262–263
intervention 112–113, 115, 118, 121, 276, 397, 413; armed 117; fiscal 16; human 66; policy **51**, 314, 398
invaders/external conflict 30–31
invasion 16, 37, 80, 94, 98, 101–102, 132, 167, 172–173, 179–180, 239, 264–265, **266**, 287, 377; Arab 132; barbarian 207; devastating 397; foreign 111; full-scale 210; Germanic **352**; human 11; Islamic 134; long-range 386; Mongol 207, 209–210, 212–215, 217–219, 221, 230; of the Northmen **354**; outside 172, 376; progressive 271; Russian 1, 5; Spanish 94

Johnson, A. W. 158
Johnson, B. 184
Jones, D. S. 184
Jordan, W. C. 196

Kaniewski, D. 99, **266**
Karamzin, N. M. 218–219
Keenan, E. 229
Kelly, W. 6
Kemp, L. 105, 113–114
Kennedy, J. F. 318
Kennedy, P. 53
Khaldûn, I. 10, 26–27
Khan, G. 11, 47, 210, 217, 221
Kievan Rus' 94, 207–210, 212–213, 215–218, 230
Kintigh, K. W. 154
Kissinger, H. 319
Kitano, H. 286
Kohler, T. A. 154
Kuznets Curve 45

Lamb, H. H. 30
Landau, M. 32
Langer, L. 220
late bronze age 61, 65, 93, 97, 265, **266**, 287, 333–334, **338**, 340, 341, 351, **352**
Latour, B. 246
Lawrence Livermore National Laboratory 325
legitimacy 12, 44, 47, 49, 129, 141, 156, 214, 219, 225, 229, 236, 245, 275, 290; political 140, 223, 226
Lehman, M. M. 387
Leon-Portilla, M. 180
Lever, J. J. 305
Levi, P. 243
Liubimov, A. V. 239, 248
Livi-Bacci, M. 182
Lockhart, J. 184
longevity 6, 42, 375, 378, *381–383*, 384–385, 388–390; civilization 375–376; institutional 383; maximum 375; societal 376; software 387

Mad Max 314, 334–337, 338, **338**, 342, 345–347, 350–351, **352–355**
Majeska, G. P. 212
malnutrition 182, 184
Malthusian: checks 199; dynamics 119; factors 118; interdependency 198; theory 194; trap 198
Mandate of Heaven 28
McNamara, R. 318, 326
measles 179–180
Mesopotamia 26, 30, 40, 80, 97, 172, 265, 272, 392
Mezentsev, V. I. 212
Middleton, G. D. 30, **31**, 170, 172

migration 101, 105, 121, 194, 287, 335, 392; climate-driven 276; forced 50, 184, 333; hostile **46**; in- **266**; large-scale 64; mass 193; out- 199, 265; peasant 197; of the Peoples 121; westward 119
Mikhailov, B. 242
Miller, D. B. 212–213, 219
Millon, R. 175
Ministry of Defence 318
Modern Analog Technique 151
Monin, P. 342, 344
monsoon 262–263, 267–268
Montesquieu, C. L. 26
morality 26–27
Motesharrei, S. 32
Mueller, T. 48
MultiPath Forecasting (MPF) 314, 398–399, 404, 407, 410, 412, 414–415
Mumford, L. 315
Muneepeerakul, R. 291

nationalism 327, **352–353**, 392
normal accident 7, 15, 377, 391
North Atlantic Oscillation 264, **266**
northern Rio Grande (NRG) 147–148, 150
nuclear: age 313, 315–316, 319–323, 326–327; -armed missiles 319; -armed states 316, 320, 327–328; arms 321; arsenals 317–318, 320–322; attacks 320; collapse 313, 316, 322–328; crisis 323; dangers 323, 327; debate 313, 323; destructive capacity 316; deterrence 66, 324–325; doomsday machine 317; exchange 77, 320; explosions 319, 324; explosives 318, 328; fallout 319; force 320–321; order 325; planning 320–321; retaliation 324; stockpiles 81; strategist 321; strategy 320; strike 320, 322, 324, 326; submarines 68; system 324; test 317; thermo- 315, 317–319; violence 328; vulnerabilities 324, 329; war 66, 69, 79, 316, 318–328; wargame 318; warheads 319; war plans 318–319, 321–323; weapons 65, 67, 80, 313, 315–328, 375; winter 68, 73, 319
Nuremberg trials 239

Obama, B. 322, 326
Officer, L. H. 402
oligarchy 38, 48, 51, 54, 109, 114
Olson, M. 45, 291
Oppenheimer, R. 61, 316–317
opportunistic 44, 253; behavior 237, 242, 253; food theft 242; habits 243; shadow

exchange 253; shadow practices 243; use
241; usurpation 120
Ord, T. 63, 79
Ortman, S. G. 150
Orwell, G. 76
Ostrowski, D. 220–221, 223

paleo-: climate 151, 153, 273–275;
environmental evidence 132, 139;
pathology 180; sciences 127
pandemic 16, 49, 75, 94, 100, 154, 201,
266, 397; engineered 66, 68, 79–80;
natural 65; outbreak 390; plague 200;
predicament 201; severe 114; worldwide
105; *see also* COVID-19
Park, J. 175
pathogens 298, 302; ancient 180; exposure
to 302; infectious 183; new 183, 260,
298; novel 16; prevalence of 267;
sensitivity to 298
Penny, D. **266**
Perestroika 244
Perrow, C. 15
perturbation 11, 155, 269, 271–272, 275,
410; climate 173, 177, 272; external 271;
major 283; random 358; resilience to
297, *303*; small 13, 269, 305; stochastic
359, 414; systemic 14
phase transitions 314, 359–362, *363*,
363–366, *367*, 367, 372
phenomena 3, 33, 359–361, 364; critical
360, *363*, 366, 372; damage 367;
ecological 10, 372; economic 368;
emergent 334, 350, 359; key 360;
macro-level 245; precursory 361, 366,
372; social 368; sociological 368
Piketty, T. 40, 289–290
Pitts, F. R. 219
plague 12, 31, 192–195, 198–201; animal
355; bacterium 267; bubonic 114, 179;
deaths 195; fiscal records post- 193;
Justinian 54, **353**; labor laws post- 198;
mortality rates 191, 193; outbreaks
200; pandemic 200; pneumonic
180–181; population pre- 192–193;
transregional 193
Podvigina, N. L. 214
poverty 75, 184, 201, 333
power failure 376–377
Pradhan, S. 369
Princeton Institute for International
and Regional Studies (PIIRS) Global
Systemic Risk 1, 62, 191
Prisoners' Dilemma 243, 245

Promethean discrepancy 322, 328
prosperity 5, 14, 193–194, 199, 201,
212–213, 333, 387; economic 211–212;
future 6
Putnam, R. 40

Quality-Adjusted Life Years (QALYs) 64

Rabi, I. I. 317
Random Field Ising Model 368, 372
recovery: capacity for 206; community
305; delayed 155; demographic
193; ecosystem 73; industrial 71–72;
likelihood of 63; negative 73, 76; no
69, 79; normative 69; ongoing 262;
plans 17; political 69; population 184,
186, 191, 200; positive 73–74, 76–78,
81; post-collapse 70; predictor of 71;
probability of 71, 81; prospect of 62,
69, 82; rapid 63; swift 207; technical 63,
69–70, 72–73, 78, 81
Red Queen hypothesis 386
redundancy 17–18, 128–129, 139, 283,
302
Rees, M. J. 66
regeneration 10, 170–171, 174, 176, 178,
282, 387
religion 6, 16, 71, 128, 209, 216, 226–228,
277, 335
religious 149, 336; aspects 229; beliefs 218;
centers 340; change 31; communities
192; dimension 117; elite 216, 228;
extremes **355**; goods 385; hierarchical
society 149; -ideological structures
126; inspiration 111; institutions 384;
leadership 153; life 216; minorities 75;
practices 230; prejudice 227; procession
125; purposes 340; responses 125;
specialists 185; systems 170, 207, 217;
values 377
Renaissance 16, 28, 71, **355**
Renfrew, C. 334, 340
resilience: accidental 236, 239, 243;
benefit of 245; building 206; capacity
for 209–210, 229; civilizational 207;
decreased 155; degree of 94, 124; drivers
of 297; dynamic of 253; empire's 139;
endogenous 94, 230; factors of 38;
falling 397; greater 1, 12; high 207;
increased 120, 277, 300, 303; inherent
125, 218; institutional 254; language of
208, 229; logic of 210; loss of 37, 155,
304–305; low 207; mechanism of 259;
medieval 196; mutualistic 304; relative

138; remarkable 191; science of 230; sectoral 125; significant 94; of the simple 247; social 399; societal 4, 38, 54, 122, 230; state's 207; strategies 260; systemic 13, 15, 17, 207; theory 26; threshold 390; toolbox of 229; unplanned 237
resources: access to 139–140; availability of 194; biotic 148; competition for 304; control of 126, 129, 264; diverting 175; dwindling 53; environmental 27; extraction of 283, 289; financial 215; floral 300, 304; flow of 116; food 300, 304; free 391; governance of 276; harvest 291; key 265; lack of 385; limited 136; loss of 140; material 110, 198; natural 259, 284, 291, **338**, 342, **354**; nutritional 296; overuse of 12; pastoral 129; pooling of 264; renewable 72, 156; shared 288; shortages of 28; significant 17; stable 307; tax-generating 132; variation of 287–288; water 139, 264, 268; withholding 122
Restall, M. 172, 177–178, 184
revolution 44, 78, 186, 253, 322, 336, 351, 358, 398–399; agricultural 70; causes of 398; China 78; components of 236; demographic 186; industrial 70–72, 77; moral 322; Neolithic 41; political 277, 368; post-Industrial 65; Russian 27; scientific 322
Rhodes, R. 326
robustness 6, 17–18, 51, 70, 104, 159, 216, 250, 282–283, 286, 288, 349; community 304; concepts of 17; consideration of 6; demand for 287; ecosystem 283; elements of 9; increasing 286; limits 260, 286, 293; local 288; loss of 283; regulatory approach to 17; tradeoffs 260, 283–284, 286, 288, 293
Rostovtzeff, M. 27
Rumsfeld, D. H. 350
Rundle, J. B. 367

Sahara 276; browning of the 262–263; sub- 276
Scheffer, M. 155
Scheidel, W. 154, 265
Schell, J. 328
Schlosser, E. 324
Schmid, B. V. **266**
Scott, J. C. 40
Second 30 Years War (1914–1956) 10
security 12, 26, 47, 66, 246, 289–290, 297, 315, 327, 335; cyber- 66; food 239, 297;

infrastructures *289*; international 328; issues 385; national 317, 327; services 241
self 246; -amplifying 269; -awareness 6; -bows 156; -conception 228; -contained 350; -damping 269, 271–272; -definition 246; -deluding 326; -destruction 27; -esteem 44; former 9; -immolation 399; -interest 17, 293; -organized 38–39, 42, 366–367, 369; -pollinating 297, 307; -propelling 272; -reflective 323; -reinforcing 76; -reliant 314; -rule 119; sense of 237, 246, 248–249; -similarity 275; -sufficiency 69, 101, 335–336, 338
senescence 26, 376, 385, 387
Shimada, I. **266**
Silfen, P. H. 209
Single Integrated Operational Plan (SIOP) 322
slavery 64, 177, 183–184, 333, **352**
smallpox 66, 71, 114, 179–181
Smith, M. E. 175
Soloviev, S. M. 219
specialization 43–44, 287, 335, 337, 342; greater 348; increase 302; of production 336; productive 150; role 139
Spielmann, K. A. 150
spinodal: criticality 366–369, 372; instability 346–369, 372–373; points 364–365, 367, 369, 372–373
Stalin, J. 74–75, 237, 240, 243, 252
Stimson, H. 315
Storey, R. 182
Sudden Catastrophic Event (SCE) 142
survivalism 392

Taagepera, R. 380, *381*
Tainter, J. A. 30, 37–39, 41, 44, 46, 47, 80, 95, 98, 140, 170, 172, 333, 376
Taleb, N. N. 104
taxation 4, 37, 40, 44, 112–113, 117, 122; breakdown of **353**; collective 226; direct 192; disproportionate 201; methods 219–221; over- 44; regime 220–221; system 221
Teller, E. 316
thermodynamic 8; equilibria 362; laws 359, 376; limit 361; quantities 361; stability 365, 372; universal applicability of 376; variables 362
Third Dynasty of Ur 26, 30–31, 48
Thompson, E. P. 315, 323
Thompson, J. M. 209, 213
Thucydides trap 13

tipping point 9–10, 13, 15, 18, 38, 65, 73, 104–105, 119, 138, 199, 238, 259–263, 269–277, 285, 296, 301, 304–305
totalitarianism 74–75, 77–78, 333
Toynbee, A. 27, 333, 376, 380, 398
trade: beneficial for 219; center 209; domination 354; flows 116; food 243; lines 230; long-distance 42, 116; networks 42, 210, 265, 266, 287–288, 372; -off 68, 283–284, 286, 288, 293; partner 213; patterns 31, 126; route 93, 99, 101, 174, 177, 208–209, 211, 213, 218, 220, 287, 313, 333, 336, 338, 340, 352–353; shadow 243–245; systems 288; transnational 381
tradition: ancient 26; historiographical 112; Hohokam 149; medical 114; Mongollon 149; of mutual responsibility 226; political 228; Pueblo 149
transformation 50, 94; civilizational 124; complex 185; cultural 128; demographic 199; dynamics of 238; economic 94; fundamental 128, 138; gradual 135; historical 124; irreversibility of 13; large-scale 142; prolonged 108; radical 156; simpler 103; social 55, 154; societal 126–128, 141, 277; systemic 10, 124, 127, 198; total 138
Trigger, B. G. 171
Triple Alliance 94, 167–168, 169, 170–171, 173–174, 176–178, 180, 182, 184–185
Truman, H. S. 315–316
trust 12, 40, 71, 222
Turchin, P. 26, 113, 400–402, 404, 407
typhus 179–181

unification 171; political 108, 171, 175; re- 354; Spanish 177, 355
United Nations 319, 327–328
Upland US Southwest (UUSS) 146–148, 151, 152, 153, 155, 157, 157–159
urbanism 43–44, 64, 69, 136; large-scale 42
US Political Violence (USPV) database 400–401

Vågene, A. J. 180–181
Vaissman, M. 209
valences 245; negative 249; positive 247
van Valen, L. 386
Vandals 110, 116, 119
Varien, M. D. 150
Vico, G. 27
Vietnam War 399
Village Ecodynamics Project (VEP) 147, 150, 153–155, 160

Villani, G. 192–193
Villani, M. 192, 195, 197
violence 13, 37, 49, 65, 115, 128, 152, 154–155, 159–160, 183, 196, 287, 290, 399, 401, 405, 407, 409, 413; competitive 148; group-on-group 401; group-on-individual 401; high 154; incidence of 159; increases in 155; interpersonal 49, 153; lethal 401; nuclear 328; organized 110; paramilitary 78; political 398, 400–401, 405–407, 412; random 401; socio-political 49; waves of 399, 411
Vladimirsky-Budanov, M. F. 213, 216
Volney, C. F. 25, 27, 32
vulnerability 39, 67, 80, 126, 265, 321, 328

war: of the Eight Princes 112; -making capacity 64, 69; prone world 321; Second 20 Years (1915–1945) 10; *see also* nuclear
Ward-Perkins, B. 335, 338
Warring States period 110, 113, 120
weapons 210, 215, 224; autonomous 66; biological 65–67, 73, 375; iron 102; of mass destruction (WMD) 63, 67, 75; systems 315; technology 223; vulnerability of 321; *see also* nuclear
Weighted Index of Social Progress 64
Weiss, H. 266
welfare 52, 69; collective 44; goal 284
wellbeing 69, 246; collective 44; decreasing 402; total 64
Wengrow, D. 43
West, G. B. 385
Western Chou dynasty 26, 28, 30, 31
Whitmore, T. M. 182, 185
Widely Applicable Information Criterion (WAIC) 370
Wild West 313, 334, 336–337, 338, 338, 342, 345–347, 350–351, 352–355
Wilkinson, D. 380, 382
Winkless, N. 30
Wohlstetter, A. 321
Woodworth, C. 221
World War I 27, 78, 252
World War II 75–78, 194, 252
Wright, A. M. 151

Yellow Turban Rebellion 111, 114, 338
Yoffee, N. 26

Zheng, J. 266
ziggurats 44

9781032363219